Praise for *Jefferson and Hamilton*

"Ferling provides valuable perspective not only on the Founding Fathers and their accomplishments but, overtly, on today, when fierce differences divide people who say they are seeking to preserve their nation and its values. Highly recommended."
                                                                    —*Library Journal*

"The author's comparative study is bold, brisk and lucid . . . From hammering out constitutional liberties and building the nation's banking system to jockeying in early elections, Ferling draws crisp, sharp delineations between his two subjects."
                                                                    —*Kirkus Reviews*

"With moments of exciting clarity, Ferling's account of two of the most famous American revolutionaries offers gossip, intrigue, and a window into their heated and turbulent relationship . . . Astute research congeals to bring the lives of Jefferson and Hamilton, Washington and Burr, and their contemporaries into our modern world. As personalities clash and egos are wounded, Ferling gives readers a chance to rediscover the birth of the United States through the characters who helped craft its most vital institutions."   —*Publishers Weekly*

JEFFERSON AND HAMILTON

JEFFERSON AND HAMILTON

· · ·

THE RIVALRY THAT FORGED A NATION

JOHN FERLING

BLOOMSBURY PRESS

NEW YORK   LONDON   NEW DELHI   SYDNEY

To Lorene Flanders
and all those in the Irvine Sullivan Ingram Library
who have provided so much assistance over the years

Published by Bloomsbury Press, New York
Bloomsbury is a trademark of Bloomsbury Publishing Plc

All papers used by Bloomsbury Press are natural, recyclable products made
from wood grown in well-managed forests. The manufacturing processes
conform to the environmental regulations of the country of origin.

LIBRARY OF CONGRESS CATALOGING-IN-PUBLICATION DATA

Ferling, John E.
Jefferson and Hamilton : the rivalry that forged a nation /
by John Ferling. — First U.S. edition.
pages cm
Includes bibliographical references and index.
ISBN 978-1-60819-528-2 (hardcover)
1. Jefferson, Thomas, 1743–1826—Political and social views.   2. Hamilton, Alexander,
1757–1804—Political and social views.   3. United States—History—1783–1815.   4. United
States—Politics and government—1789–1797.   5. United States—Politics and
government—1797–1801.   I. Title.
E332.2.F47 2013
973.09'9—dc23
2013000824

First U.S. edition published 2013
This paperback edition published 2014

Paperback ISBN: 978-1-60819-543-5

1 3 5 7 9 10 8 6 4 2

Typeset by Westchester Book Group
Printed and bound in the U.S.A. by Thomson-Shore Inc., Dexter, Michigan

Bloomsbury books may be purchased for business or promotional use.
For information on bulk purchases please contact Macmillan Corporate and
Premium Sales Department at specialmarkets@macmillan.com.

CONTENTS

CONTENTS

PREFACE

The sun struggled to peek through the scudding winter clouds as Bill and Hillary Clinton strode briskly up the steps of Monticello, Thomas Jefferson's majestic mountaintop home outside Charlottesville, Virginia. It was January 17, 1993. Just three days away from becoming America's forty-second chief executive, Clinton had chosen to embark on his inaugural festivities at the residence of his namesake, the nation's third president.

The visitors were given a tour of the mansion, after which they joined a motorcade for the journey to Washington. When Clinton took office in a festive ceremony on January 20, he spoke of Jefferson in his inaugural address, describing the Founder as an apostle of change. Jefferson, said President Clinton, had believed in democracy and knew that periodic "dramatic change" was essential in order to "revitalize our democracy" and "preserve the very foundations of our nation." To endure, Clinton said, America "would have to change," but the changes must come within the framework of "America's ideals" as set forth by Jefferson: "life, liberty, the pursuit of happiness," and the equality of all humankind. As it had been during Jefferson's time, Clinton continued, each generation was compelled to "define what it means to be an American."[1]

Clinton returned for a second visit to Monticello only seventy-five days into his presidency, and throughout his term he spoke so often of his predecessor that a national news magazine referred to Jefferson as "Bill Clinton's muse." Clinton even enlisted Jefferson in the fight for national health insurance, avowing that Jefferson would be shocked to learn that not every American had access to affordable health care. As had Jefferson, Clinton said that he believed "democracy would rise or fall not on the strength of some political elite, but on the strength of ordinary people who hold a stake in . . . how our society works."[2]

Clinton's successor, George W. Bush, said little about Jefferson. Bush was drawn more toward a different founder, Alexander Hamilton. On May 30, 2006, a spring-soft morning in the capital, Bush walked from the Oval Office to the Rose Garden to announce the appointment of a new secretary of the Treasury. In his remarks, the president said that he hoped his appointee, Henry Paulson, would follow the example of Alexander Hamilton, the first Treasury secretary, in overseeing the "management of public finances" that were crucial to "the health and competitiveness of the American economy." Above all, Bush desired that Paulson would, like Hamilton, use his talent and "wisdom to strengthen our financial markets and expand the reach of the American Dream."[3]

George Washington was the one who made things happen, but while he was the prime mover in Revolutionary America, it was Alexander Hamilton and Thomas Jefferson, more than any others, who shaped the new American nation. The strong central government, our system of finance, and the industrial vigor of the United States are Hamilton's legacy. America's bedrock belief in equality, its quest for novelty, and the continental span of the nation were bequeathed to succeeding generations by Jefferson.

Hamilton's and Jefferson's contrasting views on the shape of the new American republic—its government, society, and economy—sparked a bitter rivalry. Furthermore, the ideas and issues that divided those two Founders have persisted from generation to generation in American politics. Their opposing views are like the twin strands of DNA in the American body politic. In the nineteenth century, partisans clashed over banks, tariffs, the money supply, and workers' rights, among other things. In subsequent generations, political parties have battled over issues such as regulation of trade, the distribution of wealth and power, and government's role in health care. Always, however, the divisions in these battles stretch back to the fundamental differences that separated Jefferson and Hamilton: faith in democracy, commitment to civil liberties, trust in the wholesomeness of market forces, the availability of individual opportunities and security, toleration of dissent, the scope of the military, and above all, the depth and breadth of government intrusiveness.

Jefferson's and Hamilton's standing in the minds of Americans has hardly been constant. For decades following Jefferson's election to the presidency in 1800, a contest that spelled political ruin for Hamilton, the Virginian captured the hearts of Americans. All the while, Hamilton slid, if not into oblivion, at least into the dark shadows of history. The Democratic-Republican Party, or Democratic Party, as it was known by the 1820s, had been Jefferson's, and it was largely predominant until the mid-nineteenth century. A succession of Democratic presidents kept alive the memory of Jefferson as the author of the American creed—which he had articulated in the Declaration of Independence—while portraying their administrations as locked in battle against latter-day Hamiltonians. Andrew Jackson, who was often called the "second Jefferson," saw American history as a struggle between those who feared the people and those who resisted "the selfishness of rulers independent" of the people. Jackson called his foes "the Monarchical party," as had Jefferson, and he depicted his administration as battling the anti-democratic tools of wealthy merchants and financiers. Jacksonians toasted the "PLANTER – JEFFERSON" for sowing the "Democratic Tree of Liberty," which they insisted Jackson had brought to "blossom like the Rose."[4]

But a great shift occurred in the second half of the nineteenth century. The reputation of Jefferson, a Southerner and a slave owner, suffered nearly mortal wounds in the hearts of many Americans in the wake of Southern secession, civil war, and the repudiation of slavery. The standing of Hamilton, who had been a proponent of a strong national government, soared, and he ascended even higher in America's pantheon of heroes as the country entered the Industrial Age later in the century. While treasury secretary, Hamilton had offered an alternative to Jefferson's agrarianism, ultimately making possible the explosive growth of the American economy. As the century ended, Hamilton was touted as the creator of modern capitalism and the first American businessman, and in 1900, when New York University established a Hall of Fame to honor eminent Americans, Hamilton was the first inductee.[5]

Industrialization was a double-edged sword. It provided new social, cultural, and material opportunities, but wealth and power were soon concentrated in fewer and fewer hands. Giant corporations and important financiers exercised nearly unmatched political clout, while unprecedented numbers of Americans lived in squalor and coped with dangerous and exploitive working conditions. Jefferson's reputation rebounded, especially in the South and the Great Plains, home to farmers who saw themselves as victims of railroads, tariffs, and the fiscal policies of a national government in the grasp of corporate and financial giants. Jefferson's image took on renewed luster among those who feared his vision of an Arcadian America was vanishing before new hordes of Hamiltonians. William Jennings Bryan, the foremost spokesman for the oppressed farmers, was saluted in the 1890s as "the Jefferson of today." In hundreds of speeches, Bryan exhorted his followers to espouse "Jeffersonian principles with Jacksonian courage." He proclaimed that Jefferson had stood for "equal rights for all, special privileges for none." Others who resisted privilege, monopolies, and centralized authority reminded their followers of Jefferson's "sympathy with popular rights" and his belief that "all civil power should be . . . exercised that the interest and happiness of the great mass of the people would be secured."

In the shadow of the first laudatory biographies of Hamilton, two editions of Jefferson's papers were issued beginning in the 1890s. They were accompanied by several favorable life histories. A veritable army of historians portrayed Jefferson as having stood for advancing the liberating tendencies unleashed by the American Revolution while Hamilton had represented the forces of reaction.

Busts, statues, and memorials of Jefferson sprang up across the landscape. Democratic Clubs sponsored a Jefferson celebration at Monticello in 1896, and the next year the Democratic Party inaugurated its Jefferson Day Dinner, which thereafter has been held annually on the anniversary of the Founder's birthday. Attendees sang a song with lyrics proclaiming Jefferson the "symbol of the nation" who had stood for "the Universal Brotherhood of Man." Many of the tributes to Jefferson portrayed each federal law that aided Wall Street and corporate America as "a monument to the memory of Alexander Hamilton."

In the 1920s, countrywide fundraising efforts, including "Jefferson Week" in April 1924, raked in money as part of a generation-long campaign to make Monticello a public memorial. During the Independence Day celebrations in 1926, the sesquicentennial of America's break with Great Britain, the Thomas Jefferson Memorial Foundation formally dedicated Monticello and opened it to the public. In 1927, the gigantic sculpture at Mt. Rushmore was dedicated, a shrine to Jefferson, Washington, Abraham Lincoln, and Theodore Roosevelt as the greatest Americans.

Hamilton did not fade away during the reawakening of appreciation for Jefferson. President Theodore Roosevelt was the first occupant of the White House to openly extol Hamilton, calling him "the most brilliant American statesman who ever lived." Roosevelt also praised Hamilton as having possessed the "loftiest and keenest intellect" among the Founding Fathers, touted his "constructive statesmanship," and asserted that he had "a touch of the heroic, the touch of the purple, the touch of the gallant." Senator Henry Cabot Lodge of Massachusetts was of like mind. A biographer of Hamilton, Lodge praised his subject as an exemplary American nationalist.

Roosevelt and his followers understood that the national government had to play a role in coping with the harshness and inequities ushered in by industrialization and urbanization. Hamilton, the exponent of a strong executive branch and broad federal powers, was their hero. Some turned their scorn and malice on Jefferson, suggesting that a Jefferson government was a do-nothing government.

Roosevelt and his adherents were also ultranationalists who longed to extend the reach of American power, influence, and economic interests. They were drawn to Hamilton, the exponent of a robust, powerful United States capable not only of defending itself but also of expanding its borders. Early in the twentieth century, the admirers of Hamilton erected statues in his honor in numerous communities, organized a movement to preserve his home in Manhattan, the Grange, and in 1904 commemorated the centennial of his death. In the 1920s the Coolidge administration put Hamilton's image on the ten-dollar bill (and Jefferson's on the seldom-seen two-dollar bill).[6]

Nevertheless, Hamilton never eclipsed Jefferson in popularity in early-twentieth-century America, and admiration of the nation's first Treasury secretary vanished almost entirely during the Great Depression. In the 1930s, Franklin Delano Roosevelt governed through a New Deal coalition of farmers and urban industrial workers seeking relief from the economic collapse and eager for social and economic reforms, and he openly embraced the legacy of Jefferson. Indeed, FDR was sometimes called the "new Jefferson." FDR saw the battle waged by the New Deal against "the moneyed class" as similar to Jefferson's struggle against Hamiltonianism. "Hamiltonians we have today," FDR said, pointing to them as his implacable adversaries. Time and again, FDR decried these Hamiltonians as exponents of dominion by Wall Street and America's economic elite. New Dealers characterized their programs as built on a Jeffersonian template of opposition to oppression. They were kindred spirits of Jefferson, they said, with the similar design "to promote the interests and opportunities of the people." In hyperbole seldom matched by an occupant of the White House, FDR even labeled Jefferson the "great commoner." New Dealers willfully styled Hamilton as a "fascist" as well as "a great beast" who had evinced only loathing for ordinary citizens.

Admiration for Jefferson peaked during those years. The Jefferson postage stamp and nickel appeared in 1938, the latter with his profile on one side and an image of Monticello on the other. In 1943, on the chilly, windy bicentennial of his birth, the Jefferson Memorial in Washington was officially dedicated to America's "Apostle of Freedom" who had "sworn . . . eternal hostility against every form of tyranny over the minds of men." Merrill Peterson, a Jefferson biographer, remarked that the memorial was "the most important thing to happen to Jefferson" since his death in 1826 and proclaimed Jefferson as "the heroic voice of imperishable freedoms," standing in the "radiant center" of the American ideal.[7]

In the past half century Hamilton's reputation has been on the uptick while Jefferson's has plunged once more. As the shroud of the Cold War fell over America, Hamilton was venerated as a foreign policy wizard who had championed a firm hand in the conduct of diplomacy. Furthermore, with the first signs in the 1960s of the resurrection of conservatism from its Great Depression near-death experience, Hamilton reemerged to become what one magazine called the "patron saint" of the political right wing. His service on behalf of the financial sector and his commitment to a free market economy were applauded. The bicentennial of Hamilton's birth was widely celebrated in 1957, and five years later Congress approved a bill making the Grange a national memorial.

Meanwhile, Jefferson's reputation suffered during the civil rights era. He came to be viewed in many quarters as a hypocrite who had posed as an exponent of human rights while owning slaves and espousing racist sentiments. In the wake of DNA testing in 1998 that appeared to confirm long-standing charges that he had fathered at least one child by one of his slaves, Jefferson's reputation sank further. Many thought of him as the lecherous exploiter of a helpless woman that he owned. In some circles, Jefferson came to be seen with such contempt that movements arose to rename schools that bore his name. In 2012, an opinion essay by a prominent scholar in the normally sober *New York Times* called Jefferson the "monster of Monticello."[8]

Before President Clinton, John F. Kennedy was the last Democratic chief executive to speak often of Jefferson. Kennedy supposedly reread Jefferson's first inaugural address on the evening prior to his own inauguration and pronounced it "better than mine." At a 1962 dinner to honor Nobel Prize winners, Kennedy famously remarked that the honorees were the "most extraordinary collection of talent, of human knowledge, that has ever gathered at the White House, with the possible exception of when Thomas Jefferson dined alone."[9]

By 1980, when Ronald Reagan was elected to the presidency, nearly every vestige of Jefferson's America had disappeared. Cities had swelled. The number of farmers had shrunk to less than 5 percent of the nation's population. Jefferson's America seemed as remote as powdered wigs and silk stockings. Moreover, with Reagan's presidency, and the accompanying triumph of neoconservatism, adulation of Hamilton soared to heights nearly as lofty as reverence for Jefferson had been half a century earlier. Reagan spoke of the "wisdom of Hamilton's insight" and the "ever perspicacious Hamilton." Another wave of admiring biographies appeared, most proclaiming that the America of the late twentieth century was Hamilton's legacy. Modern-day Hamiltonians maintained that the United States' emergence as the world's greatest industrial power and the global center of high finance and central banking was due to Hamilton's creative genius and the forces he had set in motion. A PBS documentary in 2004 christened Hamilton the "forgotten father" of America. That same year the New-York Historical Society unveiled an exhibit on Hamilton's life and work. Conceived by an editor of the *National Review*, a leading conservative magazine, the show was titled "The Man Who Made Modern America." George Will, the conservative columnist, had enunciated a similar view years earlier, writing that there was "an elegant memorial in Washington to Jefferson, but none to Hamilton. However, if you seek Hamilton's monument, look around. You are living in it. We honor Jefferson, but live in Hamilton's country."[10]

If history is a guide, the lofty ascent of Hamilton's reputation and Jefferson's corresponding decline will not last forever. But one thing seems certain. Politics in its broadest framework is likely to witness continuing divisions over the competing ideas that set Jefferson and Hamilton at odds.

This book about Jefferson and Hamilton explores what shaped the thinking and behavior of each man. It inquires into their activities during the American Revolution and the war that accompanied it, their hopes for the new American nation, and the political warfare that each waged against the ideas of the other. But the book is about more than ideology and political confrontations. It aims to discover what shaped these men's temperament, to understand the character of each, and to explain the role of character in the choices that each made. It also seeks to answer not only what made each a leader but also how each met the hard tests of leadership. Finally, the book seeks to peel away their public personae to discover the private sides of Jefferson and Hamilton.

When I began this book some three years ago, I held Jefferson in higher esteem than I did Hamilton. I had not always had such a high opinion of Jefferson, but I had grown more positive toward him in the course of working on several books on the early Republic. My admiration grew as I followed the thread of his social and political thought through decade after decade. I wasn't surprised by that, but what I did find a bit startling was that I grew far more appreciative of Hamilton. I saw much that was noble in his sacrifices and valor as a soldier, much that was praiseworthy in his political and polemical skills, and much that was especially laudable in his vision for the nation and the nation's economy.

As I was beginning this project, Don Wagner, a political scientist and longtime friend, remarked to me that it would not be easy to get inside the heads of Jefferson and Hamilton. "Men like that think differently than you and me," Don said. He was correct. It was never easy, but the challenge to come to grips with men of such soaring ambition and legendary objectives, men who played for the highest stakes, made working on the book all the more exciting.

Another challenge was that Jefferson and Hamilton lived in a strikingly different period. I have sought to understand each man in the context of the time in which he lived and acted. Intriguingly, however, I found much that was surprisingly familiar, especially the ways of politics and politicians, not to mention the attraction of power and what some will do to acquire it, and keep it.

As this book took shape, I realized how much my life and thought had been shaped by Jefferson and Hamilton. My maternal ancestors had followed Jefferson's dream, one generation after another marching westward through Virginia, into Pennsylvania, and finally just across the border into West Virginia, always owning their farms and carving out for themselves the very sort of independent life that Jefferson had cherished. A third of the way into the twentieth century, my grandfather's children—including my mother—received college educations. The Ferling side of my family, which arrived in America only in the 1870s, faced a hardscrabble future, but they made their way along the path prepared by Hamilton, working in industry. My father, the son of a glass cutter, was a hard hat who worked for a large petrochemical company. I was a member of the fourth generation of the paternal side of my family in America, and the first to attend college. In the course of writing this book, I came to think that the educational opportunities that had fallen into my lap—and the laps of a great many others like me—was one of the things that Hamilton envisaged in his plans for the American economy.

A word about the book's mechanics. First, the numbered endnotes are preceded by a list of secondary sources that were especially valuable and pertinent. See the Select Bibliography—and also the "Abbreviations" section—for the full citation of each of these works. These particular sources are not otherwise cited in the numbered notes unless the author is quoted. Unfortunately, these lists of helpful secondary works do not include Jon Meacham's *Thomas Jefferson: The Art of Power* (New York, 2012), an insightful biography that appeared a few weeks after the submission of this manuscript.

Second, in the hope of conveying as much as possible about my subjects, I have preserved the original spelling in quotations from Jefferson's and Hamilton's writings.

Debts accumulate in the course of writing any book. I am particularly grateful to Matt deLesdernier and James Sefcik for reading the manuscript, pointing out errors, and offering guidance. Four good friends, Edith Gelles, Michael deNie, Keith Pacholl, and Arthur Lefkowitz, answered many questions that I posed. Lorene Flanders, who has graciously supported my research and writing, provided an office that I used daily while working on the book. Angela Mehaffey and Margot Davis in the Interlibrary Loan Office of the Irvine Sullivan Ingram Library at the University of West Georgia graciously met my frequent requests for books and articles, and Gail Smith in Acquisitions saw to the purchase of some items that were important to my work. Charlie Sicignano helped with the accession of digital copies of newspapers. Elmira Eidson and Julie Dobbs helped me out of numerous scrapes with my computer and word processing program. I owe so many debts of gratitude to Catherine Hendricks that to list them would double the length of this book.

Pete Beatty helped in many ways to bring the book to completion, all the while listening to my tales of woe about the Pittsburgh Pirates. This is my second book with Maureen Klier, who has no equal as a copyeditor, and my first with Nikki Baldauf, an excellent production editor. Geri Thoma, my literary agent, played a crucial role in the conceptualization and conception of this book. This is my seventh book with Peter Ginna, a masterful editor who, along with criticism, provides encouragement and a storehouse of wonderful ideas.

I don't think Sammy Grace, Simon, Katie, and Clementine care much one way or another about Thomas Jefferson or Alexander Hamilton, but they enrich my life, which makes the often-trying work of writing a book a bit easier.

And there is Carol, my wife, who has always been supportive of my writing, not to mention understanding and patient.

CHRONOLOGY

1743 (April 13)	Birth of Thomas Jefferson
1755 (January 11)	Birth of Alexander Hamilton
1757 (Summer)	Death of TJ's father, Peter Jefferson
1760–62	TJ studies at the College of William and Mary
1766 (?)	James Hamilton deserts his family
1767 (February 12)	TJ begins his legal practice
1768 (?)	Death of AH's mother, Rachel Levien
1769 (May 1769)	TJ enters the House of Burgesses
1772 (January 1)	TJ marries Martha Wayles Skelton
1772 (?)	AH sails for New York
1773–75	AH studies at King's College
1774 (December)	Publication of TJ's *A Summary View*
1774–75 (Dec–Jan)	Publication of AH's *A Full Vindication* and *The Farmer Refuted*
1775 (April 19)	Beginning of the Revolutionary War
1775 (June 20)	TJ enters the Continental Congress
1776 (March)	AH is appointed captain of a volunteer artillery company
1776 (March 31)	Death of TJ's mother, Jane Randolph Jefferson
1776 (June 11–28)	TJ drafts the Declaration of Independence
1776 (September)	TJ leaves Congress and reenters the House of Burgesses
1776–77 (August–January)	AH sees action in New York, Trenton, and Princeton
1777 (September–October)	AH in combat in the Battles of Brandywine and Germantown
1778 (January–May)	AH at Valley Forge encampment
1778 (June 28)	AH in combat in the Battle of Monmouth

1779 (June 1)	TJ is elected governor of Virginia
1780 (June 2)	TJ elected to a second term as governor
1780 (December 14)	AH marries Elizabeth Schuyler
1780–81 (December 31–January 6)	Benedict Arnold raids Virginia and sacks Richmond
1781 (June 4)	TJ flees from British soldiers at Monticello
1781 (October 14)	AH leads attack on Redoubt No. 10 at Yorktown
1782 (September 6)	Death of TJ's wife, Martha
1782 (November 25)	AH enters the Confederation Congress
1783 (January–March)	AH is involved in the Newburgh Conspiracy
1783 (November 25)	TJ enters the Confederation Congress
1784 (August 6)	TJ arrives in Paris as a U.S. diplomat
1786 (March 11)	TJ conducts diplomacy and visits John and Abigail Adams in England
1786 (April)	AH is elected to the New York Assembly
1786 (August or September)	TJ meets Maria Cosway
1786 (September)	AH attends the Annapolis Convention
1787 (May–Sept)	AH intermittently attends Constitutional Convention
1787 (July)	Sally Hemings arrives in Paris
1787 (October–December)	TJ and Maria Cosway are together for the final time in Paris
1789 (September)	AH becomes Treasury secretary
1789 (October 22)	TJ's family, together with Sally and James Hemings, sail for Virginia
1790 (January 14)	AH submits his Report on the Public Credit
1790 (February 14)	TJ accepts appointment as secretary of state
1790 (July)	Congress approves funding, assumption, and the Residence Act
1790 (December 13)	AH proposes an excise on spirits and the creation of a national bank
1791 (February)	AH and TJ clash on constitutionality of the bank; GW signs the bill
1791 (May 17–June 19)	TJ and James Madison undertake the "botanizing tour"
1791 (June)	AH begins affair with Maria Reynolds

1791 (October)	The *National Gazette* begins publication
1792 (December)	Frederick Muhlenberg, James Monroe, and Abraham Venable absolve AH of illegal conduct
1793 (April 22)	Washington proclaims American neutrality
1793 (September 5)	AH falls ill with yellow fever
1793 (December 31)	TJ resigns as secretary of state
1794 (October 4)	AH joins the army to suppress the Whiskey Rebellion in Pennsylvania
1795 (January 31)	AH resigns as secretary of the treasury
1795 (July)	AH speaks and writes in defense of the Jay Treaty
1796 (May 16–July 5)	AH drafts Washington's Farewell Address
1796 (December)	TJ is elected vice president of the United States
1797 (May)	Adams appoints three commissioners to negotiate with France
1798 (March–April)	Adams and Congress learn of the XYZ Affair
1798 (June 18–July 14)	Congress enacts the Alien and Sedition Acts
1798 (July 18)	Adams nominates AH to be inspector general of the new army
1800 (May 5–10)	Adams dismisses James McHenry and Timothy Pickering from his cabinet
1800 (October 24)	Publication of AH's *Letter . . . Concerning . . . Character of John Adams*
1801 (February 11–17)	The House decides the election of 1800
1801 (March 4)	TJ's inauguration as president of the United States
1804 (July 11–12)	AH's duel with Aaron Burr and death on the following day
1809 (March 11)	TJ retires to Monticello following second term as president
1826 (July 4)	Death of TJ (and John Adams)

PROLOGUE

IN THE LAST DAYS of November 1783 the British army in New York sullenly marched through the streets of Manhattan to waiting troop transports. Only a few thousand British regulars remained, some of them Americans, black and white, who had chosen to fight for the king, not for the United States. The soldiers, for the most part clad in resplendent red-and-white uniforms, did not appear to be part of a defeated army. But they were.

Slowly, inexorably, the army moved toward New York's harbor. Few New Yorkers lined the streets to watch, but the rhythmic sound of marching men, the clattering of horses on cobblestones, the stolid rattle and creaking of heavy artillery reverberated through nearby neighborhoods. At dockside, the men, burdened with equipment, struggled up steep gangplanks and onto vessels of the Royal Navy. Late in the day, as the sun sank in the western sky, the fleet sailed away from America and once it did, there could be no question that the War of Independence had finally come to an end.

A month after the departure of the enemy soldiers, General George Washington returned to Virginia, arriving at Mount Vernon on Christmas Eve in the final moments of a winter's twilight. No one had ever been happier to retire. He told acquaintances how thankful he was to be "eased of a load of public care," and of his eagerness to sit "under the shadow of my own Vine & my own Fig tree, free from the bustles of a camp and the busy scenes of public life." At last, he was free of the burden of making life-and-death decisions and of carrying the responsibility of the struggle to win American independence.[1]

Washington was sincere in his repeated insistence of wishing to live at home in peace. He had commanded the Continental army for eight trying years, and in the end he had gained victory and an iconic status. He was happy. He was with his wife, Martha, and overjoyed by the frequent visits of his four step-grandchildren, youngsters who ranged in age from three to seven and who frolicked loudly both indoors and on the emerald green lawns that splayed outward on every side of the mansion. Nothing gave him greater pleasure than his beloved estate. He was filled with plans for landscaping and gardening and with ideas for furnishing the mansion, which had been expanded during his long wartime absence. When he first arrived home, Washington rode about the estate daily, not on business, but just to savor surroundings that he found so soul stirring.

Washington was proud of what he had achieved, and he enjoyed the acclaim of his countrymen. He told numerous correspondents that he was home to stay, that he planned to spend the time allotted him gliding "gently down the stream of life, until I sleep with my Fathers." He never again wished to face the "watchful days & sleepless Nights" that were the lot of a military commander, nor did he ever again want to face trials "in pursuit of fame." It was especially nice, he said, not to have young officers circling about him hopeful "of catching a gracious smile."[2]

The United States had won the war and gained its independence, though Washington was all too aware that the young nation faced problems, mostly from what he called a "deranged" economy. Even so, he radiated optimism when he came home from the war. Yes, affairs were "unsettled," but he was convinced that the "good sense of the People" would steer the new republic toward "order & sound policy."[3] Initially, Washington was more concerned, and preoccupied, with his own troubled business affairs, which had suffered egregiously from his lengthy wartime absence.[4]

Washington's concern about the troubled financial health of the United States had crystallized during the war. Since at least the midpoint of the conflict he had urged reforms, particularly strengthening the powers of the national government so that it could raise revenue and regulate commerce. Washington's principal concern was national security—the new nation's ability to protect itself from foreign predators and to resolve pressing domestic issues before the Union imploded. An enervated United States could not forever "exist as an Independent Power." To survive, to gain respectability, what was required was self-evident: The United States must have a national government possessed of "a Supreme Power to regulate and govern the general concerns of the Confederated Republic."[5]

Washington had returned to Mount Vernon expecting the nation's problems to be swiftly resolved. When reforms had not occurred by the mid-1780s, he too expressed alarm. The United States was "tottering," he said. He knew that republican governments seldom moved in haste, and he worried that a cure might not be found in time. All that he knew for certain was that "something must be done, or the fabrick must fall."[6]

Others shared Washington's sense of a gathering crisis, though where he worried principally about national security, they were often troubled by other concerns. Creditors wrung their hands over the worthless paper money.

Debtors feared foreclosure, not to mention debtors' prison. Nearly everyone groaned under an extraordinary burden of taxation, as governments sought to continue functioning while they at the very least paid the interest on their wartime debts. Commerce languished, causing misery and apprehension. Some merchants had suffered since before the war. Many workers were out of work or feared losing their jobs. After years of sacrifice, even deprivation, many urban artisans and shopkeepers, and not a few farmers, faced an austere life.

But some were troubled not so much by economic tribulations as by democracy. The American Revolution had planted the seeds of a very different society from that which had existed in colonial days. The hierarchical society of colonial America was waning. Class distinctions, once accentuated by sharp dissimilarities in dress, were eroding. No longer were those of "middling circumstances" and the "meaner sort" as likely to defer to their social betters by bowing to them, stepping aside when passing them on the street, or doffing their hats. No longer were commoners as willing to tolerate unequal treatment before the law. No longer were they willing to acquiesce in the old belief that only gentlemen possessed the skill to hold political office. No longer were people as willing to accept the ancient notion that there was a place for each person and each person was expected to remain in his place.

The Revolution and the long war had instilled in those who had once been on the bottom the belief, stated in innumerable declarations of rights, that citizens were "equally free and independent." Many men who had been denied the suffrage before the Revolution could now vote. Men who would never have occupied positions of authority in the colonies now held public office, high office in some cases, sitting even in their state legislature. A new kind of popular leader had emerged in the United States: men who were less educated and less refined than their predecessors, men who were likely to take literally the Declaration of Independence's proclamation that "all men are born equal." But it was not only the disappearance of traditional habits and customs that was of concern. Some feared that in the emerging democracy the new politically active class would demand alternative economic policies that would benefit those in the middle and lower strata and be harmful to the wealthiest Americans. The notion of democracy and equality had taken root, and the most conservative Americans did not like it all. This was not the American Revolution that they had imagined. For them, the crisis of the 1780s included the social and political changes unleashed by the Revolution. Some looked back wistfully to colonial times, though it was unlikely that what had been done could be undone. Instead, they sought the means of removing important decisions from popular control.[7]

In the summer of 1786, New York's John Jay, the secretary of foreign affairs

under the Articles of Confederation, the first United States constitution, told
Washington of his belief that national "affairs seem to lead to some crisis—
some Revolution—something that I cannot foresee or conjecture. I am uneasy and apprehensive—more so, than during the War." French assistance had
provided hope during the war. Now there seemed to be no hope. The United
States appeared to be headed toward "Evils and Calamities," and in large
measure the nation's plight arose from entrusting authority to a new set of
men who were "neither wise nor good." Washington responded that he agreed
entirely with Jay's concerns. "I do not conceive we can exist long as a Nation,"
wrote Washington.[8]

Perhaps the earliest and most persistent voice warning that malevolent
forces were sapping life from the United States belonged to Alexander Hamilton. An aide to General Washington during the war, Hamilton had first
written on the American crisis more than three years before the conflict
ended. He was elected to the New York Assembly in 1786, and early the following year he took the floor of the legislature to deliver a ninety-minute address on America's vexations. Hamilton began by saying that the Declaration
of Independence had proclaimed that the new United States might "do all . . .
things that independent states may of right do," though in fact the national
government had never possessed the powers normally vested in sovereign
governments. Saddled with an enfeebled government, the United States had
very nearly lost the war, and since the end of hostilities it had been "in continual danger of dissolution." Matters had now reached a stage in which "national affairs . . . are left . . . to float in the chaos." The United States could not
much longer subsist, and when it collapsed, the states would be opened to
"foreign influence and intrigue." They might even make war on one another.
Large standing armies would have to be raised by each state, presenting a
greater threat to liberty than was ever likely to be posed by a redoubtable republican government. The outcome of the "dissolution of the union," Hamilton warned, was that the states would be compelled to ally with European
powers in order to survive, a step that would "plunge us into all the labyrinths
of European politics." At risk, he said, was the American Revolution and all
the hopes and dreams that had gone into it for a United States.[9]

On the day that Hamilton spoke, Thomas Jefferson was shopping in Paris,
purchasing chinaware and a door for the carriage house at his residence.[10] A
former congressman and governor of Virginia, Jefferson was the American
minister to France. He had been away from the United States for some eighteen months, but numerous friends kept him abreast of what was occurring
at home. Some were worried about America's prospects, and some saw things
in nearly as gloomy a light as did Hamilton.

But Jefferson dissented from the chorus of doom. When told that many an American longed for a restoration of colonial society and governance, he responded that if there was such a man, "send him here. It is the best school in the universe to cure him of that folly." The monarchical and aristocratic-dominated governments in Europe, he added, "are loaded with misery." When told that there were those who hated the breakdown of the colonists' hierarchical society, he replied that "the dignity of man is lost in arbitrary distinctions." Indeed, the one "germ of destruction" that he saw in America's institutions was the existence, and predominance, of aristocracy in the southern states. It was degrading, he went on, to think of a system in which "the many are crushed under the weight of a few." When Jefferson learned that some Americans were assailing the notion that the people could establish good government, he responded that he was persuaded of the overall "good sense of the people" and that he could not understand why "fear predominates over hope." Yes, there were problems, he acknowledged, but the "mass of mankind" in America "enjoys a precious degree of liberty & happiness." If American democracy was bumpy, its mistakes should be weighed "against the oppressions" on the monarchies in Europe. On the whole, said Jefferson, the constitution of the United States was "a wonderfully perfect instrument." While the U.S. government had some defects, to compare it to the governments of Europe would be "like a comparison of heaven & hell."[1]

Jefferson wrote to Washington from time to time, usually confining his remarks to European affairs. Washington always answered promptly. On one occasion, however, Jefferson discoursed briefly on American affairs, telling Washington that "the inconveniences resulting" from the problems of the national government in the United States were "so light in comparison with those existing in every other government on earth, that our citizens may certainly be considered as in the happiest political situation that exists."[2] Washington did not answer that letter.

By the time Hamilton spoke in 1787, Washington had come to share with his most conservative countrymen their dark views regarding America's troubles. Wondering now whether the people were fit for self-government, Washington concluded that "the discerning part of the community" must govern and the "ignorant & designing" must follow. It had to be this way, for most people simply would not accept "measures that are best calculated for their own good."[3] This was the prevailing sentiment regarding governance before the American Revolution.

By 1787 something else was clear. The battle lines had been drawn over determining the meaning of the American Revolution and, with it, the contours of the new American nation.

COMING OF AGE

CHAPTER I

"To make a more universal Acquaintance"

Unhappy Youths

NEITHER THOMAS JEFFERSON nor Alexander Hamilton enjoyed a happy childhood. Jefferson later characterized youth as a time of "colonial subservience." Next to slavery, he said, one's earliest years had to be the worst state imaginable.[1] At age fourteen, Hamilton denounced the "grov'ling . . . condition" which his "Fortune &c condemn[ed] him" and deplored the "weakness" that appeared to be his destiny.[2]

Thomas Jefferson was born to Peter and Jane Randolph Jefferson in 1743 at Shadwell, a sprawling country estate of 1,400 acres in the lush, mountainous terrain of frontier Albemarle County, Virginia. Young Thomas revered his father, a self-made man who, through industry, quick wits, and a good marriage, had risen to a planter's status, colonial Virginia's equivalent of aristocratic rank. Born in humble circumstances, Peter worked for years as a surveyor, growing steadily more affluent. Substance brought influence, which led in turn to a string of local posts, including justice of the peace, county surveyor, and sheriff. After marrying Jane Randolph, the daughter of a James River baron, Peter's ascent gathered momentum. Soon he was second in command of his county militia and sat in the House of Burgesses, Virginia's assembly. In the four years before Thomas's birth, Peter built Shadwell, a six-room, one-and-a-half-story farmhouse that sat atop a ridge and looked toward the Rivanna River. He modeled it on homes that were fashionable with the English gentry, though Shadwell was more modest. Peter acquired ever more land and eventually also came to possess some three hundred head of livestock, a sizable library, and scores of slaves.[3] Though Peter was not what colonial Americans considered a well-educated gentleman, Jefferson recollected his father as a man of good judgment with a keen taste for learning. In Thomas's rendering, Peter had rounded off the coarse edges of his persona and was equally at home in a gentleman's drawing room as on the untamed frontier.

Though born to a family of wealth and influence, young Thomas Jefferson thought something was missing. Because Shadwell burned in 1770, destroying nearly every letter he had written before the age of twenty-six, information on Jefferson's youth is elusive, but clues exist to the causes of his unhappy early life.

He was sent away to school at age nine, separating him for the better part of each year from Shadwell, and from his parents and his six sisters and a brother. Four years later he was separated forever from his father, who died in 1757 at age forty-nine. The two experiences may have left young Jefferson feeling abandoned and stripped of the gratification and security of a family. His mother was there, but not for him, or at least that is what he appears to have felt. Only four references to her can be found in the thousands of Jefferson's letters that have survived, none of them even remotely endearing. Whatever their true relationship, Jefferson must have felt that she did not nurture him with sufficient love and attention. A measure of his troubled sensations can be divined from his subsequent remark, "at 14 years of age, the whole care and direction of my self was thrown on my self entirely, without a relation . . . to advise or guide me." As Jefferson later recalled, lacking guidance he developed poor habits and ran with "bad company." He was amazed, he said, that he had not turned out to be "worthless." Things worked out for the best, he added, only because of his own "prudent selections" based on his "reasoning powers." Much of this sounds fanciful, and it may have been Jefferson's way of persuading himself that, like his father, he was a self-made man.[4]

Alexander Hamilton's early years were laced with material deprivation and emotional pain. Like Jefferson, he said little about his youth, and nothing that he said was in the least effusive.

Hamilton's mother, Rachel Faucette, was the daughter of a sugar planter on Nevis in the British West Indies. At age sixteen, in 1745, after inheriting what her son later called a "*snug* fortune," she moved with her mother, who was legally separated from her husband, to the nearby Danish island of St. Croix. In no time she married Johann Michael Lavien, a thirty-year-old Dane who was struggling without success to turn around an undercapitalized sugar plantation named—or, perhaps from Rachel's perspective, misnamed—Contentment. After five years, Rachel walked away from her unhappy marriage. Enraged and humiliated, Lavien had her jailed for a few weeks on what may have been trumped-up charges of adultery. As soon as she was released, Rachel fled to St. Kitts, leaving Lavien for good and abandoning her only child, Peter.

Not long passed before Rachel met James Hamilton, a thirtysomething Scotsman who had come to the West Indies to seek his fortune as a merchant.

He never found it. The reasons for his failures are not clear, though his son later attributed it to James's "indolence" and lack of the unsparing toughness and preoccupation needed to succeed in business. By the time James encountered Rachel, his career was on the descent. He was scraping by in an unskilled job, possibly that of watchman.

Rachel, who appears to have been a risk taker given to impulsive behavior and bad decisions—traits that were passed on to her son—took up with James, despite his "indigent circumstances" and the fact that she was still legally married to Lavien. Though she and James never wed, they had several children, two of whom survived childhood. James Jr. was born in 1753. His younger sibling, Alexander, was most likely born in January 1755.[5] Four years after Alexander's birth, Lavien suddenly resurfaced and filed for divorce from Rachel. Charging that she was given to "whoring with everyone," he told the court that she had "completely forgotten her duty" to her legitimate child. Lavien had no difficulty gaining the divorce. The judge, in fact, decreed that Rachel could never again legally marry and that her "whore-children" were not entitled to Lavien's property.

It is unclear what James Hamilton did to support his family during the fifteen or so years that he was with Rachel, or precisely how comfortably he and his family lived. He probably worked some of the time and Rachel may have as well. What is known is that she had inherited three of her mother's female slaves in the year after Alexander's birth and that they almost certainly were hired out to generate income for the family. Somehow, Rachel found the resources to see that Alexander—who outshone his brother as a student—received a few years of schooling. Given the prejudices of the day, young Alexander was denied formal schooling because of his illegitimate birth, but he studied with a private tutor.

In 1765, James found work in Christiansted on St. Croix and moved Rachel and the boys with him. He did not linger long. A year later, James deserted his family. Alexander, who was eleven, never again saw his father, who skipped around the Caribbean for the next three decades.

The emotional toll on young Alexander had to be considerable. He coped with the knowledge that his mother was widely seen as scandalous, with his father's desertion, and with the painful discrimination occasioned by his illegitimate birth. He never spoke ill of either parent, and when older and successful he invited his father to his wedding and sent him money.[6] But what Hamilton felt when the searing pain was fresh during his youth is unknown. The most obvious legacy of the burden that he carried was an obsessive fervor to prevail over the hand that fate had dealt him.

*   *   *

Despite his decidedly dissimilar background, Jefferson, like Hamilton, was prodded by what he later called a "spice of ambition."[7] He was the son of a father who strove to get ahead. It stretches credulity to imagine that Peter had not done his utmost to instill his habits in his son—especially as the only other male child in the family, Randolph, possessed only modest abilities. If one of the boys was to excel, it had to be Thomas. Nor is it unlikely that a youngster who clearly idolized his father would seek to equal, and probably surpass, him in many ways.

In 1752 nine-year-old Thomas completed his preparatory education at Tuckahoe, the Randolph's vast estate on the James River. Thereafter, his parents enrolled him in a Latin school run by Reverend William Douglas, a native of Scotland. The school was well to the east of Shadwell in Goochland County, the site of Douglas's Anglican parish. Jefferson spent more than five years with Douglas and was introduced to Latin, Greek, and French. This prepared him for a superior classical school run by another Anglican clergyman, James Maury. Jefferson had little good to say about his time with Douglas, but he looked on his nearly thirty months with Maury as transformative. The product of a distinguished Virginia family and a graduate of the College of William and Mary, Maury had much to offer, though the timing of Jefferson's enrollment in his academy may have been crucial. Jefferson encountered Maury at a decisive moment, scant months following Peter Jefferson's death. Jefferson boarded with Maury and his wife, and they became his surrogate family. Jefferson was impressed by his mentor's collection of books, the most extensive library he had yet seen, but what was pivotal was Jefferson's discovery that learning could be a "rich source of delight." A new world opened to him. Under the guidance of this teacher, whom he called a "correct classical scholar," Jefferson encountered the wisdom of the ancients in their own languages, which he subsequently said was a training ground for "fine composition." Perhaps most important, Jefferson was introduced to the liberating scientific and political thought of the modern European Enlightenment.[8] Young Jefferson likely had been adrift before he enrolled in Maury's small log cabin school. Thereafter, while he yet expected to spend his life on a secluded plantation, Jefferson had found a means of bringing the world, old and new, to his remote corner.

Jefferson's experience with Maury touched something else. It awakened his ambition. He wanted to be part of the wider world that he had found through Maury. All along he had been expected to follow in his father's footsteps, holding public office, possibly someday even sitting in the Virginia assembly. Jefferson still wished to take that path, and he doubtless dreamed of more. It was almost certainly at this juncture that he first coveted the qualities of a natural aristocrat, the learning, grace, and refinement that set such an individual apart from others, causing him to be seen as a natural leader because of his enlightenment, taste, and urbanity. At age sixteen, he wrote to his guardian asking that he be permitted to attend the College of William and Mary in Williamsburg. What he learned there, as well as the "more universal Acquaintance" that he would make among his classmates and professors, would "hereafter be serviceable to me," he said.[9] Jefferson had begun to wish for more from life than running a plantation.

Jefferson enrolled in the college in March 1760, just a few days before his seventeenth birthday. The institution had existed for about sixty years. Its leafy, bucolic campus consisted of three brick buildings, one of them the President's House. The president and six professors made up the faculty. There were between seventy-five and one hundred students, though some were in the prep school and around 10 percent were Indians who studied a nonclassical curriculum. Williamsburg was Virginia's capital, and over the years it had swelled to some 1,500 inhabitants. It was the largest town Jefferson had ever seen.

Jefferson was the rare student who came to college already knowing that there could be joy through study, and in Williamsburg he flourished under the tutelage of William Small, a Scotsman with a degree in medicine who was only eight years his senior. According to one student, Small was noted for his "liberality of sentiment." Jefferson was drawn to that, and he and Small forged a bond cast from their mutual delight in mathematics, science, philosophy, and rational inquiry. Above all, Small was committed to questioning conventional wisdom, and he instilled this trait in Jefferson.[10]

Years later Jefferson said that it had been his "great good fortune" to have studied with Small, whom he characterized as "correct and gentlemanly" with "an enlarged and liberal mind." To a greater degree than any other person, he said, Small "fixed the destinies of my life."[11] But Jefferson took some of the credit. He had been "a hard student," he once said, a description confirmed by classmates who remembered that he would not permit "the allurement of pleasure [to] drive or seduce him" from his studies. He was contemptuous of those who did not take learning seriously, in later years looking back on them as wastrels who had been "worthless to society." Nevertheless, Jefferson was never unsocial. He formed close, lasting relationships with several college chums. Nor did he study continuously. He adhered to a daily regimen of exercise that included walking, running, or swimming, and he allotted ample time for his violin practice.[12]

Jefferson need not have attended college. According to Peter's will, he was to receive five thousand acres and numerous slaves when he turned twenty-one, enabling him to live comfortably. Nor did he need to study further after

completing college. But his formative experiences left him yearning for something more than the life of an affluent planter. He wished for a *"very high
standing"* as a distinguished attorney or prominent public figure, someone
such as Peyton Randolph, he said, a planter-lawyer who had sat in the House
of Burgesses for years as the representative of Williamsburg and the College
of William and Mary.[13]

When Jefferson said that Professor Small had set him toward his destiny,
he did not mean that this was due solely to their classroom encounters. Small
had introduced his student to George Wythe, an esteemed Williamsburg
lawyer who was also a member of the House of Burgesses, and to the royal
governor of the colony, Francis Fauquier, whose residence was near the campus. Jefferson later said that he had been brought into their circle, dining and
playing music with the three illustrious older men. Clearly, Small saw young
Jefferson as a student of unusual talent. How Jefferson saw himself is not
known, but it could not have escaped him that his was an exceptional intellect. Not only had he outpaced the other students, but also he had been welcomed into distinguished company. Had Jefferson ever doubted his abilities, by
the time he completed his studies he had to have been convinced that he
could go places. He saw that practicing law, or at least having a thorough understanding of the law, might help in the fulfillment of his ambitions, and in
April 1762 he became an apprentice law student under Wythe. He told a friend
that he wished to become a lawyer so that he would "be admired," but he knew
that attaining recognition and eminence in the legal field might unlock the
door to an elevated position in public life, a prospect that he thought inviting.[14]

For more than a year after James Hamilton abandoned them, Rachel and her
sons lived in a two-story house in Christiansted. Her brother-in-law paid the
rent and provided some of the furnishings. The family lived upstairs, and
Rachel opened a general store on the lower level. She had inherited two additional slaves, bringing the total of her adult chattel to five, and all were likely
hired out. An inventory completed when Alexander was thirteen showed that
Rachel possessed several silver utensils, porcelain plates and basins, and a small
library. While she and the boys lived austerely, they were not impoverished.

The future may have held promise, but Alexander was star-crossed. Early in
1768 both he and his mother fell ill with a virulent fever that ravaged St. Croix.
Alexander survived. Rachel, only thirty-eight, perished. Jefferson had been
fourteen when his father died. Hamilton was one year younger when he was
effectively orphaned. Jefferson had been left with a mother with whom he apparently could not develop close emotional ties. Hamilton was left with no one.

It may have seemed as if things could not be worse, but soon they were.

The Laviens, father and son, resurfaced during the probate of Rachel's estate. They wanted everything. To get it, they gave new life to the unseemly allegations that had been aired in court years earlier during the divorce proceedings. Nine months after Rachel's death, the probate court awarded her entire estate to Peter Lavien, the son she had abandoned eighteen years before. Nothing of Rachel's was left to Alexander and his sixteen-year-old brother. The boys were placed under the guardianship of a member of their aunt's family. James was quickly apprenticed to a carpenter. Alexander, who might also have been earmarked for a life as a tradesman, was spared that fate. Perhaps before Rachel's death in February, certainly before the probate decision in November, Alexander had obtained work as a clerk for the trading firm of Beekman and Cruger—soon to become Kortright and Cruger—the New York–based company that had supplied the groceries his mother sold. As he was already employed, Alexander was not apprenticed. He continued to work for the firm's Christiansted office while living in the home of Thomas Stevens, a merchant who, together with his wife and five children, resided in Christiansted.

Hamilton worked for the company for five years. He was called a "clerk," but his work was multifaceted. In time, he kept the books, monitored shipments, stayed abreast of inventory, managed a shop and warehouse, and tended to busy ship captains. He oversaw the acquisition of commodities to be sold on St. Croix and other islands in the West Indies—mostly food, wine, livestock, and African slaves—and the sugar and its by-products that were exported to Europe and Great Britain's mainland colonies. His employment proved to be an important training ground. Hamilton subsequently referred to his years with the company as "the most useful of his education," as he learned the value of organization and discipline, perfected his command of French, and discovered how to work with others, especially impatient, bustling businessmen.[15]

Hamilton was busy, his work was varied and challenging, and he bore considerable responsibilities. Yet, he was unhappy. His formal education appeared to have come to a crashing halt before his fourteenth birthday. In addition, as he was unlikely to ever accumulate sufficient capital to open his own company, the door to upward mobility seemed permanently closed to him. He spun "Castles in the Air," as he put it, dreaming of a new lease on life.[16] More than anything, this scarred adolescent's passion appears to have been to gain renown, to surpass in distinction all those who had sneered at his mother and had looked on him with supercilious airs.

It is striking that both Jefferson and Hamilton, in their earliest surviving letter, spoke of their ambition. Jefferson, nearly seventeen, wrote of his yearning to go to college so that he might flourish in whatever he chose to do.

Hamilton, nearly fifteen, yearned to escape his dead-end job and attain a higher standing. He presumed that attending college was beyond all hope. One way out of his trap, he thought, was to make useful contacts. Another was to gain fame as a soldier. But peace prevailed. Soldiering was a dim hope unless someone started a war. "I wish there was a War," he declared.[17]

Three years after Hamilton wrote that letter, his fortunes improved. Glib and precocious, and extraordinarily bright, he caught people's attention. Older, successful men were often impressed by this industrious, enterprising, and responsible young man. Hamilton found several patrons, including Thomas Stevens, with whom he lived, and each of the three men who were his employers, Beekman, Cruger, and Kortright. However, no one was more important to him than the Reverend Hugh Knox, a Scots-Irish Presbyterian minister who took a church on St. Croix some twenty years following his graduation from the College of New Jersey, later known as Princeton. Hamilton was about seventeen when he met Knox. Quickly impressed, the pastor appears to have become something of a tutor. Knox made available his library and probably provided some direction to Hamilton's reading. He additionally helped Hamilton, who had begun to place short poetic compositions in the local newspaper, refine his writing skills. Knox's mentoring paid off. Hamilton published a dramatic and florid account of a hurricane that punished the island in the summer of 1772.[18]

Hamilton's writing helped convince his well-wishers to subsidize his college education in North America. He probably had no more than six years of schooling, two or three fewer years than most students spent preparing for admission to college, but colleges sometimes admitted deficient though promising students. If it was found that he lacked adequate preparation, Hamilton's patrons were willing, at least for a time, to underwrite his study in a preparatory school. They pooled their money, and in the fall of 1772 Hamilton sailed alone for mainland America to find his destiny.

Nearly thirty years old when Hamilton sailed, Jefferson had negotiated the shoals of youth, though his passage to maturity had been neither easy nor painless. At age nineteen, Jefferson had plunged into legal studies with Wythe. He planned to remain at Wythe's side for six or seven months, after which he would complete his training through self-study while living at Shadwell.

Jefferson remained at Shadwell for a year, but in the fall of 1763 he abandoned the rural seat and returned to the capital. He may have concluded that he needed Wythe's systematic guidance. Or, Shadwell may have seemed dismayingly isolated to a single young man fresh from three years in Williamsburg. Albemarle County was remote and primitive; a century later, a visitor described it as "wild" with "rugged and broken" roads that led to scattered homes and plantations.[19] Jefferson may also have been bothered by the constant distractions of life on a working plantation. After moving back to Williamsburg, he lived and studied with Wythe for two years, deep into 1765, reading, helping his mentor prepare for court appearances, and observing him before judges and juries.

These were not Jefferson's happiest years. He found his legal studies less than exhilarating, and complained that law books were "dull" and riddled with "jargon." Furthermore, most of his friends from college were settling into married life and the greater independence of adulthood.[20] A groomsman at many of their weddings, Jefferson appeared to be envious. They seemed blissful. He was miserable, suspended somewhere between adolescence and adulthood. That he was unsuccessful in winning the affections of his first love, Rebecca Burwell, hardly improved his state of mind.

He met Rebecca in 1762, around the time he first took up his study with Wythe, and his infatuation with her was almost surely a factor in his decision to return to Williamsburg in 1763. When they first met, Rebecca was sixteen and living at her uncle's estate near the capital. Jefferson was immediately captivated and obsessed. He must have seen her infrequently, mostly in the episodic social whirl of the town, but he could not stop thinking of her. He waxed on about her in letter after letter, confessing: "I think of her too often, . . . I fear for my peace of mind." He asked acquaintances to tell Rebecca that she was on his mind. In one of his most curious letters, Jefferson admitted that he dreamed of building a house for himself, John Page, a friend from college, and Rebecca. Despite his endless longing, he appears to have never written to her.

Though he thought of her often, in a candid moment he acknowledged, "she never gave me reason to hope." On two occasions in the fall of 1763 he sought to become a suitor. On the first occasion, at a ball, he carefully planned and rehearsed a few witty remarks and more serious palaver, but Jefferson failed miserably when he was alone with her. Overcome by a "strange confusion," the best he could do was stammer "a few broken sentences, uttered in great disorder." Later, he tried again and may even have proposed marriage, though he concocted a story of "the necessity of my going to England, and the delays which would consequently be occasioned by that." This time he was more coherent, but Rebecca rebuffed him.[21] Jefferson's behavior was that of an infatuated young man who was not ready to settle down, and who in fact must have feared that marriage would thwart his ambitions.

Within a few months Rebecca was engaged to another man, whom she married in May 1764. "Well the lord bless her I say!" Jefferson remarked when he heard the news. But he was far from over her, and he was all bluster when he told a friend that he relished being single.[22] In fact, when he learned that he had lost Rebecca, he fell ill with a crippling headache that sent him to bed in agonizing pain for several days. It was his first such bout with what some believe to have been migraines and others think were cluster, or muscular contraction, headaches. Many more would follow over the next half century, and they invariably would occur during moments of great personal stress.[23]

After a brief phase when he was rendered "abominably indolent," Jefferson returned to his studies. He grew close to Wythe, his mentor, as he had with Small, which hints that both teachers not only recognized Jefferson's remarkable intellect but also responded to his emotional needs. Jefferson came to regard Wythe as "my second father" and "most affectionate friend" as well as "one of the greatest men of the age." Later, Jefferson spoke of his law teacher as he had of Professor Small, remarking on Wythe's "salutary influence on the course of my life."[24]

Jefferson was twenty-two when he completed his studies with Wythe. In all likelihood, he passed the Virginia bar examination that same year, 1765, though he waited two additional years before commencing practice. A brief wait was not uncommon for freshly minted lawyers, though to mark time for two years was nearly unheard of. Jefferson returned to Shadwell and devoted the interim to additional study. He later claimed to have studied sixteen hours a day. While he may have exaggerated, Edmund Randolph, a relative, said that Jefferson was "Indefatigable and methodical" in his studies. James Madison later remarked with awe that Jefferson had studied the law "to the bottom, and in its greatest breadth."[25]

Jefferson felt no financial pressure to go to work, and while he studied rigorously, he craved leisure time. When he was about twenty-three, Jefferson spent two months traveling to Annapolis, Philadelphia, and New York. In part, he made the trip in order to receive the smallpox inoculation in Philadelphia. But the excursion was also, as his foremost biographer, Dumas Malone, characterized it, a "Great Tour," after the fashion of British and European aristocrats. Jefferson had never been outside Virginia, and he wanted to sightsee and shop.

However, Jefferson spent most of the five years beginning in 1765 at home, leading a life that one scholar called "monastic." He had returned to Shadwell "to reestablish himself," as historian Andrew Burstein put it, to continue his education in preparation for his adult life. Jefferson read law, but he spent more time immersed in classical philosophy, history, natural history, and the works of leading Enlightenment writers. Jefferson once said that he had a "canine appetite" for learning; Edmund Randolph conjectured that it was Jefferson's intention to acquire "great literary endowments" that could enhance his writing skills. Randolph also said that Jefferson believed his pen would lead to "advantageous connections" among the best educated men in the colonies and the mother country. What is more, Jefferson must have discovered during evenings spent in sophisticated company, as when he consorted with Small, Wythe, and Fauquier, that he was ill-equipped to keep pace with the dinner conversation. More the pragmatist than many have realized, Jefferson saw his study as indispensable to his enjoyment of a genial and cultured social life.[26]

Jefferson never looked back with affection on the seven or eight years following his graduation from college. Whereas John Adams allotted forty pages in his autobiography to that phase of life, Jefferson glossed over his early adulthood in a single sentence in his memoirs. Through 1767, Jefferson remained almost exclusively at Shadwell, and even after opening his legal practice, he lived at home with his mother for about ten months of each year. It must have been an extraordinarily solitary existence for so young a man, but it was one of his own choosing.

Throughout his life Jefferson had a proclivity to retreat from the hostile outside world, the scene of acrimony and despair, and sometimes of personal failings. In addition, he frequently showed the traits of an obsessive personality. In this instance, scarred by Rebecca's rejection, he may have fixated on not only his disappointment but also his repudiation. These would be throbbing pains for any young person to bear. It is conceivable that he shrank from the risk of further misadventures, walling himself from the cruel world in the sanctuary of home.

The loss of his earliest papers makes it impossible to understand the state of his mind. It may be that his experience with Rebecca was not that telling and that there are other explanations for his ascetic habits. Jefferson may have been more consumed with hopes for acclaim and eminence than he ever acknowledged. He had no desire to soldier, which was one possible route to prominence. Some cut a swath in politics. Patrick Henry and Richard Henry Lee had become dominant political figures in Virginia by the mid-1760s. Both were outgoing and effervescent, riveting public speakers, and fast-on-their feet debaters in rough-and-tumble legislative battles. If Jefferson was honest with himself, he must have realized that he lacked the flamboyance and extroverted qualities essential for dominating a legislative body. Early on, he likely surmised that his best hope of achieving distinction in public life was through his intellect and, possibly, his literary skills. At least in part, Jefferson isolated himself to focus on his studies, the course that seemingly offered the best hope for capturing the respect he craved.

He may even have hoped to gain renown someday in London, much as Benjamin Franklin had by the 1760s. Through Professor Small and others, and from things that he now and then saw in print, Jefferson would have known that the colonial gentry were viewed with condescension within ruling circles in the parent state. The supposedly parvenu nature of American gentlemen was a core belief among the elite in the metropolis, who snobbishly dismissed the colonials as unmannered rustics. Not a few colonial gentry worked very hard at becoming cultivated gentlemen, and Jefferson was the prime example of those who pursued gentility in all its stylizing forms, including intellectual advancement, literary and artistic fecundity, and displaying good taste in one's dwelling and its furnishings.[27]

Hurt and ambition may have gnawed at Jefferson in equal proportions. He would not have been the first to seek recognition as a balm for his pain, even to see acclaim as the means of avenging those who had wounded him. Six long years passed during which Jefferson made no attempt to court any woman. Numerous literary passages that he copied into his journal during this period reeked of enmity, even rage, toward women. Some extracts characterized women as "damnable, deceitful" and the source of untold "ills." Others suggested that "female Snares" were men's greatest "curse," and portrayed marriage as captivity.[28] Yet, while drawn to these writings, Jefferson also spoke of his married friends as the "happiest [men] in the universe" and portrayed himself as wretchedly unhappy. At age twenty-seven, years removed from his only stab at a relationship with a woman, Jefferson wrote a remarkably reckless letter to John Page, his now-married friend, a missive that laid bare his loneliness and despair. Jefferson not only gushed over Page's wife's charms, but in what he termed his "treasonable thoughts," he also mused about living with the couple so that the threesome could "pull down the moon."[29] Page did not respond for a very long time and, when he did, he ignored Jefferson's startling suggestion.

Jefferson's letter to Page was the second act of impropriety occasioned by his forlorn and disordered state of mind. In June 1768, Jack Walker, who lived at Belvoir, seven miles northeast of Shadwell, asked Jefferson to look after his young wife, Betsey, and infant daughter while he was away on a diplomatic mission for Virginia. Walker and Jefferson were old friends and classmates, and Walker's father, who had been an executor of Peter Jefferson's will, had authorized, even encouraged, Jefferson's enrollment at William and Mary.

During the four months that Jack Walker was away serving the province in the summer and fall of 1768, Jefferson frequently rode to Belvoir. His visits were more than neighborly: He attempted to seduce Betsy Walker. On more than one occasion, in fact, he made improper advances. Betsy remained silent about Jefferson's behavior for sixteen years. When she finally told her husband, Betsy claimed that during an eleven-year span beginning in 1768, Jefferson had persisted in his unseemly conduct. Nearly a quarter century passed before Jefferson was confronted with the allegations. He learned of the charges when they were splashed in the nation's newspapers during his presidency. They got into print after Walker divulged his wife's story to Jefferson's political enemies. Jefferson promptly confessed to once having "offered love to a handsome lady" while her husband was away in 1768. It occurred when he was "young and single," he said. He denied the accusation of continued misconduct toward Betsy Walker, most of which supposedly occurred while he was married.[30]

As with nearly all he-said, she-said imbroglios, it is impossible to know who told the truth. Jefferson may have lied to protect his reputation and presidency, but Betsy Walker also had a motive for fabricating her story. She wanted Jefferson removed as executor of the family's will, likely fearing the authority he might exercise over her should she be widowed. Relating the story of Jefferson's allegedly unbecoming behavior did the trick. Jack Walker changed his will, designating another executor.[31]

Jefferson may have been disconsolate and reclusive for years, but he was never dysfunctional. During his lonely years after Rebecca Burwell's rejection, he completed his legal studies and established himself as a successful lawyer. He had carefully prepared for his legal career. Aware that he was a poor public speaker, he envisaged difficulties practicing in the county courts, where success hinged on winning over juries of poorly educated small farmers. He felt that he would do better trying cases in the General Court of Judicature, where there were no juries and where verdicts were rendered by panels of judges. Greater preparation was required to practice at that level, but he was drawn to the challenge. He liked the idea of matching his intellectual skills with those of other lawyers at this level, and he found it appealing that the General Court was in session only about eight weeks of the year. That meant he would have abundant time for building and managing his own plantation and for reading, writing, and traveling.[32]

In 1767, at age twenty-four, Jefferson finally began to practice law. He could not entirely ignore the lower courts if he was to realize a substantial income, and in fact from the outset he represented numerous clients in cases concerning land claims and titles. His ascent was breathtakingly swift. Whereas John Adams had but a single client during his first year in practice, Jefferson handled sixty-eight items of business, and his caseload doubled nearly every year thereafter. By the early 1770s he averaged some five hundred cases annually and was earning about £175 a year, roughly seven times the annual income of most urban tradesmen.[33]

It was also during these years that Jefferson commenced construction of Monticello. Designing and building one's home was no more an ordinary preoccupation of a young male just beyond adolescence at that time than it is today, but as Peyton Randolph once said, Jefferson's absorption with all things pertaining to the fine arts—including architecture—"ran before the times in which he was born."[34] During his second year as a lawyer, and seven months prior to his election to the assembly, he set his slaves to work leveling the top of a tall hill on the other side of the Rivanna River from Shadwell. It was slow going. Nearly two years passed before Jefferson noted in his memorandum book: "Moved to Monticello." Actually, he moved into only "one room, which," he wrote, "serves me for parlour for kitchen and hall . . . for bed chamber and study too." He said that he hoped to have "more elbow room" shortly, but the construction of Monticello had only just begun and would require years to complete.[35]

Eighteen months after launching his legal practice, Jefferson stood for election to the House of Burgesses. It was the first election in three years, and the first since he had completed his studies in Williamsburg with Wythe. Jefferson was seeking the seat his father had held. Shy and reserved, Jefferson may not have been a backslapper or a spellbinding orator, but he hailed from an influential family and was willing to spend money to treat the voters to food and liquor. He won the election.

Jefferson entered the House of Burgesses in the spring of 1769 and immediately zoomed ahead of some who had held their seats for years. The crucial business of the assembly was performed in five committees. Some members were never appointed to one of these committees and most faced a long wait to obtain such a choice assignment. Jefferson landed on two of the plum committees on his first day as a burgess. It did him no harm that Peyton Randolph, a relative, was Speaker of the House, nor that Wythe was an influential assemblyman. Jefferson's reputation for erudition had probably also spread during the preceding two years while he practiced law. The scholar who most closely studied the practices of the House of Burgesses concluded that on occasion "a man's career in the House . . . in some measure was determined before he participated in any of its deliberations."[36] That was true of Jefferson, who rapidly emerged as chair of one of the powerful committees.

But prior to the War of Independence, which erupted six years after he entered the house, Jefferson was never part of the legislative leadership team. To some degree, he remained a second-tier legislator because his legislative responsibilities were of secondary consideration for him. He was preoccupied with his law practice and the construction of his mansion, and something

even more distracting: In the fall of 1770, Jefferson began to court Martha
Wayles Skelton.

At age twenty-seven, Jefferson was more mature and self-confident than
when he had unsuccessfully tried to court Rebecca Burwell. An assemblyman with a flourishing law practice, he had also broken away from the confining solitude of Shadwell. He had traveled to other colonies and throughout
Virginia, and between 1767 and 1770 his legal work and legislative schedule
compelled him to spend roughly a quarter of each year in Williamsburg.[37]

Jefferson courted Martha for at least fifteen months. When he first called
on her, Martha was a twenty-two-year-old widow with a three-year-old son,
John. She was living at the Forest, the estate of her father, John Wayles, about
twenty miles west of Williamsburg. Not much is known of her, as Jefferson
burned Martha's correspondence following her death. Nor did she ever sit for
an artist. One of Jefferson's slaves later described her as short and pretty,
though family members said she was "above medium height," slender with
auburn hair and large, expressive hazel eyes, good-natured, and sprightly.
Like Jefferson, she loved books and music. She played the spinet and harpsichord, he the violin, and both enjoyed singing. She was experienced in presiding over a plantation's domestic workers and in managing children. Given
his predilections, Jefferson must have thought her compliant. The icing on
the cake was that Martha was the daughter of an extremely wealthy man.
John Wayles had amassed a fortune from the practice of law, but mostly from
tobacco, slave trading, and land speculation.[38]

Jefferson was instantly smitten. Within three months he told a friend that
he was "wishing to take to himself a wife." In fact, he might have married
then, but numerous obstacles stood in the way. Shadwell had burned nine
months before he first called on Martha, and more construction was required
at Monticello if he was to have a home for himself and his bride. Jefferson also
faced another election campaign in 1771, as well as the autumn sessions of
the assembly and General Court. Waiting impatiently, he confessed that in
"every scheme of happiness" he could imagine, Martha was "in the fore-
ground of the picture, as the principal figure."[39]

He deferred marriage no longer than necessary. The couple wed on New
Year's Day 1772 in a ceremony conducted by two Anglican priests, after which
they enjoyed a traditional wedding feast that included a huge chocolate cake.
Two weeks later they set out in a phaeton on their days-long winter journey to
Monticello. In the course of their trip, the pale winter sun gave way to somber-
gray clouds, and before long snow began falling. As they approached Charlottesville, it became apparent that they were caught in a blizzard of epic

proportions. The couple decided to press onward, since they were close to their destination, though they abandoned the phaeton and switched to riding horseback. By the time the shivering newlyweds reached Jefferson's hill, the snowbanks were three feet deep. The horses struggled up the treacherous, winding road to the windswept summit, where at midnight Jefferson and his half-frozen bride alighted and dashed into his one-room, brick bachelor's cottage. As the servants had long since retired for the night, there was no fire, and the temperature in the dwelling must have hovered around freezing. Jefferson rapidly got a fire going, and he and Martha, numb and exhausted after their long and frigid ordeal, began to thaw. Martha then and ever after thought the abode a dreary place, but her husband adoringly called it their "Honeymoon Lodge." Nine months later their first child—Martha, or Patsy, as she would be called—was born.[40]

In his memoirs, Jefferson almost conveys the impression that his life began the day of his marriage. Breezing through his first twenty-nine years in four brief paragraphs, he rapturously recollected his wife as the "cherished companion of my life, in whose affections, unabated on both sides, I . . . lived . . . in unchequered happiness."[41]

While Martha gave meaning to his previously barren life, so did his role in politics. Jefferson wrote about his early political activism in his memoirs, but nearly everything he said about his service in the House of Burgesses prior to the American Revolution was misleading. Though he portrayed himself as a crusader who fought to end slavery in Virginia, his efforts were more modest. He supported a move by the assembly to end the importation of slaves into Virginia and all thirteen mainland colonies. This was not an uphill battle. Virginia had been importing slaves for more than a century and was surfeited with bondsmen. But South Carolina and Georgia, flourishing rice-producing colonies in the Low Country, had an insatiable appetite for new chattel. If the slave trade to North America was terminated, there would be shortages of labor in the rice colonies, enabling Virginia's planters to sell their excess slaves for princely sums. It was a clever move, but the king, George III, refused to play along.

Jefferson also exaggerated his influence in the assembly during his first several years in the body. In his account, the leaders included him in secret meetings to plot strategy against the royal governor and colleagues beseeched his assistance. But it is extremely unlikely that Jefferson was a legislative kingpin before the American Revolution. He served on important committees, but as was his lifelong habit as a legislator, he seldom even spoke or joined in the floor debates.[42] That he was not a leader was due somewhat to his temperament, but mostly to his absorption with private affairs.

* * *

Seventeen-year-old Alexander Hamilton arrived in the British mainland colonies less than a year after Jefferson married. Jefferson had been five years older when he had made his first long trip from home, the trek that took him as far away as New York, and he had been accompanied by at least one attendant. Hamilton, whose life of travail on St. Croix had made him incredibly self-reliant, traveled alone across the perilous sea and into a land filled with strangers. It was a venture for a hardy soul, one with an iron will and a propulsive ambition. Hamilton booked passage on a vessel bound for Boston. He barely survived the journey. Before reaching the North American coast, his ship caught fire. The crew succeeded in saving it only after taking heroic measures, and the badly damaged brig limped into Boston Harbor. Friendless, Hamilton on his own had to find transportation to Manhattan.

Hamilton's backers in Christiansted had hoped for his prompt admission to Princeton. However, given the deficiencies in his education, Princeton rejected Hamilton's application for admission, though it guided him to a preparatory academy in what now is Elizabeth, New Jersey. This schooling, and all that followed, was paid for from the subscription fund established by his benefactors on St. Croix.

Through introductory letters written by Reverend Knox, Hamilton met several influential figures in New Jersey, including William Livingston, Elias Boudinot, and William Alexander, who called himself Lord Stirling. Each would subsequently play an important role in the American Revolution. As with Hamilton's patrons in Christiansted, each must have glimpsed something extraordinary in the young West Indian, and each took Hamilton under his wing. Meanwhile, Hamilton on his own initiative bonded with others, including fellow students, with whom he was popular, and men with ties to the mercantile company that was partially bankrolling his education. Whereas Jefferson was reserved, even withdrawn, Hamilton was self-assured, gregarious, resilient, and never one to conceal his abilities.

Hamilton's assertive nature took him only so far. After several months in the prep school, he again failed to gain admission to Princeton. He later said that he had been turned down because he had requested admittance on an accelerated track, though it is possible that he remained academically deficient.[43] At some point following his second rebuff, Hamilton moved to Manhattan and prepared on his own. Finally, a year or more after his arrival in British North America—it was probably in late 1773 or early 1774—Hamilton was admitted to King's College (now Columbia University), an institution tied to the Anglican Church. It consisted of three faculty and about twenty students in a single large building on a rambling wooded campus near the outskirts of New York City, which then took up just the southern part of Manhattan Island.[44]

King's was widely seen as a conservative school with Royalist predilections, more so than William and Mary. King's president, Myles Cooper, was
an Anglican clergyman who subsequently became a leading foe of the American Revolution. Students attended chapel each morning at sunrise, vespers
after every sunset, and two worship services on Sunday. Some fellow students
later remembered Hamilton as a "zealous believer" who daily prayed "upon
his knees both night and morning," and once even composed a hymn, "The
Soul Entering into Bliss."[45]

Hamilton was admitted to King's College as a charity student, a pupil who
was fast-tracked because his financial resources were limited but who was
judged capable of handling the rigors of a heavy academic load. He was permitted to audit classes and take free tutorials. Given his formidable intellect,
incredible industry, and seemingly inexhaustible energy, Hamilton flourished, somehow even finding the time and stamina to organize a debating
club and take part in several literary societies. Like Jefferson, Hamilton gave
a wide berth to his less serious peers. His close friends were mostly the sober
and serious students who stayed out of trouble. He was closest to Robert Troup,
who hailed from a middle-rung background and went on to serve as an officer in the Continental army and ultimately as a federal judge.

From painful experience, Hamilton knew that life was filled with vicissi-
tude. A college degree would serve as a stabilizer. Though security was crucial
for him, he wanted more. Hamilton wanted to be somebody. Mere respect was
insufficient; he was driven to gain prominence, authority, and acceptance.

Anglo-American relations were quiet during Hamilton's first year or so in
the English colonies. The strains and turbulence of the mid-1760s seemed a
distant memory. Though reared on a Danish island in the Caribbean, Hamilton had worked for a firm owned by New Yorkers and had dealt with British
clients scattered through the West Indies, so he likely had some sense of the
issues that had divided the colonies and London. However, when he sailed for
the mainland colonies in 1772, Hamilton could not have known that he was
coming to a land that was about to be swept by a great revolution. As Hamilton neared the end of his first year in college, his world, like that of Thomas
Jefferson, was about to change forever.

The American Revolution

CHAPTER 2

"THE GALLING YOKE OF DEPENDENCE"

BECOMING REBELS

NEWLY MARRIED AND A FATHER, Jefferson was happy at last. At age twenty he had wondered if there was "any such thing as happiness in the world."¹ As he neared age thirty, Jefferson knew there was. He had found contentment through his family. Jefferson had given up his legal practice. He had grown contemptuous of lawyers, calling them a "disagreeable crowd" that, like "parasites" feasted off the misery of others. However, it was the additional wealth that accrued from marriage that enabled him to live on a grand scale without practicing law.² He anticipated tranquility and prosperity as a planter, and he doubtless looked toward a long career in the House of Burgesses, probably hoping that in time his intellect and pen would elevate him to a leadership role. Jefferson may have thought of writing for publication, perhaps doing as Franklin had done en route to becoming the best-known American of the era. Perhaps he too could now and then dash off a newspaper essay or write a pamphlet on a scientific matter, social criticism, or imperial policy. The last thing he expected, or wanted, was long absences from Monticello.

America's growing conflict with Great Britain intruded on Jefferson's bliss. Around the time of Jefferson's birth, the prime minister and his cabinet in London had quietly contemplated tightening control over the colonies. Britain's rulers feared that generations of distracted supervision and paltry enforcement of the imperial commercial laws might lead the American provinces to drift steadily toward independence. Nearly twenty years of warfare with Spain and France, including the Seven Years' War, which began in the colonies in 1754, thwarted Great Britain's plans to institute new colonial policies. But in 1763 hostilities ended in a magnificent British victory. In the Treaty of Paris, Great Britain acquired all of North America east of the Mississippi River, including Canada and Florida. With a long period of peace seemingly at hand, the way was clear for London to institute change. Wishing to put in place governments in the newly won territories, regulate trade with the Indians, and resolve conflicting land claims, the Crown first promulgated the Proclamation of 1763, a decree that forbade the flow of population across the Appalachians until further notice. To keep peace on the frontier, and as leverage for inducing the Indians to relinquish their lands, London left an army of several thousand troops in America. It was the first time Great Britain had deployed a sizable force in America in peacetime. However, faced with a staggering war debt and the simultaneous cost of maintaining the army in America, London needed money. Officials glimpsed two new sources of revenue. One was through a stricter regulation of colonial commerce. The other was by levying taxes on the colonists.[3]

Jefferson was twenty-one and studying with Wythe when the Stamp Act, the first direct tax that Parliament had ever imposed on the colonists, went into effect in 1765. Jefferson followed events closely. Wythe wrote the first draft of the House of Burgesses' denunciation of parliamentary taxation, asserting that it was unconstitutional. In the spring, Jefferson stood with the other spectators in the lobby outside the assembly chamber and listened as Patrick Henry delivered an impassioned speech assailing the tax. Thereafter, Jefferson not only said that Henry's oration was the best speech he had ever heard—years later, he acknowledged the enormous "impression [it] made on me"—but he also insisted that Henry's daring conduct in 1765 had launched the colonial insurgency against the parent state.[4]

Jefferson, however, did not rush into the ranks of agitators. Henry had hardly finished his celebrated speech before Jefferson returned home, embarking on two years of intense additional study. During those years, Parliament repealed the Stamp Act in the face of American protests, though it simultaneously declared its authority to legislate for America "in all cases whatsoever." In 1767, the year that Jefferson launched his legal practice, Parliament exercised the authority it claimed. It enacted the Townshend Duties, taxes on the sales of lead, tea, glass, paper, and paint in the colonies. A new wave of American resistance flared. Essays denouncing the taxes flowed from colonial presses. Several northern provinces joined in an economic boycott of British trade to force their repeal. Virginia was ready to join the embargo movement by the time the House of Burgesses assembled in May 1769, the first session in which the newly elected Jefferson served. The assembly convened and Jefferson took his seat. The royal governor, Baron de Botetourt, rode from the Governor's Palace in a handsome carriage drawn by six white horses to open the session with a brief speech. Though a newcomer, Jefferson was asked to draft the assembly's response. He did so, but his colleagues rejected his composition—possibly because its tone was not sufficiently obsequious.

The legislature instead adopted a statement that declared its "firm Attachment to his Majesty's sacred Person and Government," although the burgesses unanimously agreed to embargo British imports until Parliament rescinded the taxes.[5]

The American boycotts worked. In the spring of 1770, about the time that Jefferson began to court Martha Wayles Skelton, Parliament repealed all the Townshend duties except for its tax on tea. An air of calm settled over imperial relations, leading some to conclude that the Anglo-American tempest had ended. But the Townshend duties provoked a sea change in the thinking of even more Americans, as this second attempt to tax the colonists revealed an unmistakable pattern in London's intentions. John Adams, in Massachusetts, thought the Stamp Act had caused the "People, even to the lowest Ranks . . . [to] become more attentive to their Liberties, more inquisitive about them, more determined to defend them."[6] Some colonists were beginning to believe that a "profoundly secret, dark, and deep" plot existed among royal officials to quash the rights of the colonists.[7]

In 1770, though, no colonist imagined that the American Revolution lay on the horizon, least of all Jefferson, whose focus remained on getting his life and career on track. When he remarked in his memoirs that "our countrymen seemed to fall into a state of insensibility to our situation" during the early 1770s, it may have been a subliminal reference to his own conduct.[8]

To the surprise of most, however, imperial troubles resurfaced late in 1773. Urban protests against the lingering tax on tea culminated in December in the Boston Tea Party, an organized strike in the night on ships in Boston's harbor laden with duticd tea. Before sunrise, some ninety thousand pounds of East India Company tea had been destroyed. Imperial authorities responded with a heavy hand. In the spring, Parliament enacted the Coercive Acts, draconian measures levied solely against Massachusetts. The legislation fined the colony, shut the port of Boston until compensation was made for the destroyed tea, and made major changes to the provincial government in the Bay Colony. It was a last-ditch effort to break the back of the American insurgency by peaceful means. The colonists learned of these measures, which they called the Intolerable Acts, in May 1774.

Jefferson had by then pulled together his thoughts on the limits of British authority. He had been influenced by both Henry's stirring speech and Wythe's thinking on imperial constitutional matters. He had read deeply in the law, political theory, English history, the human condition, and the natural rights of humankind. He was also conversant with the remarkable abundance of radical tracts produced by English dissidents who styled themselves "Real Whigs," an appellation they chose in order to emphasize their attachment to the ideas of earlier English republicans. Since the late seventeenth century, these writers had produced a pugnacious literature that blended descriptions of corruption and decay in England with warnings of threats to liberty. The rot in England purportedly stemmed from the excessive powers and diabolical designs of a strong executive—the monarchy—which corrupted legislators through patronage and pensions. But England's degeneration had also allegedly occurred because its modern financial system had produced unimaginable riches for the few and deepening poverty for the many, widening the gap between rich and poor, and cursing the land with a malignant tyranny that ate away at the liberties once enjoyed by Englishmen.[9]

But more than theory composed Jefferson's thinking. While he was appreciative of his British birthright, he was also a Virginian, and proud of it. His family had lived in the province for about three-quarters of a century, and throughout his life Jefferson spoke of his homeland as "my country, Virginia." During the century and a half between the arrival of the English colonists at Jamestown and Jefferson's coming of age, each generation of Virginians had pushed westward, fighting the Indians, taking their lands, opening new frontiers. The Virginians, as Jefferson knew, had done it with little help from the mother country. Prior to the wars in the 1740s and 1750s, he said with scant exaggeration, "No shilling was ever issued from the public treasures of his majesty or his ancestors for [Virginia's] assistance."[10] He believed that Virginians, and Virginians alone, had made Virginia. But Virginians had done much for Great Britain. In the 1740s, the colony had contributed hundreds of men to an Anglo-American army that fought the Spanish in the Caribbean and South America. In the Seven Years' War, thousands served in the Virginia Regiment, fighting and dying in frontier warfare against the French and Indians.

It was indisputable as well that Virginia was a troubled colony by the 1760s, and some of its troubles arose from its colonial status. The cost of waging the Seven Years' War had left Virginia, like the parent country, saddled with steep war debts. Had it been permitted to issue its own currency, Virginia might easily have retired its debt. However, imperial authorities, who sought to protect British creditors, prohibited such a practice. Compounding matters, tobacco prices had been declining since the early 1760s, threatening some planters with ruin. Virginians might have realized higher prices had they been able to operate in a free market economy, but Britain's mercantilist system compelled them to send their tobacco to British markets. Virginia's planters were driven to borrow from British creditors. Debts piled up. As Jefferson himself later remarked, these "debts had become hereditary from father to son, for many generations, so that the planters were a species of property, annexed to certain mercantile houses in London."[11] Virginia's planters had tried to save themselves by petitioning the Crown to end the African slave trade within the British Empire. That expedient not only would have driven up the price of slaves, but also would have allowed Virginia's planters to escape their debts by selling their surplus slaves to rice-producing South Carolina and Georgia. But the king had turned a deaf ear to their entreaties, prompting one planter to exclaim that never before had Virginians felt such a "galling yoke of dependence." What Jefferson concluded from the king's conduct was that when the interests of English businessmen and financiers collided with what the colonists saw as their well-being, the Crown always sided with those in the metropolis against "the lasting interests of the American states."[12]

Something else stirred Jefferson. He thought slavery degraded and corrupted both blacks and whites, retarded Virginia's economy, and concentrated wealth and power, resulting in an oligarchy of great planters. While his views were still in gestation, he was moving toward the notion of a broader diffusion of power within Virginia. His thinking was strikingly radical. He envisaged change in the colonies' relationship with the mother country as well as fundamental change within Virginia, most of which was impossible without fundamental changes in the framework of the British Empire.[13]

John Adams once remarked, "Revolution was in the Minds of the People, and this was effected, from 1760 to 1775 . . . before a drop of blood was drawn." He was doubtless thinking of his own transformation, but he could as easily have been referring to Thomas Jefferson.[14] By 1774, Jefferson had come to favor not only greater American autonomy, he feared for the safety of "those rights which god and the laws have given equally and independently to all."[15] To his way of thinking, London's policies were all the more outrageous in light of everything the colonists had done to help expand Britain's empire.

The Coercive Acts made it clear that London had drawn a line in the sand. If the colonists failed to submit to Parliament's unlimited authority, it would mean war. Jefferson was defiant. He believed that "no other Legislature" save the House of Burgesses "may rightfully exercise authority over" the inhabitants of Virginia. Any attempt by Parliament to do so would violate the "privileges they [Virginians] hold as the common rights of mankind" to be governed by representatives of their own choosing.[16]

In the crisis brought on by the Coercive Acts, the colonists thought it essential to present a united American front and to determine their response collectively. They opted to meet in a national congress in Philadelphia in September 1774 to settle on a course of action. Jefferson fell ill en route to the August meeting of the Virginia assembly that was to select the members of its delegation to the congress. One scholar labeled it "a typical act of avoidance" on the part of Jefferson.[17] But it is more likely that he was felled by another stress-induced malady—one brought on not from fear of having to attend the Continental Congress but from anxiety that he would not be chosen as one of the province's congressmen.

Indeed, Jefferson so badly wished to attend the Congress that he drafted a set of instructions for Virginia's delegation, in the hope of improving his chances of being chosen. His composition was a lengthy treatise on imperial constitutional matters and the transgressions of both Parliament and the king. It was filled with daring assertions, which demonstrated beyond a shadow of a doubt that by the summer of 1774, some nine months before the outbreak of war, Jefferson was far more radical than most Americans. He couched what he wrote as a legal treatise that showed the way toward recon- ciliation, but the tenor of his composition suggests that he had already reached a point in his thinking where he saw American independence as preferable to any likely imperial relationship. Jefferson did not advocate independence—to have done so would have been impolitic—but his argument constituted a bridge between the common threads of radical thought prior to the Coercive Acts and the unrestrained radicalism of Thomas Paine's *Common Sense* that lay eighteen months down the road.

Since the beginning of imperial troubles, colonial protestors had main- tained that Parliament had no right to tax the colonists. Henry had said so in his flaming speech in 1765, the House of Burgesses had taken that position in its resolutions attacking the Stamp Act, and nearly every colony had followed suit. In *Letters from a Farmer in Pennsylvania*, the most popular pamphlet on imperial troubles published in America before 1776, John Dickinson of Penn- sylvania had taken a similar line. But while Dickinson had disputed Parlia- ment's right to tax the colonists, he argued that it must have the right to regulate American trade for "the common good of all."[18] Acknowledging Parliament's right to control colonial commerce was popular in the merchant- dominated northern colonies, but Jefferson had taken a different stance. He urged Virginia's delegates to Congress to declare that every piece of Ameri- can legislation passed by Parliament was "void." Parliament, he said, "has no right to exercise authority over us."

More than a few American insurgents would have agreed with Jefferson, but to this point, none had charged that the monarch was complicit in Brit- ain's allegedly iniquitous designs on America. Jefferson not only eschewed the customarily servile language the colonists used when writing of the mon- arch, but he also fumed at the king's having strayed beyond his legitimate executive role to cooperate with Parliament in its "many unwarrantable in-croachments and usurpations," especially its "wanton exercise of . . . power" in sending troops to the colonies in peacetime and in negating colonial legislation. He excoriated George III for having responded indifferently to the colonists' petitions for redress and for his heedlessness of American interests, including his refusal to permit the colonists to migrate across the Appalachians. The monarch's behavior, Jefferson wrote, threatened to stake out his reputation as "a blot in the page of history."

In what remained of his instructions, Jefferson proceeded from the radical to the bizarre. In a labyrinthine and utterly fictitious version of English history and law—one that historian Joseph Ellis characterized as "cartoonlike"—he denied the Crown's authority to dispose of land and even maintained that those who had migrated from England to America had left the jurisdiction of the mother country.[19] He sounded like a man who was desperate to stake a claim to be included in Virginia's delegation.

Jefferson's attempt failed. For one thing, nearly everything he had written was too extreme for his colleagues. Jefferson subsequently said that he had taken "our true ground," but Virginia's assemblymen understood that his views were far in advance of those of most Americans in 1774. Solidarity with the northern colonies was imperative. Only a united stand might make the imperial government back down short of war, and only a union of all the colonies could successfully implement a national boycott of British trade or effectively wage war, if it came to that. Jefferson was not chosen for still another reason. The assembly selected a star-studded seven-member delegation to send to Philadelphia. It included Patrick Henry, Richard Henry Lee, and George Washington, together with other worthies, including the Speaker of the House and a former attorney general. Jefferson had simply not done enough by this juncture to be thought the equal of the luminaries who were chosen. The delegates were instructed to agree to an embargo of British trade and to warn London that its enforcement of the tax on tea and the Coercive Acts would invite American reprisals.[20]

Nevertheless, Jefferson's impassioned scribbling was not wasted. Without his knowledge, friends in the assembly published his essay as a pamphlet, giving it a less-than-catchy title: *A Summary View of the Rights of British America*. It did not appear until near the end of the year, but in politics, timing is often everything. It was Jefferson's good fortune that by the time his treatise began to be widely read, in the spring of 1775, war with Great Britain had begun, making a wide swath of the public receptive to his condemnation of Parliament and the king. That his literary skills were a cut above the norm also attracted attention. Articulate Americans familiar with the scores of pamphlets already published on the imperial troubles were accustomed to turgid, legalistic jargon. Jefferson's writing was muscular, crisp, and lucid. For example, in discussing the limits of Britain's authority over the colonies, John Adams, in a pamphlet that appeared nearly simultaneously, wrote: "This *statum Walliae*, as well as the whole case and history of that principality, is well worthy of the attention and study of Americans. . . . '*Nos itaque*,' says King Ed. I." That was followed by an eighty-nine-word paragraph entirely in Latin. Here is how Jefferson said the same thing: "Can any one reason be assigned why 160,000 electors in the island of Great Britain should give law to four millions in the states of America, every individual of whom is equal to every individual of them in virtue, in understanding, and in bodily strength?"[21]

Jefferson added: "Single acts of tyranny may be ascribed to the accidental opinion of a day; but a series of oppressions . . . pursued unalterably thro' every change of ministers, too plainly prove a deliberate, systematical plan of reducing us to slavery." And: "The god who gave us life, gave us liberty at the same time: the hand of force may destroy, but cannot disjoin them."[22] *A Summary View* brought Jefferson a deserved reputation as a superior writer and thinker. It also led his most radical brethren in the northern colonies to see him as a soul mate.

Alexander Hamilton published his thoughts on the imperial crisis at nearly the same moment that Jefferson's *Summary View* appeared. Hamilton's knowledge of the Anglo-American dispute must have been limited before he took up residence in Manhattan, but he was a fast learner. He was also a keenly ambitious young man who had come to North America to make his mark, and when imperial tensions grew in 1774, Hamilton had to see opportunities for his ascension. There can be no doubt that he also understood that he and his world stood on the brink of a great historic moment.

Hamilton seized it. He hurriedly defended the Boston Tea Party in a short essay for a New York newspaper. After word of the Coercive Acts reached America the following spring, Hamilton, still a collegian, spoke at a mass meeting near the King's College campus. He advocated a national congress and a boycott of British trade. In November 1774 the colonists learned that the Continental Congress had defied Parliament's claim of unlimited authority. In fact, it had agreed to boycott British trade, demanded the repeal of all objectionable parliamentary legislation, and urged each colony to ready its militia for the possibility of war. As its aggressive actions appeared to make war inevitable, a number of the most conservative colonists wrote pamphlets denouncing Congress. Likely recalling the benefits he had derived from his essay on the Caribbean hurricane two years earlier, Hamilton answered one of the Tory pamphleteers, Samuel Seabury, an Anglican clergyman who had written under the pseudonym "A. W. Farmer." Hamilton's plangent rejoinder, *A Full Vindication of the Measures of the Congress*, appeared on December 15, 1774. Seabury answered with another pamphlet, prompting Hamilton, who had just celebrated his twentieth birthday, to dash off an eighty-page retort titled *The Farmer Refuted*. It was published in late February 1775.

While Jefferson's essay had an air of the meditative and philosophical about it, Hamilton's tracts had a slash-and-burn quality. Hamilton was young and seeking recognition, as well as writing to rebut a specific Tory assault on Congress. But those factors hardly mattered. Hamilton's style never changed significantly over the years. There was a no-holds-barred tone to nearly every pamphlet and essay that he penned. In these two endeavors, Hamilton characterized the foes of Congress as "Bad men" with "mad imaginations" who engaged in "sophistry" as they tried to "dupe" and "dazzle" the American public. The "Farmer" only pretended to have America's interests at heart, Hamilton charged, while in fact, those who defended Parliament and the ministry bore a "violent antipathy . . . to the natural rights of mankind." The reality was, he said, "We are threatened with absolute slavery."

Despite Hamilton's hostile tone, his argument was more temperate than Jefferson's. He recognized Parliament's right to regulate American commerce and conceded that the colonists' "dependence . . . on the King" was "just and rational." His "favourite wish," he said, was that the colonies and mother country might be reconciled.

Hamilton's compositions were redundant and overly long. His initial pamphlet was more than twice the length of *A Summary View*, and his two tracts combined were tenfold longer than Jefferson's succinct essay. Furthermore, Hamilton said nothing about the imperial crisis that was new or original, or very daring. Unlike Jefferson, he was careful to remain within the general parameters of what American protestors had been saying for the past ten years about parliamentary powers and the rights of the colonists. Hamilton was hoping to make a name for himself in New York, one of the most conservative colonies. So conservative was the province, in fact, that its assembly initially refused to ratify the actions taken by the First Continental Congress or elect delegates to the Second Congress, scheduled to meet in May 1775.[23] Viewed from that perspective, it was bold of Hamilton to write the pamphlets. And considering that he had not yet completed college, Hamilton's achievement was little short of amazing.

Moreover, while his constitutional arguments offered nothing new, he had served up something novel in the literature of the American insurgency. He may have been the first in print to maintain that Britain could not win a war with the colonists. Hamilton not only predicted that France and Spain would assist America, but he also envisioned that by using Fabian tactics America could prevent a British victory. The colonists could "evade a pitched battle" and instead "harass and exhaust the [British] soldiery" until the enemy's rate of attrition finally led it to make peace.[24]

War broke out six weeks after the appearance of *The Farmer Refuted*. The ministry of Frederick Lord North responded to the actions of Congress by ordering the use of force to suppress the colonial rebellion. Fighting began on April 19, 1775, when British regulars carried out a mission to destroy a rebel arsenal in Concord, Massachusetts. As word of the bloodletting spread, a war spirit seized America. Volunteer militia units sprouted like weeds in colony after colony. Hamilton and several fellow students joined one in Manhattan that was called the Corsicans. The proud young soldiers wore brown leather caps bearing the inscription "Liberty or Death" and skin-tight green jackets emblazoned with the words "God and Our Right." Hamilton pulsated with martial fervor, but in May, when an angry mob descended on the campus bent on roughing up the Tory-inclined president of King's College, the young student-warrior risked life and limb to address the crowd, delaying its advance until his benefactor could escape to safety.

By late June the Second Continental Congress had created an armed force, the Continental army, and appointed George Washington to be its commander. A second great battle had also been fought, this time on the grassy slopes and scarred peak of Bunker Hill, just outside Boston. Nearly one thousand British regulars were casualties in the engagement. Hamilton had been busy too. Having put aside his studies, he attacked new parliamentary legislation in two short essays for the *New-York Gazetteer*.[25] Late in the summer, he faced danger for the first time in the war. Together with more than a dozen collegiate militiamen, Hamilton came under fire from a Royal Navy warship as he and his comrades helped move cannon from the exposed Battery at the southern tip of Manhattan. The college boys fired back ineffectually with their heavy artillery.

As the leaves turned in the fall, Hamilton resumed his studies, though he did not ignore the war and colonial rebellion. Before attending class, he took part in the daily military drill, always conducted in the chilly, faint light of sunrise, on the spacious grounds of St. Paul's Church. His regimen was demanding—much as Jefferson's had been when he was the same age. Hamilton was soldiering, studying, and wielding his pen on behalf of the insurgency. Writing under the pseudonym "Monitor," he ground out fourteen essays in fourteen weeks for the *New-York Journal*. He added little to what he had said in his responses to the "Farmer," and in fact, portions of these essays were culled intact from his previous pamphlets.

Hamilton focused on the depredations of Parliament and, unlike Jefferson, said little about the behavior of the Crown. Furthermore, whereas Jefferson saw British actions as stemming from deep-rooted maladies within the British system, Hamilton saw a conspiracy at work. A "few artful men behind the curtain" in London had gained traction. Through "bribery and corruption" these miscreants had pushed the implementation of the new colonial policies. Their object had been to "enrich themselves by the plunder and spoils of their dependent colonies." If this cabal succeeded, he warned, the colonies someday would be governed by "needy courtiers" who relied on standing armies to maintain their rule. With regard to Parliament, however, Hamilton had made one giant step. Twelve months earlier he, like those in the First Congress, had acquiesced in Parliament's regulation of American trade. Now Hamilton contended that "All Parliamentary power over them [the colonists] has been mere usurpation." He was keeping step with Congress, which during the first week of December repudiated all ties to Parliament.[26]

What Hamilton had written before the war had meshed with the sentiments of most Americans. But hostilities had a jarring impact that made much in the "Monitor" series seem dated. Indeed, "Monitor's" ideas seemed antiquated next to Jefferson's in *A Summary View*, which had been penned some eighteen months earlier. With considerable justification, Jefferson once claimed that his prewar pamphlet was "the first publication which carried the claim of our rights their whole length"—that is, to the very doorstep of independence.[27] Hamilton had not gone nearly that far, and when Thomas Paine's *Common Sense* hit the streets early in 1776, in the midst of the "Monitor's" run, the young New Yorker's views seemed especially archaic.

Paine, a skilled artisan who had recently emigrated from England to Philadelphia, demystified government, which the citizenry had been taught to believe was so complex that it must be left to the educated and social elite. No good reason existed, Paine declared, why the people should not share in the governing process. He additionally demythologized monarchical rule, showing that it was a system that elevated incompetents and rogues to the throne, where they spent their time making wars and giving away titles to well-placed sycophants. For many colonists—perhaps for most—Paine drove a spike through the heart of the yearning for reconciliation. Why, he asked, should the colonists bequeath sovereignty to a "second hand government" three thousand miles away? The imperial government ruled on behalf of England's social and economic elite, giving the interests of the colonists only secondary consideration. He insisted that imperial commercial laws were harmful to colonial prosperity. Furthermore, colonial ties made it certain that Americans would forever be dragged into England's plundering wars. In contrast, American independence offered the promise of peace, prosperity, freedom, and happiness. Depicting the desperate war that was unfolding as a decisive historic event, Paine promised that victory and independence held the promise of the birthday of a new age of liberty for humankind.[28]

Hamilton had said next to nothing of American independence. Nor had he written a word about revolutionary change. Only in the wake of *Common Sense* did his gaze turn toward the British monarchy. "Monitor" suddenly mentioned the "black catalogue of royal iniquities" that dotted the historical landscape, a sad chronicle of "ambition and avarice . . . pride, caprice and cruelty." If George III was part of the "mischiefs" afflicting America, he "must be a despot." Yet, Hamilton never charged the British monarch with culpability in the alleged plot to oppress the colonists, and after one essay—the twelfth in the series—he said nothing more about royal authority. His closest approach to the topic of independence came in two oblique statements. The war, he said, had brought the imperial crisis to the "last extremity." He also said that in the past the colonists had submitted to London's hegemony "for conveniency sake," implying that Americans must be given greater autonomy, or else. But the overall tone of the series was that America was waging war to reconcile with Great Britain and its monarch, a happy and fortuitous event that would take place once the "Ministry [was] driven from the post they have occupied."[29]

Writing such a large number of essays in such a brief time was an impressive feat, all the more so as the author celebrated his twenty-first birthday in the course of his contribution. Nevertheless, circumstances—not to mention the American outlook—were rapidly changing, and Hamilton's outlook did not always keep pace. His continued insistence that America owed affection and obedience to the king was in line with the thinking of the most conservative colonists, but to a steadily increasing number of his readers it must have seemed misplaced and obsolete.

If Hamilton's ideas were slow to change, his life was transforming. Hard on the heels of his last "Monitor" essay, King's College, which was seen by many as a Tory haven, was seized by patriot forces and turned into a military hospital. At about the same time, in mid-March, Hamilton left his militia unit to enter the Continental army. He had been offered a position as an aide to Lord Stirling, a brigadier general, but Hamilton wanted no part of a desk job. He wanted action, acclaim, glory, and rapid advancement, and to achieve that he set about reading books on gunnery and received some instruction from a former "British bombardier" who lived in Manhattan. Ultimately, through the influence of well-placed New Yorkers, including John Jay and Alexander McDougall (a longtime Sons of Liberty activist who had married well and prospered), Hamilton accepted a commission as a captain and became the commander of an artillery company raised by the revolutionary government of New York. His decision to soldier was hardly surprising as, ever since he was a boy, he had longed for a war to make his name. At last, he had his war and he was committed to the cause. He was prepared, he said, to "seal with my blood the sentiments defended by my pen."[30] Passionate young Captain Hamilton was ready to serve, and to shine and win laurels.

While Hamilton donned a uniform, Jefferson worked in the House of Burgesses to get Virginia's militia mobilized, as Congress had requested.[31] He also drafted the legislature's response to a so-called peace plan offered by the British prime minister. Lord North's Conciliatory Proposal was a sham, and Jefferson treated it as such. Mindful that many legislators prayed for the empire's salvation, he tempered his composition, seeking to keep it in sync with the declarations of the Continental Congress. But Jefferson did assert that Virginia wished "a free trade with all the world," which was tantamount to demanding an end to Great Britain's century-old imperial trade regulations.[32]

When Jefferson learned in May 1775 of the bloody fighting in Massachusetts, he privately remarked that the advent of war "has cut off our last hopes of reconciliation," a more radical view than Hamilton would articulate in his *New-York Journal* essays nine months later.[33] One only had to read between the lines of *A Summary View* to see that Jefferson was ready for American independence in 1774, and his trenchant view was confirmed once Great Britain resorted to force.

Three weeks after war erupted, the Second Continental Congress convened. A couple of weeks later the Virginia assembly added Jefferson, now in his sixth year in the House of Burgesses, to the colony's delegation in Congress. Most who served in Congress were unknown to their colleagues when they arrived in Philadelphia. There were exceptions, of course, including Washington, Franklin, Dickinson, and Samuel Adams. Jefferson was now another whose reputation preceded him.

His arrival on June 20, 1775, was a bit conspicuous. He clattered along Philadelphia's cobbled streets in a handsome phaeton, accompanied by two slaves dressed in livery, four horses, and a guide he had hired in Wilmington. A Rhode Island congressman immediately wrote home that "the famous Mr. Jefferson" had entered Congress. Jefferson's fame, such as it was, was due to *A Summary View*, which had probably been read by most delegates. John Adams had perused it and called it a "very handsome public Paper" penned by "a fine Writer." Later, he recollected that Jefferson entered Congress with a "reputation for literature" and "a happy talent of composition."[34]

In 1775, Jefferson was thirty-two and in many ways a striking figure. He wore fashionable clothing, though he could not be said to be clothes-conscious. In an age when the median height of full-grown American males was five feet seven, Jefferson stood six feet two. He had reddish hair, a some-what ruddy complexion, and hazel eyes. Many remarked on his "mild and pleasing countenance." No one described him as handsome, but none thought him unattractive. Jefferson was slender, strong and sinewy, and he tended to stand ramrod straight. One of his slaves later described him as a "strait-bodied man . . . a straight-up man," and a longtime overseer at Monticello once char-acterized his posture as "straight as a gun barrel." However, he slouched badly when seated, causing some to think him ungainly and awkward. He never outgrew his boyish shyness, and with strangers he was anything but outgo-ing. Numerous new acquaintances thought him "reserved even to coldness," "serious, nay even cold," or "cool and reserved," but those who got to know Jefferson variously described him as gentle, polite, thoughtful, kind, humble, gracious, good-humored, and cheerful. He possessed "all the qualities which can arouse esteem and affection," said one observer. Nearly everyone who left a description of Jefferson was struck by his incredible intellect, and not a few thought him the most engaging conversationalist they had ever met. He was widely regarded as orderly, diligent, and industrious; John Adams thought him "prompt, frank, explicit and decisive." Many colleagues were surprised by his reluctance to join in the congressional debates. Adams served with him in Philadelphia for a year and "never heard him utter three sentences together" on the floor of Congress. Jefferson was like Washington and Frank-lin in that regard, but he was singular in other ways. Adams subsequently recalled that no congressman, not even Samuel Adams, he pointedly said, was more "prompt, frank, explicit, and decisive" than Jefferson.[35]

Around fifty members of Congress were in Philadelphia at all times in 1775–1776, and some were never asked by their colleagues to take on an im-portant assignment. Jefferson barely had time to unpack his bags before he was assigned to a committee charged with preparing a statement explaining why America was fighting this war. Above all, Congress wanted a declaration that would gin up the citizenry's willingness to serve and sacrifice. The com-mittee turned to the newcomer with the reputation as a wordsmith to write the first draft.

Jefferson, who took up this task six months before Hamilton commenced his "Monitor" series, prepared a hardy statement, which Congress titled Dec-laration on the Causes and Necessity of Taking Up Arms. Jefferson's draft went too far for John Dickinson, his cautious colleague on the committee. The leader of the congressional faction that sought reconciliation with the mother country, Dickinson responded with a draft of his own. He retained much that Jefferson had included and even took a harsher tone in his denunciation of many of Parliament's acts, but he excised Jefferson's implicit repudiation of all Parliamentary authority and added a statement denying categorically that America was fighting for its independence.[36] Jefferson did not make a fight of it, probably because his fellow Virginia delegates had coached him on their strategy of dealing with the more conservative delegates. The hard-line congressmen, which included most in Virginia's delegation, were biding their time. They believed that the war would radicalize American opinion, and when it did, the hard-liners would control Congress. In the meantime, as their leader John Adams put it: "Progress must be slow. It is like a large Fleet sailing under Convoy. The fleetest Sailors must wait for the dullest and slowest. Like a Coach and six, the swiftest Horses must be slackened, and the slowest quickened, that all may keep an even Pace."[37]

Many of the hard-liners, including Jefferson, John Adams, and Samuel Adams, covertly favored independence by June 1775. For them, the cautious progress that John Adams had alluded to was the march toward the final break with the mother country, and it was not merely slow; it was snail-like. Over a span of eleven months after Jefferson came to Philadelphia, Congress made at least three substantive moves. It resolved that Parliament had no jurisdiction over the colonies and that the colonists' fealty to the king was their sole link to the British Empire; it threw open America's ports to foreign trade; and it conducted secret talks with France leading to the receipt of military aid.

Jefferson was not on hand when all of these steps were taken. In fact, he was seldom in Philadelphia. Forty days after Jefferson's arrival, Congress adjourned and, like all of his colleagues, he went home. He was back in Philadelphia when Congress reconvened and remained there for three months, from September 30 until December 28, when he returned to Monticello to be with his family. A second daughter, eighteenth-month-old Jane Randolph, had died late in the summer and he doubtless wanted to be with Martha during this time of grief. It was not unusual for congressmen to take a hiatus of four to six weeks from their daily grind, and that was what Jefferson must have envisaged when he made the trek back to Virginia. As it turned out, his absence stretched for some seventeen weeks. In March, just as he was preparing to return north, his mother died unexpectedly. Soon thereafter, Jefferson fell ill with another migraine or stress-induced headache. He did not return to Philadelphia until mid-May, arriving just as Congress voted to ask each province to establish a government free of all ties to the Crown.[38] On the day that

Congress acted, Virginia legislators in Williamsburg instructed their delegates in Philadelphia to ask Congress to declare American independence.

Williamsburg, not Philadelphia, was where Jefferson wished to be. On his
second full day back in Congress he wrote the provincial legislature asking to
be recalled so that he could participate in the writing of the constitution that
would be needed if Virginia became an independent state. Jefferson also said
that he wished to be nearer to his wife, as he was in an "uneasy anxious state"
over her health.[39] However, his request to be permitted to return to Virginia
was denied, and Jefferson remained in the Continental Congress. This turn of
events soon enabled him to engage in a grander undertaking in Philadelphia
than could ever have been the case in Williamsburg, and one that would win
him lasting fame. It may seem strange that Jefferson preferred to serve a state
rather than play on a national stage, but Virginia was 150 years old and Jefferson's roots in the province ran deep. The United States, on the other hand,
did not yet exist—and once it was created in 1776, it would face a most uncertain future. Furthermore, while Jefferson probably knew that a Declaration of
Independence was imminent, he could not have known that he would be its
principal author. If Virginia had a member on the committee that wrote such
a document, the odds were better that it would be Richard Henry Lee, the
leader of the delegation. Even if Jefferson was selected to be among those who
prepared the Declaration of Independence, the finished document would be
the product of a committee and the Congress as a whole. Little glory was to
be derived from having participated in its drafting. In fact, no document that
Congress had produced in its first two years had been memorable, and there
was no guarantee—or much reason to think—that anyone would long remember what was said in a statement proclaiming American independence.

Life and history are filled with surprises. On June 7, Lee moved that Congress declare independence. The delegates debated his motion for two days.
Jefferson did not join the discussion. He sat quietly, taking extensive notes on
what was said. By then, three weeks after returning from Monticello, he must
have guessed that he would be appointed to the drafting committee, for Lee—
who was eager to look after his economic interests—had asked to be recalled
and was, at least figuratively, packing his bags for his journey to Williamsburg. At the conclusion of the debate, Congress postponed its decision until
July 1, but it created a committee to draft the Declaration of Independence.
Lee departed for Virginia on the day the committee was created. As Virginia
had introduced the motion for independence, it was nearly a foregone conclusion that one member of its delegation would sit on the drafting committee. Jefferson, the most renowned for his writing abilities, was selected, the
lone Southerner appointed to what the congressmen would call the Commit-

tee of Five. Two of his colleagues were New Englanders, John Adams and Roger Sherman of Connecticut; the two others were representatives of the mid-Atlantic colonies, Franklin and New York's Robert R. Livingston.

The committee met for the first time on June 11 or 12 and discussed the shape and content of the document, then selected Jefferson to be its draftsman. As Adams had been the leader in Congress of the push for independence, it might seem odd that he was passed over. He subsequently said that he declined the appointment because of his multiple responsibilities. He also recollected that he nominated Jefferson to draft the document. The evidence, though sketchy, suggests that Adams's memory was faulty on both counts. The committee turned to Jefferson from the outset, probably because of his well-known talent as a writer.[40]

Jefferson was a rapid writer. Adams subsequently recalled that Jefferson wrote the draft in one or two days. His memory might have been faulty on that score too, but at most it took Jefferson five days.[41] He worked in his apartment on the second floor of the three-story, red brick home of Jacob Graff, a successful Philadelphia mason. Jefferson wrote while seated in a revolving Windsor chair with a small, folding writing desk placed across his lap, both of which had been custom-made for him by a Philadelphia cabinetmaker. He may have worked in the early morning, when it was coolest, and he may have skipped a couple of sessions of Congress in order to have longer blocks of time for completing his task.[42]

Jefferson appears to have shown the draft to Adams and Franklin before he submitted it to the full committee. His colleagues suggested only a few alterations, all modest and stylistic, such as changing "his present majesty" to "the present king of Great Britain." It is abundantly clear that the document seen by Congress was almost exclusively the work of Jefferson.[43]

After the Declaration of Independence became an acclaimed national document, Adams jealously carped that what Jefferson had drafted was unoriginal, "a juvenile declamation" that merely rehashed what others had said. To that, he added that there was "not an idea in it, but what had been hackneyed in Congress for two years before." Though accurate, Adams missed the point. Congress did not want Jefferson to write something novel. To have done so would have been foolish. Jefferson correctly understood that he was to avoid "aiming at originality of principle or sentiment." Instead, he was to capture the "tone and spirit" of "the American mind" toward the mother country's imperial policies and the king's decision to make war on them.[44]

Scholars have written countless tomes on the sources of Jefferson's ideas. They are not that complicated. He and all well-educated colonists were familiar with Enlightenment thought, especially John Locke's concept of the social contract and the outpourings of edgy English Whig polemicists since the Glorious Revolution. Myriad statements adopted by several colonial assemblies since 1765 had drawn on these sources, and so too had Congress, local committees of public safety, extralegal provincial legislatures, and scores of pamphleteers and newspaper essayists. But nothing influenced Jefferson more than the draft of the Declaration of Rights that had been recently produced by Virginia's revolutionary provincial congress, which obviously served as the template for what Jefferson wrote with regard to human rights, the philosophy of government, and the justification of revolution in the opening paragraphs of his composition.[45]

Nonetheless, Jefferson improved on his models. He succinctly explained what Great Britain had done, or was trying to do, and why those actions violated the rights of the American people. He not only demonstrated that the colonists possessed the right to rebel but also showed that they had acted with restraint through a "long train of abuses and usurpations" until it was readily apparent that the "design" of Parliament and the Crown was "to reduce them under absolute despotism." Jefferson might have simply justified America's revolution, but he went beyond that. While the Declaration severed the colonists' ties with Great Britain, it was also the first step in the creation of a new American nation. With peerless eloquence, Jefferson launched the nation that was coming into being with a ringing commitment to the most enlightened and progressive ideas: "all men are created equal," possessed God-given "inalienable rights," including "life, liberty, and the pursuit of happiness," and the people had the right to create, alter, and abolish governments of their choosing. No nation dedicated to such munificent ideals had ever been brought into creation.

None of these concepts were new, as Adams complained, but Jefferson crisply brought them together in a mere 375 words in the two opening paragraphs. Others could have done that, but it is unlikely that any could have done so with the grace and melodic resplendence achieved by Jefferson. He seemed to move seamlessly from idea to idea, gliding like a vessel on smooth water. Effortlessly, he shifted from the rights of humankind to the right of revolution to a pithy decoding of America's reasons for dissolving its "political bands" with the mother country.

From there, Jefferson enumerated step by step the "injuries" that Americans had suffered as Great Britain's leaders conspired to establish "an absolute tyranny." It was a comprehensive, and damning, chronicle of London's despotism despite the "tyes of our common kindred." Above all, it was a stark indictment of the monarch, the sole imperial authority recognized by Congress since late 1775. It captured the deep feelings of betrayal that had taken

hold of Americans during the past decade, sentiments bred by the belief that
the mother country had repaid the colonists for their loyalty and assistance
in the Seven Years' War with taxes and arbitrary legislation. Once hostilities
erupted, that sense of betrayal was coupled with widespread rage, yet Congress in its repeated declarations and petitions had never adequately voiced
the unbridled fury that gripped the land. Jefferson articulated those super-
charged feelings. Britain's leaders had long been "unfeeling" toward their
colonists. Now they had "become the executioners of their friends & brethren." A monarch who was part of such outrages was "unfit to be the ruler" of
a free people. That sad truth had "given the last stab to agonizing affection"
on the part of the colonists. . . . We must endeavor to forget our former love
for them."

The Declaration of Independence was widely disseminated as a print document, but many listened as it was read aloud. General Washington had it
read to his troops, Abigail Adams heard it read from the balcony of the Massachusetts State House, a member of Pennsylvania's Committee of Safety
read it to a large throng gathered on the lawn of Independence Hall, and
around the country on village commons and the steps of county courthouses,
leather-lunged local officials read the document to raptly attentive audiences.[46] Those who listened discovered a magical quality to Jefferson's hand-
iwork, for he was a penman with a genius for the cadence of the written word,
a writer conversant with music who had a feel for what one scholar has called
the "rhythmical pauses . . . comparable to musical bars."[47] Nor was that all.
Historians Andrew Burstein and Nancy Isenberg have demonstrated that the
Declaration lent itself to being "read theatrically." Listeners were made to feel
the pain, disappointment, reproach, and anger that lay at the heart of Jefferson's "seductive" creation.[48]

Jefferson may have written a document to give birth to the new nation, but
first the war had to be won if the United States was to survive. With that in
mind, Jefferson consciously produced a war document. This may have been
one reason that he substituted "life, liberty, and the pursuit of happiness" for
the more conventional trilogy of "life, liberty, and property." By the summer
of 1776 it was apparent that America faced a long struggle to secure independence, and it was equally evident that, in a protracted war, many propertyless
Americans would be asked to bear arms. They, too, had to be given a reason
for serving. Furthermore, most in Congress understood that victory in a prolonged war would likely hinge on foreign help. Jefferson announced American independence to a "candid world," carefully adding that the new American
nation possessed "the full power to . . . contract alliances, establish commerce, &
do all other acts and things which independent states may of right do."

Jefferson submitted the document to Congress on Friday, June 28. On Monday, Congress took up the question of independence. John Adams anticipated the "greatest debate of all," and he was not disappointed.[49] John Dickinson was on his feet first to speak against independence, and despite the oppressive heat in Congress's closed chamber on a ninety-degree afternoon, his address lasted for nearly two hours. He warned that if the war was lost, the colonists would face the fury of British retribution. To prevent losing the war, he added, the colonists would need French help. But independence procured in that fashion would be a sham, for the autocratic, Roman Catholic French would become America's new masters following the victory. In all likelihood, he continued, the war could not be won even with French assistance. In fact, it was likely that no one could win the war. In that event, Europe's superpowers might break the stalemate by imposing peace, and by partitioning America among themselves. Dickinson wanted to continue waging war for reconciliation—not independence—and promised Congress that in a year or two Great Britain would have to make the concessions that the First Congress had sought. Americans would be left secure and prosperous, and free, within the Britain Empire. He closed by remarking that the "Book of Fate" portended a "dreadful" future for an independent America.[50]

John Adams was the first to respond to Dickinson. At some point in Adams's lengthy rejoinder, distant thunder could be heard. It came steadily closer, resounding through every nook and cranny of the State House, and soon boomed as if field artillery was being fired in the nearby street. The fleecy white clouds of morning had long since darkened, then turned a deep black. In the midst of Adams's address, the sky opened. Large drops splattered on the tall windows in Congress's chamber, and in only a moment a lashing rain slanted against the glass. The room darkened. The temperature plummeted. Candles were lit. Through it all, Adams continued to speak, arguing that the war could not be won—could not even be carried on much longer—without foreign assistance, and that no European nation would aid America so long as its objective was reconciliation within the mother country. Independence must be declared.[51]

It was late afternoon when Adams sat down. But other speakers followed. It appeared that every congressman wanted to say something. Each recognized that this was a historic day, and each wanted to be a part of history, to possibly say something that would be remembered by posterity. None succeeded in saying anything memorable. In fact, only Dickinson's speech—and merely the notes for his talk—has survived from that long day of speech making. It is not known whether Jefferson spoke, though it is probable that he did. The speeches continued until night gathered over Philadelphia. At that point, the delegates, who had not eaten since breakfast, adjourned.

The congressmen returned the next morning and, after first tending to other business, once again took up the issue of independence. No one rose to speak. Nothing was left to be said. Noon was approaching on the morning of July 2 when Congress declared American independence. The vote was 12 to 0, with New York abstaining. Its delegates had not been authorized by the authorities at home to vote for the break with Great Britain, but the authorization came a few days later and New York cast its vote for independence later in July. Congress had voted unanimously for American independence.

Immediately following the vote on July 2, the congressmen became editors, poring over Jefferson's composition. These unsparing editors made nearly forty changes to his draft. Their greatest change—and possibly the most telling deletion for the course of American history—was in striking Jefferson's magnificent, if historically inaccurate, attack on the king for having imposed slavery on the colonies. The passage was struck at the behest of Georgia and South Carolina, and with its obliteration went Jefferson's condemnation of slavery's "assemblage of horrors" and his declaration that the British monarch had violated the "sacred [natural] rights" of blacks as well as whites.

Congress pruned what Jefferson had written by a third, deleting or combining some of the twenty-seven charges that Jefferson had brought against the monarch. Jefferson fumed at what he thought was the desecration of his craftsmanship, but aside from the sentences on slavery, Congress had done him a favor. His colleagues had taken a superb draft and made it better by shortening it. The draft that Congress edited was Jefferson's document, and the Declaration of Independence that the American people, and the world, read and heard remained Jefferson's. Congress and the committee charged with preparing the draft had recognized that Jefferson was uniquely capable of producing a resplendent and awe-inspiring Declaration of Independence, and he had done just that.[52]

CHAPTER 3

"IS MY COUNTRY THE BETTER FOR MY HAVING LIVED"

MAKING THE AMERICAN REVOLUTION

SOME COLONISTS who wished to break ties with Great Britain longed for the new United States to replicate the social and political structure of the former mother country. Others, Jefferson among them, anticipated that independence would usher in sweeping reforms.

Following independence, Jefferson once again asked to be recalled to Williamsburg so that he might have a hand in drafting the state's first constitution. In part, he wanted to leave Philadelphia because it was readily apparent that Congress could not lead the reformation of America. It had been created in 1774 to meet the threat posed by London, and now its role was to be the central manager of the war effort, including American diplomacy. Even if Congress had possessed the power to initiate reforms, it would not have done so. Reforms divide, and America required unity if it was to win the war.

This time, Williamsburg complied with his wishes, and Jefferson was back in Virginia by summer's end, though too late to participate in drafting the state's first constitution. During his first three years back at home, a time of blood-drenched battles and nearly unparalleled suffering by many American soldiers, the war was mostly a faraway event for Jefferson. He seldom mentioned it in his correspondence, and it would be a stretch to suggest that he directly assisted the new nation in its life-and-death struggle. In fact, a few days after reaching home, he declined Congress's request that he join Benjamin Franklin and Silas Deane on a mission to Paris to gain French assistance. Richard Henry Lee had written a letter imploring him to go, saying that the very survival of the United States hinged on bringing France into the war. Jefferson rebuffed his friend's entreaty, pleading that his wife's health was precarious. The state of Martha's health is unknown, though Jefferson had evidently thought her well enough to leave her at home alone for four months that spring and summer. Jefferson said later that he neither wanted to be separated from his wife nor to "expose [her] to the dangers of the sea, and of capture by British ships"; he also subsequently acknowledged that he wished to remain in Virginia, "where much was to be done . . . in new modeling" the state socially and politically. Suspecting that his friend's excuse about Martha's health was spurious, Lee unambiguously told Jefferson that he should give up his "private enjoyments" at a time when so many were making enormous sacrifices.[1]

Although Jefferson relinquished little of his private life, he did not forsake all public responsibilities. He attended the meetings of the state legislature, spending up to eighteen weeks each year for the next three years in Williamsburg. The war proceeded without him, but Jefferson saw himself, and a few others of like mind, as the embodiment of the American Revolution. He was committed not just to change but also, in some instances, to such pervasive reforms that they could in truth be considered revolutionary. Furthermore, he hoped the reforms adopted by Virginia might serve as a model for all the new American states.[2]

For most, the conviction that Britain's imperial policies were tyrannical was sufficient reason to commit to the colonial rebellion. Jefferson, however, was both intellectually curious and a disciple of the Enlightenment. He took it for granted that nothing should be taken for granted. Everything was fair game for questioning and rational reassessment, and he tried to understand the reasons for London's behavior. His scrutiny led him to the conclusion that Great Britain groaned under a "vicious . . . Patrician order," an "aristocracy of wealth" that was "of more harm and danger, than benefit, to society." Over time, a "distinct set of families" had become "privileged by law." These families perpetuated their elite status through wealth in land, but also through the patronage of monarchs who "habitually selected [the] counselors of State" from the ranks of the aristocracy. It was a tailor-made system through which the monarchy gained the backing of the nobility for advancing the "interests and will of the crown." Unavoidably in this scheme of things, royalty and the aristocracy colluded first in abusing the people of England, then of Ireland. It was inevitable that someday they would similarly seek to victimize the colonists. That day had dawned, in Jefferson's judgment, when the Stamp Act was passed.

These views ignited a rage that shone through in Jefferson's writings about Anglo-American affairs, a deeper, more implacable anger than burned in the hearts of many of his fellow revolutionaries. His indignation was likely stoked as well by the belief that his years of study had made him the equal, and probably the superior, of most of the English elite, the metropolitan gentility that not only looked with condescension on colonial gentlemen but that also exploited commoners and sought to take advantage of Americans. Jefferson's writings bristled toward a Parliament that wished to "arrogate over us." He cataloged the King's and the titled nobility's long list of "treasonable crimes against their people." He denounced the Crown's repeated "unjustifiable exertion of power." Britain's elite, he charged, had "indulged themselves in every exorbitance which their avarice could dictate." It was ordained that these "worthless ministerial dependants" would prey on the people for sustenance, and it was no less inescapable that, like vultures, they would seek through Parliament's "unjust encroachment" on the rights of the people to plunder those in England and the American colonists.[3]

Jefferson was hardly the only American rebel to exhibit such fury. But he was set apart from most, both in seeing malign imperial policies as rooted in the social and political system of the mother country and in his conviction that Virginia had in some ways come to resemble Great Britain itself.[4] A handful of "great families" dominated Virginia just as their counterparts monopolized power in the mother country. He knew that in such a society, men of "virtue and talent" who were not well-born might never reach their full potential. Nor would the "interests of society" be truly served so long as an aristocracy "founded on wealth and birth, without either virtue or talents," predominated and perpetuated itself through the "transmission of [its] property from generation to generation." In the sweep of time, Virginia would mirror the decay that blighted England.

Though part of what he referred to as Virginia's "Pseudo-aristoi," Jefferson fervently believed in providing greater opportunities for all men than could ever exist in an aristocratic society. He was drawn to an alternative to aristocratic rule, a system that could provide for the well-being and personal fulfillment of a far greater percentage of the citizenry.[5] Jefferson was articulating his belief in republicanism. Historian Gordon S. Wood has called republicanism "a radical ideology, as radical for the eighteenth century as Marxism was to be for the nineteenth century." It struck at the underpinnings of the old order. For centuries, political theorists had insisted that people were too corrupt and selfish to be left to their own devices; plunder and chaos would ensue. A monarchical society was preferable, they insisted, for through it the citizenry coalesced in allegiance to the king, acknowledging their dependency on a monarch who presumably governed for the greater good of all. Jefferson and his fellow republicans rejected such thinking. Jefferson believed that "dependence begets subservience and venality, suffocates the germ of virtue, and prepares fit tools for the designs of ambition." The monarchical system was a lie. It was "treason against the people . . . against mankind in general." Like other republicans, Jefferson believed that a free citizenry could be responsible and patriotic. For republicans, as Wood put it, the American Revolution "promised nothing less than a massive reordering" of the lives of ordinary people, one that was grounded in "a fundamental shift in values and a change in the very character of American society."[6]

Jefferson never sought to unravel the reasons behind his reform proclivities. One of his best biographers, Merrill Peterson, concluded that Jefferson probably "did not understand them himself."[7] Jefferson did say that his convictions stemmed from his "life of inquiry and reflection," though he also insisted that his transforming journey had begun in college, where he "heard more good sense, more rational and philosophical conversations than in all my life."[8] But something made Jefferson receptive to the new ideas he heard from Professor Small and others, and to reconsidering old ways of thinking. His republicanism may have been nourished by his shock at recognizing that many of his dissolute and unproductive college classmates—most of whom were scions of aristocratic families—would someday be politically and socially powerful simply because of their birthright. It may have come from sitting with their ilk in the House of Burgesses, where he discovered soon enough that given the "bigoted intolerance" of most of his fellow assemblymen, nothing "liberal could expect success."[9] It is also possible that Jefferson may have sensed a contemptuous or patronizing tone among greater planters who interacted with his uneducated, parvenu father. He possibly felt that doors were shut to Peter Jefferson because he had not hailed from an elite and powerful family. Or, his republicanism may have come about in a circular manner. Critical thinking might have led him to comprehend the evil of slavery, which in turn might have led him to the conviction that republicanism offered the best hope for purging the land of that stain and, simultaneously, of improving the lot of humankind.

Jefferson had launched his reform efforts prior to independence. While trapped in Philadelphia, he had drafted a constitution and sent it to Williamsburg sometime in the spring of 1776. Much that he proposed was in step with the thoughts of others who were simultaneously contemplating constitutions for their states, but one suggestion was designed to lay "the axe to the root of Pseudo-aristocracy."[10] Believing that possession of land was the key not merely to individual freedom and the pursuit of happiness but also to the very survival of an American republic, Jefferson urged Virginia to take a step that had never previously been attempted by any American province. He suggested that Virginia give fifty acres to each free, landless man. This would immediately bestow suffrage rights on all adult, white males, and it also had the potential to launch a real social and political revolution. Most assembly-men considered such largess to be too radical. Besides, in a state where great fortunes could be made from speculating in land, and in which most of the land was owned by men of the social class that dominated the assembly, Jef-ferson's proposition never stood a chance. But he did not give up. Once he ar-rived back in Virginia in the fall of 1776 and took a seat in the legislature, Jefferson worked with others to open the west. The assembly voted to make Kentucky a county. When the war was over, settlers could look forward to crossing the mountains to the bluegrass country, where cheap—if not free—land would be abundantly available.[11]

This was just the start. Five days after reentering the legislature, Jefferson took a potentially far-reaching step. He proposed that the state's legal code be reviewed and "adopted to our republican form of government." The legisla-ture agreed and appointed him to the five-member Committee of Revisors to undertake the project. Two of the revisors, not being lawyers, rapidly dropped off the committee. The three remaining members—Jefferson, Wythe, and Edmund Pendleton—agreed to equally divide the work. They also concluded that it would be too "bold" to ask the legislature to "abrogate our whole sys-tem." Furthermore, it would delay the completion of the work for an eternity. Nevertheless, the committee from the outset saw its role as one of "modify-ing" and "modernizing" Virginia's laws. In January 1777 the three revisors "repaired to our respective homes," as Jefferson said, and took up their task. Three years passed before their work was completed.[12]

Not everything recommended by the recodification committee was espe-cially enlightened, including two areas for which Jefferson was responsible. His overhaul of the criminal code reduced a staggering number of capital crimes to just two; treason and murder. However, ignoring reforms that were already in place in some parts of Europe, he recommended a string of barbaric punishments for several crimes. So harsh was his criminal code that Jefferson himself subsequently called it "revolting" to "the modern mind." It may have been that he was boxed in by others on the committee. He later hinted at hav-ing adhered to the wishes of his two colleagues who believed that macabre punishments would deter crimes.[13] The Virginia legislature, which seldom distinguished itself as a beacon of enlightenment, was so appalled by the sav-agery of the proposed criminal code that it refused to enact it.[14]

Jefferson drafted the section on slaves and free blacks as well. Despite his resplendent and inspiring passages on liberty and equality in the Declaration of Independence, he was hardly forward-looking on matters of race. In fact, his outlook was all too conventional for the time. He admitted his abhorrence of the color black and said that he found Africans' "wooly hair" and physiques to be repugnant. Accepting abundant racial stereotypes (he called them "Deep-rooted prejudices"), Jefferson believed that blacks were slow, lazy, oversexed, less capable than whites of reasoning, and on the whole an inferior race.[15] With Jefferson taking the lead, the Committee of Revisors proposed making it illegal for slaves to be brought into Virginia, a step the House of Burgesses had unsuccessfully sought before the Revolution, but which the legislature approved in 1778.

Despite his racism, Jefferson wished to abolish slavery. He thought it an abomination for both races, and he believed its abolition would break the aristocracy's stranglehold on Virginia. However, when members of the legislature who had drafted an emancipation bill asked him to include it in the revision of the laws, Jefferson demurred, though he agreed to its submission as "an amendment . . . to be offered the legislature whenever the bill should be taken up." Scholars have criticized Jefferson for refusing to incorporate the plan in the revised statutes, but he was a savvy politician who doubtless knew that the bill had no chance of passing during the war, and that to try and fail at this juncture likely would only make it more difficult to secure passage at a more favorable moment. Nevertheless, his consent to the amendment sheds light on Jefferson's thinking with regard to ending slavery in Virginia.

The bill that he tacitly endorsed provided for the gradual end to slavery and for the removal from the state of those who were set free. It stipulated that all children born to slaves following some predetermined date were to be gradually emancipated. The females were to live with their parents until age eighteen, the males until age twenty-one; during those years, they were to be trained at public expense in farming and other pursuits. Upon reaching adulthood, they were to become "free and independent," though they were to be colonized at some undisclosed location outside the state, where they were to remain under Virginia's protection until they were self-sustaining. A couple of years after this legislation was drafted, Jefferson defended the decision to require the freedmen to leave the state on the grounds that the two races could never live together in harmony. In addition, he hinted that the expulsion of emancipated blacks was necessary for warding off race-based politics that would inevitably splinter whites.[16]

The emancipation bill was never introduced. Years later, Jefferson said that "the public mind would not yet bear the proposition," and there is little reason to doubt his assertion. However, in 1783, thinking that a state constitutional convention was about to be called, Jefferson privately prepared a draft constitution (which was published in the middle of that decade). The draft specified that Virginia was not "to permit the introduction of any more slaves to reside in this state, or the continuance of slavery beyond the generation which shall be living on the 31st day of December 1800; all persons born after that day being hereby declared free." It said nothing of colonization of those who were freed. Jefferson's constitutional thinking counted for nothing, as the proposed constitutional convention never met.[17]

Though the emancipation plans went nowhere, the Committee of Revisors—following Jefferson's lead—proposed that it be made easier for slave owners to manumit their slaves, after which those who were freed would have to leave the state. So too would white women who bore children fathered by black men, and of course they would have to take their child into exile as well. Both recommendations eventually became law. The legislature also enacted a tightened slave code that Jefferson drafted, statutes that made already unsparing laws even harsher. Neither the Committee of Revisors nor the legislature considered citizenship for free blacks, and neither contemplated bequeathing to blacks the same legal rights enjoyed by whites.[18]

Jefferson waged battles for change in three other areas: land, religion, and education. During his first days back in the assembly in 1776, he secured the repeal of the entailing of estates. Entail, a carryover from medieval England, was designed to keep the land of a family intact, and under the practice the heir to entailed land could not sell the inherited property. Though not every estate in Virginia was entailed, many were, with the result that over several generations the practice had contributed to the concentration of property in fewer and fewer hands. For example, late in the seventeenth century, John Pleasants, a Tidewater planter, had entailed his nine thousand acres among three children; a century later, at the time of independence, the property remained in the hands of just three persons. Had Pleasants's land never been entailed, some four hundred of his descendants might have owned a piece of the original estate by 1776. Jefferson was not only committed to individual freedoms; he also believed that the living should not be shackled by the practices of those who had lived in earlier times. What is more, practices such as entail facilitated the hegemony of Tidewater planters in the colonial assembly. Jefferson understood that the abolition of entail would over time weaken the aristocracy and redistribute political power in Virginia. Many of Virginia's aristocrats understood that as well, and some ranted against Jefferson's "cursed bill," exclaiming that its reform-minded author was carrying on like a "midday drunkard." Some influential Virginians hated Jefferson ever afterward.[19] But their enmity did not stop him. Once the Committee of Revisors came into being, Jefferson also went after primogeniture, which required that a father's property be bequeathed to his eldest son. Like entail, primogeniture was non-compulsory, but the recodified law proposed by the committee, and enacted in 1785, eliminated the option.[20]

Virginia had greeted independence by guaranteeing freedom of religion, though, as had been true for 150 years, the province still had an established church (the Church of England before independence, the Episcopal Church thereafter). Established churches could force all citizens to attend their services and pay tithes for their support, and they not infrequently formed an alliance with the aristocracy, standing arm in arm against change. By the time Jefferson reached Williamsburg in the autumn of 1776, the legislature had been inundated with petitions from those who urged more substantive changes in the realm of religious freedom. Conservatives fought back, hoping among other things to retain laws that required church attendance and punished heresy and blasphemy. Jefferson joined the fight for greater religious freedom, which he subsequently called the "severest contest in which I have ever been engaged."[21] The battle raged for years, and its outcome was never certain. In 1777, as part of recodification, Jefferson drafted a statute for religious freedom, but he did not feel that the time was right for its introduction. Finally, in 1779, his proposed law was introduced. It would have instituted comprehensive change, literally bringing Virginia from the premodern to the modern world in the sphere of religion. It stated that "no man shall be compelled to frequent or support" any church or religion, and that none "shall be restrained, molested, or burthened . . . on account of his religious opinions or belief." It continued: "all men shall be free to profess . . . their opinions in matters of religion" and those opinions "shall in no wise diminish, enlarge, or affect their civil capacities.[22]

After a bruising struggle, the legislature postponed action on Jefferson's bill; long after he left the assembly, his friend James Madison secured its passage. It was rapidly adopted as a model for laws of religious freedom in several states, and years later was incorporated in the U.S. Constitution through the First Amendment. Jefferson prayed that it might have some influence in Europe as well. Had "the almighty begotten a thousand sons, instead of one," they could not have eradicated the "ignorance, superstition, poverty and oppression of body and mind" that churches had inflicted, he once remarked. But he believed that a law of the sort that he had written might "emancipate the minds" of Europe's masses.[23]

Next to land reform, Jefferson believed that nothing was more crucial for sustaining republicanism than providing wider educational opportunities. To do so, he said, would establish "a system by which every fibre would be eradicated of ancient or future aristocracy." He later asserted that "a nation

[that] expects to be ignorant and free . . . expects what never was and what never will be." Should the citizenry be "inattentive to public affairs," he additionally warned, officeholders "shall all become wolves." Jefferson drafted a bill that called for three years of free public education for all white children in Virginia and for the establishment of public college preparatory schools for the most promising students. Those who excelled in the prep schools were to be the recipients of three years of free education at the College of William and Mary. While it was under consideration, Jefferson called the proposed education law "by far the most important bill in our whole code." But as was the case with his forward-looking land distribution proposal, his educational recommendations were not enacted. Nor, for that matter, did the publicly endowed state library system that he advocated come into being. Jefferson's proposals failed, he charged, because the "wealthy class [was] unwilling to incur" the expense that would result from "throw[ing] on wealth the education of the poor." Not for the last time in American history, the wealthiest in society refused to make a sacrifice from which they perceived little or nothing of benefit to themselves.[24]

Jefferson had not always succeeded as a reformer, but a real revolution had been set in motion in Virginia and other colonies. "I am surprised at the Suddenness, as well as the Greatness of this Revolution," John Adams exclaimed, adding: "Idolatry to Monarchs, and servility to Aristocratical Pride was never so totally eradicated from so many Minds in so short a Time." Jefferson said that the colonists had made the transition from monarchy to republicanism "with as much ease as . . . throwing off an old and putting on a new suit of clothes."[25] Prior to independence, Jefferson had remarked that in "truth . . . the whole object of the present controversy" was the establishment of state governments that would prevent those who held power from extinguishing liberty.[26] Before the end of 1776 a majority of the states had adopted new constitutions that severely limited the authority of state governors so they could not "corrupt"—the operative word that year—the legislative branch as the English monarch was thought to have done with Parliament. Some states broadened the electorate and based representation on population.[27] Virginia's constitution made the legislature supreme and independent, but it did little to weaken the clout of the gentry. Indeed, Edmund Randolph, who helped write the constitution, said that it "was tacitly understood" that the political leadership of the aristocracy was to continue after 1776 as it had "existed under the former government."[28]

A rankled Jefferson sought without success for three years after independence to achieve a real revolution in Virginia, both in the distribution of power and in individual freedoms. Late in life, Jefferson said, "I have sometimes asked myself whether my country is the better for my having lived at all? I do not know that it is." And with a self-effacement that would have been unimaginable for many other Founding Fathers, Jefferson went on to say that had he not lived, someone else would have done what he had done, and "perhaps, a little better."[29] On that score, he was wrong. Jefferson had not made the American Revolution alone, but his personal contribution to the blossoming of independence was staggering. He had drafted the Declaration of Independence which became for contemporaries and generations yet unborn what historian Pauline Maier has accurately described as a "scripture" crystallizing the founding ideals of the new United States.[30] But breaking Britain's chains was not enough. More than any single individual, he had struggled to diminish the power of the "Patrician order" in the hope of forming "a system" with "a foundation laid for a government truly republican."[31]

Despite all that Jefferson had accomplished, some Virginia activists in the 1770s—and many Americans in the 1790s who learned their history during the early Republic's fierce partisan warfare—came to think of Jefferson as too self-absorbed to serve in the American Revolution. The criticism began in 1776, when some in Williamsburg plotted what Jefferson thought was the "secret assassination" of his character. They assailed him for his lengthy absence from Congress.[32] Even as he drafted the Declaration of Independence, foes at home circulated the rumor that he was opposed to taking military action against Indians who helped the British army. (He countered by saying that he hoped any tribes aiding the redcoats would be driven west of the Mississippi River.)[33] Some were put off that autumn when he quit Congress after only one year's service, and others questioned his virtue when he refused to be part of the diplomatic mission to France. A year later, Richard Henry Lee wrote to Jefferson from Philadelphia, sarcasm dripping from his pen: "It will not perhaps be disagreeable to you in your retirement, sometimes to hear the events of war, and how in other respects we proceed in the arduous business we are engaged in."[34]

In later years critics portrayed Jefferson as an uncaring hedonist who had spent the trying early period of the war living in luxury and safety at Monticello, while others served in Congress or soldiered, and many died at places such as Bemis Heights, Brandywine, and Valley Forge. In truth, Jefferson's behavior was an open invitation for censure.

He spent up to nine months at home each year from the summer of 1776 until the summer of 1779, always attributing his behavior to his wife's precarious health. Martha did experience a difficult pregnancy in 1776–1777 before delivering a son who, sadly, died before he was named. Five months later she was pregnant again. The child that was born in August 1778—christened

Mary, though her father called her Maria, or Polly—survived, but Martha recovered so slowly that it is now believed that she was seriously ill for some time.[35]

Had Jefferson abandoned a spouse in perilous health, he would today justly be condemned as uncaring and self-centered. But his remaining at home was not all that provoked criticism. The manner in which he lived during the war aroused scorn. Jefferson continued building his mansion. Washington was simultaneously doubling the size of Mount Vernon, but others were overseeing the work while he served with the Continental army. Jefferson by contrast was a hands-on builder. While Washington was engaged in bitter struggles in New York, New Jersey, and Pennsylvania, Jefferson was fussing over floor plans and plantings at Monticello. Under his watchful eye, bricks were made, materials acquired, and craftsmen and laborers carefully supervised. All the while, Jefferson persistently grafted trees for his orchards, hired a gardener, and searched for a vigneron. His appetite for shopping was unflagging.

When the British and Hessian soldiers who surrendered at Saratoga in October 1777 were transferred to Albemarle County fourteen months later, Jefferson devoted his energies to making them safe and comfortable, steps that may have saved the lives of innumerable captives. Jefferson also hosted British officers at lavish dinners, opened his library to them, and invited them to his home for philosophical discussions. On many evenings, he and Martha were joined by prisoners of war for music and singing. He once wrote to a friend in Congress asking for the release from captivity of one officer, a Hessian nobleman who hoped to "return home on parole" in order to save his family's estate. Jefferson never hid his inclination to treat the captives "with politeness and generosity." In fact, from nearly the moment of the prisoners' arrival he explained his conduct to Virginia's governor.[36] But not everyone saw consorting with enemy officers in the same humane light as did Jefferson.

Jefferson also annoyed, or at least exasperated, others by imprudently talking of retiring from public life altogether in 1779. He was thirty-five years old, and his country was in the midst of a desperate struggle. France had allied with the United States a few months earlier, leading him to think that the war was nearly over—a mistaken sentiment shared by many. But peace was not at hand, and some of Jefferson's friends were angry that he would even consider retirement as this juncture. One, Edmund Pendleton, lectured him on the inappropriateness of wishing for a "happy quietus from the Public" when his services were so badly needed by his country.[37]

No one had to goad Alexander Hamilton into serving his country, and none ever questioned his courage. He had been marching and drilling with the militia for nearly ten months when, in March 1776, he took command of a volunteer artillery company and began readying it for Britain's anticipated invasion of New York. Always neat and careful about his appearance, Captain Hamilton was especially eager that his men look like soldiers. With funds that he raised, Hamilton outfitted himself and his men in blue and buff coats with buckskin trousers, and he completed the look with swashbuckling white belts crisscrossing the chest. Hamilton dressed the part of a spit-and-polish soldier, though it is unlikely that he struck anyone as rugged or tough. He was five feet seven, the average height of men in late-eighteenth-century America, but very slight, with narrow shoulders and a tiny waist. As for the past ten years he had been a clerk and a student, it was unlikely that he was mistaken for a man accustomed to hard physical work. Though twenty-one, Hamilton was so spare that his physique must have resembled that of a still-growing adolescent, probably leading some to wonder whether he possessed the stamina for the rigors of soldiering. But military officers come in all shapes and sizes, and if Hamilton's physical form was not striking, he exuded more than a few positive qualities. He moved with a supple grace, and his dedication and commitment to the cause were beyond question. Beneath thick auburn hair, his face was strong, his jaw hard and firm. His blazing azure eyes were his most prominent feature. They sparkled with enthusiasm, firmness, and intelligence, provoking a sister-in-law to remark later on that he had "a face never to be forgotten."[38] Hamilton was one of those rare individuals who, even before he said a word, conveyed a sense of courage, intelligence, and quick-wittedness. Once he did speak, he struck listeners as well educated, self-assured, and confident, a force to be reckoned with, an officer capable of leading.

Young people who have not yet proven themselves are often insecure. About to try to make a name for himself as a soldier, Hamilton was anxious. He never doubted his intellect or bravery, and he knew that he was ambitious, but he was the first to admit that he was also vain and immodest. Hamilton worried too that he lacked some of the happier traits that "embellish human nature."[39] What he meant is not clear, but he could have been pondering whether the dark side of his harsh lot in childhood had rendered him too ambitious, unfeeling, ruthless, cynical, and above all, designing.

Whatever his attributes and shortcomings, Hamilton early on understood that he would require a patron if he was to truly get ahead. Benefactors had been essential in helping him get to this point. Through ready displays of energy, intelligence, industry, loyalty, zeal, and a bright, uplifting manner, he had impressed men of influence on St. Croix. Those same qualities won over many of the well-established men he met in New Jersey and New York. Clearly, Hamilton had a facility for attracting notice and favorable judgments.

It was not due to good fortune, but the legacy of years of thought, planning, study, and hard work. Once in the army, he again called on those skills that had served him so well. To them, he added a crucial new virtue: courage under fire. The war would provide ample opportunities for Hamilton to prove his valor.

Hamilton had been in the army only about one hundred days when a British invasion fleet arrived off Long Island. The rebel army, led by General Washington, was soon boxed in by a powerful adversary, and on July 12 the British tightened the noose. Two Royal Navy frigates, the *Phoenix* and the *Rose*, sailed up the Hudson River, not only brushing past the marine obstacles the Americans had prepared but also scarcely bothered by what Washington called the "heavy and Incessant Cannonade" of the Continental artillerists. The only American casualties were several artillerymen who were killed when their own cannon exploded, the result of poor discipline and leadership.[40] All the unlucky gunners were members of Captain Hamilton's company. A tragedy of this sort can often be ruinous to one's career aspirations, but Hamilton was never disciplined, most likely because someone protected him or, as sometimes occurs in armies, blame was simply placed on someone of lower rank.

Captain Hamilton was back in action when the British landed some 20,000 men on Long Island. The brief engagement that ensued on August 27 was an American disaster. Continental losses were heavy. Those who survived did so by fleeing the battlefield and racing in wild flight for the relative safety of the redoubts in Brooklyn Heights. Part of that panicky escape, Hamilton's company lost its baggage and a field gun.[41] Heavily outnumbered and with their back to the East River, Hamilton and his trapped comrades—nearly 9,500 American Continentals and militiamen—appeared to face certain death or capture the moment that Britain's commander, General William Howe, finally attacked. But Howe was slow—and always had been. He waited for reinforcements, additional supplies, further intelligence reports. While Howe dawdled, a great storm blew up. Washington took advantage of the weather. Acting on the fog-shrouded, jet-black night of August 29, he extricated his army, bringing the wet, shaken men across the river and back to Manhattan. There was little safety there, as Hamilton quickly discovered. Posted in New York City with about 3,500 others, Washington was nearly enveloped and trapped again on September 15 following a British landing to the north at Kip's Bay. Had the redcoats moved with dispatch, they could have sealed off all escape routes from the city, and Hamilton, if he survived, would have spent the war in captivity and most likely never would have made a name for himself. Instead, the British advanced at a snail's pace, and Hamilton, for a

second time in three weeks, got away. Six hours after the British landing commenced, the last of the Americans exited the doomed city, taking unmarked
roads northward to rejoin the remainder of Washington's army in Harlem
Heights. In what one day would be seen as a strange twist of history, Hamilton was led to safety by Lieutenant Colonel Aaron Burr, a native New Yorker
who was aware of roads unknown to the British invaders.

Several weeks later General Washington and his army retreated into the
high country north of Manhattan, staying just a few steps ahead of their red-
coated pursuers. At White Plains, Washington unfurled a new strategy, the
Fabian warfare that Hamilton in *The Farmer Refuted* had predicted the rebels
would utilize to frustrate their stronger adversary. Washington would fight,
but he no longer would risk his entire army in battle. Washington's men occupied several hills and dug in. The terrain inhibited Howe from attacking all
the Continentals at once. It also compelled him to pay a heavy price for attacking in any sector. The British commander chose to direct his attack against
Chatterton's Hill. Hamilton's company was part of a thousand-man American force posted in the rocky high ground above the Bronx River and just
west of Howe's target. When the British stepped off on October 28, they first
had to cross a long stretch of russet farmland. The Continental artillery directed a murderous fire at them, so heavy in fact that the British understood
that they had to clear the defenses above the river if they were to take their
primary objective. The fighting lasted for hours until, with the slanting shadows of late afternoon gathering, Howe called off the attack. By day's end, the
Americans in Hamilton's sector had retreated, leaving Chatterton's Hill to
the British. The Fabian strategy had worked. Despite Howe's three-to-one
numerical superiority, the losses were about the same on both sides. Howe
planned another attack the following day, but rain forced a delay. By the time
the British commander could move, Washington was gone. Howe ended his
chase and marched back to Manhattan.

Not that the fighting in 1776 was over. With winter approaching, Washington divided his army. One third was sent to prepare defenses in the highlands
along the Hudson, another third was posted east of White Plains to guard
against a British invasion of New England, and Washington took the
remainder—some three thousand men—across the Hudson to defend New
Jersey. Hamilton's company was assigned to Washington's division. Choosing to go after Washington, Howe sent General Charles Cornwallis with some
ten thousand men to carry out the assignment.

Cornwallis began his pursuit on November 20. Heavily outnumbered,
Washington retreated southward, a flight that ended twelve days later when
the bedraggled Americans crossed the Delaware River into Pennsylvania.

Cornwallis might have caught the fleeing rebels, but he was delayed by bad roads and bad weather, and by the sheer size of his army, which daily foraged for tons of food, water, and firewood. Washington also did what he could to slow the enemy, destroying bridges and deploying his artillery at strategic points to lay down barrages on the advancing redcoats. The British answered with artillery salvos. Men on both sides perished. Hamilton was in the thick of things—firing, being fired at, making hurried retreats to rejoin the main army. Washington said in his reports that the British on occasion entered a town at the same "time our Rear"—the artillery in many instances—"got out."[42]

One soldier remembered seeing Captain Hamilton during the dispiriting retreat. The trooper was surprised that the company was "a model of discipline," especially as its "diminutive" commander was such "a boy [that] I wondered at his youth."[43] Another Continental who observed Hamilton thought him "a youth, a mere stripling, small, slender, almost delicate in frame, marching . . . with a cocked hat pulled down over his eyes, apparently lost in thought, with his hand resting on a cannon, and every now and then patting it as [if] it were a favorite horse or a pet plaything."[44]

All the men in Washington's force suffered during those dire days. It was cold and rained frequently. Food was scarce. No one had a tent. Even coats and blankets were in short supply. The men were ragged and unkempt. Washington said that "many of 'em" were "entirely naked & most so thinly clad as to be unfit for service." The attrition rate was heavy, though the army survived the retreat to fight another day. According to Washington, the rebel force escaped on more than one occasion because of the "smart cannonade" laid down by his artillerymen.[45]

Within a few days of crossing the Delaware, Washington's army, reinforced by militiamen and redeployed Continentals, had nearly doubled. Something of a gambler, he opted to roll the dice on Christmas night. He planned a surprise attack on the 1,500-man Hessian garrison across the river in Trenton. Washington split his army of some 5,000 men into three divisions. Each was to re-cross the Delaware and approach Trenton, one from the east, one from the south, and one from the northwest. Washington led the men who advanced from the northwest. Hamilton's company was assigned to that sector. Indeed, Washington brought along eighteen field pieces, eight heavy guns for every thousand infantrymen, a significantly larger ratio of artillery to muskets than was customary in armies of that day. Washington had learned during the fighting in New York that artillery used as a shock weapon could destroy the discipline ingrained in the enemy's professional soldiers, while at the same time emboldening his callow men.

Just as the men were about to set out, a fierce winter storm blew in. A keening wind howled. Rain, then sleet, then snow fell. The men, soaked to the skin, slogged forward for nine miles. In addition, they made a hazardous crossing of the swiftly flowing Delaware, and on both sides of the river they dragged cumbersome and heavy cannon, sometimes along uphill grades. The heaviest cannon weighed nearly a ton, as did the ammunition and trail boxes for each field piece.[46] Washington frequently rode from one end of the line to the other throughout the long, cold, difficult march. He calmly exhorted his men to keep moving and to listen to their officers. Hamilton also must have kept a close watch on the men in his company, from time to time calmly encouraging them to persevere in the face of the lashing wind and sleet, and their arduous struggles with the weapons. When his force reached the town in the final still minutes before dawn, Washington divided his men yet again. One division approached from the north, the other from the south. The rebel artillery batteries were posted in front of the division that was to advance on the tiny village from the north.

Snow was still falling from the ebony sky as the men took up their positions. Most faced an interminable wait in anxious silence until all was ready and the agreed-on time of attack at last arrived. The soldiers did what soldiers always do on the eve of battle. Some thought of their assignment. Some thought of loved ones at home. Some prayed. Not a few thought of death. Nearly every man wondered uneasily how he would perform under fire. All wanted to get on with it.

In the first pale gray light of dawn, Washington barked the order to attack. The infantrymen struck. As the surprised Germans hurried outdoors from their barracks to take up positions, the American artillery opened fire. As Colonel Henry Knox, the rebel artillery commander, later put it, "in the twinkling of an eye" the rebel cannonade "cleared the streets."[47] The Hessians tried to regroup, but they were disorganized, outnumbered, and their cannon had been captured in the first moments of the engagement. Pressed on all sides, and with artillery shells bursting among them, the Germans soon raised the white flag. The Americans had killed or captured 1,050 enemy soldiers. Washington lost only about a dozen of his men, some from exhaustion and exposure. It was the first American victory since independence had been declared.

Washington's blood was up after his victory. He easily persuaded himself that if he crossed again into New Jersey, he might inflict heavy blows on the German units that had been posted at Burlington and Bordentown. Another sensational victory might even induce Howe to abandon all of New Jersey. The last of the rebel soldiers crossed back into the lion's den on the final day of the year. But the operation took longer than anticipated, ruining Washington's plan. Not only were the Germans long gone, but Washington also learned that Cornwallis was coming after him with a considerably larger force. Abandoning his Fabian strategy, Washington decided to stand and fight. He posted his army on sloping terrain above the Assunpink Creek just outside Trenton. The Delaware River was at the soldiery's back. Retreat was seemingly impossible. Knox believed the American position was "strong, but hazardous." Some of the gray-faced soldiers, expecting the worst, described their situation as "a most awful crisis."[48]

One reason that Washington wanted to fight was that he had brought his entire complement of artillery across the river, some thirty pieces from the seven batteries raised by five states. Washington positioned his infantry in three rows on the knoll, one behind the other. Knox arranged the artillery so that it was interlocked and would fire according to a prearranged pattern. To succeed in what would become known as the Second Battle of Trenton, Cornwallis's men would have to survive the greatest massed artillery fire that the Americans had mounted to this point in the war.[49] Cornwallis did not succeed. He ordered one assault after another by shock troops who tried to cross the Assunpink. American riflemen, infantrymen, and artillery pounded away at them. It was a bloodbath. By day's end, Cornwallis had lost 8 percent of his army. American losses were a quarter of those of their adversary— about one hundred men.

Cornwallis thought he could finish off Washington the next morning, but the American commander did not give him the opportunity. Once the cold, inky night set in, the rebel army slipped away to the southeast, then turned north toward Princeton, taking a country road that today is named Hamilton Street in South Trenton. It was heavy going. The men had to trudge over partially frozen roads filled with ruts and tree stumps, and many also had to wrestle with field guns or artillery horses that slipped and slid on the treacherous ice. Some men had no shoes, and veterans later recalled that the snow was "literally marked with the blood of soldiers feet."[50] After a trek of about twelve miles, the army reached Princeton. The sun was just rising in a cloudless sky. It was going to be a glorious day. In fact, it was only then, in the first pink glint of the sun, that Cornwallis, back on the Assunpink, realized that his adversary was gone.

Washington acted on intelligence reports that Cornwallis had left only a small force to guard Princeton. With superior numbers on his side for a change, Washington wasted no time. He divided his army into two wings, each directed to advance on the college town; it is not clear where Hamilton was posted. Washington gave each division some field pieces, but he probably deployed most of his artillery at Worth's Mill, where the main Princeton-Trenton road crossed a small brook. They were to defend the army's rear should Cornwallis show up. Subsequently, the legend blossomed that Hamilton's company fought on the campus of the college that had denied him admission and that he personally fired a cannonball through the chapel, destroying the portrait of George II. It was a good story, but likely untrue. What was true was that with nearly a six-to-one majority, the rebels drove the British away, temporarily liberating Princeton. Few American military commanders have ever conducted a more risky or daring campaign than did Washington in this ten-day span. He had twice caught the British by surprise. At Princeton, he made some 450 British soldiers the victims of his Fabian strategy, now in operation once again. Altogether, the British had lost more than 2,000 men in ten days, ten times their enemy's losses.

Washington did not linger in Princeton. Learning that Cornwallis was marching north, the rebel army retreated to the west, its first step toward taking up winter quarters in Morristown, a rugged, hilly New Jersey enclave a few miles west of Manhattan. A month earlier Washington's army had been chased across the Delaware, seemingly ending a disastrous ninety-day campaign that had begun in August on Long Island. Instead, the campaign ended with the British suffering heavy losses and being forced from much of New Jersey. These stunning victories revived flagging spirits throughout America.[51]

Ambrose Serle, a secretary at British headquarters, referred to the rebel soldiery as "Raggamuffins." It was a fitting description for the tattered and exhausted men who entered Morristown. Washington told Congress that his soldiers were "bear foot & ill clad," with little food.[52] Not surprisingly, illness swept Morristown. Hamilton was among those taken sick. Spare to begin with, and exhausted by weeks of hard campaigning, he was felled with what he described as "a long and severe fit of sickness." He was fortunate to have made it this far. Only twenty-five of the sixty-eight men in his company survived their one-year enlistment.[53]

Two weeks after the army entered its winter quarters at Morristown, Washington wrote to Hamilton requesting his services as an aide-de-camp.[54] It is not clear how Washington learned that Hamilton might be good for the job. Generals Stirling and McDougall, who were acquainted with Hamilton, were with the army in Morristown, but it was more likely that Colonel Knox recommended his young gunner. As there were only about thirty officers in his artillery corps, and as Hamilton had served under Knox for nearly nine months, the two must have been in one another's presence on numerous occasions. At every crucial juncture of his life, Hamilton had stood out and been noticed by men of importance. He doubtless sought to make a favorable impression on Knox, and he must have succeeded.

Nearly six weeks passed before Hamilton accepted the commander's tender. He was ill during some of that time, though he was also uncertain about the wisdom of taking a post as an aide. Hamilton lusted after glory, which he knew was not to be had in a desk job, and that had already led him to spurn a similar offer from General Stirling. What is more, everyone knew that French assistance was on the way, including shipments of weaponry. Hamilton expected that additional regiments of artillery soon would be created. He longed to be named a regimental commander, which, as he remarked subsequently, would "in all probability . . . have led further." In other words, he might ultimately command a brigade.[55]

Neither Hamilton nor anyone else at that juncture could have imagined the stature that Washington would achieve. With the exception of Trenton-Princeton, Washington's performance in 1776 had invited criticism.[56] There was a chance that he might not remain in command of the army throughout a long war. On the other hand, if he survived as commander, and if America won the war, Washington could achieve iconic status, wielding considerable power and influence in the postwar years. For a man whose ascent at every turn had been facilitated by patrons, Hamilton had to have felt a strong pull to hitch his wagon to Washington's star. He accepted the offer, and his appointment was announced by Washington on March 1.[57] The appointment was automatically accompanied by a promotion to the rank of lieutenant colonel. He had just turned twenty-two. Only four years earlier, Hamilton had expected to spend his life working in obscurity as a clerk in the West Indies.

When Congress created the Continental army, it allotted Washington one aide-de-camp and a military secretary. But given the commander's staggering workload, the number of aides was from time to time increased. Thirty-two men eventually served in this capacity, normally about five or six at any one time. Many went on to achieve prominence, though among them Hamilton alone is widely known today. Hamilton was the nineteenth officer chosen as an aide to Washington and one of four to be appointed within a six-week period between January and March 1777. Several aides served Washington only briefly before moving on to what must have seemed to be more attractive positions. In fact, the opening that led to Hamilton's appointment came about when George Baylor left to assume command of a cavalry regiment. Hamilton must have initially imagined that something along these lines would be his fate.[58]

The aides lived at headquarters and daily interacted with Washington. As their commander said, they were "confined from morning to evening" with their assignments.[59] Ordinarily, they had two principal jobs: They helped Washington with his correspondence and from time to time were dispatched as emissaries to other field officers or civilian authorities. Washington insisted that his aides be intelligent, well educated, and skilled writers, or "ready Pen-men," as he put it. No less important, they were to be cultivated and adept at meeting and conversing with others. Washington's practice, as one of his aides subsequently revealed, was to give the aide notes for a letter; the aide then drafted the letter, Washington edited or approved it, and the aide prepared the fair copy that was to be sent off. It has been estimated that some twelve thousand letters were signed by Washington during the war and that his aides prepared some five thousand additional documents, including orders, rosters, payrolls, and the like. Washington had two further requirements: He expected his aides to respect the confidentiality of what transpired at headquarters, and he demanded their blind loyalty.[60]

Whatever Hamilton anticipated when he took the job, he quickly discovered that Washington was a demanding boss. If an aide was a disappointment, he got rid of him, usually by reassigning him to a post in the field. But Hamilton was good—very good. He was so good, in fact, that Washington soon thought him indispensable. Years later Washington characterized Hamilton as his "principal & most confidential aid."[61] Hamilton was famously bright and industrious, the most published author in the army, experienced in dealing with businessmen, and fluent in French, which proved valuable once French officers began arriving in America during 1777. (A French officer who met Hamilton in 1780 described him as an "accomplished gentleman" who spoke and wrote French "perfectly.")[62] Furthermore, as Hamilton had no family, he never left the army. Headquarters was his home. In all these ways, Washington found young Hamilton to be useful, but contrary to what many have said, the commander did not see his young aide as the son he never had. Washington may have felt paternal affection for the Marquis de Lafayette, who arrived during the summer of 1777, but he was neither tender nor friendly with others. Washington judged men according to how they could be of use to him. With Hamilton, as with his other aides, Washington never let down his guard, never tried to be a father, friend, or companion. Hamilton may never have wished for comradery with Washington, but he must have yearned for displays of warmth and approachability. When it never came, he pragmatically grew to see Washington as nothing more than his means to bigger and better things.

Life at headquarters was not all work. The main meal of the day was taken in mid-afternoon, which had been Washington's practice at Mount Vernon.

Washington and what he called his "family"—his aides—were joined on an almost daily basis by several general officers and the officer of the day, usually a young captain. Not infrequently, civilian authorities, including congressmen and governors, showed up. An important businessman might be present from time to time and, later in the war, foreign officials occasionally joined the repast. When the army was in winter quarters, generally between November and April, the families of officers often came for extended stays. At times, twenty or more were at the table. Washington did not play the host. He left that duty to his aides on a rotating basis, so that every two or three days it fell to Hamilton to preside by offering toasts and setting the conversation in motion. Hamilton required little prompting. Even as a young man, his presence filled a room. Charming and loquacious, and possessed of the gift of wit, he often was the dominant force at the table, winning over slight acquaintances and total strangers. One visitor, the wife of a cavalry officer, described Hamilton as "sensible, genteel, polite." A young Pennsylvania colonel thought he acted with "ease, propriety and vivacity." General Nathanael Greene was convinced that Hamilton's affability and good humor were akin to "a bright gleam of sunshine, ever growing brighter as the general darkness thickened."[63] A French envoy who visited the army in 1779 thought Hamilton not just "very pleasant" but also more industrious and conscientious than his cohorts. "If courage, assiduity, and penetration, mingled with a few traces of ambition, can raise a man above his equals, in a nascent republic, some day you will hear of him," the diplomat predicted.[64]

Battles were infrequent in the War of Independence, but twice in 1777 Hamilton found himself in harm's way. London planned a campaign for that summer in which General Howe was to move north from Manhattan while another British army, under General John Burgoyne, invaded northern New York from Canada. The Continentals, forced to defend the Hudson, would be caught in the pincers and destroyed. It was a superb plan, but Howe scuttled it. Envisaging few problems for Burgoyne, Howe chose to invade Pennsylvania. He thought taking Philadelphia, the seat of Congress, would deal a severe blow to American morale. Moreover, Washington would have to abandon his Fabian tactics and defend the city. Howe was convinced that if he could get the Continental army onto a battlefield, he could defeat it.

Howe was partially correct. Washington brought his army into Pennsylvania and posted it at Chadd's Ford, on the Philadelphia side of Brandywine Creek. Washington may not have believed that he could prevent his adversary from taking Philadelphia, but he intended to make Howe pay a heavy price for gaining his prize. The clash took place on September 11, a hot late-summer day. The contest was a savage, daylong fray, and the British had roughly a 2,000 man advantage. Washington spent most of the battle at a field headquarters a short distance from the battlefield. Hamilton remained at his side. However, late in the engagement, as intelligence flowed in about British movements, the commander sprang on his mount and rode like the wind to take command at the scene of the fighting. One observer said that the general's powerful charger sprang over "all the fences without difficulty," and presumably so too did Hamilton's mount, for he accompanied Washington into the midst of peril. Fighting, sharp and bloody, swirled about them for at least two hours until the sun pitched over the horizon. Mercifully for the rebels, darkness ended the battle. A British sergeant may have exaggerated when he said later that Washington's army would have faced a "total overthrow" had there been only one more hour of daylight. However, the redcoat was right in implying that things had not gone well for the Continentals. The Americans had lost more than 1,100 men, twice the number of British casualties.[65]

Washington now knew for certain that he could not prevent the British from taking Philadelphia, and he wisely chose not to risk his army a second time against Howe's entire force. But Washington remained full of fight. He suspected that some congressmen, who soon would have to flee Philadelphia, would be unhappy with his performance. He also knew that Burgoyne was in deep trouble, unable to fight through a rebel army commanded by Horatio Gates, and probably with little likelihood of retreating to Canada. Washington may have already guessed that Gates was certain to be lionized for his success, and it may have been a factor in is his decision to plan a surprise attack, an operation that might replicate his brilliant Trenton-Princeton campaign.

While planning his move, Washington ordered Hamilton to join an operation to destroy flour mills along the Schuylkill River before the enemy could take them. It was a dangerous undertaking. At one mill, redcoat dragoons attacked as Hamilton and his four comrades were crossing the river on a flat-bottomed boat. One rebel soldier was killed and another wounded, as was the boatman. Hamilton dove off the vessel into the dark, numbingly cold water and swam for safety. When he disappeared from view in the swift river current, the survivors in his party reported that Hamilton was presumed dead. Later that day, in the chilly autumn darkness of early evening, Hamilton, shivering in his wet uniform, appeared at headquarters, touching off a passionate celebration.[66]

Soon after Hamilton reported, Washington directed him to alert Congress to abandon Philadelphia "immediately without fail, for the enemy have the means of throwing a party this night into the city."[67] The congressmen were awakened in the wee hours of the morning. They fled so rapidly, and in such a state of alarm, that in his haste one New Englander forgot to saddle up before he spurred his horse.[68]

As it turned out, the British waited eight more days before marching into Philadelphia, a period when Washington once again sent Hamilton into the field. This time, Hamilton was ordered into Philadelphia to requisition blankets, clothing, and horses from the civilian population. So desperate was the situation—the commander said that without these materials "the ruin of the army, and perhaps the ruin of America" might be at hand—that Washington vested Hamilton with authority to seize that which the residents would not willingly surrender. Hamilton was put in command of upwards of 150 infantrymen and cavalry troops, and over two days the soldiers garnered a treasure trove of precious goods.[69]

Soon after Philadelphia fell, Washington struck at Germantown, north of the city, where Howe had posted about half of his army. As at Trenton, Washington had a numerical superiority, but on this occasion he failed to score a sensational victory. Unlike the Hessians, the British were not caught off guard, and that was only the start of Washington's problems. A thick morning fog shrouded entire divisions, sowing confusion among the battalion commanders. As Washington directed operations in one sector of the battlefield, Hamilton remained at his side. The fighting was intense. In three hours, both sides lost about the same number of men as at Brandywine, but at day's end the Continentals could point to no gains from their attack.[70]

A month after Germantown, Washington sent Hamilton on another mission. The American commander needed men if he was to undertake any further major initiatives before going into winter quarters. Washington knew that the victorious Gates had a surplus of manpower, for he had indeed scored a huge victory at Saratoga. (Burgoyne had surrendered 5,900 men, the so-called Convention Army that eventually would be sent into captivity in Charlottesville.) At the end of October, Washington selected Hamilton as his emissary to ride to Albany, New York, and request that Gates relinquish three brigades to the main Continental army.[71]

Choosing Hamilton for the undertaking was ill-advised. This was an errand that might require delicate negotiations, a realm in which Hamilton had no experience. Furthermore, Gates was unpopular with many New Yorkers, who loathed him for having connived with Congress to overthrow the initial Continental commander of the northern theater, Albany's General Philip Schuyler. Hamilton not only was close to many of those New Yorkers, but he was also anxious not to alienate Schuyler, who remained a powerful political figure in the state. In fact, in the midst of his talks with Gates, Hamilton slipped away and dined with Schuyler at the general's mansion, and probably reassured this possible benefactor of his loyalty. What is more, in European armies it was standard practice to send only a senior officer on a mission of this sort. Gates, who had served in the British army for years before immigrating to the colonies, was all-too-familiar with Europe's protocol. He was offended when Hamilton appeared at his door.

Predictably, that meeting, and a second session four days later, went badly. Gates had no desire to give up any of his men, especially as Congress had ordered him to retake Fort Ticonderoga, which had fallen to Burgoyne at the start of his campaign. For his part, Hamilton was apprehensive that he would fail as an envoy, and in the course of the talks he anxiously wrote to Washington: "Perhaps you will think me blameable" for not persuading Gates to relinquish the men. He argued forcefully, he said later, telling Gates that his reasons for refusing to comply with Washington's request were "unsubstantial." Gates responded "warmly," causing Hamilton to subsequently admit that at times he was "at a loss how to act." In the end, Hamilton pried loose only one brigade from Gates. He departed Albany with bitter feelings toward the hero of Saratoga.[72]

The day after Hamilton left Albany, he fell ill. He recovered quickly, only to relapse later in November with symptoms that sound like influenza, perhaps complicated by sheer exhaustion. He was bedridden for days with a high fever, chills, and aches, and more than a month passed before he regained his strength and could make the long ride in the midst of winter to rejoin his commander. Hamilton did not see Washington again until mid-January, when they were reunited at Valley Forge.[73]

A month earlier the army had taken up winter quarters there, a site at the juncture of Valley Creek and the Schuylkill River a few miles northwest of Philadelphia. By the time Hamilton arrived, all the men were housed and the horrendous scarcity of food of the first days in camp had passed, but misery remained rampant. The winter of 1777–1778 was not the coldest of the war, but it was cold enough to torment the Continentals. It snowed now and again, but more often a cold rain lashed the area. Like "a family of Beavers," as Thomas Paine put it, the soldiery had been put to constructing housing for themselves and the lower-ranking officers. Forty days passed before the last soldier was finally housed, and their quarters, as Lafayette remarked, were "scarcely gayer than dungeon cells." Twelve enlisted men were crowded into each leaky, drafty wooden hut; few of the jerry-built fireplaces drew properly and many of the men lacked a blanket. The junior officers had it a bit better. Not only were they more adequately supplied, but no more than five had to share similarly sized cabins. Nevertheless, officers and men experienced the miasmic conditions of Valley Forge. The place was a sea of mud, and the fetid reek of the stockyards and slaughter pens perpetually hung over the cantonment.

About ten days after Hamilton's arrival, food suddenly was in short supply once again. For two weeks the soldiers had only bread and water for nourishment. Washington labeled it a "fatal crisis," potentially ruinous for the survival of the army and literally lethal for many men. Still another food crisis occurred in late February, brought on, as were its predecessors, by bad weather and poor roads, shortages of wagons and teamsters, corruption in the supply system, and the proclivity of local farmers to do business with a British army that paid in specie rather than with the Continental army that paid in depreciated paper currency. The deplorable conditions spawned disease, resulting in the death of 2,500 men in about ninety days, one-seventh of those who had entered Valley Forge. The enlisted men were stranded, unless they deserted, and "desertions have been immense," Hamilton acknowledged that February. However, the officers could resign their commissions and go home, and they did so by the hundreds.[74]

The field officers, and the aides who dwelled with them, escaped the harsh deprivation suffered by the men. Washington—and Hamilton—spent the Valley Forge winter in a comfortable two-story stone house that was conveniently removed from the always-present stench that pervaded the area where the men were housed. Washington had his own bedroom on the second floor and a private office downstairs. Hamilton shared a lower floor room with his fellow aides. All officers who held ranks of major or higher succeeded in finding snug accommodations. None appears to have ever gone without meat and vegetables, and wine was always served at the main mess at headquarters, though some complained of the privation they faced. General Nathanael Greene, for instance, grumbled that he and his cohorts faced a "hard fare for people that have been accustomed to live tolerable."[75]

If Hamilton faced greater hardships than he had endured during his initial thirty months in the army, or if he carped about what he endured that winter, he never committed his feelings to paper. But Valley Forge left its indelible mark on many who survived its abhorrent conditions. For Hamilton, it was eye-opening. Beginning that winter, he struggled to learn how such misery could occur and to understand what could be done to prevent it from ever happening again. The torments and heartbreak of Valley Forge also led some who endured them, Hamilton included, to see themselves as singularly distinct from those who had not experienced that winter's travail. One day, it would be a factor in coloring how Hamilton looked at Jefferson.

CHAPTER 4

"IF WE ARE SAVED, FRANCE AND SPAIN MUST SAVE US"

THE FORGE OF WAR

DURING THE FORTY MONTHS after he returned to headquarters, Hamilton's daily routine hardly differed from that during his initial year as an aide-de-camp. Nevertheless, substantial changes occurred in his life, the conduct of the war, and the infant American nation, and each led young Hamilton in new directions.

The great American victory at Saratoga changed the war forever. France, which so far had only clandestinely aided the rebels, entered the war, concluding treaties of alliance and commerce with the United States and committing a large fleet to the conflict. London responded by sending half of its army in North America to the Caribbean to defend vital sugar islands, forcing it to adopt a new strategy for the North American theater. Largely writing off the provinces above the Potomac, the British after 1778 focused on retaking their four southern colonies, Georgia, North and South Carolina, and Virginia. If Britain succeeded, it might come out of the war with a large American empire that included Canada; the territory west of the Appalachians; the profitable tobacco and rice colonies in the south; Florida, which it had held since 1763; and sugar islands in the Caribbean.

General Washington changed as well. Thinking that the French alliance "chalk[s] out a plain and easy road to independence," Washington grew more cautious. He was willing to fight, but only to retake New York, and only then if the French fleet participated. But the French squadron that arrived in the summer of 1778 remained in American waters only briefly before departing for the Caribbean. No other French fleet was seen north of Georgia for three long years. During all that time, Washington remained inactive, convinced that time was on the side of the allies. He was certain that a stalemated war would sooner or later compel Great Britain to make peace and recognize American

independence. Year in and year out, Washington kept his army on the periphery of Manhattan to prevent the enemy from seizing control of the Hudson, but
also to be in position to campaign for New York should the French navy return.

Hamilton saw action in only one major engagement between 1778 and 1781. It
came when the British army abandoned Philadelphia in June 1778 and retreated
to New York. Washington, with an army about equal in size, shadowed the redcoats across New Jersey, looking for an opportunity to engage. From the start,
Washington was uncertain whether to hazard another full-scale battle, as at
Brandywine, or something smaller and in line with the Fabian strategy he had
off and on espoused. As the British neared New York, Washington convened a
council of war to consider the options. With abundant French assistance thought
to be imminent, nearly all the dozen general officers who were present opposed
risking a full-scale clash. Instead, they recommended that a small force of some
1,500 men—less than a tenth of the rebel army—"annoy" the British rear. Washington consented. However, when Generals Nathanael Greene and Anthony
Wayne begged him to do more, the commander waffled. Hamilton, who had
taken minutes at the council of war, sided with those who favored a bolder,
riskier action. In private, he sneered at the wariness of the majority of generals,
saying that the course they advocated "would have done honor" to a "society of
midwives." Though he did not lack in effrontery, it is unlikely that Hamilton
made known his feelings to the commander. Nevertheless, Washington, after
some deliberation, quadrupled his attack force—to 5,340 men—and ordered it to
strike the British rear on both its right and left flanks.[1]

The Battle of Monmouth was fought on June 28, 1778. The British commander, Sir Henry Clinton, may have been even more eager than Washington for a major encounter. He rushed in reinforcements. By mid-morning,
what had been a three-to-one numerical advantage for the Americans had
vanished. Not only were the numbers now on Clinton's side, but also the
British were taking the fight to their enemy. General Charles Lee, who commanded the American strike force, ordered a retreat. His plan was to find
advantageous terrain where he could make a defensive stand. Hamilton was
soon in the thick of things. Sent by Washington to the battlefield to see what
was occurring, Hamilton discovered the retreat. Although he later acknowledged that Lee's men were falling back "in tolerable good order," Hamilton
claimed to have beseeched Lee to stop the withdrawal. "I will stay here with
you, my dear general, and die with you! Let us all die rather than retreat," he
reportedly told Lee.[2] If so, General Lee, who had been a soldier for twenty
years, must have been startled to be confronted by a twenty-three-year-old
who had never commanded anything larger than a company of artillery.

The retreat ended when Washington arrived on the scene and, after a heated exchange, relieved Lee of command. Washington then proceeded to do precisely what Lee had intended. He fell back behind a ravine and made a defensive stand through a long, scorching afternoon on which temperatures climbed above one hundred degrees. Hamilton fought alongside the commander, impressing observers with his fearlessness, leading some to conclude that he was indifferent to death. He exhibited "singular proofs of bravery," said one witness. General Knox and Colonel Henry Lee, a cavalry officer, were astonished by his courage under fire, with the latter remarking on Hamilton's "*paroxysms* of bravery." Even General Lee acknowledged Hamilton's "frenzy of valor." Hamilton remained in the fight at Monmouth until, nearly prostrate from the intense heat and "considerably hurt" when his wounded horse fell on him, he was forced from the field.[3]

The contest ended inconclusively, and the following morning the British, unimpeded, resumed their retreat to New York. Hamilton was irate at General Lee's conduct, convinced that the desperate fighting on that broiling summer day had been wasted and that 360 Americans had died in vain. The young aide attributed what he thought was a lost opportunity for a magnificent American victory to Lee's "silly and pitiful" leadership. Indeed, Hamilton suspected ulterior motives for Lee's behavior.[4]

Hamilton's dark suspicions were not new. Insiders were aware that two years earlier, in the aftermath of the disastrous New York campaign, Lee had questioned Washington's abilities. Following Gates's victory at Saratoga and the simultaneous British successes in Pennsylvania—due to a series of questionable actions by Washington, or at least that was how some saw things—fresh doubts arose about America's commander. Some army officers and congressmen hoped Washington could be forced out and Gates named as his successor. Whether or not Gates was involved in any discussions among the discontented has never been determined. Nor has anyone ever conclusively established the scope of the conspiracy against Washington, but the commander thought it was widespread, and he fought back.[5] He mobilized loyal officers to court members of Congress. For instance, Hamilton's friend and fellow aide-de-camp Colonel John Laurens was dispatched to speak with his father, Henry Laurens, the president of Congress. Washington also availed himself of Hamilton's eloquent pen. Hamilton alerted high-placed New Yorkers of the "monster" plot afoot to overthrow Washington. He characterized the conspirators as "villainous" and "vermin," and he warned that should their intrigue succeed in removing Washington, it would "shake" the United States to "its center." Hamilton never specifically charged that Gates was part of the plot, though it would not have required a leap of imagination for anyone reading his letters to reach that conclusion.[6]

The cabal against Washington was foiled, but as the summer of 1778 approached, some imagined that the conspirators had turned to General Lee for help in securing Washington's removal. Lee, who had languished in captivity for nearly thirty months following his capture by the British in late 1776, had never been part of any conspiracy against Washington. However, General Greene, among others, was certain that "the junto will endeavor to debauch and poison [Lee's] mind with prejudices" against Washington. They did not have to work very hard. Lee's views about his superior's incompetence had never changed, and in fact, in April and May he recklessly carped about conditions in the army and Washington's weaknesses. Lee supposedly even told another officer that "Washington was not fit to command a Sergeant's Guard."[7] Some of this got back to Washington in the weeks preceding Monmouth, and it is likely that Hamilton was one of his sources of information. Yet, as Lee was the second-highest-ranking officer in the Continental army, Washington had little choice but to give him command of American force that was to attack the British at Monmouth.

If Hamilton had reservations about Lee before the engagement, he afterward suspected "something much worse." Hamilton told others that Lee was closely linked to the cabal against Washington, which was possible but unproven. He also conjectured that Lee's "game" was to avoid scoring a victory, hopeful that more doubts would be sown about the army and its commander. This seems far-fetched today, and it did to many then. What makes greater sense is that Hamilton, who thought of Washington as his patron, saw in this episode the means not only of eliminating a rival to the commander but also of rendering himself indispensable to General Washington.[8]

Following Monmouth, Lee, humiliated and outraged at having been removed from command during the battle, asked for a court martial to clear his name. Hamilton, of course, was summoned to testify. In his testimony, and in private letters to men of influence, Hamilton painted a dark picture of Lee, one that confirmed the wisdom of Washington's decisions during the engagement. He charged that Lee had been indecisive—the very accusation that Lee had often leveled at Washington—and also that he had not been "so calm and steady as is necessary . . . in such critical circumstances."[9]

Lee was convicted on several charges and suspended from command for a year. Incensed, the voluble Lee spent his year of penance openly assailing those whom he called the "dirty earwigs" surrounding Washington. Hamilton and young Laurens, he said, had joined in a "hellish plan" to destroy him, just as they had earlier sought to smear and annihilate everyone who questioned Washington. Lee was correct, though his own foolish and insubordinate behavior in the wake of the court martial ultimately led Congress to dismiss him from the army forever.[10]

Given what had befallen Lee and others identified as disloyal to Washington, no one thereafter dared to openly criticize America's commander.

Hamilton spent fewer years than Jefferson as a bachelor, but he too endured a lonely period when he ached for love and companionship. Jefferson was absorbed with his studies and for the most part secluded at Shadwell during his early adulthood. Hamilton was twenty-two when he moved into Washington's headquarters. Unlike Jefferson, Hamilton hardly lived in isolation, but in some ways he was terribly alone. He had no relatives to visit, and he appears to have maintained ties with only those prep school and college chums whose stars were rising and who might someday be useful to him. Indeed, he seemed wary of close attachments, remarking at the time that he wished "to keep my happiness independent [of] the caprice of others."[11] His only truly close relationships were with some of his fellow aides. They called him "Ham" or "Hammie," kidded and joked with him, and appear to have been drawn to him by genuine feelings of friendship and admiration.

The lingering image of Revolutionary War soldiers is that of grim men in the maw of extreme deprivation, like the hungry and shivering troops at Valley Forge. All too often that was true of enlisted men, but it was rarely the case for officers, and even less so for those at headquarters. In the northern states, where Washington remained until 1781, the campaign season more or less corresponded to today's baseball season. From November until the spring, when the weather was cold and wet, and America's unpaved roads were impassable, armies suspended offensive operations and went into winter quarters. That was the signal for the wives and children of many officers to come to camp, where some remained for months. While the families were present, camp life for the higher-ranking officers became more festive. The presence of women often added a spirited touch to the main mess in mid-afternoon. Furthermore, on many evenings, while the cold and at times malnourished soldiery huddled in rude cabins only a few hundred yards away, the officers enjoyed formal dinners at which bands of musicians played, gala balls that stretched deep into the night, and plays in which younger officers acted. During these surreal social seasons, older women and men might play matchmaker, introducing eligible younger officers to the daughters of senior officers and civilian officials who were in camp. No one met, or became infatuated, with more women than Lieutenant Colonel Hamilton.[12]

During the eighteen months after he returned to headquarters at Valley

Forge, Hamilton courted, or sought to woo, several young women who visited family members in the army. He so often flitted from one woman to another that Martha Washington named her tomcat Hamilton. Unlike Jefferson, Hamilton was hardly discomfited and tongue-tied in the presence of women. He boasted that he was a "renowned" lady's man, equally at ease with "a goddess" or "a mere mortal," and that "ALL FOR LOVE is my motto." However, he confessed that he found each woman to be "a most complex, intricate and enigmatical being."[13]

Hamilton may have fancied himself a lady killer, but he might more aptly be characterized as lovelorn and emotionally isolated even amid the social whirl at camp. He denied that he wished to marry. "I have plagues enough" without taking on "that *greatest of all*," he said, though he admitted that he was "willing to take the *trouble* of [women] upon myself." He may have been ambivalent toward marriage, especially given his mother's sad history with both Lavien and James Hamilton. Yet, like Jefferson, young Hamilton was profoundly lonely. He dreamed of "that most delectable thing, called matrimony," and the comforts and companionship it might bring. He yearned, he said, for a "young, handsome" woman with "a good shape," one who was genteel with "a little learning," sensible and good-natured, a believer in God, and with sufficient money "to administer to her own extravagancies."

His ideal woman was slow to turn up, and not entirely because of Hamilton's shortcomings. Whereas Jefferson had once feared that committing his heart would jeopardize the completion of his education and legal training, soldiering and warfare impeded Hamilton.[14] Alone, overworked, and overwrought by the not infrequent pressure-cooker environment in headquarters, Hamilton drew closer to Colonel Laurens, his fellow aide, than he had ever been with any other person. When Laurens, a South Carolinian, departed in 1779 to fight in defense of his state, Hamilton was crushed by his absence and often sent him missives that pulsated with homoerotic yearning. Addressing Laurens as "my Dear," Hamilton confessed that his heart was "set upon you." He added that his friend had stolen "my affections without my consent." Calling himself "a jealous lover," Hamilton made known that he was "piqued" when Laurens did not write. He exhorted Laurens to fight hard, but not to take unnecessary risks, as he could not bear to lose him. Hamilton missed Laurens so badly that he requested a leave from his duties as an aide so that he might go to South Carolina and fight alongside him. "I am disgusted with every thing in this world but yourself," he told Laurens. Washington turned down Hamilton's request.[15]

It cannot be said with certainty that Hamilton was homosexual or bisexual. Many people used the term "feminine" in describing certain of his qualities, though such a characterization hardly points to one's sexual disposition. What is more, the use of overelaborate expressions of same-sex affection was not unknown in the letter-writing style of the eighteenth century. The one thing that can be said for certain is that the erotic tone in Hamilton's missives to Laurens ended abruptly once he met Elizabeth Schuyler.

Young Hamilton had first met Elizabeth in the fall of 1777, but there had been no sparks. However, when she came to camp in the winter of 1780, Hamilton was swept off his feet. He was twenty-five; she was twenty-two. Betsey, as he soon began to call her, was petite, submissive, alluring, and the daughter of a rich and powerful New Yorker. She was everything that Hamilton had wished for. He found her attractive, especially her "fine black eyes," and he was captivated by her beauty, frankness, "innocent simplicity," "good hearted" nature, and the "sweet softness and delicacy" of her "mind and manners." He told Laurens she was "not a genius," but she had "sense enough to be agreeable." He told Betsey that she had "a lovely form" and "a mind still more lovely." Nothing was more important than her "tenderness to me," which he probably had never experienced from a woman.

Hamilton spoke of the "apprehensive . . . nature of [his] love," perhaps an admission that he was far from the self-assured paramour that he wished others to think. Or, he may simply have worried that things might not work out, especially as he could not get away to see her. They were engaged by the time she left camp late in the spring, but he did not see her again for seven months. He had often criticized other officers who left the army when an action might occur, and he would not consider such a step. In the early stages of their separation, he brooded over the meaning of her every phrase, each lapse in her correspondence, and the ever-present possibility of a rival suitor in Albany. He reminded her of his virtues—"I have talents and a good heart"— but acknowledged his shortcomings, including his immodesty and lack of wealth. He was not the most handsome man, he added, but he would bestow on her "a heart fraught with all a fond woman can wish." He wrote to her about once each week. After dashing off crucial letters for Washington, he would find the time to carefully draft his own long missive, frequently probing uncertainly to discover whether Betsey had "abated [her] affection" for him. "*I would this moment give the world to be near you only to kiss your sweet hand*," he told her after they had been apart for about a hundred days. A month later he confessed that she had given him something to live for, though he made it clear that, unlike many of his fellow aides, he would not leave the army until the war was over.[16]

Late in November 1780, accompanied by his fellow aide James McHenry, Hamilton made the long ride from Passaic Falls, New Jersey, to Albany.

Lieutenant Colonel Hamilton had been a slave to his duties. Other than trips on official business, this was his first time away from the Continental army since he had entered the service more than five years before.

On December 14 he and Elizabeth, surrounded by McHenry and members of the Schuyler family, were wed at the Pastures, the Schuylers' two-story brick Georgian mansion perched atop a hill in Albany. Hamilton had written to his father, inviting him to come from the Caribbean for the festivities. James Hamilton did not make the trip, and it is not clear whether he even answered his son's letter.[17]

The first years of war had been filled with crises of battle. After 1778, the army faced a new enemy—a great financial calamity. The value of America's paper currency had depreciated by the end of 1777, though Washington was not at first overly alarmed. Congress was taking steps to solve the problem, including appealing for action by the states, which had issued nearly half the paper in circulation. Nearly every state addressed the problem, as did numerous regional conventions, local committees, and town meetings. Furthermore, France made the first of a series of loans to its ally. Although America's economic woes remained stubbornly intractable, Washington was quietly confident through 1778 that the allies could bring hostilities to a swift end.

In January 1779, Congress summoned Washington to confer about his strategy for that year. His monthlong stay in Philadelphia produced a dramatic change in his outlook. He came away convinced that in a decentralized system that made the states sovereign, America's economic distress would never be solved. The nub of the problem was that Congress had no authority to raise and collect revenue. For years, the states had printed staggering amounts of paper currency. It depreciated rapidly, losing 75 to 80 percent of its value during the initial four years of the war. The states also piled on taxes. This toxic stew nearly brought commerce to a halt. What is more, little of the money raised by the states reached the national treasury. Congress sent stirring warnings to the states that the war might be lost because of financial insolvency brought on by "broken contracts and violated faith," but barely one-half of the $95 million that it requested was ever received by the national government.[18]

Congress had also been printing paper currency. By 1779, it had issued more than $241 million in paper. It began to depreciate in 1777, but the next year it went into free fall, the most rapid currency depreciation in U.S. history—faster than that which occurred in the Great Depression in the 1930s. By the time Congress summoned Washington to Philadelphia at the beginning of 1779, eight Continental dollars were required to purchase one dollar in specie; within a few months, the value of Continental money had

dropped to about two cents on the dollar. Congress's only immediate salvation was to borrow from the public by selling loan certificates and to seek
even more loans from France. Learning the magnitude of the financial crisis,
Washington concluded that substantive change was essential. The "cure must
be radical," was how he put it.[19]

Washington also told Congress that the collapse of the currency tied his
hands, making him unable to flesh out his battalions. He was left, he claimed,
with no choice but to remain on the defensive. The economic crisis was real,
though Washington exaggerated its impact on the army's freedom of action.
More money could have been printed, and though that would have piled up
more indebtedness and not been fiscally sound, it would have been preferable
to losing the war. Moreover, the states had some money to spend and, in fact,
in both 1779 and 1780 several northern states urged an invasion of Canada. At
one point during those years the president of the Continental Congress said
that every congressman favored an immediate invasion of Canada. But Washington was unwilling to act unless the objective was to retake New York.
Aware that many in Congress questioned the wisdom of his inactivity, Washington attributed it to the economic dilemma.[20]

Hamilton never mentioned the nation's economic problems until shortly
before Washington visited Congress, and at that time he seemed not to comprehend the deeper causes of the plight. He blamed the great scarcities on
profiteering merchants and corrupt politicians who had acted on secret information to monopolize the flour market and make windfall profits. He was
correct that "monopoly and extortion" and "arts of corruption" could produce great evils, but he did not see that the fundamental problem ran deeper.[21]

Initially, Hamilton may have derived his ideas from Washington, who believed that much of the problem was caused by big businessmen "preying
upon the vitals of this great country." Washington additionally believed that
the nation's economic ills were the result of a decline in the quality of the
delegates to Congress. The composition of Congress had changed markedly
since Washington's departure four years earlier. Three-fourths of those who
had been his colleagues in Congress in June 1775 were now gone. Some had
left for the army, and some—Benjamin Franklin and John Adams, for
instance—were abroad on diplomatic missions, but like Jefferson, most had
gone home to serve at the state level. With considerable justification, Washington thought those who were not serving the nation were shortsighted.
Early in 1779 he wrote to a fellow Virginian asking, "where are our Men of
abilities? Why do they not come forth to save their Country?" About thirty
months after Jefferson left Congress, Washington pointedly asked: Where are
"Jefferson & others" in this time of need?[22]

Hamilton concurred. A year earlier, he had complained about the "degeneracy" of those in Congress. "America once had a representation [in Congress] that would do honor to any age or nation," he stated in February 1778. But many of those "great men" had departed to serve their states, a choice that he termed a "pernicious mistake." The result had been an "alarming and dangerous" decline in the quality of congressmen. While at Valley Forge, Hamilton spoke with contempt of the gaggle of "indecisive and improvident" leaders in Philadelphia who, through "Folly, caprice, [and] a want of foresight," had caused the army to suffer horribly. A year later, he wondered whether the war might be lost as a result of the "lethargy of voluptuous indolence" on the part of those who were sitting out the war.[23] He never mentioned Jefferson in his correspondence, but it is likely that he heard Washington think out loud about him. It may be that Hamilton's contempt for Jefferson was born early in 1779.

The numerous problems that plagued the army drove Hamilton to search for their causes. Although his workday ran from early morning until nearly sundown, Hamilton squeezed in time for reading. Typically an early riser, he must have been up and reading by candlelight in the predawn darkness on many mornings, plowing through the likes of Cicero, David Hume, Thomas Hobbes, and Plutarch, gleaning what he could about human nature and the formation of new governments, but also learning economics through numerous books. He borrowed from a friend several standard economic treatises of the day. He may also have read Adam Smith's *Wealth of Nations*, but the authors he is known to have read were Hume, Wyndam Beawes, Richard Price, and Malachy Postlethwayt. The latter appears to have exerted the greatest influence on his thinking. Postlethwayt's *Universal Dictionary of Trade and Commerce* reflected at length on taxes, banking, debts, and finance. Hamilton read it through and through, and took detailed notes. The words "production," "manufactures," and "exportation" appear over and again in his notebook. Hamilton was already looking toward how the new nation might make itself economically independent.[24]

Soon after Washington returned from his eye-opening trip to Philadelphia early in 1779, Hamilton for the first time wondered whether America would win its independence. "Our affairs are in a bad way" because of economic miseries, he said. Convinced that insatiable entrepreneurial greed was at the root of America's problems, he added, "I hate money making men." But as dark as things were beginning to look only a year after the French alliance was consummated, Hamilton remained confident. Expecting continued French assistance and Spain's imminent entry into the war against Great Britain, Hamilton predicted that "Europe will save us in spite of ourselves."[25]

Hamilton had been correct about Spanish belligerency, but by 1780 America's prospects had worsened. While Washington remained inactive for a third consecutive campaign season, Great Britain was rolling up victories in the South. In 1778 it had invaded Georgia, retaken Savannah, and restored royal control. Early in 1780 the British invaded South Carolina. By June, they had retaken Charleston and a wide swath through the interior of the province.

Seeing that Washington could not, or would not, take the offensive, France—desperate to end a costly, stalemated war—announced that it was sending an army to America. Perhaps Washington would act in concert with it. Hamilton saw what the French had seen. Time was running out. If victory was not won soon, it would never be won. And if America did not win the war, hostilities would likely end in a peace negotiated in Europe and imposed on America. Hamilton urgently told acquaintances with influence in Congress that the army was in "a bad way" from lack of funds, and that not a moment could be spared.[26]

The French army arrived in stages, and later than expected. The first French soldiers, in their tight-fitting white uniforms, came ashore in Rhode Island in July 1780, but Comte de Rochambeau, their commander, was unwilling to take the field until all of his soldiery had crossed the ocean, and that would not be before the campaign season of 1781. While 1780 passed without a major campaign in the northern states, the British continued to score victories in the South, and as autumn approached, the British appeared close to conquering all of South Carolina. Hamilton's spirits collapsed. Watching helplessly as American morale waned in the face of an endless war, and one without a significant American victory since Saratoga three years earlier, Hamilton despaired that his "countrymen . . . are determined not to be free." Once again, he concluded, "If we are saved France and Spain must save us."[27]

War weariness was growing throughout America. Hamilton called it a "disgrace," but worse was to come. He was with Washington at West Point in September when Benedict Arnold's treason was discovered. It "shocked me more than any thing I have met with," Hamilton said, and he worried that it would further erode whatever spirit remained for carrying on the war. As never before, he wondered if all was lost. At best, he hoped the country was only in "a profound Sleep 'til the Cannon of the Enemy awaken us." Rallying at the last moment "is our National Character," he remarked.[28]

Driven to despair by the deteriorating military situation, Hamilton read and reflected on the national malaise over a period of eighteen months, and in all likelihood he spoke with assorted individuals who came to headquarters. By the fall of 1780 his thoughts had crystallized. They would not change substantially during the next decade.

The "fundamental defect" that Hamilton now saw was due not so much to a lack of talent in Philadelphia, as to "a want of power." Congress, now under America's first national constitution, the decentralized Articles of Confederation, was not "fit for war [or] peace," he said. Fearing an oppressive central government, the states had overreacted and, in Hamilton's opinion, had created a monster. Not only had they rendered the "union feeble and precarious," but also without "a speedy change the army must dissolve; it is now a mob rather than an army, without clothing, without pay, without provisions, without morals, without discipline." Then, in what would become a staple of Hamiltonianism, he issued a thinly veiled threat. The army's officers, he cautioned, would "begin to hate the country for its neglect of us."

Hamilton did not publish his ideas, though he communicated his views on the nation's political and economic ills to Robert Morris, a Philadelphia businessman who through much of the war was Congress's most influential member on economic matters. Hamilton urged the convening of a constitutional convention to remedy matters. He even recommended that what the convention produced need not be submitted to the states for ratification. Hamilton thought the new constitution should provide for a national government consisting of both executive and legislative branches. Of the former, he said little more than that it should be "an executive ministry," implying the existence of a prime minister and cabinet level departments. His focus was on Congress. Hamilton's remedies included vesting Congress with the authority to tax the citizenry, levy an impost on imports, and create a national bank. Indeed, a bank was critical, for Hamilton had put his finger on a key element in the nation's economic ills: The country lacked sufficient money to finance the war. But a bank could create money. Hamilton proposed that half the bank's start-up capital, a whopping two million pounds, would come from foreign loans; the remaining two million pounds would be raised through private subscriptions guaranteed by the United States. The bank would borrow money through the sale of securities and, in turn, make loans; in addition, as it would become a fountainhead of the money in circulation, the bank would provide a source of currency that could be taxed.[29] All would be lost if these remedies were not adopted. The "patient will die," was how he put it, for it was faced with "galloping consumption."[30]

The ideas broached by the fledgling economist were not entirely new. Some had probably been bandied about in private conversations among merchants, financiers, and public officials during 1779, and by late 1780 they were discussed on the floor of Congress. He must have heard some of the remedies mooted at headquarters, which likely guided his reading. But while his plan was not wholly, or even largely, original, Hamilton had done something that few others had done before late 1780: He articulated his nostrums in a lengthy, thoughtful, written argument.

In January and February 1781 Congress took several steps that Hamilton had proposed. Hamilton's advocacy was hardly the tipping point. His ideas were simply in sync with those of more powerful figures. A constitutional amendment giving Congress the authority to levy an impost on imports was sent to the states, and the Bank of North America was incorporated and supplied with capital. Congress also created four executive departments— Finance, War, Marine, and Foreign Affairs—and named Robert Morris to be the superintendent of Finance. General John Sullivan approached Washington about nominating the twenty-six-year-old Hamilton for the post, a sign that the young lieutenant colonel's advocacy had earned him attention. Washington claimed that he had never discussed economics with Hamilton, a remark that stretches credulity, but he championed his aide's intellect and patriotism, and added that no man "exceeds him in probity and sterling virtue." Ultimately, seeing that Morris was a shoo-in for the position, Sullivan dropped his plan to nominate Hamilton.[31]

Hamilton's economic recommendations, and those concerning strengthening the power of the national government, were not his only remedies for winning the war. Hamilton offered fresh ideas concerning the use of black soldiers. At the behest of the army's leadership, Congress early in the war had prohibited the enlistment of African Americans in the Continental army. Two years later, finding it difficult to obtain adequate numbers of volunteers, Massachusetts began conscripting both free blacks and slaves. Within twelve months, four other northern states permitted blacks to serve. No southern state took such a step. Indeed, Virginia and South Carolina enticed whites to enlist by offering them slaves as bounties.[32]

But once Britain retook Savannah and invaded South Carolina, Colonel Laurens, Hamilton's friend, implored Congress to raise a light infantry force composed of five thousand black soldiers to defend his province. Opposition was immediate in the South, especially in South Carolina. It was feared that not only would arming blacks lead to slave insurrections, but also that slavery might not survive the expedient.

Hamilton rapidly endorsed his friend's scheme. He recognized that if South Carolina fell, the British would almost certainly retake North Carolina. Virginia would then be imperiled. He also understood that if Great Britain reconquered the South, the United States at best would be a small, weak nation of nine states north of the Potomac River, surrounded by the British in Canada, the West, and the South. Independence would be meaningless.

But Hamilton was convinced—almost certainly correctly—that if the British were thwarted in their bid to regain their southern colonies, London would make peace. And, like Laurens, Hamilton believed that raising black soldiers was the essential ingredient to an American victory in the South. In longing for an army of blacks, Hamilton was not driven solely by a search for the means of vanquishing the enemy. His racial views were extraordinarily advanced for his time. They were an amalgam of Enlightenment thought, having been inspired by abolitionist acquaintances in Manhattan and hours of penetrating conversations with Laurens, who had returned to America from his studies in Geneva with flaming antislavery views.

In the spring of 1779, Hamilton wrote a remarkable letter to his friend John Jay, the president of Congress. "I have not the least doubt," Hamilton wrote, "that the negroes will make very excellent soldiers." Some, he said, believed that blacks were "too stupid to make soldiers." He challenged such biased thinking, saying, their "natural faculties are probably as good as ours." Americans, he told Jay, must overcome their racial bigotry. They must put national interest above "prejudices and self-interest." He closed on a pragmatic note. The Continental army needed black soldiers if it was to field a sufficient force to defend the South. Furthermore, he noted, "if we do not make use of them in this way, the enemy probably will."[33]

Opposition to the scheme advanced by Washington's two young aides was strong among southerners in Congress. However, a handful of southern congressmen defended the idea and appealed to Washington for his support, the only hope of securing congressional approval. Washington refused to join the battle. He probably feared that South Carolina, if pushed, would drop out of the war rather than risk the annihilation of slavery.[34] The plan advanced by Laurens and Hamilton was dead.

John Adams had written to Jefferson in 1777 urging his return to Congress. "We want your Industry and Abilities here," he implored.[35] Jefferson, busy with his attempts to carry out reforms in Virginia, shrugged off his friend's entreaty. But two years later Jefferson was stung by Washington's remarks about those who were not serving at the national level in the midst of America's great crisis. Jefferson admired Washington. He also knew that Washington was the most respected figure in the land. If America won the war, Washington would be a titan, powerful and dominant. No ambitious person could afford to incur his ill will.

Others besides Washington had previously beseeched Jefferson to do more. Richard Henry Lee pleaded with him "to suffer every thing rather than injure the public cause." Edmund Pendleton encouraged him to make sacrifices for the sake of "the rising Generation." An appeal from William Fleming, a friend from college who now served in Congress, was one of the more unsettling. The American cause "wear[s] a very gloomy aspect," Fleming wrote, adding, "we have . . . much to fear" both from the collapsing economy and Britain's military focus on the South, "where we are the most vulnerable." With hurt in his words, Fleming concluded his letter by saying that "Our great misfortune" was that too many had "lost sight of the great object for which we had recourse to arms, and have turned their thoughts solely to accumulating *ideal* wealth."[36]

Soon thereafter Jefferson signaled a willingness to serve as Virginia's governor. It was not solely the exhortations of others that induced him to abandon Monticello. Jefferson understood the dangers brought on by Britain's war in the South, and he knew that if the redcoats succeeded in the Lower South, they would one day come after Virginia. Besides, he believed—as Lee had put it to him—that if "we can baffle the Southern invasion," the "game will be presently up with our enemies."[37] Jefferson appreciated that this was a dangerous time to be Virginia's governor, but it was an opportune moment as well for an ambitious and idealistic individual. If the American victory was finally won on his watch, there would be laurels to be worn. What is more, a bloc in the assembly that favored domestic reform was supportive of Jefferson's candidacy. Much might be achieved if he led the state government.[38]

To be sure, Jefferson found the prospect of serving as governor to be unsettling. He worried about his abilities to handle the responsibilities of the office, especially as he had never served in an executive capacity. For that matter, Jefferson, who a year earlier had been overwhelmingly defeated in a contest to become Speaker of the House.[39] Yet, while acknowledging that a "private retirement" at Monticello was "almost irresistible," Jefferson said it "would be wrong to decline" to serve as governor.[40]

On June 1, 1779, Virginia's legislature elected Jefferson as governor, choosing him on the second ballot over two other candidates, both close acquaintances. One was John Page, perhaps his oldest, dearest friend. The other was Thomas Nelson of Yorktown, who had served in Congress and signed the Declaration of Independence, and in 1779 was the ranking officer in the state's militia.

The governor of Virginia, like most chief executives during the Revolutionary era, had little power. He existed mostly to administer legislative enactments, which he could not veto. When the governor did have to make a decision, he had to do so in collaboration with the eight-member Council of State. However, the governor could request emergency authority, and Jefferson's predecessor, Patrick Henry, had done just that when the British invaded nearby Pennsylvania in 1777. Jefferson, who believed in small, unobtrusive governments, had criticized the assembly for acceding to Henry's wishes, and throughout his two years in office he steadfastly refused to request additional powers. Jefferson did have one power that he was free to use: taking up his remarkable pen. Yet, while he had previously wielded it to shape the thinking of his countrymen—most spectacularly in the Declaration of Independence—as governor, Jefferson surprisingly never sought to rally or mold public opinion with a stirring executive address.

Jefferson was unhappy as governor. Within a month of taking office he was wistfully looking toward the day when his one-year term would end. It was bad enough holding an office that he did not relish, but Jefferson also knew when he became governor that morale was waning. As his old friend Fleming told him, the "bulk of the people . . . seem[ed] to have lost sight of the great object for which we had recourse to arms."[41] The war was four years old. The hope of imminent victory following the French alliance had faded. America had not won a significant victory in two years. Washington's army had not fought a major engagement since Monmouth, and it had not campaigned in the real sense of the term in two years.

Whatever Jefferson felt, he took his obligations seriously. In twenty-four months on the job, he returned home only twice from Williamsburg and then Richmond—which became Virginia's capital in the course of his tenure— and both visits were quite short. He coped with tons of paperwork, conferred regularly with legislators, and met almost daily with the Council of State. Almost every item of business with which he dealt was war-related. In fact, Jefferson took office in the midst of the greatest wartime crisis that Virginia had faced since the first winter of the war, when the last royal governor, aided by loyalists and runaway slaves, had waged a brief campaign against the rebels.

Three weeks before Jefferson's election, a British raiding force of more than 35 vessels and 1,800 men under Sir George Collier struck near Portsmouth. Meeting with only minimal resistance, the British sailed up the Elizabeth River to Gosport, home to one of the state's largest shipyards. Collier's men captured or destroyed at least 130 vessels and six million pounds of tobacco; laid waste to warehouses and naval supplies, including tons of seasoned wood for shipbuilding; seized large quantities of the militia's supplies; liberated up to 1,500 slaves; and plundered numerous plantations, allegedly stripping rings and jewelry from frightened women. Reeling from the magnitude of the destruction, Jefferson embarked on his new job by boldly telling the authorities in Philadelphia that Congress had forsaken Virginia. Despite the existence of a Continental navy, it had never helped the state, which had suffered from a crippling blockade imposed by only a handful of British vessels.[42]

The British did not return to Virginia for seventeen months, though Jefferson had a scare just before Christmas of 1779. Washington notified him that a huge British armada thought to contain upwards of eight thousand redcoats had sailed south from Manhattan. "Their destination [is] *reported* to be for Chesapaek bay," the commander warned. Cautioning that the enemy might invade Virginia, Washington exhorted Jefferson to "take any precautions which may appear to you necessary."[43]

Washington's warning was a false alarm. The British fleet was sailing instead for South Carolina. Virginia was fortunate. Jefferson had rushed supplies to the counties on the Chesapeake, and along the York and James Rivers that led to Williamsburg, but he had not mustered the militia. He had the authority to act but shrank from mobilization, knowing it would be costly and give "disgust" should the enemy never arrive. Besides, Jefferson gambled on a hunch: "I cannot say that I expect them," he remarked. On this occasion, he was correct.[44]

After Collier's damaging raid, Jefferson asked the state Board of War to prepare a plan of defense. In the months that followed, much of his time was consumed with establishing armories, finding weapons and powder, erecting coastal batteries, and building a network of sentinels and express riders in the hope that the state would never again be caught unaware and defenseless.[45] In addition, Virginia was to provide eleven of eighty battalions for the Continental army, about the same number as required of the two other largest states, Massachusetts and Pennsylvania. Jefferson worked tirelessly to find recruits. Virginia fell back on its age-old inducements of cash and land bounties for enlistees, and Jefferson threw his weight behind a tax increase that fell heaviest on the wealthiest. Eventually, Virginia resorted to conscription and finally, in desperation, to the proffer of a healthy male slave between the ages of ten and thirty for each man who volunteered. Still, about one-third fewer men were raised under Jefferson than by Patrick Henry. Few blamed Jefferson. Most, including Henry, attributed it to war weariness and the abundant sacrifices already made by the citizenry.[46]

Jefferson also devoted considerable time to Virginia's war in the west. A year before he became governor, the state had sent an army of 350 men under George Rogers Clark into what now is Indiana and Illinois. As the British were arming tribes in that region, Clark had been tasked with forcing the Indians to make peace. Not coincidentally, if Clark succeeded, Virginia's claim to the region—which originated in the colony's charter, granted by the Crown early in the seventeenth century—would be solidified.

By the time Jefferson took office, Clark had scored sensational victories in the Illinois country. He had captured Henry Hamilton, Britain's lieutenant governor of Detroit, thought to be the mastermind behind organizing and arming the Indians, and thousands of bushels of corn had been destroyed, a step Jefferson characterized as Clark's "happiest stroke." Believing that Clark had pacified the frontier at least temporarily, Jefferson urged a thrust against Fort Detroit, the heart of British power in the Northwest.[47] Despite Virginia's financial problems, and the possible risk the state might face from the dispersal of its limited soldiery, Jefferson acted with a bold assertiveness that he seldom displayed in dealing with threats in the east. Several factors drove him. Possession of the west in the postwar period was crucial to his dream of cheap land and widespread property ownership, which he in turn believed was crucial for the success of republicanism. Furthermore, taking Detroit before the spring would free up to eight hundred militiamen from the western counties alone, men whose service would be useful if the British ever again raided coastal Virginia. A native of a frontier county himself, Jefferson also sympathized with those in western Virginia who faced the spread of "destruction and dismay." The Indians, he said, were given to "savage irruptions" characterized by "cruel murders and devastations" visited on innocent civilians. In the end, the campaign against Detroit never materialized, in large measure because of opposition by the western militia, which had no appetite for campaigning so far from home. Jefferson let it pass. Just as he had been reluctant to hazard the displeasure of militiamen in the scare raised by the sailing of the British armada, he had no wish to provoke their anger over a crusade against faraway Detroit.[48]

Jefferson had acted responsibly, and with great vigor, in coping with the threats faced by Virginia. But the danger did not diminish. As the winter of 1780 faded, the British invasion of South Carolina began. From this point forward, the peril that Virginia faced grew greater, and the problems facing Governor Jefferson grew exponentially.

At first, few understood the significance of Britain's southern strategy when it was unfurled in 1778. Even Washington initially shrugged off the enemy's success in taking Savannah. He thought Britain's campaign in the South was no more than a sideshow, one that would have little bearing on the war. Six months later, around the time that Jefferson became governor, Washington at last comprehended that London planned the reconquest of Georgia and South Carolina, with more to follow. But so long as a British army occupied New York City, he refused to deploy any of his army to the Lower South. However, Congress acted. It ordered Continentals from the Upper South to augment the army of General Benjamin Lincoln, commander of American forces in the Southern Department. Moreover, once the British flotilla sailed from New York in December 1779—and Washington learned its destination was South Carolina, not the Chesapeake Bay—he exhorted Jefferson to send all the help he could spare to Lincoln. There "never was greater occasion for the states to exert themselves," Washington declared.[49]

Jefferson was in a bind. As Virginia had already been the target of one devastating naval raid, he could not ignore the possibility of another attack at any moment. Certain that he would receive little help from Congress, Jefferson believed that some men, and some supplies, had to be kept in Virginia for its defense. The legislature authorized the dispatch of upwards of 2,000 men to South Carolina, but Jefferson never considered giving up that many troops. Ultimately, he ordered some 400 men and some supplies to Charleston.[50] Logistical problems slowed the operation, perhaps fortunately. About the time the Virginians marched into South Carolina, the British imposed an ironclad siege on Charleston. Lincoln's army was trapped and no further reinforcements could enter the city. In May 1780 Charleston fell. The United States lost 5,500 killed and captured, but the men that Jefferson had sent south were not among them.

The news of the disaster at Charleston hit Jefferson with the impact of a body blow. With no Continentals remaining in the Lower South, at least for the time being, he feared the British army might waste no time before marching northward into Virginia. Nor was that his only concern. Shortly before learning of the debacle at Charleston, Jefferson received word from a friend in Paris that France would likely drop out of the war unless the allies soon scored a decisive victory.[51] Never had America's fortunes, or those of Virginia, looked so bleak. Given the magnitude of the crisis, Jefferson unhappily agreed to stand for a second term. The legislature reelected him in June 1780.

Jefferson worked furiously throughout that summer of 1780. Without exaggeration, he remarked that the "duties of the office I hold [are] so excessive."[52] He prepared for the defense of Virginia, but he did even more for the new Continental army in the Southern Department that was taking shape in North Carolina under the command of General Horatio Gates. Jefferson knew that if Gates stopped the British advance, Virginia might be spared further fighting. In a flurry of activity, Jefferson oversaw the outfitting of state infantry and cavalry units that were headed southward, renewed his recruiting efforts, sought "military furniture" for some "utterly unfurnished" regular battalions, and organized "a line of expresses" from Richmond to as near Charleston as possible. He calculated that his "speedy line of communication" would give him ample warning should the British army in South Carolina, now under the command of General Charles Cornwallis, plan an invasion of Virginia. In addition, he rounded up axes, tomahawks, wagons, horses, powder, flints, and cannonballs for Gates's army, and sent him two thousand

Virginia militiamen. Jefferson acknowledged that "we have not Arms" for Virginia's militia, but he advised Gates that Congress was sending three thousand muskets.[53]

Perhaps Jefferson's most remarkable step was his audacity toward General Washington. Jefferson in effect told Washington that he was wrong, something virtually no one else was willing to do. Though not confrontational—he acknowledged that Washington was "situated between two fires," a British army on Manhattan under Clinton and Cornwallis's army in South Carolina—Jefferson told the commander that the prevailing "sentiment . . . in Congress and here" was that he must yield some of his army for the defense of the South. Jefferson even urged Washington to come south and personally take command. Incredibly, Jefferson pledged to "cheerfully transfer to you every power which the executive [of Virginia] might exercise."[54] Thomas Jefferson had not quite offered George Washington dictatorial powers in Virginia, but he had come close to it. It was to no avail. Rochambeau's army landed in Rhode Island at almost the same moment that Jefferson's letter reached Washington's headquarters. Henceforth, the American commander's focus was on a joint allied campaign to retake New York.[55]

The South was a minefield for Continentals. A rebel army had been destroyed in the defense of Savannah in December 1778, and a second—Lincoln's army—surrendered in May 1780 following the siege of Charleston. In July, Horatio Gates, the victor at Saratoga as well as a rival whom Washington hated and feared, succeeded Lincoln as commander of the Continental army in the Southern Department. Gates acted rapidly—in fact, too hurriedly. Before he got the lay of the land, established an adequate intelligence network, or familiarized himself with his southern troops, Gates put his army in motion, marching southward from Hillsborough, North Carolina. (He set out just nine days after Jefferson implored Washington to come south.) Gates's target was a small British force known to be operating near Camden, South Carolina. Unbeknownst to Gates, Cornwallis was personally bringing reinforcements toward Camden. The two armies stumbled into each other and squared off on August 16. The outcome was decided when Gates's callow militiamen, including the Virginians that Jefferson had sent, broke and ran early in the engagement, setting off a contagious panic. It was a rout. One fifth of Gates's men were casualties. The remainder had taken flight, with Gates running just as hard as his frightened men. He did not stop until his sweaty mount reached Charlotte, sixty miles away.[56]

The debacle at Camden gave Hamilton the opportunity for eliminating Washington's last rival, and he made the most of it. In earlier attacks, Hamilton had sought to diminish Gates's standing by questioning his role in the victory at Saratoga, arguing that the spadework for victory been done previously by Schuyler. At Saratoga, Hamilton had argued, Gates had "hug himself at a distance" from the battlefield, leaving it to Benedict Arnold "to win laurels for him." After the Battle of Camden, Hamilton once again went after Washington's nemesis. Hamilton depicted Gates's plans for battle as a "military absurdity." With biting sarcasm, Hamilton wrote that the general "showed that age and the long labors and fatigues of a military life had not in the least impaired" his ability to run.[57] Soon after the disaster in South Carolina, Gates was removed from command. As had been the case when Hamilton helped to finish off General Lee, Hamilton had yet again done his part in the elimination of one of the commander's rivals. He had also demonstrated his value to General Washington.

Jefferson called Camden a "Misfortune," but he knew that it had been an unmitigated disaster. Once again, no American army stood between Virginia and Cornwallis, and Jefferson thought it inconceivable that Virginia could defend itself. While he had it in his power to summon and arm three thousand Virginia militiamen, he knew that powder would be in short supply and that there would be no tents for the soldiery. In addition, much of the spare clothing and wagons that he had sent to Gates now belonged to the enemy. Atop these woes, Jefferson learned that hundreds of men from several counties had enlisted in newly established Loyalist units. Should the British invade Virginia anytime soon, Jefferson told Congress late in the summer of 1780, "they would find us in a condition incapable of resistance."[58]

Jefferson's fears were realized. The blow that he dreaded, and that Virginia had expected during the seventeen months since Collier's naval raid, came in October 1780. The sortie was another raid, not an all-out invasion. It had been requested by Cornwallis, who saw the assault both as a diversion to prevent the deployment of Virginia militia farther south and as a means of interrupting the rebel supply line that ran through Virginia and into the Carolinas. As Virginia's autumn foliage burst into its gaudy colors, a British fleet of six vessels and 2,200 redcoats under General Alexander Leslie fell on the state. In the third week of October, Leslie put his cavalry and 1,000 infantrymen ashore at Portsmouth, Newport News, and Hampton. Inexplicably, the early-warning network that Jefferson had painstakingly built failed, and Leslie took Virginia by surprise. Washington had earlier cautioned that a fleet was being readied in New York for an unknown destination; however, only a week before Leslie appeared, the American commander had advised Jefferson that the British were unlikely to deploy a force of any size southward before November or December. Washington thought the British would wait until the Franco-American armies were immobilized by the winter, a view that

Jefferson too had expressed a month earlier. Such thinking likely led officials up and down the line to decrease their guard.[59]

When Leslie's raiders splashed onto Virginia soil, only the local militia was available. Poorly armed and devoid of a cavalry wing, the militiamen were ineffectual. Jefferson responded to the emergency with alacrity. He summoned thousands of militiamen from the inland counties and diverted units that had been ordered to North Carolina. He even attempted to persuade the French admiral in Rhode Island to bring his fleet to the Chesapeake, where in a joint operation the French and Virginians might trap, and doom, Leslie. There was little chance of that happening, and the possibility vanished once Leslie unexpectedly sailed away after only three weeks. His raiders had sown terror and inflicted considerable damage from below Cape Henry to the periphery of Williamsburg. With time, Leslie could have caused greater harm, but Cornwallis summoned him to the Carolinas, where the war had suddenly taken an unexpected, and ominous, turn for the British.[60]

Within a few days of the capture of Charleston, General Clinton had exulted that rebel resistance in South Carolina had been broken save for that of "a few scattering militia."[61] Clinton's claim had seemed indisputable, but in July the inhabitants of South Carolina's backcountry stirred, launching a guerrilla war. It started without help from Congress or the Continental army, and in the first months these rebels fought with little or no outside assistance. Many were Scotch-Irish Presbyterians who had come to America to escape Great Britain and its Anglican Church, though some had been radicalized by the American Revolution, and others had taken up arms in response to depredations of the British army. Guerrilla wars tend to be dirty and ferocious, and this was no exception. In time, Cornwallis's army suffered heavy attrition, the victim of partisans sustained by arms sent southward through Virginia. In part, Leslie had been sent to Virginia to interdict those supply lines, but just before he put his men ashore, the southern rebels in the Carolinas scored a sensational victory. In a battle fought on King's Mountain, near the North Carolina–South Carolina border, the British lost more than one thousand men, roughly 20 percent of Cornwallis's entire army. He ordered Leslie to South Carolina.[62]

Changes were occurring as well on the American side. Congress removed Gates following the debacle at Camden, spurred in part by the vitriol poured on him by Hamilton. Congress then asked Washington to name Gates's successor. Congress had previously made similar requests of Washington, but he had always refused to act, seeing his involvement in such personnel matters as a potential political snare. But given the desperate situation, Washington overcame his reluctance and recommended the appointment of General Nathanael Greene.

Greene, a Quaker from Rhode Island who had never soldiered before 1774, had been chosen as one of the original general officers when the Continental army was created in 1775. He quickly caught Washington's eye. An extraordinary judge of men, Washington saw things in Greene that escaped others. In time, Greene became Washington's most trusted advisor. By 1780, he had acquitted himself as a leader under fire in engagements in New England, New York, New Jersey, and Pennsylvania. If anyone could succeed in the South—and so far no one had—Washington believed it would be Greene.[63]

Following his appointment, Greene had a long meeting with Washington, then rode to Annapolis and Richmond to confer with the governors of Maryland and Virginia. He sat down with Jefferson two days after learning that Leslie had departed for South Carolina. Greene wanted immediate help, and he provided Jefferson with a lengthy shopping list of things he needed from Virginia. He told the astonished governor that he wanted ten thousand barrels of flour and five thousand of beef or pork; he also asked for two hundred hogsheads of rum or brandy, one hundred wagons, each furnished with four horses and an experienced teamster, forty skilled workers from assorted trades, and five thousand pounds in specie. He insisted that Virginia meet its quota by furnishing three thousand men to the Continental army, and he asked Jefferson to immediately provide him with an entire corps of militia adequately supplied for a winter campaign. Before leaving Richmond, Greene revealed that he had appointed General Friedrich von Steuben to command the Continentals in Virginia and to drill the state's troops.[64]

Jefferson went to work, and within thirty days most of the supplies that Greene wanted were on their way to North Carolina. But Jefferson protested to Congress that Virginia should not be expected to arm the Continentals. He acknowledged that it was the state's responsibility to arm its militia, which it had done, and he ordered the militiamen requested by Greene to march for North Carolina. However, when they arrived, Greene fumed that these men were "destitute of everything necessary either for comfort or convenience." Barely containing his anger, Greene lectured Jefferson that it served "no good purpose to send men here in such a condition. . . . There must be either pride or principle to make a soldier. No man will think himself bound to fight the battles of a State that leaves him to perish for want of covering."[65] Stung, Jefferson secured authorization from the legislature to do what Washington had done unilaterally in 1777 when he sent Hamilton to Philadelphia with authority to confiscate civilian property. If it was the only way to obtain the items, Jefferson announced that he would "provide cloathing and blankets for the troops by seizing" them.[66]

Jefferson had boldly responded to the crisis that followed Gates's defeat and Leslie's raid, but Virginia was overextended and overwhelmed. It was defending itself from invasion, helping in the struggle against Cornwallis, and waging war on the trans-Appalachian frontier. The sacrifices required in the never-ending war were taking a toll. During the fall, what Jefferson called a "very dangerous Insurrection" that aimed at thwarting militia mobilization was uncovered in two counties; both were suppressed just in the nick of time. But Jefferson presumed that the "dangerous fire" of rebellion against civil authority had not been "smothered" forever, and he was correct. Within a month, some militia officers who had been ordered to join Greene refused to march until they were paid and better supplied. The state met their demands.[67]

Jefferson privately confessed his mortification at the conduct of many Virginians. It ate at him. He grew more melancholy, a downcast turn fed by his longing to return home and pursue his "Love of Study and Retirement." Around the time of his meeting with Greene, Jefferson confided to Page that he would not accept a third term as governor and that he might immediately resign. Other Founders, including General Washington, experienced similar moments of black despair, but none resigned. Page discouraged his friend from taking a step that would finish him forever as a public official. Nearly every state official thought him "eminently qualified" for his post, Page advised. He added that it was widely acknowledged that no other Virginian could have managed the recent war crises more adroitly. Only six months remained in Jefferson's second term, Page added, and they would pass rapidly. He closed with an admonition: "Deny yourself your darling Pleasures."[68] Jefferson did not resign. But he had hardly read Page's missive before his problems worsened immeasurably.

On the last day of 1780, a Sunday, a courier brought word to Jefferson that a British flotilla of twenty-seven vessels—considerably larger than the one Leslie had commanded—had been spotted off the Virginia coast. Two weeks earlier, Jefferson had learned from Washington that a British force would soon sail from New York. It was "destined Southward," said Washington, but he could not be more specific.[69] A year earlier, Washington had sent a similar warning. Jefferson had not summoned the militia to active duty, and it had been a wise decision. When Washington's latest notification arrived, Jefferson thought it unlikely that another British fleet would descend on Virginia barely two months after Leslie's departure. Besides, he was again hesitant about calling up the militia. On that Sunday when he received word of an enemy flotilla, Jefferson weighed his choices. He made an educated guess. He guessed wrong.

For leaders, wars are filled with guesses. Inevitably, many are incorrect. Some wrong choices are forgivable. Jefferson's response in this crisis was unpardonable. Jefferson was informed at eight A.M. on Sunday, December 31, that a large fleet was sailing northward in the Chesapeake. It was already close to the mouth of the James River. The sentinel system had worked and, in light of Washington's recent warning, Jefferson should have responded with haste. Yet throughout that long Sunday, and Monday as well, Jefferson did nothing. He did not call out the militia, nor did he notify the Council of State of the possibility of an imminent threat. He did not act until he had absolute confirmation of the presence of the enemy's naval squadron. In mid-morning on Tuesday, exactly fifty hours after first learning of the potential threat, Jefferson finally summoned the militia. He later claimed that he was slow to act because he did not know whether the fleet was friend or foe.[70] It was not a persuasive explanation. When bold, decisive leadership was essential, Jefferson had failed.

He was not the only important official to hesitate in the face of peril. Washington had often acted slowly and indecisively, at times with unfortunate results. But Washington was almost always spared public criticism. That was not the case with Jefferson.

The fleet that bore down on Virginia in the closing hours of 1780 carried a force of 1,600 men commanded by Benedict Arnold. After he had turned his coat, the British rewarded him with the rank of brigadier general and gave him an army of regulars, Hessians, and American Loyalists. Arnold's objectives, like Leslie's before him, were to sow terror, wreak destruction, deflate morale, fortify the Elizabeth River, and garrison Portsmouth, from which the British could close the supply lines to General Greene.

The first of Arnold's green-clad soldiers landed in Newport News and Hampton on New Year's Eve. Before sunset the following day, the invaders had seized four vessels and their cargoes. By early January 2, the day that Jefferson at last called to arms some 4,600 militia, Arnold's force was already within five miles of Williamsburg. Two days later Jefferson was awakened before dawn and notified that Arnold's fleet was about fifty miles up the James River, roughly halfway between Portsmouth and Richmond. Jefferson summoned the "whole militia from adjacent counties" and ordered the removal of government papers from the capital. He also commanded the destruction of all arms and munitions that could not be taken from the city. For five hours, Jefferson rode about the town on horseback directing operations. Just before noon, he took Martha and his three small daughters a few miles up the James River to Tuckahoe, the estate where his mother had been raised and he had first been schooled.

On Friday afternoon, January 5, Arnold reached Richmond with some nine hundred infantry and cavalry. They marched in nearly unopposed. The militia that Jefferson had summoned the day before had not reached the capital, and those who had been called to duty earlier in the week were scattered and unable to keep pace with the raiders, who were transported by sailing vessels that glided swiftly, thanks to what Washington once called their "canvass wings." Only two hundred militiamen were in the capital when Arnold's men landed. Some bravely offered resistance, but they were heavily outnumbered.

Jefferson had returned from Tuckahoe to a safe location across the river from the beleaguered capital. Climbing a small knoll and using a spyglass, he was able to watch the marauders as they carried away their booty and set fires. Soon, a black, choking smoke hung like a blanket over the town. Arnold's men—sometimes supervised, sometimes not—acted quickly. Within twenty-four hours, the raiders destroyed two warehouses, hundreds of hogshead of liquor, a foundry, mills, stores of food, a score of carriages, twenty-six artillery pieces, several residences, stores, and a church or two. In addition, they confiscated crafts large and small, more than two thousand muskets, and large stockpiles of grain. One residence that was plundered was the home of the governor.

The raiders departed after one day, carrying off "all kinds of merchandise" in forty-two vessels of assorted sizes. Arnold got just about everything he was after, though he came away empty-handed with regard to Governor Jefferson, whom he longed to apprehend. A couple of days earlier, Arnold's men had done extensive damage to Berkeley plantation, the home of Benjamin Harrison, a signer of the Declaration of Independence. Through scuttlebutt in the Continental army, in which Arnold had been a general officer for four years after July 1776, he may have known that Jefferson was the document's principal author. Even if he did not know that, capturing the governor of Virginia would have been a great prize.[71]

Arnold's raiding expedition came to a rapid end. He had sown considerable destruction in Richmond and at plantations along the James, and he had liberated scores of slaves. However, a week after arriving in Virginia, his army went into winter quarters in Portsmouth, which he had been ordered to fortify. Arnold's plan was await reinforcements and better weather, then to strike again.[72]

Virginia had been roughed up. The damage to Jefferson had just begun. Jefferson had made mistakes, his plodding response when warned of Arnold's approach the most egregious of all. Yet, given the debilities of his office and the military challenges that Virginia faced, failure likely would have stalked any who served as the Virginia's chief executive at this juncture of the war. Nevertheless, Arnold's calamitous raid had occurred on Jefferson's watch, opening him to blistering criticism, sometimes even from old friends.

One censured him as "obstinate, lethargic," while another railed at his "neglect and supineness."[73] Jefferson was also accused of indecisiveness and incompetence. John Page ranted that the entrance to the James River had been left unfortified and the militia ill-equipped. Edmund Pendleton complained to Washington that the governor had not been "sufficiently attentive" to intelligence and did not respond to the threat until "it was too late." General Steuben intimated to Washington that a stronger, more assertive governor would have done more to prepare the state for the crisis. Jefferson did not know of all the attacks on him, or who assailed him in private, but he knew that much of the blame for the debacle was being assigned to him. He responded with the claim that poor intelligence had been to blame. Few were convinced.[74]

Angry and humiliated, Jefferson sought to get his hands on the man who had brought the troubles down on him. He approved a scheme to rig a ship with explosives and crash it into Arnold's vessel, killing or capturing him when he tried to escape the blazing craft. The plan never materialized, but Jefferson soon turned to the notion of raising a party of militiamen who were to be paid five thousand guineas apiece if they succeeded in bringing Arnold to him, dead or alive. If Arnold was brought to him alive, Jefferson pledged, he would first make a "public spectacle" of "this greatest of all traitors," then he would have him executed.[75]

CHAPTER 5

"OUR AFFAIRS SEEM TO BE APPROACHING FAST TO A HAPPY PERIOD"

GLORY FOR HAMILTON, MISERY FOR JEFFERSON

SEVERAL MOMENTS MIGHT QUALIFY as the nadir of the Revolutionary War. The best known might be Washington's seemingly hopeless retreat across New Jersey in 1776 and the dreadful Valley Forge winter in 1778. But for contemporaries, the mood may never have been blacker than at the outset of 1781. In earlier crises there had been the promise of rescue by France, but by 1781 rumors were buzzing that France wanted out of the war. Even worse, the year began with mutinies of Continental soldiers. "[W]e are bankrupt with a mutinous army," declared a Massachusetts congressman.[1]

At Washington's headquarters and in war-torn Virginia that year, the feeling was palpable that the tide had to turn or America might be compelled to return to the British Empire. In such an event, Americans might have greater autonomy than before the war, but they would not be independent and there would be no United States. No one summed up the mood better than Hamilton. The "people have lost all confidence in our public councils," he said, adding that "our friends in Europe are in the same disposition." Like others, he wondered whether "we shall after all fail in our Independence."[2]

Hamilton and Jefferson were filled with despair, and not just for America's future. Hamilton's lust for glory seemed unlikely to be fulfilled. Jefferson's public career seemed on the brink of ruin.

Hamilton had long wanted an independent command. By becoming Washington's aide and gaining his respect, he had believed he would eventually be assigned his own brigade. Then, as a field officer, he would see action and have a shot at achieving distinction. But Washington found him too useful at headquarters to let him go. Year after year, Hamilton had remained tied to a desk, and now he suspected that the war was nearly over. Hamilton anguished that at war's end he would be just another obscure soldier. He had gained notoriety among powerful figures in New York, but despite six long years of soldiering, he had failed to become an heroic figure revered for his dauntless exploits. "The stars fight against [me]," he said. "I hate Congress—I hate the army—I hate the world—I hate myself," he declared, sinking into despondency.[3]

If the war was lost, Hamilton believed that history would blame the defeat on the absurd political and constitutional system that left Congress with insufficient "powers . . . for calling forth the resources of the country." The stubborn shortsightedness of the states, he thought, was robbing America of a victory it should long since have won. Yet, while Hamilton thought that America's economic woes had prolonged the war, he was also convinced that a myriad of factors had brought the United States to the brink of the abyss. Among the failures, in his judgment, were a surfeit of mediocre army officers, the refusal of too many men of talent to serve at the national level, and a fatal overreliance on the militia.[4] Then there was the matter of General Washington. Hamilton never criticized Washington's generalship, and in fact he thought him superior to his "competitors." He never said that he thought Washington was the best man for the job, but he never said the contrary either. However, Hamilton, like quite a few others, appears to have believed that Washington shared some of the blame for the war having gone on for so long. Washington had been reluctant to send his men to the Southern Department, and he had refused to support the enlistment of African Americans, steps that might have prevented the string of defeats in Georgia and the Carolinas, and which might have brought Great Britain to the peace table. In 1779, and again in 1780, Washington had resisted Congress's pleas to invade Canada, a step that at the very least might have compelled London to withdraw its army from the South. In fact, during the thirty months since Monmouth, Washington had remained largely inactive.

Hamilton had to be guarded in expressing his views, but it was apparent that he did not like Washington. "I have felt no friendship for him and have professed none," he said, adding: "I discovered he was neither remarkable for delicacy nor good temper." Hamilton's ingrained cynicism, together with his resentment at the general's aloofness and denial of his wished-for field command, colored his opinion of Washington. Nevertheless, Hamilton had seen the unguarded and unvarnished Washington, the "ill-humor[ed]" man who was carefully hidden from public view. Like a handful of others who saw the commander up close, Hamilton came to view Washington as hard and coarse, and sometimes petty, vain, ill-tempered, inconsiderate, insecure, inelegant, and unoriginal in his thinking. Like nearly everyone else, Hamilton found Washington to be distant and cold. Although "all the world is offering incense" to Washington, Hamilton wanted no part of it. Yet for all that he disdained in Washington, Hamilton not only acknowledged that the commander was honest and honorable but he also thought it "essential to the safety of America" that the public see Washington in mythically heroic hues. What Hamilton was saying was that the cause required a fabricated Washington, one that the American people could believe in and rally round in order to sustain morale and maintain national cohesion.[5]

Hamilton once said that he had "always disliked" serving as an aide, in part because he detested "having . . . a kind of personal dependence" on any individual, whether Washington or someone else. All of his frustrations, contempt, and simmering resentments surfaced in a flash on February 15. Summoned by Washington, Hamilton was slow in getting to the commander's office. Washington, whose nerves were already stretched to the breaking point by the recent mutinies and countless other difficulties, upbraided Hamilton "in a very angry tone," telling him, "you . . . treat me with disrespect." Hamilton resigned on the spot. An hour later, Washington, who truckled to no man, sent Hamilton an apology and asked him to reconsider. Hamilton refused, though as weeks or months might be needed to find a suitable replacement, he agreed to remain on the commander's staff until his position was filled, and in fact he continued as an unofficial aide for another six months. He stayed on in part from his commitment to the cause, but also as it afforded the best prospect of fulfilling his ambition for a field command. Hamilton hoped to rejoin the artillery when a position opened or to find a post with the army in either the Carolinas or Virginia.[6]

In particular, the worsening situation in Virginia caught Hamilton's eye. He knew that Washington, in the wake of Arnold's raid on Richmond, had dispatched 1,200 men to the state under the command of the Marquis de Lafayette. In March, Sir Henry Clinton countered by sending 1,600 men under General William Phillips—who, while a prisoner of war in Albemarle County in 1779, had dined with Jefferson—to reinforce Arnold. Hamilton anticipated plenty of action in Virginia, and he wanted to be part of it.

In April, he once again asked Washington for an independent command. That more troops would be sent "to the Southward, I take . . . for granted," Hamilton added. Never short of chutzpah, Hamilton, who had been a lieutenant colonel for five years, asked to be promoted to the rank of colonel in the light infantry and sent with the deployment to the Southern Department. Washington refused. To jump Hamilton over others who had served in the field would provoke a tempest, he said. In reality, Washington thought Virginia would be a mere sideshow. He was certain that the real action would be in New York, and he wanted Hamilton near him.[7]

While Washington looked toward New York as the solution to America's dilemma, Jefferson knew that America's most pressing problem was on his doorstep. In mid-February, about six weeks after Arnold's raid, Nathanael Greene notified Jefferson that Cornwallis might soon attempt to "push through Virginia."[8] The British invasion of the South, which had commenced in Savannah two years earlier, had moved steadily northward. Virginia's turn might be next.

Ironically, it was Greene's success that brought about the likelihood of Cornwallis's descent on Virginia in 1781. Having taken command of the Southern Department late in the previous year, Greene had waged the most audacious campaign conducted by any American general since Washington's Trenton-Princeton actions four years before. Greene divided his army of some 1,400 men, sending half west of Charlotte under General Daniel Morgan while he took the remainder far to the east. It was an open invitation to Cornwallis to come into North Carolina after the rebels. Cornwallis did not need to be coaxed. In January 1781, at the very moment of Arnold's raids, Cornwallis divided his larger army and went after the two American divisions. Although each of Cornwallis's divisions was about twice the size of its counterpart, his hope of decisive victory soon went awry.

Cornwallis sent Colonel Banastre Tarleton after Morgan. Tarleton commanded the 1,200-man British Legion, a Loyalist regiment of infantry and cavalry. He almost immediately found his prey at Cowpens in South Carolina, not far from Kings Mountain. The two forces fought a pitched forty-minute battle on January 17. At its end, Morgan had won a stunning victory. The British had lost nearly one thousand men. Tarleton was one of the few to escape.[9]

Greene, meanwhile, was pursued across North Carolina by Cornwallis. Staying just a step ahead, Greene won the race, escaping across the Dan River and into Virginia on February 14. The following day, Greene wrote to Jefferson to warn that Cornwallis might push into Virginia.

Cornwallis lingered in North Carolina, regrouping after losing some 250 men in the grueling chase after Greene's tattered rebel army. Meanwhile, Greene replicated Washington's 1776 post-Trenton recrossing of the Delaware River by recrossing the Dan into North Carolina. He did not, however, immediately seek a fight with Cornwallis. Greene awaited reinforcements, including those he had demanded from Jefferson. Given "the spirit of the

Virginians," Greene wishfully told Jefferson, he was sure of receiving ample men and supplies. To this point, the campaign had unfolded "greatly to our advantage," Greene said, and with adequate numbers even greater success could be achieved. But without them, he added, North Carolina "is inevitably lost," in which case Virginia would be next on Cornwallis's list. "You will consider the necessity and act accordingly," he advised Jefferson.[10]

Greene was not alone in urging Jefferson to act. General Friedrich von Steuben besieged him with requests for tents, kettles, clothing, tools, munitions, workers, boats, and wagons that could be channeled to Greene. Jefferson did his best to comply, though when Steuben urged him to seize horses from civilians—as Washington had ordered Hamilton to do in 1777—Jefferson refused. He pleaded that the governor lacked authority for such an act, and he did not seek greater powers. He must have thought it useless to ask, as the legislature had recently refused his entreaty for harsher punishments of militiamen who refused to serve and the Council of State had not permitted Steuben to seize and outfit privately owned vessels.[11]

At this same moment, Washington himself appealed to Jefferson. The commander understood that Jefferson must be alarmed by Britain's "predatory incursions" into Virginia but asked the governor to consider the "injury to the common cause" that would result from the subjugation of the Carolinas and Georgia. The "danger to your state in particular," he told Jefferson, would be enhanced. To this, Washington added: "I am persuaded the attention to your immediate safety will not divert you from the measures intended to reinforce the Southern Army and put it in a condition to stop the progress of the enemy in that Quarter."[12]

Jefferson was in a bind. Should he send men to Greene in another state or keep the soldiers in Virginia to guard against further raids? Jefferson sent what he thought he could spare. He was active in other ways too. He drafted a proclamation to the German troops serving under Britain's flag, offering them "lands, liberty, safety" if they would desert and make their home in Virginia.[13] At the same time Jefferson begged Congress to send assistance, pointing out that most of Britain's army was in the southern theater and that General Clinton could be expected to send "still larger reinforcements" to Virginia. It was "inconsistent," he said as diplomatically as possible, for Virginia to have dispatched aid to the northern states for years, only to have those same states now ignore the plight of their brethren below the Potomac. Congress quickly ordered wagons, clothing, arms, and munitions to Virginia, but six weeks later those supplies were still gathering dust in the cargo hold of a vessel in Philadelphia's harbor.[14] However, more immediate help was on the way. It was at this moment that Washington ordered Lafayette to Virginia with 1,200 men.[15]

For an instant it appeared that Virginia's salvation was at hand. Not only did Lafayette and his men arrive, but also, at nearly the same moment in March, Jefferson learned that the French were sending a large fleet and 1,100 men under the command of Chevalier Charles-René-Dominique Sochet Destouches to the Chesapeake. Jefferson rushed 4,000 militiamen to Lafayette and rejoiced that the joint Virginia-Continental-French operation would succeed in "lopping off" the British in Portsmouth from Cornwallis's force in North Carolina. The normally pessimistic Steuben was cautiously optimistic as well. If the allies succeeded, he said, the "seat of war" would be removed "from the frontiers" of Virginia.[16]

Few operations went according to plan in this war, and this was not one of them. When Destouches reached Cape Henry on March 16, he discovered a large British squadron awaiting his arrival. The fleets clashed immediately, but as soon as the British got the better of it, Destouches broke off the fight and returned to Rhode Island. "I am truly Unhappy," Lafayette told Jefferson, and he confided to Washington that "Never has an operation been more ready (on our side) nor Conquest more certain."[17]

Arnold's force was still in Portsmouth, and Cornwallis was just south of Virginia's border. Greene had delayed acting for nearly a month after recrossing the Dan, as he gathered men and supplies. Toward the middle of March, Greene at last could report that the "Militia have flocked in," though he was "disappointed in the reinforcement" from Virginia. Nevertheless, he could wait no longer, as he knew that he would have the militiamen for only a few days. Greene maneuvered to face Cornwallis, and on March 15—the day before Destouches's abortive naval engagement—the two armies clashed in the Battle of Guilford Courthouse. Greene rightly called it a "severe conflict." At its conclusion, Cornwallis was technically the victor, as he held the blood-soaked field when the shooting stopped. But in fact the British general had won a pyrrhic victory. Cornwallis lost 550 men, twice the number lost by Greene.[18]

Greene now sensed the opportunity for a major victory. Cornwallis was hurting. "The Enemy are retireing and we advancing," he told Jefferson. He wanted Jefferson to send still more men and provisions, and to increase the length of the militia's service from six weeks to three months. If Jefferson helped, said Greene, the American army in the South might achieve something of consequence. If not, "the Army must inevitably fall a sacrifice."

Greene said that his "greatest dependence is on Virginia for support, and without her exertions I cannot keep the field." He pleaded with Jefferson to do more. "I have committed my life and reputation to your service." Be a leader, he in effect said to Jefferson. "[C]ivil polity must accommodate itself to the emergencys of war, or the people submit to the power of the enemy. There is no other alternative." With greater help from Virginia and Virginia's governor, Greene closed, he could pin down Cornwallis in North Carolina, or possibly even drive him back to South Carolina. In either case, he could keep "the war at a distance from you."[19]

But the war was already in Virginia. By the time Jefferson learned of Greene's success at Guilford Courthouse, General Phillips's large force had arrived at Portsmouth and linked up with Arnold's. There now was a British army of some 3,500 men on Virginia soil. By then, too, Steuben had concocted a bold plan. Steuben proposed that about half of the Virginia militiamen that Jefferson had summoned to protect against the British raiders, some 2,000 men, join with Lafayette's Continentals to bottle up Arnold and Phillips in Portsmouth, preventing them from rendezvousing with Cornwallis. In the meantime, the remaining 2,000 Virginia militiamen would march south and reinforce Greene. At last, Greene would have a superior force with which to fight Cornwallis. The plan had wide support. Lafayette endorsed it. General George Weedon, who commanded a militia brigade near Williamsburg signed off on it, calling it a maneuver that would catch the British by surprise and "terminate the war." Richard Henry Lee, the Speaker of the state assembly, thought it had the potential to be "one of those Master strokes."[20]

But both Jefferson and his Council of State rejected the scheme. They wanted all of Virginia's troops on Virginia soil, especially as they were unconvinced that Lafayette's force, devoid of a naval arm, could succeed in confining Arnold and Phillips. Steuben was outraged, and convinced that Jefferson failed to understand the depth of America's crisis. Weedon was no less furious, in private charging that Jefferson had "not an idea beyond local security." Though more restrained, Greene bristled at the thought of a state governor spurning a plan developed by a general in the Continental army. He thought Virginia was "lifeless," but in the same breath he complained of it being overextended, as Jefferson continued to wage war in the West. Nor could he resist telling Jefferson that Virginia's militia, by itself, would accomplish little in defending against British raiders. Southern "pride induces them [the Virginians] to wish to be thought powerful," but "they deceive themselves," he said caustically.[21]

Jefferson was bitter too. He had already told Congress that he believed Virginia had been let down by the northern states. Now, privately, Jefferson questioned Washington's acumen as a strategist, recounting how for the past three years the main Continental army had sat idle outside Manhattan while the British reclaimed Georgia and made considerable inroads toward reconquering the Carolinas. In reality, Jefferson argued, Great Britain no longer thought it could accomplish anything above the Potomac. "The Northern States are safe." Yet, while Britain's focus was entirely on the South, New York remained Washington's focal point. Washington was as obsessed with retaking New York as Spain was with reclaiming Gibraltar, said Jefferson, and he predicted that America's commander would be no more successful than had been Spain's king. As Jefferson's fury spilled forth—not unlike Hamilton's in his headquarters confrontation with Washington a month earlier—it was apparent that he believed it was Washington who had let down all who had fought in the South. But he still thought that there was a chance for victory: With proper assistance from Washington, "the Continental war would be totally changed, and [in] a single Campaign" the British could be defeated in the South and the allied victory could be won.[22]

Meanwhile, Jefferson and his fellow contemporaries were unaware that the war in the South had reached its tipping point. In the aftermath of Guilford Courthouse, Cornwallis withdrew his bloodied army to Wilmington, on North Carolina's coast, for rest and refitting. While enjoying the warm oceanside sunshine, Cornwallis wrestled with his choices. His orders were to remain in the Carolinas until both states were thoroughly pacified, but he was aware that Phillips had united with Arnold. If he marched his army northward, the number of redcoats in Virginia would exceed 5,500 men. What is more, Cornwallis knew that he could not subdue the rebels in the Carolinas as long as provisions flowed down the supply line through Virginia. Cornwallis had made his fateful decision. He and his regulars stepped off from Wilmington on the long march northward to Virginia just as April was shading into May.[23]

Phillips had already gone into action in Virginia, launching a raid of his own. This foray was up the Potomac River, and under the command of Captain Thomas Graves. Proceeding in three heavily armed schooners and several smaller craft, Graves sailed as far as Alexandria, destroying property, seizing livestock, and liberating slaves, including seventeen of Washington's chattel at Mount Vernon. Three weeks later, just as Cornwallis commenced his march toward Virginia, Phillips, with Arnold at his side, launched another raid. Taking 2,500 men, including cavalry, the British raiders yet again sailed up the unobstructed James River, this time in fourteen naval vessels. Jefferson quickly summoned the militia, but it was ineffective. In some places it responded slowly, and nearly everywhere the militiamen were poorly equipped, outnumbered, and never a match for enemy infantry with a cavalry wing. The raiders laid down what Jefferson subsequently called a "Circle of Depredation." While Phillips sowed destruction in the vicinity of Williamsburg, burned shipyards on the Chickahominy River, and torched ships and tobacco warehouses in Petersburg, Arnold captured or destroyed twenty-three vessels and burned two million pounds of tobacco up the James River. The two British divisions had planned to link up just below Richmond and lay waste to the town. They rendezvoused and sailed to Manchester, across the James from the capital, but learning that Lafayette and his Continentals were marching on Richmond—where some 500 militiamen were already posted—Phillips reconsidered. After some probes and skirmishes, the redcoat commander scrapped his plan, preferring to withdraw to Portsmouth and await Cornwallis's arrival. His raid had been a success. Indeed, the outcome had been precisely as Greene had always told Jefferson it would be. Virginia simply could not defend itself against the British raiders.[24]

Only a month remained of Jefferson's second term as governor when Phillips brought to an end his costly raid. Perhaps no Revolutionary War governor had faced greater difficulties, or had to make more burdensome decisions, than Jefferson. He led an exhausted and war-weary state. On taking office, Jefferson discovered that those free men who were willing to serve in the Continental army had long since enlisted, leaving him to lament the "difficulty, nay impossibility, . . . to get men." So widespread was what he called the "Spirit of disaffection" against military service, that by late 1780 he wondered whether the militia in much of southwest Virginia would respond to a call to arms.[25]

Jefferson also presided over a state that was averse to a strong government. Aside from his year in the Continental Congress, Jefferson had been a Virginia assemblyman for nearly a decade before becoming governor. He knew the mentality of Virginia's legislators, and he understood the limits they imposed on the state's governor. That realization restrained him from asking for emergency powers, and when he refused to confiscate the property of civilians, it was partially from personal reservations, but also from an understanding that to do so would only arouse opposition to the war in a state already suffering with war fatigue. Continentals such as Steuben and Greene thought Jefferson weak and unsuited for leadership in a time of crisis, and a case can be made for their viewpoint. However, an effective leader has to understand the governed, and from the outset Jefferson recognized that he walked a fine line in coaxing from civilians as much as possible effort without extinguishing their continued support for the war.

Could he have done more? Yes. He might have sought at least some small increase in his authority. To be sure, he might have wielded his mighty pen to rally a greater war spirit. But rhetorical appeals were not common practice among the Revolutionary War governors, or even by Congress.

Toward the end, Jefferson burned his bridges with many Continentals by refusing to support Steuben's plan for a campaign against Cornwallis in North Carolina. It might have succeeded, though war plans that look good on paper are not always successful, as the scheme for the joint Lafayette-Destouches campaign demonstrated. Nevertheless, Jefferson's opposition exposed a timidity and shortsightedness unbecoming of a leader in an emergency. His role in thwarting the Steuben plan was a greater blunder than his better-known failure of having responding languidly to intelligence that Benedict Arnold was bearing down on the state in January 1781. Even had Jefferson acted with alacrity at the news of Arnold's approach, it is difficult to imagine that Virginia could have offered a more effective resistance. Given the state's resources, Arnold's greater mobility, and the incredible expanse that had to be defended, there was little that Jefferson or any other governor could have done to lessen the damage that the raiders inflicted. Indeed, no one accused Jefferson of permitting the state to be caught off guard by Phillips's raid, yet that incursion was no less successful than its predecessors.

Jefferson took his responsibilities seriously and worked hard—very hard—and there were stretches when he toiled in the depths of despair. At times during 1781 he was on the run, separated from Martha and their three daughters—eight-year-old Patsy, two-year-old Mary, and one-year-old Lucy Elizabeth—who shuffled between Richmond and Tuckahoe. Furthermore, as the spring unfolded, little Lucy Elizabeth's health declined, and on April 15, three days after the British threatened Mount Vernon, she died. Though beset with ineffable sadness, Jefferson never ceased to be a fighter. When in 1779 the British had closed in on Charleston—with an army merely two-thirds the size of the force under Phillips—South Carolina governor John Rutledge had proposed that his state drop out of the war in return for the city being spared. Such a thought never occurred to Jefferson.[26]

By spring 1781, as his second term ebbed away, Jefferson remarked without exaggeration that Great Britain's war on America "falls at present on Virginia only."[27] Greene had made a fateful choice. A week after Guilford Courthouse, he opted to take his army into South Carolina to liberate the state from the redcoats still garrisoned there. He expected Cornwallis to follow him. He was wrong. Cornwallis turned instead toward Virginia.[28] By mid-May, Jefferson was aware that Cornwallis was in the state, and he knew that when Philips and Cornwallis united, a huge British army would be on Virginia soil. If that was not bad enough, intelligence indicated that Clinton was sending reinforcements from New York. Jefferson believed that, by the summer, there would be some seven thousand redcoats in Virginia. There were perhaps two thousand Continentals, and whatever "Ill armed and untried Militia" that could be raised, to defend Virginia against them.[29]

When Governor Rutledge in South Carolina had proposed dropping out of the war, he did so in part because he and his lieutenant governor had lost confidence in General Washington. Rutledge thought the commander's indifference to the war in the South was "scarcely credible"; his lieutenant governor, Thomas Bee, imagined that "the Southern states are meant to be sacrificed."[30] Jefferson shared Rutledge's view about Washington's strategic myopia, and on May 28, with only about a week remaining of his tenure in office, Jefferson sent Washington one final letter as governor. He pleaded yet again for Washington to come to Virginia with his army and take command of the defense of the state. "[L]end us Your personal aid.... [Y]our appearance ... would restore full confidence of salvation," he wrote. Should Washington come and bring his army, Jefferson said in closing, the only "difficulty would then be how to keep men out of the field."[31]

As April was about to turn to May, Lafayette advised Jefferson that his hands were tied unless Washington sent substantial numbers of Continentals to Virginia. Helpless to take the offensive, Lafayette said he could only pursue a Fabian strategy.[32] Not long after Jefferson read the young Frenchman's letter, General Washington, with Hamilton possibly in tow, set off from his headquarters in New Windsor, New York, for Weathersfield, Connecticut, where he was scheduled to meet with Rochambeau during the third week in May. The allies were to plan their summer campaign. What Washington would seek was hardly a mystery. For years, he had fastened on retaking New York, and he had already broached the idea to an unconvinced Rochambeau at a previous meeting in September. Rochambeau had patiently explained to Washington that the allies lacked the necessary numerical superiority and naval supremacy for either an attack or a protracted siege, but a final decision had been postponed until the expected French reinforcements arrived in the spring.

Dark, cold weather had settled over Connecticut when the allied commanders at last sat down together on May 21. Rochambeau began by saying that it was possible that the French fleet in the Caribbean might come to North America to assist the armies. He then asked Washington what he envisaged for the summer of 1781. Predictably, Washington urged a joint campaign to retake New York. Rochambeau countered with a proposal that they move their armies to Virginia. At the time, Rochambeau knew that Phillips had arrived in Virginia and that his army totaled more than three thousand men. He did not know that Cornwallis, who had set off from Wilmington, was bringing his army to Virginia as well. Washington listened, and demurred. Rochambeau subsequently recalled that his counterpart "did not conceive the affairs of the south to be [of] such urgency." The two generals argued, but Washington held his ground. Rochambeau, who had been ordered by his government at Versailles to defer to the Americans, reluctantly agreed to a joint campaign to retake New York. The moment the conference ended and Washington began the long ride back to the Hudson River, Rochambeau wrote to Commodore François de Grasse, the commander of the French fleet, and beseeched him to sail for Virginia, not New York. Unbeknownst to Washington, the wheels had been set in motion for a Virginia campaign.[33]

Hamilton could not have been happy with the agreement that Washington had secured at Weathersfield. Given his apparent feelings about the commander's limitations as a strategist, and likely aware of Rochambeau's cogent reservations about a New York campaign, Hamilton must have doubted the wisdom of what appeared to lie ahead. In fact, he suspected that operations would never commence. As late as July 10 he remarked that "there seems to be little prospect of activity," as only the most optimistic were persuaded that the French fleet would arrive. But Washington still controlled Hamilton's destiny. On the eve of the Weathersfield conference, Hamilton apologized to Washington for having "embarrassed" him by requesting an independent command. Not only did he understand why Washington had turned him down, he said humbly but he also assured the commander that his only thought was for "the good of the service."[34] Hamilton groveled. He wanted to stay in Washington's good graces, perhaps hoping against hope that some suitable position for him might turn up with Lafayette's force in Virginia, which seemed the most likely place for action in 1781.

While Hamilton brooded over the likelihood of another summer of inactivity, Jefferson faced more action than he ever wanted. By late May, with barely a week left in his term, Jefferson was at home at Monticello. Virginia's legislature had been scheduled to meet in Richmond at the beginning of May, but it had been nearly impossible to persuade the skittish assemblymen to come to the capital. Finally, several days late, a quorum was attained, but only after the governor sent assurances that Richmond was now "perfectly secure." The dubious legislators came, but were not inclined to linger in the capital. They met only long enough to agree to adjourn until May 24, when they would meet again in Charlottesville, where they could be "in full Assurance of being unmolested by the Enemy."[35]

Jefferson remained in Richmond for another week, but just as Rochambeau and Washington were sitting down together in Weathersfield, the governor arrived at Monticello. At almost the same instant, Cornwallis marched into Petersburg, Virginia, where he had ordered Phillips to bring his army. The British commander was eager for action, and victories. At about the same time that Virginia's legislature convened in Charlottesville, Cornwallis crossed the James River and set off to destroy Lafayette: "The Boy cannot escape me," he allegedly remarked. But Lafayette—as he had indicated to Jefferson—had no intention of standing and fighting. "Was I to fight a Battle I'll be Cut to pieces," he said. Retreating deep into the interior of the state, Lafayette escaped Cornwallis, much as Greene had in North Carolina. After a week of fruitless chasing about, Cornwallis changed course. He divided his force. He would continue to look for Lafayette, but he detached the Queen's Rangers to go after Steuben's small force while Colonel Tarleton, with 250 of his Green Dragoons—a troop of Tory cavalrymen—was ordered to Charlottesville to find and capture Virginia's governor and legislature.[36]

Though Jefferson and the assemblymen were aware by May 29 or 30 that a sizable body of redcoats was only thirty miles away, they continued to believe they were safe. There were some Continentals and militia between Charlottesville and Cornwallis, and besides, if a threat materialized, some imagined that Lafayette would arrive to offer protection.

The legislature met daily in the Albemarle County Courthouse and the Swan Tavern. Nearby at Monticello, Jefferson tended to his heavy official correspondence—he wrote thirty-one letters in his final ten days in office— met daily with legislators (among other things he proposed the drafting of slaves to serve as laborers in the construction of fortifications), and conducted diplomacy with John Baptiste Ducoigne, a Kaskaskia sachem from the Illinois country, who called on him at Monticello. At some point after the legislature assembled—possibly when the assemblymen were still in Richmond—Jefferson formally announced that he would not accept a third term. It hardly came as a surprise. Jefferson had long since told others of his plan to leave office, confiding even in the French chargé d'affaires in Philadelphia.[37]

Since early in the month, some assemblymen had talked of granting the governor dictatorial powers. Some thought that Patrick Henry was conspiring not only to be reelected but also to have the assembly vest him with emergency, perhaps autocratic, powers. It was a view that Jefferson came to share. In mid-May, Jefferson tacitly recommended an increase in the chief executive's authority. Nothing mattered now but managing the defense of the state, he told the assembly, adding that this was a job for which he was "unprepared by his line of life and education." As the state needed someone skilled in "the command of armies," Jefferson urged the election of General Thomas Nelson, the commander of the state's militia, as his successor. Furthermore, Jefferson proposed that Nelson be permitted to continue to command the militia while serving as governor, as "this . . . would greatly facilitate military measures." Inexplicably, the legislators did not immediately select a new governor after reconvening in Charlottesville. They scheduled the election for Monday, June 4, forty-eight hours after Jefferson's term ended.[38]

Jefferson was subsequently criticized for not having remained in office until his successor was sworn in. But he was a stickler when it came to observing the letter of the constitution, and his term was over. Besides, the legislature never asked him to stay on. His term ended on a Saturday. Had Monday been a normal day, it is conceivable that the assembly might have asked him to remain in office for a few more days until his successor arrived and took the oath of office. It is possible, too, that Jefferson would have consented. However, Monday was anything but normal.

On Sunday, Jefferson penned a few final official letters, closing the books on his tenure as chief executive.[39] He did not know that while he was at his desk, Tarleton and his green-clad horsemen had set off for Charlottesville.

The horse soldiers moved rapidly. They covered seventy miles in twenty-four hours, and might have captured Jefferson and all the assemblymen had their arrival in Charlottesville been a total surprise. But Tarleton's force was spotted sometime around midnight, when it was still about forty miles from its destination. John Jouett, a twenty-six-year-old native of Charlottesville, was enjoying the libation at the Cuckoo Tavern in Louisa when Tarleton and his men thundered past. Jouett, the son of the proprietor of the Swan Tavern, where the legislature had sometimes met, knew instantly that Jefferson and the assembly were in great peril. He leaped on his horse and rode with abandon, taking shortcuts unknown to Tarleton. Jouett won the race to Charlottesville by some ninety minutes. His first stop was at Monticello. He may have chosen to warn Jefferson first, as he thought the governor would be Tarleton's most likely target. Or Jouett may have begun at Jefferson's residence because he knew that the presiding officers of both houses of the legislature, and a few assemblymen, were lodging there.[40]

Much that happened after Jouett pounded on Monticello's front door at about four thirty A.M. remains a mystery. Over the years, Jefferson's enemies spread the story that he had fled precipitously. Friends claimed he had carelessly lingered, eating breakfast and even having his horse shod before departing.

The truth is somewhere in between. It appears that Jefferson must have remained at Monticello for around ninety minutes after he was awakened. He dressed, ordered that a carriage be readied for his wife and daughters, and probably loaded some valuables in it. He saw to the departure of his guests, either hid some precious possessions or directed trusted slaves to do so, and burned some papers while stuffing other documents in his satchel bags. Jefferson knew that the British would first have to come through Charlottesville, which he could look down on with his well-worn spyglass, and he took the precaution of posting reliable servants as lookouts along the steep road that led to his hilltop home. He knew that he did not have much time, but he had to know that he had some time. Though taken by surprise on that June 4 morning, Jefferson had known that such an emergency could happen, and he must have previously planned his escape in the event of a worst-case scenario. Martha and the girls were to go to Enniscorthy, an acquaintance's estate fourteen miles to the south, where he would later join them. They left well before he did.

As Jefferson expected, Tarleton entered Charlottesville first (where he captured seven assemblymen, who had lingered to burn papers, and Daniel Boone, who happened to be in town). Only moments after Tarleton entered the village, he ordered Captain Kenneth McLeod, with a party of twenty or more, to hurry to Monticello and seize Jefferson. McLeod and his troopers spurred their mounts, galloping toward Jefferson's mansion, never slowing as they charged up the winding and muddy road leading to it. Swinging from their sweaty horses, the troopers burst into the residence. It was empty save for Martin Hemings, a slave who was hiding his owner's silver. He likely told McLeod that Jefferson had long since departed, and the British officer must have believed him. What sort of fool would have delayed his flight until the enemy soldiers were nearly at his front door? Even if Hemings was lying, McLeod must have suspected that Jefferson was intimately familiar with myriad paths through the virgin forest. With even the slightest head start, he would be impossible to find. McLeod did ask where Jefferson was going. Hemings insisted that he had no knowledge of Jefferson's plans. Apparently finding it plausible that a master would not confide in his chattel, McLeod dropped the matter. He pursued his prey no further.[41]

Jefferson had made his getaway. Unconfirmed reports said that he departed on Caractacus, reputed to be one of the fastest horses in the state, only five minutes before McLeod arrived.[42] He probably had not cut it that closely, but Jefferson had not been gone long when the enemy reached his door.

In subsequent years, Jefferson's flight was depicted by his political enemies as a cowardly act. But if Jefferson behaved cravenly, he had plenty of company: The members of the Continental Congress had twice fled the approaching British army; Samuel Adams and John Hancock had scurried to safety from Lexington, Massachusetts, on the day in 1775 when the British army arrived and started the Revolutionary War; General Washington had retreated on numerous occasions in the face of the enemy; and Lieutenant Colonel Hamilton had taken flight after coming under fire while on his mission to destroy flour mills outside Philadelphia. In fact, none of these men had acted in a cowardly fashion. All had acted prudently. Capture meant a lengthy, possibly lethal, confinement in a British prison. Jefferson had to know that if the war was lost—and victory was far from certain in June 1781—he might never be freed. Moreover, he could only imagine what his captors might do with him if they discovered that he was the author of the Declaration of Independence.

In the pale light of early morning, Jefferson rode down the hilltop and into the cool, dark forest, heavy with the dank scent of decay brought on by spring rains. A good horseman, he rode swiftly, up steep wooded slopes, down into foggy hollows, and now and again along flush green ridges. He was hurrying toward Enniscorthy, though he had no plans to linger there; it was too close to the British army. Jefferson was reunited with Martha and the children in mid-morning, but he paused only briefly before resuming his journey. His destination now was the home of Robert Rose, an old family friend who lived some fifty miles southwest of Monticello. Jefferson remained on horseback. Martha, who had neither physically nor emotionally recovered from her last pregnancy and the recent loss of Lucy Elizabeth, rode in the carriage with the two girls. The roads were primitive, and streams had to be forded. It was not an easy trip, and to the travelers' general discomfort was added the omnipresent possibility of running upon a British patrol. But no enemy soldiers troubled them. The family stayed that Monday night at the residence of Thomas Jopling, probably a stranger, whom Jefferson paid a whopping £45 to cover their expenses. (According to Jefferson lore, another family had earlier refused them lodging, fearing reprisal by the British army.) Before finally reaching Rose's estate on Tuesday, Jefferson purchased supplies for £123 at a general store.[43]

Satisfied that his wife and children were safe with the Roses, Jefferson started back to Monticello on Thursday, anxious to learn whether the house he had lovingly constructed over the past fourteen years was still standing. On Saturday, five days after fleeing, Jefferson completed his one-hundred-mile round-trip on horseback. To his utter amazement, he found that Monticello was undamaged and his slave labor force intact. Enemy soldiers had been on his property for eighteen hours and, aside from consuming a good bit of his wine, "Captn. Mc.leod preserved every thing with sacred care," as Jefferson subsequently remarked. But not all of his properties were so fortunate.

He soon learned that his Elkhill plantation on the James River, which he had gained through marriage, had been Cornwallis's headquarters for ten days. The seven thousand redcoats and hundreds of camp followers—wives, mistresses, and freedmen—had reduced the estate to "an absolute waste" and "carried off also about 30 slaves."[44]

Jefferson and his family spent most of that summer at Poplar Forest, an estate some eighty miles southwest of Monticello that he had long before inherited. There was not the slightest possibility that the British would strike there. Still reeling from the heavy burdens and misfortunes that had been his fate as governor, Jefferson decided during that summer to take his "final leave of every thing" concerned with public life.[45] His political career had seemed to come to an end before his fortieth birthday.

But politics would not leave him be. The legislature, which had also been on the run, reconvened in Staunton on the same day that Jefferson left the Roses to return to Monticello. With passions still at a fever pitch, the assemblymen wasted no time before adopting a motion to investigate Jefferson's "Catalogue of omissions, and other Misconduct." The inquiry was to take place at the autumn session of the House of Delegates. George Nicholas had introduced the motion, but Patrick Henry, once Jefferson's friend, was the guiding light behind the probe. Jefferson was livid. He suspected that some were seeking to settle old scores and others were looking for a scapegoat. He seethed that the legislature would "stab a reputation . . . under a bare expectation that facts might be afterwards hunted up to boulster it."[46] (Ironically, two days later the United States Congress selected Jefferson to be part of the five-member team of commissioners to negotiate peace with Great Britain, if and when negotiations commenced.)[47]

During the summer, Jefferson was made aware of the details of the inquiry. The questions to be answered concerned Arnold's January 1781 raid. The legislature proposed to investigate the steps that Jefferson had taken, or failed to take, including the following: Had he put in place adequate lookouts, post riders, and a system of signals? Had he ignored Washington's warning? Had he acted slowly in summoning the militia? Had he made inadequate preparations for the transport of heavy artillery? Had he abandoned some installations without a fight? Was he responsible for a "total want of opposition to Arnold."[48]

Jefferson fumed for months as he awaited the probe. Nicholas, a "trifling" man of "natural ill-temper," was "below contempt," he said privately. But he was merely the "tool" of Henry, an individual who flourished in political "turbulence," and who had pushed the investigation to further his own ends. So indignant was Jefferson that despite his vow to leave politics forever, he successfully sought reelection to his old Albemarle County seat in the legislature. He was determined to defend his reputation and honor, and no less passionate about a face-to-face confrontation with Nicholas, Henry, and all other detractors.

What Jefferson could not know in July was that by December, a decisive military event would occur that would change everything.

About three weeks after Jefferson fled the British, Alexander Hamilton departed Albany, where he had spent a month with his pregnant wife, and rejoined Washington's army. He sped back when he learned that Rochambeau's army was marching from Rhode Island to rendezvous with its ally outside Manhattan.

Hamilton had been in limbo since quitting as Washington's aide back in February. Though no longer officially an aide, he nevertheless had continued to work for the commander through the winter and spring. But when he returned to the army in June, Hamilton had no official duties. Subsequently, he claimed to have written to Washington to resign his commission, though it seems improbable that he would have taken such a rash step, especially with the allied armies gathering and a campaign at last seemingly about to occur. True, he had told his wife that marriage had "intirely changed" him, stripping away "all the public and splendid passions," leaving him "absorbed" only with his family. But more than anything, Hamilton during the spring and summer of 1781 appears to have been conflicted, torn between a desire to be with his family and an enduring passion for acclaim. If he did write to Washington, it was probably as a last effort to persuade the commander to give him a field command. All that can be known for certain is that early in July, through an intermediary, Washington assured Hamilton that he would receive a command. Three weeks later, on the last day of the month, Hamilton was given command of a New York light infantry battalion.[49]

During the preceding six weeks, Hamilton had confessed that there was nothing of "importance to occupy my attention." However, he was never an idler.[50] He spent the time writing four long essays titled "The Continentalist" for a New York newspaper. In them, Hamilton reflected on America's decentralized political system and enervated national government. It was his first public swipe at the Articles of Confederation, and the beginning of his ceaseless endeavors to establish a more powerful national government. Composed while he anguished over the unlikely prospect of obtaining glory in the coming military campaign, Hamilton's rancor toward Washington was evident at times, though he was careful never to mention the commander by name.

When governments are too weak, he began, "the ruin of the people" was inevitable. Implying that a law of centrifugal force was at work, he said that a weak government would "continually grow weaker," destroying the "general interest" of the Union. This evil was already apparent. Even during the present desperate war, some states had not complied with Congress's demands. Worse still was the economic collapse, which had occurred because "Our whole system is in disorder." America was shackled with this toxic threat even as "a force under Cornwallis [remained] still formidable to Virginia." (Never mentioning the British in New York, Hamilton, like Jefferson, seemed to be saying that America's most pressing military concerns were in the South.) America, he continued, now found itself in its greatest crisis. In what likely was a criticism of Washington's years of inactivity, Hamilton wrote that America had underestimated "how difficult it must be to exhaust the resources of a nation . . . like that of Great Britain." Those in power had not only erroneously gambled that time was America's ally, but they had also "never calculated the contingencies" that could arise in a long war. The bright prospects brought about by the victory at Saratoga were long gone; the enemy had retaken two colonies in the Lower South. But matters could be saved if "without delay" it was agreed "to ENLARGE THE POWERS OF CONGRESS," providing it with the authority to tax and create a sovereign national government, steps which alone could lead to the "restoration of public credit."[51]

By the time Hamilton completed the four essays, he had finally received his field command. Thereafter, he turned his attention to readying his battalion for the looming campaign, wherever it might be. In May, Washington and Rochambeau had agreed on an attempt to retake New York. Six weeks later—one week after Jefferson fled from Monticello and while Hamilton vacationed in Albany—Rochambeau divulged to the American commander that de Grasse had consented to bring his fleet northward. Where, Rochambeau asked again, did Washington wish it to sail? Aware by then that Cornwallis was in Virginia with a large army, Washington was more flexible. He told his French counterpart that the Chesapeake perhaps offered the best opportunity for a decisive allied victory. Once again, Rochambeau pleaded with de Grasse to sail for the Chesapeake, not New York. But in mid-July, two weeks before Hamilton was given an independent command, Washington changed his mind. New York, he told Rochambeau, should be "our primary Object." At month's end, the indecisive American commander changed course yet again. The allies' best bet lay "to the Southward," he said."[52]

No one was sure where the fight would be, or if it would even occur. Everything hinged on where, or whether, de Grasse arrived. Any number of things might prevent, or delay, his coming. Hamilton was not confident that there would be an action, but when he took charge of his battalion, he likely guessed that if a campaign materialized, it would be to retake New York.

The sweltering days of July passed. The heavy, heat-filled days of August set in. A week passed, then another. Suddenly, on August 14, came the long-awaited word. De Grasse had sailed from Haiti eleven days earlier with a squadron of twenty-nine ships of the line. His destination: Virginia. The allied armies did not linger. Within five days French soldiers and their American brethren—7,300 strong—were on the march. Meanwhile, Washington ordered Lafayette, together with the Virginia militia, to keep Cornwallis from escaping back into North Carolina. If Lafayette succeeded, the fight would be in Virginia. In that event, the only question would be whether the allies would have to cope with only the redcoats already in Virginia, or whether Sir Henry Clinton would take his army in New York southward to rendezvous with Cornwallis. In a very short time, the allied commanders had their answer. Clinton opted to remain in New York, convinced that de Grasse lacked the naval superiority to prevent Cornwallis's withdrawal by sea. Washington and Rochambeau thought otherwise. The feeling that something very big was occurring had set in by the time the armies made the now familiar crossing of the Delaware River. By September 2, when the allied armies staged a grand parade through Philadelphia's dusty streets, Washington sensed that an epic event was playing out, for he had learned that beyond question de Grasse's fleet would be considerably larger than anything the Royal Navy could muster. Within two or three days of departing Philadelphia, Washington was beside himself with joy. He knew that Lafayette had succeeded. Cornwallis was bottled up on the peninsula below Richmond in the little village of Yorktown.[53]

As the armies marched south, past lines of curious spectators, Hamilton wrote to Betsey that his health was "perfect." His ecstasy at the prospect of battle was tempered only by his separation from her. "I am unhappy because I am so remote from you. . . . I am wretched at the idea of flying so far from you," he told her. When the armies stepped off, Hamilton thought the odds of finding Cornwallis still in Virginia were about ten to one. As the days passed, however, Hamilton, like Washington, came to think that a decisive action loomed. At Annapolis, he boarded a vessel for the voyage to the Virginia peninsula. By then, Hamilton knew there would be a siege operation in Yorktown. Not to worry, he told Betsey. Sieges are "so conducted, as to economize the lives of men." He arrived in Williamsburg late in September and was reunited with Lafayette and John Laurens. A couple of days later he was in the allied siege lines in Yorktown, from which he wrote with considerable accuracy that "our affairs seem to be approaching fast to a happy period." He predicted on October 12 that in five more days, ten at the most, Cornwallis would have to surrender.[54]

Nearly every plan, by either side, in this long war had gone awry. At Yorktown, however, everything seemed to fall effortlessly into place. With his overarching numerical superiority, de Grasse frustrated the Royal Navy's attempts to rescue Cornwallis. In the meantime, Cornwallis's men dug entrenchments while French and Continental sappers gouged the first parallel out of Virginia's sunbaked earth. It was two miles long. Once they completed their work, other soldiers dragged heavy artillery into the gun emplacements that had been burrowed. The allies, as Hamilton had tried to tell Betsey, held all the cards. De Grasse promised to stay through October. Cornwallis did not have sufficient provisions to sustain his army for such a long period. The allies had more than 19,000 men against some 8,500 men under Cornwallis. The allies possessed one-third more cannon than their adversary. As the French engineers planned the siege operation, Rochambeau assured Washington that it was "all reduced to calculation." An American general exalted that the allies had "the most glorious certainty of victory." On October 9 the thunderous allied bombardment began. A hundred field guns banged away. It continued day and night. Some 3,600 shells exploded in the tiny village of Yorktown every twenty-four hours. Cornwallis took refuge in an underground bunker. His men huddled in trenches and wet, debris-filled basements. By October 16 digging began on a second parallel closer to the tiny village, and only 150 yards from the nearest British lines.

Work on the second parallel was impeded by the existence of two British redoubts. Redoubt No. 9 was on the French side of the allied siege lines. Redoubt No. 10, a square-shaped installation defended by forty-five enemy soldiers, was on the right, or the American side, of the siege lines. Both redoubts housed a battery of mortars—which the British called "royals"—capable of lobbing shells directly into the allied parallels. Neither men nor artillery were safe so long as the redoubts functioned. Their presence was dragging out the siege. De Grasse would have to leave in a couple of weeks, and there was no time to waste.

Clearly, each redoubt would have to be taken by direct assault. The fighting would be hand-to-hand. The allied commanders decided that the French would carry out the attack on No. 9 and the Americans would conduct the strike on No. 10. Washington permitted Lafayette to select an officer to lead the American assault, and he chose his aide, Jean-Joseph Sourbader de Gimat. Lafayette's choice meant that French officers would be leading both assaults.

Hamilton stepped up. He knew that the attack on the redoubt was likely to be nearly the last act of the siege. Almost certainly, too, Yorktown would be his last venture in the war. He had told his wife that he would leave the army when this campaign concluded. "Every day confirms me in the intention of renouncing public life. . . . Let others waste their time and their tranquility in a vain pursuit of power and glory," he had told her.[55] Despite his pretense of mocking those who chased after acclaim, Hamilton was desperate to close his days of soldiering with a shot at glory. In numerous earlier engagements, he had been eager to be part of a hazardous operation. It was the price one had to pay in the quest for splendid recognition and honor. As an adolescent, he had dreamed of becoming a military hero. He had never stopped dreaming the dream. Now was his final chance.

Hamilton appealed to Lafayette to permit him to command the assault. Pleading that Washington had already approved his choice of Gimat, Lafayette refused. Hamilton went directly to Washington. One can only guess what Hamilton said, though he surely must have pointed out that he had seniority over Gimat. He likely argued, too, that it was essential for the new nation that America share the credit with the French for the pending victory at Yorktown, and he may have reminded Washington, as he had in his April letter requesting a field command, that he had loyally served his commander at a desk while others were given opportunities to be "useful to the United States" in combat roles.[56] Whatever he said, he succeeded. Washington intervened and put Hamilton in charge of the operation. Washington never said why he made the decision, but, as it would become clear on many occasions in the future, Hamilton understood the commander perfectly and was aware of how to bring Washington around to his way of thinking.

The attacks were set for the night of October 14. Hamilton would have three infantry battalions, one under Laurens. The officers would wield swords. Some men were armed with axes to clear the abatis—a tangle of logs and branches, some with sharpened ends capable of impaling a charging soldier—that ringed the breastworks. All others carried unloaded muskets. Their bayonets would be their only weapon. Hamilton's force outnumbered the enemy by nearly ten to one, but not all of his men could descend into the redoubt. For those who did, the odds would be more equal, and the fight would be desperate and infinitely dangerous.

In the final hours before the attack, before the soot-black night deepened, Hamilton wrote what could have been his last letter. Seated in a parallel redolent with the rancid scent of smoke, gunpowder, and freshly turned earth, Hamilton told Betsey how he longed to hold his child, which was due in a few weeks. "In imagination I embrace the mother and embrace the child a thousand times. I can scarce refrain from shedding tears of joy." He added that in a few days Cornwallis would have to surrender, "and then I fly to you. Prepare to receive me in your bosom. Prepare to receive me in all your beauty, fondness and goodness."[57]

October 14 was a dark, moonless night. As Hamilton's men had to race nearly five hundred yards to reach the redoubt, the sable evening was a welcome ally. When all was ready, Hamilton gave the signal to charge. The men emerged from the parallel and sped toward their target, with Hamilton in the lead. It was impossible for hundreds of men to pound noiselessly across the terrain. Some, in fact, fell with a clatter into undetected shell holes. Alerted that they were under attack, the British defenders opened fire. Men all around Hamilton were hit. But the attackers kept charging, and in an instant, the first to reach the redoubt surged inside and went after their adversaries. Hamilton must have been among the first to penetrate the abatis. The fight was brief but wild, blind, and bloody, as determined, bold, frightened, and daring men struggled at close quarters, lunging with bayonets, wielding muskets as if they were clubs, pummeling and choking other men, desperately seeking to prevail, and to stay alive. "We carried it in an instant," Hamilton said later, and in fact the fighting ended ten minutes after it began.[58] He also said subsequently that all enemy soldiers who surrendered were spared. Forty of Hamilton's men were dead or wounded. Eight of the enemy were killed and several more were casualties. Gimat was wounded, as were four other officers, two of whom were bayoneted as they scrambled into the redoubt. Hamilton escaped unscathed. Washington, in his official report, lauded the "bravery" of Hamilton and his men, adding that there had been "Few cases" during the war in which his soldiers had "exhibited stronger proofs of Intrepidity, coolness and firmness."[59]

By dawn, the second parallel had been completed. It stretched to the blood-soaked Redoubt No. 10. The allied artillery now blasted away at point-blank range. Cornwallis made his men endure the merciless bombardment for thirty-six hours, hoping against hope for a miracle. But nothing could save him and his beleaguered army. At last, having already lost 556 men in the three-week siege, the British commander signaled a willingness to talk. The negotiations were brief. The end came on October 19, six years and six months to the day since the war had begun at Lexington and Concord. On that lovely, bright, historic autumn day, while Hamilton stood watching the proceedings, the British surrendered what remained of the army that had first splashed ashore along the lower James River on New Year's Eve. In all, more than eight thousand men who had tried to crush the American rebellion in Virginia laid down their arms and went into captivity.

A few weeks after Cornwallis's surrender, Jefferson arrived in Richmond for the December meeting of the legislature. Nursing a broken wrist suffered in a recent fall from his horse, he nonetheless made the long, painful ride from

Monticello. He was driven by a bitter loathing and he also wished to defend himself in the scheduled probe into his conduct as governor. Some men would have challenged their tormentors to a duel, but Jefferson was not given to violence and he kept a tight rein on his emotions. (What is more, he, together with the "valuable part of society," condemned dueling as "knight-errantry" in defense of "imaginary honour.")[60]

There was no inquiry. "I came ... [but] found neither accuser nor accusation," Jefferson raged.[61] On the day set for the hearing, George Nicholas "withdrew from the house" and Henry sat mute. Neither they nor the assembly any longer had an ardor for going after a former official who had long served the colony and state, and the American Revolution, and who presumably would never again seek high office. Besides, after Yorktown, an investigation seemed pointless, and with America's victory the corrosive bitterness of early summer vanished like snow under a bright, warm sun.

The lack of a hearing did not assuage Jefferson. Vexed and indignant, he wanted to clear his name. He obtained the floor and "did it myself," he later said, in what must have been a tension-laced chamber. Standing erect, and mustering all the vocal force and strength he could bring to bear, Jefferson read each charge that Nicholas had presented against him the previous summer. He answered each allegation. When he was done, the legislature by a unanimous vote thanked Jefferson "in the strongest manner" for his service as governor, lauded his "impartial, upright, and attentive administration of the *powers of the Executive*," and removed from the record "all *former* unmerited Censure."[62]

Vindicated, Jefferson resigned and rode home, convinced that he would never again hold public office, and cherishing a future adorned with the "independence of private life."[63]

Hamilton, who had obtained a furlough a week after Cornwallis's surrender, had just completed an even longer ride, from Yorktown to Albany. He remained at Betsey's side through the winter, and in January was present when she gave birth to a son, Philip, who was named after her father. A few weeks later, in March, Hamilton resigned from the army. He told Washington that he hoped his service had been useful, and added that should "unfortunate events" prolong the war, he would return and "renew my exertions in the common cause."[64]

Hamilton's Revolutionary War was over. His struggle to impede revolutionary change was about to begin.

Postwar America

CHAPTER 6

"THE INEFFICACY OF THE PRESENT CONFEDERATION"

GRIEF AND INTRIGUE

LATE IN 1781, Jefferson returned to Monticello. Embittered with public life, he wanted no more of it. As Virginia's chief executive, he had coped with baffling, irresolvable difficulties. For what he called his "constant sacrifice," he had wanted nothing more than "the affection of my countrymen." Instead, he had been "arraigned for treasons of the heart and not mere weaknesses of the head," charges that had left an indelible "wound on [his] spirit."[1]

Following Cornwallis's surrender, Americans expected the war to wind down and to soon end altogether. Jefferson had never desired to be part of the team that negotiated peace, and weeks before the siege commenced at York-town, he had declined Congress's request to sail for Europe. He said that Monticello required his management, as farm operations had "run into great disorder and ruin" during his two-year absence. Privately, he confessed his longing to be with Martha and his two young daughters, who needed his "attention and instruction." He had reached a point when no office was alluring. His years of legislative service had convinced him that assemblymen spent hour after hour in "trifling [and] wordy debate," often on "unimportant questions." Much of it was "a waste and abuse of the time," which was hardly unexpected, he said, of a body filled with lawyers "whose trade it is to question everything, yield nothing, and talk by the hour." When the voters in Albemarle County reelected him to the state assembly in the spring of 1782, he refused to serve. With more than a kernel of truth, Jefferson declared that he had been "cured of every principle of political ambition." He was convinced that "public service and private misery [were] inseparably linked," and he wished to spend the remainder of his life "in mental quiet."[2]

Once at home, Jefferson returned to the contemplative life he had cherished before becoming governor, and he wrote his only book. Its genesis originated in a request by François de Barbé-Marbois, a member of the

French legation in Philadelphia, for information about the thirteen American states. Jefferson began drafting his lengthy reply shortly before Arnold's first despoiling raid, but the unrelenting crisis, and the inaccessibility of a good library, prevented him from completing his answers until he returned home. Finally, in December 1781, he sent his composition to Barbé-Marbois.[3] By then, Jefferson had begun to think of expanding the manuscript into a book. He completed a first draft within two years, but made extensive revisions thereafter, some after the manuscript was critiqued by friends. However, one suggestion that he ignored was to conceive "a more dignified title." He stuck with his first choice, and the book was published in Paris in 1785 with a less than lyrical appellation: *Notes on the State of Virginia.*[4]

Jefferson wrote about his state's geography, boundaries, climate, plant and animal life, farming, towns and counties, schools, roads, economy, and Indians. He included a segment on the legal treatment of Loyalists and, in a separate section on the law, penned a discourse on race. Much of what he wrote about race was unworthy of one who fancied himself as committed to the enlightened reconsideration of conventional thought. By contrast, Hamilton— like Jefferson, a product of a slave society and the child of a slave owner—had reassessed accepted biases and emerged as strikingly ahead of his time in his thinking on race. Jefferson, on the other hand, was unable to overcome what he acknowledged were "Deep rooted prejudices." What he wrote in the 1780s would have passed for orthodoxy among whites a century earlier in pre-Enlightenment Virginia. Jefferson contended that blacks perspired more and urinated less than whites, required less sleep, were more tolerant of heat but less of cold, and were less disciplined and reflective. Blacks, he went on, were artistically and intellectually inferior to whites, "more ardent" sexually, and physically less attractive.

Though Jefferson's racism gushed out for all to see, he denounced slavery as a "moral evil" and a "blot" on the land. His solution was gradual emancipation. All slaves born after an undesignated date should be freed upon reaching adulthood, he said. Females should be educated at public expense until age eighteen, males until age twenty-one, but thereafter they were to be colonized in some remote territory, where they would be protected by the United States until capable of independence. Jefferson justified expulsion on the grounds that it would be impossible for the two races to ever live together in harmony. White prejudice and "ten thousand recollections, by the blacks, of the injuries they have sustained," would provoke interminable "convulsions" that would inevitably "end . . . in the extermination of one or the other race."[5] It was a hopelessly pessimistic view from which he never deviated.

Still, Jefferson had excoriated slavery and called for its end at a time when only an infinitesimal number of Americans—and, save for Quakers, virtually no Southerners—were taking such a stand. His argument was courageous, and it was seen in that light by friendly contemporaries. John Adams, for instance, exclaimed that the "Passages upon Slavery, are worth Diamonds."[6]

Jefferson was bolder when it came to religion. He assailed the intolerance and barbarism of organized religion, writing that Christianity was responsible for having "burnt, tortured, fined, imprisoned" millions of innocent people. He thought it an inexplicable paradox that his fellow countrymen had been prepared to die in the American Revolution for their "civil freedom" but were willing to remain under "religious slavery." He argued passionately for freedom of religion, including the liberty to attend no church and, by implication, to be a nonbeliever. In what were to become perhaps the most-quoted sentences in the book, Jefferson asserted, "it does me no injury for my neighbour to say there are twenty gods, or no god. It neither picks my pocket nor breaks my leg."[7]

He also wrote with passion about government. Having initially been drawn to the protest against the mother country by the centralization sought by Britain's rulers, Jefferson in time came to see the purpose of the American Revolution as a struggle to enable the people to govern themselves. By the time he wrote A Summary View in 1774, he believed that the abundance of land in Virginia would permit a transition to a society of truly self-governing citizens; by the time he authored the Declaration of Independence, Jefferson was convinced that the American Revolution was an epic event that went far beyond the establishment of independence. For America, for the world, the American Revolution—captured in the vision he articulated in the Declaration of Independence—held the promise of democratization, the moment in history when humankind broke the chains of monarchical and aristocratic governance and people began to govern themselves. By 1783 he was calling for giving all free males the right to vote and basing the number of delegates allotted to each county "in proportion to the number of its qualified voters." Under the latter reform, Tidewater Virginia—which at the time was home to roughly 40 percent of the state's voters but held more than 50 percent of the assembly seats—would be stripped of its disproportionate power.[8]

Jefferson did not stop there. He pondered the relationship between governance and the socioeconomic nature of society. He had read deeply in Montesquieu and Hume, and though their views differed on many things, what he took from their writings set him to thinking. Later, he said that they had taught him how the propertyless in Europe were forced into exploitive manufacturing jobs that left them with a "want of food and clothing necessary to sustain life." Their desperate circumstances begat "a depravity of morals, a dependence and corruption, which renders them an undesirable accession to

a country whose morals are sound."⁹ Jefferson may also have feared an inexorable march toward a manufacturing society, as he thought it a rare individual who could resist the temptation of every "gewgaw held out to him,"
even if it led to indebtedness, or what he called "the keys of a prison."¹⁰ It is
possible, too, that he may already have seen trouble ahead for the American
Union, given the economic dissimilarities between the more urban and commercial northern states and the agrarian south.

In *Notes*, Jefferson condemned manufacturing states as the basest of societies for the greatest number of citizens. Jefferson believed that an inevitable
"Corruption of morals" occurred in a manufacturing state. Manufacturers
were ensnared in the demeaning vortex of a never-slackening chase after
wealth. Their unquenchable thirst for money, and their dependence on the vagaries of the marketplace, drove them inescapably to vice and venality. Moreover, all who were dependent on the success of the manufacturers—merchants,
shopkeepers, tradesmen, laborers—were compromised and shaped into "fit
tools for the designs of ambition." Cities would inevitably become manufacturing centers, he said, and just as assuredly most urban dwellers would be
fated to live in squalid surroundings. He painted a stark picture: "great cities
add just so much to the support of pure government, as sores do to the strength
of the human body."

In manufacturing societies, only those at the top of the economic structure were truly independent and more or less in control of their destiny. The
political system likely to evolve in such societies would be little different from
those in monarchical kingdoms. In both, a "heavy-handed" executive would
manage affairs on behalf of the oligarchy. The ruling elite would harbor an
"unfeeling" fear and scorn for the great mass of the citizenry, "rendered desperate by poverty and wretchedness." The lifeblood of the realm would be the
generation of fortunes for those at the top. Among other things, this dynamic
in the course of time would transform the polity into a military state. As in
ancient Rome, when Caesar said, "With money we will get men . . . and with
men we shall get money," the manufacturing state would grow ever more pugnacious and expansive. No barriers to the pursuit of riches—most assuredly
not the welfare and happiness of the great preponderance of the people—
could be tolerated.

But a rural society in which the freemen were property-owning farmers
stood in stark contrast to the "degeneracy" and "canker" of a manufacturing
society. Whereas freedom could not long exist in a manufacturing world, not
only did liberty survive among yeomen, but farming in fact kept "alive that
sacred fire" of individualism, personal independence, and liberty. "Those
who labour in the earth are the chosen people of God," Jefferson wrote, for

republicanism resided in the "spirit" of humankind. The "manners and spirit" of a free, property-owning yeomanry would preserve republicanism. He was convinced that a society composed of property-owing farmers, each in possession of roughly the same amount of land, would have a vested interest both in sustaining the "equal rights" of freemen and in perpetuating the republic that had made possible their good fortune and happiness.[11]

For Jefferson, the American Revolution had been about resisting the expansive, exploitive encroachments of a degenerate monarchical and oligarchical Great Britain, and erecting in independent America a republican system that safeguarded against those things that led to "corruption and tyranny." He was convinced that the best means of preserving republicanism—of "keep[ing] the wolf out of the fold"—was through nearly universal property ownership within an agrarian state.[12]

In April 1782, while he worked on his manuscript, Jefferson had a visitor. François-Jean de Beauvoir, Chevalier de Chastellux, a French soldier and acclaimed author, dropped in at Monticello for four days. Chastellux had come to America with the French army two years earlier, and like all of Rochambeau's men, he remained in Virginia for months after the events at Yorktown. He described Jefferson as "tall and with a mild and pleasing countenance," and he added that his host was "never spoken of here [in Virginia] without respect." Chastellux at first found Jefferson "grave and even cold," but within two hours the strangers felt as though they had "spent [their] whole lives together." Chastellux found Jefferson's conversation "always varied, always interesting," and he was somewhat astounded by the breadth of Jefferson's interests and knowledge. They conversed incessantly, and deep into the night on myriad topics, as "no object has escaped Mr. Jefferson." Jefferson lovingly showed off Monticello, leading Chastellux to conclude that the house was like no other in America, for his host had "consulted the Fine Arts" in its design. A warrior accustomed to mayhem, Chastellux nevertheless was impressed that Jefferson was not a hunter, and even more by his discovery that the estate abounded in tame deer that ate from Jefferson's hand. When Chastellux departed, Jefferson rode with him for sixteen miles, turning back only because Martha was eight months pregnant and he did not want to be away from home for even one night.[13]

Three weeks after Chastellux departed, Martha gave birth for the seventh time. The baby was named Lucy Elizabeth, the same name that had been bestowed on the little girl who had died thirteen months before—a naming practice not uncommon in eighteenth-century America. If Martha's pregnancy had been planned, it was a terribly unwise decision. She had experienced difficulties with earlier pregnancies, and she does not appear to have been in robust health since the spring of 1780. She had not only curtailed her management of household operations but also, in the summer of 1780, had begged off participating in a drive to raise and make clothing for soldiers. Little is known of Martha's health after the birth of the first Lucy Elizabeth, but the six months that followed had been harrowing: On three occasions she and her daughters had been compelled to flee approaching enemy armies. Above all else, perhaps, Martha had been pregnant about half the time that she had been married to Jefferson, rarely experiencing more than eight months between the birth of one child and the conception of the next. All knew that childbirth was fraught with risks, and no one knew this better than Martha, whose own mother had perished as a result of childbirth.

Only Thomas and Martha Jefferson knew what went into the decision to have Lucy Elizabeth. Two weeks after her birth on May 2, Jefferson said that his wife had been "dangerously ill" since the child's arrival. Martha lived until September 6, and she appears to have remained bedfast the entire time. According to one of their daughters, Jefferson supposedly stayed with her continuously and nursed her with "tenderness." By July, if not earlier, Martha's recovery was thought unlikely, and weeks before the end she seems to have known that she faced death. She was only thirty-three, and she had been Jefferson's wife for eleven years. Jefferson himself said that he was a "state of dreadful suspense" for weeks. Joined by his widowed sister, a sister-in-law, and six household slaves, Jefferson kept vigil through the last moments of what his daughter called the "closing scene."

A quarter century later, Jefferson's overseer claimed to have been told by several who were present that toward the end, Martha expressed the wish that her husband would never remarry, and that Jefferson pledged that he would not. The story seems implausible, if for no other reason than that Martha herself had remarried following the demise of her first husband. But given the emotion-laden situation, and the possibility that pain or pain medication might have dulled Martha's lucidity, it cannot be ruled out.

Just before Martha died—what Jefferson called "the catastrophe"—he "was led from the room almost in a state of insensibility." With "great difficulty," his sister "got him into his library where he fainted and remained so long insensible that they feared he never would survive." In speaking of his "long fainting fit," his daughter mentioned the "violence of his emotion," and Edmund Randolph, a relative and friend who visited him a few days later, said that Jefferson's "grief . . . [was] so violent" that he believed the "circulating report of his swooning away whenever he sees his children." His despair was so enveloping that Jefferson did not leave his room for three weeks, and he "walked almost incessantly night and day only lying down occasionally when . . . completely exhausted." After a month, he spent nearly all day every day riding about his estate, past cultivated fields and through thick forests, often seeing and talking to no one, though each day he circled back by the mansion at some point and gathered up Martha, his ten-year-old daughter, who accompanied him on horseback for a few miles. She later recollected these "melancholy rambles" as a time when she was "a solitary witness to many a violent burst of grief" by her father.[14]

Jefferson had inscribed on Martha's tombstone that she had been "torn from him by death." His bereavement was so protracted that some feared he was suicidal, and for a time he may have been. A month after his wife's death, he wrote that he was experiencing a "miserable kind of existence . . . too burdensome to bear." That he had suicidal thoughts seems confirmed by his confession that he would take his own life were it not for "the infidelity of deserting" his children. Desolated by his loss, Jefferson remained for weeks in a such a state of black depression that he was "absolutely unable" to tend to any business. Marriage and family had been crucial for Jefferson, liberating him from the reclusive and solitary existence that he had endured as a young adult. Now, he said, all "comfort and happiness" had been taken from him. He would not end his life, but his life appeared to be at an end.[15]

While Jefferson grieved, Hamilton conspired. Like Jefferson, Hamilton had gone home in 1781, and like his counterpart in Virginia, he proclaimed that he had lost "all taste for the pursuits of ambition," adding: "I sigh for nothing but the company of my wife and my baby."[16] Otherwise, Hamilton's first objective was to settle on a means of supporting his family. He had a background in business, but no appetite for it. Nor was practicing medicine, a pursuit he had considered while a college student, any longer appealing. Hamilton turned to the law. A good legal practice could support a comfortable lifestyle and, should his passion for distinction and power return, a legal career would do the most to facilitate his aspirations. After a month at home, he took up the study of the law, joking that he was "studying the art of fleecing my neighbors." Hamilton had completed his college preparatory studies and learned economics on his own. Now, he eschewed the common practice of apprenticing himself to a licensed lawyer and opted for solitary study. His friend James Duane made available his law library, and John Lansing, who had been General Schuyler's military secretary, agreed to help as need be.[17] Hamilton completed his studies with extraordinary speed. Within six months he was certified to prepare cases. After another ninety days, he was authorized to argue in court.

While still studying, Hamilton also accepted Superintendent Morris's offer to become collector of continental taxes for New York, a post that required
he lobby the state legislature to streamline the collection process. Both experiences only deepened his contempt for the Articles of Confederation, which
he had blasted in his "Continentalist" essays during the summer before Yorktown. He saw abundant evidence that the state was snatching funds that
should have gone into the national treasury. Indeed, of the eight million dollars Congress requested from the states in 1782, it received only four hundred
thousand. Hamilton additionally came away convinced that state legislatures
were repositories of "fickleness and folly." Unable to see beyond local interests,
the state legislators lacked all sense of national well-being. Hamilton rushed
out two more installments of his "Continentalist," though he added little to
what he had advocated a year earlier. He urged that Congress be given the
power of taxation, and he called for an impost of foreign imports, land and
poll taxes, taxation of certain commodities in interstate commerce, and a
national bank. America would be happy, he declared, only if it could shake
loose of the hegemony of "petty states" and create a truly "great Federal Republic." Then, it would be "tranquil and prosperous at home, respectable
abroad."[18]

Hamilton's vision was distinctly different from that of Jefferson. The Virginian's emphasis had been on the preservation and expansion of the individual's freedom and independence. Hamilton emphasized the well-being
and strength of the nation. Jefferson had become a revolutionary largely in
the hope of securing, enlarging, and sustaining personal liberties. Hamilton's
hard experience in the Revolutionary War led him to believe that liberty could
never exist unless the nation was strong and secure. From Valley Forge onward,
Hamilton had grown steadily more convinced that the nation's strength
required the consolidation of supreme power at the national level.

About a month before Martha Jefferson died, the New York assembly,
which had just adopted resolutions urging the revision of the Articles of Confederation to strengthen the powers of the national government, added Hamilton to its five-member congressional delegation in Philadelphia. His selection
was hardly a surprise. Both Hamilton and his father-in-law, General Schuyler,
had spoken openly in favor of retiring the debt owed to public creditors, those
owed money by the state and national governments for indebtedness incurred
through sustaining the cause during the Revolutionary War. Committed to
providing "compensation to the sufferers," Hamilton urged trying the "only
expedient . . . still unattempted"—vesting the national government with the
capability of raising revenue. He was a public advocate of what he termed the
"luminous" policies of Superintendent Morris, including funding the na-

tional debt as a means of establishing an enduring stream of revenue for the national government. Despite his cynical view of Congress, Hamilton was surprisingly optimistic. "I am going to throw away a few months more in public life and then I retire a simple citizen" and family man, he remarked, indicating a belief that the campaign to strengthen the national government would not be a protracted undertaking.[19]

The movement to endow Congress with authority to raise revenue had a long pedigree. During 1780 not only had some Continental army officers signed a manifesto urging an increase in congressional powers, but the Hartford Convention, composed of delegates from New England and New York, had advocated an impost—a federal tax on imports. The following year, while Hamilton penned his initial essays on economic matters, Congress sent to the states for ratification an amendment that would vest it with authority to enact an impost. Just as Hamilton arrived in Philadelphia, the amendment failed. Rhode Island's concurrence had always been doubtful, but even before it could act, Virginia rescinded its earlier affirmation. Congress was left with no means of raising revenue other than to requisition money from the states, a system that had always been ineffectual. To make matters worse, France, which had sustained the United States with a series of loans during the past several years, indicated that no further loans would be forthcoming.

Hamilton had not come to Congress to be passive. Never one to take a back seat, he emerged as a leader with remarkable speed, soon joining young James Madison to revive the campaign for an impost. Only four years older than Hamilton, Madison came from a privileged background in Virginia. A sickly youth, he had led a troubled and undirected life until the American Revolution inspired him to enter politics. Within five years he had risen from a local Committee of Safety to a seat in Congress, which he entered eighteen months before the siege at Yorktown. By the time Hamilton arrived in Philadelphia, Madison had become one of the leaders in Congress. Like Hamilton, he was bright, diligent, persistent, energetic, and above all, industrious. Temperamentally, however, the two were as dissimilar as night and day. Hamilton was outgoing; Madison reserved. Hamilton dressed in bright, colorful clothing; Madison habitually wore black. One foreign observer characterized Hamilton as "decided" and Madison as "meditative." Madison thought Hamilton "rigid" and inflexible.[20]

In 1782 both men favored a stronger national government. That had not always been the case for Madison. Like most Virginians, he had initially feared a powerful centralized government as much as he had apprehended London's absolute dominion over the colonies, but the series of military disasters in the southern theater—and the dangers they posed for the Old

Dominion—converted him into a supporter of a robust United States government. Although the war was nearly over after Yorktown, Madison remained
committed to increasing federal authority.

Soon after Hamilton reached Philadelphia, Madison declared in a speech
that to save "national independence" and the Union, Congress must have the
means of securing revenue. Hamilton could not have put it better, and at this
juncture he and Madison supported a federal impost and funded debt. Still,
differences existed. Madison was not keen on a national bank, and he probably
never agreed with the wide range of national taxes that Hamilton favored.[21]

The starting point for the collaborators was to launch a new campaign
to secure an impost amendment. Whether or not Madison knew it—and he
probably did—Hamilton wanted more, for the revenue from the impost
would simply cover the interest on the foreign debt. The impost was "a Tub
for the whale," was how Superintendent Morris put it, meaning that a tax on
imports would raise some revenue, but not enough to help the public creditors.[22] Yet it was a first step, and some among the backers of an impost conspired to find the means to win its approval. The conspirators naturally
cloaked their activities in nearly impenetrable secrecy, leaving both contemporaries and historians to guess at the dark corners of the intrigue. But two
things appear certain: Hamilton was among the conspirators, and Madison
was not. In addition, the plot came together when the schemers realized that
they might use disaffection within the corps of officers in the Continental
army to secure their ends.

The army's officers had real grievances, and for months they had been discussing remedies among themselves. Despite having "borne all that men can
bear," as they would put it, the officers had not been paid for months. They
also feared they would never receive their promised pensions. During the
Valley Forge winter, Congress had promised the officers half-pay pensions for
seven years. Two years later, pressured both by threats of mass resignations
by the officers and Washington's warnings that the "temper of the Army . . .
requires great caution," Congress extended the half-pay pensions for life. Late
in 1782, just prior to the failure of the impost amendment, the officers decided
to petition Congress for their pay and pensions. General Henry Knox drafted
their petition, which was carried to Philadelphia in January by a three-
member delegation of officers.

The delegation was headed by General Alexander McDougall, who had
taken the nineteen-year-old Hamilton under his wing during the prewar protests in New York and who may have been responsible for securing his appointment as Washington's aide in 1777. McDougall spoke with Congress
about the hardships the officers had endured and enumerated their com-

plaints. He also revealed that the officers were willing to settle for "commutation." They wanted their back pay, but were willing to accept having their lifetime half-pay pensions commuted to a five-year full-pay pension. McDougall, who had cut his teeth as a Sons of Liberty intriguer and agitator in Manhattan prior to the outbreak of the war, remained in Philadelphia for several days, all the while making sure the congressmen understood the dangers of what might occur if the officers were left empty-handed. Soon dark rumors were rampant: An officers' mutiny was pending; Washington might be overthrown and replaced with a "less scrupulous guardian of [the nation's] interests"; the army might stage a coup and establish "a military dictatorship"; mass resignations might force the breakup of the army before peace with Great Britain was concluded.[23] Fear was palpable in the halls of Congress. Arthur Lee, a Virginia congressman, wrote to Samuel Adams that "Every Engine is at work here" to increase the power of the national government. The "terror of a mutinying Army" was being held over Congress like a sword of Damocles, he said, and he added that many were apprehensive that the officers were not beyond "subverting the Revolution" to gain their ends.[24]

Hamilton likely had been aware of the discussions that had ensued among the officers during the weeks preceding McDougall's visit. But the coincidence of McDougall's arrival in Philadelphia at almost the same instant that the impost failed, and the evident apprehension that gripped Congress in the wake of the menacing warnings spread by the officers, made Hamilton and others aware that this was a heaven-sent opportunity for trying once again to strengthen the national government. Probably led by Superintendent Morris, Gouverneur Morris (who was unrelated but served as the superintendent's assistant), and James Wilson, a Pennsylvania congressman who, like Superintendent Morris, had supported American independence with considerable reluctance, a small cabal formed in January. They glimpsed the chance not only to resurrect the impost amendment but also to frighten Congress into seeking an entirely new revenue system that would permit servicing the debts of the United States and assuming the debts the states had accrued during the war. Gouverneur Morris, in a ciphered letter, revealed the conspirators' thinking: "The army have swords in their hands. I am glad to see Things in their present Train. . . . Convulsion will ensue, yet it must terminate in giving the Government that Power without which Government is but a Name."[25]

Whether Hamilton was part of the plotting from the outset, or was brought into it subsequently, is unclear. If the latter, the cabal must have seen Hamilton as especially useful. He was not only a congressman who shared their nationalistic agenda, but he also had ties with the army's officers that stretched all the way to the commander himself.

The colluders rapidly secured a portion of what they wanted. Congress agreed to resume paying the officers and to see somehow that they received their back pay. However, on February 4, the commutation scheme was rejected by Congress. The plotters now knew that commutation, and the establishment of the means of assuring adequate permanent revenue for the national government, could only be achieved if the army continued to threaten mutinous action.[26]

The pot simmered among the officers at the army's principal cantonment in Newburgh, New York. As their frustration was building toward a crescendo, Hamilton in early February wrote to Washington, his first missive to the commander in a year. His letter was a warning to Washington. While Hamilton was willing to use the army to strike fear in the hearts of congressmen, he never wanted the projected mutiny to come to fruition. A military coup would almost certainly fail, and the bitterness it aroused would be ruinous for those who hoped to strengthen the national government. Nevertheless, Hamilton was unwilling to divulge to Washington the full scope of the conspiracy, or to unmask the identity of the plotters. He couched his notice to Washington in cryptic terms, though fearing that the commander would not fully understand what he had written, Hamilton instructed him to seek clarification from Knox, an indication that the artillery chief was up to his neck in these machinations.

Hamilton spoke of the pressing need to "restore public credit and supply the future wants of government." But the heart of his letter dealt with the conspiracy among the army's officers. Hamilton alluded to the "temper . . . of the army" and how difficult it might be to confine it "within the bounds of moderation." Washington must "*take the direction*" of the army and "bring order perhaps even good out of confusion." If he did that, Hamilton added, Washington would win the hearts of his countrymen, emerging from the war as both a triumphant general and an American icon.[27]

If Washington did not at first understand all that Hamilton said, the scales fell from his eyes three weeks later when an unsigned manifesto was posted in the Newburgh cantonment. It proposed that Congress be confronted with an ultimatum: If commutation was not guaranteed, the army would disband if the peace talks failed and the war continued, but if peace broke out, the army would refuse to dissolve.[28] Treason and mutiny were intermingled in what became known as the Newburgh Address. The officers were asked to attend a meeting on March 15 to decide on a course of action.

The meeting was set for the Temple, a twenty-one-hundred-square-foot building so newly constructed by the soldiery that the smell of green wood permeated the hall. The officers gathered in an atmosphere of breathless anticipation. They were just preparing to take up the inflammatory statement to Congress when Washington, suddenly and unexpectedly, strode into the room and took the podium. Given several days to consider his response to what he knew was coming—thanks to Hamilton's advance warning—Washington read his own prepared address. He appealed to the officers to respect civilian authority and the "sovereign authority of the United States." Legislative bodies "composed of a variety of different Interests" acted slowly, he reminded his audience, and he urged patience. He also pleaded with the officers not to sully the reputation of the army, which they would surely do should they embrace the "blackest designs" advocated in the Newburgh Address.[29]

Though one of Washington's best speeches, his remarks did not sway the militants in his audience. Sensing that his appeal to reason had failed, Washington, a devotee of the theater who admired actors—and a polished thespian himself—turned to theatrics to win over his audience. Saying that he wanted to read a letter from a Virginia congressman, Washington, with suspenseful deliberation, extracted the missive from his buff-and-blue coat, meticulously unfolded it, and began reading. He stumbled over a sentence or two. With great drama, he paused and reached into his pocket once again, this time removing a pair of glasses, which with great care he put on. The men had never seen their commander wearing glasses. Without hurrying, he adjusted his wire-rimmed spectacles, paused again, then in a voice muted by despair and fatigue, told the officers: "Gentlemen, you must pardon me. I have grown gray in your service and now find myself growing blind." It was the perfect touch. In an instant, the mood in the room was transformed. As tough combat-hardened men wept openly, the mutinous defiance that had taken hold in some circles dissolved immediately. The Newburgh Address was swept aside, and its proponents were silenced.[30]

The campaign to increase the power of Congress continued, however. Washington warned Congress that the officers' forbearance had limits. The near mutiny had been quelled, he seemed to say, but next time, things might turn out differently. A few weeks later, Washington also sent to the states an address warning that the survival of the Union hinged on giving "a tone to our Federal Government." While his exhortations may have persuaded Congress to embrace commutation, the push for a general revenue system went nowhere. An impost amendment was sent to the states yet again, but it was watered down. It was to last for only twenty-five years and was to be collected by the states. A backlash against the treachery of the army's officers was partly to blame, but more important, the sense of urgency evaporated once definitive word arrived in March that a preliminary peace treaty had been signed in Paris. The long war really was coming to an end. By mid-summer 1783 the army had been reduced from some eleven thousand men to barely two thousand. It could no longer use scare tactics to stampede Congress or the states. In the new environment, those like Hamilton who favored what would be called "consolidation"—strengthening the powers of the national government and making it sovereign over the states—were voices in the wilderness. In 1785 the impost amendment, the first step toward consolidation, failed when it was spurned by New York.[31]

Hamilton had failed to achieve his goal. In some respects, however, what may have been most important for Hamilton in the long run was that the Newburgh episode had a transformative effect on his connection with Washington. Their relationship had been strained since the dustup at headquarters two years earlier, but even though Washington understood that Hamilton had sought to further the army's cause by using its officers "as mere Puppits" in order "to establish Continental funds," the commander in chief drew closer to the young congressman.[32]

As Washington said nothing about Hamilton at the time, his feelings about his former aide are hard to discern from this distance in history. Washington must have realized, if he had not previously, that Hamilton's star was ascending. Hamilton was exceptionally intelligent, a gifted writer, a man of maniacal energy, and he was well connected to those who wielded considerable influence and power in mercantile and financial circles. Hamilton seemed to possess the qualities necessary for leadership, and indeed in no time he had become a key figure in Congress. What is more, Hamilton was extraordinarily ambitious, perhaps dangerously so, for his having intrigued to use the army as leverage with civil authorities had been astonishingly risky. Washington must have been grateful to have had Hamilton on his side during the Newburgh episode. After all, it was Hamilton who had played the seminal role in making Washington appear to be the essence of moderation in contrast to the hotheads among the officers who had supported insurgency. What is more, Washington knew better than anyone the essential role that Hamilton had played in the destruction of the commander's foes, Lee and Gates. If nothing else, Washington saw with clarity that Hamilton was a force to be reckoned with.

Washington did not look for friends. He judged others in terms of whether they were enemies or could be of help to him. Hamilton had been indispensable as an aide-de-camp, and it was likely he could be crucially important to Washington in the postwar world. In fact, the commander soon opened a correspondence with Hamilton in which he carefully probed for information about what was occurring in Congress.[33] But Washington was not without feelings, and on more than one occasion he evinced a warmth toward Hamilton that was extremely rare in his other relationships. On some level, Washington may have sensed similarities between Hamilton and his own beloved older stepbrother Lawrence, who had been his role model. It may have been that Washington saw in Hamilton the man he might have become had he, too, been blessed with a formal education. Possibly, Washington was struck by the parallels between himself and his former aide. Both men burned for glory and were savvy political players, even manipulators. Washington excelled at controlling his passions, though his exceptional self-control had come only with age and experience. Hamilton, while equally canny, could be swept up by his own emotions. Possibly, Washington believed that in time Hamilton would also learn greater self-discipline, and ultimately become more like Washington himself. Perhaps Washington was simply captivated by Hamilton, as were so many others. Conceivably, too, Washington saw menacing qualities in Hamilton that nudged him to assure that his former aide remained a loyal follower, not an enemy.

Hamilton judged others more or less as did Washington. He could have left Washington to the wolves during the Newburgh episode, but instead he had alerted him to the danger. Hamilton had adroitly understood that the officers' plot would in the long run be ruinous to his ends, but he understood that Washington could be useful to him and to his cause. For his part, Washington believed that he could put his trust in Hamilton, and the general wanted this rising young star on his side.

Hamilton once let slip that he regarded the eight months he served in Congress as an "apprenticeship."[34] Despite his repeated pledges to retire from public life, Hamilton saw this first political office as a foundation for other things. Though he could not know what the future held, better than most he knew of life's vicissitudes from firsthand experience. Congressional experience, he evidently assumed, would be useful in countless ways.

Characteristically, Congressman Hamilton worked hard. Congress repeatedly turned to him for important assignments, and he served on numerous committees. None rivaled in importance the committee constituted in April to prepare for the coming peace. The new American nation would share borders with potentially hostile neighbors, for under the preliminary peace, Great Britain was to retain Canada while Florida was to be returned to Spain. There were also Indian affairs to be considered, as the vast expanse of trans-Appalachia to the Mississippi River, which was to be part of the United States, was occupied by Native Americans. The committee began its work by asking Washington for his thoughts.

Publicly, Washington and Hamilton spoke of preparing for the defense of the United States, though in fact both were adherents of what historian Richard Kohn termed a "vigorous nationalism." Washington wanted a strong United States that could rapidly open the region beyond the Appalachians, territory that had been closed to expansion for twenty years. Hamilton was more interested in strengthening the United States against possible predatory behavior by the great powers in Europe, and he likely already had dreamed of encroaching on Spanish America. Both Washington and Hamilton were mortified by state sovereignty and the new nation's "total disability" to cope with the national interest, as Hamilton put it.[35] Both knew how close the United States had come to losing the Revolutionary War. Neither wanted to chance another national emergency with an emasculated national government, and neither wanted American soldiers to suffer again as they had during the War of Independence. Both had hazarded everything during the long struggle to create the new American nation, and both fervently wished to assure its survival.

In May, Washington submitted his recommendations. He said with a straight face that he was opposed to "a large standing Army," but he advocated the maintenance of a peacetime army of 2,600, a force several times larger than Great Britain had kept in the colonies before the French and Indian War. He urged that the soldiery be garrisoned along the Canadian border, the Ohio River, here and there on the Atlantic coast, and throughout Georgia and South Carolina. He additionally suggested drastic revisions in the militia system. Washington, who had looked with contempt on militiamen since the French and Indian War, championed a plan that would compel each state's militia to conform to national standards with regard to organization, equipment, arms, and training. To see that this was done, he advised Congress to name a national inspector general to enforce the regulations. While Hamilton was pushing for economic consolidation, General Washington was doing the same with regard to the military.[36]

The lone member with a military background, Hamilton dominated the committee. It ultimately issued a report that adhered to Washington's recommendations, differing only in that it proposed a standing army even larger than the commander had recommended.[37] Hamilton rushed matters, hoping that Congress might act before word arrived of the official end to hostilities. He succeeded, but to no avail. Late in June, four days after the committee submitted its report, Congress was forced from Philadelphia by a mutiny among soldiers in the Pennsylvania line. When the congressmen reassembled in Princeton, the nationalist delegates tried to save matters by inviting Washington to town. He came and plumped for the report, but few in Congress were sympathetic. To many, it sounded as if Washington and Hamilton were espousing a peacetime garrison state, and some feared that once a standing army was sanctioned, it would inevitably grow by leaps and bounds. The nationalists' plan died. Within two years, the United States army had shrunk to a few hundred men.[38]

Hamilton was ready to leave Congress when it fled Philadelphia, but he stayed on for four additional weeks until word of the definitive peace treaty arrived.[39] He spent the month drafting a resolution urging Congress to summon a constitutional convention. Military necessity required a more robust national government, he said. He justified augmenting the powers of Congress as essential for funding commutation and compensating creditors who had "cheerfully lent their money" during the war. He proposed a new national government with separate executive, legislative, and judicial branches, and he advocated that Congress be vested with the power to levy taxes, regulate trade, and superintend military matters. He also sought the elimination of the Articles' stipulation requiring the assent of two-thirds of Congress to pass bills of "principal importance."[40]

Hamilton recorded his thoughts at nearly the moment that Jefferson, at Monticello, was writing *Notes on the State of Virginia*, a book that included his latest draft constitution for Virginia. Hamilton's emphasis could not have been more different. Hamilton was absorbed with establishing a sovereign and powerful national government capable of protecting the national interest. Jefferson, in contrast, was driving to achieve uniform representation and universal manhood suffrage for free white males, with the ultimate goal of giving every citizen "an equal voice in the direction of its concerns." As Hamilton's core conviction was that "Inequality is inherent," he believed that representation should reflect wealth, and he was silent about social justice, popular self-rule, and facilitating the realization of the will of the people.[41]

Hamilton never introduced his resolution. He knew it would be futile to do so in "the present state of things." That is not to say that he intended to abandon his quest for consolidation. He was leaving office, supposedly forever, though it seems apparent that Hamilton planned to watch for an opportunity to continue the fight, to wait on events and changing sentiments. He knew that the new American nation had "so far happily escaped" its perilous situation, as he put it in the resolution that he drafted, but "it would be unwise to hazard a repetition of the same dangers and embarrassments in any future war . . . or to continue this extensive empire under a government unequal to its protection and prosperity."[42]

In July, a month prior to Washington's arrival in Princeton, Hamilton resigned and left for home. "We have now happily concluded the great work of independence," Hamilton exalted, but he quickly added: "much remains to be done to reach the fruits of it." He knew that during his eight months in Congress he had achieved nothing to remedy "the inefficacy of the present confederation." Nothing could be done, he sighed, until there was a "return to reason."[43]

No one did more than Madison to get Jefferson back into public life. Madison believed that Jefferson had much to offer the country and also feared for the welfare of his friend, isolated at home with his dark, melancholy memories. Two months after Martha Jefferson's demise, Madison persuaded Congress to once again offer Jefferson a position among the peace commissioners in Europe, a post he had declined a year earlier. This time, Jefferson jumped at the chance for a "change of scene," telling Madison that he would "lose no time . . . preparing for my departure." He still grieved, and would for a very long time. Twenty months after Martha's death, he acknowledged his pervasive "gloom" and spoke of the "sun of life" having crested and subsided for him. Many years later, in his memoirs, Jefferson seemed to say that he had accepted the diplomatic position in 1782 more from a desire to escape Monticello than from a yearning to serve "the public interests."[44]

He reached Philadelphia just after Christmas, about two weeks before General McDougall and his fellow officers arrived from Newburgh to urge commutation and spread rumors of a possible officers' mutiny.[45] Hamilton, of course, was a member of Congress, and it is probable that he met Jefferson sometime during the Virginian's nearly seventy-five days in town, especially as both counted Madison as a friend.

When Congress had agreed to Jefferson's inclusion on the team of peace commissioners, it was already aware that negotiations were under way in Paris. In mid-February, before Jefferson could sail, news arrived that the preliminary peace accord had been signed. Congress instructed him to wait for further word. He languished for six agonizing weeks. Finally, on April 1, Congress suspended his appointment.[46]

Having gotten away from the gloom of Monticello, Jefferson was in no hurry to return home. He swung by Richmond, most likely to meet with the principal assemblymen and inquire about being added to the state's congressional delegation. He eventually arrived home in May, five months after his departure, and he remained at Monticello for six months. Jefferson need not have lingered at home for such a long time, as he learned in June that he had been appointed to Congress. He said merely that he was obliged "to stay pretty closely at home for some time to get my affairs into such a state as they may be left." Considering that only recently he had anticipated a protracted absence, one that could have lasted for years, his excuse was unpersuasive.[47]

More likely, given the talk swirling that summer that a convention was imminent for drafting a new constitution for Virginia, Jefferson—as had been the case in 1776—preferred participating in that endeavor to sitting in Congress. But when the movement for a new constitution failed, Jefferson, on October 16, at last set off for Congress. He left Polly and the infant Lucy Elizabeth with Elizabeth Eppes—his late wife's half-sister—but took eleven-year-old Patsy with him.

Jefferson traveled first to Philadelphia, where he arranged for Patsy to study with a French tutor and live with the widowed mother of a friend. On the very day he arrived in Princeton, the peripatetic Congress voted to move to Annapolis. When it reconvened on November 25, Jefferson at last became a congressman once again. He did not serve with Hamilton, who had resigned four months earlier.

Jefferson had been eager to serve in Europe, and it is possible he believed that serving in Congress would lead to his appointment to an overseas diplomatic post. Indeed, that may have been a factor in his decision to have Patsy study French. All Americans had known in early spring that the end of the war was at hand. News of the definitive peace, the Treaty of Paris—in which Great Britain recognized American independence and also terminated hostilities with France and Spain—reached Congress shortly before Jefferson took his seat. In fact, on the very day that Jefferson reentered Congress, the British army evacuated New York and General Washington led the Continental army in a victory parade down Broadway, a festive return to Manhattan, from which the rebel forces had been driven in 1776. A month later, two days before Christmas, Jefferson watched as Washington appeared before Congress and resigned his commission.[48] Jefferson was the only delegate who had been a member of Congress in 1775 on the day when Washington set off for the front to take command of the Continental army.

If Jefferson hoped Congress would quickly dispatch envoys to Europe, he was disappointed. A month after he reached Annapolis, only six states were represented. The lack of a quorum "stops all business," he reported. In January there was still an insufficient number of congressmen present to meet. Toward the end of February he yet again complained that "we cannot make a house." Congress, he said, had not met "above 3 days . . . in as many weeks."[49]

Never one to idle away his time, Jefferson toiled with his committee assignments, preparing for the day when Congress would again be able to take up business. He wrote thirty-one reports in four months, some uninvited. For instance, he drafted a paper on coinage, proposing the dollar as the unit of coinage and a simple proportional plan of values for different coins. His recommendations were adopted in 1785, a year after he left Congress.[50]

Jefferson also kept busy by planning an exacting study schedule for Patsy. "If you love me then, strive . . . to acquire those accomplishments which I have put in your power," he added. He also instructed her to at all times to be "cleanly and properly dressed. . . . Nothing is so disgusting" to men as "want of cleanliness and delicacy" in a woman, as it inevitably leads to the conclusion that the female is "a sloven or slot."[51]

In March, with a sufficient number of delegates at last present, Congress opted to grapple with one pressing issue while it was possible to do something. "We shall immediately try what we can do with the Western country" was how Jefferson put it.[52] Trans-Appalachia had suddenly become an urgent concern. Not only had the United States just received the area as far west as the Mississippi River in the Treaty of Paris, but settlers had also begun flooding across the mountains almost as soon as Cornwallis surrendered at Yorktown. Order, and possibly peace with the Indians who inhabited the region, required that some form of governance be established.

Jefferson chaired the committee that prepared a plan of government for the west. Having first considered the matter as early as 1776, and having tended to it while Congress was idled by the lack of a quorum, he was ready in no time with a plan. He recommended the creation of fourteen territories of roughly equal size. He named them in some instances for people or events from the American Revolution (Washington and Saratoga), and in some cases he combined classical and Indian nomenclature (Illinoia and Pelisipia). He proposed that the territories proceed to statehood in stages, according to the size of their population, and he urged self-government for the residents. All adult, white, male residents were to have suffrage rights, and at every stage of the progression toward statehood, the qualified voters were to choose their rulers, write their constitutions, and make their own laws. The national government was to have virtually no role in the governance of the territories. Jefferson's report contained one more controversial recommendation: After 1800, slavery and indenture servitude were to be illegal in every territory. His recommendation was silent on the matter of colonization, so that any slaves taken into the territory prior to 1800 would be permitted to remain.[53]

Congress adopted most of Jefferson's report in the Ordinance of 1784, though the national government was given somewhat more authority in the first stage of territorial governance. Furthermore, by a single vote, Jefferson's ban on slavery was deleted from the final act. Jefferson immediately understood the magnitude of Congress's decision with regard to what he called the "abominable crime" of permitting slavery's expansion beyond the original thirteen states. Two years later, he lamented that the "fate of millions unborn" would be adversely affected, and added that "heaven was silent in that awful moment!"[54]

The Ordinance of 1784 never fully took effect. When delays arose as a result of negotiating land cessions with the Native Americans, it was discovered that Jefferson's scheme for territorial boundaries, which had ignored geographical features such as rivers, was impractical. Ultimately, Congress replaced the act with the Land Ordinance of 1785 and the Northwest Ordinance of 1787, both of which incorporated sufficient numbers of Jefferson's recommendations—including the prohibition of slavery in territories north of the Ohio River—that he deserves substantial credit for envisaging the organization and governance of America's territories for generations to come. At a time when only Pennsylvania had a truly democratic constitution and many doubted that rude frontiersmen were capable of exercising self-government, Jefferson believed in the ability of people to govern themselves. In the long run, he was proven correct. Moreover, had Jefferson's recommendation concerning the prohibition of slavery in all western territories been adopted, slavery might have died a peaceful death once an adequate supply of labor existed below the Potomac River.

If Jefferson had agreed to serve in Congress as a stepping stone to a diplomatic post, his gambit succeeded. Congress had initially voted to leave three of its peace commissioners—John Adams, Benjamin Franklin, and John Jay—in Europe to seek commercial treaties. But when Congress learned on May 7 that Jay was coming home, it named Jefferson that same day to its team of envoys. No one had to twist his arm. Before evening fell on the day of his appointment, Jefferson wrote to William Short, a twenty-three-year old Virginian and graduate of the College of William and Mary, asking that he serve as his secretary.[55]

Within a week, Jefferson was on his way. He hurried to Philadelphia to retrieve Patsy and James Hemings, a nineteen-year-old slave whom Jefferson had summoned.[56] The threesome rushed to Boston in the hope of sailing with Abigail Adams and her daughter, Nabby, who were known to be crossing that summer. Jefferson's party arrived too late to enjoy their company, but he soon booked passage on the *Ceres*. It weighed anchor and sailed from America for France on July 5, 1784.

Three years earlier, Jefferson's public life seemed a thing of the past, while Hamilton, a hero at Yorktown, was positioned for greatness. But now, six months into the postwar period, Hamilton had retired from public life while Jefferson had found redemption and was embarking on what would be a transformative adventure in a foreign land.

CHAPTER 7

"THEY WILL GO BACK GOOD REPUBLICANS"

JEFFERSON IN PARIS

SOME EXPERIENCE no more than a single pivotal moment in their lives. That was not the case with Hamilton and Jefferson. The adversities of youth left an indelible imprint on Hamilton. His life changed fundamentally as a result of his move to the mainland colonies. What he encountered as a soldier reshaped his thinking, and by serving at Washington's headquarters, he came to the attention of the most influential men in America. Just as his thinking had been changed forever by the ardors of the long war, Hamilton's consolidationist perspective solidified as he grew more uneasy in the 1780s with what he found were disturbing postwar episodes and changes.

Without a doubt, Jefferson was stamped by his long years of solitary study and reflection, and by the American Revolution, which gave new meaning to his life and thought. But his plans and expectations for life after his years as governor were shattered by the loss of his wife. His years abroad, beginning in 1784, would be another pivot, as living in France widened his vision and sharpened his social skills, led to a profound personal transformation, and broadened and deepened his commitment to what he always referred to as the "principles of '76."

Jefferson was forty-one years old when he sailed for France. His Atlantic crossing was extraordinarily rapid. He landed in England after less than three weeks at sea. Before July ended, he alighted on French soil, and on the thirty-first day after departing Boston, he arrived in Paris.[1]

In large measure, Jefferson had agreed to serve in Europe in the hope of getting his life back together, though his restless curiosity enticed him to live in a strange land. He dwelled in France for five years, and in some respects it was the happiest period of his adult life, save for his time at Monticello with Martha and the girls. The life of a diplomat was good. He had ample free time, the work was challenging—and satisfying when he achieved something for his country—and he was more comfortable meeting with his diplomatic counterparts than he had ever been sitting in a legislature. Despite his well-known eulogizing of pastoral virtues, Jefferson found that he enjoyed city life. He had lived briefly in Philadelphia, but never in a city the size of Paris, a metropolis that sprawled over nearly half the area of today's city and was home to hundreds of thousands.[2] It offered countless diversions, an endless array of shops that were nirvana for an inveterate consumer, and accessibility to a rich assortment of acquaintances.

Jefferson settled in a house, which he instantly set about remodeling, but after thirteen months he moved again, renting the Hôtel de Langeac on the Champs-Élysées, where he remained for the duration of his stay. With three floors, in addition to a basement, this was a vast house, perfect for an envoy with staff and servants, and well suited for entertaining and conducting business. Its library-study was conveniently connected to a bedroom and dressing room—an arrangement that Jefferson later replicated in remodeling of Monticello. The mansion came with indoor bathrooms, and its spacious grounds included greenhouses and a large garden, where Jefferson set to work. He planted corn, sweet potatoes, watermelon, and cantaloupe and hired a gardener to tend the trees, shrubs, and grass. The Hôtel de Langeac was in a recently developed neighborhood far from downtown, but there were houses all about and a customs building just across the street. His carriage was a necessity for reaching the center of Paris, but it was walking that Jefferson really enjoyed. "A strong body makes the mind strong," he believed, and he looked on walking as both exercise and recreation. "You should . . . not permit yourself even to think while you walk," he once advised, adding that strolls helped "relax the mind." He encouraged others "to walk very far," and while in Paris he adhered to his advice, daily walking five miles or more. He even meticulously measured his walking speed, noting that he covered a mile in sixteen minutes, though because he walked faster in cold weather, he took 331 fewer steps per mile on his winter rambles.[3]

Three weeks after he arrived in Paris, Jefferson enrolled Patsy in a boarding school in a convent operated by Bernardine nuns.[4] A couple of days later he rode to Passy, a suburb, and met with his fellow commissioners, Franklin and Adams. He got on well with both, but it was with John and Abigail Adams that Jefferson established the closest relationship. Despite dissimilar backgrounds and personalities, Jefferson and Adams had enjoyed a cordial, respectful relationship while serving in Congress. In Paris, they became close friends. Each shared a passion for knowledge and conversation, and each was fascinated by politics and the theory and mechanics of governance. What unfolded between them for nine delightful months was similar to Jefferson's intellectually invigorating experience with Chastellux during his brief visit to Monticello. Abigail noted that Jefferson was "the only person with whom [her husband] could associate with perfect freedom, and unreserve." Jefferson acknowledged that he disagreed with Adams on some things, and he found him *vain, irritable.*" However, those qualities were offset by Adams's other side. He is "profound in his views: and accurate in his judgment," said Jefferson. "He is so amiable, that I pronounce you will love him," Jefferson advised Madison.[5]

Jefferson likewise developed an immediate affinity for Abigail. He had met few women like her, as she was well read and better educated than most women of the time. He was comfortable with her and enjoyed her company, and it is equally clear that she indisputably enjoyed being with Jefferson. She found him to be soft, considerate, multifaceted, and incredibly bright. She was so swept up by him that she pronounced him "one of the choice ones of the Earth," adding that he was "an Excellent Man, Worthy of his station." Abigail provided guidance about the home furnishings that Jefferson purchased, instructed him on the proper dress for a diplomat, and even shopped for some of his clothing. She also was a source of consolation for him. Jefferson was ill throughout the autumn and winter—he suffered from what travelers of the day referred to as the "seasoning," the adjustment to a strange environment—and initially, at any rate, he likely remained in the throes of grief over the loss of his wife. Furthermore, in January he was jolted by word from Virginia that little Lucy Elizabeth had perished of whooping cough. Abigail, who had lost a daughter of about the same age years earlier, understood Jefferson's pain and helped him through his bereavement. Over the year or so that he and the Adamses lived in Paris, Jefferson shared many evenings with them, sometimes entertaining them, more often as their guest, and on occasion the three were entertained by a French luminary, such as Lafayette. They went together on outings; on one occasion Abigail accompanied him to a Roman Catholic worship service at the convent where Patsy was studying. Jefferson also spent a bit of time with their seventeen-year-old son, John Quincy, and even more with nineteen-year-old Nabby, as the two enjoyed occasional shopping forays.[6]

For Jefferson, who never tired of searching for new acquisitions, living in Paris was akin to being the proverbial kid in a candy store. He purchased furnishings for his spacious residence, most of which he intended to bring home to Virginia. These included more than sixty paintings, busts (he acquired plaster copies of Jean-Antoine Houdon's busts of Washington, Franklin, Lafayette, John Paul Jones, and Voltaire), clocks, mantel pieces, cast-iron stoves, newfangled lamps, wallpaper, mirrors, and Venetian blinds, along with assorted pieces of furniture, tableware, and cooking utensils. He also bought two watches, a pair of spectacles—like Washington, he had reached the age where reading glasses had become useful—two flintlock pistols and six officers' fusils (light flintlock muskets), a harpsichord for Patsy and a violin for himself, a music stand, a Normandy shepherd and a riding horse, a large carriage, which at times was drawn by as many as five horses, and a cabriolet—a one-seat conveyance drawn by a single horse. Instruments and gadgets appealed to him, and he acquired many, including a perspective machine (which he used for making drawings in scale), a pedometer, metronome, telescope, copying machine, thermometer, solar microscope, hygrometer, and a protractor and camp theodolite, both tools used in running surveys. His greatest enjoyment may have been in shopping for books. "While residing in Paris," he later remarked, "I devoted every afternoon I was disengaged . . . in examining all the principal bookstores." He bought countless volumes for his already considerable library, and he sent home some two hundred books to Madison and a large number to a brother-in-law. The ship that brought Jefferson back to America in 1789 was jammed with eighty-six crates of his possessions and still more were shipped later on a second vessel.[7]

No traveler ever did more sightseeing than Jefferson. He purchased a map on his first day in Paris and immediately set off to see the city. In time, he visited gardens and art galleries, but Jefferson most enjoyed studying the magnificent array of architecture. Official business eventually took him to England, Holland, southern France, northern Italy, what now is Germany, and through Alsace, Lorraine, and Champagne. Everywhere he went, Jefferson sought out historic sites and the ruins of antiquity, observed the landscape (often comparing it to portions of America that he had seen), took notes on the details of provincial architectural styles, and was intrigued by the soil and farming practices. He transplanted in his Paris garden clippings from vineyards that he visited and sent samples of rice that he found in Italy to Edward Rutledge, an acquaintance from his first term in Congress, in South Carolina. Jefferson was fascinated by local culinary practices—he took comprehensive notes on the preparation of Westphalian ham, for instance—and he made such a thorough study of the numerous varieties of wine that his principal biographer concluded that he likely came to be the best-informed American on the subject.[8]

Living in a city exposed Jefferson to a new world, and he made the most of it. He spent many nights at the theater, enjoying operas, dramas, Shakespearean plays, and comedies, and frequently attended concerts and recitals. He often dined out, witnessed several hot-air balloon ascensions, and twice attended masquerade balls, which featured dancing from midnight until dawn.

He also discovered the Parisian salon, gatherings attended by both sexes and highlighted by wide-ranging discussions of literature, science, politics, and the arts. Though unaccustomed to such gender equality, Jefferson rapidly adjusted and found himself quite comfortable in the company of women. Just as he had drawn close to Abigail Adams, warm relationships emerged between him and several women. He was especially fond of Angelica Church, the sister of Betsey Schuyler, Hamilton's wife. Having eloped with an Englishman, she lived in London, but in 1787 she traveled to Paris for a two-month stay, during which she met Jefferson. Regarded by many men as singularly attractive, she was also quite intelligent, and she captivated Jefferson. He seemed to have a similar impact on her. She presented him with gifts and treasured a miniature painting of Jefferson that she acquired. Theirs was not an amorous relationship, but one in which each cherished the easy friendship of the other. He enjoyed her company so much that he beseeched her to return to Paris, invited her to Monticello, waxed on about calling on her in Albany should she ever return to visit her family, and invited her to accompany him when he prepared to return to America.[9]

Jefferson had gone to France on a diplomatic mission, and he was a diligent, if not terribly successful, envoy. He had been sent abroad to join with Adams and Franklin in seeking commercial treaties with sixteen governments in Europe and another four in North Africa. After two years, their only real success was a pact with Prussia. The other European powers remained intransigent adherents of mercantilism, an age-old doctrine that spurned free trade and emphasized national self-sufficiency. But Jefferson also rapidly discovered that many European diplomats felt that America's decentralized system, which left each state to formulate a commercial policy, posed such a barrier to trade that it was not worth their trouble to negotiate. The Barbary States of North Africa posed a different problem. Morocco, Algiers, Tunis, and Tripoli preyed on European and American commerce in the Mediterranean. They would suspend their marauding only if foreign nations paid them a tribute—or bribe—for the privilege of conducting commerce in the region. From the beginning, Jefferson thought there was little hope of success in dealing peacefully with these piratical entities, and he was correct. Rather quickly, Jefferson's experiences reshaped some of his thinking. Within a year, he became an advocate of vesting Congress with supremacy in all matters concerning foreign commerce. In addition, the Barbary pirates convinced him of the necessity for a strong navy, which by "constant cruising and cutting them to pieces by piecemeal" would solve the problem.[10]

America's greatest commercial problem, however, stemmed from recent action taken by its late enemy, Great Britain. Shortly before the Treaty of Paris was signed, London had promulgated Orders in Council signaling that it would treat the United States as it did other foreign nations. Britain would sell to the United States, but it would permit only American tobacco and naval stores to enter ports in the home islands—and then only in British vessels— and it closed altogether the ports in its West Indian colonies to United States trade. Before the Revolution, most of the exports from the American colonies had gone to Great Britain or its Caribbean possessions. American merchants, farmers, and tradesmen had expected these markets to be reopened when hostilities ended. That they were shut tightly against American commerce was a staggering blow, especially in the middle Atlantic and New England states.

The United States had concluded a treaty of commerce with its ally France in 1778, and six years later, when Jefferson arrived in Europe, three-fourths of the goods exported from the northern states went to France. Even so, the volume of that trade was small in comparison with America's prewar trade with Britain. London's retaliatory commercial policies made it imperative that the American commissioners seek ways to expand trade with France, including fully opening the French West Indies to American commerce and persuading Versailles to end lingering restrictions that had originated generations before. All this made America's minister to France the young nation's most important diplomat, and in many ways its single most important official. In May 1785, nine months after he arrived in Paris, Jefferson learned that he had been named to succeed Franklin as minister plenipotentiary to France.

Franklin, who was pushing eighty and suffered so many afflictions that he could hardly stir from Passy, had asked to be recalled. Congress complied, sent Adams to London as the first United States minister to the Court of Saint James, and named Jefferson to succeed Franklin. Jefferson knew that he would never be held in the same esteem as Franklin, who he thought was the most respected man in France. Nevertheless, Frenchmen that Jefferson had met during the war spoke positively of him to the Foreign Ministry. Lafayette, in fact, praised Jefferson as the best ambassador that the United States could appoint, and characterized him as "good, upright, enlightened" and "respected and beloved by every one that knows him."[11] Lafayette's judgment was borne out. Jefferson established an agreeable relationship with Comte de Vergennes, Louis XVI's foreign minister. Franklin had been rather passive and deferential, and Adams confrontational. Jefferson, who was always diligent and industrious, did his homework, interacted agreeably with Vergennes, and succeeded in winning the foreign minister's respect. Privately, Jefferson disparaged Vergennes's devotion to "*pure despotism*" and criticized his lack of knowledge of American affairs, but he also believed that the foreign minister's inordinate fear of Great Britain rendered him of great value to the United States.[12] However, a good rapport did not mean success. When all was said and done, Jefferson achieved little that he had set out to accomplish.

Thomas Paine in *Common Sense* had been uncannily accurate in capturing the aspirations of the colonists. "Our plan is commerce," he said of what was to be the United States, and he added that trade "will secure us the peace and friendship of all Europe; because it is the interest of all Europe to have America's free port."[13] Jefferson could not have agreed more, and he worked tirelessly to persuade the French to move toward a free trade policy. The most enlightened French officials, perhaps including Vergennes, agreed with him. But Jefferson soon saw that he was swimming upstream. The French system consisted of ancient monopolies, Byzantine restrictions, cumbersome fees and duties, and antiquated means of collecting taxes. Besides, any French official so unwary as to attempt dramatic alterations risked not only political suicide but also upsetting the fragile economic system.

Jefferson had a second goal as well. Longing to break Great Britain's near-total monopoly of the American market, he wished that France would begin exporting its manufactured goods to the United States. He was no less eager to have the French open their ports to Chesapeake tobacco, rice, and naval stores from the Carolinas and Georgia, grains from the mid-Atlantic region, and fish and oil shipped from New England. In no time, the United States could enjoy a more satisfactory balance of trade, its merchants and planters could disentangle themselves from their long-standing bondage to British creditors, and the new American Union could be bolstered. It was a vision of greater American economic independence, which if realized would only aid its political independence.

Jefferson won the approval of Vergennes and other important French officials. Hamilton's friend Gouverneur Morris, who came to France in 1789 to tend to Robert Morris's business interests, found that Jefferson was "very much Respected" by the French. Morris added that the esteem in which the American minister was held was "merited by [his] good Sense and good Intentions."[14] But Jefferson could not move mountains. Nor did he have a magic wand. For instance, even though he persuaded France to permit imports of rice from the southern Low Country, the French spurned the American product as inferior to rice from northern Italy and the Levant. For all Jefferson's work, after five years the volume of Franco-American trade had hardly changed. Not until deep into the next century would some of his dreams be realized.

Jefferson had spent thirty months in France, and his outlook regarding Franco-American relations and the security of the United States had gelled. This outlook changed little over the next quarter century. He persistently clung to the hope that, in time, the French might see their varied and ever-changing Continental trade as "of short duration" and commerce with the United States as "perpetual." In addition, he saw France as the very rock of American safety. "Nothing should be spared on our part to attach this country to us," he counseled. "It is the only one on which we can rely for support under every event. It's inhabitants love us more I think than they do any other nation of earth."[15]

In the spring of 1786, after a year's separation, Jefferson was reunited with John and Abigail Adams, if only briefly. Adams, in London, believing his negotiations on commercial treaties with Portugal and Tripoli had reached the crucial stage, asked Jefferson to come and join the talks. Jefferson came quickly, as eager to see his old friends as to conduct diplomacy. The Adamses were delighted to see him too. When leaving Paris a year earlier, Abigail had confessed that her one "regreet [was] to leave Mr. Jefferson." After moving to London, she remarked that the separation from the Virginian "left me in the dumps."[16]

Jefferson remained in England for more than six weeks, in the course of which he and Adams set off on a seven-day, three-hundred-mile tour of the English countryside. They visited gardens, took in the architecture, climbed a 115-foot observation tower for a panoramic view of five counties, walked battlefields from the English Civil War, paid admission to see Shakespeare's house—where, reprehensibly, they "Sat in the chair in which he used to Study, and cut a relic from it"—and looked over the college in Oxford.[17]

Back in London, their negotiations with Tripoli went nowhere, though the two concluded an accord with Portugal's envoy, only to learn subsequently that it had been rejected in Lisbon. Jefferson had also crossed to England filled with the misguided hope that he and Adams might jointly persuade Great Britain to budge on its trade policies toward the United States. Instead, he soon discovered—as Adams put it—that opinion in England was "high against America." Adams also remarked that the English treated him with "dry decency and cold civility." Jefferson would have relished such treatment. Throughout his stay, he felt that he was looked on with contempt. When he was introduced to the monarch, George III responded with a noticeable lack of civility. An unconfirmed story later made the rounds that the king had turned his back on Jefferson. That account was probably embellished, as Jefferson never mentioned it. Later, Jefferson said that the king and queen had been "ungracious." He added that the English people disliked Americans and "their ministers hate us, and their king more than all other men." He also remarked that the English "require to be kicked into common good manners."[18]

For the most part, Jefferson was happy to leave England and return to France. England "fell short of my expectations," he said, though in fact much that he said about England was complimentary. He thought the English were unrivaled as farmers and gardeners, and that England's "labouring poor" were better off by "about a third" than their counterparts in France. He lauded the English for their adaptability to machines, and was especially taken by their "application of . . . the steam-engine to grist mills." He even thought London was "handsomer" than Paris, though not so appealing as Philadelphia. Aside from their enmity toward Americans, the two things that he disliked most were British architecture—"the most wretched . . . I ever saw"—and the horrid "extravagance" with which the English aristocracy lived, though the British nobility hardly differed in that regard from aristocrats throughout Europe.[19]

Jefferson must also have been happy to resume his life as a diplomat, which he thoroughly enjoyed. On a day-in, day-out basis, he tended to the surprisingly large number of Americans who came to Paris, helping them as best he could. He sometimes entertained them, which he never thought an onerous part of his duties. Near the end of his mission, several Americans living in Paris paid tribute to his "particular kindness and attention to every American" who needed assistance, adding that Jefferson's "noble and generous" behavior had won their "love and admiration." Jefferson always seemed to have time to help others. When Gouverneur Morris came to Paris on business, he met with Jefferson thirteen times during his initial six weeks in the city, and on several occasions dined with him. Though they had "only a slight Acquaintance" beforehand, Jefferson showed Morris about Paris, making observations on Parisian architecture all the while, and even provided tips on shopping. Morris noted too that "Mr. Jefferson lives well, keeps a good Table and excellent Wines which he distributes freely and by his Hospitality to his Countrymen here he possesses very much their good Will."[20]

When Jefferson returned from London in the spring of 1786, almost four years had passed since his wife's death. He did not keep a diary, and in his correspondence with his closest friends Jefferson maintained a stony silence about his inner feelings. But it appears that the distractions of work and a spirited social life—and, above all, time—helped him through the canyons of anguish. Consciously or not, he was at last ready to move on with his life. All that remained was to meet the right person, and by accident, while sightseeing on a warm summer afternoon in August or September, he met her. Her name was Maria Cosway. Jefferson and his companion, the young American artist John Trumbull, stumbled upon Maria and her husband at the Halle aux Bleds, the Parisian grain market. Trumbull knew the Cosways from his days in London and introduced them to Jefferson.

Jefferson was immediately bewitched by this attractive and accomplished twenty-six-year-old blonde. She was the daughter of English parents who owned an inn in Florence. After her four older siblings were murdered by an insane nurse, Maria was sent to a convent school, where she became fluent in six languages and blossomed into an accomplished painter and musician. When she was nineteen, her mother arranged her marriage to Richard Cosway, one of London's better-known artists. He had money and the settlement was bountiful. But Cosway was nearly twice Maria's age and decidedly unattractive, with simian features. (William Hogarth, the pictorial satirist, once depicted Cosway as a hairy baboon.) Maria was not ready to marry, and to be sure, she was not eager to have Cosway as a husband. But she dutifully married and went with him to live in a four-story, twenty-six-room mansion in London, a place that soon acquired a reputation for lusty evening parties at which "dangerous Connections may be formed." That, at any rate, was the opinion of the bustling Gouverneur Morris, who met Maria in London in 1788, called on her often, and described her as "vastly pleasant." She was, in fact, a modern career woman, as she was childless and exhibited and sold her paintings.[21]

Beguiled, Jefferson begged off a prior engagement so that he could dine with the Cosways on the evening they met. That was the beginning. Over an indeterminate period, probably somewhere in the vicinity of six weeks, he spent numerous "half days, and whole days" with her. They explored Paris, visited galleries and museums, attended concerts and the theater, even ranged into the countryside. On one excursion along the Seine, Jefferson, feeling his oats and forgetting his age, attempted to bound over a fence. He did not succeed. He fell, breaking his right wrist. He underwent surgery, and for up to two weeks was confined at home with racking pain. Maria visited him throughout his convalescence. Richard Cosway's feelings are unknown. However, once he learned that his wife planned to see the recuperating Jefferson, Cosway "kill'd my project," as she put it, and suddenly cut short their stay in France. She thought her husband was more eager to return home than she had "seen him all this time."[22]

Knowing that Maria would be leaving the next day, Jefferson called for her and they rode together in his new cabriolet. That night, the pain of her imminent departure was accompanied by an excruciating throbbing in his

wrist, brought on, he said, by "having rattled a little too much over the pave-
ment." He found "No sleep, no rest" that evening.²³ The next morning, his
agony notwithstanding, Jefferson had the horse hitched to his small carriage
and accompanied the Cosways out of Paris.

Soon after returning home, Jefferson sent Maria one of the lengthiest missives he ever wrote, a four-thousand-word composition, all of it written with
his left hand. This so-called "head and heart" letter was abstruse, deliberately
so, as he was searching to learn if she thought their relationship had a future,
but at the same moment fearful of where his unbridled passion was leading.
He confessed that he had been a "mass of happiness" while with her, and that
"every moment" they shared had been "filled with something agreeable." He
waxed on about her "qualities and accomplishments," specifically her artistic
skills and "modesty, beauty, and that softness of disposition." But since the
"awful moment" of her leaving, he had sunk to the depths of sadness. "I am
rent into fragments by the force of my grief," he wrote, adding that without
her, he was "more dead than alive." He portrayed himself and Maria as similar in many ways, but especially as victims of "the same wound." Each suffered the sad, lacerating pain of loneliness, hers due to an unhappy marriage,
his the consequence of a marriage that had come to a devastating end.

The "art of life is the art of avoiding pain," he said, and one way for them to
avoid their pain was "to retire within ourselves." Though he did not say so,
this was the course he had chosen following both his disappointments as a
clumsy collegiate suitor and his wife's death. On each occasion, he had become a "gloomy Monk, sequestered from the world" and left to face "unsocial
pleasures in the bottom of his cell!" His life changed when he met Maria.
Having "felt the solid pleasure of one generous spasm of the heart," he never
wished to return to a "frigid" existence. Instead, he wanted to embrace her
"wonderful proposition"; when two lonely people were thrown together and
fell in love, she had apparently said, they should "retire" together. Sharing
their love would "insulate" them against the "dull and insipid" world of sor-
row and anguish.

Jefferson spoke of their "follies" in Paris, a married woman and single man
carrying on an affair. But the risks they had run had been "worth the price."
He had no regrets. "We have no rose without it's thorn: no pleasure without
alloy." Looking "back on the pleasures" he had found in being with her, he
assured Maria that his tender memories remained secure in the "warmest
cell" of his heart.

Reason told him that there was no hope for a permanent relationship with
her, but he contrasted his situation with that of the patriots in his country
who in 1776 had longed to be independent but knew that their dream could

only be realized through a seemingly impossible war against mighty Great Britain. Thankfully, he continued, America's rebels had sought that which they cherished. "[W]e supplied enthusiasm against wealth and numbers: we put our existence to the hazard, when the hazard seemed against us, and we saved our country."

Jefferson seemed to be saying that he and Maria should act daringly to save themselves. In the most esoteric fashion, he appeared to say that he wanted Maria to live with him at "our dear Monticello." Together on his remote hilltop, they would "ride above the storms," living happily not "in the shade but in the sunshine of life." How "sweet it is to have a bosom whereon to recline our heads."[24]

Jefferson wrote three additional times during the first weeks after Maria's return to London, routing his letters through Trumbull, so that Richard Cosway would remain unaware. In each, he probed to learn her feelings. "Write to me often. Write affectionately, and freely. . . . Say many kind things and say them without reserve," he said. A Christmas Eve missive was filled with love. He confessed, "I am always thinking of you," adding, "I am determined not to suppose I am never to see you again." And he implored her to "Think of me much, and warmly. Place me in your breast with those who you love most."[25]

Maria responded that she wanted to write "an endless letter," one in which she would presumably say all the things he wanted to hear. However, given what she called the "torments, temptations, and weariness" that had forever haunted females, she said she was unable to be straightforward. Her guarded letter was so diffuse that its meaning was difficult, if not impossible, to disentangle. One way to read it was that she was telling Jefferson of her hope to leave her husband and live with him. Though perhaps not "reasonable in [her] expectations," she said, she and Jefferson shared "trait[s] of character" and thought, and both had long been "suffering patiently" with the hand that fate had dealt them. Maria appeared to tell Jefferson that he could spend his days alone "on the beautiful Monticello tormented by the shadow of a woman"— his deceased wife—or he could live a happy and productive life with the woman he loved, a choice that would permit him to reach his full potential, so that history would remember him as a muse "held by Genius, inspired by wit."[26] No less recondite than he had been in his "head and heart" letter, Maria gave the appearance of saying that the next move was Jefferson's.

Jefferson, who had been writing to Maria roughly every three weeks, waited four months to respond, though the delay was due largely to his long trek through France and northern Italy. Either he had not understood her letter, or he wanted to make sure that he had not misunderstood what she had written, for he again delved to learn her feelings. He began by telling her that he longed to see her, and that if she came to Paris, he wanted to see her every day. During every minute they were together, he wrote, "we will . . . forget that we are ever to part again." But this too, was a letter that was more about discovering her thinking. He begged her to express the sentiments "flowing from the heart."[27]

Maria did not do that in a letter, but late in the summer of 1787 she returned to Paris, and without her husband. Officially, she had come to further her artistic aspirations, but her act was so extraordinary that in some measure she must have undertaken the trip to discover whether she and Jefferson had a future. Moreover, by acting so daringly, defiantly even, she was, as Jefferson had requested, expressing the sentiments that flowed from her heart. She arrived late in August and remained for nearly one hundred days. Though she lodged with a Polish princess on the other side of Paris, Maria and Jefferson saw each other frequently. No one knows what transpired between them, what was said, what was done. All that is known is that they were together on what was scheduled to be her last night in Paris, December 6, and that they agreed to meet the following morning for breakfast. Maria did not appear. In fact, she left Paris without saying goodbye. She subsequently pleaded both that she was "Confus'd and distracted" and that she "could not bear to take leave any more." Both explanations were probably true, but confusion, or discomfiture, was probably paramount. Something had brought matters to a head during their final night together. Indeed, she told Jefferson that she had "suspected" the evening would end as it did. She must have said that she was ready to leave her husband for him, but she must also have said that she would not divorce Cosway, a step nearly unheard of in the eighteenth century, and one forbidden by the Catholic Church.[28]

It may have been that Jefferson, like many another, could conduct an epistolary romance but could not make a face-to-face commitment. Perhaps, despite all the things he had written, he never wished for more than occasional trysts with Maria. It was possible that his feelings changed—that head triumphed over heart—during the long year that he and Maria had been separated. Or, it may have been that Jefferson would have married Maria had she been divorced but was unwilling to live with her in an adulterous relationship—which would have been scandalous and put an end to the political ambitions he still harbored.

They never saw each other again. They corresponded, but where Maria was anxious to keep alive the relationship—years later she confessed to still keeping his picture beside her bed—Jefferson's interest flagged.[29] More and more time passed between his letters, and he no longer inquired about her feelings toward him. His earlier expressions of love were replaced by banalities:

"Adieu! God bless you!"; "Be our affections unchangeable"; "think of me often and warmly, as I do of you."[30] Not until 1790, when he was back in America to stay, was he able to tell Maria what he had never ceased to feel: "I will always love you."[31]

Sometime within eighteen months of his final night with Maria Cosway, another woman entered Jefferson's life, with even more fateful consequences. During Jefferson's lifetime, the public never knew of his romance with Maria Cosway. But a dozen years after he last saw Maria, and while he still held public office, charges would be broadcast that Jefferson had long had a sexual liaison with one of his female slaves, and that he had fathered children by her. Her name was Sarah (Sally) Hemings.

Born in 1773, Sally was the child of John Wayles—Jefferson's father-in-law—and Betty Hemings, one of the slaves at the Forest. Sometime around 1776, roughly three years after Wayles's death, Jefferson brought Betty and her six children to Monticello. The Hemings family remained chattel and lived in the slave quarters, but they enjoyed a special status. The males were trained as skilled artisans, and no one in the family was ever put to work as a field hand.

Sally was three when she came to Monticello, nine when Martha died, and eleven when Jefferson, accompanied by her brother James Hemings, sailed for France. Following the death in 1785 of his infant child, the second Lucy Elizabeth, Jefferson decided that Polly, his seven-year-old daughter in Virginia, be sent to France. Planning to enroll her in the same convent school that Patsy attended, he requested that Elizabeth Eppes and her husband, with whom Polly was living, book passage for her Atlantic crossing on a vessel making for France. Jefferson also instructed them to send her in the company of a "careful negro woman," but added that Polly's attendant was to "return to Virginia directly," that is, to make a round-trip voyage. Nearly two years passed before Polly finally sailed, and when she did, the Eppeses put her aboard a vessel bound for London. What is more, they did not choose a mature woman to look after Polly, but sent fourteen-year-old Sally Hemings as her companion.[32]

Late in June 1787, Polly, now nine, and Sally arrived in London, and the ship's captain arranged to have the two girls taken to the residence of the American minister, John Adams. Abigail Adams immediately sent word to Jefferson. She added that the slave girl who had accompanied Maria was the "Sister of the Servant you have with you." She described Sally as "good naturd," but "quite like a child," and requiring "more care" than Polly, who was five years younger. She asked Jefferson to come for his daughter when it was convenient, and also inquired about sending Sally back to Virginia.[33]

One of the many mysteries of Jefferson's behavior is why he did not cross to London to retrieve the daughter he had not seen for four years. It has been suggested that Jefferson did not go to London to get Polly because "he was afraid to be in the same room with Sally and Abigail Adams," who abhorred slavery. However, Jefferson had never hidden his slaves when traveling, and in all likelihood Abigail Adams had already seen him dealing with James Hemings. Jefferson attributed his decision to the pressing business he faced in Paris, as he had only just returned from his extended trip to Italy. There is yet another explanation for his decision to remain in Paris. Maria Cosway was expected to arrive any day for her second stay in the city, and he likely wanted to be there to welcome her. Whatever the reason, Jefferson remained in Paris and dispatched his valet to fetch both his daughter and Sally Hemings to Paris. Jefferson had originally planned to send the slave who accompanied Polly back to Virginia. But the thought of sending this young girl alone on an Atlantic crossing aboard a ship filled with seamen likely gave him pause. It is also conceivable that his decision may have arisen from how her brother had blossomed during his three years in Paris. Jefferson had paid handsomely to have James Hemings trained as a French chef. Having nearly completed his apprenticeship by mid-1787, Hemings had grown so accomplished in his trade that he was about to become the *chef de cuisine* at the Hôtel de Langeac, a position that would give him responsibility for running the kitchen and supervising its staff. As Jefferson must have suspected that he would never again marry, and that public life would keep him from Monticello for long stretches, he may have thought that Sally could be trained to manage a household, a responsibility usually borne on southern plantations by the wife of the planter.[34]

During her two years in France, Sally Hemings grew from a callow adolescent who knew only country life into a young woman on the cusp of her seventeenth birthday who spoke French and had some familiarity with one of the world's largest cities. There is abundant evidence that Sally was an attractive young woman, with long, flowing black hair. Both she and her mother had white fathers, so that an acquaintance's description of her as a "bright mulatto" who was "mighty near white" rings true. Some thought she bore a distinct resemblance to Jefferson's late wife, which would not have been surprising, as they were half-sisters.

Little is known of Sally's life in Paris, and even less of her relationship with Jefferson. Initially, she probably ran errands and served as a chambermaid. In time, she may have become a seamstress. She must have accompanied Patsy and Polly to dances and dinners. It is known that Jefferson spent a considerable sum in 1789 on clothing for Sally, and she alone among his servants was lodged the previous year in a French home during a five-week period when Jefferson was away from Paris on a journey.

Otherwise, nothing conclusive is known of James and Sally Hemings's years abroad, save that slavery was illegal in France and Jefferson continued to hold both as his slaves. French law required that slave owners entering the country immediately register their chattel, after which the bondsmen were to be rapidly deported. As he clearly planned from the beginning to take both James and Sally Hemings back to Virginia, Jefferson never registered his two slaves. He was breaking the law, and he knew it. The year before Sally arrived, he had advised a fellow slave owner who was coming to France that he could probably escape notice by simply "saying nothing." Should he "attempt to procure a dispensation from the law," Jefferson added, it would likely "produce orders which otherwise would not be thought of."[35]

Jefferson's relationship with Sally Hemings would eventually be a major factor in his life. So too would his five years in Europe, which dramatically influenced his thinking. He found much that he liked about Europe. He quickly discovered that Europeans were superior to Americans in matters of art, music, architecture, science, technology, and cuisine. He even concluded that Europeans were more polite than his countrymen, and Jefferson was amazed to "have never yet seen a man drunk in France, even among the lowest of the people." While admitting that he viewed things through the prism of his American "prejudices," Jefferson proudly boasted that the most enlightened Europeans applauded the American Revolution, and when the French Revolution erupted during his final months in Paris, he was convinced that the French had been inspired by the American example.[36]

But for all Jefferson relished of European culture, he found much that he disliked, and the negatives had a profound impact on his thinking. Through his residence in France, Jefferson was able to see what absolutist rule had done to the French people and nation. What he saw further radicalized him.

Jefferson came away convinced that the freedom and opportunities enjoyed by Americans outweighed the best that Europe could offer. The "wretchedness" that he observed among France's "labouring poor" and peasants made him more appreciative than ever of what was available to America's free inhabitants. This "savage of the mountains of America," as he referred to himself, had sailed for France expecting to be swept up by the "vaunted scene of Europe." Instead, he quickly saw the "truth of Voltaire's observation that every man here must be either the hammer or the anvil." The "general fate of humanity here [is] most deplorable," he wrote, and it was due to the rigid class system and the resulting maldistribution of wealth. Not only was the "property of this country absolutely concentrated in a very few hands," but also "a very considerable proportion" of the countryside consisted of "uncultivated lands" that were deliberately "kept idle mostly for game." The consequence of this "enormous inequality" of wealth was the "misery [of] the bulk of mankind." While commoners suffered "under physical and moral oppression," lived in "hovels," and were denied the least control of their destiny, aristocrats enjoyed a splendid opulence and were attended by scores, sometimes hundreds, of servants.[37]

Jefferson was convinced that the root cause of the deplorable conditions was "a bad form of government." Monarchy, he said, was the millstone that caused the "people [to be] ground to powder." Thirty months after departing America, he was hearing that some of his countrymen had concluded that republicanism was unworkable. His response: "Send those gentry here to count the blessings of monarchy." They would find that every European monarchy was undergirded by "force."[38]

Throughout Europe, he concluded, monarchs "keep up a great standing army" and allied with an archconservative nobility and church to maintain their privileges, authority, and luxury. Force, or its threat, was reinforced by shackling "the minds of [the] subjects" with "ignorance and prejudices," through which they are induced to adore "wealth" and "pomp." Once again, Jefferson had a message for the most conservative Americans. "If any body thinks that kings, nobles, or priests are good conservators of the public happiness, send them here. . . . They will see here with their own eyes" that those who rule are a "confederacy against the happiness of the mass of people."[39]

Jefferson said that his outlook had been changed only by degrees through his experience of living abroad. "I was much an enemy to monarchy before I came to Europe. I am ten thousand times more so since I have seen what they are." While he saw that there was "scarcely an evil known in these countries which may not be traced to their king," he concluded that the "horror of evils" that surpassed all others was that the "dignity of man is lost" through the classification of "arbitrary distinctions" from the king and nobility downward. Most of humankind fell into one of "several stages of degradation," so that "the many are crouched under the weight of the few." Europe groaned beneath a system whereby the powerful had "divided their nations into two classes, wolves and sheep." Convinced that monarchy could exist under no alternative form of arrangement, Jefferson came to believe that the "evils of monarchical government are beyond remedy."[40]

He found nothing redeeming in monarchies. No king evinced the slightest degree of progressivism. None could act in a particularly enlightened manner within the system that sustained them. All kings were driven to perpetuate the exploitation of commoners. Perhaps one monarch in twenty exhibited above-average common sense, but none displayed extraordinary qualities.

There "is not a crowned head in Europe whose talents or merit would entitle him to be elected a vestryman by the people of any parish in America," Jefferson claimed. Louis XVI, France's monarch, "hunts one half the day, is drunk the other, and signs whatever he is bid," much of it thrust on him by the queen, Marie Antoinette, who "is detested" by nearly all, he reported.[41]

Jefferson advised many of his American correspondents that if they came to Europe, "they will go back good republicans." In his case, it was not only his commitment to republicanism that was strengthened but also his sense of the goodness of America. "America blesses most of its inhabitants," he rejoiced. Ninety-five percent of the French lived a "more wretched, more accursed . . . existence" than that suffered by the "most conspicuously wretched individual of the United States," he said hyperbolically. In America, government was small and unobtrusive, leaving its inhabitants to a "tranquil . . . felicity" and the opportunity to chase after happiness through whatever "pursuits . . . health and reason approve." Over and again, he exhorted friends at home to cross the Atlantic and see for themselves. "It will make you adore your country, it's soil, it's climate, it's equality, liberty, laws, people and manners. My god! How little do my countrymen know what precious blessings they are in possession of, and which no other people on earth enjoy. I confess," he added, "I had no idea of it myself."[42]

A decade earlier, just after independence was declared, Jefferson had pushed for reforms in Virginia to lessen the likelihood that the great mass of citizens might in time be downtrodden by a gentry that monopolized land, wealth, and power. The hopelessness that he beheld in Europe quickened Jefferson's radical impulses. Furthermore, appalled by the squalor and destitution that he thought endemic to cities, Jefferson became an even more fervent advocate of the agrarian way of life. Though it would be more clear in time, Jefferson lived in a Europe that was in the early throes of the Industrial Revolution. While intrigued by the possibilities offered by some of the new technology, he blanched at Europe's commercial avarice and its handmaidens, including stock markets, great banks, and monopolistic companies. He was not convinced that the captains of finance and industry were ushering in a better world. Europe's landless farmers and workers, already "loaded with misery by kings, nobles, and priests," would only become more hapless under the sway of these new, impersonal masters. Already in England, Jefferson discovered, the emerging manufacturing order had imposed land taxes that redistributed wealth in its favor while threatening ruin for many gentry and property-owning farmers.[43]

Jefferson showed no concern that the modernizing changes afoot in England, and to a lesser degree in France, posed an imminent threat to

America. His worry remained what it had always been. He feared that the tyranny of the few—the force behind the "enormous inequality producing such misery to the bulk of mankind" in Europe—would in time take hold in his country, eradicating the sparkling promise of America. During his first full year abroad, Jefferson spoke of the "earth . . . as a common stock for man to labour and live on," and he reiterated that the "small landholders are the most precious part of a state." Shaken by what he was seeing, he proposed to Madison that Virginia adopt a system of graduated property taxes, including exemptions from taxation for those "below a certain point." Not only would this lead to a redistribution of wealth, but through a more equitable "division of property" it would also preserve widespread property ownership.[44]

A measure of Jefferson's persistent, even growing, radicalism was apparent in his response to Shays' Rebellion, a protest by farmers in western Massachusetts against heavy taxation and foreclosures against their property. When the creditor-dominated state legislature refused to enact stay laws or permit an inflated currency, the farmers—most of whom had soldiered for American independence—took up arms to prevent county courts from sitting and authorizing foreclosures. The state crushed the insurgency in the autumn of 1786 by dispatching an army of 4,400 troops, raised mostly in Boston and other eastern towns.[45]

George Washington was apoplectic when he learned of the disorder in Massachusetts. "Good God," he exclaimed, and immediately expressed his fear that "combustibles" elsewhere "may set fire[s]" that could not be extinguished. John Jay denounced the "Spirit of licentiousness" that had "infected" the Yankee farmers. Madison wrote Jefferson of the "insolence" and "treason" of the insurgents. The alarm expressed by these three was shared by Abigail Adams, who in a letter to Jefferson called the farmers "a deluded multitude" of "Ignorant, wrestless desperadoes, without conscience or principals," and, for that matter, without real grievances.[46]

Jefferson's response was strikingly different. Although he did not defend the cause of the Shaysites—they had acted "in ignorance, not wickedness," he said—Jefferson remarked that the rebellion caused him no "uneasiness." "We have had 13 states independent 11 years. There has been one rebellion. That comes to one rebellion in a century and a half for each state. What country before ever existed a century and a half without a rebellion?" he asked.[47]

To assorted correspondents, Jefferson remarked that at times resistance to government was valuable. A rebellion, "like a storm in the Atmosphere," clears and refreshes the air, he said. "[A] little rebellion now and then is a good thing" if it added to the "happiness of the mass of the people." It was healthy for the people to rise up against their rulers at least once each generation. "The tree of liberty must be refreshed from time to time with the blood of patriots and tyrants. It is its natural manure."[48]

Given his outlook, it was not surprising that in 1787 Jefferson hoped that a severe financial crisis in France might lead to dramatic political changes. When Louis XVI summoned an Assembly of Notables, Jefferson thought a reduction in royal authority might be the result. Although he proved mistaken, Jefferson remained certain that liberal constitutional changes were inevitable, for the "young desire it, the middle aged are not averse, the old alone are opposed to it [and they soon] will die." What is more, he believed that revolutionary change would be achieved "without it's having cost them a drop of blood."[49] Jefferson's optimism was ultimately misplaced, though if he was wrong, so were many others, some fatally so.

When in the spring of 1789 the king summoned a meeting of the Estates General, the French parliament that no monarch had convened for generations, Jefferson was ecstatic. A "revolution in their constitution seems inevitable," he declared, including "great modifications" in the king's authority. Recognizing that Paris was "politically mad" and in "high fermentation," Jefferson followed events closely, even attending some of the legislative sessions. In high spirits, he wrote to Washington that France "has been awaked by our revolution."[50]

In fact, Jefferson was not merely an observer. Since his arrival in Paris five years before, he had grown quite close to Lafayette, with whom he had worked during his final harried year as Virginia's war governor. He liked the Frenchman and admired his intellect, but he was also convinced that Lafayette would "one day *be of* the *ministry*." Jefferson calculatingly fostered his trust and friendship. As events reached the critical stage in 1789, Jefferson received information from Lafayette about the plans and agenda of liberal aristocrats who were seeking to curb the monarchy's power, and he in turn provided advice on strategy. Imprudently, Jefferson hosted meetings at his residence and participated in the discussions, especially on the contents of a French bill of rights. He encouraged Lafayette and his confederates to demand that the Estates General meet regularly, enact all laws, and gain exclusive powers of taxation. He urged that the French "Military . . . be subordinate to the Civil authority," and he supported civil liberties for the French citizenry, including freedom of the press, trial by jury, freedom of conscience, and the right of habeas corpus. At Lafayette's behest, Jefferson also hosted a secret dinner at which an attempt was made to patch up differences among the progressive aristocrats.[51]

From nearly the beginning, Jefferson had predicted, the "fate of the nation depends on the conduct of the King and his ministers." The crisis could end in civil war or a peaceful constitutional revolution. When in June the king agreed to concessions, the Estates General was transformed into the National Assembly. Soon thereafter Lafayette introduced the Declaration of Rights in the assembly. Jefferson knew immediately that the reformers had succeeded in "cutting the Gordian knot." A great revolution had taken place, though he thought that the reformers, having kicked open the door, would seek, and obtain, more. Given France's standing as a major power, Jefferson without question hoped the French Revolution would spread across Europe and into Great Britain.

Jefferson's thinking may have been influenced by his awareness that Paris was in a "violent ferment," and in July, while out on business, he witnessed a clash between the king's soldiers and a mob. A few days later, on July 14, a mob stormed the Bastille—where for generations royal prisoners had been incarcerated, and often tortured—and in cold blood massacred the guards. Over a period of five days, inflamed mobs took control of the streets of Paris, demonstrating, plundering, and killing in a grim foretaste of horrors to come. Jefferson seems not to have been terribly outraged by the lawlessness. In his memoirs, written many years later, he said that he would "neither approve nor condemn" the actions of the Paris mobs, though he came very close to saying that people had a moral obligation to use the "power in [their] hands" for "maintaining right, and redressing wrong." From the first, he laid the blame for the "crimes and calamities" that occurred during the French Revolution at the hands of the monarch and his black-hearted advisors, whom Jefferson assailed "for the Turkish despotism of their characters."[52]

Jefferson exulted over the historic changes in France, and there can be no question that he also had no truck with those whose "polar star," as he put it, was in "preserving the ancient regime." Some who fought for the preservation of their privileges insisted, as radical conservatives are always wont to do, that only the unwary would risk tampering with the traditional "elementary principles of society." This may have been among the inspirations for the last truly significant letter that Jefferson wrote before leaving France. In the waning days of the momentous summer of 1789, Jefferson's thoughts turned to the question of "Whether one generation of men has a right to bind another." His answer was akin to an exclamation point to his ever greater commitment to republicanism and his zealous opposition to tyranny and exploitation. The "earth belongs to the living, and not to the dead," he said, to which he added: "the dead have neither powers nor rights."[53]

After five years abroad, Jefferson had changed in substantive ways. He appeared to be more self-assured, not that he had ever doubted his abilities. His liaison with Maria Cosway had broken the fetters of grief and despair that lingered long after his wife's demise, yet the heartache that attended their affair must have steeled his resolve against ever entering into another loving relationship that could lead toward marriage. What Jefferson had observed in Europe made him more respectful of the promise of America, deepened his belief in republicanism, and convinced him that the spirit and ideology of the American Revolution would spread far and wide.[54] What is more, Jefferson's reputation, which had nearly been fatally shattered by his final, disastrous months as governor of Virginia, had been rehabilitated.

Outside Virginia, Jefferson's name was not yet a household word. Few Americans knew that Jefferson had been the principal author of the Declaration of Independence. The first two histories of the American Revolution appeared in 1789, and neither addressed the authorship of the Declaration. Somewhat startlingly, Jefferson had done nothing to make the American public aware of his achievement. Franklin devoted a lifetime to self-promotion, Washington retained a biographer and helped him smooth over the military disasters that had occurred on his command, and, to be sure, Hamilton never hid from the public his valor in storming the British redoubt at Yorktown. Jefferson was cut from a different cloth. In a 1786 response to questions by a French historian, Jefferson said only that a committee had drawn up the document. A year later, when the *Journal de Paris* published a piece that credited John Dickinson with having written the Declaration of Independence, Jefferson took umbrage and drafted a letter to the editor that clarified matters. However, in the draft, he did not claim to have been the Declaration's author, and Jefferson never mailed his account of what had transpired in Congress.[55]

Jefferson was not as widely known as Washington, Franklin, and Adams, but among the politically active in America he was admired and respected as never before, both for his lengthy service to his state and nation and for his superb intellect. At an annual Independence Day gala at the Hôtel de Langeac in 1789, a group of Americans in attendance paid tribute to Jefferson, recognizing him as the author of the Declaration of Independence. Their ringing written statement acknowledged that Jefferson's "elegance of thought and expression" had "added a peculiar lustre to that declaratory act which announced to the world the existence of an empire." Word was getting out.[56]

CHAPTER 8

"TO CHECK THE IMPRUDENCE OF DEMOCRACY"

HAMILTON AND THE NEW CONSTITUTION

JEFFERSON HAD RETURNED to Congress and gone abroad in the hope of getting his life back together. In July 1783, Hamilton, who was twenty-eight, five years younger than Jefferson had been when he drafted the Declaration of Independence, left Congress to get on with his life. Hamilton could not have imagined how different the American political scene would be in just five years, or how much his life would change because of political developments. What he could see in 1783 was that peace was at hand and that he had a wife and infant son to support.

Hamilton resumed his legal practice in Albany in August, but that fall he decided to move to New York City, a large bustling port city, a center of finance, and the hub through which political power ran within the state. It was a place where a skilled attorney might flourish. His denials notwithstanding, Hamilton was hardly ready to abandon public life. By December 1, the Hamiltons had made the move and taken up residence in a rented house on Wall Street.

Hamilton may already have arrived when the British, on November 25, abandoned Manhattan and the Continental army marched in, formally retaking possession of the city in a gala parade down Broadway. General Washington remained in New York for ten happy days of ceremonies and celebratory dinners. Hamilton never called on him, and when Washington hosted a farewell luncheon for his officers at Fraunces Tavern on December 4, Hamilton did not attend, though his residence was only a short walk away. Hamilton's disillusionment with Washington had not faded, and it must have seemed unlikely to him that the general could be of further use. Now in his fifties, Washington had announced his intention of retiring, vowing never again to hold public office. Not only was Washington a man of his word, but it was also inconceivable that he would be drawn to any office that existed under the Articles of Confederation.

During his first autumn in New York, Betsey bore their second child, a daughter they named Angelica, after her sister Angelica Church—soon to be Jefferson's friend. A second son, Alexander, was born in the spring of 1786, and a third, James Alexander, in 1788. Four more children followed in the decade after 1792, and during those years the couple also took in an orphaned daughter who lived with them for ten years. Whereas the Jeffersons experienced one tragedy after another with their children—four of Martha Jefferson's six children died before reaching their third birthday, and a son from her first marriage perished at age three during the summer prior to her marriage to Thomas—all eight children borne by Betsey lived past adolescence. All signs point to Hamilton as a devoted father who lavished the care and affection on his children that he had been denied while a child.

He and Betsey were devoted to beneficent causes. Throughout her life, she worked to ameliorate the harsh conditions faced by orphans, eventually cofounding an orphanage in the city. She was a devout Episcopalian who raised her own children in the church and saw to their religious instruction. Her husband provided pro bono legal services to his parish church, though as a deist he neither took communion nor attended worship services on a regular basis. He and Betsey helped free the painter Ralph Earl, whose life of indulgence had landed him in a debtors' prison. They took in General Friedrich Von Steuben, who was down on his luck, and Hamilton persuaded Congress to award him a long-overdue land bounty. Even though the family owned one or two household slaves, Hamilton was one of the first to join the New York Manumission Society, which was founded early in 1785.[1] It pushed for the gradual end of slavery in New York and the immediate termination of the slave trade within the state. The group achieved both objectives in Hamilton's lifetime, but only after a battle lasting fifteen years. Hamilton once proposed that the members of the Manumission Society must liberate their own chattel, but he could not secure the adoption of his plan.

When Hamilton learned in 1785 that his brother James was at loose ends on St. Thomas, he sent him fifty pounds, approximately a year's income for a carpenter. Hamilton also promised that in a year or two, when his own affairs were in order, he would purchase a farm for his brother in New York and help him move to the United States. He also inquired about his father, whom he had last heard from five years earlier. He had written several letters, Hamilton said, but none had been answered. "My heart bleeds at the recollection of his misfortunes and embarrassments," Hamilton continued, adding that if his father was alive and indigent, he would give "all I have to[ward] his accommodation and happiness."[2]

Hamilton practiced law off and on for the remainder of his life, and on a full-time basis during his initial thirty months in the city. Despite beginning his practice after studying what a friend said were merely the "elementary books" of law, Hamilton swiftly flourished, though to some degree his rapid success was due to the disappearance into exile of many Tory lawyers who otherwise would have competed for clients.[3] As he never came close to knowing the law to the depth and breadth achieved by Jefferson, Hamilton owed his ascent to other qualities. Understanding the importance of presentation, Hamilton was scrupulous about his appearance. He dressed elegantly, favoring brightly colored and smartly tailored clothing, and submitted to a daily ritual with a barber who plaited, combed, and powdered his reddish-brown hair. Many observers remarked on his habit of carrying his slender frame in an erect military bearing. He was also bright, glib, combative, energetic, well connected, and ambitious. Unlike Jefferson, who soon found his legal practice to be drudgery, Hamilton enjoyed his work. He delighted in matching wits with other attorneys, took great pleasure in the theatrics useful in swaying juries, and won acclaim for his facile, extemporaneous discourses before jurors and judges. However, his greatest strength was not as a courtroom orator but in the preparation of learned written arguments. James Kent, later the chief judicial official in New York, thought Hamilton the "pre-eminent" lawyer of his day. Another veteran judge, who had observed dozens of Manhattan's lawyers over a span of a couple of generations, pronounced Hamilton unequaled in the "power of reasoning" and "creative" thinking.[4]

Yet another reason for Hamilton's nearly instant success was his willingness to defend Loyalists, who were victims of a postwar witch hunt fueled by a frenzy for retribution. Numerous factors led him to stand up for these victimized people. He believed that every citizen deserved adequate counsel and a fair trial. As many Tories had been affluent merchants before the war, Hamilton feared that their financial ruin, or exile, would have an adverse economic effect on the city. Having himself endured discrimination as a result of the circumstances of his birth, Hamilton was drawn to help those who suffered from what he called the "furious and dark passions of the human mind." But he also admitted a pecuniary interest in championing the Tories. This windfall of cases helped jump-start his practice, and led him to remark that the "folly" of prejudice "has afforded so plentiful a harvest to us lawyers . . . that we have scarcely a moment to spare from the substantial business of reaping."[5]

Hamilton won few friends by aiding those who had opposed the American

Revolution, but given his distinguished war record, he had no worries that he would be considered a closet Tory. He took on scores of cases, and toward the end of the decade, when he was again a member of the state assembly, Hamilton was instrumental in securing the repeal of all legislation that discriminated against the Loyalists.

The anti-Tory maliciousness left a stamp on Hamilton's thinking. He saw the popular vindictiveness as a foretaste of what could be expected should the United States become a democracy. In "times of heat and violence," he warned, there was always a tendency "to gratify momentary passions" with steps that "afterwards prove fatal to themselves." Furthermore, there was an ever-present danger that demagogues would both whip up hysteria—"corrupt the principles" of the people, was how he put it—and seek to capitalize on it. The governor of New York, George Clinton, was doing just that by playing on anti-Tory passions, Hamilton concluded. Hamilton had once admired Clinton, who had served as a brigadier general during the war. Back in 1782, Hamilton had called him "a man of integrity" and "a statesman." Now, however, he thought Clinton, who was in the midst of six three-year terms as the state's chief executive, was the quintessential demagogue, a "designing" man out to seize on "a prevailing prejudice" for his personal gain.[6]

The best defense against demagoguery and unrestrained popular passion, Hamilton said in two lengthy essays in 1784, was to embody Enlightenment rationalism, or what he called the "spirit of Whiggism," in American laws. This "generous, humane, beneficent and just" spirit, he added, should be sanctified in a "regular and constitutional mode." His first objective was the rule of law, but he also hoped to maintain a connection with the past. He wished for a legal code that would embody the "customs of all civilized nations" and that "cherishes legal liberty, holds the rights of every individual sacred, condemns or punishes no man without regular trial and conviction . . . [and] reprobates equally the punishment of the citizen by arbitrary acts of legislature."[7]

Jefferson would have agreed with Hamilton—to a point. He too might have been shocked by the retributive tenor of the anti-Tory legislation. However, whereas Hamilton responded with obeisance toward the law and tradition, Jefferson urged liberation from the dead hand of the past. Hamilton cherished the past as a weapon against radical innovation. Not for nothing did Hamilton tell a friend that he sought to "erect a temple to time."[8]

Banking also occupied some of Hamilton's time in the 1780s. He had urged a national bank as early as 1780, and he believed one had been created when Congress chartered Robert Morris's Bank of North America two years later. Hamilton and Morris had seen the bank as a means of stabilizing society. Both were convinced that a national bank would not only strengthen the

Union through "one general money connexion," but—as Morris had said—
would also "indissolubly . . . attach many powerful individuals to the cause of
our country by the strong principle of self-love and the immediate sense of
private interest."[9] However, the Bank of North America was undercapitalized and never became much more than a Pennsylvania bank headquartered
in Philadelphia.

In the absence of a true national bank, Hamilton played an active role in
the establishment of the Bank of New York in 1784. He served as its legal
counsel, drafted its charter for approval by the state, and sat on its board of
directors. He saw the bank's potential as a provider of seed money for merchants and entrepreneurs, and he envisaged it as the sole source of sound currency in the state. On the latter score, Hamilton's aspirations were not met,
and in mid-decade the state turned to issuing paper currency and, as a hedge
against inflation, it levied increased taxes on the wealthy. The episode was not
unimportant for Hamilton. The city's merchants became more aware of him.
For his part, Hamilton became fully conscious of their seething impatience
with shaky public credit and what they saw as the state's unsound money
policies.[10]

In what must have been nearly record time for a newly minted attorney,
Hamilton's earnings enabled his family to live comfortably. After only a year
in practice, he purchased for £2,100 in cash the Wall Street house he had been
renting.[11] Nor was he the only one who was thriving. For many, the 1780s
were a very good decade. Newspapers were filled with poems and essays describing the United States as a "blest land" with a bright future. There appeared to be opportunities at every turn. Thousands crossed the Appalachians
into what is now Kentucky and Ohio, eager to gain their own farms. Thousands of Loyalists had fled into exile, forfeiting their lands and businesses,
and creating vacancies in the public and professional offices they had held.
Before leaving to join her husband in Europe in 1784, Abigail Adams had remarked that every man in Boston who wanted a job could find one. Benjamin
Franklin returned home the following year and proclaimed that he "never
saw greater and more indubitable marks of Public Prosperity in any Country." He, too, thought that "Working people have plenty of employ and high
pay for their labour," and he added that farmers were also prospering. Similarly, Washington's letters to acquaintances in Europe painted a picture of a
bustling America in which roads and bridges were under construction, rivers
were being improved, and farms that had suffered during the war were back
in operation. Jefferson concurred, observing in 1784 that his countrymen
were "enjoying all the happiness which easy government, order and industry

are capable of giving to a people." Emigrants poured in, some twenty thousand annually to Pennsylvania alone. With the war at long last over, the future indeed looked bright.[12]

Yet, troubles existed. Commerce suffered during and after the war. Britain's decision to keep its ports closed to American exports was a punishing blow. So were the heavy taxes levied to retire state and national debts that were incurred from raising and supplying armies, and from borrowing, including foreign loans, chiefly those made by France. In 1784, the national government, needing almost one million dollars annually to service its debts, billed the states for nearly three-quarters of a million dollars. The following year it requested three million dollars from the states and stipulated that one-third was to be paid in hard money, that is, gold or silver.

Much of postwar taxation was for compensating bondholders who owned public securities, essentially the promissory notes issued during the war as IOUs to army contractors and soldiers. Because money was largely worthless after 1778, few original holders of the notes owned them any longer. Along the way, nearly all the securities had been bought up by speculators drawn almost exclusively from among the wealthiest in society. Within a few years of the end of the war, only 2 percent of Americans owned bonds. Sixteen "stockjobbers," as the speculators were often derogatorily called, owned half of Rhode Island's bonds. In Pennsylvania, a dozen "monopolizers," as the speculators were also sometimes labeled, held nearly 70 percent of that state's bonds.[13] Taxes provoke disgruntlement, and paying taxes to compensate some of the most affluent individuals in the land, few of whom had ever shouldered a weapon or been in harm's way during the war, aroused a rancor in some quarters that nearly matched the burning anti-British indignation of the war years.

The economy was not the only concern. When General Washington spoke of the "present Crisis" six months before he left the army, he was in part thinking about the new nation's military weakness.[14] He worried that the United States existed in a world filled with predatory, anti-republican, monarchical powers. Washington was equally troubled by the situation in the trans-Appalachia. Indians living beyond the mountains viewed the sudden flood of settlers as an invasion of their homeland. The Indians, moreover, were being armed by the British from Canada and western forts on American soil. According to the Treaty of Paris, the British were to relinquish those forts. But London declared that its army would not abandon those installations until the United States settled its prewar debts with British creditors, which the peace accord also required. The United States was powerless to cope. Unable to raise revenue, it could neither resolve the debt issue nor the lurking dangers in the Ohio Country.

Yet another western problem begged for a solution. The western boundary of the United States was the Mississippi River, but the peace treaty made no mention of the southern boundary. The United States claimed the 31st parallel as its southern boundary. Spain, to whom Great Britain had returned East and West Florida, claimed the 32nd parallel as the Spanish-American boundary. Following the war, Madrid closed the Mississippi River to American commerce within what it claimed as Spanish territory, roughly the one hundred miles from Natchez to the Gulf of Mexico, including New Orleans. The feeble United States was without leverage to compel Spain to open the Mississippi, a vital artery at a time when most goods moved by water.

When Washington had spoken of a crisis, he was alluding to the western threats, where "the flanks and rear of the United States are possessed by other powers." He knew the settlers wanted not only security against the Indians, but also, in order to become prosperous commercial farmers, the ability to ship their commodities to eastern and foreign markets through New Orleans. He also understood that the "Western settlers . . . stand as it were upon a pivot—the touch of a feather, would turn them any way."¹⁵ Washington was alluding to the danger of western secession, for he understood that Great Britain and Spain might offer concessions to the western settlers in return for their agreement to leave the United States. Should that occur, all hope would be dashed of a united America becoming a safe, strong land of opportunity.

When independence was declared, Americans dreamed of the fruitful commerce that would come from breaking the shackles of colonialism. The dream had not been realized. Britain and Spain largely closed their ports to American ships, and neither Franklin nor Jefferson had enjoyed much success in expanding trade with France.

John Jay, the Secretary of Foreign Affairs, sought to resolve America's difficulties with Spain through diplomacy, but his discussions with Madrid only revealed the depth of the problem. In the spring of 1786, after a year of negotiation, the secretary told Congress that Madrid was ready to sign what would be called the Jay-Gardoqui Treaty. Spain, Jay said, would open its ports to American commerce, but on the condition that the United States would renounce navigation of the Mississippi River for decades. The opening of the ports would be a bonanza for the trade-starved northern maritime states, and every one of them supported ratification. But the five southern states were opposed. They looked on what is now the southeastern United States as their territory—and in fact the southern states of Kentucky, Tennessee, Alabama, and Mississippi would ultimately be carved out of the region. But if the treaty were ratified, settlers would shun the region, for if goods could not be gotten to market, the inhabitants were destined to be dirt-poor farmers. The treaty failed only because the northern majority in Congress fell one vote short of the two-thirds majority needed to sanction the pact. Many Southerners and Westerners were outraged at the North's willingness to sell out their interests, and many Southerners saw themselves as a lonely minority in a Union in which the balance of power lay with the northern states. Those northern states, meanwhile, simmered with anger at the loss of a badly needed commercial opportunity.[16]

The exuberant pride in the new American nation that had been so manifest in 1776, and which had led many men to bear arms, was waning. Growing numbers of Northerners and Southerners were embarrassed by a Congress so enervated that it often could not meet for a lack of a quorum, and when it did meet seemed to overflow with mediocrities. A widespread feeling set in that few "men of enlarged minds" any longer wished to serve in a body that was too weak to "coin a copper," as one observer put it.[17]

"No Morn ever dawned more favourable than ours did—and no day was ever more clouded than the present," Washington declared in 1786. The "scurge" of feebleness was "shameful & disgusting," he continued, and in more than one letter he reiterated what he had said before leaving the army: "a tone" must be given "to our Federal Government, as will enable it to answer" national interests. What Washington had labeled the "present Crisis" in 1783, he was calling "the impending storm" by 1786, and he gloomily predicted that if changes were not forthcoming, the "superstructure we have been seven years, raising at the expence of much blood and treasure" was doomed.[18]

Concern over America's debility, and its nearly feckless national government, was not misplaced. But some in the newly independent United States were alarmed for reasons having nothing to do with the West, or commerce, or national pride. Long before independence, Joseph Galloway, a conservative Pennsylvanian who later turned Tory, warned Congress that a break with the mother country would unleash democracy and social disorder. America, he predicted, would be victimized by "companies of armed, but undisciplined men . . . traveling over your estates, entering your houses . . . seizing your property, and carrying havock and devastation wherever they head—ravishing your wives and daughters."[19]

Galloway's anxiety was exaggerated, but substantive political and social changes accompanied independence, just as he had forecast. Beginning in 1776, several state constitutions broadened suffrage rights, provided for more elective offices and more frequent elections, reduced the property qualifications for holding office, and corrected malapportionment in their assemblies. Men who had never before held political office ascended to positions of

authority, and in New York a substantial portion of the colonial ruling elite—
the Hudson River squirearchy, which included Hamilton's in-laws—lost
much of their pre-Revolution authority to men like Governor Clinton, who
rode to power with the backing of small farmers from upstate. What was
happening in New York was occurring elsewhere. For instance, before the
Revolution, New Hampshire's assembly consisted almost entirely of wealthy
gentlemen from the eastern coastal region; by the mid-1780s most assemblymen were ordinary farmers, and a considerable percentage came from the
western regions of the state.[20] A sense of egalitarianism also took hold. It grew
among small farmers and the propertyless, who were being asked to soldier,
and die, for the United States, but it was inspired as well by the noble ideas of
equality expressed in Jefferson's Declaration of Independence.

The traditional elite was no longer guaranteed political dominion, and some
were unhappy about it. After losing a gubernatorial race to George Clinton,
Philip Schuyler grumbled that the victor's "family and connections do not
entitle him to so distinguished a predominance." Nor were all thrilled when
their social inferiors were no longer deferential. The "spirit of independency
was converted into equality" so that each country peasant now "conceives
himself, in every respect, my equal," fumed a Virginia aristocrat.[21]

What Hamilton wrote for public consumption focused on the weaknesses
of the national government, but in private he, too, raged at the growth of
democracy. Democratic politics, he said with alarm in 1785, had brought men
and factions to power who were not "disinterested." These "new men" promoted local and selfish concerns, especially the authorization of paper money
and assorted forms of debtor-relief, including stay laws. The state assembly,
he said, was now open to increasing numbers of "the levelling kind," so that
the "despotism and iniquity of the Legislature" jeopardized "the *security of
property*."[22] Aside from Governor Clinton, no political activist bothered
Hamilton more than Abraham Yates, a man whose rise had been facilitated
by the American Revolution.

Yates's background resembled that of other Founders. Like John Adams,
Yates was raised on a small farm. Like Washington, he lacked formal education and became a self-educated surveyor. Like Hamilton, he took up the law
after limited study. But there were substantive differences as well. Yates had
never acquired the gentlemanly sheen that many realized through a liberal
education. Before the war, Yates had risen to be a sheriff, but the American
Revolution transformed him. In 1776, he was elected to New York's provincial
congress, where he helped write the state's first constitution. He pushed for
democracy and openly vowed to break the political stranglehold of the elite,
or the "high-flyers," as he called New York's wealthiest and most powerful.

Yates fought for more elective offices, annual elections, the secret ballot, graduated land taxes that fell most heavily on the wealthy, and the confiscation—and redistribution—of Loyalist estates. After the war, while a member of the state legislature, Yates resisted the augmentation of national powers, advocated inflationary monetary policies and other debtor-relief measures, and voted against the proposed impost that Congress sent to the states in 1782.

New York's conservative old guard hated Yates and other upstarts who sought to change the state politically and socially. They labeled these new men "antifederal peasants," "little folks," and "demagogues," charging that they manipulated an unsophisticated citizenry already given to believe that men of "Abilities were . . . dangerous, and learning . . . a crime." Both Hamilton and Philip Schuyler spoke of Yates's supposed "ignorance and perverseness," portraying him as a charlatan who played on class biases to gain more power.[23]

Undergirding Hamilton's assertions was a belief, common among the Founders, that their rule was disinterested. Their reasoning went like this: As they were wealthy, leisured gentlemen who were dependent on no one and no thing, they were worthy and virtuous, beholden to no sordid, local faction, and capable of governing for the greater public good. It was a noble conceit, but it was hooey. From the very first, America's congressmen had shown their stripes as representatives of disparate sections, defending the interests of the colonies and states they represented in disputes over trade embargoes, the appointment of diplomats and the army's general officers, whether or not to declare independence, what to seek from Great Britain at the peace table, and what, if anything, to accept of Spain's offer regarding trade and the Mississippi River.

Hamilton was more disinterested than most. He was neither a creditor nor a speculator in land or public securities, and though he was a shareholder in a bank, he owned exactly one share of stock. But others who railed against the likes of Yates, and who wrung their hands about democratic excesses that promoted narrow, local interests over what they presumed to be the national well-being, were hardly objective. Not a few sought to protect their wealth and investments, and to preserve the traditional social order and customary social distinctions. More and more of the most conservative Americans came to believe that the "vile State governments [were] sources of pollution," as Henry Knox put it, or grew steadily more agitated about what a Massachusetts merchant called "plebian despotism" and the "fangs" of the citizenry. Hamilton shared their concerns. "All men of respectability" and "genius," he said, "must for their own defence, unite to overset" radical, egalitarian democrats. They must ensure "that the power of government is intrusted to proper hands."[24] The sense was growing that the way to achieve this was through consolidation—the creation of a powerful national government safely under the sway of America's traditional leaders, a government capable of addressing and resolving the new nation's sundry problems, and simultaneously of foiling democratic excesses in the states.

Within eighteen months of the end of the war, a consensus was building that Congress must have more power. Early on, New York and Massachusetts formally urged that the national government be strengthened, and in 1786 Virginia's assembly proposed a "Continental Convention" to meet in Annapolis to consider "such regulations of trade as may be judged necessary." In private, James Madison, who was every bit as much a consolidationist, or Nationalist, as Hamilton, made clear that he foresaw the Annapolis Convention as only a "first instance" toward fixing the "other defects" in the Articles of Confederation. If all went well, he said, "the present paroxysm of our affairs" would in due time be resolved by "bracing the federal system." Other Nationalists thought it unwise to limit the Annapolis meeting to trade problems. A better strategy, they thought, would be to call a convention and put everything on the table. William Grayson, a Virginia congressman, thought it would be "fatal" to attempt only "a partial reformation." He presciently advised that it would be preferable to consider all "grievances . . . at the same time," as agreement on "one object will facilitate the passage of another, & by a general compromise perhaps a good government may be procured."[25]

Soon after Virginia urged the Annapolis Convention, Congress debated calling a national constitutional convention, though in the end it chose to appoint a committee to propose amendments to the Articles. In August, the committee reported seven amendments. Among other things, they would have given Congress authority to regulate trade, impose federally enforced penalties on states that did not meet national requisitions, and, as a last resort, empower the national government to collect taxes from recalcitrant states. But Congress tabled the proposed amendments. In all likelihood, the most conservative congressmen blocked their consideration. While the amendments would have given the national government the necessary authority to solve the nation's economic problems, they would not have addressed the conservatives' concerns about democracy. Furthermore, the conservatives despaired of Congress's ever tackling that matter. Only a national convention, and only a convention composed of the proper sort of delegates, could truly cope with the democratic threats unleashed by the American Revolution.[26]

By the spring, Hamilton would have known about Virginia's call for an interstate convention. During the previous year he had rebuffed those who urged him to seek a seat in the New York assembly, but in April 1786 he eagerly sought election, subsequently remarking that he was drawn back into politics by the "derangement of our public affairs."[27] He hoped to have New York's legislature endorse the convention in Annapolis, and he wished to attend it. Hamilton succeeded on both counts. In September, he was in Annapolis, where, like Madison, he was prepared to take a first step in changing the government of the United States.

The Annapolis venture failed, but it was a failure with positive consequences. Only a dozen delegates from five states attended. All stayed at the City Tavern, and with plenty of time on their hands during the week or so that most were in town, they conversed and made future plans. It is a good bet that Hamilton and Madison, reunited for the first time in more than three years, dominated the discussions, and equally likely that Hamilton, always a clever strategist, took the lead in plotting the next steps. The outcome was that the Annapolis Convention urged that another convention meet in May in Philadelphia, but that it have "enlarged powers" to take up "other" matters "as the situation of public affairs, may be found to require" in order "to render the constitution of the Foederal Government adequate to the exigencies of the Union." In addition, Hamilton and Madison knew that it was crucial to have Washington on hand, both for the respectability that his presence would bring to the meeting and to impress the public with the gravity of the nation's problems. When Madison left Annapolis for home, he swung by Mount Vernon, where he spent three days laying the groundwork for Washington to attend the Philadelphia meeting, if it in fact was to take place.[28]

What was especially needed to give the Philadelphia Convention a better chance of success was some dramatic occurrence that lent an air of immediate crisis. Like manna from heaven, Shays' Rebellion erupted just as the Annapolis Convention came to its abortive end.

The uprising aroused a sense of urgency among Nationalists, and may have contributed to their willingness to compromise once they got together in Philadelphia. The insurgency may also have convinced Washington to attend. Previously, he had tenaciously resisted all entreaties. He neither desired to risk his towering reputation in a cause that many Americans, possibly most, opposed, nor did he wish to renege on his pledge to never again hold office. Then came Shays' Rebellion, after which Washington pronounced the Philadelphia Convention "very desirous."[29]

Before Shays' Rebellion, the consolidationists had primarily focused on the dangers of national weakness, but the unrest in Massachusetts brought

economic considerations, and especially indebtedness—personal, state, and
national—front and center. This was Hamilton's bailiwick, and he responded
with a ninety-minute speech in the New York assembly in February. It was
occasioned by yet another attempt to secure a national impost, though in
some ways his address was his opening salvo on behalf of the constitution
that was soon to be drafted. Yet again, the national will had been frustrated
by a narrow provincial interest. Unless a remedy was found, powerful local
oligarchs would always have the power to thwart the national well-being. In a
contest between local and national authority, he said, "the body of the people
will always be on the side of the state governments," for local interests and
issues comprise "familiar personal concerns." During the war, localism had
played out in the form of a "universal delinquency" by the states to meet their
national responsibilities. In the five years since Yorktown, five states "have
paid nothing" to the federal treasury, while payments from the other eight
"have declined rapidly each year." This was entirely predictable. The end
game was similarly foreseeable: The national government "will never be able
to exercise power enough to manage the general affairs of the union." Such a
state of affairs renders "the confederacy . . . in continual danger of dissolution." Unless remedied, the union will be sundered, subjecting the states to
the wiles of Europe's great powers. He concluded with an appeal: Do not let
the United States perish from fears over the "imaginary dangers from the
spectre of power in Congress."[30]

Hamilton lost the battle over the impost, but he successfully moved to
have the assembly send representatives to the convention in Philadelphia. The
Clinton faction could not avoid naming Hamilton to its delegation, but by
appointing John Lansing, the mayor of Albany, and Judge Robert Yates—two
of its own—the Clintonians assured that Hamilton would be checked.

Hamilton was accustomed to dominating every room, and within days of
entering Congress in 1782 he had emerged as a leader. But Hamilton was not
a commanding figure at the Constitutional Convention. Though he was far
younger than most—thirty-two, which was ten years below the average age of
the delegates—it was not his age that was a factor. Hamilton's influence was
limited largely because his views were too radical even for this conservative
gathering. Desperate for the convention to produce something that was superior to the Articles of Confederation, Hamilton for the most part remained
on the sidelines, watching and listening, but rarely speaking.[31]

George Mason aptly described the delegates as the "first characters" in the
land, and not solely because nearly all belonged to society's top rung. Nearly
80 percent had sat in Congress, eight had been delegates to state constitu-

tional conventions, seven had been governors, and one-third had served in the Continental army. These men were experienced, but they were not disinterested. More than half were slave owners, a third were actively involved in foreign or interstate commerce, the lion's share were land speculators, and a majority owned certificates of public debt. Economic considerations were part and parcel of the deliberations. The Philadelphia Convention was also defined by who was not present. The "new men," like Abraham Yates, were conspicuously absent. Nor were vocal decentralists with democratic leanings, such as Samuel Adams and Patrick Henry, present in the East Room of the Pennsylvania State House, the same chamber in which independence had been proclaimed eleven years earlier.

While virtually every delegate came prepared to increase the powers of the national government at the expense of the states, none was willing to jeopardize the vital interests of his own state. Moreover, the larger states sought more power than they had under the Articles, while the smaller states steadfastly resisted losing their clout. These things made for problems, though it did not mean that the convention was doomed. All knew that this would almost certainly be the only opportunity in their lifetimes—and possibly the only chance ever—to fashion a truly strong national government that could cope with what they saw as deep-seated problems. These delegates were experienced politicians, skilled in the arts of bluff, bluster, and deception, but also practiced in negotiating deals. Most had come prepared to bargain, hopeful, as Grayson had predicted fifteen months earlier, that through compromise a good government could be created.

Hamilton had little experience in such things. He had sat in Congress for a few months, but at a time when it was hardly more than an idle debating society. Most of his experience had been in the army, where orders were given and followed, not disputed and haggled over. Relatively unaccustomed to the ways of legislators, he was convinced after a few weeks that "we shall let slip the golden opportunity." His "anxiety" that "the Convention . . . will not go far enough" was made all the greater by his belief that "there has been an astonishing revolution for the better in the minds of the people," and that they were now "ripe" for "a strong well mounted government."[32] During the first twenty or so sessions, he said nothing. But on June 18, his frustration and apprehension peaking, Hamilton delivered a remarkable six-hour speech in which he laid bare his most deeply held convictions, hoping to persuade the delegates to commit to a radical plan of constitutional revision.

At the time of his remarks, the convention had been presented with two working proposals. The Virginia Plan called for a new constitution that vested the national government with much greater powers, including the authority not only to enact laws "in all cases to which the separated states are incompetent," but also to "negative" state laws "contravening . . . the articles of union." The New Jersey Plan, on the other hand, proposed that the Articles of Confederation be amended to augment the powers of the federal government, though state sovereignty would for the most part be preserved.

When Hamilton rose to speak, the East Room was warm and stuffy, as it nearly always was on summer days. Following the procedure adopted by the Continental Congress, the delegates kept the room's tall windows shut, both to suppress outdoor noise and to preserve the secrecy of their discussions and transactions. Hamilton faced colleagues seated in hard Windsor chairs at round tables covered with green fabric. The tables and chairs were positioned in arcs, and the delegates sat facing the dais, where the presiding officer, General Washington, sat in the tallest chair of all. Looking out over the rather small, square room, with its gray paneled walls, Hamilton began by saying that he was "unfriendly to both plans," as under both the states would continue to "counteract" the national interest. Neither plan would solve the problems of raising adequate amounts of revenue or of raising armies before war was declared, and neither would satisfactorily check democracy. These deficiencies would mean that neither "public strength" nor "individual security" could be achieved.

What then was the solution? Hamilton said that he would like to see the "formal Extinction of State Governments," but admitted that such a step would "shock public Opinion too much." He also declared that he remained committed to republicanism, though he "despair[ed] that a republican government can remove the difficulties." In fact, the plan that he recommended was republican in only a narrow sense. Hamilton urged a national government drawn on the likeness of the British example, "the best model the world ever produced." The British government excelled because it provided for national strength, but also as it inhibited change.

Hamilton told his colleagues that every society divided into "the few and the many." The few—the "rich and well born"—having already reached society's pinnacle, had no incentive to pursue radical change. In contrast, the many were not only "turbulent and changing," but they also would "seldom judge or determine right." Therefore, it was crucial that the Constitution be designed in such a fashion to assure that the few would be the predominant force in the nation's government. This was the only safe way to "check the imprudence of democracy."

Hamilton recommended the creation of a bicameral congress, consisting of a lower house elected for three-year terms by the qualified voters, and an upper house chosen for life by an electoral college whose members had been elected by the qualified voters. He additionally urged an executive chosen by the electoral college for life. Calling the executive an "elective monarch," Hamilton said that a life term would place him "above temptation" and enable him to act solely in the national interest. He urged that the executive be vested with extraordinary powers, including unalloyed control of the military, enormous authority in the realms of foreign policy and finance, and an ironclad veto. In this layered structure of choosing the key officials, it went without saying that America's principal rulers would inevitably be drawn from society's elite. Most of those "trifling Characters" that tended to "obtrude" in republics would be screened out, he said.[33]

It was the most radical plan introduced at the Constitutional Convention, and while a great many delegates liked what they heard, all knew that the sort of constitution Hamilton favored was too impolitic to win ratification. A Connecticut delegate summed up the reaction of the Convention: Hamilton "has been praised by every body" but "supported by none."[34]

Nevertheless, speaking in what was supposed to be a secrecy-shrouded chamber, Hamilton had pulled back the curtain that concealed the true thoughts of the most conservative Americans. For them, the American Revolution had been about breaking free of the mother country and creating their own powerful nation state, one in which the entrepreneurs, speculators, exporters and importers, and men of finance would be free from London's confining shackles and oppressive hand. They had not dreamed of sweeping political or social change. But change had been unleashed, including the elevation to power of those who had been powerless in colonial days. This change aroused fear among the most conservative Americans. They yearned to stop the American Revolution, to make change more difficult, to preserve the contours of the society with which they had been familiar prior to 1776. Hamilton accepted that there would always be natural inequalities in society, and that they would increase over time. As this was the natural way of things, he was not inclined to seek any remedy for the disparities. Hamilton's way of thinking was not one of compassion. It was an expression of the elite's overarching desire to preserve their exalted status, and its class-biased, antidemocratic spirit not only would characterize Hamilton's thought for the remainder of his life, but also would remain the driving force behind much of conservative philosophy for generations to come.

Hamilton's political philosophy was strikingly unlike that of Jefferson's. Their differences were rooted in their conflicting views of human nature. Jefferson was an optimist; Hamilton was a pessimist who, in the words of one scholar, held "mankind in pragmatic distrust."[35] He saw humankind as the pawn of passion, and in numerous writings Hamilton spoke of the intractable "avarice, ambition, interest which govern most individuals." Given man's ever-present "love of power," "desire of preeminence and dominion," irresistible "low intrigue" for gaining power, and propensity for deception once in power—in order to achieve greater power and make pawns of the weak—Hamilton harbored doubts about man's capability for self-government.[36]

Later, Hamilton viewed Jefferson as a "visionary" who embraced "pernicious dreams," for the Virginian thought humankind was endowed with a moral sense that made possible affection and empathy. If man's environment could be changed so that education was widespread, social distinctions eliminated, and wealth more equally distributed, the good in mankind would predominate. Jefferson championed governments that permitted change, advocated listening to the will of the people, and denounced the oppression of the many through what he had called the tyranny of the few. His draft constitutions for Virginia bore little resemblance to the plan that Hamilton had laid out. Emphasizing the goal of maintaining the authority of the "whole body of the people," the officeholders in Jefferson's plans were to serve for brief terms, the executive was to be a weak official, and a bill of rights was to be included in order to protect the people from their government. At bottom, Jefferson's constitutional formulations sought to facilitate the desires of the governed. Hamilton emphasized the preservation of order and stability, the protection of those who had reached society's summit, and the means of restraining those who had not.[37]

Hamilton had not been a major player in the convention prior to his speech, and he played an insignificant role from that point forward. He talked at length only one other time, on June 29, in the midst of what seemed to be a crisis of indissoluble differences among the delegates. The heart of his remarks concerned the "consequences of the dissolution of the Union," though this time he emphasized the dangers from abroad claiming, "Foreigners are jealous of our encreasing greatness, and would rejoice in our" divisions. Moreover, the nation was in debt to European powers, which might drive them to gain what they were owed. If the nation is weak, he cautioned, "foreigners will invade your rights." The United States would survive only if the states remained united "for our common defence." Among his last words to the convention was an appeal to create a national government of "sufficient stability and strength" that it could provide for the national defense.[38]

Following his second speech, Hamilton went home to tend to his legal practice. Two weeks after his departure, Washington wrote to Hamilton that it seemed unlikely that the convention would produce the government that America required. "I wish you were back," he added. The convention was the first occasion, as far as is known, when Hamilton and Washington were together since Yorktown. Hamilton had not made the one-day ride from An- napolis to Mount Vernon to call on Washington the previous fall, perhaps because Betsey had given birth to the couple's third child during his absence and he was anxious to get home. But Hamilton's lingering rancor toward Washington likely played a role too, and in fact he does not appear to have associated with Washington in Philadelphia. Washington dined, drank tea, even went sightseeing with numerous others, but in his diary he never men- tioned the least contact with Hamilton. After having been in the same city with Washington for six weeks, Hamilton remarked that he had not "com- pared ideas" with Washington. The general, of course, was aware of Hamil- ton's thinking after his June speech, and he appeared not to have been put off by it. Furthermore, as Washington lodged with Robert Morris and spent considerable time with Gouverneur Morris—with whom he went fishing near Valley Forge during a weeklong recess—he was probably made aware, if he had not known previously, that Hamilton's grasp of economics was exceptional.[39]

The history of the Constitutional Convention was one of repeated compro- mises between various interests. Moreover, recognizing the difficulties that they would face in securing ratification, the Nationalists did not go as far as most would have liked. Nevertheless, the consolidationists achieved what they had long sought. Preserving the broad outlines of the Virginia Plan, the Constitution provided for an omnipotent national government, including an executive who was vested with breathtaking powers. It did not vest Congress with the authority to overrule state laws, but it accomplished the same end by prohibiting the states from exercising many sovereign powers. Despite the convention's supposed secrecy, Hamilton learned in August in New York that the proposed new government was being given "a higher tone," and he asked Rufus King to let him know when the end was near, as he wished to sign the final document. Hamilton was in his seat on the convention's last day, and he told his colleagues that while the Constitution could hardly be "more remote" from that which he had wished, he would sign it. It offered a "chance of good" and the best hope for preventing "anarchy and Convulsion," he said.[40]

Drafting the Constitution was the easy part. Ratification was far more diffi- cult. Two impost amendments had already failed, and they were less inflam- matory to many than the Constitution. Though to make ratification easier, the Philadelphia Convention stipulated that only nine states, acting through "Conventions," not state legislatures, need consent.

Deep divisions were soon apparent. The Constitution gained its stron- gest support in the urban centers and eastern counties of most states; the backcountry nearly everywhere opposed ratification. The supporters called themselves Federalists, the foes Anti-Federalists. Even the critics were divided. Some wanted to reject the Constitution and keep the Confederation, some wanted a second convention to try again to write a new constitution, some preferred to amend the Articles of Confederation, and some wished to amend the proposed Constitution. On the other hand, the Federalists were unanimous in wishing to ratify the Constitution "as it now stands."[41]

The Federalists faced a tough battle, but they entered the fight with several advantages. They offered a concrete solution to an obvious problem. Washington, the most revered and trusted American, had signed the Constitution, as had numerous other leading citizens. The nation's press, the mass medium of the day, overwhelmingly supported the Constitution. Furthermore, having waged a long fight to rid the country of the Articles, and having sat together for four months in the Constitutional Convention, the Federalists emerged from Philadelphia united, organized, and primed for the contest. They cleverly orchestrated the flow of ratifying conventions to establish a bandwagon effect. Within one hundred days of the Convention's adjournment, five states had ratified the Constitution, and eight of the necessary nine had given their approval by early spring.

New York's convention was one of the last to meet, but the battle in New York had commenced even before the Constitutional Convention ended. In July, Lansing and Yates left Philadelphia in disgust once the Constitution took shape. Once they filled Governor Clinton in on what the Constitution would almost certainly look like, he publicly predicted "a mischievous issue" from Philadelphia and was also probably behind a bevy of wild rumors in the press about what to expect. That was too much for Hamilton. He responded with an essay attacking the Articles and assailing the governor as one who had a "greater attachment to his own power than to the public good."[42] Clinton's defenders countered with vitriol of their own. One essay, signed by "Inspector," insinuated in a New York newspaper that Hamilton had "palm[ed]" himself off on Washington, whom he had served until the general realized that his aide was "a superficial, self-conceited coxcomb."[43] Another scribbler wrote of a fictitious immigrant from the Caribbean named "Tom Shit"—clearly meant to be Hamilton—who was the illegitimate offspring of a white father and a black mother. "Tom" peddled advice to a "Mrs. Columbia" about how to run her plantation, including the admonition that she appoint a superintendent for life rather than for a brief tenure.[44]

Hamilton responded to neither assault, although he asked Washington to clarify matters about his service as an aide. The general did so, and added that he had the "highest esteem and regard" for his former aide.[45] One reason that Hamilton may not have responded to the scurrilous attacks was that he had his hands full with *The Federalist Papers*, a massive undertaking that he conceived and engineered. To sway the thinking of New Yorkers, Hamilton proposed the publication of dozens of thoughtful essays on nearly every aspect of the existing Articles and the proposed Constitution. Over a period of several months, eighty-five solemn and reflective newspaper essays were penned, then collected and published as a book. Hamilton persuaded Madison, a member of Congress—which now was meeting in New York City—and John Jay to write some of the essays, and they contributed twenty-nine and five, respectively. Wielding his breathtakingly quick pen, Hamilton, as "Publius," churned out fifty-one essays in seven months, sometimes producing as many as three a week even as he tended to his legal practice. It was a Herculean effort totaling more than one hundred thousand words.

Half of Hamilton's essays covered ground that he had plowed innumerable times during the past few years, as he expanded on the imperfections of the Articles and the troubles that America faced. As always, he spoke not of problems, but of the United States having arrived at the "last stage" of "the crisis."[46] The nation would be better off with a stronger, more energetic national government, he asserted, and he emphasized how consolidation would result in abundant military might. Never mentioning national strength for the purpose of expansion, Hamilton couched his arguments in terms of finding remedies for "a nation incapacitated by its constitution to prepare for defence."[47]

Hamilton did not see the world through rose-colored glasses. A realist in touch with the darker side of human nature, he understood that commercial rivalries had spawned conflicts since the beginning of time, and that have-not nations always wanted what others had. He knew, too, that "private passions," including "bigotry," hatreds, "interests, hopes and fears," sowed bellicose designs among kings and the "leading individuals" in society. In addition, the "cries of the nation," the combative fervor of the people, sometimes "dragged their monarch into war." The world had shrunk. Europe was not as far away as it once had been, and its colonies were even closer. A weak and divided America was at risk, and would face "dangers real, certain, and formidable." But the America that would exist under the proposed Constitution would be secure. Its security would not come from the powerful new central governments having created "STANDING ARMIES." Commerce was always the driving force in the creation of national wealth, and national wealth was crucial to national power. The restoration of public credit would enhance commerce. So, too, would the construction of a robust navy capable of defending "an ACTIVE COMMERCE." A central government that regulated all commerce could retaliate against those who discriminated against the

United States, leading in turn to the inevitable expansion of American trade. A sturdy and thriving commerce would produce American prosperity and power, rendering unnecessary "Extensive military establishments." It would also permit America to "soar to ... greatness." In time, the United States would "dictate the terms of the connection between the old and the new world!"[48]

In his latter *Federalist* essays, Hamilton turned to an in-depth examination of each branch of the proposed federal government, but a theme coursed through these pieces that was quite unlike what he had said with greater candor at the Convention. For public consumption, Hamilton insisted that the Constitution had not been cobbled together so as to assure rule by one "favourite class of men." The notion that the "wealthy and well born" would predominate at the federal level was "chimerical." With three branches, and each selected by distinct "class[es] of electors," no class or faction—neither farmers, financiers, merchants, nor manufacturers—could control the government.[49]

Hamilton knew that the proposed executive branch was arousing the greatest concern among the Anti-Federalists, and he devoted more attention to it than the other branches, simultaneously endeavoring to show that the president would have adequate powers, but not so much as to endanger liberty. Hamilton took pains to demonstrate that it was a republican office that would be vastly dissimilar to the British monarchy. He also sought to persuade his readers that the chief executive not only would be unable to dominate the legislative branch, but that he could be impeached and removed by the legislators as well. In addition, Hamilton insisted that the method of electing the president reduced the likelihood of "cabal, intrigue and corruption." Indeed, it assured that the office would be filled by "men [of] the first honors" and "merit." The president's authority would be greatest in the exercise of foreign policy, but that was as it should be, for he was a national official who would best represent the national interest. Moreover, unlike a "dilatory" legislature, the chief executive would be able to act swiftly in an emergency, when the "loss of a week, a day, an hour, may sometimes be fatal."[50] Hoping always to play down the awesome powers inherent in the executive branch that the Nationalists had fashioned, Hamilton nevertheless accentuated that the presidency would be an energetic office that would serve as a counterweight to total legislative dominion or ruinous and capricious state actions.

Hamilton appeared to hold his nose when writing about the legislative branch. Among the best things he could say about the proposed Congress was that democratic excess would be kept in check through separation of powers and the grand size of the republic. The judiciary was the least noticed of the branches, but Hamilton explicitly understood that the Nationalists had fashioned judicial review as a redoubt against "the encroachments and op-pressions of the representative body." Of course, that was the last thing he wished to accentuate. Therefore, Hamilton cannily emphasized the supposed weaknesses, not the strengths, of the judiciary. It would have "no influence over either the sword [wielded by the executive] or the purse" brandished by Congress. Therefore, judges would lack the "capacity to annoy or injure" and would "take no active resolution whatever." As if judges who were unelected and held a lifetime appointment would never resort to judicial activism, the Supreme Court, as Hamilton grandly portrayed it, would have "neither FORCE NOR WILL."[51]

Hamilton envisaged *The Federalist* as crucial for securing ratification in New York, but it would be a stretch to conclude that these remarkable essays played a substantive role. Nor was *The Federalist* a significant factor in other states, as few newspapers outside New York featured the essays, and those that did published only one or two.[52] The real significance of the undertaking by Hamilton and his collaborators came years later when political scientists and historians enshrined the essays for generations of students, and judges drew on their content as the bedrock for legal judgments.

Governor Clinton may have blundered in not calling the New York assembly into special session to take up the question of the Constitution. Had he done so, the convention probably would have met early in 1788. Instead, the assembly did not meet until January 1789, at which time it scheduled the election of delegates to the ratification convention for late April and the convention's beginning date for June 17. The Anti-Federalists scored their most lopsided win in New York, capturing forty-six seats to the Federalists' nineteen. However, by the time the delegates gathered in bright, summery Poughkeepsie, a town of 2,500 about halfway between Manhattan and Albany, eight states had already ratified the Constitution.

New York's convention met for five weeks in the town's stone courthouse. Although between fifty and sixty delegates were always present, two or three on each side took on the lion's share of speaking and debating. Hamilton, Jay, and Chancellor Robert R. Livingston, who had served with Jefferson on the committee that drafted the Declaration of Independence, took charge for the Federalists. Melancton Smith, a lawyer, merchant, and congressman, together with John Lansing were the spear carriers for the other side. The sessions were characterized by lengthy speeches, sharp debate, and tough cross-examinations. Hamilton frequently took the floor. An adversary said that his speeches were "very long" and vehement and that he did not always stay on the subject. That tendency had been pointed out by Georgia's William Pierce, a colleague at the Constitutional Convention, who observed that Hamilton rambled when speaking. Pierce also concluded that, while eloquent, Hamilton's voice was "too feeble" for him to be considered a great orator. Pierce was additionally put off by the New Yorker's mien. There was an imperious streak to Hamilton's demeanor, which he did not trouble to hide. Pierce thought Hamilton "tinctured with stiffness and sometimes with a degree of vanity that is highly disagreeable." These criticisms notwithstanding, Pierce contradicted himself by judging Hamilton a "blazing Orator."[53] In Poughkeepsie, Hamilton not only mustered his talents but also, as in *The Federalist*, at times camouflaged his real thoughts. In Philadelphia, for instance, he had said that the states should be eliminated as they "are not necessary for any of the great purposes of commerce, revenue, or agriculture." In New York's Ratification Convention, he declared that the states "are absolutely necessary to the system."[54]

Nine months into the battle over ratification, it is unlikely that the speechifying changed any minds in Poughkeepsie. Other things did, however. Only a week into the convention, some delegates may have been influenced by word of New Hampshire's ratification, carried to Poughkeepsie by a courier whose services had been paid for by Hamilton. New Hampshire was the ninth state to approve the Constitution, which meant that ratification had been achieved. Nevertheless, far more delegates were swayed by the news of Virginia's ratification, which arrived a week later, and by word in mid-July that Congress had set December and January dates for the selection of presidential electors and their meetings to elect the president of the United States. After a month of deliberation, the primary question that faced the delegates had become, Would New York remain in the Union? Few New Yorkers wanted to separate from the United States, and more than a few eagerly hoped that New York City might be the national capital. In fact, on July 17, Hamilton ratcheted up the pressure on the Anti-Federalists by predicting that New York City might secede from the state if the convention did not ratify the Constitution.

But while the furious floor fights and soaring oratory provided good theater, it appeared that from the beginning a majority of the Anti-Federalists were prepared to ratify the Constitution if they could secure acceptable amendments. That certainly was their focus during the final days of the convention, and on July 26 the delegates voted for ratification, a series of "recommendatory amendments," and a convention of the states to consider the amendments to the Constitution that had been proposed by several state ratification conventions. The vote was 30–27, the smallest margin of victory in any of the eleven conventions that ratified the Constitution.[55]

*   *   *

Aside from among the most fervent Nationalists, no sense of crisis had existed in America when Jefferson sailed for Europe in mid-1784. He had departed thinking that the Articles of Confederation was "a wonderfully perfect instrument," and three years later he believed that the only change it needed was an amendment enabling Congress to regulate national commerce. Jefferson did not learn of the Philadelphia Convention until it had been sitting for a month. At the same moment he became aware of the convention, Jefferson also discovered that his young friend Madison favored granting the federal government the authority to override state laws "in all cases whatsoever." "I do not like it," Jefferson immediately wrote to Madison. However, his initial uneasiness about the convention was placated by word that Washington and Franklin were in attendance. Their presence made the convention "an assembly of demigods," persuading him that untoward changes would not be forthcoming.[56]

It was mid-November before Jefferson saw a copy of the proposed Constitution. Parts of what he read, he immediately declared, "stagger all my dispositions to subscribe" to it. He told assorted correspondents that the House of Representatives was "woefully inadequate," the "President seems a bad edition of a Polish king," and whoever became president would inevitably be "an officer for life." Quite the contrary of Hamilton, he predicted that the method of electing presidents was certain to make elections a carnival of "intrigue, of bribery, of force, and even of foreign interference." As one who was convinced that "energetic government" is "always oppressive," Jefferson thought it would have been better to have empowered Congress to enact imposts and to have "left direct taxation exclusively to the states." Indeed, it would have been better to have simply made only slight modifications to the Articles of Confederation. The Constitution, he said, was filled with "very good articles . . . and very bad," the latter having been included because too many delegates had been spooked by Shays' Rebellion. Though he did not belabor it, Jefferson, like Hamilton, understood the judiciary's potentially awesome power, and he did not like it. He must have been appalled that unelected justices who served for life could negate the will of the people as expressed by Congress, for he said it would have been better had Congress been given the authority to override the courts, as it could override presidential vetoes. He complained vociferously about the lack of a bill of rights, remarking that its omission was the document's "most glaring" defect. But he vowed to stay out of the ratification fight. Not only would it probably be over before his thoughts reached America, but also, after an absence of more than three years, he was a stranger to domestic politics. The "happiest turn the thing could take," Jefferson continued, would be for nine states to ratify the Constitution so that a new government could be put in place, but for a "respectable . . . opposition" to surface so that amendments would have to be added.[57]

During the week that New York ratified the Constitution, Jefferson learned of New Hampshire's vote, which meant that a new federal government would be created. He "sincerely rejoice[d]," he said. "It is a good canvas, on which some strokes only want retouching."[58] Meanwhile, Hamilton had gone to work on Washington to accept the presidency. Though he had written Washington only five personal letters in the nearly four years since the war's end, Hamilton dispatched three letters to the general within three months of New York's vote to ratify. He believed that Washington's presence was crucial to the success of the new government, and he secretly wanted to be part of a Washington administration.[59]

Washington was conflicted. He would be fifty-seven when he took office, and he feared that he had little time left. He wanted to spend as much of that time as possible at Mount Vernon. Moreover, if he failed as president, the colossal reputation he had won during the war might be destroyed. There was also an element of posturing to Washington's behavior. He did not wish to be seen as eager to possess power. He wanted to be asked, begged even, to accept the presidency. The newspapers were filled with essays imploring him to become president, and many people wrote to beseech him to come out of retirement. Hamilton was among those who wrote, and he understood the way Washington thought better than anyone. Washington ran a "greater hazard to that fame . . . in refusing" to serve than he would by serving as president, Hamilton said. Should the new government fail while he sat on the sidelines, he continued, the people would attribute the failure to his dereliction. Those were the magic words. Washington almost immediately agreed to serve as president, and in February 1789 he was unanimously chosen by the Electoral College, as all knew would be the case.[60]

Four months after learning that the Constitution had been ratified, Jefferson asked for a leave of absence to return to Virginia, but his wish to come home was unrelated to ratification. After Patsy had alarmed him by speaking of becoming a nun, Jefferson had initially planned to come home in 1788. He wanted his daughter, who turned sixteen in September 1788, to marry, and to marry a Virginian, but he delayed requesting a leave for a year so that Polly, his youngest child, could "perfect herself in French."[61]

A second concern drove Jefferson home, though he mentioned it to no one. He had fallen into debt, and was just beginning to understand his predicament. Jefferson's problem had its origin in his decision to accept what John

Wayles had bequeathed to his daughter, including considerable debts that were owed to overseas creditors. Jefferson had understood the risk, but he presumed that the debts could be retired through marketing the tobacco that grew abundantly on his properties and Wayles's Tidewater lands. But the Revolutionary War wrecked the tobacco trade. Nor did peace help. Not only did the Treaty of Paris stipulate that creditors were to meet with no impediments in the recovery of prewar debts, but also Britain's discriminatory trade policies were ruinous for tobacco planters. In mid-1787, Jefferson first spoke of the "torment of mind" caused by his indebtedness.[62] Thereafter, he began thinking of coming home to take charge of, and possibly rethink, operations at Monticello and his other properties.

Believing that he could restore order to his affairs quickly, Jefferson envisaged being back in Paris within six months. It was his plan—his hope—to remain in France for several more years, continuing his diplomatic mission, watching history unfold in the French Revolution, and, possibly, learning whether he had a future with Maria Cosway. Ten months elapsed before Jefferson was informed that his leave had been granted. Three weeks prior to that he had received a letter from Madison (penned shortly after Washington had assumed the presidency) that included an unsettling question: "I have been asked whether any appointment at home would be agreeable to you."[63]

Madison's query meant that he might never get back to Paris. At the very least, it probably meant that on his arrival in Virginia Jefferson would face an unpleasant choice of accepting or rejecting an office offered by Washington.

Jefferson departed Paris late in September 1789, though another month elapsed before his vessel, the *Clermont*, began its Atlantic crossing. His traveling party included his two daughters, the Normandy shepherd he had acquired in Paris, and his two slaves, James and Sally Hemings. Sally, now sixteen, may have been pregnant, as she supposedly later averred. Some historians believe that she was pregnant and that the child she was carrying was Jefferson's.[64] If so, Jefferson may have learned of her condition at the beginning of September, for at that time he suffered a migraine or cluster headache, his first in more than five years. Or, the malady may have been the result of a case of nerves triggered by his recent receipt of a missive from Maria Cosway beseeching him to stop in London. "T'is very cruel of you," she wrote, not calling on her, to which she added: "Pray take me" to America.[65]

Whether or not Jefferson had any inkling, he was on the cusp of striking life changes.

THE STRUGGLE TO SHAPE
THE NEW AMERICAN
REPUBLIC

CHAPTER 9

"THE GREATEST MAN THAT EVER LIVED WAS JULIUS CAESAR"

THE THRESHOLD OF PARTISAN WARFARE

HAMILTON AND JEFFERSON might have met in 1783 during the couple of months that both were in Philadelphia. It is certain they met in 1790, and during the next few years each was obsessed with the other.

During the winter and spring of 1789, while Jefferson was watching the frenetic early events of the French Revolution and awaiting permission to return to Virginia for a brief stay, Hamilton anxiously awaited the commencement of Washington's administration. Washington had been unanimously elected on the first Wednesday in February. John Adams received the second greatest number of electoral votes—he polled thirty-four to Washington's sixty-nine—and was to be the vice president. On April 14, Washington received official notification of his election. It was not a surprise. His bags were already packed, and in short order he was on his way to New York, home of Congress and, for the time being anyway, the capital of the United States. Despite the unambiguous concerns of many that the Constitution had created a presidency with a distinctly royal hue, Washington's journey northward from Mount Vernon befitted a monarch. Large crowds turned out to cheer him in hamlets and cities along the way, nearly every one of which feted him with some sort of regal ceremony. In Trenton, for instance, a girls' chorus serenaded him with a composition that rang out "Welcome, mighty Chief." Fully half the residents of Philadelphia lined the streets to cheer and to see the most famous American.[1]

Between September, when Hamilton had written beseeching Washington to serve as chief executive, and the president-elect's arrival in New York in April, the two had no contact. They may not have met prior to Washington's inauguration of April 30, but Hamilton was present at Broad and Wall Streets, the site of Federal Hall—New York's city hall, recently remodeled and given to Congress—when the oath of office was administered. He also attended Washington's inaugural ball a week later, and the president danced with Betsey, who found him to be grave and formal even in this relaxed environment.

Around the time he took office, Washington solicited advice on the "etiquette proper to be observed by the President." Adams and Hamilton were among those he approached. Both stressed the need for dignity, though Adams recognized that each president would behave differently according to his character and temperament. Encouraging Washington to shoot "for a pretty high tone," Hamilton urged behavior worthy of royalty: the president should receive guests at a formal weekly levee (the term used in European monarchies for royal receptions), but he should not linger more than thirty minutes; he was to host "formal entertainments" up to four times annually, though he should never "accept invitations" to visit the homes of others; he might occasionally invite six or eight congressmen or "other official characters" to dinner, but he was "never to remain long at table."[2]

Having spent years in the general's presence, Hamilton knew that his recommendations would be an ideal fit for Washington. Washington was customarily distant, solemn, and reserved. Predictably, his presidency rapidly took on a monarchical air. He was attended by servants in livery and wigs—mostly slaves brought north from Mount Vernon—traveled in a varnished, cream-colored carriage drawn by several horses and adorned with his family coat of arms, and presided over stuffy levees and dinners, occasions when he stiffly bowed, but never shook hands. The British minister, who knew royalty when he saw it, remarked that Washington was "very kingly." Those who were most conservative relished the tone that Washington set, seeing him as "a king, under a different name," as James McHenry put it, and at times when Washington appeared in public they had a band strike up "God Save the King." Not a few were put off by the royal trappings, though open criticism of Washington was a long time coming.[3]

Everything about the executive branch, about the entire federal government, was new territory. Months passed after Washington's inauguration before Congress created the last department. Congress was distracted with other business, including hashing over amendments to the Constitution to satisfy the Anti-Federalists and enacting an impost of 5 percent on imports, the revenue-raising measure the Nationalists had sought since 1782.

When Congress finally got around to the executive departments, it more or less simply replicated the three that had existed—War, Foreign Affairs (renamed "State"), and Finance (henceforth to be called "Treasury"). Its one substantive change was that whereas the president was to determine the duties of the secretaries of war and state, the secretary of the treasury was to report to Congress.[4]

Washington typically made decisions slowly, though he wasted little time in asking Henry Knox to continue in his post as secretary of war. How Washington came to his choice of a treasury secretary is not clear. Tales later circulated that he first offered the position to Robert Morris, who declined and recommended Hamilton. That unsubstantiated yarn is highly suspect. Though popular with northern, urban Nationalists, Morris was disliked—"hated" might be a better word—in many other circles. Washington fostered a persona of being above politics, but he was an adroit politician who was not about to taint his administration with one as widely despised as Morris.

Actually, the president probably settled on Hamilton early on. Washington had not been in office a month before Madison wrote to Jefferson that New York's Robert R. Livingston wanted the position, but that Hamilton, who was "best qualified for that species of business" and had considerable support among merchants and financiers, was the favorite.[5] Washington remained silent, however, until the Treasury Department was created by Congress early in September, at which time he nominated Hamilton.

Washington was drawn to Hamilton for numerous reasons. Despite the tension between them, Hamilton had been scrupulously loyal, always a selling point with Washington. The president once claimed to have never spoken with Hamilton about economics before 1789, but that stretches credulity. General Washington's habit had been to frequently surround himself with his aides at the end of the workday, and every conceivable subject was fair game for discussion. Given the often sad state of the army from 1778 onward, it is hard to imagine that Hamilton, who was publishing essays on the nation's financial woes, had not expounded on economics during those sessions. Whether or not he had, it seems probable that as far back as 1780 Washington had heard others tout Hamilton's expertise in economic matters.

No one was a better judge of others than Washington, and having spent five years with Hamilton at headquarters, corresponded with him, likely read some of his published essays, and seen him in action at the Philadelphia Convention, the president knew him well. Many who came into contact with Hamilton were appalled by what they found. But Washington admired him. Washington was aware that Hamilton was a dreamer, an intriguer, a polemicist, a relentless avenger, and a veritable storehouse of ideas; he knew, too, that Hamilton was fluent, persuasive, and nearly unequaled in guile, political dexterity, and his capacity for work. Hamilton, as Washington must have known, usually found a way to win approval of what he wanted, even if he had to scheme and conspire. Washington recognized that Treasury post was going to be both a pressure cooker and, next to the presidency, the cockpit of the new national government. The recommendations of Treasury would determine much about the shape of the new American nation, the lives of its citizenry, and the nature of its politics. Above all else, Washington was cognizant of what Hamilton wanted, and it was what he wanted. Both longed to make America what some historians have called a "fiscal-military" state, a nation with the capability of marshaling wealth and utilizing the power brought by wealth for military means.[6] Washington may not have known all the economic steps that had to be taken to get there, but he knew that Hamilton did.

Hamilton's appointment was approved by the Senate on the same day that it was submitted. Intent on avoiding all charges of iniquity, Hamilton immediately gave up his law practice, and as he owned no securities (he had only a small investment in a western land company and that single share of bank stock), he left himself without a private source of income. Neither President Washington nor any other member of his administration or of Congress did such a thing. Hamilton planned to live on his salary of $3,500 annually, a very handsome income, some ten times that of most experienced tradesmen, but considerably less than he had been earning in his legal practice.

One week after he took office, the House of Representatives gave Hamilton a deadline 110 days away to prepare a plan for coping with the nation's indebtedness. Now thirty-four, he worked daily throughout that autumn to complete his Report on Public Credit, often toiling deep into the night in his tiny, unadorned office. A foreign visitor described Hamilton, in "a long gray linen jacket," working at a pine desk covered with a simple green cloth; files were strewn about, the guest said, and the few items of furniture in the office could not have cost more than ten dollars.[7] The ideas that went into his report were not especially new, though they had to be substantiated with evidence, and he had a comptroller, assistant secretary, and thirty clerks to help with the research. (Counting inspectors, revenue collectors, and assorted other officials, the Treasury Department consisted of about 350 employees, nearly ten times the number allotted to War and State.) Clearly, Congress saw indebtedness as the nation's greatest problem.

Hamilton's forty thousand word report submitted in January 1790 was the first accurate reckoning of the extent of indebtedness. The debt of the United States totaled about $52 million. Roughly 20 percent of it—$11.6 million—was owed to foreign nations (nearly 15 percent of that in arrears of interest), while the remaining obligations were to the holders of bonds, IOUs, and currency issued by Congress and the army. Hamilton calculated the debts owed by the states to be $25 million. He estimated the total federal and state debt at a par, or face, value of $79 million. The figures provided by Hamilton were not surprising. Nor was anyone startled to learn that the annual interest payments on the national debt exceeded the revenues of the federal government. However, some were taken aback by two aspects of the plan he proposed for dealing with the debt. First, he called for the United States to assume the debts of the states, a notion that had not been widely bandied about prior to 1789. Second, instead of proposing that all indebtedness be retired, he recommended that the new federal government "fund" it—today, it would be called "refinancing"— which is to say that Hamilton urged the creation of a new debt through which to pay off the old.[8]

After years of rhetoric about a debt crisis, Hamilton had called for making the debt permanent. His idea was that new federal securities would be issued, replacing the total principal of all old securities. Investors would purchase these securities—hence they would become creditors who were making a loan to the United States—and the revenue raised from their sale would go toward retiring the old debt. The new bonds that Hamilton proposed would never mature, their average interest rate would be about 4 percent, and their holders were to receive from the Treasury a specified dollar amount annually.[9] The funding scheme that Hamilton recommended was not unheard of. It was an idea that had been discussed years before in Morris's day.

However, neither funding nor the assumption of state debts had been noised about during the campaign for the Constitution. Some of Hamilton's scheme was not as apparent then as now, or as it would come to be before the decade ran its course. He believed that consolidating state and national indebtedness would exhibit the power of the federal government. (He had said in *The Federalist* that the more the government engages in matters "which touch the most active springs of the human heart, the greater . . . it will conciliate the respect and attachment of the community.")[10] More important, Hamilton wished to attach the wealthiest Americans—those who could afford to purchase Treasury securities—to the new national government. He knew that nothing would strengthen the government more than the loyalty of wealthy and propertied creditors. That, in turn, would enhance America's credit rating and entice European investors. Finally, although Hamilton remained silent on this point, he saw consolidation and funding as merely the first step in a calibrated formula that would transform America into a powerful national state capable of defending itself and expanding its boundaries.

Jefferson had not stopped in London to see Maria Cosway, and after a twenty-six-day crossing, he landed at Norfolk late in November. On disembarking, Jefferson learned that Washington had nominated him to be secretary of state and that the Senate had already confirmed the appointment, even though he had not been consulted. Less mystery surrounds Washington's selection of Jefferson than his choice of Hamilton. Only four men had been major players in American diplomacy, and Washington easily eliminated two of them: Franklin was now eighty-three and Adams was the vice president. The third was John Jay, who had been in charge of foreign policy since shortly after the war ended. But like Hamilton, Jay was a New Yorker. Washington could not have two New Yorkers and no Southerner in his cabinet. The president nominated Jay as chief justice of the Supreme Court and turned to Jefferson, his fellow Virginian.[11]

Jefferson did not want the job. He hoped to sail for Paris in early April, after spending some seventy-five days at Monticello. He told the president that he wished to remain in his post in France, adding that he not only dreaded the public "criticisms and censures" that a cabinet officer would inevitably face but that he also feared he lacked the skills to run the Department of State. (In those days, State was responsible both for foreign policy and for what now is handled by the Department of the Interior.) However, Jefferson did not close the door. It "is not for an individual to chuse his post," he said, adding that he understood the president had to "marshal us as may best be for the public good." When Washington asked him a second time to take the position, Jefferson accepted.[12]

During his ten weeks at Monticello, Patsy married her cousin, Thomas Mann Randolph Jr., following a whirlwind courtship. Less happily, while at home Jefferson saw firsthand the deterioration his farms had suffered during his lengthy absence, and he learned that his indebtedness now totaled a staggering £7,500. As early as 1785, while he was living in Paris, Jefferson's attorney in Virginia had sold thirty-one of his client's slaves to satisfy creditors. Having seen what he called his "deranged" property, Jefferson knew that transaction had been merely the tip of the iceberg. He would have to sell more slaves, and some of his land, simply to service the interest on his debt.[13]

Jefferson finally arrived in New York on March 21, more than two months after the House of Representatives received Hamilton's plan. He rented a house on Maiden Lane, and as he had done with both residences in Paris, embarked on a remodeling project. He lived in a boardinghouse for several weeks while the house was refurbished. During this period, Jefferson drew closer than ever to Madison. When the two first met is unknown, but a relationship flowered in 1779 while Madison served on the Governor's Council, becoming one of Jefferson's trusted advisors. They grew still closer four years later when both were in Philadelphia, Madison serving in Congress and Jefferson awaiting a diplomatic appointment. Before sailing to France, Jefferson even tried to persuade Madison to purchase "a little farm" near Monticello so they could visit frequently. They corresponded during Jefferson's long stay in France, exchanging important letters concerning the French Revolution and American constitutional issues. They were reunited for the first time in nearly six years only days after Jefferson returned to Monticello in 1789, a visit that included a discussion of the post of secretary of state. Either then or soon after Jefferson's arrival in Manhattan, the two became political confederates and collaborators. Well-educated, intellectually curious Virginia planters, the two had much in common, and the warm relationship between them flourished unabated for the remainder of Jefferson's life.[14]

On arriving in Manhattan, Jefferson immediately plunged into his diplomatic and administrative responsibilities by day, while seemingly every night he enjoyed the social whirl of the capital. One occasion was a welcome-home dinner provided by the president. Hamilton and Knox attended as well, and this was probably the first time that the three cabinet members were in one another's presence. Jefferson also renewed his acquaintance with John and Abigail Adams, who were living at Richmond Hill, an elegant home situated a mile north of the city on a tall bluff overlooking the Hudson River.

Jefferson was still dressing as he had while a diplomat in Paris. Attired in "a suit of silk, ruffles, and an elegant topaz ring," he attended parties hosted by important New Yorkers nearly every evening. He was struck by how little of the American Revolution's radical spirit had taken root among Manhattan's upper crust. Filled with "wonder and mortification" at learning of their "preference of kingly over republican government," Jefferson responded by dressing in a simpler manner, donning what he called "a more republican garb."[15]

Surprisingly, Hamilton, who owned a house and entertained regularly, appears to have never invited Jefferson to his home, though once Jefferson was situated, he entertained Hamilton on a least two occasions. During one dinner, Hamilton gazed at Jefferson's portraits of John Locke, Sir Isaac Newton, and Sir Francis Bacon. He asked the identity of the subjects, to which Jefferson replied that they were "the three greatest men the world had ever produced." Hamilton responded: "The greatest man that ever lived was Julius Caesar." If he did not already know it, Jefferson discovered in that instant the yawning chasm in sensibilities that separated Hamilton and himself.[16]

Jefferson socialized with members of Congress as well, and one left a cogent description of the Secretary of State:

Jefferson is a slender man; has rather the air of stiffness in his manner; his clothes seem too small for him; he sits in a lounging manner, on one hip commonly, and with one of his shoulders elevated much above the other;

his face has a sunny aspect; his whole figure has a loose, shackling air. He had a rambling, vacant look, and nothing of that firm, collected deportment which I expected would dignify the presence of a secretary or minister. I looked for gravity, but a laxity of manner seemed shed about him. He spoke almost without ceasing. But even his discourse partook of his personal demeanor. It was loose and rambling, and yet he scattered information wherever he went, and some even brilliant sentiments sparkled from him.[17]

The social whirlwind that Jefferson enjoyed came to a sudden end around May 1. He fell ill with another headache. This bout was one of the worst he ever experienced. He was confined to his residence for nearly a month, and in bed for a good portion of that time.

Jefferson's lengthy illness and heavy workload—his duties were now far more time-consuming than his ministerial responsibilities had been—took him out of play during most of the roiling battle ignited by Hamilton's report on funding. Hamilton anticipated opposition, but he was startled when Madison, his friend and former colleague who now was the leading figure in the House of Representatives, challenged the notion of funding the domestic debt at face value.[18] Under Hamilton's plan, those who owned Continental securities were to exchange their notes for the new federal securities. Madison objected, insisting that the original holders—soldiers, farmers, and suppliers who had helped win the war—should receive a portion of the current market value of the paper. Madison was not alone. "Congress have been much divided," Jefferson said, and in fact the opposition included both northern and southern representatives. Many feared that Hamilton's program would result in an undue influence of the executive on the legislative branch, while some—recollecting the warning of radical English Whigs—saw in his plan the embryo of monarchy and aristocracy.[19]

Hamilton fought hard for his program. One observer said that no British prime minister ever worked harder, adding that Hamilton and his associates resorted to "nightly Visits" to many congressmen, offering "promises—compromises—Sacrifices—& threats." A member of the Pennsylvania delegation noted that Hamilton had built a faction within the House; it "is now established beyond a doubt," he continued, that the treasury secretary "guides the movements of the eastern phalanx," that is, the congressmen from the mid-Atlantic and New England states. It was said that Hamilton was "moving heaven and earth" to secure the adoption of his program, and that he had dispatched what various onlookers called his "gladiators," "machines," and "cabals" to lobby the members of Congress. These included those who worked in the Treasury Department, but also what one called Hamilton's "New York *junto*," important businessmen and former army officers who now were members of the Society of the Cincinnati. Robert Morris, who sat in the Senate, circulated among colleagues with whom he had rarely spoken in order to praise Hamilton, labeling him "damned sharp." Some in Congress were as alarmed by Hamilton's tactics as by his program, fearing that the end game would be the corruption of Congress, much as Parliament had supposedly been corrupted by diabolical British prime ministers. Senator William Maclay of Pennsylvania, in fact, thought some heads were being turned by offers of pecuniary gain, which led him to predict that Hamilton "will soon overwhelm us."[20]

Hamilton was doing nothing illegal. He was playing superb politics, though some were put off by him. Thinking him arrogant, Maclay referred to the treasury secretary as "his Holiness," a view seconded by a newspaper essayist who said that Hamilton would not speak to or acknowledge those he encountered on New York's busy streets. Vice President Adams regarded Hamilton as "insolent," and later claimed that only a little wine at dinner caused him to be "silly" and boastful of his exploits "like a young girl about her brilliants and trinkets."[21]

That may have been correct, but it was also true that Hamilton had learned the political arts and practiced them with an adroitness that in 1790 set him apart from most officeholders. His years in the cauldron of New York politics had been a learning experience, as had his long, uphill battle for consolidation and the ratification of the Constitution. He had learned much from General Washington, a political master who at times dispatched his well-coached aide to meet with state officials and others. Hamilton was never reluctant to bargain, and he expended much of his legendary energy in meeting after meeting, often behind closed doors, where he must have had to draw on all his arts of persuasion and manipulation. Furthermore, the treasury secretary entered this fray with a well-crafted organization and a plan of action that took his adversaries by surprise.

Nevertheless, as the long battle for consolidation had demonstrated, machinations and organization did not always lead to immediate success. As spring turned to summer, it was clear that Congress would endorse funding, but the fate of his proposed plan to assume state debts was far from certain. It was unpopular in states such as Virginia, which had already retired what it owed. With a vital cog in his program in jeopardy, Hamilton began casting about for a compromise.

The dealings of politicians are seldom transparent, and that was true of James Madison's behavior in 1790. He may never have wanted to defeat either funding or assumption. Madison was mending fences at home, where he had been damaged by his support for consolidation. It is also a good bet that he too was trolling for a compromise that would net something for Virginia. Indeed, in the early discussions over Hamilton's program, the question of the location of the national capital, an issue that had been bruited about in Congress since 1779, arose once again.[22] One of five sites seemed certain to be chosen to be the capital: New York, Philadelphia, Baltimore, somewhere on the Susquehanna River in the Pennsylvania backcountry, or some undetermined place on the Potomac River. Madison badly wanted the capital to be located on the Potomac, and he ultimately got his way through what he called a fortunate "coincidence of causes."[23] Jefferson, on the other hand, attributed the outcome of the assumption/national capital contests to a grand deal—often called the "Compromise of 1790"—that he, Madison, and Hamilton concluded.

The narrative of a bargain struck quickly and neatly had its inception in an account penned by Jefferson several years later. Sometime during the summer of 1790, Jefferson recalled, he had met a "somber, haggard, and dejected" Hamilton at the door to the president's residence. One part of his story rings true. Hamilton, he said, opened the conversation with a threat: the Union could not survive unless assumption and a "general fiscal arrangement" were approved. Supposedly, Hamilton then asked Jefferson to intercede with southern congressmen to support the Assumption Bill. Though Jefferson had remained aloof from the legislative battle, and he subsequently claimed that to this point he had not even "considered it [assumption] sufficiently," he said that he sought "conciliation" by hosting a dinner at which Hamilton and Madison were the guests.

Jefferson depicted the dinner as one at which he remained on the sideline while Madison and Hamilton bargained. The agreement that they allegedly reached called for Madison and Jefferson to persuade a couple of recalcitrant Virginia congressmen to support assumption, and for Hamilton to convince some Pennsylvania representatives, who longed for Philadelphia to be the nation's capital, to consent to locating the capital on the Potomac. On the surface, it appeared that Madison and Jefferson swallowed a bitter pill in order to get the capital, while Hamilton scuttled his friends back home who were depending on him to give them the opportunity to become very rich by making New York the national capital. "This is the real history of the assumption," Jefferson declared.[24]

Jefferson's story is true insofar as assumption was part of a bargain that involved the national capital, but the negotiations were more extensive than he recalled, or acknowledged, and a settlement was not reached until long after his famous dinner. Before the issue was settled, many congressmen, as well as the president, got into the act. Senator Maclay of Pennsylvania said that Washington exerted a "great influence in this business," and he depicted the president as Hamilton's tool, his "dishclout of . . . dirty speculation," for Washington's "name goes to wipe away blame and silence all murmuring." The senator was wrong about Washington being anyone's puppet. Washington wanted both assumption and a capital on the Potomac, and he fought to persuade Congress to select a site on the Potomac near where he owned vast amounts of property at Mount Vernon and in Alexandria. The president lobbied members of at least four state delegations. Hamilton had begun "jockeying and bargaining" well before the dinner that Jefferson hosted, and he continued to negotiate for a month thereafter, and Jefferson probably did so as well. Senator Maclay, who opposed assumption and badly wanted Philadelphia to become the capital, knew that his aspirations were doomed the moment he saw the tandem of Hamilton and Washington in action. "If Hamilton has his hand in the residence [the choice of the national capital] now, he will have his foot in it before the end of the session," Maclay predicted.[25]

The whole story will never be known, in part because Madison had long since mastered the arts of backroom negotiating and Hamilton was a maestro at intrigue. Nor was Jefferson as naïve or as dispassionate with regard to assumption as he wished others to think. Ever after, Jefferson depicted himself as a guileless innocent who was taken advantage of by Hamilton. Having been abroad for years, he claimed to have been a "stranger" both to the putative crisis that led to the overthrow of the Articles of Confederation and to the meaning of, and the need for, the "system of finances" that Hamilton advocated. "I was most ignorantly and innocently made to hold the candle," he said of the role he had played. Later, he told Washington: "I was duped into it by the secretary of the Treasury, and made a tool for forwarding his schemes, not then sufficiently understood by me; and of all the errors of my political life, this has occasioned me the deepest regret."[26] At the time, however, Jefferson said that he supported Hamilton's program from the fear that "something much worse will happen" if funding and assumption were rejected. The "something worse" was the ruin of American credit in Europe, which he believed would usher in "the greatest of all calamities." But Jefferson's tale of naïveté was not entirely a fabrication. He failed to understand that funding and assumption constituted only the foundation of Hamilton's grand design. More was to come, and it was only upon discovering that Hamilton harbored still other plans that Jefferson came to feel that he had been deceived.[27]

In the end, Congress in July enacted both the Assumption and Residence Bills. The latter moved the capital to Philadelphia for ten years while a new capital city was constructed at some site on the Potomac. The exact location was left to Washington's choosing. Not surprisingly, he selected a plot as near to Mount Vernon as possible.[28]

Soon after Congress acted, the government moved to Philadelphia. Hamilton was one of the first to find a home for his department and his family. He situated the Treasury Department in a modest two-story brick building on Third Street, between Walnut and Chestnut, just two blocks east of the Pennsylvania State House, where the Continental Congress and Constitutional Convention had met. Hamilton rented a house half a block away. Jefferson, who had resided in New York for only about one hundred days, came to Philadelphia shortly after Hamilton. He rented two new adjoining four-story brick houses on Market Street, situated only one block north and five blocks west of Hamilton's offices and residence. Jefferson's plan was to live on the ground floor—typically, he hired workers to renovate one of the houses, expanding the dining room and adding a library, stables for five horses and three carriages, and a garden house—and to utilize the remaining space for the State Department.[29] All three departments commenced operations in more or less the same size buildings, but that did not last long. While War and State each had only six employees and did not grow, Treasury's staff of ninety-three grew to more than five hundred employees before the capital moved to the Potomac in 1800. By then, its Philadelphia offices stretched from one end of the block to the other.

Jefferson returned home in mid-September, stopping en route for his first visit to Mount Vernon. He spent a busy fifty days at Monticello, during which he found a home nearby for Patsy and her husband. He also took more painful steps to cope with his indebtedness. He sold more slaves—he would sell more than fifty of his chattel during the first five years after his return from France—and he negotiated the sale of more than a thousand acres below the James River for approximately three thousand dollars. (Patsy's dowry included one thousand acres of his Poplar Forest property in Bedford County as well as twenty-seven slaves, some or all of whom he might otherwise have sold to cope with his indebtedness.)[30]

Jefferson may have begun to wrestle with his quagmire of debt, but decisions that he made in 1790 foreshadowed the losing battle that he would wage. Convincing himself that he could beat indebtedness both through altering business operations at Monticello and by selling his surplus lands and slaves, Jefferson recklessly lived beyond his means. The cost of the offices that he rented for the State Department exceeded by threefold his government allotment for rent. He had borne the expense of lavishly remodeling his New York residence, only to live in it for three months, and now he was engaged in a similar undertaking in Philadelphia. He beseeched Adrien Petit, his maître d'hôtel in Paris, to work for him in Philadelphia, not only paying him a handsome salary but covering his Atlantic crossing as well. Atop those expenditures, at year's end he was presented with a considerable bill for the cost of having shipped eighty cases of furniture, books, and assorted other items that he had left in Paris the year before, thinking that he would soon return to France.[31]

After seven weeks at home, Jefferson started back to Philadelphia. He stopped for two or three nights at Mount Vernon but was back in the temporary capital by the last week of November.[32] Years later, Jefferson recalled that strident party warfare had originated in the battle over assumption. It had indeed been what he called a "bitter and angry contest," but it was only when Hamilton unveiled the next step in his program that unbridled partisanship developed. This second phase of Hamiltonian economics sparked a jarring battle, but even more, it brought about ideological divisions that Jefferson correctly labeled "the real ground of the opposition" to Hamiltonians. These differences, and the partisanship that accompanied them, defined the first decade of the new republic.[33]

Deep within his Report on Public Credit, Hamilton had included a proposal to levy an excise tax on "every gallon of those Spirits" distilled in the United States and duties "upon all Stills employed in distilling Spirits." In short, Hamilton was proposing what would become widely known as the "whiskey tax." He had recommended such a step because he did not believe that the revenue raised from the duties on foreign imports would be sufficient for the needs of the federal government, but he also privately told Washington that he was taking this step to monopolize this source of revenue before the states latched on to it. Hamilton anticipated formidable opposition. Not only had excise taxes been denounced by the Continental Congress prior to American independence, but Hamilton himself had acknowledged in *The Federalist* that the citizenry would "ill brook" sweeping excise taxes. He was correct. In fact, when Congress passed the Funding Bill, it had stricken Hamilton's proposed excise tax from the legislation.[34]

But in December 1790, with the federal government facing a shortfall of some eight hundred thousand dollars, Hamilton resurrected his proposal for a tax on domestically distilled whiskey. (He also called for excise taxes on spirits that entered the country and rum produced in the United States from imported materials.) He thought it would produce about one-quarter of the needed revenue. Predictably, immediate and stormy opposition ensued. Five state legislatures from Pennsylvania southward denounced the proposed tax, knowing it would fall principally on farmers who distilled whiskey from the corn they raised. Their congressional delegations fought the tax, fearful that it would trigger farmers' uprisings akin to Shays' Rebellion. Skeptics also suspected hidden motives on the part of the treasury secretary. More than one was convinced that Hamilton's ultimate goal was the elimination of the states. Others were certain that he longed for a farmers' rebellion, as it would afford the administration with the pretext for raising a large American army. However, there was support for a levy on spirits in the eastern portion of many states, where merchants and the wealthy preferred a whiskey tax to its most discussed alternatives: a land tax or an increase in the impost. Hamilton's foes fought tenaciously, but once again the treasury secretary's forces were better organized. Proponents of the excise descended on Congress and soothingly told the skeptics that the whiskey tax would be devoid of the "absurdity, villainy, and deplorable effect on society" that had characterized European excises. They knew this duty would be for the best, they said, because they had "consulted Hamilton." But their finishing touch was to broadcast that Washington supported the bill. Anything "that can be fairly fixed on the President" will win support in Congress, one member murmured. On the day the Senate was to vote, Pennsylvania's Maclay cautioned against "the box of Pandora." However, the legislation passed, and in the House as well, prompting Maclay to sigh: "Mr. Hamilton is all-powerful, and fails in nothing he attempts."[35]

Jefferson and Madison had stayed out of this imbroglio, possibly because their bargain with Hamilton had committed them to support assumption as well as an excise tax.[36] However, they did not remain aloof from another battle that Hamilton set afoot with his second great report. On the day after he asked Congress to pass the whiskey tax, Hamilton boldly urged the creation of a central bank. This was the capstone of his economic "machine," as Jefferson labeled it, the "engine" that was to drive everything. And for Jefferson, it was the bank that made him understand the full meaning of Hamiltonianism.

Hamilton urged Congress to charter a Bank of the United States for twenty years "to be opened at the City of Philadelphia." At a time when the capital in the three banks in the United States totaled two million dollars, he proposed that the national bank be capitalized at ten million, with one-fifth of its start-up money provided by the government, the remainder coming through the sale of bank stock. It was to be managed by private citizens. Furthermore, federal funds were to be deposited in the bank, enabling it to issue notes that would serve as legal tender. This would significantly increase the supply of money and stimulate the economy. In emergencies, the bank could make loans to the United States, and it could routinely advance credit to private borrowers through loans for ninety days or less, which he said would stimulate investment and promote national prosperity.[37]

Over the years there had been land banks, mercantile banks, loan office banks, and, beginning in 1781, the Bank of North America, which Congress had chartered at Robert Morris's urging. None of these eased the misgivings of most Americans about banking. Much of the citizenry believed that banks promoted usury or were a swindle through which the rich cheated the poor. Senator Maclay, for instance, thought banks an "aristocratic engine" that resulted in wealth "accumulating in a few hands." Perhaps the most widespread feeling was that banks served only urban entrepreneurs, some of whom were "ignorant adventurers" or "bankrupt and fraudulent traders." Try as they might, neither the nation's ordinary husbandmen nor most planters below the Potomac could imagine how a bank could be of much assistance to them.[38] Given these endemic sentiments, Hamilton wrote his report as a veritable tutorial on banking. He contested the "jealousies and prejudices" and endeavored to show how banks had contributed to prosperity in the "most enlightened commercial nations." Otherwise, he simply insisted that the bank was essential to the establishment of the new nation's private credit and security and that sufficient controls would be built in to guard against harmful malfeasance.[39]

Hamilton's enthusiasm for banking was not new. His ideas were born a dozen years or so earlier when he had risen in the predawn quiet at headquarters and devoured the writings of English and Scots who had dilated on Great Britain's economic system that had indisputably strengthened the nation. With time, Hamilton came to understand that Great Britain, like no other nation, had found that the triad of a funded debt, a central banking system, and a market in fruitful public securities offered the means of marshaling wealth. This national treasure facilitated expansion, so that in an amazingly short time England, a small kingdom with but one-third the population of France, ruled the largest, most opulent, and splendid empire since that of Rome. What is more, the British state had achieved its status as the world's greatest political and commercial power without having imposed ruinous taxation on its citizenry. It taxed them—the landed gentry especially—but the trade in securities enabled the state to supplement its revenue raised by taxation with revenue accrued through borrowing.

However, there was a flip side to Britain's stunning success. For one thing, it had been accompanied by the propulsive growth of a centralized administration and ever more capacious bureaucracy. There had also been a resurgence in royal authority, for monarchs utilized the patronage that went hand in glove with the new reality to subtly and artfully manipulate Parliament. Furthermore, commercialization changed the fabric of the country. With its stock markets, speculation, banks, and trading companies, Great Britain seemed to be in the thrall of an insatiable quest for wealth. A new moneyed class emerged, and not infrequently its members possessed greater wealth than the aristocracy and lived more extravagantly. Not surprisingly, some public officials were servile to businesses, businessmen, and financiers.

Taxation levels may not have been oppressive, but they grew steadily, and came mostly in the form of duties on land and excise taxes on agricultural staples. At the outset of the eighteenth century, Englishmen paid twice what Frenchmen did in *per capita* annual taxation; by the end of the Revolutionary War, English taxes were three times those of France. Moreover, while Great Britain had expanded, its expansion had not occurred peacefully. The use of force was an essential ingredient in the advancement of Britain's overseas hegemony. War became commonplace. Great Britain was at war nearly 50 percent of the time between 1689 and 1783, fighting five major wars and two smaller ones. Complaints were heard in England, and some popular American figures discerned that Britain's new institutions and those who profited from them—including the king—flourished because of war, which only fed their pugnacity. Thomas Paine in *Common Sense* had written that the king had little to do but drag his country into one unnecessary war after another. Benjamin Franklin had reached the same conclusion a year before *Common Sense* appeared, telling a friend that England's "Injustice and Rapacity" drove it inevitably into "plundering Wars."⁴⁰

There can be little doubt that the English fiscal structure provided the model for Hamilton's economic plans. Several things in his experience and way of thinking drew him to the English example, but his views on human nature were crucial. His conviction that humankind was driven by ambition, cupidity, and an insatiable lust for preeminence led him to wish to equip America not just with the means of surviving in a heartless world but also with the capability of cutting a figure in that world. For this, Hamilton understood perfectly the need for ready wealth. Moreover, his conviction that people were driven primarily by their self-centered pursuit of private interests led him to seek the means of controlling humankind's selfish propensities, lest society unravel in the face of self-absorbed avarice. He was convinced that social stability required the presence of a strong central government dominated by those at the top of a hierarchical society. Through the patronage that coursed downward, multiple dependencies would result, reducing individual independence and, in Hamilton's judgment, acting as a safeguard against disorder. His viewpoint was strikingly different from that of Jefferson, who was committed to the attainment of the greatest possible measure of individual independence. Believing that people were naturally amicable, warm-hearted, and benevolent, Jefferson thought their ardor for social interactions formed a sort of glue that held society together. Indeed, he was confident that social unrest was unlikely in republics with small, unobtrusive governments, and in his judgment, monarchies inevitably created invidious class distinctions, which led to rancorous social relations.[41]

Hamilton's outlook was also shaped by the fact that his world was the commercial world. As an adolescent, he had worked for a trading company. The war years aside, his life in the mainland colonies had been spent mostly in New York, a hub of economic trafficking. He had often worked closely with public officials from the mercantile sector and represented businessmen in his legal practice. St. Croix and New York may have been inhabited largely by farmers, but for Hamilton, it was indisputable that in both places it was the merchant class that made things hum. He saw that as commerce flourished, opportunities arose for others, so that in time they and their descendants could rise socially and economically. And he believed that it was not just the wealth generated by trade that made a commercial society commendable. As with Hume, who had expounded on how "ingenuity . . . industry, knowledge, and humanity" were "linked together by an indissoluble chain" in a commercial society, Hamilton was persuaded that commercial societies produced a philanthropic, sociable, knowledgeable, enterprising people habituated to a useful work ethic. An urbanite to the core, Hamilton saw that commerce nourished cities, and cities in turn brought people together where they could intermingle in productive ways. Cities were incubators of consumerism, the arts, education, inventiveness, and enlightened thinking. People "flock into cities" in commercial societies, Hume had written—and Hamilton assented—and there they "love to receive and communicate knowledge; to show their wit . . . [and] taste in conversation and living. . . . Particular clubs and societies are every where formed: Both sexes meet in an easy and sociable manner; and the tempers of men . . . refine apace." Unlike Jefferson, Hamilton was not one to see cities as blights on humanity or to eulogize yeoman.[42]

Hamilton had the most limited knowledge of the lives of farm people. He had never lived on a farm, and even during the times that he and Betsey visited her family, it was at the Schuyler's Albany mansion. Hamilton did not denigrate husbandry, but he shared Hume's belief that farmers had "no temptation . . . to encrease their skill and industry." They raised only that which was necessary, leaving much of their land uncultivated. Theirs was a way of life that fostered a "habit of indolence," corroding the work ethic.[43]

Like many another immigrant to a new land, Hamilton was an

ultranationalist. He had come to America to escape what he had regarded as
a life without a future in St. Croix. He had succeeded spectacularly, and he
loved the country in which he had realized such good fortune. He had fought
to set his chosen land free, and he desperately wanted it to succeed as he
had succeeded. Long before he became the treasury secretary, Hamilton's
dreams of a powerful America appeared in his writing. In his first political
essay—the piece challenging the Tory Samuel Seabury nearly two years
before independence—he looked toward the "future grandeur and glory of
America," and a time when Americans would be "still securer against the encroachments" of foreign powers. In "The Continentalist" in 1782 he had longed
for a "noble and magnificent . . . great Federal Republic" that would be "respectable abroad."⁴⁴ Having endured a lonely youth embroidered with scorn
and disdain, he grew to be an adult driven by overweening aspirations of renown and glory. Though he kept his dreams to himself, it is a good bet that
whatever it was he longed to achieve, Hamilton knew that his lusty ambitions
would never be fulfilled in a frail and feeble United States. Hamilton's hopes,
together with his wartime experiences, shaped his thinking. His memory was
etched with recollections of how America's soldiers had needlessly suffered
and died, and how parochial states had shamelessly neglected the national
cause, so that the United States had come within a whisker of losing the War of
Independence. Consolidation, a powerful chief executive, and a vibrant com-
mercially driven economy—all leading to a vigorous and strapping United
States that was impervious to humiliation—were Hamilton's antidotes to the
dreadful woes he and his adopted country had experienced.

From the instant Hamilton proposed the bank, Senator Maclay knew that
Congress would approve it. "It is totally vain to oppose this bill," he sighed.
Nevertheless, the Bank's foes fought back resolutely with attacks in newspapers. There was "caballing and intrigue" on both sides in Congress, noted
Maclay. He also said that many of his congressional colleagues presumed the
president backed Hamilton, which caused them to be "borne down by . . . a
fear of being charged with a want of respect to General Washington." It soon
was apparent that Washington was actively pitching in to win approval for
the bill. Maclay thought that Washington had often slighted him in the past,
but now the president courted him, inviting the senator to dinner and be-
stowing a "marked attention" on him. Maclay was not swayed. He saw the
bank as "an aristocratic engine" that would give money interests undue influence on public policies. Among those who opposed Hamilton, some were
simply suspicious of banks, others thought too few Americans would benefit
from such a large expenditure, and the Virginians were anxious lest the

The Wren Building, one of the three buildings at the College of William and Mary when Jefferson attended the institution beginning in 1760. (Photograph by Jrcla2 via Wikimedia Commons.)

Nassau Hall at King's College (later Columbia University), where Hamilton enrolled in 1773 or 1774. (Encyclopedia Britannica/UIG/The Bridgeman Art Library.)

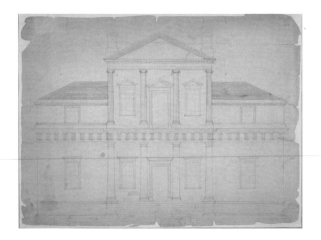

Jefferson's drawing of the original Monticello. He began construction in 1768, but demolished the dwelling in 1794 and began work on the mansion that is familiar today. (Massachusetts Historical Society, Boston/The Bridgeman Art Library.)

Thomas Jefferson in 1776 at age thirty-three. Charles Willson Peale was the artist. (The Huntington Library, Art Collections, and Botanical Gardens/The Bridgeman Art Library.)

The Pennsylvania State House, now known as Independence Hall. Congress met here while Jefferson was a member from 1775–76 and during most of Hamilton's brief stint in Congress from 1782–83. It was home to the Constitutional Convention in 1787. (Library of Congress Prints and Photographs Division.)

Alexander Hamilton (1757–1804) in the Uniform of the New York Artillery, a mid-nineteenth-century painting by Alonzo Chappel. A Continental soldier who observed Hamilton during the 1776 retreat across New Jersey described him as "a youth, a mere stripling, small, slender, almost delicate in frame, marching . . . with a cocked hat pulled down over his eyes, apparently lost in thought, with his hand resting on a cannon, and every now and then patting it as [if] it were a favorite horse or a pet plaything." (The Bridgeman Art Library.)

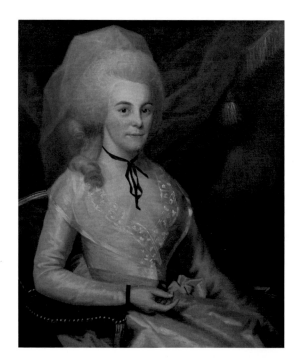

Elizabeth Schuyler Hamilton, painted by Ralph Earl. She met Hamilton in 1777. They were married on December 14, 1780, in Albany. (Museum of the City of New York/The Bridgeman Art Library.)

Philip Schuyler, Revolutionary War general, father of Hamilton's wife, and a powerful figure in New York politics. In 1791, Schuyler lost a reelection bid in the U.S. Senate to Aaron Burr. (New-York Historical Society/The Bridgeman Art Library.)

A French engraving of the British surrender at Yorktown on October 19, 1781. (Bibliothèque Nationale de France, Paris/Giraudon/The Bridgeman Art Library.)

Surrender of Lord Cornwallis, by John Trumbull. Hamilton can be seen in the front row of American soldiers, the figure closest to the horse at the far right. Washington sits on the dark horse in the background. Colonel John Laurens stands next to Hamilton. General Benjamin Lincoln, astride the white horse, is accepting the British surrender. (Hangs in the Rotunda of the U.S. Capitol. Courtesy of the Architect of the Capitol.)

Robert Morris, who as superintendent of Finance in the early 1780s advocated many of the economic policies sought by Hamilton a decade later. Painting by Charles Willson Peale. (Pennsylvania Academy of Fine Arts, Philadelphia/The Bridgeman Art Library.)

An engraving from a portrait of Abigail Adams by Gilbert Stuart, who began work on the painting in 1800 when Abigail was the First Lady. She first met Jefferson in 1785 and Hamilton some five years later. (Library of Congress.)

Thomas Jefferson sat for this portrait by Mather Brown in 1786 while in England to conduct diplomacy and to visit John and Abigail Adams. (Private collection/Peter Newark Pictures/The Bridgeman Art Library.)

Maria Cosway, a miniature painted by her husband, Richard Cosway. (© The Huntington Library, Art Collections, and Botanical Gardens.)

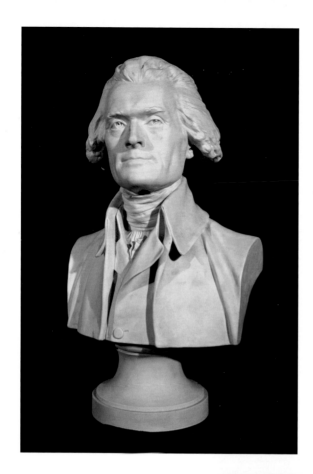

Bust of Thomas Jefferson by Jean-Antoine Houdon. The bust was made in 1789, the year that Jefferson returned from France to the United States. (Private collection/Philip Mould Ltd., London/The Bridgeman Art Library.)

George Washington, by Charles Willson Peale. The painting shows the president in 1795, the year he signed the Jay Treaty. (New-York Historical Society/The Bridgeman Art Library.)

James Madison, Jefferson's close friend and once Hamilton's as well. (Private collection/Peter Newark Pictures/The Bridgeman Art Library.)

Bird's-eye View of Federal Hall, New York, home of the U.S. Congress from March 1789 through the summer of 1790, where Hamilton's funding, assumption, and Bank bills were passed. (Painting by William Hindley (fl.1936)/New-York Historical Society/The Bridgeman Art Library.)

"What Think Ye of Congress Now." A 1790 cartoon expressing unhappiness with the deal made to move the capital and Congress to the Potomac. Congress would quit New York for Philadelphia that summer. (Historical Society of Pennsylvania.)

A mezzotint after a portrait of Alexander Hamilton by John Trumbull. The painting was done in 1792, Hamilton's third year as Secretary of the Treasury. He was thirty-seven years old at the time. (Library of Congress Prints and Photographic Division.)

Edmond-Charles Edouard Genêt, the flawed French diplomat who arrived in Philadelphia in 1793 and in the briefest time angered both Hamilton and Jefferson. (*Harper's Encyclopaedia of United States History*, vol. IV, 1905.)

"A Peep into the Antifederal Club." The earliest known Federalist cartoon attacking Jefferson, it shows Republicans as dissolute and takes some swipes at the French Revolution. (Library Company of Philadelphia.)

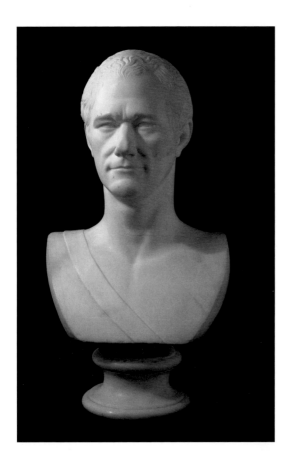

The bust of Hamilton done by Giuseppe Ceracchi in 1793, the year of Genêt's troubled embassy. The bust was Betsey Hamilton's favorite of all the works of art on her husband. (New-York Historical Society.)

John Adams, by Mather Brown. The painting was completed in 1788 while Adams was the U.S. minister to the Court of St. James. He was fifty-three years old. (Boston Athenaeum/The Bridgeman Art Library.)

"Cinque-tetes, or the Paris Monster." A 1797 cartoon satirizing France's misguided actions in the XYZ Affair. (Archives du Ministère des Affaires Étrangères, Paris/Archives Charmet/The Bridgeman Art Library.)

"The Providential Detection." Dating to the presidential election of 1800, this Federalist cartoon depicts the federal eagle preventing Jefferson from destroying the Constitution at the altar of French despotism. (American Antiquarian Society, Worcester, Massachusetts/The Bridgeman Art Library.)

An 1800 election banner that celebrates Jefferson's victory. The incoming chief executive is surrounded by the words "T. JEFFERSON President of the United States of America" and "JOHN ADAMS is no MORE." (National Museum of American History.)

Jefferson in 1800, by Rembrandt Peale. About to become president, Jefferson was fifty-seven years old. (Private collection/Peter Newark American Pictures/The Bridgeman Art Library.)

(Left) Monticello. Jefferson demolished the original dwelling in 1794 and began construction of this mansion. It likely looked more or less like this during his final retirement years, 1809 to 1826. (© Christopher Hollis/Wdwic Pictures, used under a Creative Commons 2.5 License.)

(Right) The Grange, Hamilton's home which he had constructed shortly after the election of 1800. The photograph shows the Grange as it looks in 2012, after its second relocation to St. Nicholas Park in upper Manhattan. (Photograph by Flickr user Jack and Dianne, used under a Creative Commons 2.0 License.)

Aaron Burr, by John Vanderlyn. One of many Vanderlyn paintings of Burr, this one was completed near the time of the duel. (Private collection/Peter Newark American Pictures/The Bridgeman Art Library.)

The English-made, smooth-bore, flintlock pistols used by Alexander Hamilton and Aaron Burr in their July 1804 duel. The pistols were the same used by Hamilton's son Philip in his tragic duel three years earlier. (New-York Historical Society.)

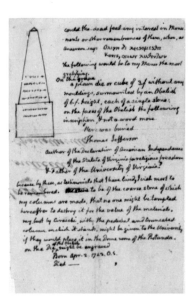

(Left) Before his death, Jefferson left explicit instructions regarding the monument to be erected over his grave, and he supplied this sketch of the marker and epitaph to be inscribed—the sketch of the marker can be seen at upper left. (Library of Congress.)

(Right) Jefferson in 1821, from a portrait painted at Monticello by Thomas Sully (this is a replica painted by Sully in 1856). The artist visited Jefferson at the behest of the faculty of the United States Military Academy, which wished to obtain a portrait of the third president. (Private collection/Photo Christie's Images/The Bridgeman Art Library.)

establishment of the bank in Philadelphia would prevent the national capital from ever being moved to the Potomac.[45]

To this moment, Jefferson had not fought any of Hamilton's proposals, and the two secretaries had maintained a cordial, though not close, relationship. The bank changed that. Jefferson was already aware of the consuming hostility in Virginia toward Hamilton's initial economic program. In fact, on almost the very day that the treasury secretary urged the bank, the state legislature denounced the assumption of state debts as unconstitutional and asserted that funding would provide the president with "unbounded influence," much like that wielded by Britain's monarch.[46] But Jefferson hardly required a nudge from the assemblymen back home. The bank proposal brought Hamilton's economic plans into sharper focus. For the first time, Jefferson understood that Hamilton was committed to crafting America on the English model. If the treasury secretary succeeded, Jefferson feared the promise of the American Revolution would be dashed.

Americans often spoke of their Revolution as a "Glorious Cause." For Jefferson, the cause had been a great republican resistance against tyrannical monarchy and centralized control by a faraway and corrupt government. He wanted minimal government in the new American nation, and he also wished to purge the land of the lingering traces of the unenlightened past, especially to wipe away those parts of the English social and political heritage that he believed continued to stain life in America.

Of late, some scholars have puzzled over Jefferson's alarm at the bank, finding his fears "obsessive and almost paranoid."[47] But Jefferson had his reasons. He looked on a bank as doing nothing to serve the interests of Virginia or most Americans, and he, too, feared that it might thwart the move of the capital to the Potomac. Consciously or not, he may also have been nettled by Hamilton's seeming influence with Washington, which Jefferson coveted. Nor did Hamilton's blatant Anglophilia sit well with Jefferson, who, like other Southerners, remembered the horror spread by the British army; and, like other planters, he chafed at not having been compensated for the slaves the redcoats had taken with them. He feared the bank would not only create a new class of speculators but also would serve as conduit for funneling largess and bribes to congressmen.[48] As much as anything, however, Jefferson's uneasiness stemmed from the fact that it was Hamilton who had proposed the bank. Through Madison, Jefferson had been made aware that Hamilton had revealed his monarchist colors and antipathy to the states at the Constitutional Convention. Now, the pieces of the puzzle came together in Jefferson's mind. Thinking that the "natural order of things is for liberty to yield and government to gain ground," Jefferson believed a national bank would only accelerate the danger. A bank would strengthen the central government, and it would assure the sway of the "financial interest" over Congress. The bank would be like a mighty "engine in the hands of the Executive . . . which added to the great patronage it possessed . . . might enable it to assume by degrees a kingly authority."[49] Taking the long view, he feared that further consolidation and the rise of a new money class—part and parcel of Hamiltonianism— would menace republicanism, decentralized government, and the agrarian way of life. He was convinced that Hamiltonianism would in time lead to the Europeanization of America, leaving Americans prey to the evils he had observed firsthand during his five years in France—monarchy, rigid social stratification, concentration of wealth, massive poverty, and urban squalor.

The Bank Bill sailed through Congress, passing with majorities of two to one in the House and three to one in the Senate, but Jefferson continued to believe that the bank would never come into being. The bill required Washington's sanction, and Jefferson remained certain that "the President is an anchor of safety to us." After all, Madison, a Virginian who had gained Washington's trust, had led the fight against the bank in the House and Attorney-General Edmund Randolph, yet another Virginian, had advised Washington that the bank was unconstitutional. Washington did not act quickly. Surprised and shaken, he asked both Jefferson and Hamilton for their opinions. Jefferson responded first with a concise memorandum. Strictly interpreting the Constitution, he argued that Congress was explicitly empowered to tax, borrow, and regulate commerce, but not to charter a bank. Should it be assumed that Congress possessed such authority because it was authorized to "provide for the general welfare of the US," congressmen would be vested with "a power to do whatever evil they pleased." Jefferson had outlined the classic argument for limited government, and he was confident that Washington, a fellow Virginian, would agree and see things in the same light.[50]

Washington immediately passed Jefferson's brief to Hamilton. Jefferson had dashed off his opinion in a few hours. Hamilton, following his customary habits, toiled for a week before submitting a paper nearly ten times longer than Jefferson's composition. Hamilton initially contemplated asserting that the minutes of the Constitutional Convention demonstrated the Framers' intention of a broad interpretation of the "necessary and proper" clause. On reflection, however, he evidently decided that should he break the vow of silence he had taken in Philadelphia in 1787, it would be an open invitation for foes who had taken extensive notes—including Lansing, Yates, and Madison—to bring to light his politically inexpedient comments on monarchy and the emasculation of state powers. In the end, Hamilton took a position that would be embraced throughout American history by those who have wished to expand the role of government: Sovereignty implies that government possesses the "right to employ all the means requisite, and fairly applicable to the ends of such power; and which are not precluded by restrictions & exceptions specified in the constitution; or not immoral, or not contrary to the essential ends of political society."[51]

Washington devoted a day to reading and reflecting on Hamilton's argument, after which he chose it over Jefferson's and on February 25, 1791, signed the Bank Bill into law. One of Hamilton's biographers wrote that Washington was overawed by the treasury secretary's "superior intellect and superior case."[52] More likely, Washington concurred because for more than a decade he and Hamilton had shared a desire to vest the national government with considerable power. For Washington, that was the whole point of the new Constitution, of having Hamilton in his cabinet, and of abandoning Mount Vernon to return to public life.

Jefferson was stunned that Washington had sided with Hamilton, and also by the treasury secretary's artful political skills. Jefferson knew that Hamilton's success during the past nine months had in some measure come from carefully organizing and managing those in Congress who shared his ideas on the future shape of America. If those who favored decentralization, an agrarian America, and possibly even republicanism itself were to win out, they too had to organize with an eye on securing "a more agricultural representation" in Congress in the elections of 1792. Jefferson began by testing the waters. He wrote activists in several states seeking to learn the depth of concern about what he called the "scrip-pomany" and "stockjobbery"—the speculative fever—unleashed by Hamiltonianism. He also inquired about whether a leader should "come forward and help" galvanize those who were uncomfortable. The responses were heartening. "I feel with you great pain" and "disgust" at the steps taken by Congress, and so do most citizens, one correspondent answered. Jefferson rapidly cobbled together a network of friendly congressmen and capital insiders who could be trusted to report to him any scuttlebutt they learned about Hamilton and his plans.[53]

Three days after Washington signed the Bank Bill into law, Jefferson launched a campaign to lure Philip Freneau, an on-again, off-again journalist who had been a college friend of Madison's, to publish a newspaper to combat Hamilton. Aware that Freneau was a noteworthy writer with a golden touch for satire, and that he shared the republican outlook of radicals such as Thomas Paine, Jefferson saw his pen as an antidote both to Hamilton and to John Fenno's *Gazette of the United States*, a newspaper that he correctly viewed as a virtual house organ of the Treasury Department. Over the course of several weeks that spring and summer, Jefferson and Madison hammered out a deal with Freneau. Jefferson agreed to put him on the State Department payroll, enabling him to supplement his earnings from the newspaper. Madison pitched in by rounding up subscribers. The first issue of Freneau's *National Gazette* appeared that autumn.[54]

Organizing those who were alarmed by Hamilton came next. From correspondents, Jefferson knew that considerable opposition existed to Hamiltonianism. From his firsthand experiences in Manhattan in 1790, he was aware that New Yorkers who hoped for the Revolution's fulfillment of progressive change were confronted by ultraconservative seigneurial families and powerful mercantile interests, some of whom had candidly told him of their preference for monarchy. Jefferson made plans to travel to the Empire State, accompanied by Madison. His purpose was not, as some later claimed, to establish a political party, and indeed it would not be until the elections of 1794 that party affiliation would be imperative for election to Congress.[55] Mostly, Jefferson simply sought to encourage those who opposed further Hamiltonian initiatives to seek seats in Congress. But as he was a member of Washington's cabinet, Jefferson could hardly divulge the real reason for his trek. Instead, he described his journey as a "botanizing tour," a vacation to study the flora and fauna in a part of the country far from his native Virginia. That was not totally untrue. Given his passion for science, Jefferson was eager to see the plants and animals in New York's backcountry and to bring cuttings of unfamiliar vegetation back to Monticello. Otherwise, the journey was designed to replicate ones that Madison had made to New York before the Constitutional Convention, when he had been intent on organizing nationalists.

Madison set off first to lay the groundwork. Two weeks later, Jefferson departed Philadelphia on what was to be a thirty-three-day journey that covered more than nine hundred miles. He traveled by carriage through Trenton and Princeton and on to Manhattan, where he linked up with Madison. They met with Chancellor Livingston, who had longed to be Washington's treasury secretary, and who suspected that the landed gentry of which he was a part would be swept aside by the financial interests being elevated by the treasury secretary's plans. Jefferson and Madison also conferred with Aaron Burr, who—aided by Governor Clinton's "twistings, combinations and maneuvers"—had recently replaced Philip Schuyler in the U.S. Senate. The Virginians guessed correctly that the overthrow of Hamilton's father-in-law was certain to put Burr and the treasury secretary at odds.[56]

From New York, Jefferson and Madison sailed up the Hudson, stopping off in Poughkeepsie and Albany, where they likely met with Clinton. Thereafter, they paused at Saratoga and Bennington to tour the battlefields of two great

American victories in the Revolutionary War. Next, they proceeded to Lake George, which Jefferson pronounced "the most beautiful water I ever saw," then to Lake Champlain. In the course of their travels, the Virginians visited Forts William Henry, Ticonderoga, and Crown Point, which Jefferson described as "scenes of blood from a very early part of our history." Nor did they ignore the plants and animals they had come to see. Jefferson was taken with a variety of species unknown in Albemarle County, thought he was seeing azaleas when in fact he was observing wild honeysuckle, inspected rock formations and waterfalls, fished a bit, watched as members of his party killed rattlesnakes, and was devoured by mosquitoes and gnats.[57]

For the most part, the travelers stuck to the backcountry, the region where the Anti-Federalists had been strongest and suspicions of Hamilton and his designs persisted. They spoke with local officials in many villages and towns. Madison and Jefferson tried to be as discreet as possible about the real reason for their journey, and they may have fooled some. But they did not hoodwink everyone. Hamilton was notified by an acquaintance that the Virginians had "scouted silently thro' the Country, shunning the Gentry, communing with & pitying the Shayites." Robert Troup, Hamilton's old college friend and fellow New York City lawyer, was even more informative. Before Jefferson was back in Philadelphia, Troup had informed the treasury secretary that the Virginians had come north to engage in "a passionate courtship" of Livingston, Burr, and Clinton, hopeful that Hamilton could be "hunted down by them."[58]

For a time, Hamilton appears to have been unconcerned, perhaps thinking that his friends exaggerated or possibly confident that his rapport with Madison, and the fact that he and Jefferson served together in Washington's cabinet, would temper the Virginians' opposition. That was not to be. In October, Freneau's *National Gazette* began publication. For a while, Freneau's tone was moderate, but in time his malice toward Hamilton shone through. As it did, cordiality between Hamilton and Jefferson waned. Soon, the two secretaries were "daily pitted in the cabinet like two cocks," as Jefferson put it.[59] The battle had been joined, a struggle over the structure of the new American nation that would shape the country's politics for the remainder of this passionate decade.

CHAPTER 10

"DEVOTED TO THE PAPER AND STOCKJOBBING INTEREST"

UNBRIDLED PARTISAN WARFARE

IT IS NOT LIKELY that Jefferson thought the bank would be the final peg in Hamilton's program. Washington, in his initial State of the Union message in January 1790, had urged the "advancement of . . . manufactures" to render the United States independent of other nations, "particularly for military supplies." Congress endorsed the president's proposal and directed the treasury secretary to act on it.[1] So, it could not have come as much of a surprise when, in the autumn of 1791, Hamilton submitted one final report, a plan for encouraging manufacturing.

Though considerably longer and less reader-friendly than his earlier reports—even Hamilton bemoaned its "great copiousness"—this was his crowning achievement, for he foretold America's industrial destiny and how to get there. Asserting that manufacturing would increase American security, he spoke of the dangerous "contrariety of interests" that existed between North and South, and made a case for how manufacturing would bring the sections closer. (Though the cotton gin would not be patented for another two years, he prophesied that northern mills would foster "the extensive cultivation of Cotton.") But his principal defense of industrialization was that national "independence and security" were materially connected with the prosperity of manufactures"; in short, a vibrant manufacturing nation could in a "future war" avoid the "extreme embarassements of the . . . late War."

Hamilton proposed that manufacturing be facilitated through federal subsidies, liberal immigration policies, national defense contracts, government-owned arms factories, publicly assisted improvements to the nation's infrastructure of roads and bridges, and the labor of women and children. (Bluntly, he wrote that in a manufacturing society, "women and Children would be rendered more useful and the latter more early useful.") He asserted that it was legally within the grasp of the national government to do these things. It required only an elastic interpretation of Congress's authority to "provide for the Common defence and general welfare." Even so, he said that most of the capital would come from private investors, whose ability to act would be aided by funding and the bank. He also believed that not only would Europeans eagerly sink their capital in American manufacturing endeavors, but also that many Old World capitalists would want to move to America to better manage their investments.[2]

Simultaneously, the Society for Establishing Useful Manufactures came into being, a body created to "concretize his report," in the words of a Hamilton biographer.[3] The society was the brainchild of Tench Coxe, the assistant secretary of the Treasury, but it was born with Hamilton's avid backing and chartered by New Jersey. It sold stock to raise capital, through which it planned to purchase seven hundred acres along the Passaic River, where it would build a town replete with factories and mills that would produce shoes, hats, fabrics, wire, pottery, carpets, and paper. It might even erect a distillery.[4] If the enterprise flourished, Hamilton envisaged capitalists rushing to emulate the New Jersey model.

Jefferson disapproved of neither manufacturing within his Arcadian America nor making the United States more independent of Europe, and he never complained about the prospect of women and children toiling in factories. However, he objected to the subsidization of manufacturing, which he saw as yet another step in dangerously expanding the reach of the national government. Madison also thought that part of Hamilton's plan was intolerable, and recommended that the "parchment had better be thrown into the fire at once." Jefferson was so troubled that for the first time he complained to Washington, telling the president that Hamilton was seeking to make the "constitution . . . a very different thing from what the people thought they had submitted to." Washington may not have understood it as such, but in retrospect, when Jefferson added that Americans were being made to ask "whether we live under a limited or an unlimited government," he was as much as telling the president that the battle lines had been drawn for partisan warfare to decide the issue.[5]

Jefferson continued to believe that Washington would see things as he did, and he fell into the unbecoming habit of complaining, even tattling, to the president about Hamilton. Jefferson was accustomed to having his way, sometimes manipulating others to gain his ends, but in Washington he met his match. Strong, savvy, and politically experienced, the president could not be engineered. Part of Jefferson's problem was that he misread Washington. Usually adroit at gauging others, Jefferson for the longest time credited the image of disinterestedness that Washington presented, and it blinded him to the reality that in matters relating to domestic America, the president and his treasury secretary marched to the same drummer.

Increasingly consumed with suspicion and immutable enmity toward Hamilton, Jefferson accepted uncritically substantial portions of the truths and untruths that made up the gossip fed to him by his intelligence-gathering lieutenants. In no time, he came to see Hamilton as a superhuman puppeteer of congressmen and diplomats. He believed the tale that Hamilton had written a pamphlet early in 1776 that took issue with Paine's *Common Sense*, and he fell for the story that his rival had left the Constitutional Convention in a fit of anger because it would not agree to his monarchical plans for America. Jefferson did not question the anecdote that Hamilton had recently raised a toast to George III at a dinner party. He gave credence to the prattle that certain New Yorkers possessed handwritten plans prepared by Hamilton for the establishment of a monarchy in the United States. Nor did he for a minute doubt the report brought by a recent visitor to London that the treasury secretary was looked on by members of Parliament as "their effective minister here." Above all, he believed the "fiscal party," with Hamilton pulling the strings behind the scenes, was seeking to manage the president.[6]

On a couple of occasions Hamilton said things that only confirmed Jefferson's suspicions. In the spring of 1791, while dining with Adams and Jefferson, Hamilton had remarked that the sway of monarchy and commercial interests over Parliament made Britain's government "the most perfect . . . which ever existed." On another occasion, Jefferson was shaken when he heard Hamilton's father-in-law, General Schuyler, express the view that "hereditary descent was as likely to produce good magistrates as election." But he was far more shocked to hear Hamilton remark that the Constitution was "a shilly shally thing, of mere milk and water, which could not last, and was only good as a step to something better."[7] Jefferson took that to mean that Hamilton and his cabal were plotting monarchy for the United States.

On at least four occasions in the six months beginning in February 1792, Jefferson met with Washington and complained about Hamilton. Jefferson's message hardly varied from one meeting to the next. He claimed that Hamilton had secretly concocted a "plan he intended to pursue" that would involve multiple initiatives and take years to complete. His "ultimate object" was America's gradual evolution into a monarchical state. Already, the Treasury Department had grown so powerful that under Washington's successors it would likely "swallow up the whole Executive powers." Jefferson insisted that Hamilton's "system" of speculation, which he characterized as "a species of gambling, destructive of morality," had corroded Congress. A "corrupt squadron" in Congress was "devoted to the paper and stockjobbing interest," he charged, adding that these congressmen were "legislating for their own interests," and those of speculators, "in opposition to those of the people." Some were so corrupted that they "formed a corps of interested persons" who acted "steadily at the orders of the Treasury." Time after time, Jefferson reiterated the charge that Hamilton had already made great strides in laying the groundwork for "transforming the government into a monarchy."

Washington steadfastly defended Hamilton. He told Jefferson that he approved "the treasury system" and added that the secretary of state's fears of monarchy were delusional. On two occasions, Washington offered to be "the Mediator to put an end" to the battling between his cabinet members, but Jefferson would have none of it. Early in 1793, Jefferson told Washington that he would not rest until Congress was "cleansed of all persons interested in the bank or public stocks," leaving America with a "pure legislature."[8]

Jefferson's initial visit with Washington to carp about Hamilton's program had come when the treasury secretary proposed his plan for manufacturing. As it turned out, Jefferson could have saved himself the trouble. The House of Representatives turned aside the proposition and it was not enacted, convincing Jefferson that the tide had turned and that "things were returning into their true channel." Indeed, as historian Lance Banning pointed out, "the political mood of the country had undergone a radical change" during 1791, as criticism of Hamiltonianism grew more pronounced. Jefferson thought the turnabout was due to his organizing efforts, including his assistance in enabling Freneau. He exaggerated his influence, though it had been enormous. Given the change, Jefferson was confident that the agrarian interests would win control of Congress in the congressional elections of 1792. That alone, he said, would keep "the general constitution of it's true ground."[9]

Hamilton knew that Jefferson and Madison had opposed parts of his economic program, but was slow to realize that they had taken steps to piece together a concerted opposition. He discounted warnings about the hidden intent behind their botanizing tour and dismissed hearsay that Madison had "insinuate[d] unfavorable impressions of [him]."[10] Although he and Jefferson had often disagreed in cabinet meetings, Hamilton did not at first suspect his counterpart. Jefferson's refinement and loathing of confrontation had led him to remain polite and gentlemanly, but Hamilton was misled even more because both were serving the same president. Hamilton was not alone in his shortsightedness. It was not until eighteen months after the dustup over the bank, and a half year after Jefferson first complained to him about Hamilton's program, that Washington said he was aware of "a personal difference" between his two cabinet members. However, everyone else appears to have known what was occurring by the spring of 1792, when Abigail Adams remarked on the "Rage" of the Virginians against Hamilton. Spring was in full bloom when Hamilton finally deduced what was afoot. Like Jefferson, Hamilton received a combination of news and gossip from what he characterized as "many channels," and by May everything pointed toward Jefferson and Madison as the instigators of the growing opposition to his economic designs.[11]

Hamilton was startled by Madison's opposition. They had become friends a decade earlier and were colleagues in the campaign to achieve consolidation and the impost. Besides, Hamilton had not thought it possible that Madison, a Virginian, could oppose policies supported by Washington. Like some historians, the treasury secretary may have privately attributed Madison's turnaround to jealousy occasioned by Hamilton's having captured Washington's favor, but he also now concluded that Madison, while "a clever man," was "very little Acquainted with the world."[12]

Hamilton was also convinced that Madison's "exalted opinion of the talents, knowledge and virtues of Mr. Jefferson" largely accounted for his former friend's transformation. Hamilton now saw Jefferson as a "man of profound ambition & violent passions" who was guided by an "unsound & dangerous" philosophy. Drawing on the tidbits provided by his informants, Hamilton's impression of Jefferson was a tangle of truths, half-truths, and misconceptions. He believed that Jefferson had from the first opposed the Constitution (partially true); that he shared the "temperament" of the radical French revolutionaries, whom "he had had a share in exciting" to act (true in part, though mostly an exaggeration); that he had returned to America hoping to become the treasury secretary (incorrect); that from the first he had secretly disapproved of funding (inaccurate); and that, above all, Jefferson was consumed with an "ardent desire" to succeed Washington as president (badly mistaken). Hamilton thought Jefferson was dangerous. If he succeeded in rousing the states to "narrow the Federal authority," the entire system of consolidation that had been achieved might unravel. It put Hamilton in mind of a "very just, though a course saying—That it is much easier to raise the Devil than to lay him."[13]

Aware of the danger, Hamilton as always took the offensive. In six essays churned out in rapid succession during the summer of 1792—mostly for Fenno's *Gazette of the United States*—Hamilton dispelled any doubt that Jefferson was responsible for the *National Gazette* or that he was the "head of a party." He contended that Jefferson disliked the Constitution and believed the president had "administered injudiciously and wickedly" in signing the

Bank Bill. Hamilton painted Jefferson as seeking nothing less than the reduction of the national government to "the skeleton of Power," with states elevated "upon its ruins." If Jefferson succeeded, Hamilton warned, he would tear down a strong United States and the "reinvigoration" of the economy achieved during the past few years. In its place, a victorious Jefferson will have substituted "National disunion, National insignificance, Public disorder and discredit."[14]

Hamilton knew that his biting essays would bring a response, and he imagined that Jefferson would author the rejoinders. He was wrong. Jefferson covertly assisted Freneau in framing some of his visceral essays, plied the editor with restricted Department of State materials, and persuaded Madison to take up his pen. Seldom able to say no to his friend, Madison contributed at least nineteen unsigned essays to the *National Gazette* before the fall elections in 1792. In the process, Madison and Freneau reframed the debate from a battle over the scope of government to an epic contest between republicans and monarchists. From this point forward, the Jeffersonians portrayed Hamilton and his faction as favoring an elitist system in which the citizenry remained deferential and acquiescent while the "true republicans" sought to fulfill the American Revolution.[15]

Madison defended political parties, which to this juncture had been almost universally condemned as existing to advance factional interests rather than the general good. Though he never said so explicitly, Madison offered a blueprint for democratic politics. He came close to embodying Jefferson's precept that the earth belonged to the living, and that one generation could not be held in check by its forebears. Madison defended parties because they provided representation to the hitherto unrepresented, and in so doing they offered the promise of spreading wealth and power. He charged that Hamiltonianism was not only directed "less to the interest of the many than of a few" but also bottomed on the hope that control of the national government would "by degrees be narrowed into fewer hands" until it ultimately "approximated . . . an hereditary form." But those who opposed Hamilton believed "that mankind are capable of governing themselves." They hated "hereditary power as an insult to the reason and an outrage to the rights of man." Underscoring what he and Jefferson saw as the fundamental difference in their outlook and that of their foes, Madison reminded readers that the American Revolution had been an assertion of the people against monarchical and aristocratic tyranny. He proclaimed that the Revolution, and the war that secured independence, had not been for the purpose of creating an all-powerful state, much less to perpetuate rule from the top down. The American Revolution had been a struggle against British consolidation and a battle to save liberty. Liberty had been saved, and "liberty [was] the great end, for which the Union was formed." It was not the government but the "people themselves" who were the "best Keepers of the People's Liberties." With pride, Madison referred to the anti-Hamilton faction as the "Republican party." (It was a name that stuck, though throughout the 1790s the Jeffersonians would also sometimes be called the Democratic-Republican Party, and beginning early in the nineteenth century the faction became the Democratic Party.)[16]

Jefferson may not have written any essays, but in May he sent a remarkable letter to Washington in the hope of shaking the president's confidence in Hamilton, and possibly even persuading him to cut his ties with the treasury secretary. Though he never mentioned Hamilton by name, Jefferson told the president that Hamiltonianism was pushing the nation toward annihilation. Funding's "artificially created" debt necessitated higher taxes, duties that would turn the citizenry against the government and provoke such "clamour" that they could only be collected "by arbitrary and vexatious means." Nor would the people sit by idly while Hamiltonianism turned society into a "gaming table" and corrupted Congress so that it consented to the decimation of the "limitations [on government] imposed by the constitution." The people were beginning to understand that the "ultimate object" of Hamiltonianism was to "prepare the way for a change, from the present republican form of government, to that of a monarchy, of which the English constitution is to be the model," Jefferson said. The country was divided between what he called the "republican party" and the "Monarchical federalists," and increasingly too between North and South. As the divisions deepened, the "incalculable evil" of the "breaking of the union" could not be ruled out.[17]

Washington waited nearly six weeks to respond, but finally did so in a face-to-face meeting. He ignored Jefferson's complaints about Hamiltonian economics, a sign that he continued to approve Hamilton's ideas, and brushed aside the allegations that Hamilton was bent on establishing a monarchy, though he acknowledged that some of the gentry in the largest northeastern cities—the bedrock of the treasury secretary's support—might desire an American king. They were a tiny minority, Washington said, adding that most Americans were "steadily for republicanism." But, he warned, if extremists such as Freneau provoked disunion and anarchy, that would "produce a resort to monarchical government."[18]

Washington was more troubled than he let on to Jefferson. Concerned for the survival of Hamiltonianism, which he supported, the president was additionally beginning to worry that the American Union might not survive the tempestuous partisanship. (Startlingly, Washington subsequently confided to Edmund Randolph that if the United States broke up, "he had made up his mind to remove [from Mount Vernon] and be of the northern" states.)[19] Like most, Washington knew little about economics. But he did know his treasury secretary, and from experience the president was fully aware of Hamilton's propensity for intrigue. Despite what he told Jefferson, Washington found the talk about monarchy to be worrisome. What is more, by this time some of Jefferson's warnings about the corrosive effects of speculation had been borne out. Trading in bank script had been so frenzied in the summer of 1791 that in no time its value increased twelvefold. But after just five weeks, the bubble burst and America experienced its first crash in government securities. The pattern was replicated a few months later when three new banks opened and speculators rushed to get rich quick. Once again, only five weeks elapsed before another collapse occurred. On this occasion, many of the desperate speculators tried to save themselves by preying on the gullible from the lower economic classes, borrowing their money to fend off creditors. Instead, all went bust, including "Widows, orphans, merchants[,] mechanics &c.," as one of Hamilton's friends informed him.[20] Many of those who were ruined were stockholders in the Society for Establishing Useful Manufacturing, dooming the planned industrial experiment on the Passaic.

A few days after his conversation with Jefferson, Washington, in need of reassurance, wrote to Hamilton. After making clear that he believed Hamilton's program had left the "Country . . . prosperous & happy," the president passed along a list of twenty-one complaints about Hamiltonianism that he had allegedly heard on a recent trip to Mount Vernon. In fact, Washington had heard everything from Jefferson, and much that he transmitted to Hamilton was word for word from his secretary of state.[21]

Typically, Hamilton responded in detail, his letter running ten times the length of that which he had received from the president. He explained public debts and banking, falsely claimed that not a single member of Congress was a speculator (though he acknowledged that some owned "a pretty large amount" of bank stock) and flatly denied that he sought a monarchy for America. Whatever Hamilton desired in his heart of hearts—and the circumstantial evidence points to his monarchist bent—he knew that his countrymen would not tolerate a crowned head in their government, and he presented a compelling argument showing why there would never be a serious conspiracy to replace the presidency with monarchy. "[N]one but a madman" could attempt such a thing, he said. "If it could be done at all, which is utterly incredible, it would require a long series of time, certainly beyond the life of any individual to effect it. Who then would enter into such a plot? For what purpose or ambition?" Unless brought on by "convulsions and disorders," or "popular demagogues," an American monarchy would never exist, he declared. Next, he went after Jefferson, who he correctly assumed was the author of the complaints that Washington had passed along. Jefferson's unquenchable ambition had led him to "mount the hobby horse of popularity," Hamilton charged, and he added the hint that Jefferson's dismissal from the Cabinet might be necessary to save the strong national government.[22]

Washington soon wrote to both of his cabinet officers asking for "forbearances and temporizing," and reminding Hamilton that Jefferson was a "zealous" patriot. He did not feel the need to point out Hamilton's patriotism to Jefferson, but he did tell the secretary of state that he regarded the attacks on Hamiltonianism as attacks on himself that "filled me with painful sensations."[23] Washington's concern for the safety of the Union was genuine, and there can be no doubt that he hoped the partisan fighting would be brought to an end. Yet, what he had said during the past year to Jefferson and what he had not said to Hamilton made clear that he fixed the blame for the inflammatory partisanship solely on Jefferson and his faction.

Misled by his respect for Washington, Jefferson continued to believe that the president had an open mind. Hamilton, however, excelled at understanding Washington. Among other things, he knew that Washington not only listened to him but also embraced his economic policies. Hamilton shrewdly acknowledged his recent retaliatory essays against Jefferson and Madison, telling Washington that after years as "a silent sufferer," he felt that he could no longer remain still. His foes, he charged, were seeking nothing less than the "undoing of the funding system," a step that would "prostrate the credit and the honor of the Nation." Confident that Washington was anchored to him more than to Jefferson, Hamilton advised the president to purge his cabinet should the unbridled partisanship persist. Jefferson replied in one of his longest, and least impressive, letters. Rehearsing his familiar allegations, Jefferson contended that much of the treasury secretary's program had been enacted through corruption and because its supporters had "swallowed his bait." That made it sound as if Jefferson was suggesting that the president had been "duped by the Secretary of the treasury, and made a tool for forwarding his schemes." This was not the sort of thing that someone as proud as Washington was happy to hear. Furthermore, whereas Jefferson usually denounced Hamilton in the judicious language of a proper diplomat, his boiling anger got the best of him as he penned page after page. Jefferson poured out his venom in the manner of a haughty, well-born gentleman who scorned a social upstart. Blinded to the reality that Hamilton fit perfectly the description of the less fortunate but meritorious young man whom he had once been eager to assist through enlightened educational reforms, Jefferson, in a gust of disdain, proclaimed to Washington that Hamilton was "a man whose history, from the moment at which history can stoop to notice him, is a tissue of machinations against the country which has not only received him and given him his bread, but it's honors."[24]

Foreign policy rarely surfaced in Washington's dialogues with his secretaries over partisanship, aside from when the president expressed his concern that "our enemies will triumph" should "internal dissentions" tear apart "our vitals."[25] Yet, striking differences over American policy toward Great Britain were part of the factional conflict, and they surfaced even before Washington's inauguration and long before Jefferson returned to America. They first became apparent when Madison in 1789 asked Congress to enact the impost that twice had failed in the days of the Confederation. He proposed a 5 percent duty on most imports, but discriminatory rates against Great Britain, which was responsible for 90 percent of all American imports. Madison saw discrimination as the only means available for compelling London to open its ports, including those in its West Indian colonies, to American vessels. Madison was challenged by representatives from the northern merchant-dominated states, and he lost the battle. On very nearly the same day that the nomination of Hamilton to be treasury secretary was approved, Congress enacted the impost without discriminatory features.[26]

The northern merchants had feared that Madison's plan would drive them out of business. Though he had not played a public role in the contest, Hamilton found the initiative distasteful for a different reason. The lion's share of federal revenues would come from the impost on British imports. Its yield would be important to the operation of the new government, but pivotal to the success of Hamilton's funding system. Should discrimination provoke British retaliation, and that was a distinct possibility, revenue would dry up. Hamilton desperately wished to avoid discrimination against British trade. In fact, he longed for a commercial treaty with London, knowing that such a pact not only would enhance American trade, but rekindle fondness for all things British.

Nineteen days after Hamilton became the treasury secretary, in September 1789, George Beckwith, a British official en route from London to Quebec, paused in New York. His Manhattan breather was planned. Beckwith was under orders to communicate to Washington's administration that London would retaliate should the United States discriminate against British trade. In the absence of both a British minister to the United States and a secretary of state—Jefferson was just leaving Paris on the first leg of his journey home— Beckwith delivered his message to Senator Schuyler, who arranged a meeting with Hamilton.

Washington would have been better served had someone else spoken with Beckwith. Hamilton not only was desperate to stabilize and enlarge the American economy, but he also believed that close ties with the former mother country would further the political and social agenda he had pursued for years. In addition, the president was less interested than Hamilton in immediately expanding commercial ties with London, and far more eager to have Great Britain relinquish its western posts within the United States. Washington also fervently wanted London to provide compensation for the slaves its army had taken from the country at the end of the Revolutionary War—yet another mandate of the Treaty of Paris that the British were ignoring. Hamilton's one experience with diplomacy had been his mission to General Gates in 1777. He had not shined. In dealing with Beckwith, Hamilton's Anglophilia was palpable. After falsely assuring Beckwith that the sentiments he expressed were those of President Washington, Hamilton gushed that he had "always preferred a Connexion" with Great Britain, political as well as economic. "*We think in English*, and have a similarity of prejudices, and of predilections." What is more, Hamilton remarked that Britain's intransigent position on the slavery question was "perfectly satisfactory" and told Beckwith that the United States would acquiesce "to limitations of size of vessels" if it was permitted to trade in the British West Indies. Not surprisingly, Beckwith concluded that the United States was desperate for Britain's friendship.[27]

Unaware of the liberties Hamilton had taken, Washington dispatched Gouverneur Morris to London as a special envoy. His discussions got nowhere, and Hamilton was partly to blame for that. During a portion of the time that Morris was in England, Hamilton was busily engaged in further talks with Beckwith, who returned to Manhattan in the summer of 1790. By then, Jefferson was on the scene and was aware of Hamilton's talks with Beckwith, though he did not object. His quarrel with Hamilton had not yet begun; besides, it would have been unconventional for the nation's principal diplomat to engage in talks with such a low-level official as Beckwith. However, had Jefferson been privy to the conversations, he would doubtless have been appalled to hear Hamilton once again reassure Beckwith that "a connexion" with Great Britain was "infinitely Important" to the United States.[28] Furthermore, when the talks proceeded to the possibility that a British minister would be sent to the United States, Hamilton inappropriately divulged that Jefferson, while "a gentleman of honor," was given to "predilections" respecting Great Britain and France—in other words, the secretary of state was allegedly an Anglophobe and a Francophile. Should difficulties arise with Jefferson, Hamilton brazenly added, he "should wish to know them" so that he could do his best to "be sure they are clearly understood, and candidly examined."[29] Having as much as questioned Washington's judgment concerning who headed the State Department, Hamilton did not reveal to the president everything that he had told Beckwith.

Britain's first minister to the United States, George Hammond, a chubby twenty-eight-year-old eager-beaver, arrived in Philadelphia in October 1791 and rapidly entered into discussions with Jefferson. He ran up against a more wary American diplomat than Beckwith had encountered. Having read Morris's dispatches from London, Jefferson had found that they confirmed both what Adams had reported during the previous decade and what he had learned during his visit to England five years earlier. Britain's government, Jefferson had said at the time, was "averse to all arrangements with us" and committed to maintaining Anglo-American relations "on their ... terms." Indeed, anti-American sentiment was so strong that opposition politicians "dare not open their lips in favor of a connection with us." Not only did the British have no intention of evacuating their frontier posts, but also the price that London demanded for a general commercial accord was a formal alliance, a step that would scuttle America's ties with France, the one country that had come to its defense and the only nation capable of posing a threat to Great Britain.[30]

Jefferson had no interest in an Anglo-American alliance. Like Washington, he thought a commercial accord was secondary to the resolution of the frontier posts issue and securing restitution for the slaves. Nor was Jefferson in any hurry to negotiate a trade agreement. With significant changes occurring in revolutionary France, he was more hopeful than ever that Paris might be willing to agree to lift trade restrictions adhered to by the *ancien régime*. He was happy to allow time for the French to come around. In addition, Jefferson agreed with Madison that commercial discrimination was essential for forcing London to agree to a decent trade pact, but he knew that such legislation was inconceivable unless the composition of Congress changed in the elections in 1792. Moreover, while willing to enhance trade with the former mother country, Jefferson longed to expand trade with France. He understood that the more Britain monopolized American commerce, the greater its influence would be culturally, politically, and economically within the United States. In that respect, Jefferson's foreign policy outlook, like that of Hamilton's, was ideological and sprang from his dreams for the shape of the new American nation. Yet, while Jefferson has been limned by many historians as a diplomat hopelessly in the thrall of Anglophobia, the foreign policy that he practiced in his dealings with Hammond was closer than Hamilton's to the thinking of the president they served. Like Washington, Jefferson strove for true American independence, vigilant lest the United States should ever find itself alone and friendless in the face of the world's greatest naval power, and equally watchful against slipping back toward a semi-colonial status with its former mother country.

If not inhospitable toward Hammond, Jefferson was only barely cordial, and with the practiced hand of a veteran diplomat he proceeded at a leisurely pace, deliberately slowing matters by insisting that all communication be in writing rather than in face-to-face discussions. Furthermore, Jefferson customarily dragged his feet in responding to Hammond's replies.[31] Hammond was irritated. Aware of what Hamilton had told Beckwith, Hammond had crossed the Atlantic expecting to find that the United States craved the normalization of relations with London, so much so that it was willing to pay a high price to achieve a general agreement. He blamed Jefferson for the lack of progress, remarking that "J. is in the Virginia interest and that of the French, and it is his fault that we are at a distance." (Hammond's secretary reported Jefferson's "rancorous malevolence" to London.) After two months in Philadelphia, Hammond turned to Hamilton, whom he thought "more a man of the world than J." noting, "I like his manners better."[32] The treasury secretary was all too willing to enter into private talks with the British minister, a step that went beyond imprudence. Hamilton's behavior was treacherous, for he had to know that he risked subverting the diplomacy of his nation's chief diplomat.

Hamilton soon enough secretly apologized to Hammond for Jefferson's "intemperate violence," falsely depicted the secretary of state as staking out positions that were not in accord with those of Washington, communicated confidential information regarding the status of United States negotiations with Spain, and divulged that despite the State Department's renewed talks with France concerning a new commercial agreement, "the scale . . . preponderated in favor of the *commercial* encouragements afforded by Great Britain." With "much force and emphasis," Hamilton conceded that the United States so thirsted after trade in the West Indies that it was willing to accept the "restrictions and regulations as Great Britain might require." As he had done with Beckwith, Hamilton deceptively volunteered that there were deep divisions within the administration on the matter of restitution for slaves who had been taken.[33] Hamilton's conduct was scandalous and indefensible, and had the president known of it, Washington might have had no choice but to cashier his treasury secretary. In the end, however, Hamilton's betrayals made little difference. Britain and the United States were far apart on most issues, and London was not willing to open the West Indies to American trade. Barring an American capitulation, which was not going to happen under President Washington, no accord could have been reached with or without Hamilton's perfidy.

*   *   *

Early in 1792 Washington began to speak privately of retiring at the end of his first term, and in May he asked Madison to draft his farewell speech. Washington had a habit of disavowing his intention of seeking public office until a wide array of important figures beseeched him to serve, but in this instance his desire to return home was genuine. He turned sixty early that year and would be sixty-five when a second term ended, if he lived that long. He had survived serious illnesses in 1789 and 1790, maladies which he believed had left him "sensibly more infirm." Feeling "himself growing old," troubled by hearing and memory loss, and having long since wearied of the "fatigues and disagreeableness" of the presidency, Washington desperately wished to enjoy his last good years at Mount Vernon.[34]

The president's retirement was the last thing that either Hamilton or Jefferson wanted. Both thought him the adhesive that held together the Union, and Hamilton had unfilled plans that required Washington's aegis. Keenly aware of how Washington thought, Hamilton advised him that the consensus of public opinion was that his retirement would be the "greatest evil, that could befall the country." The "affairs of the national government are not yet firmly established," he warned, adding that in Washington's absence the champions of state sovereignty would tear down all that had been achieved since 1789. Knowing that Washington's immeasurable pride would find intolerable anything but a unanimous vote in the electoral college, Hamilton advised that a handful of "fanatical individuals" might not vote for him, but that the final tally would reveal a "general confidence and attachment towards you." But as always in such instances with Washington, Hamilton's trump card played on the president's vanity. Hamilton counseled that it would be "critically hazardous" to Washington's lasting reputation if he did not accept a second term.[35]

When Washington in February 1792 first informed Jefferson of his intention of retiring, the secretary of state did not attempt to dissuade him. In fact, Jefferson responded that he too wished to leave his post and return home. Washington, who could spread treacle as handily as Hamilton, immediately beseeched Jefferson to stay on, telling him that he was "much more important" to his administration than any other officer. Some ten weeks later, fearful of unrest, and possibly even secessionist movements, Jefferson had come to "tremble" at the thought of Washington's retirement. He urged him to accept a second term, saying: "North and South will hang together, if they have you to hang on."[36]

Months passed before Jefferson again raised the matter. All along, however, he reiterated his intention of resigning as soon as he could "wind up the business of my office," telling Washington that he looked forward to retiring "with the longing of a wave-worn mariner, who has at length the land in view."[37] In the autumn, with the electoral college due to meet in about sixty days and Washington still not having agreed to a second term, Jefferson called on him at Mount Vernon and beseeched him to stay on. His argument remained unchanged: Washington was "the only man in the U.S. who possessed the confidence of the whole." After one more term, the people's habit of "submitting to the government and . . . thinking it a thing to be maintained" would be ingrained. Washington listened to Jefferson's lengthy soliloquy, after which he conceded that he "would make the sacrifice" should his "aid [be] thought necessary to save the cause."[38] In December the presidential electors unanimously reelected Washington.

Throughout 1792, Washington had appealed to Hamilton and Jefferson to abandon their partisan sniping, and it is not inconceivable that the president's threatened retirement was at least partially designed to silence his warring cabinet rivals. If so, his strategy was an abysmal failure. Hamilton and Madison were writing polemical pieces for newspapers, and Freneau's *National Gazette* had gathered a head of partisan steam as the elections of 1792 approached. Freneau portrayed Hamilton's program as beneficial only to wealthy Northerners, equated the secretary's style with that of British prime ministers who served their king, called Hamilton's followers "Noblesse and Courtiers," preached on the "Injustice of the Excise Law," warned that Hamiltonianism threatened American independence by making the new nation a client state of Great Britain, and savaged Adams for his purported affinity for monarchy. Washington remained off-limits until after his reelection, but thereafter his supposedly royal habits came under fire. Freneau blasted the "*monarchical prettiness*" of his administration, focusing on its "*levees, drawing rooms, stately nods instead of shaking hands, titles of office*, seclusion from the people."[39]

Washington was mortified by the attacks. When Jefferson had called on him in October, the president and his guest walked about Mount Vernon's sparkling gardens and lush and verdent lawn in the chill of early morning. When they reentered the mansion, Washington escorted Jefferson to a parlor and opened the conversation by declaring that the partisan warfare had gone too far. Jefferson listened, but did not back down. Instead, he launched into another tirade about Hamilton's monarchical bent. This was too much for Washington. He snapped that there were not "ten men in the U. S. whose opinions were worth attention who entertained such a thought" of "transforming this government into a monarchy." Jefferson responded that there were "many more than he imagined," but before he could expand his argument, they were called to breakfast. Sensing Washington's anger, Jefferson "avoided going further into the subject." It was the last time he attempted to enlighten the president about Hamilton in a face-to-face meeting, in large measure because Jefferson at last understood how inextricably bound Washington was to the treasury secretary.[40]

But Jefferson did not desist in his efforts to force Hamilton out of the government, and a few weeks after visiting Mount Vernon, a veritable treasure trove of intelligence reached the secretary of state. The story—at least the story that Hamilton eventually told—began during the summer of 1791. Betsey, with her four children in tow, had fled oppressively hot Philadelphia for her parents' home in more summer-friendly Albany. Hamilton remained at work in the city, however, and one day, while home alone, a visitor called on him. It was an attractive, twenty-three-year-old woman named Maria Reynolds. She poured out a tale of woe about the mistreatment she had experienced at the hands of her husband, James Reynolds, who in the end had abandoned her for another woman, leaving her destitute. She asked Hamilton for financial assistance. Captivated, and likely reminded of his mother's similar plight following her abandonment, Hamilton agreed to help. He promised to bring money to Maria's residence that night. Taking along bills issued by his Bank of the United States, Hamilton arrived at her apartment as darkness descended on the city. It was very late when he left, and more than a financial transaction had occurred.

He returned on other nights, though with Betsey away, Hamilton's home became their favorite trysting place. Their affair continued for some time, even after Maria broke the news that her miscreant husband had returned and the couple had reconciled. She also divulged for the first time that James Reynolds had profited handsomely by speculating in government securities. The magic elixir that led to his success, she added, had been inside information peddled by the assistant secretary of treasury, William Duer. The supposedly worldly Hamilton could not see the trap he was heading into, or perhaps his carnal desires overwhelmed his good sense. Persuading himself that Maria had a "real fondness" for him, Hamilton, the master of intrigue, had fallen into the snares of a consummate grifter.

Throughout the summer, Hamilton wrote his "beloved Betsey," telling her, "I cannot be happy without you." Stoically, he awaited his wife, he wrote, "with all the patience I can . . . for your return." He told Betsey that he was in "good health & only want you with me," but he advised her "not to precipitate your return," as the "native air" in Albany was superior to the unwholesome heat of the city. He could hardly wait to behold "that sweet bloom in your looks," he wrote a few weeks later, but added that his "extreme anxiety" for her health prompted him to beseech his wife to stay on in Albany at bit longer.[41]

In September, after a two-month absence, Betsey and the children returned home. Hamilton continued his extramarital affair, simply meeting Maria at her apartment when her husband was elsewhere. In December, Maria confided that her husband had learned of their affair. Two days later, James Reynolds confronted Hamilton and demanded "satisfaction." He wanted one thousand dollars. If he did not receive it, Betsey and the world would learn of Hamilton's affair with Maria. Hamilton paid the hush money. Yet, incredibly, he continued his relationship with Maria, and for five additional months he made more and more blackmail payments. All the while, Betsey was pregnant with their fifth child. Reynolds made his final stab at extortion in August 1792, but by then Hamilton had at last quit seeing Maria and refused to make further payments. The blackmail ended, at least for a time.

The world might never have known of Hamilton's tawdry behavior had not James Reynolds and a companion, Jacob Clingman—once a clerk to the former Speaker of the House, Pennsylvania's Frederick Muhlenberg—been arrested in November 1792 and charged with perjury and defrauding the U.S. government. As they were being prosecuted by Oliver Wolcott, the comptroller of the treasury, Reynolds and Clingman plotted a possible way to make the government abandon the case. Through the intercession of Muhlenberg, Clingman was released on bail, after which he obligingly advised the congressman that Reynolds and Hamilton had been partners in illegal speculation in treasury securities. Clingman passed along some enigmatic letters that Hamilton had sent to Reynolds, but the biggest potential bombshell was his suggestion that Reynolds possessed sufficient evidence to "hang the secretary of the Treasury." Muhlenberg knew the charges had to be looked into, and he easily persuaded Abraham Venable, a fellow representative, and Senator James Monroe—both Virginians and, like the former speaker, opponents of Hamilton—to help him investigate.

The threesome spoke with Reynolds in his jail cell and interviewed his wife at her residence. Three days later, they confronted Hamilton at his home. The treasury secretary immediately told the story of his extramarital affair and the blackmail he had paid Reynolds, showing them his letters to the husband-and-wife embezzlement team. Convinced that Hamilton was blameless with regard to misusing public money, the three congressmen not only dug no further but also pledged not to go public with the story. However, they brought in John Beckley, another Virginian and the clerk of the House, to make copies of the documents that Hamilton had provided. Hamilton believed the matter would never come to light. The congressmen had given him their word. Besides, they had readily agreed that the matter was nothing more than what Hamilton himself later called "a plain case of a private amour," and this was not an age when sexual escapades were fodder for partisan politics.[42]

But four individuals, none friends of Hamilton, were privy to sensational information about one of the most powerful men in America. Today, such information would in all likelihood not remain secret for very long. Nor did it remain under wraps in 1792. Jefferson appears to have heard the news within forty-eight hours of the congressmen's conversation with Hamilton. He probably was told of it by Beckley, who was a cog in his machine of informants.[43]

Jefferson remained silent about Hamilton's illicit affair and blackmail, but the astonishing news of his adversary's improper behavior left him more certain than ever that the treasury secretary was utterly corrupt. Already convinced that Hamilton had turned the nation into a casino, replete with malicious repercussions for its institutions and the habits of its citizenry, it was not much of a leap for Jefferson to think the man himself must be dishonorable. With a bit of digging, Jefferson expected that further evidence of Hamilton's malfeasance would turn up. He must also have hoped that when faced with the threat of a formal inquiry, Hamilton would resign in order to prevent word of his affair with Maria Reynolds from being made public. Working behind the scenes with William Giles, a young, blindly loyal Virginia congressman, Jefferson helped craft a set of resolutions designed to compel Hamilton to make an accounting of America's loans, which in turn would initiate a House investigation into the treasury secretary's conduct. It was a fishing expedition in search of Hamilton's financial improprieties, outright misconduct, or questionable behavior. Jefferson must have been certain that he could not lose. He might be rid of Hamilton, but even if that did not occur, the hearings would awaken the citizenry to the "extent of their danger." Jefferson had previously tried to stop the advance of Hamiltonianism. Now, he sought its rollback.[44]

The congressional inquiry that Jefferson hoped for never took place. Hamilton answered five of the resolutions, easily disposing of the questions of improper procedures. He also tutored friendly congressmen, enabling them to run circles around their congressional foes in the debates on the remaining nine charges. It was over by late winter 1793, with Congress having repudiated Giles's resolutions by heavy majorities. Hamilton had eluded an in-depth investigation.

But Jefferson was not terribly disappointed. Things had taken a turn his way. He rejoiced that the outcome of the congressional elections had been "favorable to the republican candidates" from Pennsylvania southward. The "Monocrats (who are few tho' wealthy and noisy) are *au desespoir*," he exclaimed, as the Republicans' victory will "turn the balance" in Congress. He thought the election results "turned out to be what was expected." Jefferson was also convinced that his faction's victories over the Federalists, as the devotees of Hamiltonianism were calling themselves, were the result both of the opposition press he had established and the spadework he and Madison had done with their botanizing tour. The people, once given "faithful accounts of what is doing here," had made the right choices. Jefferson was reassured. As 1793 began, Jefferson predicted that "the tide of this government . . . will . . . subside into the true principles of the Constitution."[45] Jefferson believed that Hamilton had been stopped and that he had won.

CHAPTER 11

"A LITTLE
INNOCENT BLOOD"

TO THE MOUNTAINTOP AND TO THE
TOP OF THE MOUNTAIN

EARLY IN 1792, Jefferson informed Washington of his plans to retire after one more year, and at the same time he told Patsy that the "ensuing year will be the longest of my life." Not only would he have served three years as secretary of state, a post he had never aspired to, but also he had spent little time at Monticello since he entered Congress nearly a decade before. Jefferson was eager to exchange "labour, envy, and malice, for ease, domestic occupation, and domestic love and society." In the spring, and again in the fall, he reminded the president that he was "bent irresistibly on the tranquil enjoyment of my family, my farm, and my books." But in February 1793, when Jefferson told Washington that he would be leaving office in six weeks, the president pressed him to stay on. Reluctantly, Jefferson consented to serve "perhaps till summer, perhaps autumn." In mid-summer, he wrote to Washington that September 30 would be a "convenient" moment for his retirement, whereupon the president took an extraordinary step. He called on the secretary of state at his residence, which may have been the only time that Washington paid a visit to the home of one of his cabinet officers, and yet again asked Jefferson to stay on longer. Remain in office through the end of the year, he pleaded, by which time the "affairs of Europe would be settled." As if to sweeten the pot, Washington confided that Hamilton had informed him of his intention of retiring in the spring of 1794. Jefferson pondered the request for five days before consenting, though on the condition that he be permitted to return to Monticello to tend to private matters in the fall.[1]

By 1793, events in Europe, and especially in France, had gone in directions that Jefferson could not have imagined at the time he left Paris. In 1789, he had believed that the establishment of a constitutional monarchy had nearly brought the French Revolution to an end. He rejoiced in what had occurred, and so did most Americans, who believed the French revolutionaries had been inspired by the American Revolution. Washington proudly and prominently displayed the key to the Bastille, sent to him by Lafayette, at Mount Vernon, and Hamilton supposedly remarked that the electrifying events in Paris had moved him as had nothing else since Lexington and Concord. Well into 1792 the French Revolution remained so popular in the United States that some Americans referred to themselves as Jacobins—the name adopted by a faction in France—and some even followed the practice of the French revolutionaries by addressing one another as "citizen" and "citess," a deliberate stab at blurring class distinctions. When several conservative nations allied against republican France and invaded the country, nearly every American prayed for a French victory, and when word arrived in December 1792 that the French had repelled the invasion, spontaneous celebrations erupted throughout the United States.[2]

But enthusiasm waned among the more conservative Americans when they learned of terror, bloodshed, and social upheaval in France. Hamilton became alarmed when France's aristocratic ruling class lost power. Thereafter, he warned that French "excesses" and "enormities" put at risk "the foundations of right security and property, of order, morality and religion."[3] Word of the "September Massacres" in 1792 was especially important in transforming conservative friends of the French Revolution into foes. Well over a thousand executions had occurred in Paris, and perhaps four hundred others died in regional capitals. Many of the victims were clergy, and the frenzied killing spree was followed by a campaign of de-Christianization that included the spoliation of churches and desecration of sacred relics. By the spring of 1793, around the time of Washington's second inauguration, Americans learned that Louis XVI, who had befriended them during the War of Independence, had died on the guillotine. By then, Americans also knew that France's revolutionaries were out to overturn not just the monarchy but also society itself. Titles that had set apart the nobility from the commoners were banished. Soon, the knee britches and silk stockings that had distinguished elite males from those who were not well born were replaced by long trousers, a fashion revolution that instantly obliterated discernable signs of rank. Formal bowing fell out of favor as well, and was replaced by handshakes. Many American conservatives were aghast at what John Adams decried as France's "democratical hurricane." Traditionalists took umbrage at the disappearance of the familiar, scorning what they labeled as the "hugging and rugging . . . addressing and caressing" that was the new custom in France. Hartford's Chauncey Goodrich, a devotee of Hamilton's, worried that America's "noisy set of demagogues" would imitate the Parisian "contagion of levelism" that threatened to make French aristocrats the "equal to French barbers." Above all, America's conservatives feared that the French example would inspire rampant democracy within the United States.[4]

Washington may have hung the key to the Bastille in the hallway of his mansion, but from the beginning he feared that the revolution would unleash radical change. Once it commenced, he had nothing good to say about events in France.[5] Nor did Hamilton. He insisted that the "horrid and disgusting scenes" and the "atrocious depravity" of the French "assassins" caused every person of "reason and humanity [to] recoil." He publicly defended Louis XVI following word of his execution, calling him "a humane kind-hearted man" whose "magnanimous policy" had helped the Continental army win the Revolutionary War.[6]

Jefferson saw things differently. Years later, Jefferson said that had he been a member of the French assembly, he would not have voted to kill the king and queen.[7] But at the time, early in 1793, he defended regicide, asserting that the experiment in constitutional monarchy had failed and that "despotism" would have been reinstated had the king not been executed. He added that sending Louis XVI to the guillotine might "soften" royal rule elsewhere by demonstrating that monarchs were "amenable to punishment like other criminals." Jefferson was personally gentle and pacific, but he was also a true revolutionary. He had sought political and social changes in America and longed for the republican ideology of the American Revolution to spread throughout Europe. Change in America had come with relatively little social upheaval, but Jefferson understood that given its ancient and entrenched ruling classes, reform in Europe would inevitably be accompanied by radical revolutionary upheaval. He did not shrink from the bloodshed that would ensue. To him, it was like a just war. Some had to die in pursuit of a worthy cause.

Jefferson believed that if the oppressed in France succeeded in improving their lot, the liberation of "the whole earth" would follow. But if the French Revolution failed, unwelcome consequences would be the result even in the United States, where a "falling back to that kind of Half-way-house, the English constitution" would be the least of the unfortunate results. Liberty was worth a "little innocent blood," he declared. Indeed, even if "half the earth [was] desolated," the destruction would be worth it in order to bring an end to monarchy's victimization of the great mass of humanity. "Were there but an Adam and Eve left in every country, and left free, it would be better than as it now is," he said. Jefferson's defense of killing to attain ideological ends has shocked many in subsequent generations, but truly radical change seldom occurs bloodlessly. The Founders had spilled blood in the American Revolution, and some among them understood that carnage would inevitably accompany the French Revolution. Even the humane Franklin, who was alive when the earliest bloody mob violence occurred in Paris, thought the "disagreeable" savagery was justifiable "if by the struggle she [France] obtains and secures for the nation its future liberty, and a good constitution."[8]

Hostilities in what would be known as the Wars of the French Revolution began in the spring of 1792. Initially, France was at war with Prussia and Austria, but in 1793 Great Britain entered the conflict, and that sent passions soaring within the United States. Just weeks after news of Franco-British fighting reached America, Jefferson remarked that the "war has kindled ... the two parties with an ardour which our own [domestic] interests ... could never excite."[9] In most eighteenth-century European wars, the outcomes perhaps altered the balance of power, but had little impact on the lives of most people. This war was different. The Franco-British war was a life-and-death struggle between rival ideologies. The fate of ruling classes hung in the balance, convincing many Americans that the war's outcome was vitally important to the future of the United States. Sometimes portraying England as "fighting the battle of the civilized world," Federalists craved the defeat of the French radicals, and some would not have been displeased by the restoration of the monarchy. Republicans drank toasts to the French and yearned for "liberty ... [to] assume a predominating influence" as "every monster" of despotism was destroyed.[10] Partisanship, already venomous, moved to another level, prompting scholars to observe that in all of American political history the "bitterness of the division" was exceeded only by the frenzied malice of the Civil War era.[11]

All the key players in Washington's administration agreed on one thing: The United States must remain neutral in this war. Washington, Hamilton, and Jefferson may have agreed on little else, but each was convinced that another war so soon after the War of Independence would be economically ruinous and possibly fatal to the American Union. The cabinet officers skirmished, however, over whether to maintain the Treaties of Alliance and Commerce with France. Hamilton wished to suspend the accords, Jefferson to preserve them. Behind the infighting was the desire of each to aid one side or the other without injuring the interests of the United States. In the end, Washington sided with Jefferson, who argued persuasively—and correctly—that the United States could safely abide by the treaty's stipulation that it must permit French warships and privateers to utilize American harbors as a refuge, a privilege that would be denied England. Though excoriated later as a Francophile, Jefferson always put America's interests first. In that spirit, he advised Washington that the alliance did not extend to France the right to equip its privateers or sell its prizes in American ports, and he counseled that the United States should not waver on that point. It was an opinion that required a broad, legalistic reading of the treaty, and it was one with which Washington concurred. On April 22, the president, eschewing the word "neutral," declared that the United States was "impartial" toward all belligerents. This would be "a disagreeable pill" to many Republicans, Jefferson allowed, but it was "necessary to keep us out of the calamities of a war."[12]

The cabinet additionally discussed whether Washington should receive the first minister sent to the United States by the French Republic, an envoy who was known to have already begun his Atlantic crossing. Once again, all agreed that he must be received. By the time the cabinet made that decision, Citizen Edmond-Charles-Edouard Genêt, the twenty-nine-year-old French minister, was in Charleston, where he had landed ten days earlier.

Genêt came to a United States that was blazing with partisanship, and his impetuous manner only added fuel to the fires already raging. France could not have chosen a worse envoy. Genêt was rash and stubborn, and in the grip of a feverish revolutionary zeal. Yet, the problems that befell his mission were not entirely his fault. France had stuffed Genêt's pockets with inflammatory instructions. He was directed to use propaganda, secret agents, and hired American adventurers to arouse fervor for the French Revolution among the residents of Spanish Florida and Louisiana, as well as British Canada, steps aimed at helping France in its war against Britain and its Spanish ally. The envoy was also to play a pivotal role in the privateering war on British shipping. Genêt was not only to recruit American sailors for those vessels but also to see that the privateers were outfitted in American ports and permitted to sell their prizes in those havens. Aside from these inevitably provocative undertakings, there was an aspect of Genêt's mission that held the promise of substantive gain for the United States. Genêt was to reveal that France was opening its ports, and those of its colonies, to American commerce, the goal that Franklin and Jefferson had unsuccessfully sought throughout the 1780s. This was a pot-sweetener. Genêt's final task was to negotiate a new Franco-American treaty of commerce, one with enticing benefits to Americans. However, it would come with the condition that United States must discriminate against any nation (such as Great Britain) that pursued a mercantilistic policy toward America.

The ecstatic greeting that Genêt received in Charleston put Washington on guard against potential troubles in pursuing a neutral course. A huge crowd welcomed the envoy ashore, after which he commissioned four vessels as French privateers. That was merely the beginning. Throughout Genêt's month-long journey to Philadelphia, town after town hailed him with banquets, the pealing of bells, artillery salutes, and addresses that pulsated with love for France. Philadelphia welcomed him with open arms on May 16. Two days later, the president, a formidably reserved, cold individual to begin with, received Genêt with glacial formality while standing beneath portraits of Louis XVI and Marie Antoinette.[13]

The reception extended by Jefferson could not have been more different. Hoping that the voice of the people would melt the "cold caution of their government," Jefferson saw that, through Genêt, the United States might gain its long-sought commercial ends with France, a step that might weaken Great Britain and set in motion the death rattle of the British monarchy. One other thing. Jefferson interpreted the receptions lavished on Genet as evidence that "the old spirit of 1776 is rekindling," which he was convinced would be to the detriment of the Federalist Party. Genêt, he believed, could be useful for partisan political reasons.[14]

Jefferson was eager for Genêt to succeed, and as a result of things that the secretary of state said, or through his tone and manner, the Frenchman may have surmised that he would be given extraordinary latitude. Early on, Jefferson shared things with Genêt as he had never done with George Hammond. For instance, he divulged that Washington was influenced by the Anglophiles in his cabinet. Jefferson additionally coached Genêt, advising patience, as a more friendly Congress—the one elected the previous autumn—would convene near the end of the year. However, Jefferson also told Genêt what the United States would not tolerate, and he defended and elucidated his country's position in a lengthy and learned discourse on international law.

Genêt refused to listen, and he rapidly wore out his welcome. He answered Jefferson with impertinence, threatened to go over Washington's head to the American public to get what he wanted, and ignored United States policy by arming a privateer in the port of Philadelphia. Hamilton, who labeled Genêt the "most offensive" diplomat imaginable, was so sufficiently worried—"panick struck," was how Jefferson characterized him—that he met secretly with Hammond to assure him of his efforts to prevent the French envoy from dragging the United States into war with Great Britain. Through conduits such as the influential Federalists John Jay and Rufus King, Hamilton leaked to the press word of Genêt's threat to appeal to the public. And he launched yet another newspaper campaign, a series of nine essays that he penned that summer under the signature "No Jacobin." His objective was to turn public opinion against Genêt by publishing details of the envoy's behavior, and in fact Hamilton's initial sentence trumpeted: The "Minister of the French Republic has threatened to appeal from the President of the United States to the People." Within fifty days, Jefferson was equally dismayed, having on his own

come to see Genêt as a detriment to Franco-American relations. Condemning Genêt as a "Hotheaded . . . disrespectful and even indecent" blunderer,
Jefferson "saw the necessity of quitting a wreck which could not but sink
all who should cling to" him. He agreed with Washington and Hamilton
that the administration must demand Genêt's recall.[15]

Genêt was gone, but the firestorm aroused by the European war blazed on.
The French minister had stirred the pot, but most of the heat directed toward
the Washington administration had been provoked by American neutrality,
which was assailed in Republican quarters as a betrayal of France and republicanism, and as a pro-British policy. To this point, Washington had largely
escaped criticism. No longer. He was ripped in the Republican press for his
"cold indifference" toward America's Revolutionary War ally and a republic at
war with a monarchical tyrant, and blasted for listening only to those Tory-
inclined members of his cabinet rather than to public opinion. The criticism
did not sit well with the notoriously thin-skinned president. At one cabinet
meeting, his volcanic temper erupted, causing Jefferson to note that the "President . . . got into one of those passions when he cannot command himself."[16]

However, nothing bothered Washington and Hamilton more than the
emergence of the Democratic-Republican Societies that sprang up after Great
Britain entered the war. Hamilton was sure that Genêt, or possibly French secret agents, had orchestrated their creation, but in fact they mushroomed
spontaneously to give voice to the pulsating popular mood. They were, as their
name suggested, the manifestation of the democratizing spirit that was part
and parcel of Revolutionary America, and that in itself excited pangs of anxiety in Hamilton.

The first Democratic-Republican Society was formed in Philadelphia in
1793, but within a few months some fifty others had come into being in several states. The membership was galvanized by alarm at the growing reach
and power of the national government, and particularly by signs of presidential omnipotence and the monarchical overtones of Washington's presidency.
Manhattan's Society, for instance, sprang into being in the course of a campaign to protect a local printer accused by Federalists of sedition for having
criticized the Washington presidency. But it was the French Revolution, and
the threat it faced from Europe's monarchical powers, that really fueled the
movement. Members often wore red, white, and blue cockades in imitation of
French radicals, frequently addressed one another as "fellow citizen" rather
than with the class-imbued "sir," and on occasion actively mobilized voters for
the Republican Party. Now and then a fiery orator urged republicans everywhere to "unite with France and stand or fall together." But on the whole,
few advocated American involvement in France's war, though they were

clearly bent on making it difficult for the Washington administration to aid London.[17]

Hamilton feared the clout of the Democratic-Republican Societies, which mimicked the Sons of Liberty and other radical organizations that had played an important role in organizing the insurgency against Great Britain during the American Revolution. His most immediate concern was the danger they posed to American neutrality, and during the summer of 1793 he authored seven newspaper essays on the subject. He defended Washington and his authority to proclaim neutrality. He insisted that since France had started the European war, the United States was not obligated by the Treaty of Alliance to come to its assistance. Hamilton argued that it was not in the best interests of the United States to enter the war on the side of France. Surrounded by British and Spanish possessions, faced with hostile Indians along its frontier, and lacking a navy, the new American nation would find itself in an "unequal contest." And in what would be a staple of right-wing politics for generations to come, Hamilton painted those who questioned American foreign policy as disloyal. However, the lengthiest portions of his essays were devoted to extinguishing America's sense of obligation toward France. Only weeks after his lachrymose essays praising Louis XVI for his magnanimity in providing assistance during the American Revolution, Hamilton asserted that "the interest of France had been the governing motive of the aid afforded us" after 1775.[18] Eighteenth-century politicians and polemicists were decidedly modern in that not every word they uttered was to be taken as forthright.

At the height of the partisan furor, Philadelphia was invaded by a more dangerous foe than any foreign adversary. Yellow fever struck in August, and for weeks it gripped the city. Transmitted by mosquitoes, Philadelphia's outbreak commenced along the waterfront, a low-lying, swampy region that was a breeding ground for the insects. It quickly spread across the city. In no time, nearly 150 people were dying each week, and the epidemic continued until autumn's first frosts destroyed the mosquitoes. By then, nearly five thousand had perished, roughly 8 percent of the population.

Philadelphians assumed the disease was spread by human contact, leading them to avoid others as much as possible. "Every body who can is flying" from the city, Jefferson said, and in fact upwards of twenty thousand did flee, but neither he nor Hamilton took that expedient. Jefferson never fell ill, which he attributed to his remoteness from the "filth" and heat of the city. Thinking that he would retire at the conclusion of Washington's first term, Jefferson had given notice that he would be abandoning his Market Street home. However, when the president persuaded him to stay on, Jefferson had to find another residence, and in April he had moved beyond the city to a summer cottage on the east bank of the Schuylkill River. That reduced his risk, but did not eliminate it, as he commuted daily to his office.[19] Fortune smiled on Jefferson, and he escaped the malady.

Hamilton was not so lucky. He fell ill on September 5, and Betsey contracted the illness a few days later. Like all the afflicted, both suffered excruciating headaches, nausea, chills, and aches. They were attended by Edward Stevens, the son of St. Croix's Thomas Stevens, who had taken in young Hamilton when he was orphaned. Edward Stevens had eventually immigrated to the mainland and was now a Philadelphia physician. Most physicians prescribed purges, or rubbed their patients with ointments and wrapped them in blankets soaked with vinegar. Those treated by Stevens received quinine, cold baths, wine, a concoction to stop the vomiting, and laudanum, a painkiller consisting mostly of opium. At the height of the epidemic, Jefferson said that about two in three victims survived, and the Hamiltons not only pulled through but also were on the mend within five days, a far more rapid recovery than most experienced. Stevens's therapies were of doubtful benefit. But because the Hamiltons could afford a physician, it is likely they were never dehydrated, and that was probably crucial in their deliverance.[20]

Jefferson was aware that Hamilton had been taken ill, but his hatred for his counterpart was so suffocating that he never sent a note of sympathy or well-wishing. In fact, he told Madison that he doubted the treasury secretary was actually suffering from yellow fever. Jefferson thought it possible that Hamilton might have caught cold, but more likely that he was merely a hypochondriac. In one of his cruelest utterances, Jefferson added that Hamilton "had been miserable several days from a firm persuasion he should catch it [the yellow fever]. A man as timid as he is on the water, as timid on horseback, as timid in sickness, would be a phaenomenon if the courage of which he has the reputation in military occasions were genuine."[21]

Jefferson finally left for Monticello in mid-September, six weeks into the epidemic. This was his planned autumn leave, though several days before his carriage rattled out of the city, the government had shut down. Jefferson remained at home for a month, where he scrupulously tended to his State Department correspondence, but never wrote a personal or partisan letter. It was the beginning of the end of this phase of Jefferson's public service, and when he returned to Pennsylvania on November 1—to Germantown, actually, where the government met for several weeks—his pace seemed to wind down. In part, this was because Jefferson was initially challenged to find a space for his work; for two weeks he shared a public room in a tavern with numerous other refugees. However, because of his stature, or perhaps because he could afford it, he secured a bed while most others slept on the floor.[22]

Jefferson's final cabinet dustups with Hamilton occurred during his stay in Germantown. In June, the British government had issued an Orders in Council directing the captains of Royal Navy vessels to seize American ships bound for French ports with cargoes of grain. While Hamilton and Jefferson agreed that the United States must protest London's action, Jefferson wanted Washington to denounce this malevolent action in the harshest tones in his annual State of the Union address. This was not their only dispute over the contents of the president's address. Washington wished to report on a wide range of the administration's actions since Congress's adjournment in March, including the proclamation of neutrality and the dismissal of Genêt. The cabinet fought over both what Washington should say and, as he could not cover everything in an oral address, what documents—if any—should be made public. Hamilton insisted on keeping all documents secret, declaring that it would provoke a "serious calamity" should Washington divulge the French offer to negotiate a commercial accord. He also bristled over the language that Jefferson recommended in responding to the Orders in Council. His "draught . . . amounted to a declaration of war" against England, Hamilton asserted. Jefferson "whittled down the expressions" in the draft he had prepared for Washington, but they remained tough. No one was more surprised than Jefferson when Washington took his side. The president, Jefferson said, expressed "more vehemence" toward London "than I have seen him shew." It was one of the first times that Jefferson could remember Washington siding with him against Hamilton.[23]

Making public Jefferson's correspondence with Genêt vindicated him even in the eyes of some of his harshest critics, many of whom—taken in by Hamilton's partisan assaults—had presumed the secretary of state had acted slavishly toward the French envoy. Even Hamilton's close friend and confidant, Robert Troup, told the treasury secretary that having been made aware of Jefferson's tenacity had "blotted all the sins . . . out of the book of our remembrance." Doubtless to Hamilton's consternation, Troup even expressed his "regret that he [Jefferson] should quit his post."[24]

Jefferson's final major act as secretary of state was to report to Congress on American commerce, an accounting that Congress had requested nearly three years earlier. In 1791, Hamilton had persuaded him to delay his report, lest it jeopardize negotiations over London's yielding of its western posts. Thereafter, it was Jefferson who dragged his feet, awaiting a more friendly Congress. In December 1793, when the Congress that had been elected in 1792 finally assembled, he acted.

Jefferson's report was the culmination of twenty years of his thinking, and the final salvo on behalf of much that he had sought to accomplish as secretary of state. The author of the Declaration of Independence was seeking to make the United States truly independent, to terminate the commercial dependence on Great Britain that had prevailed in the colonial era and continued despite the American victory in the Revolutionary War. Jefferson was privy to secret, and accurate, information from intelligence sources that the British ministry was unrelenting in its policy of denying American trade in the West Indies, and that it harbored malign intentions toward America's shipbuilding and fishing industries. Armed with this knowledge, he saw little to lose through a more confrontational policy toward London. Indeed, he remained convinced that reciprocity offered the best hope of compelling Great Britain to trade more fully and equitably with the United States. Jefferson longed to break Britain's commercial domination of Europe and North America. At the same moment, he looked for ways to forestall the evils that he imagined would ensue from Hamiltonian economics, to indefinitely sustain America's agrarian republic, and to bring about closer relations with France. In one way or another, his commercial report was aimed at achieving these objectives.

Jefferson opened with statistical data calculated to show the dangerous degree to which Britain dominated American commerce. This was a prelude to the heart of his message: his call for free trade. Instead of the prevailing "piles of regulating Laws, Duties, and Prohibitions" that "shackles" world commerce, Jefferson dreamt of each nation being free "to exchange with others mutual surpluses for mutual Wants." Free trade was crucial for the American economy, he said, but it was also "essential" as a "resource of Defence." Free trade would not only lead to economic independence, it would also result in a robust commerce, which in turn would produce a flourishing commercial fleet that would serve as a nursery of sailors for the American navy. Some nations, he went on, wanted free trade, and in an accompanying letter he advised the Speaker of the House that France was ready to negotiate a commercial treaty "on liberal principles." But for those nations such as Great Britain that would not abandon systems that discriminated against American commerce, he said, "it behooves us" to retaliate with countermeasures. Very nearly the last word that Jefferson uttered as secretary of state was that the United States should adopt similarly restrictive commercial policies toward Great Britain, imposing punishing taxes on English imports, or forbidding their importation altogether, until London agreed to admit American exports to British ports.[25]

With that, Jefferson was ready to go home. He had remained in Washington's cabinet a year longer than he had wished, and he was not swayed when, just before Christmas 1793, the president made a final attempt to persuade him to stay on. Jefferson told him that he was "immoveable." With sadness, Washington relented. He wrote to Jefferson thanking him for his "integrity and talents," and added that all the reasons that had led him to nominate his fellow Virginian to serve as secretary of state had been vindicated by the expertise "eminently displayed in the discharge of your duties."[26]

On January 5, after visiting his Philadelphia barber for the last time and purchasing several items for Monticello, Jefferson set off for home and what Hamilton snidely called another "permanent" retirement. (Actually, to this point Jefferson and Hamilton had each "retired" twice.) Jefferson rode the public stage most of the way, and on the eleventh day after departing the capital, he reached his hilltop mansion. He was fifty-one and convinced that he would never again leave Monticello for any extended time. "The little spice of ambition, which I had in my younger days, has long since evaporated," he contended. The "length of my tether is now fixed for life from Monticello to Richmond," he remarked two weeks after he came home, and in fact, during the next three years his longest journey was his lone trip to Richmond. Jefferson likely reasoned that he had about fifteen years left, perhaps twenty if he was especially fortunate. He was the leading light of what was coalescing into an organized political party, which had to have made him aware that someday he might be called on to stand for election to the presidency. Then again, that might never occur, for in 1794 it was far from certain how long Washington would occupy the office, and the feeling was widespread that Vice President Adams was the heir apparent.[27]

Jefferson's happiness at escaping politics was readily apparent. Ten weeks after coming home he said that he had not seen a Philadelphia newspaper since he left the capital, and he had no wish to see one. Eight months into his retirement he was asked to serve as envoy extraordinary to Madrid. He declined, remarking that his only regret about retirement was that he had not entered into it years earlier. He added that every day increased his "inflexibility" about ever returning to public life. He did not write to Washington until he had been home for four months, and nearly the entirety of his letter was about farming, which he said he had embraced "with an ardour which I scarcely knew in my youth." When he completed his initial year at home, Jefferson exclaimed that it had been the most tranquil of his life, one in which he had enjoyed excellent health, save for a brief but "violent attack of the Rheumatism." At last, he was surrounded by his family. Maria, now fifteen, lived with him, and Martha, whose home was nearby, visited often, sometimes leaving her two children with their grandfather. Relatives and friends called, especially in the summer when the roads were more likely passable. Serenity "becomes daily more and more the object of my life," he proclaimed. "Master of my own time," he now "look[ed] back with wonder and regret over my useless waste of time" in politics. Even Jefferson's correspondence fell to a fraction of what it once had been. "I put off answering my letters now, farmer-like, till a rainy day, and then find it sometimes postponed by other necessary occupations."[28]

Jefferson portrayed himself as a committed farmer who lived a simple life, telling friends that he had become "too much attached to the plough," had his "hands full" with farming, and was "the most ardent farmer in the state. I live on my horse."[29] There was considerable truth in what he said. He boasted of rising daily before the sun. After a light breakfast (hot bread and cold ham, along with coffee or tea), he spent much of each day riding about his far-ranging estate, vetting his crops and shops, and supervising his laborers. He also rode for exercise, and if the weather permitted, he tried to spend a couple of hours each day in the saddle. His focus on a healthy lifestyle extended into other areas. He did not smoke and he avoided hard liquor. He usually drank a glass or two of wine with dinner and, though not a vegetarian, he insisted that vegetables be the staple of his diet. Like many in his time, he took just two meals a day, sitting down to dinner at three thirty in the winter, at five during the longer days of summer. It seemed like an unadorned life, but Jefferson was a walking contradiction. While some of his tastes were simple, he owned a capacious mansion stuffed with richly upholstered European furniture, a vast collection of art, and perhaps the nation's largest collection of natural history artifacts. He dined on food prepared by a trained chef—James Hemings until late in 1795 and thereafter a chef that he had tutored—was waited on by slaves, and, when indoors, was never more than a few steps from one of the largest libraries in North America.[30]

The one dark cloud that intruded on Jefferson's unruffled existence was his mounting indebtedness. It exceeded £8,500 in 1795, roughly a 15 percent increase since his return from France, despite his sale of land and slaves during every year that he had been home. He had even been driven to leasing portions of his estate. But now that he was home, Jefferson believed he could resolve his problem through his personal management of operations at Monticello. He instituted numerous changes, gradually transforming the plantation into a small industrial village where nails, textiles, and charcoal were made, and tinsmiths and coopers labored. The nailery was the largest of those enterprises. It was tended by about a dozen young males who toiled long hours over the blazing forge, making upwards of ten thousand iron nails daily, from which Jefferson grossed $2,000 in 1796. The nails were sold mostly in Philadelphia and Richmond, and for a time Jefferson was able to boast that the nailery provided "completely for the maintenance of my family." It generated sufficient profits every two months to pay for a year's worth of luxury comestibles—coffee, tea, chocolate, sugar, molasses, rice, rum, and brandy—that he had shipped to Monticello.

But agriculture remained the heart of operations at Monticello. He largely replaced tobacco cultivation with more profitable grain production, especially wheat, which required only 20 percent of the labor needed by tobacco (he sold some of his surplus labor and reassigned the remainder to industrial pursuits). Jefferson devised a seven-year crop rotation plan that one visitor thought so innovative it could only have come from a "contemplative mind." He began to offer a variety of incentives to improve the work habits of his laborers, and he micromanaged the annual harvest, not only mapping out the tasks for each of the roughly seventy chattel assigned to the fields but also seeking to create a festive atmosphere fueled in part by generous allotments of food and liquor.[31]

Jefferson might have provided incentives and sought to make the work more cheery, but the barbarity of slavery could not be hidden. Its existence ultimately depended on the use—or the threat of the use—of force. That was as true at Monticello as at any other plantation. One study concluded that "the Monticello machine operated on carefully calibrated violence," but others have concluded that Jefferson mitigated violence or that his slaves were not treated badly according to the standards of the time. What is clear is that Jefferson diligently sought to apprehend runaway slaves, tolerated the flogging of his chattel, and sometimes ordered whippings. He also bought and sold slaves, fully aware that he was sundering families. Moreover, from the 1780s onward, Jefferson employed a score of overseers; some were not just harsh but also cruel, an unpleasant truth of which he was likely aware. Jefferson once remarked that he loathed "severity," and there is no credible evidence that he ever personally whipped a slave. Indeed, one of his longest-serving overseers described him "always very kind and indulgent to his servants." Yet, he was a slave owner, and a cold-blooded harshness was necessary for keeping people enslaved and exacting labor from them. What is more, by the 1790s his obsession with his debt problems may have led him to brook more stringent measures. It appears to be an unpleasant truth that Jefferson, as historian Henry Wiencek has written, was all too aware of the brutal nature of slavery and that he "distanced himself from the ugly reality of his system."[32]

For all of Jefferson's thought and work, and the severity that he tolerated, he remained only a marginally successful farmer. Droughts, floods, and unexpected early freezes took their toll, as did an infestation of Hessian fly, an insect that devastated wheat crops. Furthermore, Jefferson's land was not the best. He lived and farmed in a mountain range, and the soil his laborers worked was not the rich, bottomland variety.[33]

If bad luck and poor land did nothing for Jefferson's debt problem, his extravagant lifestyle exacerbated his plight. Addicted to home remodeling, Jefferson decided to tear down, and rebuild, the original Monticello. The structure had "never been more than half finished," he claimed, and during his nearly unbroken absence between 1783 and 1794, it had "gone into almost total decay." But there was more to it than that. He had he been inspired by architectural styles he had observed in Paris, probably wished for a dwelling that differed from the one he had shared with his late wife, and sought a larger house to accommodate his children, grandchildren, and visitors during his retirement years.[34]

Jefferson had probably decided to reconstruct his mansion before leaving France, and within two years of returning to the United States, he had conceived a plan for the new Monticello. The house was to be twice the size of the original dwelling, and it was designed to conform to Palladian principles, but with ample allowances made for convenience and privacy. More than a year before he resigned from Washington's cabinet, Jefferson set his laborers to making bricks and hauling stone up the long hill to the site of the original Monticello. Construction began in earnest when he came home, leaving him to feel that he was "living in [a] brick-kiln" amid incessant "noise, confusion and discomfort." Work proceeded very slowly. Thirty months after coming home, all the while living in a small portion of the original structure, the cellars had been dug and work had begun on the foundation, but six long years passed before the house was under roof. Even then, scaffolding for the carpenters, plasterers, and painters stood in most rooms, leaving one visitor to describe the house as "grand & awful," with an ever-present "general gloom."[35]

Early in 1795, Jefferson heard from Maria Cosway, the first word from her since about the time he entered Washington's cabinet. He had answered at once in 1790, telling her that should she come to Monticello it would be "all I could desire in the world," adding that his greatest wish was "to enjoy the affections of my heart." She had not responded. Years passed. Along the way, he heard that she had become a mother. Halfway through his final year in Philadelphia, Jefferson asked a mutual acquaintance for word about Maria, even intimating that he wished to resume his correspondence with her. Just before leaving the capital, he learned that Maria had entered a convent in Genoa. Stunned, he exclaimed that he thought she "would rather have sought the *mountain-top*."[36]

Jefferson had been at home for a year when two letters from Maria arrived, a short one and a longer one penned about ten days apart. She had recently returned to London, she said, and had learned that Jefferson had inquired about her nearly a year earlier. She was pleased to learn that he had often mentioned her in his letters to Angelica Church, their mutual friend, but Maria's tone was guarded and the language cryptic. Nevertheless, she made clear that through Angelica she knew that as late as 1793 Jefferson had seemed to suggest that he yet wished her to come to Monticello. Making no attempt to hide her melancholy feelings, she acknowledged her "wish to come" to that "smal spot unknown to Misery, trouble, and Confusion." To that she asked: "Why Can I not come?"[37]

Jefferson did not respond for nine months, a sure sign that his feelings were not what they had once been. When he finally wrote, he spoke of his desire to travel with her through Italy, but did not invite her to Monticello. When "I think of you," he said, "I am hurried off on the wings of imagination into regions where my fancy submits all things to our will." Perhaps he was suggesting that while in Paris together, he wished they might have overcome the obstacles that kept them apart.[38]

Undeterred, Maria responded at once, writing with lyric sadness that she kept his picture in her bedroom. She would prefer to see him in person, she added, and again spoke of her desire to come to Monticello.[39] Jefferson did not answer her letter.

When he had heard from Maria in 1795, eight years had passed since they had last seen each other. Much had changed. Indeed, when Jefferson responded to her letter that autumn, he was involved in an intimate relationship with another woman who was carrying his child. That woman was Sally Hemings, his chattel and the half-sister of his late wife, Martha.

Hemings subsequently attested that Jefferson had fathered children by her, and the preponderance of circumstantial evidence and recent DNA testing bear her out. She supposedly said that she had become Jefferson's "concubine" while in Paris, and that he was the father not only of a child that she was carrying when she left France in the fall of 1789 but of the six additional children that she subsequently bore. That first child, she said, had been born soon after she returned to Virginia, but died shortly thereafter. She added that she had not wished to return to America with Jefferson, as "in France she was free, while if she returned to Virginia she would be re-enslaved." However, Jefferson "induce[d]" her to come home with him by promising her "extraordinary privileges" and making the "solemn pledge" that all her children would be freed at age twenty-one.[40] She told her story to one of her sons, Madison Hemings, but it is unlikely that she would have done so until he was at least well into adolescence, more than thirty years after 1789. Furthermore, Madison did not share her testimony with the world until about half a century after he heard it. Every word of the story that Madison told may have been true, though there are sufficient red flags to give pause to a circumspect scholar. One has to consider whether Madison Hemings, whose standing would have been enhanced by having been sired by a Founding Father, was motivated by a self-serving penchant. In addition, human memory is treacherous under the best of circumstances, and it is especially hazardous to give credence to every detail in a secondhand account provided by Madison Hemings some fifty years after he first heard his mother's story.

Little in Hemings's narrative can be verified. There is no way to prove that Jefferson and Sally were intimate while in Paris, or that he was the father of the child she was allegedly carrying in 1789, or even that she was pregnant when they sailed for America. Jefferson did not make an inventory of his chattel until 1794, and when he did, he did not record that Sally was the mother of a four-year-old. It is possible that her 1789 pregnancy was not carried to term; or the child may have died in infancy, as she supposedly said; or the child may have been freed by the time Jefferson first compiled a list of his slaves. Or, she may not have been pregnant in 1789. Her allegation that Jefferson wanted her to return to Virginia is doubtless true. He had an economic stake in her, and the experience and skills she had acquired in Paris would be useful at Monticello. He may even have envisaged a mature Sally Hemings taking on many of the responsibilities that ordinarily fell to the mistress of a large southern plantation. He probably wanted her to come home to Monticello so badly that he promised her preferential treatment.

Jefferson was a manipulative sort who, according to one scholar, had "a great ability, as genuinely smart and sensitive people do," to disarm others in order to "bind them to himself."[41] He may well have employed his guile to coax this reluctant, sixteen-year-old girl to abandon freedom for a lifetime of slavery, even to become his mistress. On the other hand, little artfulness may have been required to persuade her to return to Virginia. It may never have occurred to her to go against Jefferson's will. Not only was he one of the most powerful men in America, but also she may have thought herself utterly dependent on him. Or, aware that as the unmarried black mother of an infant she would likely have faced incredible hardships had she chosen to remain in Paris, she may have welcomed a return to Virginia. Her older brother James agreed to return to Virginia and he may have persuaded her not to stay in France. What is more, as her mother and siblings lived at Monticello, where she had been raised, she may have felt the tug to come home. It is even conceivable that she was the more cunning of the two. She may have utilized the threat of remaining in Paris to pry bountiful pledges from Jefferson. There are at least two additional explanations for her decision to sail for America with the Jeffersons. As Jefferson came home in 1789 expecting to be in Virginia only briefly, it is conceivable that Sally wished to visit relatives, after which she would return with him to Paris. Still another possibility is that she may have been so in love with Jefferson that she was eager to return home with him.

It is likely that Jefferson and Sally Hemings did not begin their intimate relationship until 1794, when he returned to Monticello following his departure from Washington's cabinet. It was not until sometime in that period that his passion for Maria Cosway appears to have burned out. Furthermore, between March 1790 when he left Monticello to become secretary of state and January 1794 when he retired and came home, Jefferson and Hemings were seldom together. She was never in New York or Philadelphia with him, and he spent less than six of the forty-six months that he served in Washington's cabinet at Monticello. When Jefferson resigned his cabinet post, he believed he would never again hold public office nor stray far from home. If fear of a scandal ruining his political ambitions had previously been a concern, that no longer was the case. Moreover, beginning in 1794 he rebuilt Monticello in such a way as to protect his privacy in a house that was frequently occupied by relatives and guests.

Sally Hemings was pregnant early in 1795 and in October gave birth to a daughter, Harriet. There can be little doubt that Jefferson was her father, or that he sired two other daughters (born in 1799 and 1801) and three sons (born in 1798, 1805, and 1808). Madison Hemings was the child born in 1805. Jefferson was home at least nine months prior to the birth of each of these children, many visitors remarked on how the male children resembled him, and talk was rife in Charlottesville that Jefferson had a slave mistress who was bearing his children. He set these children free at a young age, as he supposedly had pledged to do. Though Jefferson owned some six hundred slaves during his long life, the children he sired with Sally, and two men from the Hemings family, were the only chattel he liberated.[42]

If their intimate relationship began in 1794, Jefferson would have been fifty-one and Hemings twenty-one at its inception. Jefferson's feelings may be more easily fathomed. Abundant evidence indicates that Hemings not only was attractive, but that she bore a decided resemblance to her half-sister, Jefferson's late wife. Furthermore, in his "head and heart" letter to Maria Cosway, Jefferson had intimated that he could never again surrender his heart to someone who could break it. That was highly unlikely to occur with Sally Hemings. As his slave, she was bound to him. In addition, given the excessive

Phoenix Books Rutland

2 Center St. Suite 1
Rutland, VT 05701
(802) 855-8078
www.phoenixbooks.biz

Cust: **None**

08-Oct-15 1:13p	Clerk: R2REG
Trns. #: 70000728	Reg: 2

9781608195435	*Jefferson And Hamilt*
1 @ $20.00	$20.00

Sub-total:	$20.00
Tax @ 6.000%:	$1.20

Total:	**$21.20**

* Non-Tax Items

Items: 1	Units: 1

Payment Via:

CASH	$22.00

Change (Cash)	**$0.80**

racism in Virginia, and indeed throughout the United States, she had little prospect of a better life than she had at Monticello. She was most unlikely to abandon him.

A world away from Monticello, Alexander Hamilton remained deeply involved in politics. In the summer of 1793, just before Jefferson told the president of his unequivocal plans to retire, Hamilton had informed Washington of his intention to leave the cabinet once he submitted some "propositions" to Congress. Hamilton wanted to stay on until he had removed all suspicions about his conduct as treasury secretary. He was doing just what Jefferson was at that moment. Jefferson feared that to step down in the summer of 1793 would leave the impression that he had been driven from office by Hamilton, who was whaling away at him in essays about Genêt and neutrality. Similarly, Hamilton worried that to retire in mid-1793 would cause some to suspect that he had fled office before Congressman Giles, with more "time for due examination," could resume his inquiry into the treasury secretary's possible misconduct. Taking the rarest of rare steps in American political history, Hamilton asked Congress to reopen Giles's investigation, adding that "the more comprehensive it is, the more agreeable it will be to me."[43]

There must have been many times when Hamilton regretted the step he had taken. Congress opened its weeks-long hearings in March 1794. Hamilton was compelled to make one report after another to prove that he had never acted improperly, especially in stock speculation and the use of monies designated for settling the domestic debt. Hard-pressed, Hamilton on one occasion appealed to Washington to certify that he had acted with the president's approval. Washington's response disappointed him. Instead of a ringing defense, the president merely said that he had authorized what Hamilton had proposed to do, so long as he acted legally. Hurt by the president's tepid answer, Hamilton once again beseeched Washington's help in his battle against the "false and insidious" congressmen, begging the president to do more to show that his treasury secretary was "a man of honor." Nothing more came from Washington, who was more accustomed to being shielded than to risking his reputation in the defense of others. Washington's ambivalence notwithstanding, Hamilton was fully vindicated by Congress.[44]

It is somewhat surprising that Hamilton did not quit once he was exonerated. Given his consuming emphasis on personal honor and the many times he had come to Washington's defense, Hamilton must have been furious with the president's less-than-resilient backing. Yet, Hamilton stayed on, serving for nearly another year. By the time the congressional inquiry ended, the Washington administration was enmeshed in its most crisis-laden twelve-month period, a time of both peril and opportunity for Hamiltonianism. What is more, with Jefferson gone—and succeeded by Edmund Randolph, a relative lightweight—Hamilton was able to dominate the cabinet as never before.

While Hamilton coped with the congressional investigation, he was embroiled in the battle over imposing discriminatory rates on British imports, the step that Jefferson had urged in his final act as secretary of state. Madison had followed Jefferson's report by reintroducing his 1789 resolution to discriminate through tariffs and restrictions against nations that had not signed a commercial treaty with the United States. British commercial hegemony was making America dangerously dependent on London, Madison declared, adding that in time "our taste, our manners, and our form of Government itself" would be shaped by British influences. Madison faced determined opposition and resistance by Federalist representatives. Fisher Ames of Massachusetts and William Loughton Smith of South Carolina led the fight against reciprocity, though Jefferson, at Monticello, had only to read Smith's fifteen-thousand-word speech assailing the measure to know in an instant that Hamilton was "its true father." (The content was so "ingenious," Jefferson said, that Smith's extemporaneous reply to Madison on the House floor demonstrated that he had not comprehended what Hamilton had prepared for him.)[45]

Through Smith, Hamilton couched his argument against discrimination largely in terms of American national security. The thrust of his reasoning was that discrimination would provoke retaliation, ending British investment in America, the fuel driving the new nation's economic growth. Leaving nothing to happenstance, Hamilton appealed to a wider audience through two newspaper essays. As always, his arguments were canny, not to say misleading. (Jefferson applied the term "sophistry" to them.) Contending that the purpose of discrimination was to weaken the British war effort against France, Hamilton engaged in a philippic against the "atrocious depravity" of the French Revolution, which should preclude "material service to the cause of France." Hamilton's rhetorical brilliance was not solely responsible for winning the battle, but in the final days of winter, America's farmers and city workers—envisaging uncultivated fields and barren harbors—lost their taste for discrimination. Sensing that victory was slipping away, Madison played for time. He postponed a vote in the House, telling Jefferson that their best hope was that London take some provocative step that "would strengthen the arguments for retaliation."[46]

London obliged. The British fleet in the Caribbean immediately enforced the Orders in Council, which kicked in at the outset of the year. By March, newspapers bulged with listings of American merchant ships and cargoes that had been seized. In no time, 250 American vessels had fallen victim to the British navy. Numerous American seamen had also been taken captive and impressed into the British navy. War fever swept the country. Madison wished to avoid war in 1794 as much as Jefferson had a year earlier during the neutrality crisis, but reciprocity aside, the House leader seemed not to know what to do. He sorely missed Jefferson, who was more adroit both at recognizing the broad contours of an issue and at sensing the vulnerabilities of an adversary.

Hamilton and the Federalists filled the vacuum, seizing the initiative with greater success than at any time since the bank fight more than three years before. Fearing that London's policy would nourish Anglophobia, which could result in the destruction of his financial system, Hamilton thought it essential that the Federalists control America's response to Britain's provocations. But there was more. From the beginning, he had sought the creation of a fiscal-military state, and over the years, his party had pushed with success to increase the size of the American army. In the five years since Washington's first inauguration, America's army had grown from five hundred to five thousand men. Hamilton now asserted that a "respectable military posture" required the expansion of the army by an additional twenty thousand men. Madison knew that augmenting the army was "absurd," as there was no prospect of a British invasion. He divined that the Federalists were employing an "old trick," one that he knew well from his days as a Nationalist. The Federalists were magnifying the sense of crisis in order to turn "every contingency into a resource for accumulating force in the Government," much as they had done with Shays' Rebellion and other purported emergencies. Jefferson saw things in the same light: "Not that the Monocrats and Papermen . . . want war; but they want armies and debts," he said.[47]

Given what he called America's "antient hatred of Gr. Britain," Jefferson thought war was possible unless the crisis was quickly resolved. Neither he nor Madison wanted war and both continued to believe that only trade discrimination would compel London to back down. As such a policy was never tried, it cannot be known whether it would have been effective, but as trade with America was merely one-sixth of Britain's total commerce, the odds against its success were considerable. In the end, it was the Federalists who had Washington's ear, and they coalesced around seeking a negotiated settlement. While Federalist spokesmen took a hard line, party leaders met with Washington and beseeched him to send an envoy to London. There were dangers in that course. As America would have little leverage, the settlement might be undesirable, or if negotiations broke down, nothing might be left but commercial discrimination or war. But negotiations also offered hope. Talks could result in the termination of the Royal Navy's ruinous practices, and they might finally settle the differences left unresolved since the war. Hamilton told Washington that time was of the essence. If the Republicans were permitted to "excite and keep alive irritation and ill humour" toward Great Britain until they achieved reciprocity, an accommodation with London would be out of the question. To follow Jefferson's course, he added, would be to back Britain into a corner, leaving it to choose between war or "disgrace or disrepute," and London would never acquiesce in the latter.[48]

Washington must have known Hamilton well enough to know when he embroidered. Nevertheless, the president preferred an honorable peace. He was willing to give diplomacy a chance. Initially, Washington leaned toward dispatching Hamilton, who was backed by every major Federalist. But the Republicans howled. One Virginian told the president straightaway that "more than half America" would think it "unsafe to trust power in the hands of this person," and James Monroe warned Washington that because of Hamilton's well-known Anglophilia, his appointment would not only provoke the "strongest . . . dissatisfaction" in France but also taint any treaty that he negotiated. Privately, Jefferson allowed that Hamilton's selection would be "degrading." He thought the only reason that Washington was considering Hamilton was to remove him from the country, saving him from the "disgrace and . . . public execrations" that would ensue when his economic system collapsed, as surely it would.[49]

Aware of the firestorm, and possibly of the damage his long-term ambitions would suffer should the mission to London end in failure, Hamilton removed himself from consideration. He cited the "collateral obstacles" that his appointment would entail. Washington quickly named John Jay instead. The selection outraged most Republicans, who dismissed Jay as a clone of Hamilton. One Democratic-Republican chapter in western Pennsylvania questioned whether Washington realized there were competent men available besides New York Anglophiles. It added that the president had so sequestered himself from the public that he had become akin to the "grand sultan of Constantinople." Madison correctly told Jefferson that this was "the most powerful blow ever suffered by the popularity of the President," as he had never before been so savagely attacked.[50]

The fury provoked by Jay's appointment was not the only cause of western resentment toward the Washington administration. Hatred of Great Britain was intense among frontier settlers who vividly remembered the Revolutionary War and were all too aware that the British government continued to occupy its western posts and arm the Indians in the Ohio Country. Large numbers of these frontiersmen were tenant farmers who lived hardscrabble lives, and they reasoned that if the British had been made to quit their posts, the fertile lands in trans-Appalachia would have been safe for settlement. But after five years of Washington's presidency, the British and their Indian allies were still there. Moreover, if Spain had been compelled to open the Mississippi River to American commerce, the frontiersmen would by now have transitioned from dirt farmers to commercial farmers, as they could be exporting their goods downriver to the West Indies, Europe, and America's East Coast cities. They knew that Genêt had offered a plan for opening the Mississippi, but Washington had sent him packing and the great river remained closed. Now, Washington's envoy extraordinary to London was John Jay, who a decade earlier had been willing to surrender his country's claims to the Mississippi River. Given their plight, the one thing that might have provided these farmers with a discretionary income had been the sale of the whiskey they distilled, but Washington's administration had levied the so-called whiskey tax on them. The feeling was rife among these surly westerners that Washington's government was dominated by elite northeastern speculators who were indifferent to the predicament facing those who lived on the frontier.[51]

In reality, no one wanted to resolve the problems that faced the western settlers more than Washington, and he tried to do so with the limited resources at his disposal. From the outset of his administration, the president had set both Hamilton and Jefferson to discussing with London's envoys the end of British occupation of the western post. Those talks were unavailing. What is more, the president had sent two armies beyond the mountains to pacify the Indians, but both had suffered mortifying defeats. A third army was gathering in 1794, to be led by Anthony Wayne, a former Continental army general.

But if Washington had diligently sought to resolve those deep-seated problems, the policies of his administration contributed to the western difficulties that he faced in 1794. That year's crisis was sparked by the excise on distilled liquor. To pay for the assumption of state debts, Hamilton had advocated, and obtained, the whiskey tax three years earlier. The levy imposed a heavy burden on western farmers. Staggering overhead costs prevented them from transporting their corn across the mountains to eastern markets, but a couple of mules could carry several kegs of their corn whiskey to those same markets, where its sale to thirsty city dwellers would net a nifty profit. Those profits, however, would largely be wiped out by the whiskey tax. In addition, the farmers saw the legislation as unfair on several counts. For one thing, large distillers—all in the East—paid less than small farmers, for they were assessed a per-gallon tax while farmer-distillers paid according the gallon capacity of their still. For another, the small western farmers who paid the excise on spirits knew that the ultimate beneficiaries of the duties imposed on them would be wealthy easterners who owned the federal securities sold to pay for funding and assumption. Nothing about the whiskey tax was accidental. Within the interstices of Hamilton's plan was a scheme not merely for transferring wealth from the least affluent to the most prosperous but also for the transference of economic and political power from the west, which had been solidly anti-Federalist, to northern and eastern cities, the Federalist base.[52]

When Congress considered the excise on spirits, Jefferson had warned the president that it was "odious" to take from the lowly and give to the stockjobbers. He added that the tax would produce "clamour [and] evasion" and that its collection would require "arbitrary and vexatious means," including possibly making "war on our own citizens." Five state legislatures condemned the proposed tax, with some asserting—as Washington acknowledged—that the legislation "could never be executed in the Southern states." Some in Congress predicted that "war and bloodshed" would result if the tax was enacted. Nor was Washington unaware that many believed Hamilton supported the excise on whiskey as the means of provoking western resistance, affording the administration with a golden opportunity to demonstrate the power and authority of the new government. Both Washington and Hamilton knew that numerous alternative sources of revenue existed, among them a land tax, a stamp tax, or an increase in the impost. Hamilton did not favor them, as they would have fallen heaviest on speculators, eastern merchants, and the most affluent in general. Moreover, the president, who was trying to sell the thousands of acres he owned in the West, was not interested in taxing land. In the end, Washington listened to Hamilton rather than Jefferson and nearly a third of the states. The whiskey tax passed a deeply divided Congress, in large measure because of the president's backing.[53]

Trouble was not long in coming. The first tax collectors sent to western Pennsylvania in 1791 were beaten or tarred and feathered, or both. Federal officials were assaulted throughout the South and in Kentucky, a new federal territory, but Pennsylvania witnessed the greatest violence and the most intemperate public protest. Democratic-Republican Societies everywhere denounced the excise, but the Mingo County chapter near Pittsburgh took steps to foster an organized resistance to the tax. Eighteen months after the law went into effect, not one cent in revenue had been collected in western Pennsylvania.

The dissidents knew there was danger in protest, but they saw their struggle as a battle on behalf of democracy, and some of their leaders believed that democracy involved more than just voting. Democracy included the more general right to take a stand against oppressive government. It was not long before the Federalist press took aim on the anti-tax insurgents. Indeed, Federalists seized on the disorders in western Pennsylvania as a pretext for savaging the Democratic-Republican Societies as traitors. As early as 1792 rumors buzzed through the mountains and hollows in western Pennsylvania that Hamilton "wishe[d] to make us examples." This rumor was well grounded, for in private Hamilton was urging the president to use force. He counseled that "vigorous & decisive measures" were necessary, lest the "spirit of disobedience . . . extend" and render the government "prostrate." He added: "Moderation enough has been shewn." Hamilton never understood farmers and their problems, or if he did, he remained indifferent toward those whom he knew would never support the Federalist agenda. Washington had a different perspective. Although he shortsightedly attributed the western resistance to those who had always opposed a strong national government, he feared that a harsh response might destroy their loyalty to the United States. Before he resorted to force, the president wished to try "lenient & temporizing means" to dampen the "daring and unwarrantable" defiance. Otherwise, the public would say: "The cat is let out." That is, the citizenry would be confirmed in their suspicion that the law had originated from a wish to crush the anticipated rebellion with armed might.[54]

Spurning Hamilton's heavy-handed approach, Washington got the duty on spirits lowered, tried other taxes, and dispatched emissaries to the frontier to offer both reason and cajolery. The West cooled down for a year, but by 1794 it had combusted again, ignited by Britain having gone to war against France, its seizure of American ships and seamen, and Washington's selection of Jay as his envoy to London. Not only had no revenue been collected in western Pennsylvania during the twelve months prior to mid-1794, but also the Democratic-Republican Societies were savaging the administration, accusing Washington of having surrounded himself with aristocrats and Anglophiles.[55]

In August 1794, Washington convened his cabinet, together with Pennsylvania's governor and assorted state officials, for one final discussion. The governor pleaded with the president not to use force, arguing that the western farmers trusted the state and could be brought to terms peacefully. Knox and Hamilton, on the other hand, demanded "an immediate resort to Military force." The following day, at Washington's behest, Hamilton submitted a written opinion. Labeling the frontiersmen's defiance as nothing less than "Treason," he advised that "the very existence of Government demands" that the rebellion be crushed. Hamilton urged the president to raise a military force of 12,000 men. Washington listened to his treasury secretary. After issuing a proclamation couched in language that resembled George III's declaration in 1775 that the colonists were rebels, the president summoned 12,950 militiamen to active service, appointed Virginia's governor and former Continental army cavalry officer Henry Lee to command the force, and turned loose Hamilton to rip the whiskey rebels in the press. Hamilton's hyperbole reached new heights in the four "Tully" essays that followed. He alleged that westerners were engaged in a "dark conspiracy" to force the United States into war with Great Britain. Their rebellion must be crushed, he said, in order to preserve "every thing . . . dear to a free . . . people."[56]

Leaving behind his pregnant wife—who suffered a miscarriage in his absence—Hamilton on October 4 donned full military regalia and rode west with the president.[57] At Carlisle, Washington took charge of a larger army than he had commanded much of the time during the Revolutionary War. Being back in military surroundings was an intoxicant for Hamilton. He was swept up by cadence of marching soldiers, the stirring sounds of drums and fifes, and the sight of Washington in his familiar old uniform astride his white charger. Hamilton, on his mount, was ready for glory.

Washington did not linger with the army. Unwilling to tarnish his reputation by killing American citizens, the president soon departed for Mount Vernon, surrendering command to Governor Lee. Hamilton displayed no reluctance to spill blood. He vengefully called those who defied federal law "madmen" and "wicked insurgents." Denying that he was "a quixot," Hamilton loudly proclaimed that every whiskey rebel must be "skewered, shot, or hanged on the first tree." He even pressed fellow Federalists in Congress to enact a "law regulating a process of outlawry" so that the insurgents' property might be confiscated and those who fled could be hunted down and legally killed. The utmost "vigour" was essential, he said, in order to root out the "political putrefaction of Pennsylvania."[58]

The pomp and ceremony of the first days at Carlisle soon gave way to reality. Once the army began its westward march, appalling supply shortages persisted. The "troops are every where a head of their supplies," Hamilton complained. Not long passed before he called what was happening an embarrassment. Next, he began to suspect chicanery on the part of teamsters and businessmen. "I directed some Cloathing to be forwarded. Not an iota of them has arrived," he fulminated a week into the march. For that matter, "Not a shoe, blanket or ounce of ammunition" had reached the men. Pennsylvania's autumn nights were chilly, and men suffered from "nakedness," just as their predecessors had in the War of Independence. Frantically, Hamilton wrote to authorities in Philadelphia: "For God's sake . . . Let some cloathing come forward."[59] The officers, of course, lived more comfortably, just as in the last war. It was a pattern that prompted the author of the most complete history of the Whiskey Rebellion to write: "The journals of officers often read like tourist guides to taverns and scenery along the route, while enlisted men's diaries recounted weeks of hunger and cold."[60]

The campaign provided Hamilton with little glory, as the insurgents did not put up a fight. The army rounded up some 150 suspected rebels, many of whom were treated harshly before being released. Only 20 were held for prosecution, and they were forced to make a pitiless winter's march across Pennsylvania to Philadelphia to stand trial. Hoping they would be treated unsparingly, Hamilton confided to the president that he longed for the judiciary to make examples of them as "traitors." Ultimately, just 2 of the whiskey rebels were convicted. One was an imbecile, the other a madman. Washington pardoned both.[61]

Jefferson neither defended nor assailed the whiskey rebels, but he was appalled by Washington's decision to send "such an armament against people at their ploughs." He saw hypocrisy in the administration's patience in the face of "the kicks and scuffs of our [British] enemies" on the high seas, yet its haste at "arming one part of the society against another." It was clear to him that Hamilton was behind the use of force. Raising the army, said Jefferson, answered the treasury secretary's "favorite purposes of strengthening government and increasing the public debt; and therefore an insurrection was announced and proclaimed and armed against, and marched against, but could never be found."[62]

Jefferson was not surprised that in his absence Hamilton had come close to becoming America's equivalent of a prime minister, but he was shocked by what came next. In his annual State of the Union address, Washington defended his action, attributing the insurgency to the Democratic-Republican Societies, which through the "arts of delusion" had "fostered and embittered" the "passions" of the western farmers.[63] It was a theme that would be repeated throughout American political history by those who cried that dissent was unfounded and due to the manipulation of the likes of "reds" and "outside agitators."

Republicans were furious. In its official response to the speech, the House of Representatives pointedly refused to censure the Democratic-Republican Societies. Jefferson was no less outraged, as he saw Washington's remarks as a direct assault on free speech. Believing he had long since divined Hamilton part and parcel, Jefferson now understood something else. As Madison put it to him, the president's actions and speech amounted to the "final triumph" of the Federalists, for they had brought Washington into their camp. Jefferson concurred.[64]

CHAPTER 12

"A COLOSSUS TO THE ANTIREPUBLICAN PARTY"

THE ELECTION OF 1796

SOON AFTER RETURNING from western Pennsylvania, Hamilton notified Washington of his intention to leave the cabinet at the end of January 1795. As the treasury secretary had already postponed his retirement for eighteen months, Washington made no attempt to dissuade Hamilton, though the president acknowledged that he had always wished to prevent his leaving. Thereafter, in a nearly identical letter to the one he had written when Jefferson departed, Washington thanked Hamilton for his steadfast service and loyalty.[1]

Skepticism greeted newspaper accounts that Hamilton was forced to return to private life by his "poverty," but it was true.[2] He was in debt. Unlike a host of today's public figures, Hamilton had not grown rich from public service. But he estimated that within five or six years of reopening his law practice, he would be on his feet again.[3]

Friends understood his plight, though even they doubted Hamilton when he said that he never planned to return to public life.[4] He was only forty, three years younger than Washington had been when he had taken command of the Continental army and the same age as Jefferson when the war ended. Moreover, Hamilton confided to acquaintances that he expected his legal work to be "much less" satisfying than his years as treasury secretary. Attentive friends saw him as restless and ambitious, not especially interested in personal wealth but obsessed with the power and authority of the national government. They had heard him admit that Jeffersonianism "haunts me every step I take" and remark that a part of him believed that Jefferson would not long remain in retirement. They had also heard him express concern that public opinion was swinging away from the Federalists. Some had heard him state that it was "Torture" to watch Madison and Aaron Burr, among other Republicans, as they "sported with" the destruction of the *good footing* he had fabricated for the nation through his funding and banking systems.

Friends knew that Hamilton was convinced that the Jeffersonians would harm the nation, even that they loved the United States less than he did. They heard him wonder: "Am I then more of an American than those who drew their first breath on American Ground?"[5]

Hamilton spent several leisurely weeks with his family in Albany, but as summer approached he rented a house and office in Manhattan and resumed his legal practice. He had been tending to the law only a month before Washington reached out to him.

Just days after Hamilton departed Philadelphia, the president received the treaty that John Jay had negotiated. Washington was disappointed. One look at the Jay Treaty must have convinced him that Jefferson had been correct all along in saying that Great Britain would not alter its stance toward America. While London agreed to pay compensation for the damages that had resulted from its seizure of American ships and cargoes, it refused to liberalize its trade policies with America. Nor would London shorten its outlandishly lengthy list of contraband items, indemnify slave owners for their chattel taken away by British armed forces during the late war, or recognize the right of neutrals to trade with whomever they wished in wartime. Furthermore, Jay's negotiations produced nothing new with regard to America's western problems. His accord replicated the terms of the Treaty of Paris of 1783: Britain was to evacuate the northwest posts and Americans were to pay the prewar debts owed British creditors. The president was most disappointed by Article XII. He had hoped that London would open its West Indian ports to American shipping. Instead, only small American ships—vessels about one-fifth the size of ordinary merchant ships—would be permitted to trade in those ports, and in addition, America's merchants were forbidden to re-export goods from the West Indies to other parts of the world.

Washington knew the Jay Treaty would trigger a firestorm. He also knew that the pact's rejection might set in motion a trail of events leading to war with Britain and its ally Spain, two powerful nations whose colonies stretched along the flanks and hindquarters of the United States. Washington wanted peace, fearing disaster for the weak, strife-torn United States in another round of warfare. He opted to submit the treaty to the Senate, where the Federalists held precisely the two-thirds majority needed for ratification. To help assure this outcome, the president kept the terms of the treaty secret until the Senate met. It was a savvy move that prevented a lengthy onslaught in the Republican press prior to Senate action, and it worked. Voting along political and sectional lines, the Senate ratified the Jay Treaty, though its approval was conditional on the exclusion of Article XII. Every Federalist voted for ratification, every Republican against it; 90 percent of those voting for ratification represented northern states, and 70 percent who voted against it were from southern or western states.

Once ratification was out of the way, Washington had to decide whether to accept the treaty. He first asked Hamilton to assess the accord. It was the president's first communication with Hamilton in the four months since the treasury secretary had left his cabinet. Washington had not inquired about Hamilton's well-being in retirement—nor had he asked Jefferson how he was doing—and in a businesslike letter devoid of niceties, he simply requested Hamilton's opinion.[6]

Hamilton responded within a couple of days with a six-thousand-word answer. He analyzed the treaty article by article, quibbling about much of the wording, as if to say that he might have done a better job, though on the whole he was positive. In 1789 Hamilton had told Colonel Beckwith that the United States would agree to trade in the British West Indies even if London restricted the size of America's vessels; however, he now objected to Article XII, calling it "unprecedented & wrong." Even so, he urged acceptance of the treaty, asserting that it "closes . . . as reasonably as could have been expected the controverted points between the two countries." Hamilton added that the Jay Treaty not only assured that the United States would regain its western posts, "an object of primary consequence in our affairs," but also, and above all, it would enable the United States to escape "the dreadful war which is ruining Europe."[7]

On very nearly the same day that Hamilton first saw the treaty, Jefferson received a copy from one of Virginia's two senators. Jefferson's reaction could hardly have been more different. Though he did not speak out publicly, Jefferson told correspondents that the accord was "infamous," "a monument of folly or venality," and a "treaty of alliance between England and the Anglo-men of this country against . . . the people of the United states." Even at the risk of war, Jefferson said he preferred reciprocity to the Federalists' treaty with their "patron-nation."[8]

Hamilton meanwhile wasted little time before publicly defending the treaty. His action was part of another astute strategy on the part of the president. Washington might have accepted the treaty in mid-July, as there is no reason to believe that his views differed in the least from those of Hamilton, but he wanted public opinion to form in support of the treaty before he acted. Washington claimed that he was awaiting the advice of "dispassionate" men before making up his mind, but Hamilton was the only person he consulted, and the president had his answer within three weeks of the Senate's vote. Having gotten Hamilton's opinion, Washington as much as asked his former secretary to publicly defend the Jay Treaty against its attackers, who he said were howling "like . . . a mad-dog." Washington even coached him on what to say in defense of the treaty.[9]

Hamilton required neither mentoring nor arm twisting to spring into action. The Jay Treaty was crucial for his economic program. In mid-July, he spoke at a public meeting outside New York's City Hall, a gathering called by Republicans who wished to draft a statement beseeching Washington not to sign the treaty. A rowdy crowd of some five hundred mostly anti-treaty proponents were still present when Hamilton spoke late in the afternoon. Hecklers had a field day. Some tried to shout him down, others to silence him by "hissings, coughings, and hootings." Rocks were hurled at him. According to a suspect story that circulated, Hamilton was struck in the head, after which he responded: "if you use such knock-down arguments, I must retire." He did angrily storm off the speaker's stand and soon thereafter came close to fisticuffs with some in the crowd. Still later on this busy, hot day, Hamilton challenged two men who verbally assaulted him to duels. One had slandered him by accusing him of cowardice for once having refused to fight a duel. Both accepted Hamilton's challenges, though in the end cooler heads prevailed and the combatants never faced off on the dueling ground.[10]

Hamilton subsequently spoke to friendlier audiences of merchants and Federalists, but his principal activity was to do as Washington wished. He wrote polemics that sought to alter public opinion. Hamilton collaborated with Senator Rufus King of New York to produce thirty-eight pieces in a series titled "The Defence." Hamilton penned almost three-fourths of the essays, often churning out three a week, and he rushed his first into print only eight days after hearing from the president.

Hamilton opened with his familiar slash-and-burn tactics. The foes of the Jay Treaty, he charged, were Francophiles who for years had been "steadily endeavouring to make the United States a party in the present European war." What is more, the treaty's opponents wished to prevent a normalization of relations with London in order to improve Jefferson's chances of succeeding Washington. Thereafter, he largely elaborated on the points he had made privately to Washington. His most crucial argument was that the United States would not be adequately prepared for war for at least another decade. The beauty of the Jay Treaty was that it prevented immediate hostilities while buying time to resolve other issues that strained Anglo-American relations. It offered hope that "we may . . . postpone war to a distant period."[11]

Washington was pleased, and after reading the partisan assault on the Jeffersonians, the president congratulated Hamilton on the "satisfactory manner" of his response. By the time Hamilton's eighth essay appeared, Washington had signed the treaty into law and privately told his confederate that he "sincerely regret[ted]" that he no longer was part of the cabinet. It was a sentiment the president never expressed to Jefferson.[12]

Hamilton was unaware of perhaps the greatest compliment paid to him. It came from Jefferson, who recognized that Hamilton was at least in part responsible for a shift in public opinion toward the treaty. Even the merchants, Jefferson said, had originally been "open-mouthed . . . against the treaty," but Hamilton had brought them around. Through what Jefferson called Hamilton's "boldest act," the "hue and cry" against the pact had been redirected onto its foes. To these tributes, Jefferson lauded what his adversary had been able to achieve: "Hamilton is really a colossus to the antirepublican party. Without numbers, he is an host within himself."[13]

Jefferson encouraged Madison to take on Hamilton in the press. Though Madison demurred, he fought the treaty in the House of Representatives by attempting to block the appropriations needed to implement the accord. Jefferson neither criticized nor endorsed such a strategy, though in a sense he had encouraged Madison, telling him that the Federalists "have got themselves into a defile."[14] Jefferson reasoned that in time, when the public understood that the Jay Treaty imperiled France, opinion would turn against the act. Madison gambled on that premise, but lost. He stretched out the battle deep into the spring of 1796, but ultimately lost the contest when the House agreed by a three-vote margin to appropriate the funds.

During the nip-and-tuck battle, Washington had again encouraged Hamilton to "shew the impropriety" of Madison's action. Hamilton immediately rushed out a broadside arguing that the House had no constitutional authority on the subject of treaties. The issue was stark: The "CONSTITUTION and PEACE are in one scale—the overthrow of the CONSTITUTION and WAR in the other." Madison, he charged, was acting on behalf of a "VIRGINIA FACTION, constantly endeavoring" to plunge the United States into one of Europe's "most dreadful Wars." Jefferson and Madison thought that Washington's foursquare support of the treaty had saved it, but with votes up for grabs even in New York's delegation in the House, and the outcome razor-thin, Hamilton's last-ditch essay may have been no less crucial.[15]

The long battle over the Jay Treaty was important in another sense. To this point, neither the Federalists nor the Republicans were true political parties, but the life-and-death issues at stake in this foreign policy clash caused both to begin construction of what one historian has called "national policy machinery."[16] The emergence of something resembling modern political parties may have been about to occur anyway. Rumors abounded that Washington, who would turn sixty-five just as his second term ended, planned to step down. If so, the election of 1796 would be the first real presidential election and party organization could be the difference between victory and defeat.

Washington was ready to go home. He was physically and emotionally exhausted, and enraged by the steady drumbeat of criticism in the press for his support of the Jay Treaty. He had also achieved everything he had set out to accomplish. The Union was intact, the once-sagging economy was doing well, and at last the West would be opening to a massive influx of settlers. The latter was due to the Jay Treaty and General Anthony Wayne's victory over the Indians in the Battle of Fallen Timbers in 1794. But the West would also be opening because Spain, apprehensive that the Jay Treaty signaled an Anglo-American alliance, had agreed in the Pinckney Treaty in 1795 to open the Mississippi River and New Orleans to American commerce. (The treaty was the result of the mission to Madrid that Jefferson had declined in the summer of 1794.)

When Washington made up his mind to retire, he called on Hamilton one last time. While Hamilton was in Philadelphia in February 1796 to argue a case before the Supreme Court of the United States, Washington asked him to draft his farewell address.[17] Hamilton not only knew how Washington thought; he also knew that he had often helped to shape the president's thinking. In this instance, Hamilton prepared a carefully crafted valedictory address that highlighted what he knew to be on Washington's mind, while at the same time advancing the interests of the Federalist Party in the looming presidential election, a contest that he believed the president hoped the Federalists would win. Washington altered the wording, if not the meaning, of some sections in the drafts presented to him, and he curtailed Hamilton's verbosity and bombast, giving the speech a more statesmanlike sheen. Once the work was done, the president thanked Hamilton with uncustomary warmth, signing his final letter: "With true respect & attachment." Washington issued the Farewell Address in September.

The final product of the Washington-Hamilton collaboration stressed the importance of the Union and the necessity of obeying the government. By branding dissenters as "cunning, ambitious and unprincipled men" who threatened to "impair the energy of the system," it included a thinly veiled defense of Hamilton's fiscal program. It warned of the danger of foreign alliances and made a camouflaged appeal to the citizenry to overcome their enmity toward Great Britain.[18]

Republicans construed the address as unvarnished partisanship. They were sure it revealed that Washington was "completely in the snares" of the Federalist Party, as they put it. Furthermore, as Washington issued his "Adieu"—as Jefferson called it—six months before the end of his term, Republicans also saw the Farewell Address as the Federalists' first shot in the presidential election of 1796.[19]

Hamilton may have thought about running for president, and if so, it was likely a fleeting thought. He knew that New England believed its turn had come to have one of its own in the presidency, and Vice President John Adams was a New Englander. Besides, Adams had served long and well. He had spent three years in Congress, where he led the fight for independence, and almost a decade abroad as an American diplomat before his eight aimless years in the vice presidency. In the minds of many, Adams's service made him Washington's heir apparent. It was now or never for Adams, who was twenty years older than Hamilton, and New England wanted it to be now. So did Adams. The moment that Washington informed his cabinet that he planned to step down, Adams told his wife that he would be a candidate.[20]

Soon thereafter Adams wrote to Jefferson. It was unusual for Adams to write the Virginian, for their once-close relationship had been a casualty of political passions. When Jefferson became secretary of state, he and the Adamses had picked up where they had left off during their days in Europe. They socialized frequently, often arguing vehemently about politics, especially after Adams in 1790 published essays in which he appeared to defend monarchical government. Yet, not even those disagreements corroded their affection for each other. However, when a private letter written by Jefferson that criticized Adams was published, their relationship was sundered. Jefferson had complained about "the political heresies that have sprung up," and it was clear that he was alluding to Adams, among others, as a republican heretic. Adams was outraged, Jefferson horrified. Adams felt betrayed. It was one thing for Jefferson to say something like that in private, but quite another for him to slander Adams behind his back. Jefferson tried to make amends. Adams would have none of it. Their friendship died.[21]

When Adams wrote to Jefferson early in 1796, he was fishing to discover his former friend's intentions in the pending election. Both were cordial but insincere in their brief correspondence, and both knew it. Adams waxed on about his longing to retire; Jefferson replied that he hated politics.[22] Jefferson knew that Adams would seek the presidency. Adams assumed that Jefferson could not avoid seeking it.

For some time Jefferson had encouraged Madison to run for the presidency when Washington retired. In turn, Madison asked Jefferson to run, once beseeching him not to "abandon [his] historical task." Madison wrote, "You owe it to yourself, to truth, to the world." Jefferson evinced no interest. He would not abandon retirement to become the emperor of the universe, he once said, and fifteen months after leaving Washington's cabinet, he declared that returning to public office was a "question [that] is for ever closed with me." The springs of ambition that once had driven him, he added, have long since withered."[23]

Madison and others who visited Monticello throughout 1796 implored Jefferson to enter the race, but they did so gently, fearing that if pushed too hard, he would bind himself with an unequivocal refusal. Jefferson's mind on this subject remains impenetrable, though if his correspondence is a guide, at this juncture he was genuinely uninterested in the presidency. It is true that he was disturbed by the unchecked successes of the "Anglomen" since he had retired. He told a correspondent that there were two American political parties, "One which fears the people most, the other [fears] the government." That which feared the people, the Federalist Party, had enjoyed a resurgence. In the past two years it had suppressed the Whiskey Rebellion, nearly silenced the Democratic-Republican Societies and others who applauded the French Revolution, and ratified the Jay Treaty. Disconcertingly, it had grown more popular in the process. But Jefferson attributed its success to having Washington—whom he called "the colossus"—on its side, and now the president was stepping down.[24]

Jefferson's reluctance to enter the contest in 1796 may also have stemmed from a belief that Adams was virtually assured of winning. The vice president seemed certain to capture all the electoral votes from New England, New York, and New Jersey, giving him fifty-eight of the seventy needed for victory. As the Federalists were also strong in Pennsylvania, Delaware, and Maryland, Adams was likely unbeatable. The prospect of Adams's election did not trouble Jefferson. The two disagreed on important issues, but Adams was neither an extremist nor an adventurer, and as a solid Yankee, he could be depended on to harbor no wish of shaping the United States on the template of Great Britain. However, from Jefferson's point of view, Adams's greatest virtue was his fierce independence. Unlike Washington, Adams would not be dominated by Hamilton or anyone else.

The election in 1796 was to be the nation's first contested battle for the presidency, although four years earlier the vice presidency had been an object of contention. Alarmed by Adams's pro-monarchical writings, some Republicans had conspired in 1792 to prevent his reelection, "removing the monarchical rubbish of our government," as one put it.[25] For the vice presidency, Pennsylvania's Republicans backed Aaron Burr, while the Republican leaders in Virginia preferred George Clinton.

Burr's political rise had been rapid. Following a stint in the state assembly, Governor Clinton named him attorney general of New York. Two years later, in 1791, Burr became a U.S. senator, unseating Hamilton's father-in-law,

Philip Schuyler. Paradoxically, his surging popularity may have cost him the vice presidency in 1792. It at least sank him with Madison and James Monroe. Fearing Burr as a looming rival to a Republican Party led by Jefferson, both did what they could to block the New Yorker's candidacy. As little escaped Jefferson's attention, and as Madison and Monroe consulted with him regularly, it is probable that Jefferson was aware of their activities, and not inconceivable that he was behind what they did.[26]

But the Southerners had not been Burr's only problem in 1792. Earlier that year, Hamilton had worked behind the scenes to thwart Burr's hopes of becoming governor of New York, and in the autumn he acted covertly to blacken Burr's reputation before the Electoral College met to vote in the presidential election. Hamilton assailed Burr as "unprincipled both as a public and private man" and the "worst sort" for high office, as he purportedly stood for nothing but that which "suits his interest and ambition."[27]

In some respects, the rivalry that had developed between Hamilton and Burr was odd, as the lives and careers of these two were strikingly similar. Both were orphaned—Burr while still a baby—and both became soldiers soon after college. During the Revolutionary War, each had seen considerable action and each had served as aides-de-camp—to Israel Putnam and Alexander McDougall in Burr's case. Each endured the grim winter at Valley Forge and each fought at Monmouth, where Burr suffered a serious heatstroke that ended his military service. Like Hamilton, Burr had married and started a family by the early 1780s, and at about the same time as Hamilton, he had opened a law office in Manhattan. At times, the two crossed swords in the courtroom, but on occasion they partnered to form a defense team. The two even bore something of a resemblance. They were nearly the same age and height—Burr was one year younger and one inch shorter—both were slightly built, and both impressed others as being noticeably striking, dashing even, in appearance.

But political activists make enemies. Once Burr captured Schuyler's Senate seat, his relationship with Hamilton changed. That same year, 1791, Burr met with Jefferson and Madison when the Virginians passed through Manhattan on their botanizing tour. From that moment forward, he was the target of "Hamilton's relentless political and personal attacks," as Burr's biographer Nancy Isenberg put it. During the presidential contest in 1792, Hamilton's sharp attacks on Burr were inspired by the realization that his rival loomed as a more serious threat than was Clinton to siphon votes from John Adams in the mid-Atlantic states.[28]

In the end, the Republicans in 1792 had backed Clinton for the vice presidency. He ran a distant second to Adams. Burr received only a single electoral vote.

In 1796 both the presidency and vice presidency were up for grabs. That year, and for some time thereafter, the nominees were selected by caucuses of each party's congressmen. As the Constitution mandated that each member of the Electoral College was to "vote by Ballot for two Persons" for the presidency, each party nominated two candidates. The Constitution also stipulated that the recipient of the greatest number of electoral votes, if a majority, was to become president; whoever received the second most votes, whether or not a majority, was to be the vice president. The Federalists in 1796 selected Adams and South Carolina's Thomas Pinckney, who had negotiated the recent treaty with Spain. Jefferson, the best-known Republican, had always been the first choice of the party's leaders. He never said that he would run for the presidency, but he never said unconditionally that he wouldn't, and in the end, the Republican caucus picked him. Burr had actively sought to be selected as one of the nominees. He politicked in Boston and Portsmouth, New Hampshire, after which he took the stage south to Pennsylvania and Virginia. He lingered in Virginia for three months mending fences, and made a one-day visit to Monticello to call on Jefferson.

Only Burr actively campaigned that autumn, spending six weeks in New England. It was a counterproductive tactic, as many southerners, especially Virginians, concluded that his objective was to beat out both Jefferson and Adams for the presidency.[29] The other nominees, following what had been the customary practice in the colonial era, remained at home throughout the campaign, trying their best to appear disinterested. But while most of the candidates were inactive, others were busy. Somewhere in the vicinity of 60 percent of all adult white males could vote in 1796, and they were courted by party activists with liquor and food at banquets and rallies that usually featured political speeches.[30] Above all, voters were wooed through broadsides, pamphlets, and newspapers.

Republican screeds depicted Jefferson as experienced and trustworthy, and as a champion of human rights. They assailed the Federalists as Anglophiles and aristocrats who wished to preserve a society with limited opportunities for commoners, and they portrayed Adams as a monarchist, limning the portly vice president as the "His Rotundity" and the "Duke of Braintree." The Federalists responded by calling Washington one of their own and painted Adams as a hero of the American Revolution. They boosted Adams as Washington's logical successor and depicted the Republicans as democrats, a term that had long been associated with social unrest and radical change. Federalists attacked Jefferson as "weak, wavering, indecisive," more a philosopher than a politician. He was probably suited to be a college president, it was said, but not the president of the United States. Some Federalists

twisted Jefferson's commitment to religious liberty to mean that he was secretly an atheist and a danger to Christianity. Jefferson was likely most disturbed by the tactics of Virginia Federalists, who dredged up his record as a
wartime governor and represented him as inept and timorous and as a leader
who had left the state in the lurch when he fled the enemy raiding party that
descended on Monticello. Jefferson did not respond to any of the attacks, but
supporters in Virginia rushed into print depositions defending his conduct as
governor, touting his bravery, and in one instance, arguing that in 1781 "the
government had abandoned Jefferson rather than the reverse."[31]

Hamilton remained in the shadows during this campaign, but he was a
major player nonetheless. His dictum was: " 'Tis all-important to our country
that [Washington's] successor shall be a safe man" and "that it shall not be Jefferson. We have every thing to fear if this man comes in. . . . [E]very thing
must give way to the great object of excluding Jefferson."[32] Driven by fear and
loathing, Hamilton in October and November rushed out twenty-five newspaper essays under the pen name "Phocion." He maligned Jefferson from
pillar to post, but especially sullied his character. Hamilton charged that in
three "critical moments"—in 1776, 1781, and again in 1794—Jefferson had
"skulked to a snug retreat," abandoning the nation in its hour of peril, fleeing
danger, failing to lead. Hamilton not only lauded Washington, but also insisted that Jefferson had "greatly disapproved and perseveringly opposed" the
first president's policies. He portrayed Jefferson as having "countenanced"
Genêt's malignant behavior, backing off only when public opinion turned
against the "meddling and crafty foreigner." He contended that Jefferson had
sought "to entangle the United States into altercations with England." Hamilton additionally vilified Jefferson for having "vindicated the horrors and
cruelties" of the French Revolution, claimed that he had plagiarized others
when preparing a report on weights and measures, and blasted the criminal
code that Jefferson had conceived in the 1770s as filled with "atrocious and
sanguinary cruelties."[33]

Almost alone, Hamilton raised questions about Jefferson and race. He
drew on passages from *Notes on the State of Virginia* to demonstrate Jefferson's racism. His objective was to reveal "the confusion of ideas which pervaded" the Virginian's thinking—son of the Enlightenment, yet a racist—and
to question Jefferson's right to be considered a "moral philosopher." However,
Hamilton did blast Jefferson's proposal that liberated slaves be uprooted and
colonized elsewhere, saying that, rooted in racism, such a practice would be
nearly as inhumane as slavery itself. The heart of his assault focused on Jefferson's seeming obsession with "preserving the beauty" of the white race, a
topic that led Phocion to bring up the allegedly rampant sexual exploitation

of female slaves on southern plantations. Miscegenation inevitably led to race mixing, or the "*stain of blood* of . . . her . . . master," to which Hamilton added: "He [Jefferson] must have seen all around him sufficient marks of this *staining of blood*."[34]

Knowledge of Jefferson's relationship with Sally Hemings was a topic of conversation in Charlottesville and among Virginia's politicians, and it was probably through his contacts with the latter that Hamilton had been made privy to the rumors. However, the general public outside Virginia was unaware of the gossip, and they could not have understood the meaning of Hamilton's swipe. So why did he allude to Jefferson's relationship with Sally Hemings? In all likelihood, he was telling the Jeffersonians that he was aware of the story and would make it public if they revealed his tryst with Maria Reynolds. Neither Hemings nor Reynolds surfaced in this campaign.

Hamilton was active in other ways, just as he had been during the two previous presidential elections. In 1789, Hamilton had labored behind the curtain to see that Washington was unanimously elected and that no second-choice candidate received an equal number of votes. In 1792, he had worked undercover to wreck both Burr's and Clinton's hopes of being chosen vice president. Adams knew little or nothing about Hamilton's intrusiveness in those campaigns, but he was aware of the rumors of the New Yorker's machinations in 1796.

Hamilton's greatest worry in 1796 was that some northern Federalist electors would withhold their second vote from Pinckney in order to assure Adams's election. If that occurred, Jefferson might slip in, capturing either the presidency or vice presidency. Hamilton wanted neither. He doubtless shared the view of Oliver Wolcott, who had succeeded him as treasury secretary, that Jefferson as chief executive would destroy the Constitution, as well as be "fatal to our independence." Like Wolcott, Hamilton may also have believed that Jefferson could do even greater harm as vice president, for in that office he would "become the rallying point of faction and French influence," sowing divisions and subverting Adams's presidency.[35] Acting on these presumed threats, Hamilton declared that his foremost objective was "the exclusion of Jefferson." He advised party stalwarts that "good calculation [and] prudence" dictated the avoidance of "unfortunate" risks. His wish, he said, was that every Federalist elector would cast his two votes for Adams and Pinckney. But Hamilton often had a hidden agenda, and that was the case in the election of 1796. He preferred Pinckney to Adams, as the South Carolinian might be more easily manipulated than the fiercely independent Yankee. Moreover, Hamilton believed that Pinckney had a better chance than Adams of accumulating some votes in the South. By calling for every Federalist elector to vote for Adams and Pinckney, Hamilton in reality was trying to engineer Pinckney's election as president.[36]

Rumors abounded regarding what Madison termed Hamilton's "Jockeyship" of electoral votes, leading Jefferson to conclude that Adams would be "cheated" out of the presidency by what he said was Hamilton's trickery. Madison even predicted that the New Yorker's scheming would force the issue into the House of Representatives, either from a tie or because no candidate received a majority of the votes. Throughout, Jefferson appeared unenthusiastic. "I had rather be thought worthy" of the presidency than to be elected president, he declared. Late in the fall, he told Madison that he hoped he would be defeated or, at worst, be elected vice president. One outcome "would leave me at home the whole year, and the other two thirds of it," he said. However, in the event that Adams finished in a dead heat with any candidate, Jefferson instructed his friend to use his influence in the House to secure Adams's election.[37]

The presidential electors met in December, and even before Christmas the public learned that Adams had been elected by a bare majority. Jefferson had finished second with three fewer votes, and was to become the vice president. As Jefferson had thought likely, Adams won every vote from New England, New York, and New Jersey. However, eighteen New England electors, fearful that Hamilton's intrigue would deny victory to Adams, cast their second vote for assorted Federalists other than Pinckney. That opened the door for Jefferson, who ran well in the South—he swept every vote from South Carolina, Georgia, Kentucky, and Tennessee—and captured fourteen of the fifteen votes from Pennsylvania.

The outcome of the contest turned on two things. Adams won two electoral votes below the Potomac, one in Virginia and one in North Carolina. Had Jefferson won those votes, he would have nosed out Adams by a margin of seventy to sixty-nine. But had all the Yankee Federalists cast their second vote for Pinckney, the South Carolinian would have received seventy-seven votes, making him the second president of the United States, the outcome that Hamilton had longed to see. Yet, it was Hamilton's connivance that may have cost Pinckney the election and put John Adams into the presidency.

Though it did not have an impact on the outcome, Burr's fate in the contest had ominous long-term implications. Virginia's twenty Republican electors were angered and disenchanted by Burr's campaigning in New England, and only one of them voted for him. Much later, Burr angrily remarked that "Virginians . . . are not to be trusted," and he emerged from the election with an ineradicable bitterness over what he believed had been his betrayal.[38] Burr had also struck out in New England, failing to win any of its thirty-nine votes. Success there had always been problematic, but if any one individual was responsible for snatching votes away from him, it was Hamilton, who had worked hard to keep the Federalist electors in line and who now was crowing that the electoral results "will not a little mortify *Burr*."[39] In all likelihood, the former treasury secretary's gloating got back to Burr, who could only conclude that for the third time in four years, Hamilton had played a major role in foiling his electoral ambitions.

Jefferson was the least disappointed loser of all time. If "I [have to] reappear at Philadelphia," he said, it was best to return as vice president. "I have no inclination to govern men," he told one correspondent. To another, he wrote: "Neither the splendor, nor the power, nor the difficulties, nor the fame, or [the] defamation" of the presidency held any appeal for him.[40]

Was Jefferson being truthful? Without a doubt. He was happy at home. He was aware that the Jay Treaty would likely damage relations with France, possibly bringing on a crisis with which he was not anxious to cope. And he knew that Washington's presidency would be a tough act to follow. For the time being, it was better to leave the presidency to Adams.

CHAPTER 13

"THE MAN IS STARK MAD"

PARTISAN FRENZY

HAMILTON DID NOT ATTEND Adams's inauguration. Jefferson considered not attending, but in the end thought he must appear "as a mark of respect to the public," and to silence the inevitable accusation that he considered "the second office as beneath my acceptance."[1]

After an eleven-day journey, Jefferson reached Philadelphia two days prior to the inaugural ceremony. He called on Adams that same afternoon. It was their first meeting in four years, and it was friendly, though nothing of great substance was said. Back in December, on learning the outcome of the election, Jefferson had written a missive of great importance to the president-elect. Although he did not expect that Adams would believe him, Jefferson insisted that he had not wanted to win the contest. "I leave to others the sublime delights of riding in the storm," Jefferson wrote. He predicted turbulent days ahead. The Jay Treaty would make an enemy of France, he warned, bringing on the gravest crisis since the Revolutionary War. Jefferson wished the incoming chief executive well. He advised that the extreme Federalists would demand war with France, but added that if Adams could "shun for us this war," the "glory will be all your own." Above all, Jefferson cautioned Adams about Hamilton, a man of great subtlety whose "spies and sycophants" abounded, and who would try to control the new administration.

Unfortunately, Adams never read Jefferson's letter. Before mailing it, Jefferson asked Madison to read it. Madison was aghast. The "general air" of the letter might tie Jefferson's hands in the event that he subsequently wished to speak out against Adams's policies, Madison thought. As for Hamilton's anticipated machinations, let Adams cope with that problem. Jefferson relented. The letter was never sent, and possibly because of that a closer relationship between the incoming vice president and president, one filled with many candid discussions, was aborted. Relations between Jefferson and Adams were destined to be distant and ill-tempered during the next four years.[2]

Though it may not have made a difference, it is possible that had Adams read Jefferson's warning about Hamilton's spies and toadies, the incoming president might have made different choices when selecting the members of his cabinet. Instead, Adams retained those who had served Washington, a collection of individuals whose first loyalty was to Hamilton. Adams's decision was baffling, as he had to know of their affinity for Hamilton. James McHenry, who stayed on as secretary of war, had been the best man at Hamilton's wedding, and Treasury Secretary Oliver Wolcott had served for four years as comptroller of the Treasury under Hamilton. Timothy Pickering, the disputatious secretary of state, had never been as close to Hamilton as the others, but the two had known each other since their days as fellow officers in the Continental army. From innocence and inexperience—Adams had never served in an executive capacity—the new chief executive never suspected that these men, two of whom were fellow Yankees, would betray the president they served. But if Adams could not see his folly, Jefferson could. He immediately concluded that the "Hamiltonians by whom he is surrounded . . . are only a little less hostile to him than to me."[3]

On the day after their pleasant meeting, twenty-four hours prior to his inauguration, Adams called on Jefferson. The incoming president wanted to talk about relations with France. The Directory, revolutionary France's latest government, regarded the Jay Treaty as an abrogation of the Franco-American alliance, and it soon announced its intention of seizing neutral vessels carrying British goods. Word of French confiscations on the high seas had begun to reach America. During their second visit, the incoming president asked Jefferson to sail to Paris and, as Jay had done in London, seek to negotiate an accommodation. Jefferson immediately declined, pleading not only that he was "sick of residing in Europe" but also that it would be improper for the vice president to be away for what would be at least a year. Adams next proposed Madison for the assignment. Madison's appointment would have launched Adams's presidency on a nonpartisan note, but given the Virginian's solid Republican credentials, his embassy might have reassured France's leaders of America's friendship. Jefferson approached his friend, but Madison, who was frightened of sailing, declined.[4] Had it not been for Madison's twin negatives—his counsel against Jefferson's demonstration of solidarity with Adams and his refusal to undertake the diplomatic mission—the course of the next four years might have been quite different.

On Inauguration Day—prior to learning of Madison's decision—Adams informed his treasury secretary that he had indirectly approached the Virginian about a diplomatic mission to France. Wolcott exploded, telling Adams that he and his cabinet colleagues would resign if Madison was appointed. Three weeks earlier, Hamilton had confided to a member of his party that any display of nonpartisanship by Adams would be resisted. Hamilton wanted "a united and a vigorous administration," he said, and to this he added a stunning admission: "If Mr. Adams has Vanity"—that is, should he attempt to chart an independent course—"a plot has been laid to take hold of it." Wolcott's action laid bare the intrigue that Hamilton had entered into with the cabinet. Hamilton and his devotees had conspired to bend the president of the United States to their will.[5]

Hamilton won the initial skirmish. Adams relented, telling his cabinet that he would instead appoint a three-member commission to sail for France. The president deferred a decision on the commission's composition for sixty days, until Congress gathered for a special session that he had called. All three cabinet members quickly wrote to Hamilton to learn his thoughts on the commission, and one even sent along the rough draft of the president's speech to the looming session of Congress. "I beg you . . . to communicate to me your ideas," Pickering pleaded. McHenry implored Hamilton to consider himself still a member of the cabinet, beseeching him to provide advice so that "I might avail myself of your experience, knowledge and judgment." Wolcott confided that he respected Hamilton's opinion and would adhere to whatever his former boss advised.[6]

Hamilton replied to each of his allies, giving them surprising marching orders. He recommended the inclusion of a Republican, even possibly Madison, on the president's three-member commission. (Wolcott was now amenable to Madison sailing for France, though with the "utmost reluctance.") Hamilton also wanted the navy augmented and the army expanded by twenty-five thousand men. As the Republicans would respond that these measures were being taken "to *provoke* a war," he advised the cabinet officers to take the line that these national security measures were being "done towards preserving peace."[7]

While Hamilton pulled strings in the cabinet, friends voiced his foreign policy views in Congress. Hamilton's uneasiness shined through. He feared that France was winning the land war in Europe and that the Bank of England—what he called Great Britain's "vital part"—was teetering on the edge of collapse. Should such an "evil" transpire, London likely would be compelled to make peace, which would "leave us alone to receive the law from France." Moreover, with Britain out of the war, Hamilton claimed that France, driven by "a spirit of *domination* and *Revenge*," and shackled with a huge army "that she will be glad to get rid of," would invade the United States. The scenario that Hamilton envisaged may have been wildly improbable, but it was designed to foster military preparedness, an objective he had long relished to consummate his fiscal-military state.[8]

At nearly the same moment, Jefferson outlined his thoughts on what he called the "awful crisis." His ideas had hardly changed since he had left Washington's cabinet. They were driven by the dominion that he believed London exercised over America. Great Britain had always "wished a monopoly of commerce and influence with us," he said, and it had "in fact obtained it." He labeled America's merchants "false citizens." They "thr[e]w dust into the eyes" of "their dependants" in northern port cities and farm towns, hoping to convince them that it was in their best interest to perpetuate America's servile relationship with Britain. He called the merchants and financiers the "most influential characters" in the northern states, and charged that they "possess[ed] our printing presses," that is, that they controlled the lion's share of the newspapers across the land. Through that "powerful engine," they not only wielded incredible national influence but also hoped to "force" the president "to proceed in any direction they dictate." Had the Jay Treaty been rejected, Jefferson believed that they would have destroyed the Union rather than gone to war with Britain. Had they not feared being left to stand alone, they would already have taken the United States to war with France. Jefferson yearned to avoid war, to "keep out of the broils of Europe." He supported sending a commission to France to negotiate a settlement, and prayed that Adams would have the freedom to do so. In the meantime, he appealed to northern friends, as he had done when he undertook his botanizing tour, to join with southern Republicans in the search for "some means of shielding ourselves . . . from foreign influence, commercial, political, or in whatever other form it might be attempted." Overstatement danced throughout what Jefferson said, but at bottom he understood his foes perfectly, and he could not have been more on target in his fears that Hamilton would after all succeed in controlling Adams.[9]

Jefferson doubted that Adams could withstand the powerful forces that hoped to control his foreign policy, and in the spring of 1797 the vice president met several times with Joseph Philippe Létombe, the French consul-general at Philadelphia. In essence, Jefferson cautioned about the Federalist extremists and how they might force Adams to their side. But he also advised that Adams would likely be president for only one term, an indication perhaps that Jefferson was already contemplating building an effective Republican opposition and seeking the presidency in 1800. Time was on the side of improved Franco-American relations, he said. "It is for France, great, generous, at the summit of her glory, to pretend to take no notice, to be patient, to precipitate nothing, and all will return to order" after the Adams presidency.[10]

As the spring dragged on, the crisis deepened. Between his inauguration and the convening of the special session of Congress in May, Adams learned that France had refused to accept Charles Cotesworth Pinckney, whom Washington had dispatched to Paris—much as he had sent Jay to London. Adams required no coaching from his cabinet to greet Congress with a pugnacious speech, and he asked for all that Hamilton had urged as part of a military preparedness campaign, save for enlarging the army. But Adams wished to give negotiations one more chance. He proposed sending a three-member commission to Paris that included the rebuffed Pinckney, together with John Marshall of Virginia and Elbridge Gerry of Massachusetts. The cabinet exploded when Adams suggested Gerry, a Republican, and pushed instead for Rufus King, whom Hamilton wanted. But in the end, the secretaries acquiesced. Two of the three were Federalists, just as Hamilton had wished.[11]

Jefferson, who was unaware of what had transpired between the president and his advisors, was satisfied with Adams's handling of the crisis. Moreover, Jefferson appeared contented with his decision to return to public life. As he had expected, the vice presidency was a "tranquil and unoffending station" that enabled him to spend up to eight months each year at Monticello.[12] With ample free time, he accepted the presidency of the American Philosophical Society, which Franklin had created to encourage scientific inquiry. The vice president corresponded and met with others who were interested in science, and even prepared a paper that contrasted the size of European and American animals, a study based on fossil remains. In Philadelphia, Jefferson lived in Francis's Hotel, where he rented a suite of rooms, and dined twice daily at a common table with several congressmen and senators, both Republicans and Federalists. (Jefferson said he "never deserted a friend for differences of opinion." Were people to mingle only with those of like mind, he said, "every man would be an insulate being.")[13] From his residence, Jefferson had only a short walk to Congress Hall, where he presided over the daily meetings of the Senate, sitting behind a desk in a red morocco chair atop the dais. Hour after hour, he listened to speech after interminable speech, saying nothing. He could vote only in the event of a tie, and as the Federalists held a lopsided majority in the Senate, voting was not in the offing.

But Jefferson's experiences were not entirely pleasant. As the political battles grew more passionate, he remarked that unlike previous days when friendships had persisted despite "warm debates and high political passions," now "Men who have been intimate all their lives cross the streets to avoid meeting, and turn their heads another way, lest they should be obliged to touch their hat." Jefferson grieved that many had erected an impenetrable "wall of separation" between themselves and former friends, and sadly noted that numerous old acquaintances now "declined visiting me." He lamented the changed atmosphere. It "is afflicting to peaceable minds," he declared, adding, "passions are too high . . . to be cooled in our day."[14]

The incendiary political atmosphere grew from a sense that the choices to be made in the 1790s were life changing. For instance, many who had long enjoyed a privileged social standing feared the loss of their elite status if French Jacobinism—supposedly embodied by Jefferson and espoused by the Republican Party—triumphed in America. There were businessmen, and those who clung parasitically to them, who were certain that their prosperity was inextricably tied to Britain's victory in the European war. Against them, at least half the population prayed for a French victory, fearful that a triumphant Britain would result in the slow, steady erosion of American independence, and also that London's victory would ensure that the conservative elements predominant in America before 1776 would reestablish their mastery.

During the rancorous special session of 1797, congressmen fought over every preparedness measure that Adams recommended, though in the end the president got nearly everything he wanted. In this white-hot environment, newspapers and pamphlets were filled with scurrilous attacks. No one was immune. Jefferson unwittingly contributed to the vehemence—and reaped the harvest—through yet another wayward private letter. Early the previous year, during his despair at the Jay Treaty, Jefferson had written to Philip Mazzei, a former neighbor who had moved to Italy, to bring him up to date on American affairs. He reported that "an Anglican, monarchical and aristocratical party has sprung up, whose avowed object is to draw over us the substance" of the British system. This was the staple of Republican rhetoric, and had Jefferson stopped there, his comments would not have caused a ripple. But he added: "It would give you a fever were I to name to you the apostates who have gone over these heresies, men who were Samsons in the field and Solomons in the council, but who have had their heads shorn by the harlot England."[15]

Unfortunately for Jefferson, Mazzei had the letter published in a Florence newspaper. Just as the special session of Congress began, the letter appeared, as was inevitable, in a Federalist newspaper in New York, then in seemingly every Federalist paper in the land. Republican editors fought back, accusing the New York printer who had first made the letter public in America of having descended to the "*Sink Pot of Malignity.*"[16] But the damage was done, and could not be repaired. Nearly everyone who read the letter reached the same conclusion: the "Samson in the field" whom Jefferson had accused of being partisan and an Anglophile—and anti-republican to boot—could be none other than George Washington. Jefferson had assailed the most sacrosanct of Americans.

Federalist screeds had a field day with Jefferson. It was now undeniable that he and his party were more loyal to France than to America, they said. Some even tossed around words such as "treasonable" and "traitorous." Jefferson had a thick skin and was accustomed to attacks in the press, but he was mortified that his comments about Washington, whom he revered, had been made public. Washington was not a forgiving person. A full year before the Mazzei letter was made public, Henry Lee, the Federalist governor of Virginia and commander of the army sent out to crush the Whiskey Rebellion, had gossiped to Washington of Jefferson's supposed antipathy. Jefferson got wind of it and asked Washington not to believe "the slander of an intriguer, dirtily employed in sifting the conversations of my table."[17] Washington believed Jefferson's denials. But when the Mazzei letter hit the press, followed shortly thereafter by more tales of Jefferson's alleged infidelity—malicious stories conveyed to the ex-president by Federalists—Washington would not be mollified and cut his ties with his former secretary of state. He never again invited Jefferson to Mount Vernon, nor did he write to him, and following her husband's death, Martha Washington likewise would have nothing to do with Jefferson.

Jefferson had previously criticized Washington's policies from time to time, beginning with his questioning of the general's strategic thinking in the final troubled years of the war. But Jefferson had never doubted Washington's abilities. Long years after the Mazzei letter incident, Jefferson continued to exalt Washington. Indeed, his praise of Washington exceeded the most favorable comments that Hamilton ever committed to paper about the general. Jefferson lauded Washington's "great and powerful" mind, prudence, integrity, sound judgment, and above all his courage, asserting in 1814 that he was "incapable of fear." Though declaring that Washington's "heart was not warm in its affections," Jefferson late in life wrote: "He was, indeed, in every sense of the words, a wise, a good, and a great man."[18]

Hamilton was also a victim of the malice of the times during that steamy summer. To his horror, a Republican writer in 1797 published some details of Hamilton's sordid involvement with Maria and James Reynolds, an episode that had occurred years earlier. The author was James Thomas Callender, a Scotsman whose scurrilous writings had forced him to flee from Britain to Ireland and eventually, in 1793, to Philadelphia. By means that were never ascertained, Callender came into possession of copies of the documents compiled by Frederick Muhlenberg, Abraham Venable, and James Monroe during their 1792 inquiry into Hamilton's conduct. Callender published the material at very nearly the same moment that the Federalists were enjoying the bonanza made possible by the Mazzei letter. The revelations first appeared in pamphlets, then in a volume titled *The History of the United States for 1796*.

Callender did not care much about Hamilton's sexual escapades. Indeed, he was skeptical of the story that Hamilton had told the congressmen about having had an affair with Maria Reynolds, even believing that the treasury secretary had forged her supposed letters. Instead, Callender was persuaded that Hamilton, privy to insider information, had used Treasury Department funds to speculate in government securities. He had, to use today's terminology, laundered the money through James Reynolds. To Callender's way of thinking, Hamilton's yarn about paying blackmail was a smokescreen to mask his improper conduct at the Treasury.

Needless to say, Hamilton was furious, and mortified. His answers in the congressional inquiries had long since satisfied most fair-minded observers that suspicions of his financial misconduct were baseless. Now, yet again, charges of his supposed peculation were being ginned up. Worse still, Hamilton's "wenching," as Callender alluded to it, had become public knowledge. Among those who learned of his infidelity for the first time were Betsey Schuyler Hamilton and the children.

In an instant, Hamilton understood that Callender's publication threatened him with enormous personal and political damage. He yearned for public vindication. Consumed with the need for respect, Hamilton feared being seen as not only "unprincipled but a fool."[19] In addition, he was clearly worried that the allegations, and revelations, would ruin his public aspirations. Hamilton had always had a propulsive ambition, and nothing in his correspondence or behavior—unlike that of Jefferson's in the first years following his departure from Washington's cabinet—suggests that it had slackened. Economic necessity had contributed to both men's decision to return to private life, but Jefferson quite obviously relished time with his family and longed for greater freedom for intellectual pursuits. Those were not discernable factors in Hamilton's abandonment of office, and given his voracious appetite for polemics and the energy he expended to control the Adams presidency, it appears that his political ambitions were unchecked.

Having spent years at the highest level of the national government, Hamilton would not have been tempted by many political offices. However, he had always yearned for military glory, and his behavior in years to come demonstrated that those dreams remained alive. Given his avidity for power and fame, it is likely that in moments of reverie Hamilton thirsted for the presidency. He was still quite young. In 1804, the earliest moment that Hamilton could have imagined that the presidency was a possibility, he would be only forty-nine years old, eight years younger than Washington had been when he became president. Even at the time of the election of 1816, Hamilton would be the same age that Adams had been in the recent presidential contest. In the summer of 1797, Hamilton was desperate to thwart the damage that might be caused by Callender's malice. An air of madness characterized his behavior, as he fought yet again to lay to rest all suspicions of financial malfeasance. His inability to do so marked this as a watershed event for him, leaving him more fearful than ever that the door to his further political ascendancy had been impenetrably sealed against him.

Silence would have been his best option. That was what Wolcott advised, in essence telling Hamilton to simply say that the congressmen who conducted the inquiry had at the time acknowledged finding nothing that could "affect [his] character as a public Officer or impair the public confidence in [his] integrity." Hamilton was accustomed to directing others, not to taking advice. He did not listen. As with so many other choices made by the impulsive Hamilton, a man driven inexorably by a compelling need for esteem, his response was ill-judged. "I am obliged to publish every thing," he said, and he did just that.[20]

Hamilton answered the "Jacobin Scandal-Club," as he put it, by offering his account of his tawdry relationship with Maria and James Reynolds in a lengthy pamphlet, hoping to convince the public that his part in the affair had been driven by carnal lust, not by greed. He pointed out that on three occasions, members of Congress had absolved him of financial misdeeds. To this, he added that had he stolen from the Treasury, he would have pilfered more than the few hundred dollars that had passed from him to James Reynolds. Then came the bombshell: "My crime is an amorous connection with his wife." Reynolds's "design [had been] to extort money from me," Hamilton confirmed, saying he had become the "dupe of the plot." He had been ensnared by their "most imposing art." Maria had seduced him. He had been moved by her supposed plight, though he all but said that he had been swept off his feet by her many charms.

It was a sordid, and salacious, confession, and he begged for forgiveness, crying out: "I can never cease to condemn myself."[21] But in all of American political history, perhaps no figure ever acted as unwisely as did Hamilton in coming clean. His was a tale of having been a slave to passion, a disclosure of having been bamboozled by a couple of unsavory con artists, and a shocking admission that he had persisted in sleeping with Maria even after her husband was aware of what was occurring. Friends stuck by him, but many others greeted his avowal with ridicule. Callender gushed ecstatically that Hamilton's admission was "worth all that fifty of the best pens in America Could have said against him." In no time, Hamilton was spoofed in a New York theatrical production. Many thought the revelations raised troubling questions about his character and judgment. Others, like Jefferson's financial agent in Philadelphia, thought it tawdry of Hamilton to air his story in such a manner that "poor Mrs. H . . . must be severely injured."[22] (They might have found it even more shocking had they known that Hamilton drafted his pamphlet at the moment that Betsey was giving birth to their sixth child.) What is more, his story struck many as so wildly implausible as to lend credence to Callender's charges. Jefferson, for instance, concluded that Hamilton's "willingness to plead guilty as to the adultery seems rather to have strengthened than weakened the suspicions that he was in truth guilty of the speculations." Others said that Hamilton had sought "to creep under Mrs. R's petticoats" in order to hide what he had really been up to.[23]

Skepticism would have been even more widespread had the public known the circumstances under which Hamilton drafted his confession. He hurried to Philadelphia, where he composed his pamphlet while lodging in a rented room in a boardinghouse. It had never been his practice to leave home to draft his essays and pamphlets, and this departure in his behavior raises questions. Hamilton's best biographer attributed his uncustomary conduct to an unwillingness to "face his family" as he "confessed his sins."[24] Another explanation is that Hamilton wished to peruse the Treasury Department's ledgers. It is unlikely that the slavish Wolcott would have objected, and there was little danger that he would blow the whistle should emendations be made.

Hamilton wanted redemption, but he was also determined to find who had leaked the documents to Callender. He knew that Muhlenberg and his colleagues who had investigated the matter in 1792 had made copies of the materials they turned up in their probe. Within a few weeks of that initial investigation, Hamilton also knew that "whispers" were circulating in Virginia about the affair, and he must have suspected that William Giles's investigation, launched merely three months after Muhlenberg's inquiry, stemmed from knowledge of the payments he had made to Reynolds.[25] Someone in Virginia who knew of the affair was talking. Both Venable and Monroe, who had joined with Muhlenberg to look into the matter, were Virginians. Of the two, Monroe had a motive for retribution. The year before, President Washington had recalled Monroe as American minister to France, a humiliating end to his embassy. The president had acted on the advice of an entirely Federalist cabinet, and he had dispatched a Federalist in Monroe's stead.

Actually, there was another possible suspect. Venable told Hamilton that he did not know how "these papers got out, unless by the person who copied them," John Beckley, at the time the clerk of the House of Representatives, and a Virginian. Wolcott said the same thing to Hamilton. But from the outset Hamilton focused exclusively on Monroe. Of the three congressmen who had investigated the matter in 1792, Monroe was the most important politically, and he was close to Jefferson. Hamilton burned with desire to secure his absolution, but at the same moment he wanted to harm Monroe by revealing that he had been the culprit who leaked the documents to Callender.[26]

Hamilton immediately called on Monroe, who by happenstance was visiting relatives in Manhattan. Though Hamilton had long dominated others through his combative manner, it did not work when he confronted Monroe, a gritty Southerner. Like Hamilton, Monroe had soldiered for several years, first in the infantry, where he saw considerable combat (and received a life-threatening gunshot wound in the attack on Trenton), before serving as an aide-de-camp to General Stirling. Hamilton and Monroe had met during the war, and in fact Hamilton had recommended him for a field command in the African American regiment that Colonel Laurens hoped to raise. But they split in the partisan 1790s. Monroe, a Republican senator, fought tenaciously against what he called the "monarchy party." The Federalists' payback came when they induced Washington not only to recall him from France—it was Hamilton who had actually persuaded the president to summon Monroe home—but to do so in a letter so harsh that it threatened his political career.[27] It is not likely that Monroe would have truckled to anyone, especially any Federalist in the summer of 1797, and he most certainly was not going to permit Hamilton to push him around.

Their meeting was stormy. An observer described Hamilton as "very much agitated" when he entered the house. He wasted little time before accusing Monroe of turning over the documents to Callender. Both men spoke with "some warmth." At one point, Monroe said that if Hamilton "would be temperate or quiet for a moment," he would "answer him candidly." That silenced Hamilton long enough for Monroe to point out that he had only returned from France two weeks earlier. He acknowledged that Muhlenberg and Venable had asked him to keep the sealed packet containing the papers from their inquiry, and he added that he had entrusted it to a "friend in Virginia." Hamilton responded by calling him a liar, and Monroe in turn replied that his accuser was a "Scoundrel." Hot-tempered as always, Hamilton shot back: "I will meet you like a Gentleman." Monroe did not flinch. In a flash, he replied: "I am ready get your pistols." Only the intervention of friends who were present prevented an immediate duel.

Hamilton, who remained "extremely agitated" while Monroe was "quite cool," shifted gears. If he could not persuade Monroe to acknowledge his role in passing along the documents to Callender, then Hamilton demanded that the Virginian at least repudiate the remarks made in a deposition he had taken from Jacob Clingman, Reynolds's confederate, back in 1792. Clingman had stated that Hamilton's supposed romance with Maria Reynolds was an artifice designed to conceal the treasury secretary's crimes. Monroe had copied the statement and passed it on to Venable and Muhlenberg without comment. Callender had made it public. Indeed, for Callender, it was the heart of his case against the former treasury secretary. Hamilton pressed Monroe to discredit Clingman's allegation. Monroe was evasive. He agreed only to ask Muhlenberg and Venable to join him in a letter acknowledging that their inquiry had produced no evidence of financial impropriety by Hamilton.[28]

Within a week, Hamilton had such a letter, but he thought it insufficient.[29] During the next half year, he deluged Monroe with letters demanding that he formally refute Clingman. Monroe demurred. This was his retaliation against an old political foe, one who had repeatedly insulted him. In letter after letter, the desperate Hamilton charged Monroe with responsibility for Callender's publications, alleged that the Virginian had done so from a "design to . . . drive me to the necessity of a formal defense"—which, if true, was successful, for Hamilton did not publish his account of the Reynolds affair until six weeks after his confrontation with Monroe—and assailed him as "malignant and dishonourable." In December, Monroe came close to formally challenging Hamilton to a duel, and announced that Aaron Burr would be his second. But Burr thought a duel pointless, especially as Monroe never believed, or charged, that Hamilton had acted illegally while treasury secretary. Furthermore, by refusing to deliver some of the correspondence between Monroe and Hamilton, Burr prevented the rhetoric from mushrooming to an intemperate level that would have made a duel inevitable. In the end, the imbroglio withered away. No duel was fought. Burr, in 1797, may have saved Hamilton's life.[30]

At the outset of 1798, Adams asked his cabinet to consider what steps he should take if the news from the three envoys he had sent to France was bad. McHenry immediately turned to Hamilton for direction, then passed along the advice to his colleagues, each of whom recommended to the unsuspecting president what the former treasury secretary had outlined. Hamilton desired military preparations, including the augmentation of the army, which he had failed to obtain in 1797, and the suspension of the treaties with France, which he had unsuccessfully sought in 1793. He wanted the regular army increased to twenty thousand men and an additional, or *provisional* army" of thirty thousand also to be raised. Hamilton told the cabinet that he did not want war, as the United States was not prepared for hostilities with a major power and there was "a strong aversion to war in the minds of the people." Besides, there was nothing to gain—neither trade nor territory—from a war with France. He coached his minions to tell Adams that the military build-up would induce France to negotiate, and he even encouraged them to advise the president to declare a national day of prayer, which he said would be "very expedient" politically.[31]

About a month after the cabinet advocated Hamilton's covert recommendations, Adams heard from his three diplomats in Paris, and the news was indeed bad. The French government had not received Marshall, Gerry, and Pinckney. Instead, it sent out agents, later identified as "X, Y, and Z," to demand that the United States apologize for Adams's truculent speech to the special session of Congress, abandon claims for French spoliations on the high seas, and pay bribes to leading officials. Only after these conditions were met would France open talks with the envoys. France's conduct was outrageous, and Adams was duly outraged. He consulted his cabinet, which again secretly touched base with Hamilton. His advice remained the same as it had been a month earlier, save that Hamilton now urged the cabinet to implore Adams to make a "*temperate*, but *grave solemn* and *firm* communication" to Congress. It was to be premised on the far-fetched notion that American independence was threatened by France's conduct.[32]

After listening to his cabinet, Adams shredded the first draft of a rage-filled speech to Congress and replaced it with one that was more moderate. Even so, Adams declared that no hope existed for reaching an accommodation with Paris, and he proceeded to recommend everything his cabinet—and Hamilton—wanted, save for a call to increase the size of the army. (Privately, Adams remarked that "there is no more prospect of seeing a french Army here, than there is in Heaven.") Wishing to prevent a wave of war hysteria, Adams revealed only that France had refused to accept America's envoys.[33]

Jefferson listened to the speech and exploded with anger. Thinking Adams had been astonishingly provocative, Jefferson said the president's remarks were "insane." Adams, he concluded, had become the "stalking horse" of the "war gentlemen" within the Federalist "war-party," extremists who were manufacturing a crisis that would lead to hostilities, and who knew what else. Jefferson thought the Republicans should play for time, insisting that no steps be taken until the congressmen could go home and meet with their constituents. That would defer any action until December, by which time, he reasoned, France would have won the war, or be on the cusp of victory, and the "Hamilton party" would not dare go to war.[34]

But Jefferson's plan was thwarted when Giles and other alarmed Republicans in the House demanded the release of the communiqués sent home by the commissioners. That was a drastic mistake. Once the documents were made public, the nation was made aware of France's provocative actions. Outrage swept the land. Even Jefferson condemned France's behavior as "very unworthy of a great nation," though he did not think it cause for war, in part because he believed that much of John Marshall's account was a fabrication. (He spoke of "the XYZ dish cooked up by Marshall" and "Marshall's XYZ romance.") However, Jefferson was not sanguine that hostilities could be averted, as the revelations had caused such a "shock on the republican mind" that many members of his own party had jumped on the war bandwagon. But what really plunged Jefferson into gloom was his belief that Hamilton was not only more powerful than Adams among Federalists but also bent on hurrying the United States into war before "Great-Britain will be blown up."[35]

Jefferson had painted the Federalists with a broad brush. In fact, not all Federalists thought alike, any more than all Republicans marched in lockstep. As has not infrequently been the case with American political parties, there were at least two factions among Federalists, and one—sometimes called the Ultra Federalists, sometimes the High Federalists—consisted of conservative extremists, Anglophiles bent on frustrating the Republicans' alleged hopes of radical social and political change. Hamilton was both a High Federalist and an opportunist, and he saw in what Adams called a "half war with France"— what historians have ever after referred to as the Quasi-War—a fortuitous vehicle for achieving ends that he had long desired.[36] Hamilton did not want war, but he desired a more militarized state and the severance of all ties with revolutionary France. To be sure, he was more than willing to play on the popular anger and fear for partisan advantage.

What had been an affront to the United States was made into a crisis by leading Federalists. As historian John Miller wrote, "the party elders . . . induced hysteria and then turned it to party purposes."[37] The Federalist press went into overdrive to whip up anti-French fury and convince the public that thousands of untrustworthy, potentially dangerous, pro-French "serpents" lived within the United States. Hamilton did his part, rushing out a seven-part series titled "The Stand." "[O]ur independence is menaced" by France, he declared. To that, he added: "'Tis not in their power" to harm America, unless internal enemies provoked an "abject submission to their will." Those enemies were real, he claimed. There were "tools of France" and "satellites of France" within the United States, and they "prostituted to a foreign enemy." Through "treasonable and parricidal sentiment," they were "willing that their country should become a province to France."[38]

Adams joined in with numerous addresses bristling with bellicose language. His motivation was not to heighten the crisis, but to mold public opinion behind the dogged steps he saw as necessary to bring France to the negotiating table. Adams had long been respected for his protracted service to the nation, but his tenacity in this critical period transformed him into a revered figure. Abigail Adams remarked that nearly all of her countrymen were now happy that her husband had won the election in 1796, as under Jefferson "all would have been sold to the French."[39] Swept off his feet by his newfound popularity, Adams went along with nearly everything the Federalists could push through Congress.

In rapid-fire succession that spring and summer the Federalists abrogated the treaties with France, authorized American vessels to attack French predators, spent more on the navy than the nation had spent in the past ten years combined, and against Adams's wishes expanded the army from 4,173 to 14,421 officers and men, quadrupling the number of infantry regiments and increasing the cavalry sixfold. (Many, including Hamilton, referred to the original army as the "Old Army" and considered it a "frontier constabulary," while they labeled the newly created force the "New Army.") In addition, Congress authorized the president to incorporate into the army those companies of volunteers that organized as units. Finally, Congress sanctioned the creation of both a "Provisional Army" and an "Eventual Army"—the two would have totaled some forty thousand men—which the president could activate in the event of "imminent danger." (Adams never perceived such a danger, and those portions of the army never truly came into being.) Finally, Congress levied land and stamp taxes to pay for the steps it had taken.[40]

The congressional Federalists did not stop there. During that scorching summer, they enacted the punitive Alien and Sedition Acts, claiming them a wartime necessity. In fact, the legislation was enacted almost entirely for the purpose of making political gains. Not for the last time in American political history did conservative extremists who feared change exploit a perceived foreign threat to, in the words of historian James Roger Sharp, "consolidate their strength and destroy their political opposition."[41] The High Federalists went after what one called the "democrats, mobocrats & all other kinds of rats."[42] Partisanship was never far from their thoughts. They wished, historian Ron Chernow has written, "to muzzle dissent and browbeat the Republicans into submission."[43]

The repressive Federalist legislation tripled the period that immigrants had to wait in order to become citizens. This was an unmistakable attempt to weaken the Republican Party, home to the "hordes of wild Irishmen" and other putative Jacobins who were, as a Federalist charged, the "grand cause of all our present difficulties." To deal with what a High Federalist claimed was the "army of spies and incendiaries scattered through the continent," two acts authorized the deportation of aliens who were already in the country.[44]

Jefferson called those laws "detestable" and "worthy of the 8th or 9th century," but he saw them coming. He thought the Sedition Act was the essence of the Federalist program, and long before it was introduced, he prophesied that sooner or later the opposition would seek "the suppression of the whig presses."[45] Actually, the Sedition Act aimed at all free speech, for it was made a crime to "write, print, utter or publish" anything "scandalous, and malicious" about the United States government, or to bring into "contempt or disrepute" the Congress or the president. Now and then, a High Federalist was candid enough to acknowledge what his party was up to. South Carolina's Robert Goodloe Harper virtually admitted on the floor of Congress that Federalists sought to keep from the public the ideas of their political opponents. The Sedition Act, he said, was designed to prevent the "filthy streams" of the opposition party's principles from "gain[ing] a credit with the community."[46] Once these harsh laws were enacted, an outraged Jefferson proclaimed that in less than ten years the federal government "has[d] swallowed more of the public liberty" than had England before 1776.[47]

Claiming that he did not wish to be "cruel," Hamilton nevertheless advocated the deportation of aliens. Though once an alien himself, he now declared that the great majority of them "ought to be obliged to leave the Country." He also endorsed the Sedition Act. He not only spoke out against immoderate criticism of presidential policies but also said that "approbation of . . . France" was "portentous" and required "every human effort" to prevent it. Whereas Jefferson attested that the Alien and Sedition Acts flew "so palpably in the teeth of the constitution as to shew they [the Federalists] mean to pay no respect to it," Hamilton's only concern was that the laws might be politically counterproductive.[48]

By June, Hamilton had gotten nearly everything he wished from the Quasi-War crisis, though one great plum had eluded him. He had done much for his country; now, he wanted his country to do something for him. In his earliest surviving letter, the adolescent Hamilton had dreamed of rising from the depths through military service. He still equated soldiering with ascension, and he continued to yearn for eminence, perhaps more than ever in the wake of Callender's revelations and his own ill-judged response. Despite his talk three years earlier of facing a lengthy period of practicing law in order to cope with indebtedness, Hamilton hungered for a leading position in the New Army. Holding high command could facilitate his enduring dream of glory. It could also be useful for partisan political reasons.

Adams first appealed to Washington to assume command. Adams expected him to ascent readily to the nation's call, but Washington equivocated. He appeared to say that his acceptance hinged on his ability to select the leading general officers. The only thing he said with clarity was that those officers should be younger, energetic men.[49] Perplexed, Adams sent McHenry to Mount Vernon to discover what was on Washington's mind. During three of the hottest days of the summer, the secretary of war conferred with Washington. When their discussions were completed, Washington wrote Adams that he would serve on the condition that he would not have to leave home unless a French invasion was probable. As he would seldom, if ever, be with the army, the inspector general, the second in command, would in reality hold the reins of power. Washington recommended the appointment of Hamilton to this post.[50]

Adams was dumbfounded, and angry. He had wished to respect the seniority among the veteran officers of the Revolutionary War. Under this formula, he could appoint Massachusetts's Henry Knox to the post of inspector general. He informed Washington of his desire. Washington responded that he would not serve unless Hamilton was appointed immediately beneath him. Not daring to defy Washington, Adams buckled. In an instant, Colonel Hamilton became Major General Hamilton.[51]

Washington's behavior, as was often the case in his relationship with Hamilton, was extraordinary. In this instance, though a private citizen, Washington had dictated policy to the president of the United States, an act he would never have tolerated while he held the office. A year earlier, not long after he had broken with Jefferson, Washington learned of Hamilton's scandalous behavior with James and Maria Reynolds. He immediately sent his former treasury secretary a gift and a note expressing his sincere regard and friendship. Later, Washington told Hamilton of the "very high esteem" in which he held him.[52] For Washington, among the least compassionate of men, such behavior was nearly without precedent. Hamilton had not even responded to Washington's second note. But in May 1798, as the Quasi-War heated up, Hamilton thought the former president could be of use. He fancifully told Washington that the Republicans were plotting to change the Constitution at the behest of France. He additionally urged Washington to undertake a tour of Virginia and North Carolina—"under some pretense of health," he artfully suggested—to speak out in favor of defensive preparations. Washington swallowed the yarn about the Republicans, but declined to go on the road. That prompted a second letter from Hamilton breaking the news that the New Army would be created and revealing his hope to be its inspector general. Indeed, he implied that it was the only rank he would accept.[53]

Washington knew Hamilton well. He knew his strong points. He was also mindful of his weaknesses, including his hot-tempered impulsiveness, penchant for intrigue, and obsession with winning glory. In addition, Washington was fully aware that Hamilton was devoid of command experience. It is unthinkable that Washington would have backed any other unseasoned man with such a long list of reproachful attributes. He may have dared to support Hamilton from a belief that he could control his former aide, or doubtful that a French invasion would occur, Washington may also have felt that Hamilton could do little harm to himself or his country. There was also a gambler's streak in Washington, and in 1798 he may have been willing to run the risk that Hamilton's strengths would override his darker traits.

More important, Washington was Federalist in all but name, as Jefferson had slowly come to realize. Washington knew that no one had done more than Hamilton to advance the core principles of the Nationalists, later called Federalists. Hamilton had labored tirelessly to strengthen the national government, overthrow the Articles of Confederation, and win ratification of the Constitution. It was Hamilton above all others who had forged the contours of the new American nation. Washington had shared Hamilton's hopes of achieving these ends. He believed in Hamilton and wanted him to have a political future, and putting him in a position to win glory—as Washington himself had achieved an exalted status through warfare—might be essential for the furtherance of Hamilton's political future. Washington saw in Hamilton the greatest likelihood of maintaining Federalist domination, of keeping the Jeffersonians from gaining control of the national government. Washington understood that by backing Hamilton in 1798, he was helping not just his former aide but also the fortunes of the Federalist Party.

Having commanded the Continental army, Washington also knew full well that Inspector General Hamilton would be able to name hundreds of junior officers. Armed with such power, Hamilton could establish a potent Federalist base in every state, as well as create a solid phalanx of provincial leaders who would be personally indebted and loyal to him. (Indeed, six months after his appointment, Hamilton acknowledged that he had been "very attentive to the importance of appointing friends of the Governt. to Military stations.")[54] Like Jefferson, Washington knew that Hamilton was the colossus who drove the Federalist Party and accounted for its greatest successes. He was intent on Hamilton's ascent to the loftiest heights in American politics, and by forcing the president of the United States to accept his choice for inspector general, Washington had done what he could to afford Hamilton the opportunity to become America's predominant political figure early in the nineteenth century, much as he himself had been in the late eighteenth century.

Nothing since the enactment of Hamilton's economic program had so troubled Jefferson as events in the summer of 1798. Eighteen months earlier, he had believed the tide was running against the Federalists. Their successes, he believed, had been due to the citizenry's overweening wish for the Union to survive, Washington's "irresistible influence," and "the cunning of Hamilton." Even after fifteen months in the vice presidency, Jefferson remained confident that the Federalists' anti-republicanism would be the death knell of the party. In a brief time, he predicted, "we shall see the reign of witches pass over."[55]

He was wrong. Despite the supposed departure of both Washington and Hamilton from the national stage, Federalist achievements in 1798 were startling. They had brought the nation to the cusp of war, enacted draconian legislation threatening civil liberties and political dissent, drastically expanded the army, and secured Hamilton's appointment as its day-to-day commander. Furthermore, the Federalists were doing well in the scattered off-year congressional elections. (In fact, the party was en route to retaining control of the Senate and sweeping to a twenty-vote majority in the House.)[56]

As the vice president gathered gossip and intelligence from his customary network of capital insiders—he knew the details of the Federalist military plans six weeks prior to the XYZ revelations, for instance, and was told that Hamilton had privately described the presidency as a monarchy, "for a monarchy it is"—Jefferson trembled for the future.[57] The "delusion of the people" had been necessary for every Federalist achievement, Jefferson believed, and he felt they had achieved their ends through dominance of the press and presidency. Now that what he called "the Hamilton party" was firmly "in possession of the revenues & the legal authorities of the U.S.," Jefferson predicted that there "is no event . . . however atrocious, which may not be expected." If the citizenry acquiesced in the Alien and Sedition Acts, Jefferson feared the Federalists would next push for hereditary monarchy and "the establishment of the Senate for life." If the Federalists succeeded in taking the country to war, they would argue the necessity of endowing the federal government with "a power under whose auspices every thing fatal to republicanism is to be apprehended."[58]

During the ratification struggle, foes of the Constitution had warned that the document was "made like a Fiddle, with but few Strings," so that those in power could "play any tune upon it that they pleased."[59] Jefferson was certain that the Federalists had done just that, and would do it again, utilizing the implied powers clause and other elastic provisions to stretch the Constitution and claim legal sanction for their actions. Aware that Hamilton had told the Constitutional Convention that he desired a government modeled on that of Great Britain, Jefferson believed that at every step since 1789 the "Tory party"—as he sometimes called his adversaries—had emulated British policy.[60]

Jefferson may have been most concerned about the newly swollen army under total Federalist domination. He and his party saw no need for the New

Army. "[N]obody pretends . . . there is . . . the least *real* danger of invasion," Jefferson remarked. Other Republicans doubted the value of the army even if there was a war. They pointed out that not even an army of several hundred thousand could defend the thousands of miles of American coastline. Only the militia could handle that job, they said. Consequently, many Republicans, Jefferson included, feared from the outset that the real purpose of the army—patronage aside—was to suppress dissent, possibly even to invade states that were Republican strongholds.[61]

Other Virginians shared Jefferson's fears. For some, the existence of "standing armies" meant "oppressive taxation" and endless wars.[62] Others, like Senator Stevens T. Mason, worried that the Federalists might use the army "to attain their favorite object of crushing . . . Republicanism."[63] In 1798 Virginia embarked on defensive preparations, reorganizing its militia, purchasing arms, building an armory in Richmond, and increasing taxes by 25 percent to secure the revenue needed for those measures.[64]

Jefferson was convinced that only a bold, dramatic step might stop the High Federalists before the army was used. He played with fire, though just as Hamilton in the Newburgh Conspiracy had built in safeguards by alerting General Washington, Jefferson in 1798 told confidants that his "passive firmness" was a ploy, a tactic in a game of bluff that he hoped would never be implemented. To do so, he knew, would destroy the constitutional settlement of 1787–1788, and with it the Union. Merely putting his concept on the table was to risk alienating Republican allies in New York and Pennsylvania. But he felt something had to be done. To save the Union, the foes of the extreme Federalists must demonstrate the lengths to which they were willing to go. Only then, might moderates—centrists—step forward to stop Hamilton and those in his thrall.[65]

In the heat and languor of late summer, Jefferson working at his desk at Monticello, conceived a doctrine of state interposition, or nullification. He began by asking who was to judge the limits of federal power. He answered by saying it was inconceivable that federal authorities be permitted to judge what powers they possessed. Instead, Jefferson said that each state must decide if federal authorities had exercised powers that the states had not granted at the Constitutional Convention. Each state must have the authority to declare federal acts null and void within its domain.

Jefferson was a devoted defender of the sphere of state authority who feared ever-greater concentrations of power in the national government, but he favored neither nullification nor secession. He loved the Union. He was convinced that Hamilton and his ilk were bent on the evisceration of republicanism and the states, and he believed that if they persisted, the result would be a backlash that would destroy the Union. Jefferson understood that the Union brought national security, which in turn was essential for the preservation of freedom and republicanism. He would loyally support a war, he remarked during the Quasi-War crisis, adding that in the event of hostilities, "we must give up political differences of opinion & unite as one man to defend our country." But there were limits to his forbearance. He could not stand by idly and watch the Federalists crush republicanism. Already, he thought, Federalist extremists had sundered the compromise of sorts that had been reached between the consolidationists and their adversaries at the time of ratification. They could not be permitted to go even further.[66]

Once Jefferson committed his doctrine of state interposition to paper, a friend who carefully protected the author's identity shepherded a modified version through the legislature of Kentucky, which in 1792 had become the fifteenth state. Once the Kentucky Resolutions passed, Jefferson induced Madison, who years before had led the fight for consolidation, to prepare a similar, though not identical, statement for the Virginia assembly. It was enacted as the Virginia Resolutions. While the tenor of both sets of resolves was that state interposition was a proper remedy, they asked the other states to join with them only in resolving that the Alien and Sedition Acts were unconstitutional. None did so. Some states were critical, others deprecatingly silent. Jefferson knew that he had gone too far for his political allies in the mid-Atlantic states, whom he desperately needed if the Hamiltonians were to be stopped.[67]

When Adams, in November 1798, returned to the capital from a lengthy vacation at home, he detected a change in popular temperament, a tempering of the militant mood of summer. Jefferson also discerned the change when he traveled from Monticello to Philadelphia a month later. The vice president thought it stemmed from hostility toward the Federalists' assault on civil liberties, tax increases, and their standing army.[68]

Adams's discovery may have led him to reconsider the course of his presidency, though the bruising episode over the appointment of the inspector general had already shaken him to the core. In its wake, Adams had become certain of his betrayal by the cabinet, which he now believed had exaggerated the French threat in order to obtain an army headed by Hamilton. Furthermore, Adams was convinced that Hamilton's intrigue knew no bounds. Even before he became president, Adams had been put off by what he described as Hamilton's "proud, spirited, conceited, aspiring" qualities. Thinking Hamilton as "great a Hypocrite as any in the U. S.," Adams entered office vowing "to keep him [Hamilton] at a distance."[69] After eighteen months on the job, Adams had come to see Hamilton as operating "underground and in darkness" to achieve his ends. He now believed that Hamilton had plotted incessantly throughout his public career "to get rid of" his enemies, and those of Washington as well. Hamilton, Adams believed, had worked tirelessly behind the scenes during the election of 1796 to secure Pinckney's election and his defeat. He felt assured that Hamilton had been the puppeteer pulling Washington's strings in order to secure appointment as inspector general. As he looked back, Adams concluded that Hamilton had been the real power in Washington's cabinet, though he was just as certain that the former treasury secretary had merely been the point man for America's archconservatives. "Washington . . . was only viceroy under Hamilton, and Hamilton was viceroy under the Tories," Adams remarked. His anger rising, the president understood at last that he had been made "the dupe" of Hamilton's intrigue. In private, he referred to Hamilton as "Caesar." He also alleged that Hamilton was a "libertine," a womanizer who had been involved in many extramarital affairs, a widely shared view. Within his close circle of friends, Adams called Hamilton the "bastard brat of a Scottish peddler" who was "devoid of moral principle" and who had corrupted his age by his remorseless quest for power and fame.[70]

Abigail Adams told her husband that Hamilton aspired to be another Napoleon. She called him "a second Buonaparty." (Jefferson used identical terminology, privately labeling Hamilton "our Buonaparte.") Calling Hamilton "Spair Cassius" and "that cock sparrow," the First Lady added that Hamilton was evil: "O I have read his Heart in his wicked eyes many times, the very devil is in them," she advised.[71]

Beyond a doubt, Hamilton had hidden motives. He had gotten his army and he wanted to use it. He was an ultra-nationalist, and he had to know that this was likely his last hope of achieving military glory. He confided to McHenry his dream of joining with Great Britain to wrest from Spain its South American empire. Initially however, his gaze focused closer to home. "All on this side [of] the Missippi must be *ours* including both Floridas," he told the secretary of war, who immediately stepped forward and urged Adams—without success—to ask Congress for "full powers" to send an army to seize Florida in order to "counteract" France's supposed designs on the region.[72]

After becoming inspector general during the eventful summer of 1798, Hamilton plotted moves against beleaguered Spain, France's hard-pressed ally. He dispatched military supplies to the Florida border, confiding to trusted officers that the measures he took "looks to offensive" action. He added: "If we are to engage in war our game will be to attack where we can. France is not to be considered as separate from her ally. Temping objects will be within our grasp."[73] He not only inveighed allies in Congress to resolve that a state of war with France would exist if negotiations had not succeeded by November 1799, but also urged legislation sanctioning a preemptive strike for "taking possession of the Floridas and Louisiana" before France took those areas from its Spanish ally. Hamilton declared that he had long considered "the acquisition of those countries as essential to the permanency of the Union." Nor was that all. He looked far beyond the borderlands. He advised the High Federalists on the need to seize this moment of Europe's woes and "detach South America from Spain."[74] Hamilton was mesmerized with the notion of an Anglo-American campaign to liberate Venezuela from Spanish rule. While Rufus King, now the minister to Great Britain, sought London's cooperation, General Hamilton talked with Francisco de Miranda, a Venezuelan soldier of fortune, about sending the army to South America, if England and Adams's administration approved "so good a work."[75]

Hamilton prepared Washington for his foreign adventures when the old general came to Philadelphia late in 1798 to organize the army. Though he dared not breathe a word of what he was contemplating, Hamilton coyly sold Washington on the notion that the army was essential in order "to preserve us from being overwhelmed in [the] ruins" of the "falling empires" that would occur because of the European war.[76] Hamilton was more candid in his conversations with High Federalists, prevailing on some Massachusetts congressmen to cultivate Adams's support of American jingoism.[77] Their talks with the flabbergasted president did not go well. Saying he did not know whether to laugh or cry, Adams roared that he would not engage "myself or my country in most hazardous and expensive and bloody experiments to excite similar horrors in South America."[78] Adams soon enough traced the adventurous schemes to Hamilton, reaching the conclusion that the inspector general's plan was to use the army to establish monarchy in America, make himself the chief executive, and restore full ties with Great Britain.[79] To that, Adams added: "The man is stark mad."[80]

Conditions in the army nearly drove Hamilton mad. His New Army existed largely on paper. No more than five thousand men ever enlisted. Furthermore, numerous slots for officers went unfilled, partly because Adams deliberately obstructed the appointment process, but also because in five southern states no qualified Federalists could be found. (Hamilton preferred Federalists, but he was more flexible than Adams, who rejected several Republican applicants; Hamilton counseled that it was inadvisable to "give to appointments too absolute a party feature.") The army's supply service rapidly broke down, men went without pay for months, and crucial equipment never materialized. In the Union Brigade there was one flint for every four men and one shovel for every seventy-five. Large numbers throughout the army either had no muskets or defective ones that could not be fired safely.[81]

Plagued with these tangles, Hamilton worked valiantly to rectify matters, though it soon was clear that he lacked General Washington's skills as an army administrator. In no time, Hamilton was plunged into a swamp of micromanagement, issuing bloated directives that sometimes took on the air of the Mad Hatter. Convinced that "smart dress [was] essential," the inspector general came unhinged when he saw the hats worn by one regiment, saying he was "disappointed and distressed." Washington, he noted, had recommended "cocked-hats." Hamilton specified: "This always means hats cocked on three sides. I was assured that cocked hats were provided. I repeated the assurance to the officers. But the hats . . . are only capable of being cocked on one side; and the brim is otherwise so narrow as to consult neither good appearance nor utility. They are without cockades and hoops." Hamilton additionally devoted hour upon hour compiling lists of field grade and junior officers to the lowest rank in every state, even rating those who were to be captains and lieutenants as "bad," "probably good," "good," "unworthy," "tolerable," "Wont do," "not much of anything," "well enough," "perhaps," "respectable," "not strong," "strong," and "very respectable."[82]

If Hamilton pondered sending his army into foreign lands, he also contemplated using it to put down disorders in the United States, just as Jefferson and the Republicans feared. Hamilton knew that what he wrote on this subject was extremely sensitive, so much so that on occasion he dictated his letters to his ten-year-old son in order to camouflage his identity as the author. Grasping at far-fetched rumors, he told his closest political allies that the army had to be increased because of "the possibility of internal disorders."[83] He passed along the tattle of a Richmond Federalist who advised not only that Virginia Republicans sought "Nothing short of DISUNION, and the heads of JOHN ADAMS, and ALEXANDER HAMILTON" but also that the state could be brought to heel only through "*open war*."[84]

Filled with suspicion, Hamilton believed the Virginia and Kentucky Resolutions were the signal that secession was imminent. If "well managed," he said, the Federalist response would "turn to good account," presumably meaning that the threat of nullification could be used to justify intervention and secure political gains.[85] Hamilton instructed congressional Federalists to conduct hearings, and he advised what the committee's conclusion should be: With "calm dignity united with pathos," the committee should declare that as Virginians were conspiring with "a hostile foreign power" to "overturn the government," the United States "must not merely defend itself but must attack and arraign its enemies."[86] Hamilton appeared to be proposing nothing less than a federal invasion of Virginia and the arrest and trial of the dissidents.

Hamilton had lost his bearings. Or, perhaps the true Hamilton at last was shining through. Consumed with hatred of Jefferson and his adherents, and mad for glory, Hamilton's ego appeared to have run amok.

Word of Hamilton's grandiose hopes and dreams could not be kept secret. Philadelphia was a small place and people talked. In time, the inevitable happened. Adams learned of at least some of the things that Hamilton was contemplating. Someone, possibly an alarmed Federalist who thought Hamilton dangerous or delusional, or both, showed the president a copy of a letter Hamilton had written on the subject of invading Virginia. On his own, Adams put together enough of the pieces to confirm his suspicions of collusion between the inspector general and the High Federalists. More than ever, the president was convinced that Federalist extremists, including those in his cabinet, harbored a secret agenda that included relentlessly pushing him to take a hard line toward France. Their end, he had concluded, was war with France. Serendipitously, as the president was reaching this conclusion, he was also receiving tantalizing intelligence from numerous sources that pointed toward France's desire for peace.

Adams acted cautiously. In his annual address in December 1798, Adams revealed that he had discerned some evidence of French moderation, and added cryptically that he remained committed to a "humane and pacific policy." Jefferson bridled at the overall belligerence of the speech, convinced that Adams wanted a war but was unable to discover "the cause for waging it." Many High Federalists had an opposite reaction. They were convinced that Adams was inching toward a settlement that would destroy their well-laid plans. Hamilton soon was in touch with leaders of the faction in Congress, telling them that "these precarious times" demanded that the army be recruited and expanded.[87]

In January and February, Adams received more evidence of France's willingness to reach an accommodation. He faced difficult personal and political choices. Adams believed peace was imperative for the survival of the Union. But he feared that by merely agreeing to talks with France, he risked the rupture of his party, likely destroying his chances of reelection. The national interest won out. Without warning, on February 18, 1799, Adams sent Congress a message announcing that he was sending a new team of envoys to Paris in the hope of opening negotiations. Congressional High Federalists were apoplectic. Witnesses heard shouting in closed-door meetings between them and the president.[88]

Jefferson thought Adams had acted "grudgingly and tardily," but even so he was cautiously optimistic that Paris would "find dispositions to bury the tomahawk." All "I ask from France . . . is peace & a good price for our wheat and tobacco," Jefferson said.[89] Recognizing at once that a rapprochement would be a crumpling blow to his plans, Hamilton was distraught. In his black mood, he grew peevish, even treating the loyal McHenry with an uncustomary acerbity. Hamilton made one overt stab at thwarting Adams's peace initiative. He sought to persuade one of the envoys, Judge Oliver Ellsworth, not to sail. That would delay negotiations for nearly a year, as the Senate could not appoint Ellsworth's successor until it met again late in the fall, and the replacement envoy would face the time-consuming Atlantic crossing. But Hamilton's desperate ploy failed. Ellsworth embarked for France.[90]

For the first time in a decade, Hamilton had no influence over events. He could only watch as his dreams vanished. But Hamilton never sidestepped a fight. In October, the president came south, ending an elongated stay at home in Massachusetts. As Philadelphia lay in the grip of another siege of yellow fever, Adams's destination was Trenton, where he was scheduled to meet with his cabinet for the first time in more than six months. Adams was drawn and haggard, ill with a cold, and exhausted by his long journey. Seldom in a good mood, Adams was especially out of sorts when he sat down with his cabinet. In several meetings over five days, the last one a stressful session that continued until nearly midnight, Pickering, Wolcott, and McHenry fought the president over engaging in talks with the French. Adams held his ground. Next, the cabinet officers attempted to draft instructions to the envoys in such a manner that the talks would virtually be doomed before they began. Once again, Adams stood firm.[91]

Doubtless learning what had occurred, Hamilton, who had brought so many to his way of thinking, mounted his horse at headquarters in Newark and rode hard to reach Trenton. An air of desperation sped Hamilton on his mission. Three days before the inspector general saddled up, Jefferson had predicted that "we may expect peace" to stem from the negotiations in Paris.[92] Hamilton must have also believed that would be the outcome of the talks. He called on Adams on the pretense of discussing issues concerning the army, but Hamilton's real objective was to persuade the president to abort the peace talks in Paris.

Hamilton was shown into the parlor that Adams was using as a temporary office. As the president was staying at the home of two maiden aunts, the room was likely simply furnished. Given his illness and the trying deliberations with his cabinet, Adams's disposition, already sulky and resentful, was not improved by Hamilton's presence. For his part, Hamilton knew beforehand that he was not a favorite of Adams, but he had no idea of the depth of the president's hatred for him. Hamilton had only infrequently been in Adams's company, and the inspector general may never have previously called on this president as a supplicant. Standing before Adams, who sat smoking a cigar and listening with exemplary patience, Hamilton likely fell back on the manner that had worked so well for him on so many occasions, and especially with Adams's predecessor. Hamilton manifested an air not merely of authority but also of infallibility.

Hamilton began with a lengthy monologue on the state of Europe. He spoke condescendingly, or so Adams thought. In fact, Hamilton reminded the president, who recognized few as his intellectual equal, of a teacher addressing a callow student. Adams also thought Hamilton came across as "an impertinent ignoramus." As Hamilton proceeded, he grew more frenzied. He spoke louder, flailing with agitation. Years before, army officers had told Adams that Hamilton often grew more impassioned as he argued, so that the president, for whom this was a novel experience, was prepared. In fact, Adams subsequently said that he enjoyed this "paroxysm" on the part of his nemesis. While Hamilton argued that the Bourbons would be back on the throne by Christmas, making Adams's mission unnecessary, the president listened with delight to this desperate, "[over]wrought . . . little man."

When Hamilton concluded his discourse, Adams respectfully but assertively rejected his predictions for Europe, remarking that it was more likely that "the sun, moon & stars will fall from their orbits." (The president was the more accurate of the two. The Bourbons did regain power in France, but not until more than fifteen years after the autumn of 1799.) Thereafter, Hamilton switched course. He asserted that the peace mission would trigger war with Great Britain. Once again, Adams—correctly, as it turned out—demolished the logic of Hamilton's argument piece by piece. Adams had thoroughly beaten Hamilton, and he had done so, he later claimed, without ever losing his temper.[93]

Hamilton's world was collapsing. He had been bested by Adams, and many observers, including Jefferson and probably Hamilton as well, expected the Republicans to make considerable gains in both houses of Congress in the following year's elections.[94] Near Christmas, Hamilton received the worst news of all. Washington had died unexpectedly at Mount Vernon. Some Federalists had already begun to importune Washington to stand for the presidency in 1800, telling him that Adams was unelectable and that Jefferson surely would become the next chief executive.[95] Hamilton had not approached Washington on the matter, though it is not difficult to imagine him having a hand in the nascent campaign to lure the general back into public life. Hamilton was overcome on learning of Washington's demise. No "man . . . has equal cause with myself to deplore the loss," he said, adding: "My imagination is gloomy my heart sad." But Hamilton grieved not so much the loss of a man he loved as one who had been "an Aegis very essential to me," as he put it.[96]

Adams got in one more dig against Hamilton. He left the post of commanding officer of the army, which Washington had held, unfilled. Adams could not bring himself to elevate Hamilton to that position. It made little difference. In February 1800, two months almost to the day after Washington's death, Congress suspended enlistments in the New Army. Three months later, the army disbanded.[97]

Hamilton never gave up. He told High Federalists that Republican "sentiments dangerous to social happiness" necessitated further strengthening of the national government. Hamilton contemplated several steps, including legislation even more harsh than the Sedition Act and unspecified "Vigorous measures of counteraction" to curb the "incendiary and seditious practices" that he imagined.[98]

To achieve his ends, Hamilton knew, the Federalists must win the election of 1800, and unseat John Adams in the process.

CHAPTER 14

"THE GIGG IS UP"

THE ELECTION OF 1800

FROM THE START of the Quasi-War, and the repressive Federalist legislation that followed, it is likely that Jefferson planned to run for president in 1800.
In fact, he may never have considered not being a candidate. But, like Washington and many another of that time, Jefferson wanted to convince others that he
was a reluctant candidate. He said repeatedly that he did not want to be president. He allowed that a man's ambition raged between the ages of fifteen and
thirty-five, but thereafter one's "principal object" became a "sigh for tranquility." He was "sated with public life" by age thirty-eight, Jefferson claimed, the
time his unhappy gubernatorial years ended. Some older men continued in
public life until an advanced age, though "not from a passion for pre-eminence."
They were driven by avarice, partisan passions, or "to promote the public good
or public liberty." Of course, he stressed the latter as his reason for running.[1]

Federalist "bigots" had "dishonored our country" through their "delirium"
of looking "backwards instead of forwards," Jefferson declared. In his mind, the
election of 1800 would be a contest between those who longed for the change
heralded by the American Revolution and reactionaries who sought to revert to
a dark, static past when monarchs had held sway and those in the lower social
orders knew their place and were impounded in that place. If his side prevailed,
Jefferson believed the American Revolution would be fulfilled and the United
States would become "the asylum for whatever is great and good."[2]

Jefferson was confident. He sensed a "growing detestation" of all that the
Ultra Federalists stood for, including the "heroes of the party." The party's
demise, and with it Hamilton's downfall, would be the "last act of the federal
tragedy." Jefferson believed the Republicans could regain control of the House
of Representatives and make substantive inroads against the majority that
the Federalists had long enjoyed in the Senate.[3] The signs also looked good
for a Republican victory in the presidential election. Even an indifferent
observer—and Jefferson was not that, but a seasoned politician who followed
such things closely—could see that Republican prospects were promising.[4]

In 1796, Adams had squeaked past Jefferson by three electoral votes, winning every vote from New England, New York, New Jersey, and Delaware. Four years earlier, Jefferson had received all but two of the electoral votes from south of the Potomac, all of the votes from Kentucky and Tennessee, and four of Maryland's ten votes. Jefferson believed he could do as well, if not better, in those states in 1800.

Informed observers, including Jefferson and Hamilton, believed the election's outcome would be determined in New York, Pennsylvania, and South Carolina. Even though New York had given its twelve electoral votes to Adams and Pinckney in 1796, Jefferson radiated optimism about a shift in that state. In January 1800 he met in Philadelphia with Aaron Burr, who told him that there was "no doubt" that the Republicans would win every legislative seat at stake in April's elections in Manhattan. That, said Burr, would give the party control of the assembly, and as the assembly chose the state's presidential electors, that would mean the two Republican nominees would win all twelve of New York's electoral votes in 1800.[5]

While his prospects in New York were favorable, Jefferson knew that he would not do as well in Pennsylvania as he had in 1796, when he had won fourteen of the Keystone State's fifteen votes. The difference was that in 1800 the lower house of the state assembly was controlled by the Republicans and the upper chamber by the Federalists, and the two parties differed over the selection of presidential electors. Republicans favored a winner-take-all system, which had worked well for them in 1796. Federalists preferred to have the electors chosen in districts, through which the party seemed certain to win three or four electoral votes. If the two houses could not concur on how the electors were to be chosen, Pennsylvania would not cast any electoral votes. That would help the Federalists. If there was a compromise, it was inconceivable that the Federalists would agree to a solution that awarded Jefferson more than eight or nine votes. It was certain that Jefferson would win fewer votes in Pennsylvania than he had in the last election.

In 1796, South Carolina had done something unique. Its legislature had decreed that each of the state's presidential electors was to cast one vote for Jefferson, the Republican, and one for the favorite son Thomas Pinckney, a Federalist. What the state's electors would do in 1800 hinged on whether the Federalists once again nominated a South Carolinian and on which party controlled the assembly. The composition of the legislature would not be determined until the autumn elections.

Through the early months of 1800, Jefferson continued to tell friends that he hoped to remain the vice president, as the office enabled him to spend most of each year at home. His friends responded by telling him that they wanted him to become their president, and they expected him to be elected, as the "tyde of the Political affairs" had changed. If the chief executive was chosen by a popular vote, said one, Jefferson would receive 75 percent of the votes.[6] Like Washington in 1788 and 1789, Jefferson in 1800 was genuinely conflicted. He wanted to be president to shape America's future, but he longed to stay at home "where all is love and peace." What is more, he thought of the presidency as a "splendid misery." Nothing else that he said so encapsulated his ambivalence over the price he would have to pay to hold the office.[7]

While Jefferson was torn over the presidency, Hamilton knew that his chances of holding meaningful power in the near future were slim. On the occasion of his forty-fifth birthday in 1800, Hamilton appeared to say that he might have chosen a more promising political course. After leaving Washington's cabinet, he might have agreed to a European diplomatic assignment, or perhaps he could have served in Congress. Instead, he "had left every thing else to *follow the Drum*," to soldier. Yet, through an "Injustice," his "sacred" service had, if anything, diminished his standing. Never denying his obsessive ambition, Hamilton looked toward a distant future for vindication: "I feel that I stand on ground which, sooner or later, will ensure me a triump over all my enemies."[8]

Hamilton had intrigued in the three previous presidential elections. He intended to do so again. In 1800, he would seek Adams's political destruction, "even though the consequence should be the election of *Jefferson*."[9] Hamilton seethed with hatred for Adams, who had resisted the creation of the New Army and his appointment as inspector general. He was embittered that Adams had pursued negotiations to end the Quasi-War crisis. What he must have regarded as his belittling treatment at the hands of the president during their meeting in Trenton only further infuriated Hamilton. It was Hamilton's hope that General Charles Cotesworth Pinckney, brother of the 1796 nominee and second in command of the fading New Army, would be one of the Federalist nominees. And Hamilton planned to do all he could to ensure Pinckney's election, as it offered the best hope of his speedy return to some powerful position.

Hamilton's task of electing any Federalist grew more formidable in the wake of the New York assembly elections in April. Just as Burr had forecast, the Republicans won all the lower house seats up for grabs in Manhattan and seven of the nine that were contested in the upper house. The outcome gave the party control of the legislature. Shut out in New York in 1796, the Republicans were now guaranteed all twelve of the state's electoral votes in 1800.

What had occurred in New York disclosed a looming seismic shift in American politics. New York City had been a Federalist stronghold for the past dozen years. Manhattan had supported the ratification of the Constitution and thereafter the lion's share of its residents consistently embraced Hamiltonian economics, which both the city's tradesmen and unskilled workers viewed as the facilitator of trade, jobs, and prosperity. But in the late stages of the 1790s, those who worked with their hands turned away from the Federalist Party, increasingly seeing politics—as Hamilton discerned in an analysis in 1796—as "a question between the Rich & the poor."[10] Workers saw the Federalist Party as the home of the gentry, and viewed its tight money policies as securing the "advantage of the Few," but offering nothing to the cash-hungry members of society's lower strata. Growing numbers were put off by the party's social traditionalism and its national policies, especially the Alien and Sedition Acts, its standing army and seeming lust for war with France, and the new taxes levied to pay for the army. Some even noted that following Jefferson's departure from the State Department, the Federalists had removed from the federal currency all symbols of liberty, such as the Liberty Tree or the Liberty Cap.

The growing disenchantment with Federalist attitudes and programs, which Jefferson and others had noticed as early as 1798, had to be politically harnessed. That was precisely what Burr did in Manhattan in 1800, displaying a nearly unmatched awareness of what was soon to become standard urban political practice. He organized an operation in which decisions flowed down from a central committee to small councils at the ward level. The Republican Party published its message and held street rallies at which leaders, including Burr, addressed the crowds. Party workers campaigned door-to-door and got the voters to the polls on election day. Burr also picked legislative candidates with name recognition, including former Governor Clinton and General Horatio Gates, to run against the Federalist slate of bankers and lawyers from elite law firms. The only thing that was not modern about the Republican campaign was that—as Burr told Jefferson—it had been conducted in a "highly honorable" manner with "no indecency, no unfairness, no personal abuse."[11]

When Jefferson learned of the results in New York, he remarked that the Republican triumph went "far towards deciding the great election." Indeed, he thought it would have determined the outcome of the general election had it not been for the "peculiar circumstances" in Pennsylvania.[12] For Hamilton, however, South Carolina was now the crucial battleground. He urged his party to choose General Pinckney, a South Carolinian, as one of its nominees. Moreover, fully aware that in 1796 eighteen New England electors—fearing anti-Adams intrigue, chiefly by Hamilton—had cast their second vote for someone other than Thomas Pinckney, Hamilton appealed to the party's leaders to pledge in "a distinct & solemn concert" to "support *Adams & Pinckney*, equally." This, he added, "is the only thing that can possibly save us from the fangs of *Jefferson*."[13]

Hamilton took an additional step, one that not only laid bare his gnawing disdain for America's emerging democratic practices but that also exposed him as a relic of an earlier era. He beseeched Governor John Jay to override the recent legislative elections by summoning the current Federalist-dominated assembly into a special session to draw up a new set of rules for the selection of presidential electors. Ever the schemer, Hamilton's shocking plan was to have the outgoing legislature vote that the electors be chosen according to the popular vote in each congressional district, and for this arrangement to be retroactive. Through this ploy, the Federalists would win perhaps ten of New York's twelve electoral votes. It "will not do to be over-scrupulous" when striving "to prevent an *Atheist* in Religion and a *Fanatic* in politics from getting possession of the helm of the State," Hamilton reasoned. Jay refused to be part of such a contemptible scheme.[14]

Soon after New York's election, congressional Federalists caucused and named Adams and General Pinckney as their candidates. Thinking along the same lines as Hamilton, Jefferson observed that Pinckney's selection was one of the Federalists' typical "hocus-pocus maneuvers" to siphon Republican votes in both of the Carolinas, as they had done in 1796.[15] A few days later, the Republicans in Congress chose their candidates. Jefferson's selection was never in question, but some preferred George Clinton as the other nominee, thinking him more popular than Burr with Southerners. However, Clinton endorsed Burr, who was chosen. This time the Republican caucus stipulated that Jefferson was the party's first choice for the presidency.[16]

Burr's selection was just one of the rip currents set off by the pivotal New York election. Soon thereafter, and within hours of again receiving his party's nomination, Adams settled old scores with the disloyal McHenry and Pickering. He fired both men. His action was premeditated and vengeful, but it was political as well. Needing Connecticut's votes if he was to have any chance of winning, Adams did not oust Wolcott, whose treachery had been as great as that of his colleagues. What is more, in ridding himself of McHenry and Pickering, Adams sought to demonstrate his independence and commitment to an honorable peace, and to show that he was unfettered by the radical right wing of his party. Trolling for support in the South, more crucial than ever now that New York was lost, Adams named Virginia's John Marshall as Pickering's successor.

When the president dismissed McHenry, his bitterness toward his disloyal secretary of war, and his hatred of Hamilton, gushed forth. Near nightfall on May 5, Adams summoned McHenry from dinner to discuss a trivial federal appointment. The conference ended quickly, but as McHenry was leaving the president's office, something he said—or perhaps his tone of voice—brought Adams's volcanic rage to the surface. He accused McHenry of having deceitfully conspired with Hamilton to hamper his presidency. When the secretary tried to object, Adams silenced him. In the grip of long pent-up passions, Adams lashed out. With a burst of incivility, Adams told McHenry that he was inept and two-faced, and called him a toady of "the greatest intriguant in the World," meaning Hamilton, of course. With a head of steam, Adams insisted that Hamilton was largely responsible for the erosion of Federalist strength in Manhattan and the party's almost-certain loss of the presidency in 1800. The president did not stop there. Hamilton, he told McHenry, was "devoid of every moral principle—a Bastard, and . . . a foreigner." In what Adams must have thought would be the cruelest blow of all, he added: "Mr. Jefferson is an infinitely better man; a wiser one, I am sure, and, if President, will act wisely. I . . . would rather be Vice President under him . . . than indebted to such a being as Hamilton for the Presidency."[17]

After learning from McHenry of Adams's tirade, Hamilton set out on a three-week tour of New England. Officially, he went north "to disband Troops." No one was fooled. His "visit was merely an Electioneering business," Abigail Adams reported, and she and many others assumed he was beating the bushes on behalf of Pinckney. Soon enough, word reached the President's House in Philadelphia that Hamilton and some of his officers had encouraged political leaders in Connecticut and Rhode Island to see to it that some electoral votes were withheld from the president.[18] For months, Hamilton had been saying privately that Adams was given to capricious and irrational behavior, and that he was "very *unfit* and *incapable*." Most party leaders despised the president, he had said. In the spring, Hamilton had gone so far as to tell some of his fellow Federalists that the party might be better off if it lost the election, after which it could regroup in opposition to Jefferson's foreordained "foolish and bad measures." Once McHenry dutifully reported the president's uncivil comments, Hamilton responded that Adams was "as wicked as he is mad."[19] There can be no doubt that he aired these feelings in his talks with the Yankee activists.

There is also no question that Hamilton's trip did not go well. Time and again, New Englanders told him straightaway that they were "decidedly for the re-election of Mr. Adams," and some warned that if Hamilton persisted in his plot against the president's reelection, electoral votes would be withheld from Pinckney. Getting word of this, some South Carolinians tried to restrain Hamilton, telling him that his behavior was counterproductive and widely seen as stemming from "private pique" rather than principle.[20]

For weeks thereafter Hamilton abandoned his open vendetta against Adams, which had been as unwise as it was unnecessary. Based on the information at this disposal, Hamilton knew that Pinckney stood a good chance of outscoring the president. For one thing, South Carolina's congressional delegation had given "every assurance" that "such was the popularity of General Pinckney," that he would receive all of the state's electoral votes even if the Republicans controlled the state assembly. In other words, in a worst-case scenario, Jefferson and Pinckney would divide South Carolina's electoral votes. Furthermore, Hamilton was convinced that once it was widely perceived that Adams probably could not win, two or three Federalist electors in Connecticut and New Jersey would withhold their vote from him in the hope of securing Pinckney's election.[21]

But while Hamilton refrained from openly going after Adams, during the summer he took the extraordinary step of writing to the president. His letter was composed along the lines of a first communiqué leading to a challenge to duel. Declaring that he was "injured" by Adams's alleged assertions that he was part of a "British Faction" within the Federalist Party, Hamilton asked the president of the United States to avow or disavow his remarks. When Adams did not respond, Hamilton fired off a second letter, in which he branded the president's supposed comments to McHenry as a "wicked and cruel calumny," as well as the product of a depraved mind. Adams did not respond to that letter either. In his second missive, Hamilton had pointedly defended himself as one "who without a stain has discharged so many important public trusts." Knowing there would never be a duel, Hamilton may have engaged in this exercise in the hope of causing uneasiness in a hated nemesis who had sullied his character.[22] Whatever the reason, Hamilton's judgment was at best clouded, and this was only his most recent instance of imprudence. As Hamilton disparaged Adams's soundness, his own volatility, even irrationality, was growing more evident.

Jefferson returned home from Philadelphia in May and remained at Monticello for the duration of the campaign. Of the four candidates, only Burr openly electioneered, trekking to New England and New Jersey in a vain search for a Federalist elector or two who might be persuaded to vote for the Republican candidates.[23] The others sought to convey to the public that they awaited a call to the presidency that they would not seek. Despite their posturing, Adams and Jefferson stealthily courted voters. Adams's purge of his cabinet was done with an eye on the election, and late in May he also rode south to inspect the new Federal City on the Potomac—or Washington, as everyone was calling it—which was slated to become the national capital on June 15. Adams took a roundabout route through the backcountry of Pennsylvania and Maryland, states in which he had garnered only eight of a possible twenty-five electoral votes in 1796. In the course of his peripatetic journey, the president stopped in one dusty village after another to deliver a brief speech. He repeatedly emphasized his commitment to national independence, his role in the American Revolution, and his blood ties to his acclaimed cousin, Samuel Adams.[24]

Jefferson had also taken a circuitous route on his trip home earlier that same month, swinging through Richmond, which he had not previously visited during his vice presidency.[25] The detour permitted him to shore up the Republican base in the face of recent Federalist successes. Jefferson delivered no speeches that summer or fall, but he wrote a campaign autobiography, the first presidential candidate to do so. He listed achievements that he had "been the instrument of doing": writing the Declaration of Independence, terminating the foreign slave trade in Virginia, sending a "great number of olive plants . . . to . . . S. Carola"—that most crucial of states—and seeking a "more general diffusion of knowledge" in Virginia.[26] Jefferson additionally wrote numerous letters in which he spelled out his convictions, producing a party platform of sorts. He articulated his belief in reserving to the state those powers not expressly given to the national government, and he added that he wished to retire the national debt, limit the president's encroachment on congressional authority, eliminate the standing army, keep the navy small, and rely on the militia to safeguard national security. He opposed foreign alliances—"let our affairs be disentangled from those of all other nations, except as to commerce"—and wished for free trade with all nations. He favored freedom of religion and the press, and opposed "all violations of the constitution to silence . . . our citizens."[27]

While most of the candidates avoided the hustings, party activists were busy. For the most part, both sides spread their message through pamphlets, broadsides, and newspapers. The Federalists had a decided edge in the press, but Republican newspapers had climbed from about 15 percent of the total in 1796 to nearly one-third by 1800. The Republicans were better organized for disseminating information, as they established committees of correspondence to funnel publications to the hinterland. Each party's campaign literature proclaimed its policies, but much of it also consisted of what today is called "negative" or "attack ads," bitter, often scurrilous invective directed toward the other side.[28]

Some Republican penmen limned Adams as a monarchist and portrayed Pinckney as a mediocrity, but their essayists mostly focused on the Federalist program. One writer after another attacked the Alien and Sedition Acts, the taxes levied to pay for the debt and the New Army, and the very existence of the standing army. Much of their ink was spilled on Hamilton's economic program, and, indeed, almost as many barbs were directed at the former treasury secretary as at the president. The "ambitious, amorous little Hamilton," said one Republican, was responsible for having run up a twenty-million-dollar national debt in peacetime, roughly one-third as much as had been accumulated in the entire Revolutionary War. Funding was the "most memorable piece of imbecility and impudence that was ever imposed on a nation," said another. Calling their foes the "Anglo-federal party," many scribblers emphasized the link between Federalist and British economics. In time, they argued, Hamiltonianism would transform America into a land dominated by corrupt stockjobbers who saw peace as their greatest enemy. Federalist opposition to political and social change was another focal point of the Republican message. Party writers insisted that there was little to distinguish the Federalist Party and the Tories who in 1776 had opposed breaking with Great Britain. In this vein, Republicans repeatedly broadcast Hamilton's pro-monarchy speech to the Constitutional Convention.

Republicans also defended Jefferson. His Declaration of Independence was "the most sublime production of genius which either the ancient or modern world has exhibited." He was the friend of small farmers and American commerce, the foe of high taxes, standing armies, and any who sought to impose their religious beliefs on others. Jefferson would preserve the peace. He would save the American Revolution. Asserting that the real meaning of the election concerned the fulfillment of the "Spirit of 1776," it was said: "If your independence was worth achieving, it is worth preserving," and Jefferson was the candidate who would do so.

New England Federalists made a case for Adams as a trenchant thinker and prudent statesman who had resisted the temptation to rush madly to war. As the campaign unfolded, however, other Federalists openly insisted that Pinckney's chances of winning were better than those of the president. They defended the South Carolinian as a moderate with a distinguished war record, a public figure without a blot on his record, a soldier who had won the esteem of General Washington.

Federalists took credit for the nation's economic well-being since 1789 and trumpeted that Washington had sympathized with what the party stood for. Their principal tactic was to take the offensive, and they were good at it, so good that few future mudslingers surpassed them. Federalists painted the Republicans as indistinguishable from radical French Jacobins, and stamped their adversaries as democrats, atheists, and wild-eyed revolutionaries who would not rest until they dragged the United States to war against Great Britain.

The abuse that Republicans directed against Hamilton paled in comparison to the calumny heaped on Jefferson. Jefferson was said to have gulled his clients while a practicing attorney. His war record was one of "uninspiring patriotism." He lived sumptuously while others sacrificed during the war,

322 JEFFERSON AND HAMILTON

acted as a coward when Tarleton's soldiers descended on Monticello in June 1781, and thereafter never "peeped out of his hermitage" until the war ended. Nor had he authored the Declaration of Independence; it was the work of a committee. Federalists charged that Jefferson's residence in France had transformed him into a dangerous radical, so that when he returned to America his head was filled with a "stock of visionary nonsense." A Federalist newspaper in Virginia alleged that Jefferson had a slave mistress. The closest the charge came to receiving any attention elsewhere, however, came when a New York paper enigmatically called him "a libertine." Federalists twisted Jefferson's advocacy of religious freedom in *Notes on the State of Virginia* to brand him an atheist. New Englanders were warned to hide their Bibles should Jefferson become president, and across the land Federalists cautioned that Jefferson's election would call down God's vengeance on the United States. Voters were told that their choice was between "A RELIGIOUS PRESIDENT or . . . JEFFERSON—AND NO GOD." Federalists had a field day with the Mazzei letter, which led them to charge that Jefferson hated Washington. They rebuked him as a "Solomon of Jacobinism." Speaking at a Federalist gathering that summer in Boston, Hamilton said he hoped American tradesmen would "never act as the *Journeymen* of Jacobinism; nor as *Master-workmen* in the Mazzeian *Babel*."[29]

That was not all that Hamilton said during this election. Early in the summer, Hamilton encouraged his closest political allies to spread word of Adams's "unfitness." His entreaties fell on deaf ears. When he told them of his plans to publish a tract that chronicled "in detail" the president's supposed shortcomings, many advised against it, cautioning that it would divide the party. With pitiless honesty, one friend warned that such a tract would constitute "new proof that you are a *dangerous man*." Still churning with resentment at Adams, and driven by a recklessness that had recently grown more pronounced, Hamilton could not be dissuaded. By late summer he had completed his draft of a pamphlet that he intended to have circulated only in South Carolina, hoping it would discourage that state's electors from voting for Adams. Once his draft was complete, Hamilton passed it along to acquaintances for criticism. Someone in possession of the manuscript turned it over to a Philadelphia editor, who, seeing a major story, published extracts. A few days later, just a few weeks before the electors were to vote, the *Letter from Alexander Hamilton, Concerning the Public Conduct and Character of John Adams, Esq. President of the United States*, appeared as a pamphlet.[30]

Hamilton filled fifty-four pernicious pages with venom about Adams's allegedly wrongheaded behavior as a congressman, diplomat, and chief executive. The heart of his indictment was that Adams's virtues were offset by his "distempered jealousy," "extreme egotism," "vanity without bounds," "ungovernable indiscretion," and "ungovernable temper," traits that had led the president to spurn the "prudent" advice of his cabinet and to act impetuously and injudiciously. Already, Adams had torn down much that President Washington had achieved, Hamilton claimed. Given four more years, he might bring the Union to the brink of doom.[31]

Hamilton's published rejoinder to Callender in 1797 had been harmful. His public assault on Adams was ruinous. Hamilton's standing was already in decline. His junket to New England had failed, the Federalist governors of New York and Maryland—and some party regulars in Congress—condemned his intrigue to defeat the president, and when word leaked out of Adams's barbed comments to McHenry about Hamilton's character, not a few Yankees were inclined to agree. In July, Hamilton acknowledged that he no longer could sway the "second class" Federalists, the lesser, mostly younger, members of his party.[32] When the *Letter from Alexander Hamilton* appeared, perceptive observers such as Madison instantly realized that the pamphlet's "recoil" would hurt Hamilton more than it would Adams, and in fact it was not long before Noah Webster, a New York Federalist editor, countered with a tract charging that the former treasury secretary's "ambition, pride, and overbearing temper" were leading the party, and possibly the Union, to devastation. Even Robert Troup, Hamilton's friend since college, candidly told him: "Not a man . . . but condemns it."[33]

Some of the traits that Hamilton attributed to Adams were true, but some aptly described his own character, as his former adherent, George Cabot, a Massachusetts senator, told him.[34] Disregarding sound advice, Hamilton's rancor and thirst for power and fame—as well as revenge—had driven him to act rashly. Some signs of Hamilton's flawed temperament were apparent years earlier. In some respects, it is surprising that he rose as far as he did. It is even more astonishing that so many other public figures permitted themselves to become satellites orbiting about him, or like Washington to believe so deeply in him. For Jefferson, on the other hand, Hamilton's latest act was merely further confirmation that he was indeed "the evil genius of this country."[35]

People spoke of December 3 as "Election Day." They were referring to the day designated for the presidential electors to meet and vote. There was no single day when voters went to the polls. The electors were chosen by popular vote in only five of the sixteen states. Elsewhere, state legislatures chose them, and the assembly elections were conducted throughout the year. However, by autumn, as the Pennsylvania and South Carolina elections approached, the likely outcome had come into sharper relief.

All along, many assumed that Adams had been mortally wounded by the Republicans' springtime victory in New York, but the president never entirely lost hope, and in the fall his cause was helped immeasurably by events in Pennsylvania. The state's October 14 elections resulted in a stunning victory for the Republicans, who captured fifty-five of the seventy-eight seats in the lower house of the assembly, won six of the seven seats up for grabs in the upper house, and carried ten of the thirteen congressional districts. Nevertheless, even though three-fifths of Pennsylvania's voters had demonstrated a preference for Republican candidates, the Federalists still clung to a narrow majority in the statehouse's upper chamber, and they used it to block a decision on the choice of presidential electors. The deadlock dragged on for weeks. With Election Day on the horizon, it appeared that Pennsylvania might be unrepresented in the electoral college. But at the last moment the two parties reached an agreement, each hopeful that its presidential candidate would ultimately triumph, and each lusting after the spoils of office should their party be victorious. The compromise awarded eight electoral votes to the Republicans and seven to the Federalists.[36]

As the heavy skies of November set in, Adams knew that he would win six more votes in Pennsylvania, Jefferson six fewer, than in 1796. But both knew that Jefferson's total from New York and Pennsylvania would be six votes more than he had garnered four years earlier. In 1796, Adams had won nine votes in Maryland, North Carolina, and Virginia, and he might win that many again in 1800. Still, that would leave him short of a majority. For a Federalist to win this election, Adams or Pinckney had to capture all, or most, of South Carolina's eight electoral votes. What is more, Jefferson, who had won all eight of South Carolina's votes in 1796, had to be shut out, or nearly so, in that state.

Thanks to the sun-seared South Carolina backcountry—whose inhabitants hated the Bank of the United States, had never cottoned to a strong national government, and were roiled by the taxes levied by the Federalists in 1798 to pay for the army—the Republicans piled up a majority in that autumn's assembly elections. It now was certain that Adams could not win. On the face of it, the assembly elections suggested that the next president would be a Republican, but nothing was ever so simple in the election of 1800. As Jefferson put it, "considering local & personal interests & prejudices," it "is impossible to foresee how the juggle will work" in South Carolina's assembly.[37] He was referring to the fact that many of his followers were also devoted to General Pinckney. If the assembly directed the state's electors to give their two votes to Jefferson and Pinckney, the latter's vote total would likely exceed seventy, more than a majority of the electoral votes and possibly more than the seventy-one Adams had received in his winning bid in 1796.

On the eve of Election Day, South Carolina's legislature acted. About a dozen Republican assemblymen refused to buckle to pressure to support Pinckney. "[B]elieving the fortune of America to depend on our vote," one of the legislators wrote to Jefferson, the electors were directed to vote for the "republican *candidates only*." To that, the legislator added: "Our state has done itself immortal honour." Another South Carolinian reported to Jefferson that the electors had agreed to withhold one vote from Burr; one elector would cast his vote for George Clinton. As late as December 12, Jefferson believed he had won the election, and he told a friend: the "votes will stand probably T.J. 73. Burr about 70. mr. Adams 65. Pinckney probably lower than that."[38]

Jefferson's assessment was informed, but incorrect. While dead-on with regard to Adams and Pinckney, he was startled to learn in mid-December that South Carolina's electors had given all of their votes to Jefferson and Burr. The result was that the two Republicans had finished in a dead heat with seventy-three electoral votes apiece. The vote had been along sectional lines. Adams had won 86 percent of his votes in the North. Jefferson had garnered nearly 73 percent of his votes in the South.

Despite the fury of the campaign, no one had yet won. The House of Representatives would have to choose the president. The Constitution stipulated that in the event two candidates tied with a majority of electoral votes, the House was to determine the winner with each state casting one vote. The Congress in session had been elected in 1798, and the Federalists had a sixty-four to forty-two majority. That was inconsequential. What mattered was that the Republicans had a majority in eight delegations, and the Federalists in seven, while Vermont's two congressmen were split along party lines. In keeping with the convoluted nature of this election, a Maryland Federalist announced his intention of voting for Jefferson, a decision that left that state's delegation, like Vermont's, equally divided. With sixteen delegations, nine votes would be needed to win. The Republicans lacked a majority, and that, said Jefferson, produced great "exultation in the federalists," who saw an opportunity for intrigue.[39]

Early in December, thinking he had won the election, Jefferson sent a carefully written letter to Burr. Saying that he wished "to compose an administration," Jefferson made clear his belief that he was to become the chief executive. More cryptically, he appeared to make an offer: Should Burr not contest the election in the House, Jefferson would give him greater powers than Washington and Adams had bestowed on their vice presidents. Burr's response, written when he also believed Jefferson had won the election, was reassuring. He not only spoke of "your administration," but also expressed a yearning for an "Active station." In other published letters in December, Burr pledged to "disclaim all competition."[40]

The House could not act until the election results were opened and tabulated in the Senate, which was set by law for February 11. That gave the Federalists two months to discuss their options. Some wished to challenge the
outcome in several states, hoping to invalidate a sufficient number of electoral votes to award victory to Adams. Others wanted to prevent the House
from reaching a decision, which would leave executive authority in the hands
of the Federalist pro tempore of the Senate until the newly elected Republican
Congress assembled late in 1801. Bolder spirits proposed calling for a second
election, grounding their argument on a 1792 presidential succession act stip-
ulating that a special election be held if both the presidency and vice presidency were vacant. A few Federalists were swept up by a January newspaper
essay written by "Horatius." It proposed that in the event of a House deadlock, Adams should appoint, with congressional consent, an "officer of the
United States" to serve as president during the next four years. Helpfully, the
author suggested that the designated official should be Secretary of State John
Marshall—who in all likelihood was the essayist who offered the solution.
Some Federalists viewed the House contest as a heaven-sent opportunity to
sow fatal divisions within the Republican ranks. Perhaps the majority, seeing
this as a choice "among Rotten Apples," as one put it, advocated stringing
things out until either Jefferson or Burr agreed to a brokered deal. Some,
whose enmity toward Jefferson had deep roots, wanted to back Burr, who,
after all, hailed from a northern mercantile state. A few—very few—thought
it only right to concede the victory to Jefferson, the clear-cut popular choice.[41]

Hamilton immediately jumped in. He backed Jefferson over Burr, portraying the Virginian as the lesser of two evils. Despite acknowledging that with
"Burr I have always been personally well," Hamilton in the next breath said:
"As to Burr, there is nothing in his favour." Hamilton called him a "profligate"
and an "unprincipled . . . voluptuary." He charged that Burr was consumed
with "extreme & irregular ambition" and given to "infinite art [and] cunning."
He would plunder the country, destroy the Constitution, and erect in its stead
a "system . . . sufficient to serve his own ends," including probably "simple *despotism*." Jefferson was a hypocrite whose "politics are tinctured with fanati-
cism," but he was "*able* and *wise*," whereas Burr was shifty and "*dexterous*."
Burr, said Hamilton, was the "most dangerous man of the Community."[42]

A Federalist here and there might have shared Hamilton's feelings about
Burr, but his overheated views were not typical. Senator Cabot, for instance,
thought Burr safer than Jefferson, who would cause "the roots of our Society
[to be] pulled up & a new course of cultivation substituted."[43]

Hamilton's vilification of Burr was consistent with the abuse he had frequently directed at his antagonist. For a decade, Hamilton had portrayed

Burr as unscrupulous, devoid of principles, rash and irresponsible in his private affairs, and given to intrigue. Hamilton regarded his assaults as part and parcel of politics, and claimed that notwithstanding the savagery of his allegations, he and Burr had an amicable relationship. If it was as friendly as Hamilton insisted, it may in part have been so because Burr had never responded with even a fraction of his rival's hostility, and he refrained from questioning Hamilton's character and temperament.[44]

Hamilton's obsession with Burr stemmed from his understanding that if Burr was elected through the connivance of the Federalists, the party—which Hamilton regarded as his own—would never be the same again. Federalists who contemplated a bargain with Burr during the contest in the House might believe they could subsequently control him. Hamilton knew better. "We can never have him fairly in our power," he said, for Hamilton recognized that Burr was a very modern politician who believed in and practiced democratic politics. He would use the enormous powers of the presidency to build his base. To "My Mind," Hamilton said, "the elevation of Mr Burr by Federal Means to the Chief Magistracy of the U. States will be the worst kind of political suicide" for the Federalist Party and all that it had stood for.[45]

Hamilton's analysis was astute, but his voice no longer carried the weight it once had. Some Federalists reached out to Burr, and he listened. Burr had assured Jefferson of his loyalty, but that was before he knew the election had failed to produce a victor. Thereafter, while not openly seeking the presidency, he was willing to listen to what the Federalists had to offer.[46] Though Burr was within a whisker of winning the biggest prize in American politics, he never came to Washington and bargained directly with the Federalists who would cast the deciding votes, and that may have been his undoing if he really intended to betray Jefferson. He wrote numerous letters from New York, but the machinations in Washington were so fast-moving that Burr's communiqués, and the ones he received, were nearly always outdated.

Much of what was undertaken, including by Jefferson, was swathed in mystery. But not everything could be kept secret. Thanks to his long-standing intelligence network, Jefferson was aware early on that the Federalists were seeking to "debauch" Burr with an offer of some sort, and he knew, too, of Hamilton's preference for him over Burr. A week into January—about three weeks after the electoral college vote was public knowledge—Jefferson still believed that Burr's "conduct has been honorable & decisive." Not long thereafter, however, he discovered that "Burr . . . ha[d] agents here at work." That prompted a letter to Burr in Albany, warning that the Federalists were seeking "to sow tares between us." Later, when Burr would not openly disavow the presidency, Jefferson seethed with anger. Much later, Jefferson declared that Burr had "inspired me with distrust" from nearly their first meeting.[47]

Jefferson felt that he was "surrounded by enemies & spies catching & per-verting every word which falls from my lips," and he added that he longed to "fly from [this] circle of cabal, intrigue & hatred." Given the carnival of con-spiracy and deceit playing out in Washington, Jefferson could not be certain that he knew of each and every maneuver, but of one thing he was absolutely sure: he was approached by some Federalists with an offer. If he would agree to a deal, Vermont's Federalist congressman would switch sides and vote for him on the first ballot. That would give Jefferson nine states and victory. What they wanted in return is not known, but Hamilton had been pushing the Federalists in the House of Representatives to offer a bargain: in return for Federalist votes, Jefferson must assure them that the fiscal system would remain intact; United States neutrality in Europe's wars would continue; the navy would be preserved and gradually augmented; and with the exception of the cabinet, Federalist officeholders would be kept in place. Hamilton's plan, or something very close to it, likely comprised the tender offered to Jef-ferson. He rejected it. He was running an incredible risk, but Jefferson had a deft feel for politics that was reinforced by information from party activists. He was convinced that the eight states with Republican majorities were sol-idly in his column. That left Burr with the six Federalist-dominated delega-tions: the four older New England states plus Delaware and South Carolina. Jefferson was one vote short. Burr was three votes short.[48]

February 11 was the day set for officially counting the electoral votes, after which the House would decide the election of 1800. It was a Wednesday, three weeks prior to Inauguration Day. Residents of Washington awakened that morning to a driving snowstorm. Members of Congress and the vice presi-dent left their warm lodgings late in the morning and hazarded icy walks and windblown snowdrifts on their climbs up Capitol Hill. Precisely at noon, the Senate convened and the electoral college ballots were tabulated.[49] As soon as Jefferson, who was constitutionally responsible for counting the votes, an-nounced the outcome that all had known for weeks, the House members hur-ried to their chamber.

The House vote on the first ballot, taken at one P.M., was exactly what had been expected: Jefferson eight, Burr six, two states—Maryland and Vermont—deadlocked. Jefferson was one vote short of victory. As rumors had circulated that a vote or two might change after the initial ballot, the House quickly voted again. It is now known that a scheme had been hatched—which Burr was aware of, and had not quashed—to have congressmen from New York, New Jersey, and Vermont switch from Jefferson to Burr on the second ballot.⁵⁰ The plan fizzled. The second House vote was identical to the first. The House continued to vote. By six o'clock, fifteen ballots had been taken. The tally never changed. As darkness gathered over the capital, the House adjourned so that its members could have dinner. Returning around nine o'clock, the congressmen began to vote again, thereafter balloting more or less every hour on the hour until eight A.M.—with the same result each time. Many congressmen grabbed some sleep between votes, groggily rising from their cots when summoned to cast their ballot; some even voted while wearing a nightcap. As a gray dawn spilled over the capital at eight A.M., the House leadership called a temporary halt for breakfast. Twenty-seven ballots had been cast in a span of nineteen hours. The congressmen returned around noon and cast a twenty-eighth ballot. It was identical to all the others. At that point, the House called it quits for the day, and the members made their cold, slippery walk home.⁵¹

The House balloted only once on Friday. The vote had not changed. On Saturday, three ballots were taken. Still no change. When the members departed for their lodgings in the chilly dusk of Saturday evening, they had voted thirty-three times in four days.

Jefferson had once expressed little interest in the presidency, but no longer. He wanted the victory that he knew he had won and believed he deserved. He had not been home from France long before he took up the fight against those who, as he saw it, wished to frustrate the true meaning of the American Revolution. Throughout the 1790s he fought what he believed was a reactionary effort to reestablish what had existed in pre-Revolutionary Anglo-America. At last, in 1800 he had beaten them, yet as day after day passed, and ballot after deadlocked ballot was cast, victory eluded him.

Jefferson was a fighter for what he believed in, and that winter, with his presidency and the triumph of the American Revolution in jeopardy, he fought back, and with no holds barred. Washington buzzed with rumors that Virginia would secede if Jefferson was denied victory. Jefferson never made such a threat explicitly, but he warned that Federalist intrigue threatened "a dissolution" of the Union, and he said simply that he could not restrain his supporters. Nor did he quash talk that Pennsylvania and Virginia would unleash armies of militiamen to prevent his election from being stolen, even after Federalist newspapers countered that New England would field sixty thousand militiamen to meet Pennsylvania's "factious foreigners" and the "*fighting* bacchanals" from the South. Jefferson also visited Adams, probably on the Saturday of the House balloting. Without success, he urged Adams to veto any Federalist legislation that would foil the Republican victory; Jefferson additionally warned that what he called a Federalist coup d'état might be resisted with force. Other Republicans took up the cudgel, "openly and firmly" warning their foes that "the middle States would arm" and resist with force Federalist "usurpation." However, the tipping point may have been Republican talk of calling another constitutional convention to "re-organize the government, & to amend it" so that it reflected the "democratical spirit of America." The threat of rewriting the Constitution aroused great concern among the Federalists. Jefferson said it "shook" them and gave "them the horrors."[52]

The break that Jefferson had hoped for came on Saturday night or Sunday morning. Delaware's lone congressman, James Bayard, who had voted for Burr on every ballot, told Federalist leaders that on Monday he would vote for Jefferson. Subsequently, Bayard claimed to have changed sides only after Jefferson, through an intermediary, entered into "a deal" such as Hamilton and others had been advocating.

All that is known for certain is that the Federalists caucused twice on Sunday and that Bayard was showered with invective by colleagues who were holding out for Burr. Bayard characterized the verbal assaults as "reproaches vehement."[53] He bowed to the pressure, agreeing to continue voting against Jefferson until word arrived from Burr as to whether or not he would agree to a deal with the Federalists. Word from Burr had not reached the capital by noon on Monday, when the House convened and balloted twice. There was no change in the tally. Following the second ballot—its thirty-fifth—the House adjourned and the congressmen scattered. Later on that cold winter day, Burr's letter arrived. After reading his communiqué—which was soon destroyed—Speaker Sedgwick declared: "the gigg is up." Burr had refused the terms demanded by the Federalists. Burr was "determined not to shackle himself with federal principles," Bayard remarked, and in disgust added: "Burr has acted a miserable paultry part. The election was in his power, but he was determined to come in as a Democrat."[54] Burr had not just lost the election; he had ruined himself politically by refusing from the start to acknowledge Jefferson as the victor. He had alienated his own party by intriguing with the Federalists, and infuriated the Federalists with his last-minute failure to strike a deal. He would hold the office of vice president, but henceforth he was a pariah in the South, which in 1801 was the heartland of the Republican Party, and an enemy of Jefferson, the party's leader.

The following day, February 17, the House on its thirty-sixth ballot decided the election of 1800. Bayard, together with South Carolina's all-Federalist delegation, abstained in the final vote, while Maryland and Vermont balloted for Jefferson, who received the votes of ten states.

Jefferson was, at last, the president-elect. He had been the first to take the lead in organizing opposition to Hamiltonianism, and he was the symbol around which those who hated the Federalist Party rallied, the figure above all others who had articulated the dreams of political and social change that all along had been part of the American Revolution. The Federalist leadership, including Hamilton, had failed to comprehend the new political culture that had been materializing during the past quarter century—and especially in the 1790s—and in time the party came to be seen as representing interests disconnected from much of the citizenry. Once the party was thought to have been taken over by extremists, it was doomed.

No one contributed more to the Federalist Party's demise than Hamilton. In his quest for glory he had created an army that much of the citizenry feared and hated; in his scorn for Adams, Hamilton had sundered a party in which many members both continued to believe in the president and yearned for the honorable peace that he sought. Adams, in fact, had done better than his party in the election of 1800. The president was defeated in a squeaker, while other Federalists were drubbed in numerous congressional contests, losing control of the House and for the first time the Senate as well.

The Nationalists—the conservatives—had written a Constitution in 1787 that aimed at making change difficult, and the election of 1800 demonstrated just how hard change could be. Jefferson won by a slender margin, and despite his oft-repeated denials, it is likely that he had agreed to a bargain with the Federalists in order to win the election. Burr was told at the time by friends in Washington that Jefferson had struck a deal. Furthermore, a Maryland congressman gave credence to the story, and Bayard's correspondence—and the subsequent testimony under oath by two participants in the purported negotiations—point toward a bargain having been made.[55] In addition, Jefferson's actions as president lend credence to the allegations. Despite his decade-long fight against Hamiltonianism, President Jefferson never touched the Bank of the United States, continued borrowing by the federal government, and never sought the wholesale removal of Federalist officeholders.[56]

But if Jefferson had agreed to a secret bargain, he had not acted disgracefully. Indeed, by doing so, he may have prevented civil war and saved the Union.

CHAPTER 15

"THIS AMERICAN WORLD WAS NOT MADE FOR ME"

A GLORIOUS BEGINNING AND A TRAGIC END

JEFFERSON SPENT THE FIFTEEN DAYS between the House's decisive vote and Inauguration Day, March 4, putting together his cabinet, contemplating diplomatic assignments, and working on his forthcoming address.

Sometime before Abigail Adams departed for home—she left on the Friday that the House cast its twenty-ninth ballot—Jefferson called on her to say goodbye. Sadly, the warmth she had once felt for him was a casualty of several years of partisan rancor, and the atmosphere of what would be their final visit must have been cold and formal. Her feelings were shared by her husband, who refused to call on and congratulate his newly elected successor.[1]

Jefferson was living at Conrad and McMunn's, where he had taken lodgings in November. The boardinghouse, on the south side of Capitol Hill, was home to thirty residents, all Republicans, including a couple of congressmen who had brought their wives to Washington. The boarders joined Jefferson every day for breakfast and dinner at a common dining table. For the most part, the other lodgers had a small room or shared accommodations "like scholars in a college or monks in a monastery," as Adams put it. Jefferson lived more commodiously. He had rented a private room, parlor, and reception room. Hardly posh, they were convenient for greeting visitors, of which there was no shortage.[2]

On the Monday before Wednesday's inaugural celebration, Jefferson rented a carriage. Where he rode is not known, but if he toured Washington, he saw a work in progress. It was mostly a construction zone littered with piles of building materials, rude shacks for the free and slave work crews, and unpaved roads that long since had been turned to a fetid ooze by winter snows and rains and heavily laden wagons. Five hotels, a few inns, several boardinghouses, and a sprinkling of shops dotted the landscape. The two-story brick Treasury was the only completed federal building. The Capitol and the President's House, like the buildings for the State and War Departments, were usable, though unfinished.[3] Jefferson spent Tuesday in his apartment, probably making the final changes to the inaugural address which had already undergone at least two drafts.

A creature of habit, Jefferson arose as usual before dawn on March 4. He wrote a single letter, tending to private business in Richmond, and enjoyed breakfast with the usual clan at the congested dining table. Mostly, he waited for the ceremonies to begin. At ten o'clock the Washington artillery company began firing its field pieces, and soon thereafter a company of riflemen from Alexandria paraded in the muck before the president-elect's boardinghouse.

Around eleven o'clock Jefferson emerged. Like his predecessors, he had chosen to wear a plain suit, but unlike them, he eschewed a ceremonial sword. There was another striking difference. Washington had ridden to his first inaugural in his luxurious coach, and Adams had been conveyed to his in a splendid carriage drawn by six huge horses. Jefferson chose to walk, the simple and commonest means of getting about for most Americans, who found carriages, and in some instances even horses, beyond their means.

The little procession was led by United States marshals and officers of Alexandria's militia, who marched with swords drawn. Jefferson was joined by all the Republicans in Congress and two members of Adams's cabinet. Adams himself was not present. Misguidedly construing the festivities as a celebration of his defeat, Adams refused to join in. He had caught the four A.M. stagecoach out of town.[4]

As the ceremony began in Washington, celebrations were occurring elsewhere. News of Jefferson's election by the House had already triggered cannonading and spontaneous parades, bonfires, and the pealing of bells in many towns. The *Aurora*, a Republican newspaper in Philadelphia, had declared: "The Revolution of 1776 is now, and for the first time, arrived at its completion." Until now, it went on, much that Americans had sought in throwing off British domination had been held in check by "the secret enemies of the American Revolution." But Jefferson's election meant nothing less than the triumph of "the true . . . Republican principle." Now, on Inauguration Day, a second round of celebrating commenced in many cities and hamlets. A float in Philadelphia's parade featured a young woman dressed as Liberty who was harassed by kings, soldiers, and clergy, but was saved by a man playing Jefferson.[5]

Jefferson's mud-splattered walk up gently sloping Capitol Hill took only a few minutes. When he arrived at the Capitol, still under construction, nearby artillery rang out and his militia honor guard saluted smartly. Passing through a scrum of curious onlookers and well-wishers, he entered the building and was escorted into the Senate chamber. Some Federalist congressmen had stayed away, unable to endure the sight of Jefferson taking office, but seemingly everyone else in Washington was there. A newspaper reported that 1,140 people, including 154 women, were packed into the tiny chamber. Burr, of course, was present, and had taken his oath of office earlier in the morning. He surrendered his chair to Jefferson. Following an introduction by the vice president, Jefferson rose and read his address in a barely audible voice, described by one observer as "almost femininely soft."[6]

Of the first four inaugural addresses, only Jefferson's was memorable. Much of it was a lyrical paean to the new president's belief that America's revolutionary heritage had at last been fulfilled. But there was more. Hoping to defuse passions and restore unity in the fractured land, he began by attempting to reassure the losers. He spoke of his hopes for a restoration of "harmony and affection without which liberty, and even life itself, are but dreary things." He insisted that the vanquished in the recent election "possess their equal rights." Americans have differed over policies, he added, "but every difference of opinion is not a difference of principle. We have called by different names brethren of the same principle. We are all republicans: we are all federalists." He did not capitalize the terms, as he was not referring to political parties. He meant that members of both parties embraced republicanism and federalism, in which the national government possessed some powers and the states other powers.

Summarizing his ideology and expectations, Jefferson declared that the sum of good government was restraint in spending and commitment to the liberty and equality of all free persons. He added that the nation's rulers must focus on this "chosen country," not any foreign nation. The best government would seek peace through commerce and avoid "entangling alliances." Such a government would have no reason to impose onerous taxes on its citizenry. It "shall not take from the mouth of labor the bread it has earned," was how he put it. He acknowledged that some worried that such a government would be too weak to secure the interests of the United States, but he declared that America possessed "the strongest government of earth." It was the world's only government, he said, "where every man, at the call of the law, would fly to the standard . . . and meet invasions of the public order as his own personal concern."

In closing, Jefferson expanded on how his presidency would carry out the ideals of the American Revolution. He was committed to "a jealous care of the right of election by the people"; the "absolute acquiescence in the decisions of the majority"; the conviction that "a well disciplined militia [is] our best reliance in peace"; the "supremacy of the civil over the military authority"; the "honest payment of our debts"; "equal and exact justice to all men"; and the preservation of the rights and liberties of free men. "The wisdom of our sages, and blood of our heroes have been devoted" to attaining these ends. They should be the "creed of our political faith [and] . . . touchstone by which to try the services of those we trust."[7]

When Jefferson finished, Chief Justice John Marshall administered the oath of office. Thereafter, Jefferson returned to his boardinghouse, where he lived for two more weeks until all of the Adamses' possessions had been removed from the President's House. According to legend, it was mealtime at Conrad and McMunn's when Jefferson returned to his residence, and he stood with his fellow boarders awaiting a chair so that he might have his dinner.[8]

Alexander Hamilton was not in Washington for Jefferson's inauguration. In fact, he never set foot near the District of Columbia, something he likely would have done had he ever visited Mount Vernon.

Reading Jefferson's speech in the newspapers, Hamilton agreed with the more moderate Federalists who thought it "better than *we* expected." He publicly remarked that the address provided "a ray of hope" that Jefferson would not pursue a "violent and absurd" course. He was especially happy that Jefferson had neither designated funding nor the Jay Treaty as "abuses."[9]

Not many cared any longer what Hamilton thought. During his first week in office, Jefferson smugly noted that Hamilton was "almost destitute of followers." Hamilton was all too aware of that, and no less aware of the malevolence "which friends as well as foes are fond of giving to my conduct." Calling himself a "disappointed politician," Hamilton had to wonder whether he had the slightest hope of ever again being an important figure on the national stage.[10] At times, he seemed resigned to spending the remainder of his days in private pursuits. On occasion, he declared that the "passions" that had driven him to grasp power and win fame had waned because of the "triumphant reign of Decomocracy," as he spelled it. At other times, however, he confessed that his dismal prospects spread "gloom" to "the bottom of my soul," and he confided to close friends that he was waging a struggle "to abstract my self from" public affairs. If Burr was a capable judge, Hamilton's inner turmoil was intense. In April, the vice president told Jefferson that Hamilton "seems to be literally Mad with spleen and envy and disappointment."[11]

Hamilton often maintained that nothing any longer mattered to him but his wife and children, and that he could "find true pleasure" only through them.[12] "What can I do better than withdraw from the [public] Scene," he said a year after Jefferson became president. Yet, he grew despondent observing the swirling social and political changes of Jefferson's world all about him, and he was suffused with melancholy when he lamented, "Every day proves to me more and more that this American world was not made for me."[13]

As if to show that family mattered most, Hamilton began construction of a country estate, an undertaking that had never especially interested him before. He visualized the dwelling as "a fine house," and named it "The Grange" after his clan's ancestral home in Scotland. At times, he implied that the house was to be a "refuge" for one with no future in public affairs.[14] He acquired thirty-five acres above Harlem Heights—between 140th and 147th Streets on today's Upper West Side—for the stupendously expensive sum of fifty-five thousand dollars. Though a cottage, with barns and sheds, had been built on the property by a previous owner, Hamilton's sylvan tract was still virgin woodlands in the bucolic northern reaches of Manhattan. It was nine miles from downtown, a ninety-minute carriage ride in his day, a problem for a lawyer who practiced in the city, though the distance also provided sanctuary from the recurrent yellow fever outbreaks that swept the urban center.

Hamilton hired a distinguished local architect and builder who completed the work with a speed that would have astonished Jefferson. By the summer of 1802 the Hamiltons were living in their new Federal-style clapboard house. The exterior was painted yellow and ivory, and included verandas and piazzas on two sides. A library, parlor, dining room, and two guest rooms made up the first floor. Six rooms with eight fireplaces were upstairs, including the family's private living room, which opened onto a balcony with a breath taking view of the Hudson River, some two hundred feet below. Hamilton hung a Gilbert Stuart painting of Washington in the first-floor hallway, likely the first thing seen by visitors, and he furnished his home with Louis XVI sofas and chairs.[15]

The house, and the acres of landscaping that Hamilton almost obsessively planned, cost about twenty-five thousand dollars. He had poured some eighty thousand dollars into his estate. His annual income was roughly twelve thousand dollars.[16] As with his adversary from Monticello, Hamilton's suddenly lavish lifestyle had plunged him into debt. Like it or not, Hamilton gave the appearance of one who understood that his days in public office were behind him. Still relatively young, and with many years left to practice law, retiring his debts would not be difficult. But everything about his having embarked on this endeavor was uncharacteristic, from his wish for a mansion, to his captivation with gardening, to his sudden spendthrift habits. Perhaps he saw redemption in it, recompense to a wife and children who had been overshadowed by politics and betrayed in marriage. Perhaps he really believed the estate offered asylum from the cruel world he had failed to conquer. Or, perhaps, this was his statement to the world that although defeated in politics, he was still a winner, a man who had risen from nothing to this crowning material success. It may not have been a coincidence that Hamilton launched his spending spree almost immediately after learning that President Adams had called him an immoral foreign bastard.

Hamilton's all-consuming passion had been to hold great power and win glory, and from adolescence he had never thought it hopeless to dream that dream. Time and again, he had learned that adversity could be overcome. On repeated occasions, he had discovered how unpredictable the future could be. Only four or five years after finding himself stuck in a dead-end job in Christiansted, he had become the aide-de-camp to the most important soldier in North America. It was a post that filled his future with bright promise, and he had capitalized on the opportunities that came along. His political fortunes had plummeted in 1799 and 1800, but who could know what the future held. Hamilton turned forty-six in 1801, still a young age for one in public affairs. At that age, John Adams had been sixteen years away from becoming president. General Washington anguished at Valley Forge in his forty-sixth year, not yet an iconic figure and not even certain his position as commander of the Continental army was secure. Jefferson was a few months short of turning forty-six when he was offered the position of secretary of state, an opportunity that came a decade after his political career appeared to have ended disastrously in his wild flight from Colonel Tarleton's soldiers. Hamilton knew the vagaries and vicissitudes of American politics, and he clung to the hope that in time the Federalists might regain the presidency or that the political parties might be reshuffled. Someday, somehow, he might again be on top.

In 1801, Hamilton joined with friends to found a Federalist newspaper, the *New-York Evening Post*, which published its first issue in November.[17] A month later, in his initial effort to claw his way back into political prominence, he placed the first of eighteen essays attacking Jefferson in his paper. In search of an issue that Federalists might ride back into power, Hamilton mostly blasted the Jeffersonian Republicans for removing a few Federalist officeholders and repealing the Judiciary Act of 1801, the Federalists' last-ditch effort to pack the courts with their own judges before the opposition party took control. "The Examination," as Hamilton's acrid series was titled, attracted little attention. His pieces were turgid and painfully repetitive, his ideas shopworn, his style smacking of pettiness. (He chose to launch his enterprise with a shrill assault on a matter of little consequence: Jefferson's decision to report on the state of the union in a written report rather than in a formal address to Congress.)[18] That the country was prospering hardly aided

Hamilton's cause. "Go where you will," observed his old friend Troup, and "you will behold nothing but the smiling face of improvements and prosperity."[19] Above all, Hamilton's essays aroused no controversy because his stature had sunk so low that even fellow Federalists were largely indifferent to his polemics. His striving for political rehabilitation had failed. A wiser course might have been to abandon public affairs entirely for a few years, hoping that someday his party would summon him back to the playing field as an elder statesman.

That he wrote these essays was peculiar, grotesque perhaps, for his eldest son, Philip, had been killed in a duel scant days before Hamilton composed the first piece in the series. The fatal duel had arisen from Philip's outrage at an Independence Day speech delivered in lower Manhattan by George Eacker, a Republican lawyer who practiced in the city. Eacker had censured Federalist policies during the XYZ Affair, including the creation of the army under Inspector General Hamilton. Months after the speech, Philip confronted Eacker during a play at the Park Theater, causing an embarrassing disturbance and provoking Eacker to issue a challenge. There was never the slightest doubt that Philip would accept, and the duel was fought two days later, on November 22, at Paulus Hook, New Jersey. Eacker shot and killed young Hamilton.

General Hamilton, who had not been present at the duel, was so "completely overwhelmed with grief," according to an observer, that he attended the funeral only through the support of others. Hamilton described his loss as "the most afflicting of my life."[20] That he persisted in writing essay after essay of "The Examination" at such a time may have been because he saw it as a therapeutic distraction during his bereavement. But it may have been that his obsession with his crumbling political forces was such that nothing, not even the tragic death of his son, could stay his hand. The latter seems all too likely, and in retrospect, Hamilton's character, his long-nourished hatreds, and his gnawing ambition provided the impetus that long since had placed him on the course leading inexorably to his own tragic end.

Hamilton's foundering fortunes were the legacy of his intemperate behavior in the political contest of 1800. Aaron Burr found himself in a similar situation. He, too, had done great harm to himself through his unwise choices when the House resolved the election. The misjudgments made by these two during the campaign put them on a fatal collision course.

Burr soon found himself without power or even patronage in Jefferson's administration. As the 1804 presidential election approached, he called on the president to learn where he stood. When the conference ended, Burr knew he would not be part of the Republican ticket in the coming election.[21] On the outs nationally, he looked on the governor's contest in New York as a restorative.

Early on, Hamilton sensed that the clash between Burr and Jefferson was "absolutely incurable," thinking it "founded in the breasts of both in the rivalship of an insatiable and unprincipled ambition."[22] Hamilton saw the split as a double-edged sword. He welcomed it as likely to be ruinous to Burr's political career, and he rejoiced at the prospect of ineradicable divisions among New York's Republicans. Hamilton must have dared to hope for a Republican fracture that could pave the way for the Federalists to recapture the state in the presidential election of 1804.

His joy was tempered, however, by the fear that Burr, who had intrigued with Federalists during the deadlocked election, would be driven to do so again. When he learned that Burr had attended a Federalist banquet in the capital to commemorate Washington's birthday in 1802, Hamilton was convinced that the vice president was exploring a switch to the Federalist Party. Should Burr change parties, and should that lead—as seemed certain—to the restructuring of New York's Federalist Party, Hamilton's influence in the party would decline even further. The possibility also existed that Burr might form a new party. That was not an idle concern. Burr had shot his bolt within the Republican Party, and like other astute politicos, he could readily see the dire plight of the Federalist Party in the face of America's continuing democratization. After the congressional elections in 1802, for instance, Federalists held barely one-third of the seats in both the House and Senate. When Burr, in 1802, started his own newspaper in New York City, Hamilton was convinced that the vice president's plan was to draw both Federalists and disgruntled Republicans into his camp.[23]

In 1804, Burr entered the governor's race, running as a Republican. He was repeatedly slandered in the press, including by some Republicans who could not forgive his perfidy in the 1800 presidential election. Federalist penmen blasted away as well. Hamilton was active, slashing at his nemesis. Burr could not know who penned each tract, but some charges sounded strikingly similar to allegations that Hamilton had made earlier. For instance, someone averred that Burr was given to "abandoned profligacy," a defamation that strayed across the line from criticism of political ideas and practices to matters of private character. It is not difficult to imagine Burr thinking that Hamilton, long his caustic rival, was responsible for the smear.[24]

That Hamilton played an active role in the campaign must also have struck many, including the vice president, as inspired solely by the wish to prevent Burr's election. After all, the Federalist Party in New York was moribund. Having lost the state in 1800, and suffered worse defeats in 1802, the Federalists did not even nominate a candidate in 1804. Instead, large numbers of Federalists "embarked with zeal in support of Mr. Burr," as Hamilton remarked with alarm.[25] Without success, Hamilton beseeched Rufus King to run against Burr. When that initiative failed, Hamilton reluctantly supported Morgan Lewis, New York's Republican chief justice, a candidate he did not think could win.

Hamilton spoke out in favor of Lewis and against Burr. Displaying his customary lancing invective, he portrayed Burr as given to "Jacobinic principles," slavish to "popular prejudices and vices," and having a propensity toward "pernicious extremes." What really troubled Hamilton, as he divulged to a Federalist caucus in Albany, was his fear that if Burr was elected, Yankee High Federalists would rally round this "man of talents intrigue and address," seeing him as the captivating leader who could form a confederation of several northern states separate from the United States. In private, Hamilton depicted Burr as "skillful adroit and able," and sufficiently unscrupulous to lead a movement to dismember the Union.[26]

Hamilton's comments were mild compared with some charges in the press. Burr, who had remained single since the death of his wife a decade earlier, was savaged as sexually promiscuous, a consort of prostitutes both male and female, and the host of racially integrated parties. Calling these soirées "nigger ball[s],"one writer alleged that Burr had turned his home into a bordello where he sometimes engaged in sexual relations with black women. One scandalmonger, James Cheetham, a newspaper scribbler who had immigrated to New York from England six years earlier, was the worst of the bunch. No sleazy charge was beyond the bounds for him, and Cheetham often dredged up questions that Hamilton had raised years before about Burr's character, always carefully identifying the former treasury secretary as the first to have made the allegations.[27]

The mudslinging did its work. Burr was defeated, a crushing loss that likely spelled the end of his political aspirations in New York. Burr knew of Hamilton's involvement in stymieing his vice presidential aspirations back in the 1790s. He also was aware that no one was more responsible than Hamilton for undermining his shot at the presidency in the House contest in 1801. Now, in 1804, Burr likely thought Hamilton had contributed substantively to his ruinous loss in New York's governor's race.

It was while in this frame of mind that Burr in June learned of malicious comments that Hamilton had purportedly made about him during a dinner party in Albany some five or six months earlier. Through newspapers, Burr discovered that Dr. Charles Cooper, a guest at the dinner, had written in a private letter in March that "Gen. Hamilton . . . *spoke of [Burr] as a dangerous man . . . who ought not to be trusted.*" Cooper's letter somehow found its way into the press, prompting a rebuttal from Philip Schuyler, who observed that as Hamilton had chosen to remain neutral in the Burr-Lewis contest, he could not have made such a comment. Schuyler's retort was unconvincing—after all, Hamilton had publicly denigrated Burr at the Federalist caucus in Albany in February. And it outraged Cooper, who responded publicly by defending what he said. Indeed, Cooper inflamed the situation further by adding, "I could detail to you a still more despicable opinion which General HAMILTON has expressed of Mr. BURR."[28]

Some sixty days later, having finally learned of Cooper's letters, Burr wrote to Hamilton. He did not raise the matter of having been called dangerous. That was politics as usual. He was disturbed by Hamilton's supposedly "more despicable opinion of him," suggesting that Burr believed Hamilton had denigrated his character and private behavior, the very sort of venomous accusations that had been levied against him with devastating effect in the recent gubernatorial election. Burr demanded of Hamilton "a prompt and unqualified acknowledgment or denial."[29]

Hamilton might have denied the allegation, as had Schuyler, and the matter would have ended. Or, he might have challenged the blabbermouth Dr. Cooper for having spread malicious stories, a step that almost certainly would have satisfied Burr. He did neither, probably because he knew that numerous individuals had heard him make the deleterious comments at the Albany dinner. Instead, Hamilton responded disingenuously, and in a quibbling, hair-splitting tone. For instance, he asked what exactly Burr meant by "despicable." He refused to acknowledge or deny having said anything.[30] Burr shot back that Hamilton's reply was insincere. He spelled out that he would regard as despicable any comment that questioned his honor.[31] Burr had given his adversary a second chance to bring the matter to an end, but Hamilton replied: "I have no other answer to give than that which has already been given.[32] Surprised and outraged, Burr penned one final letter. He said he had expected Hamilton to display the "frankness of a Soldier and the Candor of a gentleman," yet instead had received evasive responses, which Burr characterized as bristling with "defiance." "[Y]ou have invited the course I am about to pursue," Burr wrote.[33]

The correspondence had been hand delivered by intermediaries. William Van Ness, a blonde ruddy-faced New York congressman, acted on Burr's behalf, while Nathaniel Pendleton, a former aide to General Nathanael Greene and an ex-federal judge who had (with Hamilton's assistance) entered into private law practice in Manhattan, was the courier for Hamilton. Both men sought to defuse what was occurring, but when a peaceful solution proved elusive, Van Ness delivered to Pendleton the formal request for what contemporaries referred to as an "interview"—a duel. As Hamilton had legal cases pending before the state supreme court, the duel was scheduled for July 11, more than two weeks away.[34]

It is impossible to fathom the dark recesses of the souls of either Burr or Hamilton, but it appears that at the outset of this imbroglio, Burr never imagined a duel would be fought. He subsequently said that on two previous occasions, Hamilton, understanding that his "improper and offensive" remarks about Burr's "character" might result in a challenge to duel, had prevented such an occurrence by coming "forward voluntarily" and making "apologies and concessions." Furthermore, while serving as a mediator during Hamilton's dust-up with James Monroe in 1797, Burr had advised his man that Hamilton "would not fight." Sure enough, in that case Hamilton had found a way to avoid a duel that Monroe was prepared to fight. Yet, while Burr may not have expected this feud to end on the field of honor, there can be no doubt that he had been driven to the breaking point. He was weary of Hamilton's "setled & implacable malevolence," frustrated that his adversary had "long indulged himself in illiberal freedoms with my character," and enraged by the former treasury secretary's unrelenting "support of base Slanders." Furthermore, Burr was convinced that Hamilton would "never cease in his Conduct."[35]

Burr had ample reasons for hating this man who had played a considerable role in frustrating his political dreams, but Hamilton was not in the grip of a seething rage. He did not even seem to dislike Burr. He feared Burr's political success, distrusted him, and saw deep character flaws that in his judgment rendered Burr unfit for the highest offices.[36] But though Hamilton was, in Samuel Johnson's phrase, "a very good hater," remarkably, Burr was not among those he hated.

Duels were fought for all sorts of absurd reasons, but if one should have been aborted, this was it. Two years earlier, Hamilton had mused that "Men are . . . for the most part governed by the impulse of passion." That might be the best explanation for what led Hamilton to the dueling ground.[37] So, too, might be the explanation offered by Gouverneur Morris, who quipped in the aftermath of the interview: "If we were truly brave we should not accept a challenge; but we are all cowards."[38] Some have even fancifully conjectured that a suicidal Hamilton welcomed the duel. According to this theory, he kept the appointment on the dueling ground from the belief that he had nothing to live for, or that he wished to die in repentance for the harm he had done to Burr, or from the conviction that in death he would gain the glory that had eluded him in life.[39]

In fact, Hamilton wished to live, for his family and himself, but he was seized with the conviction that what Burr demanded put his honor at stake.

He refused to display any sign of what he saw as weakness. He told his wife, in a letter that she did not see until after the duel, that it was impossible to "have avoided the interview . . . without sacrifices which would have rendered me unworthy of your esteem." He implied, too, that it would "unman me" to permit Burr's challenge to pass uncontested.[40] An obsession with honor was not new for Hamilton. Dishonored by the circumstances of his birth—as so many believed in his day—Hamilton was driven throughout his life to win acclaim, to act worthily, to defend his honor. When this compulsiveness was blended with his passionate, headstrong, manner, it could be a toxic brew. Indeed, for this man who was drawn to battle, given to daring intrigue, liberal with calumny, and increasingly reckless, the dueling ground seems almost to have been his inexorable destiny.

During the days before the duel, Hamilton prepared his will and put his affairs in order.[41] He also drafted what he knew might be his final testament. Hamilton said that he bore "no ill-will to Col Burr, distinct from political opposition," but he admitted having on numerous occasions said "extremely severe" things about Burr, including "very unfavourable criticisms . . . of the private conduct of this Gentleman" which "bore very hard on him." He even admitted that some things he had said had been "falshoods." To this, Hamilton added that while he deplored dueling on "religious and moral principles," his honor compelled him to accept the challenge, as Burr's "tone" had been "unnecessarily peremptory and menacing, and . . . positively offensive." Nevertheless, as he could not "shed the blood of a fellow creature in a private combat," Hamilton declared his intention "to *reserve and throw away* my first fire, and I *have thoughts* even of *reserving* my second fire."[42]

Hamilton was a master at imagery. He could be harsh and cruel, as in his portrayals of Gates, Adams, and Burr. He could be sparklingly positive, as in his defenses of Washington during the war and his representation of Pinckney in the presidential election. In his last testament, Hamilton sought to project a flattering image of himself to contemporaries and succeeding generations. No one can ever know what was really in Hamilton's mind, though readers of his apologia should be wary. For instance, Hamilton portrayed himself as an implacable foe of dueling who was being dragged reluctantly to the field of honor; yet, since 1779 he had issued ten challenges.[43] All that can be known for certain is that he anticipated his testament being made public in the event of his death. If neither man was injured, or if he killed Burr, Hamilton would have the option of destroying his testament or, in the wake of adverse publicity, of issuing it as his vindication.

With considerable truth, Hamilton remarked that he could "gain nothing by the issue of the interview."[44] For that matter, neither could Burr. In fact,

Burr seemingly stood to lose the most. In all likelihood, Hamilton's public fortunes would not be destroyed should he kill his opponent. But Burr, whose slim hopes for political resurgence rested on fashioning an alliance with northern Federalists, stood to lose everything by killing a man who continued to be venerated by some party stalwarts in the northern states. Indeed, that realization may have lulled Hamilton into the belief that Burr would never shoot to kill.

During the interlude leading to the duel, Burr and Hamilton saw each other on one occasion. They shared a banquet table at Fraunces Tavern during an Independence Day party. A day or two later, the Hamiltons hosted a ball attended by seventy guests. On the Sunday before Wednesday's scheduled duel, Hamilton supposedly read the Morning Prayer and a liturgical worship service in the Episcopal Book of Common Prayer. Afterward, he and his family walked about the estate, then sat together for hours under a large shade tree. The next morning, after saying goodbye for the last time to his wife and the children, he rode to the city. Hamilton spent Monday and Tuesday at his town house, tending to his legal practice and writing letters. According to witnesses, Burr slept soundly on the night before the duel, but sleep eluded Hamilton. In the last hours before dawn, he composed a hymn to Betsey.

Wednesday, July 11, dawned humid and summery in the city. As New York tended to be more unsparing toward dueling, the prearranged plans called for the combatants to leave at five A.M. from separate docks, and to be rowed by unarmed oarsmen up the Hudson to Weehawken on the Jersey side of the river.[45] Pendleton and Dr. David Hosack, a respected physician and professor of medicine and botany at Columbia, likely arrived at Hamilton's Cedar Street home as the first blotchy pink rays of morning light splashed over Manhattan. A few blocks away, and at nearly the same moment, Van Ness, who was to be Burr's second, called on his man. With little wasted time, both parties set off for the river, commencing the long journey to the dueling ground. Pendleton thought Hamilton appeared to be relaxed.

Burr was the first to arrive at the interview site, disembarking some twenty minutes ahead of Hamilton. Leaving the oarsmen at the river's edge, Burr and Van Ness had a short walk across a sandy beach to a narrow, forlorn path that led to a flat, rocky shelf about twenty feet above the river. The ledge—the dueling ground—was a small area, perhaps thirty feet by fifteen feet. A cedar tree grew on the ledge, which was littered with dead branches, the legacy of winter and spring storms.

Hamilton's barge docked a few minutes before seven o'clock. He and Pendleton climbed the incline to the ledge. Upon arriving, they "exchanged salutations" with Burr and Van Ness. As the seconds stepped off ten paces, marking the spots where the duelists were to stand, the combatants manifested an air of unruffled calm. When lots were drawn to determine where the men would stand, Pendleton made the lucky draw. Oddly, he selected the northern position for Hamilton, though that meant he would be looking into the streaming morning sunlight. Burr and Hamilton walked to their positions. The seconds loaded and cocked the smooth-bore pistols selected by Hamilton, and handed them to their men. Each man then assumed the duelist's stance: the right foot about two feet in front of the left, the face looking over the right shoulder, the stomach severely retracted in the mostly forlorn hope of shrinking the target by a few fractions of an inch.[46] One of the seconds repeated the rules that had been agreed on days before.

Van Ness, in a subsequent statement, chronicled what occurred as the last of the preliminaries played out. Hamilton, bothered by the sun, "levelled his pistol in several directions, as if to try the light; then drew from his pockets & put on, a pair of spectacles, and again levelled his pistol in different directions," including "once at Mr. Burr, who was all this time silent." After several seconds, Hamilton announced: "this will do; now you may proceed." The long wait was over.

One of the seconds asked whether each man was ready. Each uttered the agreed on affirmative reply: "Present." Only a second or two elapsed before the first shot was fired.

The oarsmen had lingered at the water's edge and Dr. Hosack remained out of sight in nearby woods, all hoping that in the event that New York pressed charges, they could truthfully testify to have seen nothing. The seconds were the only witnesses. Subsequently, they agreed on what happened prior to the shooting, but offered different versions of events thereafter.[47] Pendleton initially attested only that the two pistols were "discharged successively." Two days later, as friends and followers busily crafted an image of the former treasury secretary that they hoped would live on, Pendleton asserted that Hamilton "did not fire first—and that he did not fire at all at Col. Burr." Instead, he insisted, Hamilton's pistol discharged only because of an "involuntary exercise of the muscles" caused by having been wounded. He also made the uncorroborated claim that he found the bullet's path in the cedar tree some twelve feet above ground level and about fourteen feet to one side of where Burr had stood. Van Ness saw things differently. He believed Hamilton fired first and missed. Burr took aim and fired.[48] He did not miss. His bullet smashed through Hamilton's rib cage on his right side before slicing through his liver and diaphragm and piercing his spine.

Hamilton fell immediately. Dr. Hosack, hearing the shots, rushed to the scene. In an instant, he knew that Hamilton had been mortally wounded. So, too, did Hamilton, who had learned in the Revolutionary War that there was no hope for one who had sustained the grievous damage of what soldiers called having been "gut shot." He had begun the descent to a slow, agonizing, and thoroughly unnecessary death. Hamilton immediately said to his physician: "This is a mortal wound, Doctor." Little time elapsed before he was unconscious. His breathing was undetectable and Hosack could not find a pulse. The doctor and Pendleton gathered up Hamilton's seemingly lifeless body and rushed downhill to the waiting barge. During the long passage back to Manhattan, Hamilton regained consciousness and spoke. His vision was unclear, he said, and he had lost all feeling in his legs.

When they reached New York, Hamilton was taken to an upstairs bedroom in a house on Jane Street, near the waterfront. Hosack administered wine and water, and laudanum to minimize pain.[49] Betsey and the children were summoned and arrived in the afternoon. Hamilton slept much of the time during the thirty-one hours that he lived after being shot, but while awake he asked to be given Holy Communion. Two pastors refused. An Episcopalian priest spurned Hamilton because he had not regularly attended his church. A Presbyterian minister rebuffed his entreaties because it violated the church's practice to privately administer the sacrament. Finally, under pressure, the Episcopalian relented late on Wednesday. The next day, July 12, Hamilton's life ebbed away in the presence of twenty or so doleful friends and family who crowded into his room, some standing, some on their knees praying.

At about one forty-five P.M. he lost consciousness for the last time. Fifteen minutes later Hamilton died quietly.

Exactly what occurred in the duel, and what raced through the combatants' minds in the final breathless seconds before firing their pistols will never be known. Pendleton and Van Ness initially composed a joint account, though admitting that they did not fully agree on what had transpired. Subsequently, each second fleshed out his chronicle, though each provided an account in which accuracy likely gave way to a desire to defend the reputation of his man. However, if Van Ness was correct in contending that Hamilton donned glasses and sighted in on his target—an assertion that Pendleton never denied—Burr would have had to have believed that his adversary intended to kill him. Moreover, Hamilton's behavior makes it extremely difficult to give credence to his last testament claim that he intended to throw away his first shot, or to Pendleton's emended contention that he had done so.

One can only imagine the emotional intensity that must have engulfed the combatants as they stood a few paces apart, staring at an armed bitter rival. Their hearts must have raced. Adrenalin must have pumped. For a few seconds, reasoned thought must have been impossible.

No one can know what either duelist intended as he climbed the ledge in Weehawken. But once Hamilton drew down on his man and, in all likelihood, was the first to fire his weapon, Burr, a frenzy of nerves, gripped with unimaginable emotions and certain that Hamilton had just tried to kill him, must have shot to kill.

RECKONING

JEFFERSON LEARNED of Hamilton's death five days after the duel and simply mentioned it to Patsy and a correspondent as a "remarkable" occurrence.[1] At the time, he was absorbed with grief over the death of his daughter Polly, who at age twenty-five had died two months earlier from complications of childbirth.[2]

As the years passed, Jefferson said little about Hamilton, and his few comments mostly concerned his old adversary's political philosophy.[3] Not even Adams could entice Jefferson to speak critically of his former rival. Reunited through the efforts of a mutual friend, Adams and Jefferson began to correspond in 1812, writing mostly about philosophy and theology, but sometimes about history, and occasionally about the American Revolution and the turbulent early days of the Republic. Adams told Jefferson that Washington and Hamilton had been "Jugglers behind the Scene" who manipulated his cabinet, and he portrayed Hamilton as a puppeteer pulling Washington's strings.[4] Refusing to take the bait, Jefferson merely remarked that he and Hamilton had "thought well" of each other.[5] Late in his life, when he believed "the passion of the time" had cooled, Jefferson recalled Hamilton as "a singular character" of "acute understanding" who was "amiable in society," valued "virtue in private life," and was "disinterested, honest, and honorable in all private transactions."[6]

Jefferson was forty months into his presidency when the Hamilton-Burr duel was fought. Nearly twenty years later, when he was seventy-six, Jefferson referred to his election as "the revolution of 1800." In *Common Sense*, in 1776, Thomas Paine had said that by declaring independence, the American colonists would have it within their "power to begin the world anew." That encapsulated Jefferson's thinking, and when he became president, he envisaged a new "chapter in the history of man." He once said that his presidency was about realizing "as real a revolution in the principles of our government as that of 1776 was in its form." He took office expecting not the completion of the American Revolution but in some respects its beginning.[7]

To Jefferson, the American Revolution had never been solely about breaking away from Great Britain. It had been about enhancing the liberties of free people, reducing social inequality, and making it possible for individuals to be more independent. Within days of entering the presidency, Jefferson wrote to friends who had played major roles in 1776, likening the American Revolution—by which he meant the period from Congress's declaration of independence to his election—to a bark sailing in severe weather and rough seas that threatened its destruction. Federalist "Charlatans" had tried every trick, seized on every uncertainty and anxiety, he charged, to secure the "abandonment of the principles of our revolution." They had failed. With his election, he wrote, the "storm is over, and we are in port."[8]

Thomas Paine, who was about to sail for America after an absence of some fifteen years, was one acquaintance to whom he wrote, and Jefferson ebulliently told him that he would "find us returned generally to sentiments worthy of former times." The election, as Jefferson understood it, had gone against those who favored consolidation and the creation of a mighty fiscal-military nation. The victors believed in a national commitment to the "just & solid republican" principles of the American Revolution and they also were driven by a sense of "duty" to "all mankind" to make republicanism work.[9]

Jefferson's presidency ushered in change. The centralizing tendencies of recent years came to a halt. His administration cut back on federal expenditures, drastically slashed the number of officeholders (including 40 percent of the Treasury Department's employees), made drastic cuts in the size of the navy, and reduced the army to 3,287 men, the same size it had been at the conclusion of Washington's presidency. Jefferson left intact the Bank of the United States—that may have been the bargain he struck with Bayard—but the program of fiscal austerity that he pursued reduced the federal budget, slashed taxes (the excise on whiskey was eliminated), and reduced the national debt. By 1810 the debt was half of what it had been in 1801. These very real changes were accompanied by symbolic changes. Jefferson comported himself with a determined republican simplicity. He rode about the capital on horseback rather than in a carriage tended by liveried servants, jettisoned levees altogether, generally eschewed state dinners heavy with pomp and ceremony, dressed casually, and at times even answered the door at the President's House.

Committed to the preservation of an agrarian way of life, Jefferson hoped that for generations, even centuries, most Americans would live outside cities and would farm the land they owned. As president, he did what he could to facilitate that life-long dream. He set in motion the practice of making it easier to purchase federal land, until in 1820 a farmer could buy 80 acres of western land for a bit more than one hundred dollars (down from a high of having to purchase 640 acres at two dollars per acre). Through the Louisiana Purchase, Jefferson bloodlessly doubled America's frontier, which thereafter stretched hundreds of miles west of the Mississippi River and abutted the Rocky Mountains. The percentage of the labor force in farming increased from 75 percent in 1800 to 80 percent in 1820.[10]

Jefferson had spoken of a revolution of 1800, and politically and socially, Jeffersonianism was truly revolutionary. After 1800, suffrage rights were broadened. Property qualifications were gradually phased out and universal manhood suffrage—the right of all adult, white males to vote—took hold. Changes in voting rights were accompanied by the nearly complete end to the requirement for meeting property qualifications in order to hold office. Furthermore, whereas the presidential electors had been chosen by state legislatures in three-fourths of the states in 1800, they were popularly elected in three-fourths of the states a quarter century later. A breathtaking egalitarianism burst forth as well. The deference patterns of colonial times—and of eons in Europe before American colonization commenced—were largely gone before the nineteenth century was very old. Men stopped bowing to their social betters and began shaking their hands, and badges of social distinction, such as silk stockings and silver-buckled shoes, faded from view. As a British traveler in America noted during Jefferson's presidency: Americans "have a spirit of independence, and will brook no superiority. Every man is conscious of his own political importance, and will suffer none to treat him with disrespect."[11]

The day when there had been a place for everyone, and everyone knew his place, was vanishing. Within a few short years of Jefferson's inauguration, little was left of the eighteenth-century hierarchical society that had been in place when the Revolutionary War began, and that many Federalists had so fervently cherished. The new world that Paine and Jefferson longed for had come into being, and as it did, the pre-Revolutionary past into which Jefferson and Hamilton were born had indeed become an alien world not unlike that imagined by the British writer L. P. Hartley in his mid-twentieth century novel The Go-Between: "The past is a foreign country: they do things differently there."[12]

Hamilton had not lived to witness the sweeping transformation in America's political and social fabric, but he lived long enough to understand that crucial aspects of the world he had inhabited were disappearing, and he understood the cause of the sea change all about him. In his last letter, written on the day before he was rowed to Weehawken, Hamilton wrote that "our real Disease . . . is DEMOCRACY." He called it a "poison" and presciently foresaw it as certain to grow only "more violent."[13]

Had he lived to 1826, the fiftieth anniversary of the Declaration of Independence—he would have been seventy-one that year—Hamilton would have been aware of more than political and social change. Though Jeffersonian America was overwhelmingly agrarian, Hamilton would have seen evidence of the nation's transformation into a modern capitalistic society. The number of towns with more than 2,500 inhabitants had more than doubled since 1800, banks had sprung up like toadstools (more than three hundred existed by 1800), and with investors at home and abroad seeding American enterprise, manufacturing was flourishing. There was hardly a cotton mill in America in 1800; within fifteen years there were nearly 250. Twenty years after Jefferson's inauguration, one-fourth of the labor force in New England and the mid-Atlantic states worked in factories that churned out hats, shoes, textiles, and a great deal more. In rural townships such as Dudley and Oxford, Massachusetts, virtually every inhabitant had been a farmer in 1790; but fifty years after independence, residents were three times more likely to work in a factory than to own a farm. Factory towns seemed to materialize out of thin air, as did Slatersville, Rhode Island, which had not existed when Jefferson took office, but had a population of some 500 a dozen years later, and nearly all its residents worked in mills.[14]

Hamilton would have been dismayed by much that he beheld, though he might not have been appalled at discovering that Americans, in the words of one historian, had become a "people totally absorbed in the individual pursuit of money." If Hamilton might have thought his countrymen were on the right track, Jefferson was unhappy both with America's emerging business culture and the volcanic exuberance for evangelical Christianity that had gathered force during his presidency. Though he never acknowledged it, both were the products of the democracy nourished by the American Revolution, and both had been unfettered by his revolution of 1800.[15]

Jefferson had opposed much that he found in his world, and he knew that his successors would seek to change the world he had helped to make. "We might as well require a man to wear still the coat which fitted him when a boy, as civilized society to remain ever under the regimen of their . . . ancestors," he said late in life. While some things that were unsavory to him had taken root, as an old man he thought it "a good world on the whole." He was especially buoyed by the conviction that "the flames" of the American Revolution "have spread over . . . much of the globe," setting alight fires that threatened to consume tyranny. "[L]ight and liberty are on steady advance," he proclaimed shortly before his death. In his final letter, Jefferson rejoiced that his countrymen still believed that the choice made in 1776 had been the proper one, and he remained confident that, in time, humankind everywhere, inspired by the ideals of the American Revolution, would "burst the chains" of despotism and superstition, and secure the "rights of man."[16]

In his last years, Jefferson's optimism was tempered by a disquieting recognition that his younger countrymen did not understand their elders who had made the American Revolution. The old Revolutionaries, he said, were "left alone amidst a new generation whom we know not, and who knows not us."[17] He was aware that Franklin and Adams had penned autobiographies, but Jefferson declared in 1816 that to "become my own biographer is the last thing in the world I would undertake." With some truth, he told Adams that he liked "the dreams of the future better than the history of the past," while in 1817, with an abundance of dissimulation, he informed another friend that the skills for writing history were "not to be found among the ruins of a decayed memory."[18]

Yet, Jefferson desperately wished to be remembered by posterity, and he wanted future generations to understand his side of the story of his life and times. He carefully preserved eighteen thousand letters he had written and another twenty-five thousand he had received, and he even indexed his correspondence. There can be no doubt that he hoped they would be published following his death.[19] Beginning in 1818, Jefferson also gathered together his journal entries and a collection of memoranda dating from his time in Washington's cabinet down to late in his own presidency. In a lengthy introduction, Jefferson acknowledged that he had made a "calm revisal" of these records, and even that he had "cut out" portions. He was candid about his intent. Though he did not publish the "Anas," as he called the aggregation, Jefferson knew that subsequent generations would see these documents and compare them with the papers left by Hamilton and Washington. Cautioning readers that "we are not to suppose that every thing found" in the materials left by those individuals "is to be taken as gospel truth," he said that the availability of his "Anas" would enable subsequent generations to come to a more accurate understanding of the early years of the American Republic.[20]

Despite his earlier disclaimer, Jefferson in 1821 set to work on an autobiography, though he could not bring himself to call what he was writing by its real name. Instead, he said that he was making "some memoranda" for his "own more ready reference, and for the information of my family." He carried the story down to his arrival in New York to join Washington's cabinet, stopping there, as he evidently believed the "Anas" adequately recorded the years that followed.[21] But he feared that all of this might be insufficient for the preservation of his reputation. In one of his last letters, Jefferson beseeched Madison to "take care of me when dead."[22]

Jefferson's reputation would have been better served, and so would humanity, had he devoted his last years to the eradication of slavery. Before the Revolution, he had acted nobly to terminate the foreign slave trade, a possible first step toward ending slavery in Virginia. His Declaration of Independence, with its lyrical passages on liberty, inspired many in his time, and later, to rethink slavery. Had Congress retained his paragraph attacking slavery, all of subsequent American history might have been different, as it also would have been had Congress approved Jefferson's proposal in 1784 to prohibit slavery in the western territories. Jefferson did not seek to end slavery when modernizing Virginia's legal code during the war. Manumissions increased Virginia's free black population by sixfold in the 1780s, and the number of manumissions tripled in the twenty years after 1790, but this was also a period when slavery was "fixed more securely on the Virginians," in the words of historian Robert McColley. Jefferson understood the times better than most, and he knew that any attempt to end slavery in Virginia during the 1780s was doomed to fail.[23]

Jefferson's concerns about slavery were subsumed by other matters during his five years in France, and resisting Hamiltonianism became his overarching concern once he returned home. After 1784, not only did slavery consume less of his thought than it had a decade earlier, but also, in the wake of Santo Domingo's bloody slave insurrection in the 1790s, Jefferson saw whites in slave Virginia in the proverbial position of the man riding the back of tiger. (Or, as he put it: "We have the wolf by the ear.")[24] In *Notes on the State of Virginia*, he had written that prejudice among whites, and a lust for revenge on the part of blacks, meant that emancipation would be followed by race conflicts, even racial extermination. The ghastly slaughters in the Caribbean slave revolts confirmed his fears. Thereafter, Jefferson felt that Virginia had two choices: maintain slavery as a means of race control or end slavery and banish all African Americans from Virginia.

He believed "the revolutionary storm now sweeping the globe"—the tempest he had played a vital role in unleashing—was the cause of the slave revolt in the West Indies. He predicted that a "combustion must be near at hand" in Virginia, adding that "only a single spark is wanting to make that day tomorrow." In 1797, he said that Virginia's leaders must do something, and quickly, to prevent a catastrophe. If nothing was done, wrote Jefferson from his lonely mountaintop in an Albemarle County in which nearly 50 percent of the inhabitants were enslaved, "we shall be the murderers of our own children."[25]

Bringing slavery to a gradual end, followed by the expulsion of the freed slaves, was what he wanted done. But he did nothing toward that end in the 1790s. Furthermore, as president he declined to act in 1802 when the Virginia assembly, in response to the discovery and suppression of a planned slave insurrection in Richmond, contemplated legislation calling on the United States to set aside western lands as an asylum for emancipated slaves. Though Governor James Monroe thought the idea might succeed with the backing of the president, Jefferson refused to entertain such a notion. Insisting that the West was for white yeomen only, he instead endorsed the notion of sending liberated slaves "out of the limits of the US," an impractical expedient given both its cost and the revulsion with which it was greeted by many. (Jefferson himself estimated in 1824 that the joint cost of compensating slave owners who liberated their chattel and resettling a million and a half freedmen to the Caribbean would run some $900 million, at a time when the annual budget of the United States was merely a fraction of that amount.)[26]

Five years after Jefferson's presidency, in 1814, Edward Coles, once Madison's private secretary, appealed to Jefferson to speak out against slavery. Coles planned to free his slaves and give them land in the Illinois Territory, and he asked Jefferson to assist in the eradication of slavery by formulating and "getting into operation" a plan of emancipation. Although Jefferson acknowledged "our . . . moral and political reprobation" at not having already acted to banish slavery, he refused to take up the fight. In fact, he inexplicably told Coles that this battle was "an enterprise . . . for the young," not for those of his generation. What is more, he insultingly, and dismayingly, lectured this ardent young man who was about to take a personally sacrificial step that Jefferson had never contemplated. Jefferson reproached Coles's generation for not having "proved their love of liberty" by fighting to eradicate slavery, and he also heaped blame for slavery's continued existence on the shoulders of Coles and his brethren.[27]

Despite his inaction, Jefferson told Coles that "love of justice" and "love of country" required that something be done to end the heinous institution.[28] But five years later, in 1819, when the Missouri Crisis provided Jefferson with another chance to take a courageous stand against slavery, he failed to seize the moment. The crisis came about when a New York congressman introduced legislation providing for the gradual end to slavery in the new state of Missouri. Congress had previously prevented the expansion of slavery into territories, but it had never attempted to terminate its existence within a state. While the proposed legislation triggered talk of the South's secession, John Adams, now eighty-four years old, believed that if Congress stopped slavery's expansion, slavery—hemmed into a few southeastern states—would in time die out.

Acting on his conviction, Adams did something he had not done previously. He gently raised the slavery question with Jefferson. Adams hoped Jefferson would dare to risk his eminent standing, using his influential voice to warn the South that slavery's expansion posed a great danger to the future of the American Union. Jefferson understood the threat. He said that his reaction to the introduction of the slavery issue into the political arena was akin to being awakened by "a fire-bell in the night," leaving him "filled . . . with terror" for the future of the United States. In his heart of hearts, Jefferson may even have suspected that the Union was doomed. Yet, he refused to denounce the spread of slavery, and in private he made it clear that he would stand with the South in defense of slavery.[29]

In recent years, Jefferson has been criticized by historians who have nearly unanimously concluded that he bore a greater responsibility than any other Founder for "having failed to place the nation on the road to liberty for all."[30] Though Jefferson could hardly have made the nation or the southern slaveocracy do his bidding, he was, with the exception of Washington, the Founder who might have spoken, and acted, against slavery with the greatest influence. Yet, despite his recognition that human bondage was wicked, and his acknowledgement of a moral imperative to end slavery, Jefferson steadfastly refused to consider emancipation during the half century following independence unless it was linked to the exile of the freedmen.

Worse, perhaps, Jefferson refused to free his own slaves. An established lawyer, he might have freed his slaves during the American Revolution and lived comfortably from his law practice, as did his mentor, George Wythe, who liberated his chattel following his wife's death. Like Hamilton, Jefferson in the 1780s and 1790s might have alternately held office and practiced law. Moreover, his salary as a government official after 1790 was substantial. He derived an annual salary of $3,500 as a member of Washington's cabinet. His salary increased by about forty percent when he became vice president and multiplied another fivefold when he ascended to the presidency. During the fifteen years that he held national office between 1790 and 1809, Jefferson's average annual salary was nearly sixteen thousand dollars, several times that of a skilled tradesmen in one of the more lucrative crafts.

However, by the time Jefferson entered Washington's cabinet, his independence was circumscribed. From the moment in 1773 that he accepted the fortune that John Wayles had bequeathed to his daughter, Jefferson was shackled by debt. Thereafter, it was infinitely more difficult for him to cut his ties to slavery, as his income as a planter offered his best hope of solvency. But there was something else. Coveting the accoutrements of wealth, he never attempted to live austerely. Like Washington, Jefferson made a conscious decision to keep others enslaved so that he might live the sumptuous life.[31]

Mystery surrounds Jefferson's thoughts and actions concerning emancipation, though historians have offered abundant conjectures. It has been asserted that he was never interested in ending slavery, and that he believed the denial of freedom to slaves offered the best chance of extending liberty and equality to all white Virginians. One historian has argued that in 1792 Jefferson came to the conclusion that the "births of slave children produced capital at the rate of 4 percent per year," a transformative assessment that led him to abandon his earlier antislavery inclinations. It has also been suggested that while Jefferson thought slavery was morally repugnant, he believed that morality could not be imposed from the top down; therefore, he presumed that slavery would end only when the citizenry came to think of it as intolerable. Historian Jack Rakove has wisely reminded us that the past really is an unfamiliar place to succeeding generations, and that Jefferson was born into a world that was not only accustomed to slavery but also in which the most enlightened were "only beginning to understand that slavery was an evil of a kind radically different from the other wrongs of life."[32]

Jefferson himself offered some clues concerning the decisions he made about slavery. He once said that the slavery debates in Virginia's House of Burgesses before 1776 convinced him that "nothing was to be hoped" concerning slavery's eradication in his lifetime. He additionally said that those who had sought to end the slave trade in Virginia in the 1760s had been "treated with the grossest indecorum."[33] Already buried under an avalanche of Federalist invective, he may have flinched in the 1790s at the thought of inviting even more personal attacks. Furthermore, just as many historians have remarked that one war was sufficient for the Founders, causing them to walk the extra mile for peace rather than face hostilities again with a major European power, it may have been that one American Revolution was enough for Jefferson. With his acute anxieties about race relations, he may have been unwilling to pry the lid off the Pandora's box of slavery. What is more, good leaders need to have both a feel for what is possible and knowledge of how to prioritize their battles. During the 1790s, already embroiled in the fight against Hamilton, Jefferson must have shrunk from introducing other matters that would have increased his difficulties, possibly even assuring the success of Hamiltonianism.

When Jefferson came home at the conclusion of his presidency, a few years before Coles approached him, he was sixty-six years old, tired of politics, and eager for tranquility. He was also consumed with the plague of indebtedness, which eventually exceeded one hundred thousand dollars and forced him to sell his most treasured possession: his library of some 6,700 volumes. Had he freed his chattel, he would have lost Monticello, leaving him without "even a log hut to put my head into," as he said it with considerable exaggeration.[34]

Those things may have accounted for his silence concerning slavery. But something else may have played a role as well. James Callender, the newspaper scribbler whose lacerating pen Jefferson had once subsidized, turned on his patron in 1802, furious that he had not been rewarded with a comfortable federal job following the election of 1800. Beginning that September, Callender—writing in the *Richmond Recorder*, a Federalist paper—announced to the world that Jefferson "keeps, and for many years has kept, as his concubine, one of his slaves. Her name is SALLY.... By this wench Sally, our president has had several children."[35] Callender's allegations about Jefferson and Hemings continued into the spring of the following year, and in addition, he broke the story of Jefferson's improper advances toward Betsy Walker nearly forty years earlier. Both stories were picked up by other Federalist editors, who gleefully published them. While savagely attacking Callender, some Republican editors acknowledged that Sally Hemings was a slave living at Monticello who had borne children, though not by Jefferson.

Aside from one opaque denial, Jefferson maintained a stony silence concerning the sensational allegation about his relationship with Hemings.[36] Callender's revelations may also have silenced any inclination that Jefferson felt to speak out against slavery, as he must have feared that the public would inevitably interpret his remarks as confirmation of his protracted intimacy with one of his female slaves. Indeed, while Jefferson took steps to liberate some slaves in his final days, he shrank from emancipating Sally Hemings. In March 1826, Jefferson prepared his will, in which he stipulated that five of his slaves were to be freed. All were from the Hemings family, and two were sons borne by Sally. (Her other living children, both daughters, had left Monticello in 1822 with Jefferson's apparent consent, going off to live as white people.) To prevent their banishment from Virginia, which after 1806 was required of those who were manumitted, Jefferson successfully appealed to the assembly for permission for the five to live within the state. However, he knew that if he petitioned the legislature on behalf of Sally Hemings, it would be interpreted by many as bearing out the stories that she had been his mistress. Instead, when he died, Sally, who was fifty-three, moved with her sons to Charlottesville and lived as a free person. Eight years later, she was freed by Jefferson's daughter Martha.[37]

Jefferson was about to turn eighty-three when he drafted his will. He had lived at home in retirement for seventeen years, for the most part enjoying good health and delighting in the steady parade of admirers who came to the mountaintop to meet him. During all that time, he said, he followed a "regular routine of the day. From sunrise till breakfast only I allot for all my pen and ink work. From breakfast to dinner I am in my garden, shops, or on horse back in the farms, and after dinner I devote entirely to relaxation or light reading."[38] Throughout those years he worked with his farm manager in the hope of making his plantation more profitable, but the place was unsuited to good farming. He invested heavily in two mills, expanded the manufacturing of cloth, and continued operations at the nailery, but while these enterprises increased his income, they contributed little toward the reduction of his indebtedness. During his presidency, Jefferson began construction of an octagonal getaway house in Bedford County, ninety miles away. Finally completed in 1816, he named it Poplar Forest and escaped to it from time to time in the final decade of his life. But he spent most of each year at Monticello, which he shared with Martha—who during her middle years largely lived apart from her husband—and his several grandchildren. His was a busy schedule for a retiree, and a part of it was given over to a voluminous correspondence, including the exchange of hundreds of letters with John Adams.

Jefferson largely avoided politics in these years, but he remained an active reformer, resuscitating the plans for education he had conceived forty years earlier. He drafted legislation for a state system of elementary, secondary, and college education, but once again his reach exceeded his grasp, though the assembly was willing to invest in higher education. For years, Jefferson had contemplated the creation of a university, and at about the midpoint of his retirement he surveyed property in Charlottesville and prepared architectural drawings of a novel "academical village," as he called it. The assembly eventually approved the creation of the University of Virginia. As a member of its Board of Visitors, he was active in the hiring of its president and faculty, and even drew up plans of class schedules, faculty bylaws, and degree requirements. Classes commenced a year before he died, prompting this man who had spent a lifetime shaping the thought of others to remark that his last great act was to provide "for the instruction of those who are to come after us."[39]

During the next twelve months, Jefferson's health declined, and as spring faded into summer in 1826, he sensed that the end was near. He did not dread death. He believed that behind the creation of the universe and life there was "a conviction of design" by a "superintending power." He expected "to ascend in essence to an ecstatic meeting with the friends we have loved and lost and whom we shall still love and never lose again." Though ready to go, he drew on the last reserves of his formidable willpower and managed to stay alive until July 4, the fiftieth anniversary of the Declaration of Independence. That same day, John Adams died in Quincy, Massachusetts. They had outlived Hamilton, their nemesis, by twenty-two years.[40]

Hamilton and Jefferson had been major players in provoking substantive changes, though Hamilton, the outsider from the West Indies, had sought to preserve much of the political and social contours of the world that he found when he alighted in America. He failed, of course, and in his final years he believed that his dreams for his country had come to grief. Indeed, nearly everything that he had stood for was being rejected by the American people. By the jubilee of independence in 1826, if not long before, few in the country mourned his absence. Late-nineteenth-century politicians, financiers, and industrialists would breathe new life into his economic programs, but by then much that Hamilton had stood for had become commonplace in the modern industrial states in Europe. One can wonder if the American economy from the Gilded Age forward might have taken the shape it assumed even had Hamilton never been the treasury secretary.

However, it would be a mistake to undermine Hamilton's legacy. Next to Washington, Hamilton was the most important figure in the establishment of the American Republic. He played a key role in the Nationalists' campaign to overthrow the Articles of Confederation, and his Herculean efforts helped secure the ratification of the Constitution. The consolidation he championed, the funding system he introduced, and the bank he fathered were pivotal in restoring the nation's tattered credit, unfettering commercial activity, and returning prosperity to a new nation that had long endured a languid economy. Much of the capital that helped create the mills and factories that sprang up in the early nineteenth century was available because of Hamilton's economic programs, as was the financial underpinning for the Erie Canal, which officially opened in 1825, linking the East and the West, the dream that Washington had cherished. There were perils in Hamilton's vision, as Jefferson never tired of pointing out, but his financial system proved to be an amazing vehicle for the spread of wealth and opportunity, for enabling sons and daughters to achieve more than their parents had, and for the facilitation of the arts, philanthropy, inventiveness, and education on a scale that would have been unimaginable in Jefferson's Arcadia.

That Hamilton achieved these ends was all the more remarkable in that his recommendations flew in the face of the accepted economic wisdom of his day, and that he espoused innovative commercial and industrial programs in a thoroughly agrarian country. He succeeded through nearly unmatched political aplomb and adeptness. However, with time his reactionary bent was more visible, and by the end of the 1790s his political instincts failed him in the wake of his support of the Alien and Sedition Acts, his lust for military glory, and his egregiously misguided attack on the president during the election of 1800. Even so, his successes as treasury secretary were decisive in bonding powerful northern merchants and financiers to the new national government with a glue that was indissoluble. Their attachment to the Union was crucial in overcoming northern separatist movements that sprang to life up in the face of Jefferson's election. What is more, his commitment to rapprochement with Great Britain was central to opening the West and preserving the peace, and both were absolutely critical to the preservation of the Union. Jefferson once called Hamilton "a colossus" to his party. It could be said that he was a colossus in the founding, shaping, and survival of the early Republic.

Jefferson was the more revolutionary of the two. He was drawn to the resistance movement against Great Britain at least in part by the hope of bringing fundamental political, social, and economic change to his native America. Sensing a historical significance in the revolutionary fervor in the colonies, Jefferson came to see the American Revolution as the dawning of a new era symbolized by fresh ways of thinking and the remodeling of the world. His Declaration of Independence was an eloquent expression of his revolutionary outlook. In a very few rhapsodic words, his majestic composition provided Americans with a sense of identity as would nothing else framed by any of his contemporaries or by leaders in succeeding generations, save perhaps for the rhetoric of Abraham Lincoln, Franklin Delano Roosevelt, and Martin Luther King Jr. Jefferson also saw his presidency as a voyage into new waters. He was looking forward, not backward, he declared, and on taking office he proclaimed the advent of a new era launched by the "mighty wave of public opinion," a notion that would not have resonated with his predecessors.[41]

Jefferson may have been forward-looking, but it was Hamilton who sought to construct what later generations would see as the modern nation state. Jefferson resisted that trend, preferring a loose, decentralized union of states, sufficient for mutual protection against foreign predators and for the facilitation of commerce, and with just enough military clout to see to the opening of the West.

Jefferson saw Hamilton as a counterrevolutionary, which was neither entirely correct nor totally incorrect. More than any other figure in the early years of Washington's presidency, Jefferson mobilized the resistance and provided the ideology against the darker things for which Hamilton stood. With his unsurpassed grasp of political reality, Jefferson was instrumental in stopping Hamiltonianism. No one knows what the United States might have become by the fiftieth anniversary of independence had Hamilton and the High Federalists had their way. What we do know is that the sweeping democracy and propulsive egalitarianism of 1826 America owed more to Jefferson than to any other Founder.

While Hamilton's focus was on a strong and independent United States, Jefferson dreamed of making the world a better place. He divined that what

he called the "corrupt squadrons of stockjobbers" were the inevitable handmaidens of Hamiltonianism, and he understood that once such forces were
unleashed, it would be doubtful at best that those who governed would act to
achieve the greatest good for the greatest number. Empathetic toward those
who faced the miseries wrought by manufacturing, ambitious entrepreneurs,
and capricious market forces, Jefferson also feared that, in time, the world
Hamilton sought would consist of a prosperous few who lived sumptuously
while the great majority remained propertyless and mired in squalor. Jefferson's agrarian idyll, the polar opposite of Hamiltoniansim, envisaged a promised land of virtuous, republican, property-owing farmers who had little need
of a powerful centralized government, who would never yearn for the rule of
"angels, in the form of kings," and who would be independent of the long and
awesome clout of the social and economic elite. Such a society, overseen by
republican governance, was the "world's best hope," he said in his inaugural
address.[42] It was a dream, and dreams do not always come true, but for most
members of the several generations following Jefferson's death, America more
closely resembled Jefferson's dream than it did the reveries of Hamilton.

Today's America is more Hamilton's America. Jefferson may never have
fully understood Hamilton's funding and banking systems, but better than
most he gleaned the potential dangers that awaited future generations living
in the nation state that Hamilton wished to bring into being. Presciently,
and with foreboding, Jefferson saw that Hamiltonianism would concentrate
power in the hands of the business leaders and financiers that it primarily
served, leading inevitably to an American plutocracy every bit as dominant
as monarchs and titled aristocrats had once been. Jefferson's fears were not
misplaced. In modern America, concentrated wealth controls politics and
government, leading even the extremely conservative Senator John McCain
to remark that "both parties conspire to stay in office by selling the country
to the highest bidder."[43] The American nation, with its incredibly powerful
chief executive, gargantuan military, repeated intervention in the affairs of
foreign states, and political system in the thrall of great wealth, is the very
world that Jefferson abhorred.

Hamilton and Jefferson had their champions and detractors in their lifetimes, and both have been lionized and criticized by politicians and scholars
ever since. The exaltation of Hamilton began immediately after his shocking
demise. Two days later, as bells pealed throughout Manhattan, Hamilton's
body was conveyed to Trinity Church along city streets lined with the grieving and the curious. Mourners streamed in for two hours to pay their respects, after which the doors to the church were closed for a formal service

attended by those with whom Hamilton had most closely associated. His family was present, of course, and so too were officers from the Continental army and the New Army, and several Manhattan lawyers, merchants, and bankers. Columbia's faculty and students were also admitted. The ubiquitous Gouverneur Morris delivered an extended, sorrowful eulogy. Morris ignored Hamilton's years in the West Indies and omitted mentioning what he had recently confided to his own diary: Hamilton not only was "indiscreet, vain and opinionated," but he was also "on Principle opposed to republican and attached to monarchical Government." Morris hit his stride when he spoke of Washington taking Hamilton as an aide: "It seemed as if God had called him suddenly into existence that he might assist to save a world!" The "single error" of Hamilton's life had been his belief that the Constitutional Convention had not created a sufficiently powerful national government. Calling Hamilton the most "splendid" member of Washington's cabinet, Morris attributed the nation's "rapid advance in power and prosperity" to Hamilton's economic policies. Morris admonished the audience, when faced with difficult choices, to ask: *Would Hamilton have done this thing*? He closed with an appeal: "I CHARGE YOU TO PROTECT HIS FAME—It is all he has left."[44]

In Charlottesville, Virginia, bells rang when Jefferson died. The students at the university, and many residents of the village, donned black crepe armbands. All businesses in town remained closed on July 5, the day of the funeral. Though it rained, the service was held outdoors at the family burial plot at Monticello. Students and faculty from the university, many neighbors and residents of Charlottesville, and some who had been Jefferson's slaves attended. All stood in the wet, emerald green grass listening to the rector of the local Episcopal church. When he was done, the coffin was lowered into a freshly dug grave next to that of Jefferson's wife. A month or so later, a six-foot obelisk headstone was placed atop a three-foot-square slab that rested on the grave.[45] The gravestone bore an inscription composed by Jefferson:

HERE WAS BURIED THOMAS JEFFERSON
AUTHOR OF THE DECLARATION OF AMERICAN INDEPENDENCE
OF THE STATUTE OF VIRGINIA FOR RELIGIOUS FREEDOM
& FATHER OF THE UNIVERSITY OF VIRGINIA.

His coffin had been made by John Hemings, the fifty-year-old half-brother of Sally.

No one knows where Sally Hemings is buried.

Select Bibliography

The correspondence of Jefferson and Hamilton, as well as nearly all of Hamilton's published essays, are available in modern collections in which specialized editors have provided useful introductory essays and clarifying footnotes. In addition, users are helped immensely by generally excellent indexing.

The modern edition of Jefferson's papers has been dribbling out since 1950, and at the completion of this manuscript had reached nearly the midpoint of his presidency. One should see Julian P. Boyd et al., eds., *The Papers of Thomas Jefferson* (Princeton, N.J., 1950–). Fortunately, in 2004 a second Jefferson papers project commenced that will span his seventeen-year retirement following his presidency. See J. Jefferson Looney et al., eds., *The Papers of Thomas Jefferson: Retirement Series* (Charlottesville, Va., 2004–). At the completion of this manuscript, the retirement series had progressed through the first half dozen years after Jefferson returned for good to Monticello. Two older multivolume series include most of Jefferson's correspondence after 1815. These are Paul Leicester Ford, ed., *The Writings of Thomas Jefferson* (New York, 1892–99); and A. A. Lipscomb and A. E. Bergh, eds., *The Writings of Thomas Jefferson* (Washington, D.C., 1900–4).

Jefferson's correspondence with John and Abigail Adams, which continued on and off for four decades, has been collected in two volumes. See Lester J. Cappon, ed., *The Adams-Jefferson Letters: The Complete Correspondence Between Thomas Jefferson and Abigail and John Adams* (Chapel Hill, N.C., 1961). Jefferson's letters to and from his daughters and other family members can be found in E. M. Betts and J. A. Bear Jr., eds., *The Family Letters of Thomas Jefferson* (Columbia, Mo., 1966). The financial record books that Jefferson kept are available. See James A. Bear and Lucia Stanton, eds., *Jefferson's Memorandum Books: Accounts, with Legal Records and Miscellany, 1767–1826* (Princeton, N.J., 1997). A massive single-volume compilation of Jefferson's letters and writings can be found in Saul K. Padover, *The Complete Jefferson: Containing His Major Writings, Published and Unpublished, Except His Letters* (Freeport, N.Y., 1969).

Single-volume editions of Jefferson's most important letters and writings have been edited by Merrill D. Peterson. See *The Portable Thomas Jefferson* (New York, 1977) and *Thomas Jefferson, Writings* (New York, 1984).

The modern edition of Hamilton's papers has long since been completed and spans twenty-seven volumes. See Harold C. Syrett and Jacob E. Cooke, eds., *Papers of Alexander Hamilton* (New York, 1961–79). A fine one-volume collection of his most important writings is also available. See Joanne B. Freeman, ed., *Alexander Hamilton, Writings* (New York, 2001).

Historian Noble Cunningham edited a documentary study that outlines the lives of the two men, and America's founding, around forty crucial documents. See Noble E. Cunningham Jr., *Thomas Jefferson versus Alexander Hamilton: Confrontations That Shaped a Nation* (New York, 2000).

Biographies of Jefferson and Hamilton abound. The most comprehensive on the life of Jefferson is the six-volume, encyclopedic effort by Dumas Malone, *Jefferson and His Time* (Boston 1948–81). Alf J. Mapp Jr. authored a two-volume life history: *Thomas Jefferson: A Strange Case of Mistaken Identity* (Lanham, Md., 1987) covers the period through the election of 1800, while the subsequent years are detailed in *Thomas Jefferson: Passionate Pilgrim—The Presidency, the Founding of the University, and the Private Battle* (Lanham, Md., 1993). For longer single-volume treatments that emphasize his public side, see Merrill D. Peterson, *Thomas Jefferson and the New Nation* (New York, 1970); Noble Cunningham, *In Pursuit of Reason: The Life of Thomas Jefferson* (Baton Rouge, La., 1987); Willard Sterne Randall, *Thomas Jefferson: A Life* (New York, 1992); and Jon Meacham, *Thomas Jefferson: The Art of Power* (New York, 2012). The modern biography that reshaped the discussion on Jefferson is Fawn M. Brodie, *Thomas Jefferson: An Intimate History* (New York, 1974). For a semibiographical character study of Jefferson, see Joseph J. Ellis, *American Sphinx: The Character of Thomas Jefferson* (New York, 1997).

For good short biographies see Page Smith, *Jefferson: A Revealing Biography* (New York, 1976); Norman K. Risjord, *Thomas Jefferson* (Lanham, Md., 2002); and Richard B. Bernstein, *Thomas Jefferson* (New York, 2003).

All other Hamilton biographies are overshadowed by Ron Chernow's massive and resplendent single volume, *Alexander Hamilton* (New York, 2004). For an older, though useful, two-volume life history, see Broadus Mitchell, *Alexander Hamilton* (New York, 1957, 1962). Several more brief biographies are available. See Richard Brookhiser, *Alexander Hamilton: American* (New York, 1999); Jacob E. Cooke, *Alexander Hamilton* (New York, 1982); Noemie Emery, *Alexander Hamilton: An Intimate Portrait* (New York, 1982); Robert A. Hendrickson, *Hamilton* (New York, 1976); Forrest McDonald, *Alexander Hamilton: A Biography* (New York, 1982); John C. Miller, *Alexander Hamilton: Portrait in Paradox* (New York, 1959); Willard Sterne Randall, *Alexander Hamilton: A Life* (New York, 2003); and Nathan Schachner, *Alexander Hamilton* (New York, 1957). Hamilton's life through the American Revolution is told in detail in James Thomas Flexner, *The Young Hamilton: A Biography* (Boston, 1978).

Far more has been written on Jefferson than on Hamilton, perhaps because of his longer life and greater abundance of papers. In fact, so many books and essays have poured forth on Jefferson that a comprehensive list of those works published prior to 1992 fills two large volumes. See Frank Shuffelton, ed., *Thomas Jefferson: A Comprehensive Annotated Bibliography of Writings About Him* (New York, 1983) and Shuffelton, *Thomas Jefferson: An Annotated Bibliography* (New York, 1992). Unfortunately, no such bibliography of works on Hamilton has been compiled.

A few previous comparative studies are available. The earliest was written by a journalist and political activist and reads like a campaign advertisement for Jefferson. See Claude Bowers, *Jefferson and Hamilton: The Struggle for Democracy in America* (Boston, 1925). A more scholarly treatment is Roger G. Kennedy, *Burr, Hamilton, and Jefferson: A Study in Character* (New York, 2000), though this book begins with the Hamilton-Burr duel and focuses largely on Jefferson's relationship with Burr after 1804. For a thoughtful and provocative analysis, see Darren Staloff, *Hamilton, Adams, Jefferson: The Politics of Enlightenment and the American Founding* (New York, 2005), a study that emphasizes how the Enlightenment guided and transformed these Founders.

Both Jefferson and Hamilton have been the subject of numerous works that probe specific aspects of their life, thought, ideas, and policies. Readers can find many cited in the notes for this book.

ABBREVIATIONS

AH	Alexander Hamilton
AJL	Lestor J. Cappon, ed., *The Adams-Jefferson Letters: The Complete Correspondence Between Thomas Jefferson and Abigail and John Adams*. 2 vols. Chapel Hill, N.C., University of North Carolina Press, 1959.
Bernstein, *TJ*	R. B. Bernstein, *Thomas Jefferson*. New York, Oxford University Press, 2003.
Brodie, *TJ*	Fawn M. Brodie, *Thomas Jefferson: An Intimate History*. New York, W. W. Norton, 1974.
Brookhiser, *AH*	Richard Brookhiser, *Alexander Hamilton: American*. New York, Free Press, 1999.
Chernow, *AH*	Ron Chernow, *Alexander Hamilton*. New York, Penguin Press, 2004.
Cooke, *AH*	Jacob Ernest Cooke, *Alexander Hamilton*. New York, Charles Scribner's Sons, 1982.
Cunningham, *TJ*	Noble E. Cunningham Jr., *In Pursuit of Reason: The Life of Thomas Jefferson*. Baton Rouge, Louisiana State University Press, 1987.
DAJA	L. H. Butterfield et al., eds., *The Diary and Autobiography of John Adams*. 4 vols. Cambridge, Mass., Harvard University Press, 1961.
Ellis, *American Sphinx*	Joseph J. Ellis, *American Sphinx: The Character of Thomas Jefferson*. New York, Alfred Knopf, 1997.
ESH	Elizabeth Schuyler Hamilton
Flexner, *Young Hamilton*	James Thomas Flexner, *The Young Hamilton: A Biography*. Boston, Little, Brown and Company, 1978.
FLTJ	E. M. Betts and J. A. Bear, Jr., eds., *The Family Letters of Thomas Jefferson*. Columbia, Mo., University of Missouri Press, 1966.
Ford, *WTJ*	Paul Leicester Ford, ed., *The Writings of Thomas Jefferson*. 10 vols. New York, G. P. Putnam's, 1892–99.
GW	George Washington
JA	John Adams
JM	James Madison
JMB	James A. Bear and Lucia Stanton, eds., *Jefferson's Memorandum Books: Accounts, with Legal Records and Mis-*

cellany, 1767–1826. 2 vols. Princeton, N.J., Princeton University Press, 1997.

L & B, *WTJ* A. A. Lipscomb and A. E. Bergh, eds., *The Writings of Thomas Jefferson.* 20 vols. Washington, D.C., Thomas Jefferson Memorial Association of the United States, 1900–04.

LDC Paul H. Smith, ed., *Letters of Delegates to Congress, 1774–1789.* 29 vols. Washington, D.C., Library of Congress, 1976–2000.

McDonald, *AH* Forrest McDonald, *Alexander Hamilton: A Biography.* New York, W. W. Norton, 1982.

Malone, *TJ* Dumas Malone, *Jefferson and His Time.* 6 vols. Boston, Little, Brown and Company, 1948–81.

Miller, *AH* John C. Miller, *Alexander Hamilton: Portrait in Paradox.* New York, Harper and Brothers, 1959.

Mitchell, *AH* Broadus Mitchell, *Alexander Hamilton.* 2 vols. New York, Macmillan Company, 1957, 1962.

Padover, *CTJ* Saul K. Padover, ed., *The Complete Jefferson: Containing His Major Writings, Published and Unpublished, Except His Letters.* Freeport, N.Y., Books for Libraries, 1969.

PAH Harold C. Syrett and Jacob E. Cooke, eds., *The Papers of Alexander Hamilton.* 27 vols. New York, Columbia University Press, 1961–87.

Peterson, *TJ* Merrill D. Peterson, *Thomas Jefferson and the New Nation.* New York, Oxford University Press, 1970.

PGWC W. W. Abbot et al., eds., *The Papers of George Washington: Colonial Series.* 10 vols. Charlottesville, University Press of Virginia, 1983–95.

PGWCfed W. W. Abbot et al., eds., *The Papers of George Washington: Confederation Series.* 6 vols. Charlottesville, University Press of Virginia, 1985–97.

PGWP Dorothy Twohig et al., eds., *The Papers of George Washington: Presidential Series.* Charlottesville, University Press of Virginia, 1987–.

PGWR Philander Chase et al., eds., *The Papers of George Washington: Revolutionary War Series.* Charlottesville, University Press of Virginia, 1985–.

PGW: Ret. Ser. Dorothy Twohig et al., eds., *The Papers of George Washington: Retirement Series.* 4 vols. Charlottesville, University Press of Virginia, 1998–99.

PJA Robert J. Taylor et al., eds., *Papers of John Adams.* Cambridge, Mass., Harvard University Press, 1977–.

PJM William T. Hutchinson et al., eds., *The Papers of James Madison.* Chicago and Charlottesville, University of Chicago Press and University Press of Virginia, 1962–.

PTJ Julian P. Boyd et al., eds., *The Papers of Thomas Jefferson.* Princeton, N.J., Princeton University Press, 1950–.

PTJ: Ret. Ser.	J. Jefferson Looney et al., eds., *The Papers of Thomas Jefferson: Retirement Series.* Princeton, N.J., Princeton University Press, 2004–.
TJ	Thomas Jefferson
WW	John C. Fitzpatrick, ed., *The Writings of Washington.* 39 vols. Washington, D.C., U.S. Government Printing Office, 1931–44.

NOTES

PREFACE

1. William Jefferson Clinton, Inaugural Address, January 20, 1993, in *Public Papers of the Presidents of the United States: William J. Clinton, Book 1, 1993* (Washington, D.C., 1994–2002), 1:1–2.

2. President Bill Clinton, *Between Hope and History: Meeting America's Challenges for the 21st Century* (New York, 1996), 127.

3. George W. Bush, "Remarks Announcing the Nomination of Henry M. Paulson, Jr., to Be Secretary of the Treasury," May 30, 2006, in *Public Papers of the Presidents of the United States: George W. Bush, 2006, Book 1, 2006* (Washington, D.C., 2010), 1:1043–45.

4. Andrew Burstein, *The Passions of Andrew Jackson* (New York, 2003), 223–28. The quotation is on page 223.

5. Gordon S. Wood, *Revolutionary Characters: What Made the Founders Different* (New York, 2006), 121–22.

6. Ibid., 122.

7. Merrill D. Peterson, *The Jeffersonian Image in the American Mind* (New York, 1960), 457.

8. Francis D. Cogliano, *Thomas Jefferson: Reputation and Legacy* (Charlottesville, Va., 2006), 199; Paul Finkelman, "The Monster of Monticello," *New York Times*, November 30, 2012.

9. Arthur M. Schlesinger Jr., *A Thousand Days: John F. Kennedy in the White House* (Boston, 1965), 1, 733.

10. Unless otherwise noted, the foregoing survey of Jefferson and Hamilton in popular thought draws on Peterson, *Jeffersonian Image in the American Mind*; Stephen F. Knott, *Alexander Hamilton and the Persistence of Myth* (Lawrence, Kan., 2002); and William Hogeland, "Inventing Alexander Hamilton: The Troubling Embrace of the Founder of American Finance," *Boston Review*, November/December 2007, *http://bostonreview.net/BR32.6/hogeland.php*. Quotations from Peterson can be found on pages 72, 74, 253, 260, 261, 263, 352, 356, 360, 377–78, and 385. Quotations from Knott can be found on pages 6, 49, 72, 74, 87, 88, 102, 139, 161, 190, and 203.

PROLOGUE

1. *WW* 27:287–88; GW to Marquis de Lafayette, February 1, 1784, *PGWCfed* 1:87–88.

2. GW to Lafayette, February 1, 1784, *PGWCfed* 1:88; GW to Philip Schuyler, January 21, 1784, ibid., 1:68.

3. GW to Jonathan Trumbull Jr., January 5, 1784, *PGWCfed* 1:12.

4. GW to Henry Knox, January 5, 1785, *PGWCfed* 2:253; Ron Chernow, *Washington: A Life* (New York, 2010), 465; Woody Holton, *Unruly Americans and the Origins of the Constitution* (New York, 2007), 59.

5. GW, "Circular to the States," June 8, 1783, *WW* 26:483–96.

6. GW to John Jay, May 18, 1786, *PGWCfed* 4:56.

7. The foregoing draws on Gordon S. Wood, *The Radicalism of the American Revolution* (New York, 1992), 11–243; and Terry Bouton, *Taming Democracy: "The People," the Founders, and the Troubled Ending of the American Revolution* (New York, 2007), 61–104.

8. Jay to GW, June 27, 1786, *PGWCfed* 4:131; GW to Jay, August 15, 1786, ibid., 4:212.

9. AH, New York Assembly. Remarks on an Act Granting to Congress Certain Imposts and Duties, February 15, 1787, *PAH* 4:71–93. The quotes are on pages 77, 83, 91, and 92.

10. *JMB* 1:653.

11. TJ to George Wythe, August 13, 1786, *PTJ* 10:244–454; TJ to Edward Carrington, January 16, August 4, 1787, ibid., 11:48–49, 678; TJ to JM, January 30, 1787, ibid., 11:92–93; TJ to GW, November 14, 1786, ibid., 10:533; TJ to Benjamin Hawkins, August 4, 1787, ibid., 11:684; TJ to Joseph Jones, August 14, 1787, ibid., 12:34.

12. TJ to GW, August 14, 1787, *PTJ* 12:36–37.

13. GW to Lafayette, May 10, 1786, *PGWCfed* 4:42; GW to Henry Lee Jr., October 31, 1786, ibid., 4:318; GW to Jay, August 15, 1786, ibid., 4:212.

CHAPTER 1: "TO MAKE A MORE UNIVERSAL ACQUAINTANCE": UNHAPPY YOUTHS

Malone, *TJ*, 1:3–165; Peterson, *TJ*, 3–31; Brodie, *TJ*, 86–94; Chernow, *AH*, 7–53, 147–48, 203, 209, 226–27; Cooke, *AH*, 1–8; Flexner, *Young H*, 9–63; Mitchell, *AH*, 1:1–60; Brookhiser, *AH*, 13–28; Miller, *AH*, 3–8.

1. John Ferling, *Setting the World Ablaze: Washington, Adams, Jefferson, and the American Revolution* (New York, 2000), 7.

2. AH to Edward Stevens, November 11, 1769, *PAH* 1:4.

3. Susan Kern, *The Jeffersons at Shadwell* (New Haven, Conn., 2010), 1–40. An inventory of Peter Jefferson's library as of 1757 can be found in ibid., 261–62.

4. TJ to Thomas Jefferson Randolph, November 29, 1808, *FLTJ*, 362–63.

5. This and all previous quotations above in the saga of AH's life are from AH to William Jackson, August 26, 1800, *PAH* 25:89–90.

6. AH to James Hamilton Jr., June 22, 1785, *PAH* 3:617.

7. Quoted in Brodie, *TJ*, 71.

8. TJ to Joseph Priestley, January 27, 1800, *PTJ* 31:340. See also Kevin J. Hayes, *The Road to Monticello: The Life and Mind of Thomas Jefferson* (New York, 2008), 31–42.

9. TJ to John Harvie, January 14, 1760, *PTJ* 1:3. This paragraph draws in part on Gordon S. Wood, "The Trials and Tribulations of Thomas Jefferson," in Peter S. Onuf, ed., *Jeffersonian Legacies* (Charlottesville, Va., 1993), 402–3.

10. Hayes, *Road to Monticello*, 50–56; Silvio A. Bedini, *Thomas Jefferson: Statesman of Science* (New York, 1990), 23–29. The "liberality of sentiment" quotation can be found in Hayes, *Road to Monticello*, 54.

11. TJ, Autobiography, in Padover, *CTJ*, 1120.

12. TJ to Vine Utley, March 21, 1819, Ford, *WTJ* 9:126; TJ to William Duane, October 1,

1812, Lipscomb and Berg, *WTJ* 2:420; Malone, *TJ*, 1:56–57; Harry S. Randall, *The Life of Thomas Jefferson* (New York, 1858), 1:37, 41–42.

13. Quoted in Trevor Colbourn, ed., *Fame and the Founding Fathers: Essays by Douglass Adair* (New York, 1974), 7.

14. TJ to John Page, December 25, 1762, *PTJ* 1:5; TJ, Autobiography, in Padover, *CTJ*, 1120.

15. Quoted in Robert Hendrickson, *Hamilton* (New York, 1976), 1:26.

16. AH to Stevens, November 11, 1769, *PAH* 1:4.

17. Ibid.

18. AH to the *Royal Danish American Gazette*, April 6, 1771, September 6, October 17, 1772, *PAH* 1:6–7, 34–38, 38–39.

19. Quoted in Andrew Burstein, *The Inner Jefferson: Portrait of a Grieving Optimist* (Charlottesville, Va., 1995), 14.

20. TJ to Page, December 25, 1762, July 15, 1763, *PTJ* 1:5, 10.

21. TJ to Page, December 25, 1762, July 15, October 7, 1763, January 19, 1764, *PTJ* 1:11, 13–14.

22. TJ to William Fleming, March 20, 1764, *PTJ* 1:16.

23. Jon Kukla, *Mr. Jefferson's Women* (New York, 2007), 34–36. Consult Kukla's extensive endnotes for the literature on tension headaches in general and TJ's problems in particular.

24. TJ to Ralph Izard, July 17, 1788, *PTJ* 13:372; TJ to Thomas Jefferson Randolph, June 14, 1806, Lipscomb and Bergh, *WTJ* 12:197–98; TJ, Autobiography, in Padover, *CTJ*, 1120; Randall, *Life of Thomas Jefferson*, 47; Brodie, *TJ*, 61; Page Smith, *Jefferson: A Revealing Biography* (New York, 1976), 23.

25. Randall, *Life of Thomas Jefferson*, 58–65; Edward Dumbauld, *Thomas Jefferson and the Law* (Norman, Okla., 1978), xi.

26. The "monastic" quote and many of the ideas in this paragraph draw on Peter S. Onuf, "Making Sense of Jefferson," in Peter S. Onuf, ed., *The Mind of Thomas Jefferson* (Charlottesville, Va., 2007). The "reestablish himself" quotation is from Burstein, *Inner Jefferson*, 12. The "canine appetite" quotation is from William Howard Adams, *The Paris Years of Thomas Jefferson* (New Haven, Conn., 1997), 125. See also Edmund Randolph, "Essay on the Revolutionary History of Virginia," *Virginia Magazine of History and Biography* 43 (1953): 123.

27. This paragraph draws on Michal J. Rozbicki, *The Complete Colonial Gentleman: Cultural Legitimacy in Plantation America* (Charlottesville, Va., 1998), 7–126.

28. Kenneth A. Lockridge, *On the Sources of Patriarchal Rage: The Commonplace Books of William Byrd and Thomas Jefferson and the Gendering of Power in the Eighteenth Century* (New York, 1992), 47–102; Douglas L. Wilson, ed., *Jefferson's Literary Commonplace Book*, in *Papers of Thomas Jefferson*, 2nd set (Princeton, N.J., 1989), 19, 70–71, 72, 76–77, 82, 98–99, 117–18, 126–27. See also, Kukla, *Mr. Jefferson's Women*, 37–40.

29. TJ to Page, February 21, 1770, *PTJ* 1:34–35.

30. The text of Walker's 1802 allegation and TJ's confession can be found in Malone, *TJ* 1:448–50. See also Kukla, *Mr. Jefferson's Women*, 41–63.

31. Kukla, *Mr. Jefferson's Women*, 55–56.

32. Dumbauld, *Thomas Jefferson and the Law*, 66–83; Frank L. Dewey, *Thomas Jefferson, Lawyer* (Charlottesville, Va., 1986), 9–14; Randall, *Life of Thomas Jefferson*, 85–86.

33. John Ferling, *John Adams: A Life* (reprint, New York, 2010), 26–28.

34. Quoted in Adams, *Paris Years of Thomas Jefferson*, 78.

35. *JMB* 1:212; TJ to James Ogilvie, February 20, 1771, *PTJ* 1:63.

36. Charles Sydnor, *Gentlemen Freeholders: Political Practices in Washington's Virginia* (Chapel Hill, N.C., 1952), 100.

37. *JMB* 1:xlv–xlvi.

38. Randall, *Life of Thomas Jefferson*, 1:62–64; Brodie, *TJ*, 88.

39. TJ to Ogilvie, February 20, 1771, *PTJ* 1:63; TJ to Robert Skipwith, August 3, 1771, ibid., 1:78.

40. Randall, *Life of Thomas Jefferson*, 1:64, 160. For a good summary of the family legends concerning the newlyweds' adventures, see Virginia Scharff, *The Women Jefferson Loved* (New York, 2010), 89–90.

41. TJ, Autobiography, in Padover, *CTJ*, 1121, 1151.

42. Ibid., 1120–22.

43. "Narrative of Hercules Mulligan of the City of New York," [n.d.], *William and Mary Quarterly* 4 (1947): 209.

44. Flexner, *Young Hamilton*, 60.

45. On AH's habit of praying daily, see "Narrative of Colonel Robert Troup," March 22, 1810, in *William and Mary Quarterly* 4 (1947): 213.

CHAPTER 2: "THE GALLING YOKE OF DEPENDENCE": BECOMING REBELS

Malone, *TJ*, 1:91–97, 128–42; Peterson, *TJ*, 32–79; Cunningham, *TJ*, 23–51; Chernow, *AH*, 54–74; Miller, *AH*, 3–16.

1. TJ to Page, December 25, 1762, *PTJ* 1:5.

2. Frank L. Dewey, *Thomas Jefferson, Lawyer* (Charlottesville, Va., 1986), 83–93.

3. Lawrence Henry Gibson, "The American Revolution as an Aftermath of the Great War for Empire," *Political Science Quarterly* 55 (1950): 86–104; Jack P. Greene, "An Uneasy Connection: An Analysis of the Preconditions of the American Revolution," in Stephen G. Kurtz and James H. Hutson, eds., *Essays on the American Revolution* (Chapel Hill, N.C., 1973), 32–80; Gordon S. Wood, *The American Revolution: A History* (New York, 2003), 17–18.

4. TJ to William Wirt, April 12, 1812, in Padover, *CTJ*, 898; Kevin J. Hayes, *The Road to Monticello: The Life and Mind of Thomas Jefferson* (New York, 2008), 75.

5. Resolutions for an Answer to Governor Botetourt's Speech, May 8, 1769, *PTJ* 1:26–27; Virginia Nonimportation Resolutions, May 1769, ibid., 1:27–30.

6. JA, Diary, December 18, 1765, *DAJA* 1:263.

7. On the evolution of JA's thinking, see JA to Hezekiah Niles, February 13, 1818, in Charles F. Adams, ed., *The Works of John Adams, Second President of the United States: With a Life of the Author* (Boston, 1850–1859), 10:285–86; JA to William Tudor, June 1, 1817, July 9, 1818, ibid., 10:259, 327; JA to Tudor, November 16, 25, December 7, 1816, Adams Family Papers, Massachusetts Historical Society, Boston, 1954–1959, microfilm edition, reel 123; JA to Sheldon Jones, March 11, 1809, ibid., reel 118; JA to TJ, July 15, 1813, July 9, 1818, *AJL* 2:237, 594; JA, Diary, March 22, 1773, *DAJA* 2:80; JA to Benjamin Rush, February 27, 1805, May 1, 21, 1807, in John A. Schutz and Douglass Adair, eds., *The Spur of Fame: Dialogues of John Adams and Benjamin Rush, 1805–1813* (San Marino, Cal., 1966), 35–36, 80, 88.

8. TJ, Autobiography, in Padover, *CTJ*, 1122.

9. Bernard Bailyn, *The Ideological Origins of the American Revolution* (Cambridge, Mass., 1967), 22–54. See also the excellent summaries in Lance Banning, *The Jeffersonian Persuasion: Evolution of a Party Ideology* (Ithaca, N.Y., 1978), 21–90; and David N. Mayer, *The Constitutional Thought of Thomas Jefferson* (Charlottesville, Va., 1994), 19–24.

10. [TJ], *A Summary View of the Rights of British America* (Williamsburg, Va., 1775), *PTJ* 1:122.

11. Quoted in Peterson, *TJ*, 40.

12. H. Trevor Colbourn, *The Lamp of Experience: Whig History and the Intellectual Origins of the American Revolution* (Chapel Hill, N.C., 1965), 3–56, 158–60; Bernard Bailyn, *Ideological Origins of the American Revolution*, 55–143; Gordon S. Wood, *The Creation of the American Republic, 1776–1787* (Chapel Hill, N.C., 1969), 10–45; Gordon S. Wood, "Conspiracy and the Paranoid Style: Causality and Deceit in the Eighteenth Century," *William and Mary Quarterly* 39 (1982): 401–2; TJ, Autobiography, in Padover, *CTJ*, 1122; [TJ], *A Summary View*, *PTJ* 1:135.

13. Darren Staloff, *Hamilton, Adams, Jefferson: The Politics of Enlightenment and the American Founding* (New York, 2005), 244–56.

14. JA to TJ, August 24, 1815, in *AJL* 2:455.

15. Quoted in Woody Holton, *Forced Founders: Indians, Debtors, Slaves, and the Making of the American Revolution in Virginia* (Chapel Hill, N.C., 1999), 72.

16. Draft of Declaration of Rights, July 26, 1774, *PTJ* 1:119; TJ, Draft of Instructions to the Virginia Delegates to the Continental Congress, [July 1774], ibid., 1:121.

17. Joseph J. Ellis, *American Sphinx*, 29.

18. John Dickinson, *Letters from a Farmer in Pennsylvania* (1768), in Merrill Jensen, ed., *Tracts of the American Revolution, 1763–1776* (Indianapolis, Ind., 1967), 128–63. The quotation can be found on page 140.

19. TJ, Draft of Instructions to the Virginia Delegates in the Continental Congress, [July 1774], *PTJ* 1:121–35. The quotations are on pages 125 and 129. For Ellis's characterization, see Ellis, *American Sphinx*, 41. The literature on TJ's composition is extensive; see Stephen A. Conrad, "Putting Rights Talk in Its Place: *The Summary View* Revisited," in Peter Onuf, ed., *Jeffersonian Legacies* (Charlottesville, Va., 1993), 254–80; David Mayer, *The Constitutional Thought of Thomas Jefferson* (Charlottesville, Va., 1994), 28–37; Kristofer Ray, "Thomas Jefferson and *A Summary View of the Rights of British America*," in Francis D. Cogliano, ed., *A Companion to Thomas Jefferson* (Chichester, England, 2011), 32–43.

20. TJ to John W. Campbell, September 3, 1809, Ford, *WTJ* 9:258; Instructions by the Virginia Convention to Their Delegates in Congress, 1774, August 1–6, 1774, *PTJ* 1:141–43; John E. Selby, *The Revolution in Virginia, 1775–1783* (Williamsburg, Va., 1988), 10.

21. JA, "Letters of Novanglus," *PJA* 2:339–40; [TJ], *A Summary View*, *PTJ* 1:126.

22. [TJ], *A Summary View*, *PTJ* 1:125, 135.

23. Jack N. Rakove, *The Beginnings of National Politics: An Interpretive History of the Continental Congress* (Baltimore, 1979), 67.

24. [AH], *A Full Vindication of the Measures of the Congress* ... (New York, 1774), in *PAH* 1:78; [AH], *The Farmer Refuted* ... (New York, 1775), ibid., 1:81–165. The quotations from these two pamphlets can be found in ibid., 1:46, 52, 59, 77, 82, 90, 91, 151, 158, and 165.

25. [AH], "Remarks on the Quebec Bill," June 15, 22, 1775, *New York-Gazetteer*, in *PAH* 1:165–76.

26. [AH], *New-York Journal*, "The Monitor," Nos. I, IV, XI, XIV, November 9, 30, 1775, January 18, February 8, 1776; Worthington C. Ford, et al., eds., *Journals of the Continental Congress* (Washington, D.C., 1904–1937), 3:410.

27. Quoted in Hayes, *Road to Monticello*, 153.

28. Philip S. Foner, ed., *The Complete Writings of Thomas Paine* (New York, 1945), 1:3–46.

29. [AH], *New-York Journal*, "The Monitor," Nos. IV, VII, XII, XIV, November 30, December 28, 1775, January 25, February 8, 1776.

30. The "bombardier" quote can be found in John Hamilton, *The Life of Alexander Hamilton* (New York, 1840), 1:52, and the "seal my blood" quotation is in Chernow, *AH*, 72.

31. Report of Committee to Prepare a Plan for a Militia, [March 25, 1775], *PTJ* 1:160–61.

32. Virginia Resolutions on Lord North's Conciliatory Proposal, [June 10, 1775], *PTJ* 1:170–74. The quotation is on page 172.

33. TJ to William Small, May 7, 1775, *PTJ* 1:165.

34. *JMB* 1:396–99; Samuel Ward to Henry Ward, June 22, 1775, *LDC* 1:535; JA, Autobiography, *DAJA* 3:335–36; JA to Timothy Pickering, August 6, 1822, Adams, *Works of John Adams*, 2:512.

35. Some quotations are from Malone, *TJ*, 1:203, 295, 392, and 420. Some are from John Ferling, *Setting the World Ablaze: Washington, Adams, Jefferson, and the American Revolution* (New York, 2000), 49. See also James A. Bear, ed., *Jefferson at Monticello* (Charlottesville, Va., 1967), 11, 13, 18, 71–73; JA, Autobiography, *DAJA* 3:335–36; JA to Pickering, August 6, 1822, Adams, *Works of John Adams*, 2:513–14.

36. TJ, Composition Draft, ND, *PTJ* 1:193–98; TJ, Fair Copy for the Committee, [n.d.], ibid., 1:199–203; John Dickinson's Composition Draft, [n.d.], ibid., 1:204–12; The Declaration of the Causes and Necessity of Taking Up Arms, Ford, *Journals of the Continental Congress*, 2:128–57.

37. JA to Abigail Adams, June 11, 1775, in Lyman H. Butterfield et al., eds., *Adams Family Correspondence* (Cambridge, Mass., 1963–), 1:216.

38. JA to Warren, May 15, 1776, *PJA* 4:186; JA to AA, May 17, 1776, Butterfield, *Adams Family Correspondence*, 1:410. For TJ's itinerary, see *JMB* 1:xlvi–xlvii.

39. TJ to Thomas Nelson, May 16, 1776, *PTJ* 1:292.

40. Nothing is certain about how and why TJ was chosen to draft the Declaration of Independence. JA and TJ left conflicting accounts of what transpired in the committee. See JA, Autobiography, *DAJA* 3:336–37; JA to Timothy Pickering, August 6, 1822, Adams, *Writings of John Adams*, 2:512–14n; TJ to James Madison, August 30, 1823, Ford, *WTJ* 10:267–69. See also Pauline Maier, *American Scripture: Making the Declaration of Independence* (New York, 1997), 99–105; and John Ferling, *Independence: The Struggle to Set America Free* (New York, 2011), 299–300.

41. On the time that TJ devoted to the draft, see Ferling, *Independence*, 309. JA's recollection is in JA, Autobiography, *DAJA* 3:336.

42. Nathan Schachner, *Thomas Jefferson: A Biography* (New York, 1951), 118; David McCullough, *John Adams* (New York, 2001), 120.

43. Carl Becker, *The Declaration of Independence: A Study in the History of Political Ideas* (reprint, New York, 1960), 151–52; TJ to Madison, August 30, 1823, Ford, *WTJ* 10: 267–69; "Jefferson's 'original Rough draught' of the Declaration of Independence," *PTJ* 1:423–28, and the editorial note on the evolution of the text, ibid., 1:413–17; "John Adams' Copy of the Declaration of Independence, [ante June 28, 1776], *PJA* 4:341–51. See also Julian Boyd, *The Declaration of Independence: The Evolution of the Text as Shown in Facsimiles of Various Drafts by Its Author* (Washington, D.C., 1943).

44. JA to Pickering, August 6, 1822, *WJA* 2:514n; John Ferling, *John Adams: A Life* (reprint, New York, 2010), 148; TJ to Henry Lee, May 8, 1825, Lipscomb and Bergh, *WTJ* 7:407.

45. Maier, *American Scripture*, 124–28. The draft of Virginia's Declaration of Rights can be found in Peter Force, ed., *American Archives*, 4th series (Washington, D.C., 1837–46), 6:1537.

46. David Freeman Hawke, *A Transaction of Free Men: The Birth and Course of the Declaration of Independence* (New York, 1964), 207–8; John Hazleton, *The Declaration of Independence: Its History* (New York, 1906), 242; 156–57, 258–81; Maier, *American Scripture*, 157–59; Elbridge Gerry to Joseph Trumbull, July 8, 1776, *LDC* 4:406; JA to Samuel Chase, July 9, 1776, *PJA* 4:372; AA to JA, July 21, 1776, Butterfield, *Adams Family Correspondence*, 2:56; GW, General Orders, July 9, 1776, *PGWR* 5:246; ibid., 5:247n; GW to John Hancock, July 10, 1776, ibid., 5:258; Lt. Col. Thomas Seymour to Gov. Jonathan Trumbull, July 11, 1776, Peter Force, ed., *American Archives* 5th series (Washington, D.C., 1847–1853), 1:205; Col. Thomas Hartley to Gen. Gates, July 28, 1776, ibid., 1:630.

47. Jay Fliegelman, *Declaring Independence: Jefferson, Natural Language, and the Culture of Performance* (Stanford, Cal., 1993), 4–28. The quotation can be found on page 10.

48. Andrew Burstein and Nancy Isenberg, *Madison and Jefferson* (New York, 2010), 36–39. The quotation can be found on page 37.

49. JA to Archibald Bulloch, July 1, 1776, *PJA* 4:352.

50. For Dickinson's speech, see John Dickinson's Notes for a Speech in Congress, [July 1, 1776], *LDC* 4:351–58, 356n.

51. On JA's speech, see Ferling, *Independence*, 324.

52. Maier, *American Scripture*, 235–41; Carl Becker, *The Declaration of Independence: A Study in the History of Political Ideas* (reprint, New York, 1960), 160–71; Ferling, *Independence*, 318–41; TJ to Lee, July 8, 1776, *PTJ* 1:456. For a good, short essay on the Declaration, see Robert G. Parkinson, "The Declaration of Independence," in Cogliano, *A Companion to Thomas Jefferson*, 44–59.

CHAPTER 3: "IS MY COUNTRY THE BETTER FOR MY HAVING LIVED": MAKING THE AMERICAN REVOLUTION

1. Hancock to TJ, September 30, 1776, *PTJ* 1:523–24; Lee to TJ, September 27, November 3, 1776, ibid., 1:522–23, 590; TJ to Hancock, October 11, 1776, ibid., 1:524; TJ, Autobiography, in Padover, *CTJ*, 1151; John Ferling, *Setting the World Ablaze: Washington, Adams, Jefferson, and the American Revolution* (New York, 2000), 151; *JMB* 1:425–37, 447.

2. Andrew Burstein and Nancy Isenberg, *Madison and Jefferson* (New York, 2010), 51.

3. [TJ], *A Summary View of the Rights of British America* (Williamsburg, Va., 1774), 122, 123, 124, 127.

4. TJ exaggerated the similarities between colonies and mother country. See Gordon S. Wood, *The Radicalism of the American Revolution* (New York, 1992), 115–18.

5. The foregoing paragraphs draw largely on TJ to Samuel Kercheval, July 12, 1816, Ford, *WTJ* 12:4; TJ, Autobiography, in Padover, *CTJ*, 1139–40; TJ to JA, October 28, 1813, *AJL* 2:388.

6. Gordon S. Wood, *The American Revolution: A History* (New York, 2003), 91–93. The TJ quotation can be found in Thomas Jefferson, *Notes on the State of Virginia*, ed. William Peden (Chapel Hill, N.C., 1955), 128.

7. Peterson, *TJ*, 45.

8. TJ to JA, October 28, 1813, *AJL* 2:391. TJ's "more good sense" quotation can be found in Peterson, *TJ*, 14.

9. TJ, Autobiography, in Padover, *CTJ*, 1121.

10. TJ to JA, October 28, 1813, *AJL* 2:389.

11. TJ, Third Draft by Jefferson of a Constitution, [before June 13, 1776], *PTJ* 1:362; TJ to JA, October 28, 1813, *AJL* 2:389.

12. TJ, Autobiography, in Padover, *CTJ*, 1144–46.

13. TJ to Wythe, November 1, 1778, *PTJ* 1:230.

14. TJ, *Notes on the State of Virginia*, 144–45; TJ, Autobiography, in Padover, *CTJ*, 1140, 1144–47; TJ, Bill Nos. 64–76, *PTJ* 2:492–522, 505–6n; John Selby, *The Revolution in Virginia* (Charlottesville, Va., 1980), 160; Bernstein, *TJ*, 38–40.

15. TJ, *Notes on the State of Virginia*, 137–43.

16. Ibid., 137–38. See also Paul Finkelman, "Jefferson and Slavery: 'Treason Against the Hopes of the World,'" in Peter S. Onuf, ed., *Jeffersonian Legacies* (Charlottesville, Va., 1993), 196.

17. Jefferson's Draft of a Constitution for Virginia, [1783], *PTJ* 6:298 and the editorial note on pages 278–84. See also TJ, Autobiography, in Padover, *CTJ*, 1149–50; John Chester Miller, *The Wolf by the Ears: Thomas Jefferson and Slavery* (New York, 1977), 20–21; Robert McColley, *Slavery and Jeffersonian Virginia* (Urbana, Ill., 1973), 2–3, 72, 115–16, 120, 132–35, 143–59.

18. TJ, Bill Nos. 51, 53, *PTJ* 2:2:470–72, 475–76.

19. Holly Brewer, "Entailing Aristocracy in Colonial Virginia: 'Ancient Feudal Restraints' and Revolutionary Reform," *William and Mary Quarterly* 54 (1997): 307–46. The quotes can be found on page 341.

20. TJ, Bill No. 20, *PTJ* 2:391–93, 393n.

21. Quoted in Selby, *Revolution in Virginia*, 145.

22. TJ, Bill No. 82, *PTJ* 2:545–47. The quotation can be found on page 548. See also, ibid., 2:547–53n.

23. TJ to JM, December 16, 1786, *PTJ* 10:603–4; TJ to Wythe, August 13, 1786, ibid., 10:244; Merrill D. Peterson, "Jefferson and Religious Freedom," *Atlantic Monthly* 272 (December 1994): 113–24; Burstein and Isenberg, *Madison and Jefferson*, 56.

24. TJ, Bills Nos. 79, 80, 81, *PTJ* 2:526–45; TJ to Edward Carrington, January 16, 1787, ibid., 11:49; TJ to Wythe, August 13, 1786, ibid., 10:244; TJ, *Notes on the State of Virginia*, 146–49; TJ, Autobiography, in Padover, CTJ, 1149, 1150; TJ to JA, October 28, 1813, *AJL* 2:389; Garrett Ward Shelton, *The Political Philosophy of Thomas Jefferson* (Baltimore, 1991), 65.

25. JA to Abigail Adams, July 3, 1776, Lyman H. Butterfield et al., eds., *Adams Family Correspondence* (Cambridge, Mass., 1963–), 2:28; JA to Richard Cranch, August 2, 1776, ibid., 2:74; TJ to Benjamin Franklin, August 13, 1777, *PTJ* 2:26.

26. TJ to Nelson, May 16, 1776, *PTJ* 1:292.

27. Wood, *The American Revolution*, 65–70.

28. Quoted in Selby, *Revolution in Virginia*, 116.

29. TJ, "Jefferson's Services to His Country," [1800?], Padover, *CTJ*, 1288.

30. Pauline Maier, *American Scripture: Making the Declaration of Independence* (New York, 1997), 175–208.

31. TJ, Autobiography, in Padover, *CTJ*, 1140, 1150.

32. TJ to Fleming, July 1, 1776, *PTJ* 1:412.

33. TJ to Page, August 5, 1776, *PTJ* 1:486.

34. Lee to TJ, August 25, 1777, *PTJ* 2:29.

35. Fawn M. Brodie, *Thomas Jefferson: An Intimate History* (New York, 1974), 152–53, 159; Annette Gordon-Reed, *The Hemingses of Monticello: An American Family* (New York, 2008), 129–30, 132; On Martha Jefferson's health, see Virginia Scharff, *The Women Jefferson Loved* (New York, 2010), 118–20. Scharff depicts Martha as fighting for her life during these difficult pregnancies.

36. TJ to Lee, April 21, 1779, *PTJ* 2:255; TJ to William Phillips, [April ?, 1779], ibid., 2:261; TJ to Henry, March 27, 1779, ibid., 2:237–44.

37. TJ to Lee, August 30, 1778, *PTJ* 2:210–11; Edmund Pendleton to TJ, May 11, 1779, ibid., 2:266.

38. The "never to be forgotten" quote is in Gordon S. Wood, *Revolutionary Characters: What Made the Founders Different* (New York, 2006), 127.

39. AH to ESH, October 2, 1780, *PAH* 2:449.

40. GW to John Hancock, July 12, 1776, *PGWR* 5:284, 285n.

41. John C. Hamilton, *The Life of Alexander Hamilton* (New York, 1840), 1:54.

42. GW to Hancock, November 30, 1776, *PGWR* 7:233.

43. Quoted in Hamilton, *The Life of Alexander Hamilton*, 1:57.

44. Quoted in Mitchell, *AH*, 1:96.

45. GW to Hancock, November 27, December 1, 16, 1776, *PGWR* 7:223, 245, 352.

46. On Washington's artillery, and the ratio of artillery to infantry for the engagement at Trenton, see David Hackett Fischer, *Washington's Crossing* (New York, 2004), 223–25.

47. *PGWR* 7:458–59n.

48. The quotes are in William M. Dwyer, *The Day Is Ours! November 1776–January 1777: An Inside View of the Battles of Trenton and Princeton* (New York, 1983), 320; Robert Beale, Memoirs, in Dennis P. Ryan, ed., *A Salute to Courage: The American Revolution as Seen Through Wartime Writings of Officers of the Continental Army and Navy* (New York, 1979), 57; *PGWR* 7:526n.

49. Dwyer, *The Day Is Ours!*, 315–20; North Callahan, "Henry Knox: American Artillerist," in George A. Billias, ed., *George Washington's Generals* (New York, 1964), 247–48.

50. Quoted in Fischer, *Washington's Crossing*, 321.

51. The narrative of the campaign of 1776 draws on John Ferling, *Almost a Miracle: The American Victory in the War of Independence* (New York, 2007), 120–86; and Fischer, *Washington's Crossing*, 94–345.

52. Edward J. Tatum, ed., *The American Journal of Ambrose Serle* (New York, 1969), 158; GW to Hancock, January 5, 1777, *PGWR* 7:523.

53. AH to the Convention of the Representative of the State of New-York, March 6, 1777, *PAH* 1:200.

54. *PGWR* 8:117n.

55. AH to GW, July 29[–August 1], 1798, *PAH* 22:37.

56. See John Ferling, *The Ascent of George Washington: The Hidden Political Genius of an American Icon* (New York, 2009), 104–23.

57. GW, General Orders, March 1, 1777, *PGWR* 8:468.

58. Arthur S. Lefkowitz, *George Washington's Indispensable Men: The 32 Aides-de-Camp Who Helped Win American Independence* (Mechanicsburg, Pa., 2003), 5, 15, 99–100.

59. Quoted in Brookhiser, *AH*, 29.

60. Lefkowitz, *George Washington's Indispensable Men*, 7–14. Washington's "Pen-men" remark can be found on page 8.

61. GW to JA, September 25, 1798, *PGW: Ret. Ser.* 3:41–42. On GW's handling of disappointing aides, see Lefkowitz, *George Washington's Indispensable Men*, 28.

62. Howard C. Rice Jr., ed., *Travels in North America in the Years 1780, 1781 and 1782 by the Marquis de Chastellux* (Chapel Hill, N.C., 1963), 1:344.

63. The quotations can be found in Flexner, *Young Hamilton*, 148–49.

64. Quoted in Lefkowitz, *George Washington's Indispensable Men*, 193.

65. Ferling *Almost a Miracle*, 187–93, 242–43, 245–51.

66. *PAH* 1:326–27n.

67. AH to John Hancock, September 18, 1777, *PAH* 1:326.

68. "The Diary of Robert Morton," *Pennsylvania Magazine of History and Biography* 1 (1877): 3–4.

69. GW to AH, September 21, 22, 1777, *PAH* 1:330–31, 332–33; AH to Hancock, September 22, 1777, ibid., 1:331–32; AH to William Livingston, September 22, 1777, ibid., 1:334; AH to Lt. Col. Anthony Walton White, September 23, 1777, ibid., 1:334–35.

70. Ferling, *Almost a Miracle*, 253–56.

71. GW to AH, October 30, 1777, *PAH* 1:347–48.

72. AH to Horatio Gates, November 5, 13, 1777, *PAH* 1:351–53, 362–63; AH to GW, November 6, 10, 12, 15, 1777, ibid., 1:353–55, 357–60, 360–62, 363–64.

73. AH to GW, November 12, 15, 1777, *PAH* 1:360, 363.

74. GW to William Buchanan, February 7, 1778, *PGW:R* 13:465; AH to George Clinton, February 13, 1778, *PAH* 1:426; Ferling, *Almost a Miracle*, 274–82. For the Paine and Lafayette quotes, see Ferling, page 276.

75. Thomas Fleming, *Washington's Secret War: The Hidden History of Valley Forge* (New York, 2005), 33; Nathanael Greene to GW, January 1, 1778, *PGWR* 13:99.

CHAPTER 4: "IF WE ARE SAVED, FRANCE AND SPAIN MUST SAVE US": THE FORGE OF WAR

Malone, *TJ*, 1:301–69; Peterson, *TJ*, 166–240; Chernow, *AH*, 126–66; McDonald, *AH*, 17–43; Mitchell, *AH*, 1:143–221.

1. AH to Elias Boudinot, July 5, 1778, *PAH* 1:510.

2. Quoted in Flexner, *Young Hamilton*, 231.

3. Proceedings of a General Court-Martial for the Trial of Major General Charles Lee, July 13, 1778, *PAH* 1:520–21; ibid., 23:547n. The Lee quotation can be found in William S. Stryker, *The Battle of Monmouth*, ed. William Starr Myers (reprint, Port Washington, N.Y., 1970), 199.

4. AH to Boudinot, July 5, 1778, *PAH* 1:510–11.

5. James Craig to GW, January 6, 1778, *PGWR* 13:160–61; Patrick Henry to GW, February 20, 1778, ibid., 13:609; John Ferling, *Almost a Miracle: The American Victory in the War of Independence* (New York, 2007), 282–86. On Lee's 1776 comments about GW's inability, see *PGWR* 7:237–38n.

6. AH to George Clinton, February 13, 1778, *PAH* 1:428.

7. Charles Lee to Joseph Reed, November 24, 1776, in *Lee Papers, Collections of the New-York Historical Society for the Year 1871, . . . 1872, . . . 1873, . . . 1874* (New York, 1872–1875), 2:305–6; Nathanael Greene to Griffin Greene, May 25, 1778, in Richard K. Showman et al., eds., *The Papers of Nathanael Greene* (Chapel Hill, N.C., 1976–2005), 2:406; Elias Boudinot, "Exchange of Major-General Charles Lee," *Pennsylvania Magazine of History and Biography* 15 (1891): 32–33.

8. AH to Lord Stirling, July 14, 1778, *PAH* 1:522; AH to Boudinot, July 5, 26, 1778, ibid., 1:510, 528.

9. Proceedings of a General Court-Martial for the Trial of Major General Charles Lee, July 13, 1778, *PAH* 1:520–21; AH to Boudinot, July 26, 1778, ibid., 1:528; AH to Stirling, July 14, 1778, ibid., 1:522.

10. Lee to Gouverneur Morris, July 3, 1778, *Lee Papers*, 2:457; Lee to Reed, July 22, 1778, ibid., 2:479; Lee to the President of Congress, April 22, 1780, ibid., 3:424; Lee to Greene, Sep-

tember 12, 1782, ibid., 4:35; "General Lee's Vindication to the Public," *Pennsylvania Packet*, December 3, 1778, ibid., 3:255–65; [Charles Lee], "A Short History of the Treatment of Major General Conway . . . ," *Pennsylvania Packet*, December 3, 1778, ibid., 3:265–69; [Charles Lee], "Some Queries, Political and Military, Humbly Offered to the Consideration of the Public," *Maryland Journal and Baltimore Advertiser*, July 6, 1779, ibid., 3:341–45.

11. AH to John Laurens, April 1779, *PAH* 2:35.

12. Ferling, *Almost a Miracle*, 328; Holly A. Mayer, *Belonging to the Army: Camp Followers and Community During the American Revolution* (Columbia, S.C., 1996), 147–49.

13. AH to Catherine Livingston, April 11, May [?], 1777, *PAH* 1:225–27, 258–60; ibid., 2:262n, 521n.

14. AH to Laurens, April 1779, *PAH* 2:37–38.

15. AH to Laurens, April [?], September 11, 1779, January 8, March 30, 1780, *PAH* 2:35, 165, 255, 304.

16. AH to ESH, June–October [?], July 2–4, 20, August [?] and 31, September 3, 6, October 2, 13, 27, 1780, *PAH* 2:350, 351, 361, 388, 399, 419, 423, 449, 474, 493; AH to Laurens, June 30, 1780, ibid., 2:348.

17. AH to ESH, June–October, 1780, *PAH* 2:350.

18. Thomas K. McGraw, *The Founders and Finance: How Hamilton, Gallatin, and Other Immigrants Forged a New Economy* (Cambridge, Mass., 2012), 47, 66; Richard B. Morris, *The Forging of the Union, 1781–1789* (New York, 1987), 34–37. The quotation from Congress's Circular Letter to the states can be found in Morris, page 35.

19. GW to John Augustine Washington, May 12, 1779, *PGWR* 20:462; McGraw, *The Founders and Finance*, 65.

20. Richard Buel Jr., *In Irons: Britain's Naval Supremacy and American Revolutionary Economy* (New Haven, Conn., 1998), 129–32; Richard Buel Jr., *Dear Liberty: Connecticut's Mobilization for the Revolutionary War* (Middletown, Conn., 1980), 103, 171; E. James Ferguson, *The Power of the Purse: A History of Public Finance, 1776–1790* (Chapel Hill, N.C., 1961), 32, 35–39, 44–47, 126; GW to the President of Congress, July 9, 1779, *WW* 15:391–92; GW to Marquis de Lafayette, September 30, 1779, ibid., 16:372; GW to John Armstrong, May 18, 1779, *PGWR* 20:517–19.

21. AH, Publius Letters, nos. 1–3, October 16, 26, November 16, 1778, *PAH* 1:562–63, 567–70, 580–82.

22. GW to George Mason, March 27, 1779, *PGWR* 19:627–28; GW to Burwell Bassett, April 22, 1779, ibid., 20:161; GW to Gouverneur Morris, May 8, 1779, ibid., 20:384–86; GW to William Fitzhugh, April 10, 1779, ibid., 20:30–31; GW to Lund Washington, May 29, 1779, ibid., 20:688–89.

23. AH to George Clinton, February 13, 1778, *PAH* 1:425; AH to Laurens, September 11, 1779, ibid., 2:167.

24. AH, Pay Book of the State Company of Artillery, [1777], *PAH* 1:373–411; McGraw, *The Founders and Finance*, 61–62.

25. AH to Laurens, May 22, September 11, 1779, *PAH* 2:53, 166–67; AH to James Duane, September 14, 1779, ibid., 2:173.

26. AH to Laurens, May 22, 1779, March 30, 1780, *PAH* 2:53, 303.

27. AH to Laurens, March 30, June 30, 1780, *PAH* 2:303, 347; AH to Duane, May 14, 1780, ibid., 2:321.

28. AH to Laurens, June 30, 1780, *PAH* 2:347; AH to ESH, September 25, 1780, ibid., 2:441; AH to Isaac Sears, October 12, 1780, ibid., 2:473.

29. For Hamilton's proposed remedies, see AH to [?], [December 1779–March 1780], *PAH* 2:234–51; AH to Duane, September 3, 1780, ibid., 2:400–18; AH to Sears, October 12, 1780, ibid., 2:472–73; AH to Robert Morris, April 30, 1781, ibid., 2:604–35. The quotations can be found on pages 401, 402, 406, and 605.

30. AH to Laurens, September 12, 1780, *PAH* 2:427.

31. GW to John Sullivan, February 4, 1781, *WW* 21:181, 180–81n; Jack N. Rakove, *The Beginnings of National Politics: An Interpretive History of the Continental Congress* (Baltimore, 1979), 282–83, 302.

32. Joyce Lee Malcolm, "Slavery in Massachusetts and the American Revolution," *Journal of the Historical Society* 10 (2010): 429–34.

33. AH to John Jay, March 14, 1779, *PAH* 2:17–19. See also Ferling, *Almost a Miracle*, 65, 113, 341–42.

34. Henry Laurens to GW, March 16, 1779, *PGWR* 19:503; GW to Laurens, March 20, 1779, ibid., 19:542; ibid., 504–5n.

35. JA to TJ, May 26, 1777, *PJA* 5:204.

36. Lee to TJ, May 3, 1779, *PTJ* 2:263; Pendleton to TJ, May 11, 1779, ibid., 2:266; Fleming to TJ, May 10, 11, 22, 1779, ibid., 2:264, 265, 267–69.

37. Lee to TJ, May 3, 1779, *PTJ* 2:262.

38. John Selby, *The Revolution in Virginia, 1775–1783* (Williamsburg and Charlottesville, Va., 1988), 209.

39. Alf Mapp, *Thomas Jefferson* (New York, 1987–1991), 1:128–29.

40. TJ to Lee, June 17, 1779, *PTJ* 2:298; TJ to William Phillips, June 25, 1779, ibid., 3:15.

41. TJ to William Phillips, June 25, 1779, *PTJ* 3:15; Fleming to TJ, May 22, 1779, ibid., 2:269.

42. TJ to John Jay, June 19, 1779, *PTJ* 3:5; Michael Kranish, *Flight from Monticello: Thomas Jefferson at War* (New York, 2010), 114–17; Michael A. McDonnell, *The Politics of War: Race, Class, and Conflict in Revolutionary Virginia* (Chapel Hill, N.C., 2007), 343–44.

43. GW to TJ, December 11, 1779, *PTJ* 3:217.

44. Board of War to TJ, December 23, 1779, *PTJ* 3:238–40; TJ to Benjamin Harrison, December 23, 1779, ibid., 241; TJ to Lee, January 2, 1789, ibid., 3:260.

45. TJ to the Board of War, November 15, 18, December 23, 1779, January 19, 1780, *PTJ* 3:186, 193–94, 240, 264; Board of War to TJ, November 15, 16, December 11, 16, 23, 1779, March 23, 1780, ibid., 3:187–89, 215, 223, 238, 330; TJ, Instructions to Inspector of Stores and Provisions, January 25, 1780, ibid., 3:269.

46. McDonnell, *Politics of War*, 277, 393–94, 411–19; L. Scott Philyaw, "A Slave for Every Soldier: The Strange History of Virginia's Forgotten Recruitment Act of 1 January 1781," *Virginia Magazine of History and Biography* 109 (2001), 367–86; Kranish, *Flight from Monticello*, 130; TJ to GW, December 16, 1779, *PTJ* 3:228; TJ, Form of Recruiting Commission, [November 28, 1780], ibid., 3:330; Henry to TJ, February 15, 1780, ibid., 3:293.

47. TJ to Lee, June 17, 1779, *PTJ* 2:298; TJ to GW, June 19, 1779, ibid., 3:6; TJ to George Rogers Clark, January 1, 1780, ibid., 3:258.

48. TJ to GW, September 26, 1779, December 13, 1780, *PTJ* 3:665; 4:204; TJ to Clark, December 25, 1780, February 19, 1781, ibid., 4:233, 653.

49. GW to Lafayette, March 8[–10], 1779, *WW* 14:219; GW to Committee of Conference, January 8, 1779, ibid., 13:485–91; GW to TJ, April 15, 1779, *PTJ* 3:352; Ferling, *Almost a Miracle*, 347.

50. TJ to GW, February 17, 1780, *PTJ* 3:297.

51. TJ to Philip Mazzei, May 31, 1780, *PTJ* 3:405.

52. TJ to Lee, September 13, 1780, *PTJ* 3:642.

53. TJ to Samuel Huntington, June 9, 1780, *PTJ* 3:427; TJ to GW, June 11, 1780, ibid., 3:432; TJ to Horatio Gates, August 4, September 3, 1780, ibid., 3:526, 588.

54. TJ to GW, July 2, 1780, *PTJ* 3:478.

55. GW to TJ, July 18, 1780, *PTJ* 3:489–90.

56. Ferling, *Almost a Miracle*, 437–43.

57. AH to Boudinot, July 5, 1778, *PAH* 1:512; AH to James Duane, September 6, October 18, 1780, ibid., 2:420–21, 479; AH to ESH, September 6, 1780, ibid., 2:422.

58. TJ to Gates, September 3, 1780, *PTJ* 3:588; TJ to Huntington, September 3, 14, 1780, ibid., 3:589–90, 647–48; TJ to North Carolina Board of War, September 23, 1780, ibid., 3:659; TJ to GW, September 23, 1780, ibid., 3:660.

59. TJ to Huntington, October 25, 1780, *PTJ* 4:67; GW to TJ, September 11, October 10, 1780, ibid., 3:639; 4:27. TJ also thought the British unlikely to send a large force southward so long as the French fleet, superior in size to the Royal Navy in the Chesapeake region, remained in North American waters. See TJ to Huntington, September 14, 1780, ibid., 3:647.

60. Thomas Nelson to TJ, October 21, 1780, *PTJ* 4:54–55; TJ, Steps to Be Taken to Repel General Leslie's Army, October 22[?], 1780, ibid., 4:61–63; TJ to Gates, October 28, 1780, ibid., 4:78; Ferling, *Almost a Miracle*, 477.

61. Quoted in Carl P. Borick, *A Gallant Defense: The Siege of Charleston, 1780* (Columbia, S.C., 2003), 230, 233.

62. Ferling, *Almost a Miracle*, 451–63.

63. See Theodore Thayer, *Nathanael Greene: Strategist of the Revolution* (New York, 1960); Terry Golway, *Washington's General: Nathanael Greene and the Triumph of the American Revolution* (New York, 2005); Gerald M. Carbone, *Nathanael Greene: A Biography of the American Revolution* (New York, 2010).

64. General Greene's Requisition for the Southern Army, November 20, 1780, *PTJ* 4:133–34; Greene to TJ, November 20, 1780, ibid., 4:130–32.

65. TJ to Friedrich von Steuben, December 4, 6, 8, 21, 30, *PTJ* 4:178, 185, 188–89, 219–20, 250; Steuben to TJ, December 28, 1780, ibid., 4:244; Greene to TJ, December 6, 1780, ibid., 4:183.

66. TJ to Steuben, December 21, 1780, *PTJ* 4:219.

67. TJ to Virginia Delegates in Congress, October 27, 1780, *PTJ* 4:4:77; Kranish, *Flight from Monticello*, 138–39.

68. TJ to GW, October 22, 1780, *PTJ* 4:60; Page to TJ, December 9, 1780, ibid., 4:192. On GW's despair in the dark days of the New York campaign in 1776, see GW to John Augustine Washington, September 22, 1776, *PGWR* 6:371–74.

69. GW to TJ, November 8, December 9, 1780, *PTJ* 4:105, 195.

70. TJ, Diary of Arnold's Invasion and Notes on Subsequent Events in 1781 [The 1796? Version], December 31, 1780, January 1, 1781, *PTJ* 4:258; Arnold's Invasion as Reported by TJ in the *Virginia Gazette*, January 13, 1781, ibid., 4:269.

71. For the account of Arnold's invasion and raid on Richmond, see TJ, Diary of Arnold's Invasion, January 2–5, 1781, *PTJ* 4:258–59; TJ, *Virginia Gazette*, January 13, 1781, ibid., 4:269–70; Depositions of Archibald Blair, Daniel Hylton, and James Currie, October 12, 1796, ibid., 4:271–72; TJ to GW, January 10, 1781, ibid., 4:333–35; TJ to George Weedon, January 10, 1781, ibid., 4:335–36; Kranish, *Flight from Monticello*, 167–99; Selby, *Revolution in Virginia*, 222–25.

72. Willard M. Wallace, *Traitorous Hero: The Life and Fortunes of Benedict Arnold* (New York, 1954), 274.

73. Quoted in McDonnell, *Politics of War*, 402.

74. Selby, *Revolution in Virginia*, 223–24; John Ferling, *Setting the World Ablaze: Washington, Adams, Jefferson, and the American Revolution* (New York, 2000), 232. The Page and Pendleton quotes can be found in Kranish, *Flight from Monticello*, 203–4.

75. Kranish, *Flight from Monticello*, 216–17; TJ to J. P. G. Muhlenberg, January 31, 1781, *PTJ* 4:487.

CHAPTER 5: "OUR AFFAIRS SEEM TO BE APPROACHING FAST TO A HAPPY PERIOD": GLORY FOR HAMILTON, MISERY FOR JEFFERSON

Chernow, *AH*, 154–66; Miller, *AH*, 62–79; Flexner, *Young AH*, 330–74; Mitchell, *AH*, 1:222–61; Malone, *TJ*, 1:330–69; Peterson, *TJ*, 203–40.

1. James Lovell to JA, January 2, 1781, *LDC* 16:537; John Ferling, *Almost a Miracle: The American Victory in the War of Independence* (New York, 2007), 468–69, 476.

2. AH to Robert Morris, April 30, 1780, *PAH* 2:605, 633.

3. AH to Laurens, September 12, 16, 1780, *PAH* 2:428, 431.

4. AH to Laurens, February 4, 1781, *PAH* 2:550; AH to Duane, September 6, 1780, ibid., 2:421.

5. AH to Schuyler, February 18, 1781, *PAH* 2:565–67, 566n; AH to James McHenry, February 18, 1781, ibid., 2:569.

6. AH to Schuyler, February 18, 1781, *PAH* 2:563–68; AH to Greene, April 19, 1781, ibid., 2:595.

7. AH to GW, April 27, 1781, *PAH* 2:600–601; GW to AH, April 27, 1781, ibid., 2:601–3.

8. Greene to TJ, February 15, 1781, *PAH* 4:615.

9. Lawrence E. Babit, *A Devil of a Whipping: The Battle of Cowpens* (Chapel Hill, N.C., 1998).

10. Greene to TJ, February 15, 28, March 10, 1781, *PTJ* 4:615–16; 5:23, 111–12.

11. GW to TJ, February 6, 1781, *PTJ* 4:543–44; TJ to Steuben, January 14, February 7, 12, 16, March 10, 1781, ibid., 4:357–58, 555, 592–93, 633; 5:117–20; Michael Kranish, *Flight from Monticello: Thomas Jefferson at War* (New York, 2010), 224–26.

12. GW to TJ, February 6, 1781, *PTJ* 5:543.

13. TJ to Huntington, January 15, 1781, *PTJ* 4:399; TJ, Circular Letter to the Members of the Assembly, January 23, 1781, ibid., 4:433–34; TJ to Steuben, January 29, 1781, ibid., 4:477; TJ, Proclamation, February 2, 1781, ibid., 4:505.

14. TJ to Huntington, January 15, 1781, *PTJ* 4:370.

15. GW to the Marquis de Lafayette, February 20, 1781, in Stanley J. Idzerda, ed., *Lafayette in the Age of the American Revolution: Selected Letters and Papers* (Ithaca, N.Y., 1977), 3:333–34.

16. GW to TJ, February 21, 1781, *PTJ* 4:683; TJ to Lafayette, March 2, 1781, ibid., 5:43; Lafayette to TJ, March 3, 1781, ibid., 5:49–51; Steuben to TJ, March 5, 1781, ibid., 5:66.

17. Ferling, *Almost a Miracle*, 502–3; Lafayette to TJ, March 26, 1781, *PTJ* 5:261; Lafayette to GW, March 26, 1781, Idzerda, *Lafayette in the Age of the American Revolution*, 3:417–18.

18. Greene to TJ, March 10, 16, 1781, *PTJ* 5:112, 156; Lawrence E. Babit and Joshua B. Howard, *Long, Obstinate, and Bloody: The Battle of Guilford Courthouse* (Chapel Hill, N.C., 2009).

19. Greene to TJ, March 23, 31, 1781, *PTJ* 5:215, 301–2.

20. Steuben, Proposal for an Expedition Against Cornwallis, March 27, 1781; Idzerda, *Lafayette in the Age of the American Revolution*, 3:419–20; Lafayette on Steuben's Proposed Expedition, March 27, 1781, ibid., 420–21; Lee to TJ, March 27, 1781, *PTJ* 5:252; George Weedon to TJ, March 27, 1781, ibid., 5:267; Harry M. Ward, *Duty, Honor or Country: General George Weedon and the American Revolution* (Philadelphia, 1979), 177–82.

21. Greene to TJ, April 6, 1781, *PTJ* 5:361. The Weedon quotation is in Peterson, *TJ*, 226. Greene's "lifeless" quotation is in Kranish, *Flight from Monticello*, 204.

22. TJ to Chevalier la Luzerne, April 12, 1781, *PTJ* 5:421–22.

23. For a general account of Greene's war in the South, see Ferling, *Almost a Miracle*, 463–66, 477–500, 505–16.

24. TJ to Speaker of the House of Delegates, May 10, 1781, *PTJ* 5:626; Selby, *Revolution in Virginia*, 272–74; Kranish, *Flight from Monticello*, 233, 240–51.

25. TJ to James Wood, October 5, 1780, *PTJ* 4:14–15; TJ to the Virginia Delegates to Congress, October 27, 1780, ibid., 4:76–77; TJ to Lee, September 13, 1780, ibid., 3:642.

26. See David Ramsay, *The History of the American Revolution* (reprint, Indianapolis, 1990), 2:27; and Ferling, *Almost a Miracle*, 386–87.

27. TJ to la Luzerne, April 12, 1781, *PTJ* 5:421.

28. Ferling, *Almost a Miracle*, 508–9.

29. TJ to Those Appointed by Lafayette to Remove Horses out of the Route of the Enemy, [May 15, 1781], *PTJ* 5:655; TJ to GW, May 9, 1781, ibid., 5:623.

30. The quotations can be found in James Haw, *John and Edward Rutledge of South Carolina* (Athens, Ga., 1997), 123–24.

31. TJ to GW, May 28, 1781, *PTJ* 6:33.

32. Lafayette to TJ, April 25, 1781, *PTJ* 5:554.

33. Baron Ludwig von Closen, *The Revolutionary Journal of Baron Ludwig von Closen, 1780–1783*, ed. Evelyn Acomb (Chapel Hill, N.C., 1958), 86; Conference with Rochambeau, May 23, 1781, *WW* 22:105–7; GW to Greene, June 1, 1781, ibid., 22:146; Edward G. Lengel, *General George Washington* (New York, 2005), 329–30. The quotations are in James T. Flexner, *George Washington and the American Revolution, 1775–1783* (Boston, 1968), 429, 430.

34. AH to ESH, July 10, 1781, *PAH* 2:647; AH to GW, May 2, 1781, ibid., 2:636–38.

35. TJ to the Members of Assembly for Fluvanna and Certain Other Counties, May 1, 1781, *PTJ* 5:585. The "unmolested" quotation is in Kranish, *Flight from Monticello*, 269.

36. Lafayette to GW, May 24, 1781, Idzerda, *Lafayette in the Age of the American Revolution*, 4:130–31; Ferling, *Almost a Miracle*, 511–12.

37. TJ, Diary of Arnold's Invasion [The 1796? Version], *PTJ* 4:260–61; TJ, Speech to Jean Baptiste Ducoigne, June 1, 1781, ibid., 6:60–63; TJ to François de Barbé-Marbois, March 4, 1781, ibid., 5:58.

38. TJ to the Speaker of the House of Delegates, May 10, 1781, ibid., 5:627; Michael A. McDonnell, *The Politics of War: Race, Class, and Conflict in Revolutionary Virginia* (Chapel Hill, N.C., 2007), 462.

39. TJ to Joseph Reed, June 3, 1781, *PTJ* 6:74; TJ to the Surveyor of Monongalia County, June 3, 1781, ibid., 6:76.

40. TJ, Diary of Arnold's Invasion [The 1796? Version], *PTJ* 4:261.

41. Annette Gordon-Reed, *The Hemingses of Monticello: An American Family* (New York, 2008), 138–39.

42. Kranish, *Flight from Monticello*, 283–84.

43. *JMB* 1:510, 510–11n; Kranish, *Flight from Monticello*, 286.

44. *JMB* 1:511; Kranish, *Flight from Monticello*, 284; TJ to William Gordon, July 16, 1788, *PTJ* 13:363.

45. TJ to Edmund Randolph, September 16, 1781, *PTJ* 6:118.

46. John Beckley to TJ [Enclosing a Resolution of the House of Delegates], June 12, 1781, *PTJ* 6:88; Archibald Cary to TJ, June 19, 1781, ibid., 6:97; TJ to George Nicholas, July 28, 1781, ibid., 6:105.

47. Huntington to TJ [Enclosing a Resolution of Congress Appointing Peace Commissioners], June 15, 1781, *PTJ* 6:94–95.

48. George Nicholas to TJ, July 31, 1781, *PTJ* 6:105–6; Charges Advanced . . . with Jefferson's Answers [After July 31, 1781], ibid., 6:106–8.

49. AH to ESH, July 10, 13, *PAH* 2:647, 652–53; GW, General Orders, July 31, 1781, ibid., 2:658.

50. AH to ESH, July 13, 1781, *PAH* 2:652.

51. AH, "The Continentalist," nos. 1, 2, 3, and 4 [July–August 1781], *PAH* 2:649–52, 654–57, 660–65, 669–74. The quotes can be found in ibid., 2:651, 652, 661, 663, 673.

52. Lengel, *General George Washington*, 332; GW to Rochambeau, June 13, 1781, *WW* 22:208; Conference at Dobbs Ferry, July 19, 1781, ibid., 22:396–97; Donald Jackson et al., eds., *The Diaries of George Washington* (Charlottesville, Va., 1976–1979), 3:397, 399, 404–5.

53. Jackson, *Diaries of George Washington*, 3:406, 407, 409, 413, 414–16; Richard M. Ketchum, *Victory at Yorktown: The Campaign That Won the Revolution* (New York, 2004), 151, 159; Lengel, *General George Washington*, 333, 335; Ferling, *Almost a Miracle*, 523–30; Flexner, *George Washington and the American Revolution*, 441, 444; Douglas Southall Freeman, *George Washington: A Biography* (New York, 1948–1957), 5:314, 525–28; GW to Lafayette, August 21, September 10, 1781, *WW* 23:11, 34; Lafayette to GW, August 25, 1781, Idzerda, *Lafayette in the Age of the American Revolution*, 4:357.

54. AH to ESH, August 16, 22, September 6, 15–18, October 12, 1781, *PAH* 2:666, 667, 675, 678.

55. AH to ESH, September 6, 1781, *PAH* 2:675.

56. AH to GW, April 27, 1781, *PAH* 2:601.

57. AH to ESH, October 12, 1781, *PAH* 2:678.

58. AH to ESH, October 16, 1781, *PAH* 2:682.

59. AH to Lafayette, October 15, 1781, *PAH* 2:679–82. For GW's laudatory comments about AH's bravery, see Mitchell, *AH*, 1:259.

60. TJ to Thomas Mann Randolph Jr., July 13, 1806, Ford, *WTJ* 8:459.

61. TJ to Lafayette, August 4, 1781, *PTJ* 6:111–12; TJ to Isaac Zane, December 24, 1781, ibid., 6:143.

62. TJ, Diary of Arnold's Invasion [The 1796? Version], *PTJ* 4:262; Resolution of Thanks to Jefferson by the Virginia General Assembly, December 12, 1781, ibid., 6:135–36.

63. TJ to Lafayette, August 4, 1781, *PTJ* 6:112.

64. AH to GW, March 1, 1782, *PAH* 3:4, 5.

CHAPTER 6: "THE INEFFICACY OF THE PRESENT CONFEDERATION": GRIEF AND INTRIGUE

Brodie, *TJ*, 184–232; Cunningham, *TJ*, 84–89; Peterson, *TJ*, 241–96; Malone, *TJ*, 1:373–423; Chernow, *AH*, 167–84; McDonald, *AH*, 43–48.

1. TJ to James Monroe, May 20, 1782, *PTJ* 6:184–86.

2. TJ to McKean, August 4, 1781, *PTJ* 6:113; TJ to the Speaker of the House of Delegates, May 6, 1782, ibid., 6:179; TJ to Monroe, May 20, 1782, ibid., 6:184–86; TJ, Autobiography, in Padover, *CTJ*, 1156–57.

3. TJ to Marbois, December 20, 1781, *PTJ* 6:141–42.

4. Quoted in Kevin J. Hayes, *The Road to Monticello: The Life and Mind of Thomas Jefferson* (New York, 2008), 240.

5. Thomas Jefferson, *Notes on the State of Virginia*, ed. William Peden (Chapel Hill, N.C., 1955), 87, 137–40.

6. JA to TJ, May 22, 1785, *AJL* 1:21.

7. TJ, *Notes on the State of Virginia*, 157–61. The quotation can be found on page 159.

8. Ibid., 118–29, 209–22; TJ, Draft of a Constitution for Virginia, [May–June 1783], *PTJ* 6:294–308. On TJ's three constitutional drafts in 1776, ibid., 1:337–65. Some in this paragraph draw on Peter S. Onuf, "Jefferson and American Democracy," in Francis D. Cogliano, ed., *A Companion to Thomas Jefferson* (Chichester, England, 2011), 397–418.

9. TJ to Mr. Lithgrow, January 4, 1805, L & B, *WTJ* 11:55–56.

10. TJ to Thomas Pleasants, May 8, 1786, *PTJ* 9:473.

11. TJ, *Notes on the State of Virginia*, 117–29, 164–65. My section on TJ and manufacturing draws on the insightful section in Jean M. Yarbrough, *American Virtues: Thomas Jefferson on the Character of a Free People* (Lawrence, Kans., 1998), 71–77.

12. TJ, *Notes on the State of Virginia*, 121.

13. Howard C. Rice Jr., ed., *Travels in North America in the Years 1780, 1781 and 1782 by the Marquis de Chastellux* (Chapel Hill, N.C., 1963), 1:2–24; 2:389–96.

14. TJ to Monroe, May 20, 1782, *PTJ* 6:186; TJ to Chastellux, November 26, 1782, ibid., 6:203. The accounts left by Randolph and TJ's daughter Martha can be found in ibid., 6:186–87n. On Martha Jefferson's health and final illness, see Jon Kukla, *Mr. Jefferson's Women* (New York, 2007), 78–85; and Virginia Scharff, *The Women Jefferson Loved* (New York, 2010), 142–50.

15. TJ to Elizabeth Wayles Eppes, October 3[?], 1782, *PTJ* 6:198. For the inscription on the tombstone, see Andrew Burstein and Nancy Isenberg, *Madison and Jefferson* (New York, 2010), 93.

16. AH to Richard Kidder Meade, March 1782, *PAH* 3:69.

17. AH to Lafayette, November 3, 1782, *PAH* 3:192; Duane to AH, May 5, 1782, ibid., 3:88.

18. AH to Robert Morris, July 13, August 13, 1782, *PAH* 3:108, 135; AH, "The Continentalist," nos. 5 and 6 [April 18 and July 4, 1782], ibid., 3:75–82, 99–106. The "great Federal Republic" quotation is on page 106.

19. AH to Richard Kidder Meade, August 27, 1782, *PAH* 3:151; Morris to AH, September 12, 1782, ibid., 3:164, 164n; AH to Morris, September 28, 1782, ibid., 3:170; AH to the Public Creditors of the State of New York, September 30, 1782, ibid., 171–76. On the assembly's resolution, see ibid., 3:241n.

20. On JM's background, see Burstein and Isenberg, *Madison and Jefferson*; Lance Banning, *The Sacred Fire of Liberty: James Madison and the Founding of the Federal Republic* (Ithaca, N.Y., 1995); and Jack Rakove, *James Madison and the Creation of the Federal Republic* (Glenview, Ill., 1990). The foreign observer is quoted in Brookhiser, *AH*, 52. On JM's view, see JM to TJ, April 22, 1783, *PTJ* 6:263.

21. Banning, *Sacred Fire of Liberty*, 21–39. JM's quotes can be found on pages 29 and 30.

22. Superintendent Morris's quote can be found in Miller, *AH*, 87.

23. Worthington C. Ford et al., eds., *The Journals of the Continental Congress* (Washington, 1904–1937), 24:291–93; Richard H. Kohn, "The Inside History of the Newburgh Conspiracy: America and the Coup d'Etat," *William and Mary Quarterly* 27 (1970): 187–220; Woody Holton, *Unruly Americans and the Origins of the Constitution* (New York, 2007), 67; Thomas Fleming, *The Perils of Peace: America's Struggle for Survival After Yorktown* (New York, 2007), 264.

24. Arthur Lee to Samuel Adams, January 29, 1783, *LDC* 19:639.

25. Quoted in Richard B. Morris, *The Forging of the Union, 1781–1789* (New York, 1987), 46.

26. The preceding paragraphs draw on Richard H. Kohn, *Eagle and Sword: The Federalists and the Creation of the Military Establishment in America, 1783–1802* (New York, 1975), 20–24.

27. AH to GW, February 13, 1783, *PAH* 3:253–55.

28. Ford, *Journals of the Continental Congress*, 24:295–97.

29. GW, To the Officers of the Army, March 15, 1783, *WW* 26:222–27.

30. Josiah Quincy, ed., *The Journal of Major Samuel Shaw* (Boston, 1843), 101–5.

31. John Ferling, *A Leap in the Dark: The Struggle to Create the American Republic* (New York, 2003), 252.

32. GW to AH, April 4, 1783, *PAH* 3:315–16.

33. GW to AH, March 31, April 4, 16, 22, 1783, *PAH* 3:309–11, 315–16, 329–31, 334–37; AH to GW, April 8, 1783, ibid., 3:317.

34. AH to John Jay, July 25, 1783, *PAH* 3:417.

35. AH to Clinton, January 12, 1783, *PAH* 3:240; Kohn, *Eagle and Sword*, 49.

36. GW, "Sentiments on a Peace Establishment" (1783), *WW* 26:374–98; GW to AH, May 2, 1781, *PAH* 3:346–47.

37. Continental Congress Report on a Military Peace Establishment, June 18, 1783, *PAH* 3:378–97. These paragraphs draw on Kohn, *Eagle and Sword*, 40–48.

38. GW to Duane, September 7, 1783, *WW* 27:133–40; GW, Observations on an Intended Report of a Committee of Congress on a Peace Establishment, September 8, 1783, ibid., 27:140–44; Kohn, *Eagle and Sword*, 50–62.

39. AH to ESH, July 22, 1783, *PAH* 3:413.

40. AH to Jay, July 25, 1783, *PAH* 3:416; AH, Unsubmitted Resolution Calling for a Convention to Amend the Articles of Confederation" (July 1783), ibid., 3:420–26.

41. TJ to Samuel Kercheval, July 12, 1816, in Merrill D. Peterson, ed., *The Portable Thomas Jefferson* (New York, 1975), 553–54; AH to Clinton, February 24[–27], 1783, *PAH* 3:268–74.

42. AH to Robert R. Livingston, July 23, 1783, *PAH* 3:414; AH, Unsubmitted Resolution Calling for a Convention, (July 1783), ibid., 3:425.

43. AH to Jay, July 25, 1783, *PAH* 3:416–17.

44. TJ to JM, November 26, 1782, *PTJ* 6:207; TJ to G. K. van Hogendorp, May 4, 1784, ibid., 7:208; TJ, Autobiography, in Padover, *CTJ* 1151.

45. *JMB* 1:525.

46. Resolution of Congress Releasing Jefferson from His Commission to Negotiate Peace, April 1, 1783, *PTJ* 6:259; Ferling, *A Leap in the Dark*, 247–48. TJ was in Philadelphia from late December until late January, when he journeyed to Baltimore, where he planned to sail for Paris on a French vessel. When Congress put him on hold, he returned to Philadelphia on February 26 and remained in the city until April 12. It was during that period of approximately seventy-five days that AH and TJ might have met. See *JMB* 1:525–30.

47. TJ to Isaac Zane, June 17, 1783, *PTJ* 6:317.

48. GW, Address to Congress on Resigning His Commission, December 23, 1783, *WW* 27:284–85.

49. TJ to Harrison, December 24, 1783, *PTJ* 6:419; TJ to JM, January 1, February 20, 1784, ibid., 6:436, 546.

50. Jefferson's Notes on Coinage, *PTJ* 7:175–85, 150–60n.

51. TJ to Marbois, December 5, 1783, *PTJ* 6:374; TJ to Martha (Patsy) Jefferson, November 28, December 11, 22, 1783, January 15, February 18, March 19, 1784, ibid., 6:360, 380, 465, 543–44; 7:43–44.

52. TJ to William Short, March 1, 1784, *PTJ* 6:569.

53. TJ, Report of the Committee, March 1, 1784, *PTJ* 6:603–5. See also the editorial note in ibid., 6:581–600n.

54. TJ, Observations on [Jean Nicolas] Démeunier's Manuscript, June 26, 1786, *PTJ* 10:58.

55. TJ to William Short, May 7, 1784, *PTJ* 7:229.

56. Annette Gordon-Reed, *The Hemingses of Monticello: An American Family* (New York, 2008), 156–60.

CHAPTER 7: "THEY WILL GO BACK GOOD REPUBLICANS": JEFFERSON IN PARIS

Malone, *TJ*, 2:3–255; Brodie, *TJ*, 233–318; Peterson, *TJ*, 297–389.

1. *JMB* 1:554–57, 556–57n.

2. Howard C. Rice Jr., *Thomas Jefferson's Paris* (Princeton, N.J., 1976), 3.

3. TJ to Mme de Corny, June 30, 1787, *PTJ* 11:509–10; TJ to Peter Carr, August 19, 1785, ibid., 8:407; Rice, *Thomas Jefferson's Paris*, 52, 103; Edward Dumbauld, *Thomas Jefferson, American Tourist: Being an Account of His Journeys* (Norman, Okla., 1946), 14–15; Annette Gordon-Reed, *The Hemingses of Monticello: An American Family* (New York, 2008), 225–26, 231.

4. *JMB* 1:560, 560n.

5. Abigail Adams to John Thaxter, March 20, 1785, in L. H. Butterfield et al., eds., *Adams Family Correspondence* (Cambridge, Mass., 1963–), 6:80; Abigail Adams to TJ, June 6, 1785, *AJL* 1:28; TJ to JM, January 30, 1787, *PTJ* 11:94–95.

6. Edith B. Gelles, *Abigail and John: Portrait of a Marriage* (New York, 2009), 165–66; David McCullough, *John Adams* (New York, 2001), 328; Abigail Adams to Cotton Tufts, March 8, 1785, in Butterfield, *Adams Family Correspondence*, 6:78; Abigail Adams to Mary Smith Cranch, May 8, 1785, ibid., 6:119. On Abigail Adams shopping for TJ, see ibid., 6:391, 414–16, 422–23, 463, 496, 497. For an excellent account of an American's struggles to adjust to French culture and society—in this instance, Abigail Adams—see Gelles, *Abigail and John*, 168–74.

7. See the entries, and often the editorial notes, in *JMB* 1:559, 566, 576, 577, 594, 607, 615, 630, 636, 646, 651, 652, 686, 710, 712, 714, 726, 728, 731, 736, 738, 740, 741, and 743. See also Rice, *Thomas Jefferson's Paris*, 122. Jefferson's remark about shopping in bookstores almost daily is quoted in Kevin J. Hayes, *The Road to Monticello: The Life and Mind of Thomas Jefferson* (New York, 2008), 283.

8. See Malone, *TJ*, 2:118.

9. *JMB* 1:561, 563, 567, 600, 604, 609, 611, 626, 630, 635, 638, 648, 651, 683, 684, 693, 729, 731, 732, 734; TJ to Angelica Schuyler Church, February 17, July 27, August 17, 1788, *PTJ* 12:60–1; 13:422–23, 520–21; Andrew Burstein, *The Inner Jefferson: Portrait of a Grieving Optimist* (Charlottesville, Va., 1995), 107–9.

10. TJ to James Monroe, November 11, 1784, June 17, 1785, *PTJ* 7:512, 8:229–31.

11. Quoted in Peterson, *TJ*, 316.

12. TJ to JM, January 30, 1787, *PTJ* 11:95–96.

13. Thomas Paine, *Common Sense* (1776), in Philip S. Foner, ed., *The Complete Writings of Thomas Paine* (New York, 1945), 1:20.

14. Quoted in Max M. Mintz, *Gouverneur Morris and the American Revolution* (Norman, Okla., 1970), 207.

15. TJ to John Jay, February 1, 1787, *PTJ* 11:101; TJ to JM, January 30, 1787, ibid., 11:96.

16. Abigail Adams to Elizabeth Smith Shaw, April 24, 1786, Butterfield, *Adams Family Correspondence*, 7:149; Abigail Adams to TJ, June 6, 1785, *AJL* 1:28. Abigail Adams's "in the dumps" quotation can be found in John Ferling, *Adams vs. Jefferson: The Tumultuous Election of 1800* (New York, 2004), 28.

17. *DAJA* 3:184–86, 187n.

18. JA to Jay, June 26, July 19, 29, October 21, November 1, 1785, February 14, 1788, in Charles Francis Adams, ed., *The Works of John Adams* (Boston, 1850–56), 8:274–75, 282, 289, 331, 336, 476; TJ to Page, May 4, 1786, *PTJ* 9:446; TJ to William Stephens Smith, September 28, 1787, ibid., 12:193.

19. TJ to Page, May 4, 1786, *PTJ* 9:445–46.

20. A Fourth of July Tribute to Jefferson, July 4, 1789, *PTJ* 15:239; Beatrix Cary Davenport, ed., *A Diary of the French Revolution by Gouverneur Morris* (Boston, 1939), 1:8, 10, 14, 16, 18, 23, 29, 34, 37, 46, 48, 49, 50, 159n; Morris to GW November 12, 1788, ibid., 1:xxxii; *JMB* 1:726.

21. Davenport, *A Diary of the French Revolution*, 1:197, 488; Jon Kukla, *Mr. Jefferson's Women* (New York, 2007), 86–92.

22. TJ to Maria Cosway, April 24, 1788, *PTJ* 13:104; Maria Cosway to TJ, September 20, October 5, 1786, ibid., 10:393–94, 433.

23. TJ to Maria Cosway, October 5, 12, 1786, *PTJ* 10:431–32, 448.

24. TJ to Maria Cosway, October 12, 1786, *PTJ* 10:443–53.

25. TJ to Maria Cosway, November 29, December 24, 1786, *PTJ* 10:555, 627. On Trumbull as courier, see Burstein, *The Inner Jefferson*, 76–79.

26. Maria Cosway to TJ, February 15, 1787, *PTJ* 11:148.

27. TJ to Maria Cosway, July 1, 1787, *PTJ* 11:520.

28. Maria Cosway to TJ, December 10, 25, 1787, *PTJ* 12:415, 459–60.

29. Maria Cosway to TJ, November 13, 24, 1794, December 4, 1795, *PTJ* 28:201, 209–10, 543–44.

30. TJ to Maria Cosway, January 31, April 24, 1788, May 21, 1789, *PTJ* 12:540; 13:103–4; 15:143.

31. TJ to Maria Cosway, June 23, 1790, *PTJ* 16:551. The nature of TJ's relationship with Maria Cosway has been variously interpreted. For good accounts, which do not always tally with my interpretation, see Kukla, *Mr. Jefferson's Women*, 92–114; Virginia Scharff, *The Women Jefferson Loved* (New York, 2010), 204–8; Burstein, *The Inner Jefferson*, 75–107; and William Howard Adams, *The Paris Years of Thomas Jefferson* (New Haven, Conn., 1997), 222–35.

32. On the delay in sending Polly, and the other decisions of the Eppeses, see the account in Scharff, *The Women Jefferson Loved*, 166–80.

33. Abigail Adams to TJ, June 26, 27, July 6, 1787, *AJL* 1:178, 179, 180–82.

34. For the background of Sally Hemings and the Hemings family, and for James

Hemings's life and training in Paris, see Gordon-Reed, *The Hemingses of Monticello*, 153–209; and Annette Gordon-Reed, *Thomas Jefferson and Sally Hemings: An American Controversy* (Charlottesville, Va., 1997), 158–69. On TJ being afraid to be in Abigail Adams's presence with one of his slaves, see Conor Cruise O'Brien, *The Long Affair: Thomas Jefferson and the French Revolution, 1785–1800* (Chicago, 1996), 23–24.

35. TJ to Paul Bentalou, August 25, 1786, *PTJ* 10:296. The account of Sally Hemings's background and residence in Paris, as well as on France's slave laws, draws on Gordon-Reed, *The Hemingses of Monticello*, 209–325. For the quotations describing Sally Hemings, see ibid., 271.

36. TJ to Charles Bellini, September 20, 1785, *PTJ* 8:569; TJ to GW, December 4, 1788, ibid., 14:330.

37. TJ to Bellini, September 30, 1785, *PTJ* 8:568; TJ to JM, October 28, 1785, ibid., 8:681–82; TJ to Lafayette, April 11, 1787, ibid., 11:285.

38. TJ to Eliza House Trist, August 18, 1785, *PTJ* 8:440; TJ to Joseph Jones, August 14, 1787, ibid., 12:34; TJ to JM, January 30, 1787, ibid., 11:92–93.

39. TJ to Wythe, August 13, 1786, *PTJ* 10:244.

40. TJ to GW, May 2, 1788, *PTJ* 13:128; Jefferson's Observations on Demeunier's Manuscript, [February (?)–June 22, 1786], ibid., 10:52; TJ to David Ramsay, August 4, 1787, ibid., 11:687; TJ to Edward Carrington, January 16, 1787, ibid., 11:49.

41. TJ to Jay, October 8, 1787, *PTJ* 12:218; TJ to JM, August 2, 1787, ibid., 11:664; TJ to Benjamin Hawkins, August 4, 1787, ibid., 11:684.

42. TJ to Ramsay, August 4, 1787, *PTJ* 11:687; TJ to Trist, August 18, 1785, ibid., 8:404; TJ to Bellini, September 30, 1785, ibid., 8:569; TJ to Monroe, June 17, 1785, ibid., 8:233.

43. An excellent analysis of TJ's outlook on the iniquities inherent in an urban manufacturing society can be found in Peter Onuf, *Jefferson's Empire: The Language of American Nationhood* (Charlottesville, Va., 2000), 69–79. For a good overview of his ideas, see Drew McCoy, "Political Economy," in Merrill D. Peterson, ed., *Thomas Jefferson: A Reference Biography* (New York, 1986), 106–12.

44. TJ to JM, October 28, 1785, *PTJ* 8:682.

45. See Daniel P. Szatmary, *Shays' Rebellion: The Making of an Agrarian Insurrection* (Amherst, Mass., 1980).

46. GW to Henry Knox, December 26, 1786, *PGW:Cfed* 4:481–83; Jay to TJ, October 27, 1786, *PTJ* 10:488; JM to TJ, March 18, 1787, ibid., 11:222–23; Abigail Adams to TJ, January 29, 1787, *AJL* 1:168.

47. TJ to William Stephens Smith, November 13, 1787, *PTJ* 12:356.

48. TJ to AA, February 22, 1787, *AJL* 1:173; TJ to JM, January 30, 1787, *PTJ* 11:93; TJ to Ezra Stiles, December 24, 1786, ibid., 10:629; TJ to Smith, November 13, 1787, ibid., 12:356.

49. TJ to John de Crèvecoeur, August 6, 1787, *PTJ* 11:692; TJ to Jay, January 9, June 21, 1787, ibid., 11:31–32, 489; TJ to Monroe, August 9, 1788, ibid., 13:489.

50. TJ to Jay, May 23, August 3, 1788, *PTJ* 13:190, 464; TJ to Anne Willing Bingham, May 11, 1788, ibid., 13:151; TJ to GW, December 4, 1788, ibid., 14:330; TJ, Autobiography, in Padover, *CTJ*, 1176.

51. TJ to JM, January 30, 1787, *PTJ* 11:95; TJ to Lafayette, June 3, 1789, ibid., 15:165–66; TJ to Rabaut de St. Etienne, June 3, 1789, ibid., 15:166–67; TJ, Draft of a Charter of Rights, [June 3, 1789], ibid., 15:167–68; TJ, Autobiography, in Padover, *CTJ*, 1177, 1182. I am indebted to Conor Cruise O'Brien, who noted that JM had advised TJ in 1784 that as Lafayette's "future friendship" might be helpful to the United States, "prudence requires us to cultivate" his

affection. See O'Brien, *The Long Affair*, 333n. For good accounts of TJ's activities, see Philipp Ziesche, "Exporting American Revolutions: Gouverneur Morris, Thomas Jefferson, and the National Struggle for Universal Rights in Revolutionary France," *Journal of the Early Republic* 26 (2006): 437–40; and Adams, *Paris Years of Thomas Jefferson*, 251–95.

52. TJ, Autobiography, in Padover *CTJ*, 1183, 1185, 1188.

53. Ibid., 1190; TJ to JM, September 6, 1789, *PTJ* 15:392–97.

54. TJ, Autobiography, in Padover, *CTJ* 1187.

55. TJ, Answers to [François] Soulés's Queries [September 13–18, 1786], *PTJ* 10:380; TJ, To the Editor of *Journal de Paris*, August 29, 1787, ibid., 12:61–65.

56. A Fourth of July Tribute to Jefferson, July 4, 1789, *PTJ* 15:239–40. See also, Pauline Maier, *American Scripture: Making the Declaration of Independence* (New York, 1997), 169–70.

CHAPTER 8: "TO CHECK THE IMPRUDENCE OF DEMOCRACY": HAMILTON AND THE NEW CONSTITUTION

Chernow, *AH*, 184–273; Brookhiser, *AH*, 55–74; Miller, *AH*, 120–215; McDonald, *AH*, 71–115; Cooke, *AH*, 31–72; Mitchell, *AH*, 329–465; Malone, *TJ*, 2:203–13.

1. *PAH* 3:597.

2. James Hamilton to AH, May 31, 1785, *PAH* 3:612; AH to James Hamilton, June 22, 1785, ibid., 3:617–18.

3. Nathan Schachner, ed., "Alexander Hamilton Viewed by His Friends: The Narratives of Robert Troup and Hercules Mulligan," *William and Mary Quarterly* 4 (April 1947): 209.

4. Quoted in Cooke, *AH*, 38.

5. [AH], "A Letter from Phocion to the Considerate Citizens of New York" (January 1784), *PAH* 3:483–97; [AH], Second Letter from Phocion (April 1784), ibid., 530–58; AH to Gouvernor Morris, February 21, 1784, ibid., 3:512. The quotations on prejudice and discrimination can be found in AH's first Phocion letter, ibid., 3:484.

6. AH, "A Letter from Phocion," *PAH* 3:485, 486.

7. Ibid., 3:486, 488; AH, "Second Letter from Phocion," ibid., 3:550. See also, Bernard Bailyn, *The Ideological Origins of the American Revolution* (Cambridge, Mass., 1967), 26–54, 175–81; H. Trevor Colbourn, *The Lamp of Experience: Whig History and the Intellectual Origins of the American Revolution* (Chapel Hill, N.C., 1965), 6–9.

8. AH to Gouverneur Morris, February 21, 1784, *PAH* 3:513.

9. Quoted in Lawrence S. Kaplan, *Alexander Hamilton: Ambivalent Anglophile* (Wilmington, Del., 2002), 63.

10. John P. Kaminski, *George Clinton: Yeoman Politician of the New Republic* (Madison, Wisc., 1993), 96–105.

11. AH to ESH, March 17, 1785, *PAH* 3:599.

12. Merrill Jensen, *The New Nation: A History of the United States During the Confederation, 1783–1789* (New York, 1950), 114–15, 125, 133–34, 145–48, 192, 196, 200–202, 211, 215; Abigail Adams to JA, May 2, 1784, L. H. Butterfield, et al., eds., *Adams Family Correspondence* (Cambridge, Mass., 1963–), 5:330; Benjamin Franklin to Ferdinand Grand, January 29, March 6, 1786, in A. H. Smyth, ed., *Writings of Benjamin Franklin* (New York, 1905–7), 9:482–93; Franklin to David Hartley, October 27, 1785, ibid., 9:472; Franklin to Jonathan Shipley, February 24, 1786, ibid., 9:489; GW to la Luzerne, August 1, 1786, *PGWCfed* 4:186; Jefferson's Reply to the Representations of Affairs in America by British Newspapers, [November 20, 1784], *PTJ* 7:540.

13. Woody Holton, *Unruly Americans and the Origins of the Constitution* (New York, 2007), 26–45, 65–66, 136.

14. GW, "Circular to the States," June 8, 1783, *WW* 26:486.

15. GW to Benjamin Harrison, October 10, 1784, *PGWCfed* 2:92.

16. On postwar western issues, see John Ferling, *A Leap in the Dark: The Struggle to Create the American Republic* (New York, 2003); and Richard B. Morris, *The Forging of the Union, 1781–1789* (New York, 1987), 232–44.

17. Charles Thomson to TJ, May 19, 1785, *PTJ* 7:273; David Ramsay to Benjamin Rush, February 11, 1786, *LDC* 23:148.

18. GW to Henry Lee, October 31, 1786, *PGWCfed* 4:318; GW to William Grayson, July 26, 1786, ibid., 4:169; GW to JM, November 5, 1786, ibid., 4:331; GW, Circular to the States, June 8, 1783, *WW* 26:486.

19. [Joseph Galloway], *A Candid Examination of the Mutual Claims of Great Britain, and the Colonies: With a Plan of Accommodation on Constitutional Principles* (New York, 1775), 32–33.

20. Gordon S. Wood, *The American Revolution: A History* (New York, 2003), 140; Sean Wilentz, *The Rise of American Democracy: Jefferson to Lincoln* (New York, 2005), 13–31.

21. Merrill Jensen, *The American Revolution Within America* (New York, 1974), 50–166. The quotations are on pages 101 and 104–5.

22. AH to Robert Livingston, April 15, 1785, *PAH* 3:609.

23. AH to Robert Morris, August 13, 1783, *PAH* 3:139; AH to Livingston, April 15, 1785, ibid., 3:608–9; Alfred F. Young, *The Democratic Republicans of New York: The Origins, 1763–1797* (Chapel Hill, N.C., 1967), 9, 21, 29–30, 44, 62, 572; E. Wilder Spaulding, *New York in the Critical Period, 1783–1789* (reprint, Port Washington, N.Y., 1963), 185; Roger Champagne, *Alexander McDougall and the American Revolution* (Schenectady, N.Y., 1975, 211–12; Thomas Cochran, *New York in the Confederation: An Economic Study* (reprint, Clifton, N.J., 1972), 136–37, 149, 170; Wood, *American Revolution*, 139–42; Kaminski, *George Clinton*, 104; Jensen, *American Revolution Within America*, 102; E. Wilder Spaulding, "Abraham Yates," in *Dictionary of American Biography* (New York, 1929–1937), 20:597–98; Abraham Yates to Robert Yates, June 9, 1787, *LDC* 24:320; Yates to Henry Oothoudt and Jeremiah Van Rensselaer, August 29, 1787, ibid., 24:411; William Blount to Richard Caswell, January 28, 1787, *LDC* 24:76.

24. AH to Livingston, April 25, 1785, *PAH* 3:609. The preceding paragraphs draw on Gordon S. Wood, "Interests and Disinterestedness in the Making of the Constitution," in Gordon S. Wood, *The Idea of America: Reflections on the Birth of the United States* (New York, 2011), 127–69. The Henry Knox quotation is in Wood, page 134, while the "plebian despotism" and "fangs" quotations are in Jensen, *American Revolution Within America*, 155.

25. William Grayson to JM, May 28, 1786, *PJM* 9:64; JM to Monroe, January 22, March 14, 18, 1786, ibid., 8:483, 497–98, 505–6.

26. The two preceding paragraphs draw on Jensen, *New Nation*, 418–20; and Morris, *Forging of the Union*, 252–53.

27. AH to William Hamilton, May 2, 1797, *PAH* 21:77–78.

28. AH to ESH, September 8, 1786, *PAH* 3:684; Address of the Annapolis Convention, September 14, 1786, ibid., 3:686–90; Stuart Leibiger, *Founding Friendship: George Washington, James Madison, and the Creation of the American Republic* (Charlottesville, Va., 1999), 61–62.

29. GW to Knox, December 26, 1786, *PGWCfed* 4:481–82.

30. AH, New York Assembly. Remarks on an Act Granting to Congress Certain Imposts and Duties, February 15, 1787, *PAH* 4:71–92. The quotations can be found on pages 83–84, and 91.

31. For those who predominated in the Philadelphia Convention, see Clinton Rossiter, *1787: The Grand Convention* (New York, 1966), 138–56, 241–54.

32. AH to GW, July 3, 1787, *PAH* 4:224.

33. Four delegates at the Philadelphia Convention took notes on AH's presentation: Madison, Robert Yates, John Lansing, and Rufus King. Though varying in detail, the four sets of notes are in general agreement on what AH said. See *PAH* 4:187–207. Outlines that AH prepared to guide him in making his remarks can also be found in ibid., 4:178–87, 207–9.

34. Max Farrand, ed., *The Records of the Federal Convention of 1787* (New Haven, Conn., 1937), 1:363.

35. Richard K. Matthews, *The Radical Politics of Thomas Jefferson: A Revisionist View* (Lawrence, Kan., 1984), 102.

36. AH, Speech on a Plan of Government, June 18, 1787, *PAH* 4:189, 193; *The Federalist*, no. 6 and 68, ibid., 4:310, 311, 312, 589.

37. Some of this paragraph draws on Gordon S. Wood, "The Radicalism of Thomas Jefferson and Thomas Paine Considered," in Wood, *Idea of America*, 213–28. AH's "pernicious dreams" quotation can be found in Wood, 222. See TJ's three drafts of a proposed constitution for Virginia in 1776, as well as his 1783 draft, in *PTJ* 1:337–64; 6:294–305. The quotation is from TJ, Albemarle County Instructions Concerning the Virginia Constitution [1783], ibid., 6:287.

38. Constitutional Convention. Remarks on Equality of Representation of the States in the Congress, June 29, 1787, *PAH* 4:220–21, 221–23n.

39. For GW's diary while attending the Constitutional Convention, see Donald Jackson et al. eds., *The Diaries of George Washington* (Charlottesville, Va., 1976–1979), 5:156–86.

40. AH to Rufus King, August 28, 1787, *PAH* 4:238; Constitutional Convention, AH's Remarks on Signing the Constitution, September 17, 1787, ibid., 4:253. For a good summary of the convention, see Wood, *American Revolution*, 151–58.

41. Pauline Maier, *Ratification: The People Debate the Constitution, 1787–1788* (New York, 2010), 93.

42. AH, To the [New York] *Daily Advertiser*, July 21, 1787, July 21, 1787, *PAH* 4:229–32. The quotes can be found on pages 229 and 232.

43. *PAH* 4:281n.

44. The quotations are in Chernow, *AH*, 245.

45. AH to GW, October 11–15, 1787, *PAH* 4:280–81; GW to AH, October 18, 1787, ibid., 4:284–85.

46. *The Federalist*, nos. 1 and 15. The quotations can be found in *PAH* 4:301 and 357.

47. *The Federalist*, nos. 25. The quotation can be found in *PAH* 4:425.

48. *The Federalist*, nos. 6, 8, 11, and 24. The quotations can be found in *PAH* 4:310–11, 314, 328, 332, 340, and 346.

49. *The Federalist*, no. 60. The quotations can be found in *PAH* 4:545.

50. *The Federalist*, nos. 67–77. The quotations can be found in *PAH* 4:587, 589, and 627.

51. *The Federalist*, nos. 27, 66, and 78. See the Gottfried Dietze, *The Federalist: A Classic on Federalism and Free Government* (Baltimore, Md., 1960), 141–75; and Jill Lepore, "Benched," *New Yorker* (June 18, 2012): 77–82.

52. Maier, *Ratification*, 84.

53. Melancton Smith to Nathan Dane, June 28, 1788, in Merrill Jensen, John P. Kaminski et al., eds., *The Documentary History of the Ratification of the Constitution* (Madison, Wisc., 1976–), 22:2015–16; Jane Butzner, comp., *Constitutional Chafe: Rejected Suggestions of the Constitutional Convention of 1787* (reprint, Port Washington, N.Y., 1970), 162.

54. For AH's numerous speeches and his comments in the debates, see *PAH* 5:14–34, 36–60, 62–89, 92–135, 138–40, 141–47, 149–60, 163–77, 178–85, and 188–96. His contradictory comments on the states can be found in AH, Speech on a Plan of Government, June 18, 1787, ibid., 4:191; and AH, Remarks to the New York Ratifying Convention, June 27, 1788, ibid., 5:100.

55. For the best account of the long, complicated New York ratifying convention, see Maier, *Ratification*, 340–400, upon which my account draws, but also see John Kaminski, "New York: The Reluctant Pillar," in Stephen L. Schecter, ed., *The Reluctant Pillar: New York and the Adoption of the Federal Constitution* (Troy, N.Y., 1985), 48–117.

56. TJ to Demeunier, June 24, 1786, *PTJ* 10:14; JM to TJ, March 19, 1787, ibid., 11:219–20; TJ to JM, June 20, 1787, ibid. 11:480–81; TJ to JA, August 30, 1787, *AJL* 1:196.

57. TJ to JA, November 13, 1787, *AJL* 1:212; TJ to JM, December 20, 1787, *PTJ* 12:439–42; TJ to William Stephens Smith, November 13, 1787, February 2, 1788, ibid., 12:356–57; TJ to John Rutledge Jr., February 2, 1788, ibid., 12:557; TJ to Francis Hopkinson, March 13, 1789, ibid., 14:650; TJ to Edward Carrington, December 21, 1787, ibid., 12:446. The "energetic government is always oppressive" quotation is in Malone, *TJ*, 2:169.

58. TJ to JM, July 31, 1788, *PTJ* 13:442.

59. AH to GW, August 13, 1788, *PAH* 5:201–2.

60. AH to GW, September [?], November 18, 1788, *PAH* 5:220–22, 233–34; John Ferling, *The Ascent of George Washington: The Hidden Political Genius of an American Icon* (New York, 2009), 273–75.

61. TJ to Jay, November 19, 1788, *PTJ* 14:214–15; TJ to Elizabeth Wayles Eppes, December 15, 1788, ibid., 14:355; TJ to JM, August 28, 1789, ibid., 15:368–69.

62. TJ to Nicholas Lewis, July 29, 1787, *PTJ* 11:640.

63. JM to TJ, May 27, 1789, *PTJ* 15:153.

64. Annette Gordon-Reed, *The Hemingses of Monticello: An American Family* (New York, 2008), 326–27; "The Memoirs of Madison Hemings," in Annette Gordon-Reed, *Thomas Jefferson and Sally Hemings: An American Controversy* (Charlottesville, Va., 1997), 246.

65. Maria Cosway to TJ, August 19, 1789, *PTJ* 15:351. TJ received her letter on August 27.

CHAPTER 9: "THE GREATEST MAN THAT EVER LIVED WAS JULIUS CAESAR": THE THRESHOLD OF PARTISAN WARFARE

Chernow, *AH*, 270–390; McDonald, *AH*, 117–236; Miller, *AH*, 219–321; Cooke, *AH*, 73–96; Brookhiser, *AH*, 75–100; Malone, *TJ* 2:242–370 and 3:198–206; Peterson, *TJ*, 390–446; Cunningham, *TJ*, 131–70.

1. John P. Kaminski and Jill Adair McCaughan, eds., *A Great and Good Man: George Washington in the Eyes of His Contemporaries* (Madison, Wisc., 1989), 117–21.

2. JA to GW, May 17, 1789, *PGWP* 2:312–141; AH to GW, May 5, 1789, *PAH* 5:335–36; Ron Chernow, *Washington: A Life* (New York, 2010), 577.

3. Kenneth R. Bowling and Helen E. Veit, eds., *The Diary of William Maclay and Other Notes on Senate Debates* (Baltimore, Md., 1988), 342, 349; Worthington C. Ford, *The True*

George Washington (Philadelphia, 1896), 174; John Ferling, *The Ascent of George Washington: The Hidden Political Genius of an American Icon* (New York, 2009), 278–80; Douglas Southall Freeman, *George Washington* (New York, 1948–1957), 6:77–78; Forrest McDonald, *The Presidency of George Washington* (Lawrence, Kans., 1974), 28–30; John C. Miller, *The Federalist Era, 1789–1801* (New York, 1960), 5–10; Stanley Elkins and Eric McKitrick, *The Age of Federalism* (New York, 1993), 49; Gordon S. Wood, *Empire of Liberty: A History of the Early Republic, 1789–1815* (New York, 2009), 75–85; John Ferling, *The First of Men: A Life of George Washington* (reprint, New York, 2010), 377. The McHenry quote can be found in Wood, *Empire of Liberty*, 75.

4. McDonald, *Presidency of George Washington*, 36–38; Chernow, *Washington*, 619; Wood, *Empire of Liberty*, 91.

5. JM to TJ, May 27, June 30, 1789, *PTJ* 15:153, 228.

6. Wood, *Empire of Liberty*, 93–94.

7. Quoted in Thomas K. McCraw, *The Founders and Finance: How Hamilton, Gallatin, and Other Immigrants Forged a New Economy* (Cambridge, Mass., 2012), 92.

8. AH, Report on Public Credit, January 9, 1790 [submitted on January 14, 1790], *PAH* 6:65–168; McCraw, *The Founders and Finance*, 95.

9. Mark Schmeller, "The Political Economy of Opinion: Public Credit and Concepts of Public Opinion in the Age of Federalism," *Journal of the Early Republic* 29 (2009): 49; McCraw, *The Founders and Finance*, 97–98.

10. Quoted in Wood, *Empire of Liberty*, 103.

11. Chernow, *Washington*, 598.

12. TJ to GW, December 15, 1789, February 14, 1790, *PTJ* 16:34–35, 184; GW to TJ, January 21, 1790, ibid., 16:116–18.

13. TJ to Jean Nicolas Démeunier, April 29, 1795, *PTJ* 28:341; TJ to Robert Lewis, October 5, 1791, ibid., 22:186; Henry Wiencek, *Master of the Mountain: Thomas Jefferson and His Slaves* (New York, 2012), 89.

14. JM to GW, January 4, 1790, *PGWP* 4:536–37; TJ to JM, February 20, *PTJ* 6:550. For a full account of the evolution on the relationship between TJ and JM, see Andrew Burstein and Nancy Isenberg, *Madison and Jefferson* (New York, 2010), 65–217.

15. TJ, Anas, February 4, 1818, in Padover, *CTJ*, 1207–8. On TJ's clothing styles and his switch to a more republican attire, see Deborah Norris Logan, ed., *Memoir of Dr. George Logan of Stanton* (Philadelphia, 1899), 50.

16. TJ to Benjamin Rush, January 16, 1811, *PTJ: Ret. Ser.* 3:305.

17. William Maclay, *The Journal of William Maclay: United States Senator from Pennsylvania, 1789–1791* (New York, 1927), 265–66.

18. On the break between JM and AH, see Lance Banning, *The Sacred Fire of Liberty: James Madison and the Founding of the Federal Republic* (Ithaca, N.Y., 1995); Alan Gibson, "The Madisonian Madison and the Question of Consistency: The Significance and Challenge of New Research," *Review of Politics* 64 (2002): 311–38; Gordon S. Wood, *Revolutionary Characters: What Made the Founders Great* (New York, 2006), 143–72; and Michael Schwarz, "The Great Divergence Reconsidered: Hamilton, Madison, and U.S. British Relations, 1783–1789," *Journal of the Early Republic* 27 (2007): 407–36.

19. TJ to David Howell, June 23, 1790, *PTJ* 16:553; Lance Banning, *The Jeffersonian Persuasion: Evolution of a Party Ideology* (Ithaca, N.Y., 125–51.

20. Benjamin Rush to JM, April 10, 1790, *PJM* 13:146; Maclay, *Journal of William Maclay*, 184, 189, 204, 205, 267, 301, 325. The "eastern phalanx" quote is in Chernow, *AH*, 327.

21. JA to Benjamin Rush, January 25, 1806, in John Schutz and Douglass Adair, eds., *The Spur of Fame: Dialogues of John Adams and Benjamin Rush, 1805–13* (San Marino, Cal., 1966), 48. The newspaper essay on AH as arrogant is cited in Joanne Freeman, *Affairs of Honor: National Politics in the Early Republic* (New Haven, Conn., 2001), 46.

22. Burstein and Isenberg, *Madison and Jefferson*, 211–41; John Ferling, *A Leap in the Dark: The Struggle to Create the American Republic* (New York, 2003), 320–23. The following are excellent works on the life and thought—including the changing thought—of JM: Banning, *Sacred Fire of Liberty*; and Jack N. Rakove, *James Madison and the Creation of the American Republic* (New York, 1990).

23. JM to Edmund Pendleton, June 22, 1790, *PJM* 13:252–53.

24. Jefferson's Account of the Bargain on the Assumption and Residence Bills," [1792], *PTJ* 17:205–7.

25. Maclay, *Journal of William Maclay*, 285, 286, 296, 304, 319, 326–32. The quotations can be found on pages 296 and 319. See also Josiah Parker to JM, June 15, 1790, *PJM* 13:246.

26. TJ, Anas, February 4, 1818, in Padover, *CTJ*, 1208–9; TJ to GW, September 9, 1792, *PTJ* 24:352.

27. TJ to John Harvie Jr., July 25, 1790, *PTJ* 17:271; TJ to Monroe, June 20, 1790, ibid., 16:537.

28. The literature on the Compromise of 1790 is considerable. For a good starting point, see Jacob E. Cooke, "The Compromise of 1790," *William and Mary Quarterly* 27 (1970): 524–45; Kenneth R. Bowling, "Dinner at Jefferson's: A Note on Jacob E. Cooke's 'The Compromise of 1790,'" ibid., 28 (1971): 629–48; Elkins and McKitrick, *Age of Federalism*, 146–61; John Ferling, *A Leap in the Dark*, 321–26; and Burstein and Isenberg, *Madison and Jefferson*, 217–20. On GW's selection of the site for the Federal City, see Ferling, *Ascent of George Washington*, 294–95; and Ferling, *The First of Men*, 397–98.

29. *JMB* 1:770n; William Temple Franklin to TJ, July 20, 1790, *PTJ* 17:236–39; TJ to William Temple Franklin, July 25, 1790, ibid., 17:267–69.

30. Wiencek, *Master of the Mountain*, 89–90. On Patsy's dowry, see Marriage Settlement for Martha Jefferson, February 21, 1790, *PTJ* 16:189–91.

31. *JMB* 1:765–71.

32. *JMB* 1:768–69.

33. TJ, Anas, February 4, 1818, in Padover, *CTJ* 1209, 1211.

34. AH, Report on Public Credit, January 9, 1790, *PAH* 6:102–3; Thomas P. Slaughter, *The Whiskey Rebellion: Frontier Epilogue to the American Revolution* (New York, 1986), 95–97. Slaughter is also my source for Hamilton's *Federalist* comment on excise taxes; see the quotation on page 97.

35. AH, First Report on the Further Provision Necessary for Establishing Public Credit, December 13, 1790, *PAH* 7:210–36; Slaughter, *Whiskey Rebellion*, 96–105; *Journal of William Maclay*, 370–72, 374–79, 386, 387. The quotations are from *Journal of Maclay* and can be found on pages 375, 376, 379, and 387.

36. William Hogeland, *The Whiskey Rebellion: George Washington, Alexander Hamilton, and the Frontier Rebels Who Challenged America's Newfound Sovereignty* (New York, 2006), 62.

37. AH, Final Version of the Second Report on the Further Provision Necessary for Establishing Public Credit (Report on a National Bank), December 13, 1790, *PAH* 7:305–42; AH, Draft of an Act to Incorporate the Bank of the United States [December 1790], ibid., 7:399–406; McCraw, *The Founders and Finance*, 115.

38. *Journal of William Maclay*, 345; *PAH* 7:244–46n; AH, Second Report on the Further Provision Necessary for Establishing a Public Credit (Report on a National Bank), December 14, 1790, ibid., 7:311.

39. AH, Report on a National Bank, *PAH* 7:305–42. The quotes are on page 306.

40. Wood, *Empire of Liberty*, 93–94; Gordon S. Wood, "Illusions of Power in the Awkward Era of Federalism," in Gordon S. Wood, *The Idea of America: Reflections on the Birth of the United States* (New York, 2011), 257–59; Bernard Bailyn, *The Ideological Origins of the American Revolution* (Cambridge, Mass., 1967), 35–54. Thomas Paine, *Common Sense* (1776), in Philip S. Foner, ed., *The Complete Writings of Thomas Paine* (New York, 1945), 1:20–21; Franklin to Joseph Galloway, February 25, 1775, in Leonard W. Labaree et al., eds., *The Papers of Benjamin Franklin* (New Haven, Conn., 1959–), 21:509. On the changes wrought in England, including the levels of taxation, see John Brewer, *The Sinews of Power: War, Money and the English State, 1688–1783* (New York, 1989), 29, 89, 118, 175, 193–96, 199, 200, 203.

41. Wood, *Empire of Liberty*, 102–4; Gordon S. Wood, "The Radicalism of Thomas Jefferson and Thomas Paine Considered," in Wood, *The Idea of America*, 217–19, 222–23; Wood, *Revolutionary Characters*, 129–30.

42. David Hume, *Essays Moral, Political and Literary* (1742), edited and with a forward, notes, and glossary by Eugene F. Miller (Indianapolis, 1987), 206, 255, 261, 263, 271–73. This paragraph additionally draws on Elkins and McKitrick, *Age of Federalism*, 92–131.

43. Hume, *Essays Moral, Political, and Literary*, 261, 419–20. For an excellent assessment of AH's thinking on humankind, society, and government, see Clinton Rossiter, *Alexander Hamilton and the Constitution* (New York, 1964), 113–84.

44. [AH], "The Continentalist," no. 6, July 4, 1782, *PAH* 3:106; [AH], *A Full Vindication of the Measures of the Congress, &c.*, December 15, 1774, ibid., 1:56. See the longer essay in Gerald Stourzh, *Alexander Hamilton and the Idea of Republican Government* (Stanford, Cal., 1970), 189–205.

45. Elkins and McKitrick, *Age of Federalism*, 229; *Journal of William Maclay*, 242, 243, 249, 341, 345–62; Banning, *Jeffersonian Persuasion*, 148–54. The quotations can be found in Maclay's *Journal* on pages 341, 353, and 358; and in Banning, *Jeffersonian Persuasion* on page 148.

46. Wood, *Empire of Liberty*, 145; Virginia Resolution on the Assumption of State Debts, December 16, 1790, in Henry Steele Commager, ed., *Documents of American History* (New York, 1968), 155–56.

47. The quotation is from Joseph J. Ellis, *American Sphinx: The Character of Thomas Jefferson* (New York, 1997), 131.

48. Sean Wilentz, *The Rise of American Democracy: Jefferson to Lincoln* (New York, 2005), 46, 48.

49. TJ, Notes on the Letter of Christoph Daniel Ebeling, [after October 15, 1795], *PTJ* 28:507. The "natural progress of things" quotation is from David N. Mayer, *The Constitutional Thought of Thomas Jefferson* (Charlottesville, Va., 1994), 84.

50. Ferling, *A Leap in the Dark*, 337; TJ, Opinion on the Constitutionality of the Bill for Establishing a National Bank, February 15, 1791, *PTJ* 19:275–80. The quote about empowering Congress to do evil is on page 277.

51. AH, Draft of an Opinion on the Constitutionality of an Act to Establish a Bank, [n.d.], *PAH* 8:64–97; AH, Final Version of an Opinion on the Constitutionality of an Act to Establish a Bank, February 23, 1791, ibid., 8:97–134. The quotation can be found on page 98.

52. The quotation can be found in McDonald, *AH*, 209.

53. TJ to George Mason, February 4, 1791, *PTJ* 19:242; TJ to Edward Rutledge, August 25, 1791, ibid., 22:74; TJ to Robert R. Livingston, February 7, 1791, ibid., 19:241; TJ to Henry Innes, March 13, 1791, ibid., 19:542–43; Livingston to TJ, February 20, 1791, ibid., 19:296; TJ, Anas, February 4, 1818, and July 10, 1792, in Padover, *CTJ*, 1211, 1224–25.

54. TJ to Philip Freneau, February 28, 1791, *PTJ* 19:351; TJ to JM, May 9, July 21, 1791, ibid., 20:293, 657; Noble E. Cunningham, *The Jeffersonian Republicans: The Formation of Party Organization, 1789–1801* (Chapel Hill, N.C., 1957), 17. See the lengthy editorial note on "Jefferson, Freneau, and the Founding of the *National Gazette*" in *PTJ* 20:718–53.

55. For the slow formation of parties, see Cunningham, *Jeffersonian Republicans*, 33–49, 63–64, 71–77.

56. Nancy Isenberg, *Fallen Founder: The Life of Aaron Burr* (New York, 2007), 105–7. For TJ's ongoing efforts to mount an opposition to the Hamiltonians, see the introductory essay Todd Estes, "Jefferson as Party Leader," in Francis D. Cogliano, ed., *A Companion to Thomas Jefferson* (Chichester, England, 2011), 128–44.

57. Jefferson's Journal of the Tour, May 21–June 10, 1791, *PTJ* 20:453–56; Jefferson's Notes on the Hessian Fly, May 24–June 18, 1791, ibid., 20:456–62; TJ to Martha Jefferson Randolph, May 31, 1791, ibid., 20:463–64; TJ to GW, June 5, 1791, ibid., 20:466–67; Jefferson's Table of Distances and Rating of Inns, May 17–June 19, 1791, ibid., 20:471–73; *JMB* 2:818–23.

58. Nathaniel Hazard to AH, November 25, 1791, *PAH* 9:534; Robert Troup to AH, June 15, 1791, ibid., 8:478–79.

59. TJ to Walter Jones, March 5, 1810, *PTJ: Ret. Ser.* 2:272.

CHAPTER 10: "DEVOTED TO THE PAPER AND STOCKJOBBING INTEREST": UNBRIDLED PARTISAN WARFARE

Chernow, *AH*, 360–430; McDonald, *AH*, 211–61; Miller, *AH*, 296–342; Cooke, *AH*, 97–120; Malone, *TJ* 2:420–88; Peterson, *TJ*, 459–79; Cunningham, *TJ*, 167–77.

1. GW, To the United States Senate and House of Representatives, January 8, 1790, *PGWP* 4:544, 545; *PAH* 10:230n.

2. AH, Final Version of the Report on the Subject of Manufacturers, December 5, 1791, *PAH* 10:230–340. The quotations can be found on pages 253, 291, 302, and 313. See also, the four drafts of this report prepared by AH in ibid., 10:23–339, and the draft composed by Tench Coxe, the assistant secretary of the Treasury, in ibid., 10:15–23.

3. Quoted in Cooke, *AH*, 102.

4. Prospectus of the Society for Establishing Useful Manufactures, [August 1791], *PAH* 9:144–53. No copy of the prospectus exists in AH's handwriting, but the editors of his papers attribute it to him.

5. JM to Henry Lee, January 1, 1792, *PJM 14:180*; TJ, Memoranda of Conversations with the President, March 1, 1792, *PTJ* 23:186–87.

6. TJ, Anas, March 11, 12, September 30, November 19, 1792, June 7, 12, 1793, in Padover, *CTJ*, 1220, 1221, 1226, 1227, 1231, 1244, 1245, 1246. The quotations are on pages 1244 and 1246.

7. TJ, Anas, February 4, 1818, and October 1, 1792, in Padover, *CTJ* 1211, 1228; TJ to Benjamin Rush, January 16, 1811, *PTJ: Ret. Ser.* 3:305.

8. The preceding paragraphs are based on TJ, Memoranda of Conversations with the President, March 1, 1792, *PTJ* 23:184–87; TJ, Notes of a Conversation with George Washington, July 10, 1792, ibid., 24:210–11; TJ, Notes of a Conversation with George Washington, October 1, 1792, ibid., 24:433–36; TJ, Anas, February 7, 1793, in Padover, *CTJ*, 1234–35. The

quotations can be found in *PTJ* 23:186-87; 24:211, 434, and 435; and Padover, *CTJ*, 1234 and 1235.

9. TJ, Memoranda of Conversations with the President, March 1, 1792, *PTJ* 23:187. The "ultimate object" quotation can be found in TJ to GW, May 23, 1792, ibid., 23:537. For Banning's quote, see Lance Banning, *The Jeffersonian Persuasion: Evolution of a Party Ideology* (Ithaca, N.Y., 1978), 159.

10. AH to Edward Carrington, May 26, 1792, *PAH* 11:429.

11. TJ, Notes of a Conversation with George Washington, October 1, 1792, *PTJ* 24:434; Abigail Adams to Mary Cranch, March 29, 1792, in Stewart Mitchell, ed., *New Letters of Abigail Adams, 1788-1801* (Boston, 1947), 80-81; AH to Carrington, May 26, 1792, *PAH* 11:430.

12. AH, Conversation with George Beckwith, [October 1789], *PAH* 5:488.

13. AH to Carrington, May 26, 1792, *PAH* 11:426-45.

14. AH in the *Gazette of the United States*, July 25, August 4, 11, 18, 1792, and in the *National Gazette*, September 11, 1792, *PAH* 12:107, 157-64, 188-93, 193-94, 224, 361-65. The quotations can be found on pages 159, 161, 162, 163, and 362.

15. Conor Cruise O'Brien, *The Long Fuse: Thomas Jefferson and the French Revolution, 1785-1800* (Chicago, 1996), 119; Joyce Appleby, *Capitalism and the New Social Order: The Republican Vision of the 1790s* (New York, 1984), 73-74; Gordon S. Wood, *Empire of Liberty: A History of the Early Republic, 1789-1815* (New York, 2009), 148-51. TJ later told GW that he could pledge "in the presence of heaven, that I never did by myself, or any other, directly or indirectly, say a syllable" in Freneau's newspaper, "nor attempt any kind of influence" over the editor. See TJ to GW, September 9, 1792, *PTJ* 24:356.

16. For JM's series of *National Gazette* essays, see *PJM*, vol. 14. The quotes can be found in *PJM* 14:370-72.

17. AH to GW, May 23, 1792, *PTJ* 23:535-40.

18. TJ, Notes of a Conversation with George Washington, July 10, 1792, *PTJ* 24:210-11; ibid., 23:540-412n.

19. TJ, Notes of a Conversation with Edmund Randolph, [after 1795], *PTJ* 28:568.

20. Robert Troup to AH, March 19, 1792, *PAH* 11:157.

21. GW to AH, July 29, 1792, *PAH* 12:129-34; GW to Henry, March 28, 1778, *PGWR* 14:336.

22. AH to GW, August 18, 1792, *PAH* 12:228-58. The quotations can be found on pages 250, 251, and 252.

23. GW to TJ, August 23, 1792, *PTJ* 24:317; GW to AH, August 26, 1792, *PAH* 12:276-77. GW's remarks about regarding the attacks on AH as attacks on himself can be found in TJ, Notes of a Conversation with George Washington, July 10, 1792, *PTJ* 24:210.

24. AH to TJ, September 9, 1792, *PAH* 12:347-50; TJ to GW, September 9, 1792, *PTJ* 24:351-59.

25. GW to TJ, August 23, 1792, *PTJ* 24:317.

26. Stanley Elkins and Eric McKitrick, *The Age of Federalism* (New York, 1993), 65-74, 124.

27. AH conversation with George Beckwith, [October 1789], *PAH* 5:482-90. The quotations can be found on pages 483, 484, and 487. The surviving notes of the discussion are those of Beckwith, not AH.

28. AH to GW, July 8, 15, 1790, *PAH* 6:484-85, 493-95; AH conversations with George Beckwith, July 15, August 7-12, 8-12, 1790, ibid., 6:497-98, 546-48, 550-51; Elkins and McKitrick, *Age of Federalism*, 212-21. The quotation can be found in Elkins and McKitrick, on page 219.

29. AH conversation with George Beckwith, [July 15, 1790], *PAH* 6:497.

30. TJ to GW, December 15, 1790, *PTJ* 18:301–3; TJ to John Jay, April 23, 1786, ibid., 9:402; TJ to William Temple Franklin, May 7, 1786, ibid., 9:466. See also the exhaustive editorial note in ibid., 18:220–83. Morris's reports of April 7, May 29, July 3, and August 16, September 18, 1790, can be found in ibid., 18:285–300.

31. TJ to George Hammond, October 26, November 29, December 5, 12, 13, 15, 28, 1791, January 28, February 2, 25, March 30, 31, April 12, 13, May 29, June 2, 6, July 6, 9, 12, 1792, February 16, April 18, May 3, 15, June 5, 13, 19, 25, 26, August 1, 4, 7, 8, September 5, 10, 11, 12, 13, 22, November 13, 14, December 26, 1793, *PTJ* 22:234, 352–53, 378–79, 394, 399, 409–11, 467; 23:82, 97, 148–49, 352–53, 357, 406, 417, 551–602; 24:18–19, 37, 164, 202–3, 221; 25:206–7, 563–64, 644; 26:38–40, 197–98, 290–91, 321, 322, 361–62, 375–76, 378, 596, 612–13, 634–35, 639–40; 27:35–37, 82–83, 89, 99–100, 106, 143, 353, 368–71, 620–22. A succinct account of TJ's diplomacy with Hammond can be found in Elkins and McKitrick, *Age of Federalism*, 244–56.

32. Memorandum of Conversation between Philemon Dickinson and George Hammond, March 26, 1792, *PTJ* 23:344–45; S. W. Jackman, "A Young Englishman Reports on the New Nation: Edward Thornton to James Bland Burges, 1791–93," *William and Mary Quarterly* 18 (1961): 85–121.

33. Conversations with George Hammond, December 15–16, 1791, January 1–8, 2–9, March 31, April 30–July 3, May 28–29, May 29–June 2, July 1–2, 1792, *PAH* 10:373–76, 493–96, 498–99; 11:212–14, 347–48, 446–49, 454–55; 12:1–3. See also ibid., 10:350–51.

34. TJ, Memoranda of Conversations with the President, March 1, 1792, *PTJ* 23:185; Notes of a Conversation with George Washington, July 10, 1792, ibid., 24:210; Madison's Conversations with Washington, May 5, 1792, *PGWP* 10:351. On GW's health concerns, see John Ferling, *The Ascent of George Washington: The Hidden Political Genius of an American Icon* (New York, 2009), 305.

35. AH to GW July 30 [–August 3], 1792, *PAH* 12:137–38.

36. TJ, Memoranda of Conversations with the President, March 1, 1792, *PTJ* 23:185–86; TJ to GW, May 23, 1792, ibid., 23:535–40. The quotations can be found on pages 185 and 539.

37. TJ to GW, September 9, 1792, *PTJ* 24:358.

38. TJ, Notes of a Conversation with George Washington, October 1, 1792, *PTJ* 24:434.

39. Lewis Leary, *That Rascal Freneau: A Study in Literary Failure* (reprint, New York, 1964), 196–223. The quotations can be found on pages 203 and 223.

40. TJ, Notes of a Conversation with George Washington, October 1, 1792, *PTJ* 24:433–35.

41. AH to ESH, August 2, 9, 10, 21, September 4, 1791, *PAH* 9:6–7, 24, 25–26, 87–88, 172–73. The quotations can be found on pages 7, 24, 26, and 87.

42. AH, *Observations on Certain Documents Contained in No. V & VI of "The History of the United States for the Year 1796," in Which the Charge of Speculation Against Alexander Hamilton, Late Secretary of the Treasury, Is Fully Refuted, Written by Himself* (Philadelphia, 1797), *PAH* 21:238–85. See also the lengthy editor's note on the subject in ibid., 21:121–44. The quotations can be found in AH's account of the affair in ibid., 21:266 and 288.

43. TJ, Notes on the Reynolds Affair, December 17, 1792, *PTJ* 24:751.

44. TJ to GW, May 23, 1792, *PTJ* 23:537; TJ to Thomas Mann Randolph Jr., March 3, 1793, ibid., 25:314.

45. TJ to Thomas Mann Randolph Jr., November 2, 16, 1792, March 3, 1793, *PTJ* 24:556, 623; 25:314; TJ to Thomas Pinckney, December 3, 1792, ibid., 24:696.

CHAPTER 11: "A LITTLE INNOCENT BLOOD": TO THE
MOUNTAINTOP AND TO THE TOP OF THE MOUNTAIN

Chernow, *AH*, 431–81; Cooke, *AH*, 121–57; Miller, *AH*, 364–414; Malone, *TJ*, 3:39–242; Peterson, *TJ*, 479–543; Cunningham, *TJ*, 178–94; Brodie, *TJ*, 361–95.

1. TJ, Notes of Conversations with George Washington, March 1, October 1, 1792, February 7, August 6, 1793, *PTJ* 23:184–87; 24:434; 25:154; 26:627–30; TJ to GW, May 23, September 9, 1792, July 31, August 11, 1793, ibid., 23:539; 24:358; 26:593, 659–60; TJ to Thomas Mann Randolph Jr., January 1, 1792, ibid., 23:8; TJ to Martha Jefferson Randolph, January 15, March 22, 1792, ibid., 23:44, 326; TJ to William Short, January 28, 1792, ibid., 23:84.

2. TJ to John F. Mercer, December 10, 1792, *PTJ*, 24:757; John Ferling, *A Leap in the Dark: The Struggle to Create the American Republic* (New York, 2003), 356–57.

3. AH, "The French Revolution," (1794), *PAH* 17:586.

4. Simon Schama, *Citizens: A Chronicle of the French Revolution* (New York, 1989), 633, 776; Fisher Ames, "[Untitled] Against Jacobins," [1794?], in Seth Ames, ed., *Works of Fisher Ames*, edited and enlarged by W. B. Allen (Indianapolis, 1983), 2:974–84; Ames to Theodore Dwight, August [?], 1793, ibid., 2:964; David Waldstreicher, "Federalism, the Style of Politics, and the Politics of Style," in Doran Ben-Atar and Barbara B. Oberg, eds., *Federalists Reconsidered* (Charlottesville, Va., 1998), 115–16; Chauncey Goodrich to Oliver Wolcott, February 17, 1793, in George Gibbs, ed., *Memoirs of the Administrations of Washington and Adams, Edited from the Papers of Oliver Wolcott* (New York, 1946), 1:88; Gordon S. Wood, *Empire of Liberty: A History of the Early Republic, 1789–1815* (New York, 2009), 177–78. The JA quotation can be found in John R. Howe, *The Changing Political Thought of John Adams* (Princeton, N.J., 1966), 171–72.

5. Ron Chernow, *Washington: A Life* (New York, 2010), 658.

6. AH, "Americanus," no. 1, January 31, 1794, *PAH* 15:670–71; AH, "Pacificus," no. 5 (July 13–17, 1793), ibid., 15:92–95.

7. TJ to Joseph Fay, March 18, 1793, *PTJ* 24:402; TJ, Autobiography, in Padover, *CTJ*, 1188.

8. TJ to William Short, January 3, 1793, *PTJ* 25:14; TJ to Mason, February 4, 1791, ibid., 19:241. The Franklin quote can be found in H. W. Brands, *The First American: The Life and Times of Benjamin Franklin* (New York, 2000), 705–6.

9. TJ to James Monroe, June 4, 1793, *PTJ* 26:190.

10. The quotations can be found in Joyce Appleby, *Capitalism and a New Social Order: The Republican Vision of the 1790s* (New York, 1984), 57.

11. Lance Banning, *The Jeffersonian Persuasion: Evolution of a Party Ideology* (Ithaca, N.Y., 1978), 208–9; Wood, *Empire of Liberty*, 209.

12. TJ, Opinions on the Treaties with France, April 28, 1793, *PTJ* 25:608–18, 597–602n; TJ to JM, April 28, 1793, ibid., 25:619; TJ, Anas (April 18, May 6, 1793), in Padover, *CTJ*, 1242–43; Stanley Elkins and Eric McKitrick, *The Age of Federalism* (New York, 1993), 340–41.

13. The two preceding paragraphs draw on Elkins and McKitrick, *Age of Federalism*, 330–36, 341.

14. TJ to JM, April 28, 1793, *PTJ* 25:619; TJ to Monroe, May 5, 1793, ibid., 25:661.

15. TJ to Monroe, May 5, 1793, *PTJ* 25:661; TJ to JM, July 7, August 11, 1793, ibid., 26:444, 652; AH conversation with George Hammond, June 10–July 6, 1793, *PAH* 14:525–26; AH, "No Jacobin," July 31–August 24, 1793, ibid., 15:145–51, 184–91, 203–7, 224–28, 243–46, 249–50, 268–70, 281–82, 304–6; Christopher J. Young, "Connecting the President and the People: Washington's Neutrality, Genêt's Challenge, and Hamilton's Fight for Public Support," *Jour-*

nal of the Early Republic 31 (2011): 454; Andrew Burstein and Nancy Isenberg, *Madison and Jefferson* (New York, 2010), 262. The "most offensive" remark by AH can be found in Elkins and McKitrick, *Age of Federalism*, 348, while the source for the "No Jacobin" quote is *PAH* 15:145.

16. TJ, Anas (August 2, 1793), in Padover, *CTJ*, 1256. See also TJ to JM, June 9, 1793, *PTJ* 26:241. On the press attacks on GW, see Chernow, *Washington*, 693.

17. Eugene Link, *Democratic-Republican Societies, 1790–1800* (New York, 1942), 44–70; Matthew Schoenbachler, "Republicanism in the Age of Democratic Revolution: The Democratic-Republican Societies of the 1790s," *Journal of the Early American Republic* 18 (1998): 237–61; Jeffrey L. Pasley, "Thomas Greenleaf: Printers and the Struggle for Democratic Politics and Freedom of the Press," in Alfred F. Young, Gary B. Nash, and Ray Raphael, eds., *Revolutionary Founders: Rebels, Radicals, and Reformers in the Making of the Nation* (New York, 2011), 364. The quotations can be found in Philip S. Foner, ed., *The Democratic-Republican Societies, 1790–1820: A Documentary Sourcebook* (Westport, Conn., 1976), 19; and Appleby, *Capitalism and a New Social Order*, 55–56.

18. AH, "Pacificus," nos. 1–7, June 29–July 27, 1793, *PAH* 15:33–43, 55–63, 65–69, 82–86, 90–95, 100–106, 130–35. The quotations can be found on pages 67 and 105.

19. *PTJ* 25:xlii; ibid., 27:xlix; TJ to William Carmichael and William Short, September 11, 1793, ibid., 27:88; TJ to JM, September 1, 1793, ibid., 27:7; TJ to Thomas Mann Randolph Jr., September 2, 15, 1793, ibid., 27:21, 121; TJ to Martha Jefferson Randolph, September 8, 1793, ibid., 27:64.

20. *PAH* 15:325n, 332n; AH, To the College of Physicians, September 11, 1793, ibid., 15:331; Alan Brodsky, *Benjamin Rush: Patriot and Physician* (New York, 2004), 329.

21. TJ to JM, September 8, 1793, *PTJ* 27:62.

22. TJ to JM, November 2, 1793, *PTJ* 27:297; TJ to Randolph, November 2, 1793, 299.

23. TJ, Notes of Cabinet Meeting on the President's Address and Messages to Congress, November 28, 1793, *PTJ* 27:453–55; TJ to GW, December 2, 1793, ibid., 23:471–72; GW to TJ, December 2, 1793, ibid., 27:473.

24. Robert Troup to AH, December 25, 1793, *PAH* 15:588.

25. TJ, First, Second, and Final State of the Report on Commerce, [August 23, 1791–April 13, 1792, February 5–23, 1793, December 16, 1793], *PTJ* 27:535–78. The quotations can be found on pages 574 and 575. See also the editor's note, ibid., 27:532–35; and Elkins and McKitrick, *Age of Federalism*, 378–81; Doran S. Ben-Atar, *The Origins of Jeffersonian Commercial Policy and Diplomacy* (New York, 1993), 17–133. The quotation can be found in *PJT* 27:574. As for ministerial intentions toward America, TJ had read Lord Sheffield (John Baker Holroyd), *Observations on the Commerce of the American States* (London, 1784), and he had received from William Temple Franklin the secret communiqué of Lord Hawkesbury (Charles Jenkinson) that formed the basis of British commercial policy toward the United States.

26. TJ to Martha Jefferson Randolph, December 22, 1793, *PTJ* 27:608; GW to TJ, January 1, 1794, ibid., 28:3.

27. *JMB* 2:910–12; TJ to JM, April 27, 1795, *PTJ* 28:339; TJ to Gates, February 3, 1794, ibid., 28:14. The AH quote can be found in Ferling, *A Leap in the Dark*, 366.

28. TJ to JM, April 3, October 30, 1794, *PTJ* 28:50, 337; TJ to JA, April 25, 1794, February 6, 1795, ibid., 28:57, 261; Edmund Randolph to TJ, August 28, 1794, ibid., 28:117–19; TJ to Randolph, September 7, 1794, ibid., 28:148; TJ to GW, May 14, 1794, ibid., 28:74–75; TJ to Robert Morris, February 19, 1795, ibid., 28:268.

29. TJ to Wythe, April 18, 1795, *PTJ* 28:337; TJ to William Branch Giles, April 27, 1795,

ibid., 28:337; TJ to JA, May 27, 1795, ibid., 28:363; TJ to Alexander Donald, May 30, 1795, ibid., 28:366.

30. Jack McLaughlin, *Jefferson and Monticello: The Biography of a Builder* (New York, 1988), 9–10, 20–25, 162–63, 228–34, 356–59, 361–68. On life at Monticello, see the account by Margaret Bayard Smith in Merrill D. Peterson, ed., *Visitors to Monticello* (Charlottesville, Va., 1989), 49.

31. TJ to John Bolling, October 7, 1791, *PTJ* 22:198–99; TJ to Randolph, January 8, 1792, January 24, 1793, ibid., 23:33; 24:91; TJ to James Lyle, April 15, 1793, ibid., 25:550–51; TJ to Jean Nicolas Démeunier, April 29, 1795, ibid., 28:341. On TJ's farming plan, see the account of the duc de La Rochefoucauld-Liancourt, who visited Monticello in 1796. It can be found in Peterson, *Visitors to Monticello*, 23–27. The "contemplative mind" quote is in ibid., page 23. For a short, informative essay, see Lucia Stanton, "Thomas Jefferson: Planter and Farmer," in Francis D. Cogliano, ed., *A Companion to Thomas Jefferson* (Chichester, England, 2011), 253–70. On the industry at Monticello and TJ's earnings from the production of nails, see Henry Wiencek, *Master of the Mountain: Thomas Jefferson and His Slaves* (New York, 2012), 92–93.

32. Wiencek, *Master of the Mountain*, 113, 149; William Cohen, "Thomas Jefferson and the Problem of Slavery," *Journal of American History* 56 (1969): 503–26; Lucia Stanton, "'Those Who Labor for My Happiness': Thomas Jefferson and His Slaves," in Peter S. Onuf, ed., *Jeffersonian Legacies* (Charlottesville, Va., 1993), 158–60; Lucia Stanton, *"Those Who Labor for My Happiness": Slavery at Thomas Jefferson's Monticello* (Charlottesville, Va., 2012). To contrast TJ's treatment of his slaves with practices elsewhere, including at GW's Mount Vernon, see John Ferling, *The First of Men: A Life of George Washington* (reprint, New York, 2010), 476–78; and Henry Wiencek, *The Imperfect God: George Washington, His Slaves, and the Creation of America* (New York, 2005), 46–48, 348–49.

33. TJ to James Lyle, July 10, 1795, *PTJ* 28:405–6; TJ to Démeunier, April 29, 1795, ibid., 28:341. On TJ's labor-management plans, see Stephen B. Hodin, "The Mechanisms of Monticello: Saving Labor in Jefferson's America," *Journal of the Early Republic* 26 (2006): 377–418.

34. TJ to Constantin Volney, April 10, 1796, *PTJ* 29:61.

35. TJ to Wythe, October 23, 1794, *PTJ* 28:181; TJ to Volney, April 10, 1796, ibid., 29:61. On the rebuilding of Monticello in these two paragraphs, see McLaughlin, *Jefferson and Monticello*, 239–338. The "general gloom" and "grand & awful" quotes are from the recollection left by Anna Thornton. See her account in Peterson, *Visitors to Monticello*, 34–35.

36. TJ to Maria Cosway, June 23, 1790, *PTJ* 16:550–51; Maria Cosway to TJ, April 6, 1790, ibid., 16:312–13; TJ to Angelica Church, June 7, November 27, 1793, ibid., 26:215; 27:449; Church to TJ, August 19, 1793, ibid., 26:723.

37. Maria Cosway to TJ, November 13, 24, 1794, *PTJ* 28:201, 209–11.

38. TJ to Maria Cosway, September 8, 1795, *PTJ* 28:455–56.

39. Maria Cosway to TJ, December 4, 1795, *PTJ* 28:543–44.

40. "The Memoirs of Madison Hemings" (March 13, 1873), in Annette Gordon-Reed, *Thomas Jefferson and Sally Hemings: An American Controversy* (Charlottesville, Va., 1997), 245–48. All of the quotations from his account can be found on page 246.

41. Annette Gordon-Reed, *The Hemingses of Monticello: An American Family* (New York, 2008), 269, 294, 304, 315, 382, 477. The quotations can be found on pages 269 and 304.

42. The best secondary sources on Jefferson and Sally Hemings are the two books by Annette Gordon-Reed—*Thomas Jefferson and Sally Hemings* and *The Hemingses of Monticello*— and Fawn Brodie, *TJ*, 361–95. This study draws extensively on those three important works. On DNA testing to determine the possibility of TJ's paternity of at least one of Hemings'

children, see Eugene Foster, "Jefferson Fathered Slave's Last Child," *Nature* 396 (November 5, 1998): 27–28; and Foster's response to letters in ibid., 397 (January 7, 1999): 32. The DNA tests were conducted on male-line descendants of two sons of Field Jefferson, who was TJ's paternal uncle, and a male-line descendant of Eston Hemings, who was Sally Hemings's last child, and others. The tests divulged a link with the male descendants of Field Jefferson, meaning that one of the eight Jeffersons alive in 1808 could have been the father of Eston Hemings, and might have fathered Sally's other children. The eight were TJ, his brother Randolph, the five sons of Randolph, and a cousin, George Jefferson. While the tests did not categorically establish TJ's paternity, circumstantial evidence points toward him as the most plausible father of her children. He owned Sally Hemings, she lived at Monticello, he was home nine months before the birth of each of her children, and late in life he freed all of her children, a rarity for TJ. Although I believe that TJ was the father of the six children that Sally Hemings bore between 1795 and 1808, there are skeptics. For a collection of essays by doubters, see Eyler Robert Coates Jr., ed., *The Jefferson-Hemings Myth: An American Travesty* (Charlottesville, Va., 2001). On TJ having owned six hundred slaves in his lifetime, see Cassandra Pybus, "Thomas Jefferson and Slavery," in Cogliano, *A Companion to Thomas Jefferson*, 272.

43. AH to GW, June 21, 1793, *PAH* 15:13; AH to Frederick A. C. Muhlenberg, December 16, 1793, ibid., 15:461–62; TJ to GW, July 31, 1793, *PTJ* 26:593.

44. AH to GW, April 7, 8, 1794, *PAH* 16:245, 249–53; GW to AH, April 8, 1794, ibid., 16:249.

45. TJ to JM, April 3, 1794, *PTJ* 28:49. The JM quotation can be found in Elkins and McKitrick, *Age of Federalism*, 384.

46. AH, "Americanus," no. 1 and 2, January 31, February 7, 1794, *PAH* 15:669–78; 16:12–19; TJ to JM, April 3, 1794, *PTJ* 28:49; JM to TJ, March 2, 1794, ibid., 15:269–70. The quotations in AH's essays can be found in *PAH* 15:671, 675; 16:13.

47. AH to GW, March 8, 1794, *PAH* 16:134–36; editor's note, ibid., 16:130–34; JM to TJ, March 12, 14, 26, 1794, *PTJ* 28:35, 38, 43–44; TJ to JM, April 3, 1794, ibid., 28:49–50.

48. AH to GW, April 14, 1794, *PAH* 16:266–79; TJ to JM, April 3, 1794, *PTJ* 28:49; Wood, *Empire of Liberty*, 193.

49. The comments on AH can be found in the editor's note, *PAH* 16:263–64. TJ's comment is in TJ to Monroe, April 24, 1794, *PTJ* 28:55.

50. AH to GW, April 14, 1794, *PAH* 16:278; Resolution of the Democratic Society of Pennsylvania, May 8, 1794, Foner, *Democratic-Republican Societies*, 105; Resolution of the Democratic Society of the County of Washington, June 23, 1794, ibid., 134; JM to TJ, May 11, 1794, *PTJ* 28:73.

51. Link, *Democratic-Republican Societies*, 54; Foner, *Democratic-Republican Societies*, 18, 36; Thomas P. Slaughter, *The Whiskey Rebellion: Frontier Epilogue to the American Revolution* (New York, 1986), 67, 88, 106–7; Elkins and McKitrick, *Age of Federalism*, 471.

52. William Hogeland, *The Whiskey Rebellion: George Washington, Alexander Hamilton, and the Frontier Rebels Who Challenged America's Newfound Sovereignty* (New York, 2006), 62–69; Terry Bouton, "William Findley, David Bradford, and the Pennsylvania Regulation of 1794," in Young et. al., *Revolutionary Founders*, 233–51.

53. TJ to GW, May 23, 1792, *PTJ* 23:536; TJ, "Notes of Agenda to Reduce the Government to True Principles," [ca. July 11, 1792], ibid., 24:215; Slaughter, *Whiskey Rebellion*, 95–105, 113–14; John Steele to GW, May 23, 1792, *PGWP* 7:181, 182n; GW to David Humphreys, July 20, 1791, ibid., 8:359. On taxation, see Robin L. Einhorn, *American Taxation, American Slavery* (Chicago, 2006), 158–174, 187.

54. AH to GW, September 1, 1792, *PAH* 12:311–12; GW to AH, July 29, August 5, September 7, 17, 1792, ibid., 12:129–30, 166–67, 331–33, 391–92. See also Sean Wilentz, *The Rise of American Democracy: Jefferson to Lincoln* (New York, 2005), 63–64. The "make us examples" quotation is in Bouton, "William Findley, David Bradford, and the Pennsylvania Regulation of 1794," Young et. al., *Revolutionary Founders*, 243.

55. Foner, *Democratic-Republican Societies*, 94, 127–28, 132, 133, 135, 136; Link, *Democratic-Republican Societies*, 131, 133. Wilentz, *Rise of American Democracy*, 63.

56. Conference Concerning the Insurrection in Western Pennsylvania, August 2, 1794, *PAH* 17:9–13; AH to GW, August 2, 5, 1794, ibid., 17:15–19, 24–58; GW, Proclamation, August 7, 1794, *WW* 33:475–76. AH's "Tully" essays can be found in *PAH* 17:132–35, 148–50, 159–61, and 178–80.

57. Knox to AH, November 24, 1794, *PAH* 17:392. Knox told AH of Betsey's miscarriage, adding that "she is extremely desirous of your presence in order to tranquilize her."

58. AH to Angelica Church, October 23, 1794, *PAH* 17:340; AH to Rufus King, October 30, 1794, ibid., 17:348. AH's bombast about skewering and hanging insurgents is quoted in Chernow, *AH*, 475.

59. AH to Samuel Hodgdon, October 7, 1794, *PAH* 17:309, 310; AH to Knox, October 8, 1794, ibid., 17:312–13; AH to Mifflin, October 17, 1794, ibid., 17:327.

60. Slaughter, *Whiskey Rebellion*, 217.

61. AH to GW, October 29, November 8, 15, 1794, *PAH* 17:347, 361, 372; Slaughter, *Whiskey Rebellion*, 217–20.

62. TJ to JM, October 30, December 28, 1794, *PTJ* 28:182, 229; TJ to Monroe, May 26, 1795, ibid., 28:359.

63. GW, Sixth State of the Union Address, November 19, 1794, *WW* 34:29–35. The quotations can be found on pages 28–29.

64. TJ to JM, December 28, 1794, *PTJ* 28:228–30; TJ to Giles, December 17, 1794, ibid., 28:219; JM to TJ, November 30, 1794, ibid., 28:212.

CHAPTER 12: "A COLOSSUS TO THE ANTIREPUBLICAN PARTY": THE ELECTION OF 1796

Malone, *TJ* 3:261–94; Peterson, *TJ*, 542–60; Cunningham, *TJ*, 199–205; Chernow, *AH*, 482–516; Cooke, *AH*, 158–83; Miller, *AH*, 415–50.

1. AH to GW, December 1, 1794, *PAH* 17:413; GW to AH, February 2, 1795, ibid., 18:247–48.

2. JM to TJ, January 11, February 15, 1795, *PTJ* 28:245, 265.

3. AH to Angelica Church, March 6, 1795, *PAH* 18:288.

4. JM to TJ, January 26, 1795, *PTJ* 28:251.

5. AH to Rufus King, February 21, 1795, *PAH* 18:278–79; AH to Angelica Church, December 8, 1794, March 6, 1795, ibid., 17:429; 18:288.

6. GW to AH, July 3, 1795, *PAH* 18:398–400.

7. AH, Remarks on the Treaty of Amity Commerce and Navigation lately made between the United States and Great Britain, [July 9–11, 1795], *PAH* 18:404–54. The quotations can be found on pages 407, 411, 418, 432, and 451. See also AH conversation with George Beckwith, [October 1789], ibid., 5:484.

8. TJ to Thomas M. Randolph, August 11, 1795, *PTJ* 28:435; TJ to JM, September 21, 1795, ibid., 28:476; TJ to Edward Rutledge, November 30, 1795, ibid., 28:542.

9. GW to AH, July 13, 29, August 31, 1795, *PAH* 18:461–63, 524; 19:205.

10. Joanne B. Freeman, *Affairs of Honor: National Politics in the New Republic* (New Haven, 2001), xiii–xv, 171. The "hissings" quote is on page xiii.

11. AH's "Defence" series can be found in *PAH*, vols. 18, 19, and 20. The publication date for each essay can be found in the editor's note in ibid., 18:476. The quotations can be found in ibid., 18:481 and 499.

12. GW to AH, July 19, August 31, 1795, *PAH* 18:524; 19:205.

13. TJ to JM, September 21, 1795, *PTJ* 28:475.

14. Ibid.

15. GW to AH, March 31, 1796, *PAH* 20:103; AH, "To the Citizens Who Shall be Convened this Day in the Fields in the City of New York," ibid., 20:131–34.

16. Rudolph M. Bell, *Party and Faction in American Politics: The House of Representatives, 1789–1801* (Westport, Conn., 1973), 191.

17. *PAH* 20:169n; GW to AH, June 26, 1796, ibid., 20:239.

18. GW, Farewell Address, September 19, 1796, *WW* 35:214–38; AH to GW, May 10, June 1, July 5, 30, August 10, September 4, 5, 8, 1796, *PAH* 20:173–74, 214–15, 246–47, 264–65, 293–94, 316, 317–18, 320–211; GW to AH, May 15, June 26, August 10, 25, September 1, 6, 1796, ibid., 20:174–78, 237–40, 292–93, 307–9, 311–14, 318–19; AH, Abstract Points to Form an Address [May 16–July 5, 1796], ibid., 20:178–83; AH, Draft of Washington's Farewell Address [July 30, 1796], ibid., 20:265–88; AH, Draft on the Plan of Incorporating, [August 10, 1796], ibid., 20:294–303.

19. JM to James Monroe, September 29, 1796, *PJM* 17:403; TJ to JM, December 17, 1796, *PTJ* 29:223.

20. GW to John Jay, May 8, 1796, *WW* 35:37; JA to Abigail Adams, January 5, 1796, Adams Family Papers, Massachusetts Historical Society (Boston, 1954–1959), microfilm ed., reel 381.

21. TJ to JA, July 17, August 30, 1791, *PTJ* 20:302–3, 310–11; JA to TJ, July 29, 1791, ibid., 20:305–7; "The Rights of Man," editor's note, ibid., 20:268–90; TJ to JM, May 9, 1791, ibid., 20:293.

22. JA to TJ, January 31, April 6, 1796, *PTJ* 28:600; 29:58–59; TJ to JA, February 28, 1796, ibid., 28:618–19.

23. TJ to JM, December 28, 1794, April 27, 1795, *PTJ* 28:230, 338–39; JM to TJ, March 23, 1795, February 7, 1796, ibid., 28:315, 607.

24. TJ to Constantin Volney, December 9, 1795, *PTJ* 28:551; TJ to JA, February 28, 1796, ibid., 28: 619; TJ to Monroe, July 10, 1796, ibid., 29:147.

25. Quoted in Nancy Isenberg, *Fallen Founder: The Life of Aaron Burr* (New York, 2007), 116.

26. On the opposition of JM and James Monroe to Burr in 1792, see Isenberg, *Fallen Founder*, 115–18; Noble Cunningham, *The Jeffersonian Republicans: The Formation of Party Organization, 1789–1801* (Chapel Hill, N.C., 1957), 45–49.

27. AH to [?] September 21, 26, 1792, *PAH* 12:408, 480.

28. On the life of Burr, see Isenberg, *Fallen Founder*. For her excellent appraisal of Hamilton's savage attacks on Burr in 1792, see pages 118–20.

29. On Burr's campaigning in 1796, see Isenberg, *Fallen Founder*, 145–48.

30. Chilton Williamson, *American Suffrage: From Property to Democracy, 1760–1860* (Princeton, N.J., 1960), 84–86, 89, 100, 107, 117, 122–24; Alexander Keyssar, *The Right to Vote: The Contested History of Democracy in the United States* (New York, 2000), 6–10, 21, 29; Isenberg, *Fallen Founder*, 144–54.

31. Edmond Berkeley and Dorothy Smith Berkeley, *John Beckley: Zealous Partisan in a Nation Divided* (Philadelphia, 1973), 146; Theodore Sedgwick to Rufus King, March 12, 1797,

Sedgwick Letterbook, Massachusetts Historical Society; Cunningham, *Jeffersonian Republicans*, 97–103; David Sisson, *The American Revolution of 1800* (New York, 1974), 243–46; Robert M. S. McDonald, "Was There a Religious Revolution of 1800?" in James Horn, Jan Ellen Lewis, and Peter S. Onuf, eds., *The Revolution of 1800: Democracy, Race, and the New Republic* (Charlottesville, Va., 2002), 175–80; "Documents Relating to the 1796 Campaign for Electors in Virginia," *PTJ* 29:193–99. The quotation on TJ as weak and wavering can be found in Bernstein, *TJ*, 115. The quotation on the government abandoning TJ is the editor's wording and can be found in *PTJ* 29:194.

32. AH to [?], November 8, 1796, *PAH* 20:376.

33. AH's twenty-five "Phocion" essays appeared in the *Gazette of the United States* between October 14 and November 24. The quotations in this paragraph can be found in the essays appearing on October 14, 19, 25, November 1, 4, 10, and 19, 1796. These essays do not appear in *PAH*, but his biographer, Ron Chernow, convincingly demonstrates AH's authorship. See Chernow, *AH*, 511–12.

34. [AH], "Phocion," *Gazette of the United States*, October 14, 15, 1796.

35. Quoted in James Roger Sharp, *American Politics in the Early Republic: The New Nation in Crisis* (New Haven, Conn., 1993), 149.

36. AH to [?], November 8, 1796, *PAH* 20:376–77.

37. JM to TJ, December 5, 1796, *PTJ* 29:214; TJ to William Cocke, October 21, 1796, ibid., 29:199; TJ to JM, December 17, 1796, ibid., 29:223; TJ to JA, December 28, 1796, ibid., 29:235.

38. The quotations can be found in Isenberg, *Fallen Founder*, 148, 152, and 154.

39. AH to King, December 16, 1796, *PAH* 20:445.

40. TJ to Volney, January 8, 1797, *PTJ* 29:258; TJ to James Sullivan, February 9, 1797, ibid., 29:289.

CHAPTER 13: "THE MAN IS STARK MAD": PARTISAN FRENZY

Malone, *TJ*, 3:295–458; Peterson, *TJ*, 543–625; Cunningham, *TJ*, 206–20; Chernow, *AH*, 517–602; Miller, *AH*, 451–508; Cooke, *AH*, 184–208.

1. TJ to JM, January 22, 1797, *PTJ* 29:270.

2. TJ to JA, December 28, 1796, *PTJ* 29:235; TJ to JM, January 1, 1797, ibid., 29:247–48; JM to TJ, January 15, 1797, ibid., 29:263–64.

3. TJ to Elbridge Gerry, May 13, 1797, *PTJ* 29:362.

4. TJ, Anas, March 2, 1797, in Padover, *CTJ*, 1271. On JM's fear of the sea, see JM to TJ, April 27, 1785, *PTJ* 8:115. JM mysteriously said that a long voyage would "be unfriendly to a singular disease of my constitution."

5. TJ to King, February 15, 1797, *PAH* 20: 515–16.

6. Timothy Pickering to AH, March 26, 1797, *PAH* 20:549; Oliver Wolcott to AH, March 31, 1797, ibid., 20:573; McHenry to AH, April 14, 1797, ibid., 21:48.

7. AH to Pickering, March 26, 29, 1797, *PAH* 20:549, 557.

8. AH to Smith, April 10, 1797, *PAH* 21:29–41. See also AH's much shorter version in his letter of March 30 to Wolcott. It can be found in ibid., 20:567. His "receive the law" remark is in that missive.

9. TJ to Gerry, May 13, 1797, *PTJ* 29:363–64.

10. Quoted in Stanley Elkins and Eric McKitrick, *The Age of Federalism* (New York, 1993), 566.

11. AH to Pickering, May 11, 1797, *PAH* 21:82; John Ferling, *John Adams: A Life* (Knoxville, Tenn., 1992), 345.

12. TJ to Benjamin Rush, January 22, 1797, *PTJ* 29:275.

13. TJ to Henry Knox, April 8, 1800, *PTJ* 31:488; TJ to William Hamilton, April 22, 1800, ibid., 31:534.

14. TJ to Edward Rutledge, June 24, 1797, *PTJ* 29:456; TJ to William Hamilton, April 22, 1800, ibid., 31:534; TJ to Angelica Church, January 11, 1798, ibid., 30:23.

15. TJ to Philip Mazzei, April 24, 1796, *PTJ* 29:82.

16. See the lengthy editor's note on the "Mazzei Letter" in *PTJ* 29:73-81. The "treasonable" quote is in editor's note, ibid., 29:76.

17. TJ to GW, June 19, 1796, *PTJ* 29:127-28.

18. TJ to Walter Jones, January 2, 1814, in Padover, *CTJ*, 924-25.

19. AH to John Fenno, [July 17-22, 1797], *PAH* 21:167.

20. Wolcott to AH, July 3, 1797, *PAH* 21:144-45; AH to Jeremiah Wadsworth, July 28, 1797, ibid., 21:187.

21. AH, *Observations on Certain Documents Contained . . . In Which the Charge of Speculation Against Alexander Hamilton . . . is Fully Refuted, Written by Himself* (Philadelphia, 1797), in *PAH* 21:238-85. The quotations can be found on pages 243 and 252.

22. John Barnes to TJ, October 3, 1797, *PTJ* 29:542.

23. Callender to TJ, September 28, 1797, *PTJ* 29:536-37; TJ to John Taylor, October 8, 1797, ibid., 29:546. The "creep under Mrs. R's petticoats" quote is in Nancy Isenberg, *Fallen Founder: The Life of Aaron Burr* (New York, 2007), 167.

24. Quoted in Chernow, *AH*, 533.

25. Henry Lee to AH, May 6, 1793, *PAH* 14:416.

26. Venable to AH, July 9, 10, 1797, *PAH* 21:153-54, 159. Wolcott to AH, July 3, 1797, ibid., 21:145. Venable's quotation is in ibid., 21:159.

27. Harry Ammon, *James Monroe: The Quest for National Identity* (New York, 1971), 81-156. The "monarchy party" quote is on page 103.

28. David Gelsen's Account of an Interview between Alexander Hamilton and James Monroe, July 11, 1797, *PAH* 21:159-62.

29. James Monroe and Muhlenberg to AH, July 17, 1797, *PAH* 21:168-70. Venable was out of town and played no part in the response to AH.

30. AH to Monroe and Muhlenberg, July 17, 1797, *PAH* 21:170-72; AH to Monroe, July 17, 18, 20, 22, 28, August 4, 9, January [?], 1798, ibid., 21:172-73, 174-75, 176-77, 180-81, 186, 200, 208, 346; Isenberg, *Fallen Founder*, 164-66.

31. JA to his cabinet, January 24, 1798, *PAH* 21:339-40; McHenry to AH, January 26, 1798, ibid., 21:339; AH to McHenry, [January 27-February 11], 1798, ibid., 21:341-46.

32. AH to Pickering, March 17, 1798, *PAH* 21:364-66.

33. JA, Message, *Adams Papers*, 1639-1889, microfilm edition, 608 reels (Boston: Massachusetts Historical Society, 1954-1959), reel 387; JA to McHenry, October 22, 1798, ibid., reel 391; JA, "Message to Congress," March 19, 1798, in James D. Richardson, ed., *A Compilation of the Messages and Papers of the Presidents* (New York, 1897-1917), 1:264-65.

34. TJ to JM, March 21, April 5, 1798, *PTJ* 30:189-90, 191-92, 244-45. TJ penned two letters to JM on March 21. The quotations can be found on pages 189, 191, and 245.

35. TJ to JM, April 6, 1798, *PTJ* 30:250-51. On TJ's fears for the survival of Republicanism, see Gordon S. Wood, *Empire of Liberty: A History of the Early Republic, 1789-1815* (New York,

2009), 241. On TJ's belief that John Marshall fabricated some of his reports on the French government's behavior, see TJ to Edmund Pendleton, January 29, April 22, 1799, *PTJ* 30:661; 31:97.

36. Quoted in Alexander DeConde, *The Quasi-War: The Politics and Diplomacy of the Undeclared War with France, 1797–1801* (New York, 1966), 328.

37. John C. Miller, *Crisis in Freedom: The Alien and Sedition Acts* (Boston, 1951), 22.

38. AH, "The Stand," nos. 1–7 [March 30–April 21, 1798], *PAH* 21:381–87, 390–96, 402–8, 412–18, 418–32, 434–440, 441–47. The quotations are on pages 383–84 and 446. The "satellites of France" quotation is from a separate essay by AH titled "A French Faction." It, too, appeared in April 1798 and is in ibid., 21:452–53. That quote can be found on page 452.

39. John Ferling, *A Leap in the Dark: The Struggle to Create the American Republic* (New York, 2003), 424–25. The Abigail Adams quote is on page 425.

40. Wood, *Empire of Liberty*, 245–46, 263–64. On the army from 1789 through the creation of the New Army, a succinct overview is available in *PAH* 22:384–85n, though the best account of its creation, and the Federalists' motives in bringing it into being, can be found in Richard H. Kohn, *Eagle and Sword: The Federalists and the Creation of the Military Establishment in America, 1783–1802* (New York, 1975), 224–29. See also TJ to JM, February 5, 1799, *PTJ* 31:9. The term "frontier constabulary" is that of Kohn, *Eagle and Sword*, 244.

41. James Roger Sharp, *American Politics in the Early Republic: The New Nation in Crisis* (New Haven, Conn., 1993), 176.

42. Quoted in John C. Miller, *The Federalist Era, 1789–1801* (New York, 1960), 228.

43. Chernow, *AH*, 570.

44. The quotations can be found in Wood, *Empire of Liberty*, 249, 250.

45. TJ to JM, April 26, 1798, *PTJ* 30:300; TJ to Thomas Mann Randolph Jr., May 9, 1798, ibid., 30:341.

46. Quoted in James Morton Smith, *Freedom's Fetters: The Alien and Sedition Laws and American Civil Liberties* (Ithaca, N.Y., 1956), 120. The texts of the four laws can be found in ibid., 435–42.

47. TJ to John Taylor, November 26, 1798, *PTJ* 30:589.

48. AH to Pickering, June 7, 1798, *PAH* 21:495; AH to GW, May 19, 1798, ibid., 21:467; AH to Wolcott, June 29, 1798, ibid., 21:522; TJ to JM, June 7, 1798, *PTJ* 30:393.

49. JA to GW, June 22, 1798, *PGW: Ret. Ser.* 2:351–52; GW to JA, July 4, 1798, ibid., 2:368–71.

50. GW to JA, July 13, 1798, *PGW: Ret. Ser.* 2:402–4; GW, Suggestions for Military Appointments, July 14, 1798, ibid., 2:414–15.

51. JA to McHenry, August 29, September 30, 1798, *PAH* 22:8n, 16; GW to JA, September 25, 1798, *PGW: Ret. Ser.* 3:36–43.

52. GW to AH, August 21, October 8, 1797, *PAH* 21:214–15, 298–99.

53. AH to GW, May 19, June 2, 1798, *PAH* 21:466–68, 479–80; GW to AH, May 27, 1798, ibid., 21:470–74.

54. AH to McHenry, February 6, 1799, *PAH* 22:467.

55. TJ to John Taylor, June 4, 1798, *PTJ* 30:388, 389; TJ to William Strickland, March 23, 1798, ibid., 30:212–13.

56. Manning J. Dauer, *The Adams Federalists* (Baltimore, 1953), 233.

57. For an example of TJ's intelligence system, see Notes on Conversations with Abraham Baldwin, John Brown, and John Hunter, [March 11, 1798], *PTJ* 30:172–73.

58. TJ to Samuel Smith, August 22, 1798, *PTJ* 30:484–85; TJ to Stevens Thomson Mason, October 11, 1798, ibid., 30:560; TJ to Taylor, November 26, 1798, ibid., 30:589; TJ to Tadeusz Kosciuszko, June 18, 1798, ibid., 30:416.

59. Quoted in Saul Cornell, *The Other Founders: Anti-Federalism and the Dissenting Tradition in America, 1788-1828* (Chapel Hill, N.C., 1999), 229.

60. TJ to John Wise, February 12, 1798, *PTJ* 30:98.

61. TJ to JM, February 5, 1799, *PTJ* 31:9; Kohn, *Eagle and Sword*, 225.

62. John Taylor to TJ, May 13, 1798, *PTJ* 30:348.

63. Quoted in Kohn, *Eagle and Sword*, 225.

64. Sharp, *American Politics in the Early Republic*, 203-5.

65. TJ to JM, November 17, 1798, January 30, 1799, *PTJ* 30: 580, 666; TJ to Gerry, January 26, 1799, ibid., 30:646.

66. TJ to Hugh Williamson, February 11, 1798, *PTJ* 30:94; TJ to Kosciuszko, February 21, 1799, ibid., 31:52; TJ to Page, January 24, 1799, ibid., 30:641; TJ to Taylor, November 26, 1798, ibid., 30:589. When John Taylor of Caroline County, Virginia, advocated secession rather than remain in a Union in which the South was subordinate to an anti-republican northern majority, TJ urged "a little patience" as "the body of our countrymen is substantially republican through every part of the union." See Taylor to TJ, May 15, 1798, ibid., 30:348; TJ to Taylor, June 4, 1798, ibid., 30:388-89.

67. TJ's Fair Copy of the Kentucky Resolution, [before October 4, 1798], *PTJ* 30:543-49; Resolutions Adopted by the Kentucky General Assembly, November 10, 1798, ibid., 30:551-55; JM to TJ, December 29, 1798, December 29, 1799, ibid., 30:606; 31:278; editor's notes, ibid., 30:529-35; 31:279-80n; Sharp, *American Politics in the Early Republic*, 188-200.

68. Ferling, *A Leap in the Dark*, 442; TJ to JM, January 3, 1799, *PTJ* 30:610.

69. Quoted in Kohn, *Eagle and Sword*, 230.

70. JA to McHenry, August 29, September 13, 1798, Charles Francis Adams, *The Works of John Adams, Second President* . . . (Boston, 1850-1856), 8:588, 594; JA to John Trumbull, July 23, November [?], 1805, *Adams Papers*, microfilm edition, reel 118; JA to F. A. Vanderkemp, August 23, 1806, April 3, 1815, Simon Gratz Collection, Historical Society of Pennsylvania; JA to Rush, August 23, September 30, December 4, 1805, January 25, 1806, September 2, November 11, 1807, April 18, 1808, August 28, 1811, in John A. Schutz and Douglass Adair, eds., *The Spur of Fame: Dialogues of John Adams and Benjamin Rush, 1805-1813* (San Marino, Cal., 1966), 35, 42, 45, 47-48, 94-95, 98-99, 113, 192; JA to Benjamin Waterhouse, July 12, 1811, in Worthington C. Ford, ed., *Statesman and Friend: Correspondence of John Adams and Benjamin Waterhouse, 1784-1822* (Boston, 1927), 65; JA to William Cunningham, October 15, 1808, in *Correspondence between the Hon. John Adams . . . and the Late William Cunningham* (Boston, 1823), 44.

71. Abigail Adams's "second Buonaparty" quote is in DeConde, *Quasi-War*, 97. See also TJ to Thomas M. Randolph, February 2, 1800, *PTJ* 31:358; the additional comments by the First Lady can be found in Edith B. Gelles, *Abigail and John: Portrait of a Marriage* (New York, 2009), 240.

72. AH to McHenry, [January 27-February 11], 1798, *PAH* 21:345. The McHenry quote can be found in Page Smith, *John Adams* (Garden City, N.Y., 1962), 2:989.

73. AH to James Gunn, December 22, 1798, *PAH* 22:389.

74. AH to Harrison Gray Otis, January 26, 1799, *PAH* 22:440-41.

75. AH to Francisco de Miranda, August 22, 1798, *PAH* 22:156.

76. GW to McHenry, December 13, 1798, *PGW: Ret. Ser.* 3:253.

77. Quoted in Chernow, *AH*, 567-68.

78. Quoted in DeConde, *Quasi-War*, 119.

79. Quoted in Elkins and McKitrick, *Age of Federalism*, 617.

80. Quoted in David McCullough, *John Adams* (New York, 2001), 518.

81. Kohn, *Eagle and Sword*, 246–48. The AH quotation can be found in William B. Skelton, *An American Profession of Arms: The Army Officer Corps, 1784–1861* (Lawrence, Kans., 1992), 24.

82. On AH and hats, see AH to McHenry, May 18, 1799, *PAH* 23:122; Skelton, *An American Profession of Arms*, 96–98. The *PAH*, vols. 22 and 23, are filled with similar instances of micromanagement. For the lists ranking the officers, see ibid., 22:89–146, 270–312, and 317–39. On the army, and JA taking no steps to recruit it, see ibid., 22:387–88n.

83. AH to Otis, December 28, 1798, *PAH* 22:394.

84. William Heth to AH, January 14, 18, 1799, *PAH* 22:413–15, 422–24, The quotations are on pages 415 and 423.

85. AH to King, February 6, 1799, *PAH* 22:465.

86. AH to Theodore Sedgwick, February 1, 1799, *PAH* 22:452–53.

87. JA, Second Annual Address, December 8, 1798, Richardson, *Messages of the Presidents*, 1:261–65; TJ to Randolph, December 20, 1798, *PTJ* 30:604; AH to Otis, December 27, 1798, *PAH* 22:393–04; AH to Gunn, December 22, 1798, ibid., 22:388–89; DeConde, *Quasi-War*, 168–69.

88. JA to GW, February 19, 1799, *PGW: Ret. Ser.* 3:388; Elkins and McKitrick, *Age of Federalism*, 615–41; Ferling, *John Adams*, 372–85; DeConde, *Quasi-War*, 142–22.

89. TJ to Randolph, February 19, 1799, *PTJ* 31:50; Henry Remsen, March 4, 1800, ibid., 31:415; TJ to Everard Meade, April 8, 1800, ibid., 31:489.

90. DeConde, *Quasi-War*, 221–22.

91. Elkins and McKitrick, *Age of Federalism*, 639–40; DeConde, *Quasi-War*, 220.

92. TJ to Remsen, October 14, 1799, *PAH* 31:212.

93. *Correspondence between the Hon. John Adams . . . and the Late William Cunningham*, 29–30. The "impertinent ignoramus" quote can be found in John Ferling, *Adams vs. Jefferson: The Tumultuous Election of 1800* (New York, 2004), 124. A nearly identical version of AH's meeting with the president was provided by Abigail Adams, who was relating what her husband told her soon after the episode. See Abigail Adams to Mary Cranch, December 30, 1799, in Stewart Mitchell, ed., *New Letters of Abigail Adams, 1788–1801* (Boston, 1947), 224–25. Both JA's and the First Lady's versions can also be found in *PAH* 23:546–47n.

94. TJ to Monroe, January 12, 1800, *PTJ* 31:301.

95. John Trumbull to GW, June 22, August 10, 1799, *PGW: Ret. Ser.* 4:144, 236; Gouverneur Morris to GW, December 9, 1799, ibid., 4:452–53. Morris's letter arrived at Mount Vernon after GW's death.

96. AH to Tobias Lear, January 2, 1800, *PAH* 24:155; AH to Charles Cotesworth Pinckney, December 22, 1799, ibid., 24:116; AH to Martha Washington, January 12, 1800, ibid., 24:184–85. AH marched in the state funeral ceremony in Philadelphia on December 26. After a sojourn at home, TJ was unable to reach the capital in time to participate in the funeral.

97. *PAH* 22:386–88n.

98. AH to Jonathan Dayton, [October–November, 1799], *PAH* 23:599–604.

CHAPTER 14: "THE GIGG IS UP": THE ELECTION OF 1800

1. TJ to Benjamin Rush, September 12, 1799, *PTJ* 31:183.

2. TJ to Joseph Priestley, January 27, 1800, *PTJ* 31:341.

3. Ibid.; TJ to JM, May 12, 1800, ibid., 31:579; TJ to Charles Pinckney, November 4, 1800, ibid., 32:243.

4. For a good example of TJ's analysis of the likely outcome of the 1800 presidential election, see TJ to JM, March 4, 1800, *PTJ* 31:408-9.

5. TJ to James Monroe, January 12, 1800, *PTJ* 31:300-301.

6. TJ to Robert R. Livingston, April 30, 1800, *PTJ* 31:550; Joseph Barnes to TJ, October 25, 1799, March 4, 10, 1800, ibid., 31:330, 405, 226, 427; TJ to Mary Jefferson Eppes, February 15, 1801, ibid., 32:593; TJ to Monroe, January 12, 1800, ibid., 31:301.

7. TJ to Mary Jefferson Eppes, February 15, 1801, *PTJ* 32:593; TJ to Elbridge Gerry, May 13, 1797, ibid., 29:362.

8. AH to Rufus King, January 5, 1800, *PAH* 24:167; AH to Henry Lee, March 7, 1800, ibid., 24:299.

9. AH to Theodore Sedgwick, May 10, 1800, *PAH* 24:475.

10. AH to King, May 4, 1796, *PAH* 20:158.

11. Burr to TJ, May 5, 1800, *PTJ* 31:557. The foregoing paragraphs on the New York contest draws on Alfred Young, *The Democratic Republicans of New York, The Origins: 1763-1797* (Chapel Hill, N.C., 1967), 474-76; William Merrill and Sean Wilentz, eds., *The Key of Liberty: The Life and Democratic Writings of William Manning, "A Laborer," 1774-1814* (Cambridge, Mass., 1993), 59, 63-64, 73-74, 112, 126; Linda Kerber, "The Federalist Party," in Arthur M. Schlesinger Jr., ed., *History of U.S. Political Parties* (New York, 1973), 1:3-29; Gordon S. Wood, "The Enemy Is Us: Democratic Capitalism in the Early Republic," *Journal of the Early Republic* 16 (1996): 293-308; David Waldstreicher, "Federalism, the Style of Politics, and the Politics of Style," in Doran Ben-Atar and Barbara B. Oberg, eds., *Federalists Reconsidered* Charlottesville, Va., 1998), 99-117; Steven Watts, "Ministers, Misanthropes, and Mandarins: The Federalists and the Culture of Capitalism," ibid., 157-75; Alan Taylor, "From Fathers to Friends of the People: Political Personae in the Early Republic," ibid., 225-45; John Ferling, *Adams vs. Jefferson: The Tumultuous Election of 1800* (New York, 2004), 128-31; Nancy Isenberg, *Fallen Founder: The Life of Aaron Burr* (New York, 2007), 196-200; David Hackett Fischer, *The Revolution of American Conservatism: The Federalist Party in the Era of Jeffersonian Democracy* (New York, 1965); 9, 52, 95-96, 161, 308. Fischer deals with the election of 1800 throughout his book, including in the appendix.

12. TJ to Tadeusz Kosciuszko, May 7, 1800, *PTJ* 31:560.

13. AH to Sedgwick, May 4, 1800, *PAH* 24:453.

14. AH to Jay, May 7, 1800, *PAH* 24:464-66, 467n.

15. TJ to Thomas Mann Randolph Jr., May 7, 1800, *PTJ* 31:561.

16. Ferling, *Adams vs. Jefferson*, 132; Isenberg, *Fallen Founder*, 201-2.

17. McHenry to AH, June 2, 1800 [with McHenry to JA, May 31, 1800, enclosed], *PAH* 24:550-65. The quotations are on pages 555 and 557.

18. JA to Thomas Boylston Adams, July 14, 1800, *PAH* 24:574n; Abigail Adams to Thomas B. Adams, July 16, 1800, ibid., 24:575-76n.

19. AH to King, January 5, 1800, *PAH* 24:168; AH to Sedgwick, May 10, 1800, ibid., 24:475; AH to McHenry, June 6, 1800, ibid., 24:573.

20. Joseph Hale to King, July 9, 1800, *PAH* 24:577n; John Rutledge Jr. to AH, July 17, 1800, ibid., 25:30.

21. Sedgwick to King, September 26, 1800, *PAH* 24:451; AH to Charles Carroll of Carrollton, July 1, 1800, ibid., 25:1-2.

22. AH to JA, August 1, October 1, 1800, *PAH* 25:51, 125-26.

23. Thomas N. Baker, "'An Attack Well Directed': Aaron Burr Intrigues for the Presidency," *Journal of the Early Republic* 31 (2011): 560.

24. William Shaw to Abigail Adams, June 8, 1800, in *Adams Family Papers, 1639–1889*, microfilm edition, 608 reels (Boston, Massachusetts Historical Society, 1954–1959), reel 398; JA to James Lloyd, March 31, 1815, ibid., reel 122; Stephen G. Kurtz, *The Presidency of John Adams: The Collapse of Federalism, 1795–1800* (Philadelphia, 1957), 398; John Ferling, *John Adams: A Life* (reprint, New York, 2010), 402–3; Noble E. Cunningham Jr., "Election of 1800," in Arthur M. Schlesinger Jr., ed., *History of American Presidential Elections, 1789–1968* (New York, 1971), 1:115–16.

25. *JMB* 2:1019.

26. TJ, Summary of Public Service, [after September 2, 1800], *PTJ* 32:122–24.

27. TJ to Elbridge Gerry, January 26, 1799, *PTJ* 30:645–50; TJ to Amos Alexander, June 13, 1800, ibid., 32:6; TJ to Gideon Granger, August 13, 1800, ibid., 32:95–97; TJ to Jeremiah Moore, August 14, 1800, ibid., 32:102–3; TJ to Caesar A. Rodney, December 21, 1800, ibid., 32:336–37; TJ to John Vanmetre, September 4, 1800, ibid., 32:136; TJ to Samuel Smith, October 17, 1800, ibid., 32:227; Cunningham, "Election of 1800," in Schlesinger, *History of American Presidential Elections*, 1:114, 118–19. TJ's quote about disentangling from other nations can be found in *PTJ* 32:96.

28. Jeffrey L. Pasley, *"The Tyranny of Printers": Newspaper Politics in the Early Republic* (Charlottesville, Va., 2001), 157; Noble E. Cunningham, *The Jeffersonian Republicans: The Formation of Party Organization, 1789–1801* (Chapel Hill, N.C., 1957), 153–60.

29. For an expanded treatment of the campaign rhetoric in 1800, and the sources for the quotations in the foregoing paragraphs, see Ferling, *Adams vs. Jefferson*, 144–56. For the AH quotation regarding "Mazzeian Babel," see the editors' note, *PTJ* 29:79. Bernard Weisberger, *America Afire: Jefferson, Adams, and the Revolutionary Election of 1800* (New York, 2000); and Edward J. Larson, *A Magnificent Catastrophe: The Tumultuous Election of 1800: America's First Presidential Campaign* (New York, 2007), also treat the campaign in considerable detail. For the allegation about TJ and Sally Hemings, and the charge that he was a "libertine," see Brodie, *TJ*, 427.

30. AH to Wolcott, July 1, 1800, *PAH* 25:4–5; George Cabot to AH, August 21, 1800, ibid., 25:74–75. See also the editors' note in ibid., 25:169–85.

31. AH, *Letter from Alexander Hamilton*, *PAH* 25:186–234. The quotations are on pages 190, 192, 196, 210, 214, 226, 222, and 233. Historian Joanne Freeman, who has written extensively on dueling and its code, has suggested that when JA did not respond to AH's intemperate August letters regarding his alleged leadership of a British faction—which she said "contemporaries well recognized" as nothing less than the "ritualistic opening of an affair of honor"—AH believed the "code of honor entitled [him] to "post the president, condemning him before the world." See Joanne B. Freeman, *Affairs of Honor: National Politics in the New Republic* (New Haven, Conn., 2001), 149.

32. Kurtz, *The Presidency of John Adams*, 400–401; AH to Charles Carroll of Carrollton, July 1, 1800, *PAH* 25:2.

33. JM to TJ, January 10, 1801, *PTJ* 32:436–37. Webster's and Troup's quotations can be found in Ralph Adams Brown, *The Presidency of John Adams* (Lawrence, Kans., 1975), 185.

34. Brown, *The Presidency of John Adams*, 185.

35. TJ to Burr, December 15, 1800, *PTJ* 32:307.

36. TJ to Rush, December 14, 1800, *PTJ* 32:306; Thomas McKean to TJ, December 15, 1800, ibid., 32:307–10; TJ to Charles Pinckney, November 4, 1800, ibid., 32:242–43. For a good account of Pennsylvania imbroglio, see Jacob E. Cooke, *Tench Coxe and the Early Republic* (Chapel Hill, N.C., 1978), 380–89.

37. TJ to JM, November 9, 1800, *PTJ* 32:250; TJ to Randolph, December 5, 1800, ibid., 32:271.

38. Charles Pinckney to TJ, December 6, 1800, *PTJ* 32:279–80; Peter Freneau to TJ, December 2, 1800, ibid., 32:265–66; TJ to Thomas Mann Randolph, December 12, 1800, ibid., 32:300.

39. TJ to JM, December 19, 1800, *PTJ* 32:322.

40. TJ to Burr, December 15, 1800, *PTJ* 32:307; Burr to TJ, December 23, 1800, ibid., 32:342–43; Ferling, *Adams vs. Jefferson*, 178. For TJ's residence in Washington, see *JMB* 2:1031n.

41. Michael A. Bellesiles, "'The Soil Will Be Soaked with Blood': Taking the Revolution of 1800 Seriously," in James Horn et al., eds., *The Revolution of 1800: Democracy, Race, and the New Republic* (Charlottesville, Va., 2002), 67; Bruce Ackerman, *The Failure of the Founding Fathers: Jefferson, Marshall, and the Rise of Presidential Democracy* (Cambridge, Mass., 2005), 41–45; James Gunn to AH, December 18, 1800, *PAH* 25:263; Sedgwick to AH, January 10, 1801, ibid., 25:310–13; Gouverneur Morris to AH, January 16, 26, 1801, ibid., 25:324–25, 329–30; John Rutledge Jr. to AH, January 10, 1801, ibid., 25:308.

42. AH to Wolcott, December 16, 1800, *PAH* 25:257; AH to James Bayard, December 27, 1800, January 16, 1801, ibid., 25:276–77, 319–24; AH to John Rutledge Jr., January 4, 1801, ibid., 25:293–98; AH to James Ross, December 29, 1800, ibid., 25:280–81; AH to McHenry, January 4, 1801, ibid., 25:292.

43. Cabot to AH, August 10, 1800, *PAH* 25:64.

44. The foregoing on Burr draws on Isenberg, *Fallen Founder*.

45. AH to Bayard, April 6, 1802, *PAH* 25:588.

46. Burr to Samuel Smith, December 29, 1800, in Mary-Jo Kline and Joanne Wood Ryan, eds., *Political Correspondence and Public Papers of Aaron Burr* (Princeton, N.J., 1983), 1:478–79. In the words of historian Joanne Freeman, Burr "left things open," saying nothing about "*declining* the office if offered." See Joanne B. Freeman, "A Qualified Revolution: The Presidential Election of 1800," in Francis D. Cogliano, ed., *A Companion to Thomas Jefferson* (Chichester, England, 2011), 145–163. The quote is on page 155 of Freeman's essay.

47. TJ to Randolph, January 23, 1801, *PTJ* 32:500; TJ to Mary Jefferson Eppes, January 4, 1801, ibid., 32:391; TJ to Burr, February 1, 1801, ibid., 32:528; TJ, Anas (April 15, 1806), in Padover, *CTJ* 1286–87.

48. TJ to Eppes, February 15, 1801, *PTJ* 32:593; TJ, Anas, (February 12, 14, 1801, January 26, 1804), in Padover, *CTJ*, 1282, 1285; AH to McHenry, January 4, 1801, *PAH* 25:292–93; AH to Wolcott, December 16, 1800, ibid., 25:258; AH to Bayard, December 27, 1800, ibid., 25:277.

49. There were problems with Georgia's ballot, now thought to have been caused by carelessness or incompetence by those who certified the results in Savannah. Jefferson wisely, and correctly, concluded that the irregularities were due to frontier lawyers, and he counted the state's votes for himself and Burr. Had he done otherwise, no one would have received a majority of the electoral votes, and the House would have had to pick the winner from the five candidates who had received electoral votes. See Ackerman, *Failure of the Founding Fathers*, 55–76.

50. Baker, "'An Attack Well Directed,'" *Journal of the Early Republic* 31:555–56.

51. *PTJ*, editorial note, 32:578n; Sharp, *Deadlocked Election of 1800*, 149–53; Ferling, *Adams vs. Jefferson*, 186–89.

52. TJ to Monroe, February 15, 1801, *PTJ* 32:594; TJ to JM, February 18, 1801, ibid., 33:16; TJ, Anas (April 15, 1806), in Padover, *CTJ*, 1286–87; Ackerman, *Failure of the Founding*

Fathers, 87–88; James E. Lewis Jr., "'What Is to Become of Our Government': The Revolutionary Potential of the Election of 1800," in Horn, *Revolution of 1800,* 20; Bellesiles, "'The Soil Will Be Soaked with Blood,'" ibid., 65; James Roger Sharp, *American Politics in the Early Republic: The New Nation in Crisis* (New Haven, Conn., 1993), 267–71; Sharp, *Deadlocked Election of 1800,* 153–56. The "factious foreigners" and "*fighting* bacchanals" quotations are in Ackerman, *Failure of the Founding Fathers,* 3.

53. Quoted in Sharp, *Deadlocked Election of 1800,* 159.

54. "Deposition of James A. Bayard," April 3, 1806, in *Memoirs of Aaron Burr: With Miscellaneous Selections from His Correspondence,* Matthew L. David., ed. (New York, 1971), 2:122–33; John S. Pancake, *Samuel Smith and the Politics of Business, 1752–1839* (Tuscaloosa, Ala., 1972), 57; Franck A. Cassell, *Merchant Congressman in the Young Republic: Samuel Smith of Maryland, 1752–1839* (Madison, Wisc., 1971), 99–101; Bayard to Richard Bassett, February 16, 1801, *Annual Report of the American Historical Association for the Year 1913* (Washington, D.C., 1915), 126; Bayard to Samuel Bayard, February 22, 1801, ibid., 131–32; Morton Borden, *The Federalism of James Bayard* (New York, 1955), 84–93; Bayard to AH, March 8, 1801, *PAH* 25:344. The Sedgwick quotation can be found in Ferling, *Adams vs. Jefferson,* 193.

55. TJ, Anas (April 15, 1806), *CTJ,* 1287; Burr to Albert Gallatin, February 25, 1801, in Kline and Ryan, *Political Correspondence and Public Papers of Aaron Burr,* 1:509; Bayard to Allan McLane, February 17, 1801, *Annual Report of the American Historical Association for the Year 1913,* 128; "Deposition of Bayard," *Memoirs of Burr,* 2:122–33; "Deposition of Samuel Smith," ibid., 2:133–37.

56. For a good introduction to the topic of TJ's presidency, accompanied by an excellent bibliographical guide, see Robert M. S. McDonald, "The (Federalist?) Presidency of Thomas Jefferson," in Cogliano, *A Companion to Thomas Jefferson,* 164–83.

CHAPTER 15: "THIS AMERICAN WORLD WAS NOT MADE FOR ME": A GLORIOUS BEGINNING AND A TRAGIC END

Chernow, *AH,* 640–709; Cooke, *AH,* 225–43; Miller, *AH,* 533–76; Brookhiser, *AH,* 197–217.

1. TJ to Henry Knox, April 8, 1800, *PTJ* 31:488.

2. Susan Dunn, *Jefferson's Second Revolution: The Election Crisis of 1800 and the Triumph of Republicanism* (New York, 2004), 191; James Roger Sharp, *The Deadlocked Election of 1800: Jefferson, Burr, and the Union in the Balance* (Lawrence, Kans., 2010), 125. JA's quote can be found in Thomas Froncek, ed., *The City of Washington: An Illustrated History* (New York, 1977), 87.

3. *JMB* 2:1035. The quotation is in Dunn, *Jefferson's Second Revolution,* 191. For a good description of the new capital, see David McCullough, *John Adams* (New York, 2001), 541–42, 550–51.

4. John Ferling, *John Adams: A Life* (reprint, New York, 2010), 413.

5. Malone, *TJ,* 4:29–32; Dunn, *Jefferson's Second Revolution,* 213–17; David Waldstreicher, *In the Midst of Perpetual Fetes: The Making of American Nationalism, 1776–1820* (Chapel Hill, N.C., 1997), 187–93. The *Aurora* quotations can be found in McCullough, *John Adams,* 562.

6. Editor's note, *PTJ* 33:134. The "femininely soft" voice quote is in Margaret Bayard Smith, *The First Forty Years of Washington,* ed., Gaillard Hunt (New York, 1906), 26.

7. TJ, First Inaugural Address, March 4, 1801, *PTJ* 33:148–52. TJ's two earlier drafts can be found in ibid., 33:139–47.

8. Bernstein, *TJ,* 136.

9. James Bayard to AH, March 8, 1801, *PAH* 25:344; AH, *An Address to the Electors of the State of New-York*, March 21, 1801, ibid., 25:365.

10. TJ to Gates, March 8, 1801, *PTJ* 33:215; AH to Gouverneur Morris, February 29, 1802, *PAH* 25:544; AH to Richard Peters, December 29, 1802, ibid., 26:69.

11. AH to ESH, January 26, May 24, 1800, *PAH* 24:220, 525; AH to Charles Cotesworth Pinckney, December 29, 1802, ibid., 26:71; Burr to TJ, April 21, 1801, *PTJ* 33:627.

12. AH to ESH, January 26, [1800], *PAH* 24:220.

13. AH to Gouverneur Morris, February 29, 1802, *PAH* 25:544.

14. AH to William Cooper, September 6, 1802, *PAH* 26:52; AH to Peters, December 29, 1802, ibid., 26:69.

15. Editor's note, *PAH* 25:38–41.

16. AH, Alexander Hamilton's Explanation of His Financial Situation, [July 1, 1804], *PAH* 26:289.

17. *PAH* 25:450.

18. The eighteen essays of AH's "The Examination," published between December 17, 1801–April, 8, 1802, are interspersed between pages 453 and 597 in volume 25 of *PAH*.

19. Quoted in Miller, *AH*, 542.

20. Editor's note, *PAH* 25:436–38; AH to Benjamin Rush, March 29, 1802, ibid., 25:583–84; AH to John Dickinson, March 29, 1802, ibid., 25:583.

21. TJ, Anas (April 15, 1806), in Padover, *CTJ* 1286.

22. AH to King, June 3, 1802, *PAH* 26:13–14.

23. AH to Gouverneur Morris, March 4, 1802, *PAH* 25:559; AH to Bayard, April 6, [16–21], 1802, ibid., 25:588, 605.

24. Quoted in Chernow, *AH*, 661.

25. AH to King, February 24, 1802, *PAH* 26:195.

26. AH, Speech at a Meeting of Federalists in Albany, February 10, 1804, *PAH* 26:187–90; AH to Harper, February 19, 1804, ibid., 26:191–92.

27. Nancy Isenberg, *Fallen Founder: The Life of Aaron Burr* (New York, 2007), 243–56. The "nigger ball" quotation can be found in Chernow, *AH*, 675.

28. Cooper's two letters, which were published in the *Albany Register* in April, can be found in *PAH* 26:243–46 and 244n.

29. Burr to AH, June 18, 1804, *PAH* 26:242–43.

30. AH to Burr, June 20, 1804, *PAH* 26:247–49.

31. Burr to AH, June 21, 1804, *PAH* 26:249–50.

32. AH to Burr, June 22, 1804, *PAH* 26:253–54.

33. Burr to AH, June 22, 1804, *PAH* 26:255–56.

34. William P. Van Ness's Narrative of Events, June 18–22, 21–22, 22, 22–23, 25, 26, 27–28, 1804, *PAH* 26:241–42, 246–47, 249, 251–52, 254–55, 257–58, 261–62, 264, 267, 274–75; Nathaniel Pendleton's Narrative of Events, June 22, 23, 23–25, 25, 27–28, 1804, ibid., 26:252, 259, 260, 263, 274–76; Aaron Burr, Instructions to Van Ness, June 22–23, 1804, ibid., 26:256–57; Burr to Van Ness, June 25, 26, 1804, ibid., 26:265, 266–67; Van Ness to AH, June 23, 1804, ibid., 26:257, 258; AH to Van Ness, June 23, 1804, ibid., 26:259; Van Ness, Disclaimer for AH Prepared by William P. Van Ness, June 25, 1804, ibid., 26:265–66; Pendleton, Nathaniel Pendleton's First and Second Accounts of AH's Conversation at John Taylor's House, June 25, 1804, ibid., 26:260–61, 263; Pendleton to Van Ness, June 26, 1804, ibid., 26:270–71; Van Ness to Pendleton, June 27, 1804, ibid., 26:272–73. On Van Ness and Pendleton, see Thomas Fleming, *Duel: Alexander Hamilton, Aaron Burr and the Future of American Politics* (New York, 1999), 60, 125.

35. Editor's note, *PAH* 26:240; Burr, Instructions to Van Ness, June 22–23, 1804, ibid., 26:157. On Burr's advice to Monroe in 1797, see Roger G. Kennedy, *Burr, Hamilton, and Jefferson: A Study in Character* (New York, 2000), 69.

36. AH to Bayard, April 6, 1802, *PAH* 25:587.

37. AH to Bayard, April [16–21], 1802, *PAH* 25:605.

38. Quoted in Joanne B. Freeman, *Affairs of Honor: National Politics in the New Republic* (New Haven, Conn., 2001), 196.

39. J. Lee Schneidman and Conalee Levine-Schneidman, "Suicide or Murder: The Burr-Hamilton Duel," *Journal of Psychohistory* 8 (1980–81):159–81. For an excellent account of AH's thinking, and one that does not buy into the psychohistory theory, see Joseph J. Ellis, "The Duel," in Joseph J. Ellis, *Founding Brothers: The Revolutionary Generation* (New York, 2000), 20–47.

40. AH to ESH, July 4, 1804, *PAH* 26:293.

41. AH, Statement of my property and Debts, July 1, 1804, *PAH* 26:283–87; AH, Alexander Hamilton's Explanation of His Financial Situation, [July 1, 1804], ibid., 26:287–91; AH, Deed of Trust . . . , July 6, 1804, ibid., 26:297–300; AH, Assignment of Debts . . . , July 9, 1804, ibid., 26:301—4; AH, Debts Owed for Services Not Rendered, July 10, 1804, ibid., 26:307; AH, Last Will and Testament of Alexander Hamilton, July 9, 1804, ibid., 26:305–6.

42. AH, Statement on Impending Duel with Aaron Burr, [June 28–July 10, 1804], *PAH* 26:278–80.

43. For a compilation of AH's earlier dueling activities, see Freeman, *Affairs of Honor*, 326–27. The compilation can be found in endnote number thirteen.

44. AH, Statement on Impending Duel, [June 28–July 10, 1804], *PAH* 26:279.

45. William P. Van Ness's Regulations for the Duel, July 9, 1804, *PAH* 26:306–7; Nathaniel Pendleton's First Statement of the Regulations of the Duel, July 4, 1804, ibid., 26:295–96; Nathaniel Pendleton's Second Statement of the Regulation for the Duel, July 10, 1804, ibid., 26:308–9

46. Fleming, *Duel*, 323–24.

47. Freeman, *Affairs of Honor*, 180.

48. For the conflicting accounts offered by the seconds, see Joint Statement by William P. Van Ness and Nathaniel Pendleton on the Duel . . . , July 17, 1804, *PAH* 26:333–34; Nathaniel Pendleton's Amendments to the Joint Statement . . . , July 19, 1804, ibid., 26:337–39; William P. Van Ness's Amendments to the Joint Statement . . . , July 21, 1804, ibid., 26:340–41; editor's notes, ibid., 26:334–36n.

49. David Hosack to William Coleman, August 17, 1804, *PAH* 26:344–47.

RECKONING

1. TJ to Martha Jefferson Randolph, July 17, 1804, *FLTJ*, 261; TJ to Philip Mazzei, July 18, 1804, L & B, *WTJ* 11:41.

2. See Virginia Scharff, *The Women Jefferson Loved* (New York, 2010), 306–9.

3. TJ to John Melish, January 13, 1813, in *PTJ: Ret. Ser.* 5:563–64. See also TJ to Walter Jones, March 5, 1810, January 2, 1814, ibid., 2:272; 7:102–3; TJ to Joel Barlow, January 24, 1810, ibid., 2:176–77; TJ to Rush, January 16, 1811, ibid., 3:305; TJ to William Worthington, February 24, 1810, ibid., 2:252.

4. JA to TJ, June 30, July 3, 22, November 15, 1813, September 3, 1816, *AJL* 2:346, 349, 363, 488.

5. TJ to Barlow, January 24, 1810, *PTJ: Ret. Ser.* 2:177.

6. TJ, Explanations of the 3 volumes bound in marbled paper, February 4, 1818, in Padover, *CTJ*, 1211.

7. TJ to Spencer Roane, September 6, 1819, Ford, *WTJ* 12:136, 140; TJ to Priestley, March 21, 1801, *PTJ* 33:394; Thomas Paine, *Common Sense* (1776), in Philip S. Foner, ed., *The Complete Writings of Thomas Paine* (New York, 1945), 1:45.

8. TJ to Dickinson, March 6, 1801, *PTJ* 33:196; TJ to Samuel Adams, March 29, 1801, ibid., 33:487; TJ to Barlow, March 14, 1801, ibid., 33:274; TJ to Short, March 17, 1801, ibid., 33:337. TJ to Paine, March 18, 1801, ibid., 33:358–59.

9. TJ to Paine, March 18, 1801, *PTJ* 33:358–59; TJ to Priestley, June 19, 1802, ibid., 37:625–26.

10. The foregoing draws on Gordon S. Wood, *Empire of Liberty: A History of the Early Republic, 1789–1815* (New York, 2009), 286–356; Gordon S. Wood, *The Radicalization of the American Revolution* (New York, 1992), 312; Susan Dunn, *Jefferson's Second Revolution: The Election Crisis of 1800 and the Triumph of Republicanism* (Boston, 2004), 273–82; Darren Staloff, *Hamilton, Adams, Jefferson: The Politics of Enlightenment* (New York, 2005), 332–50; and William B. Skelton, *An American Profession of Arms: The Army Officer Corps, 1784–1861* (Lawrence, Kans., 1992), 8.

11. Quoted in Wood, *Empire of Liberty*, 712. See also Robert M. S. McDonald, "The (Federalist?) Presidency of Thomas Jefferson," in Francis D. Cogliano, ed., *A Companion to Thomas Jefferson* (Chichester, England, 2011), 164–83.

12. L. P. Hartley, *The Go-Between* (New York, 1958), 7.

13. AH to Theodore Sedgwick, July 10, 1804, *PAH* 26:309.

14. Wood, *Empire of Liberty*, 702–3; Wood, *Radicalization of the American Revolution*, 310–25; Joyce Appleby, *Inheriting the Revolution: The First Generation of Americans* (Cambridge, Mass., 2000), 57–59; Jonathan Prude, *The Coming of Industrial Order: Town and Factory Life in Rural Massachusetts, 1810–1860* (Cambridge, Eng., 1983), 71.

15. Wood, *Radicalization of the American Revolution*, 325, 366–69.

16. TJ to Samuel Kercheval, July 12, 1816, in Merrill D. Peterson, ed., *The Portable Thomas Jefferson* (New York, 1976), 559; TJ to JA, April 8, 1816, September 12, 1821, *AJL* 2:467, 575; TJ to Roger Weighman, June 24, 1826, Ford, *WTJ* 10:390–92.

17. TJ to Van De Kemp, January 11, 1825, Ford, *WTJ* 10:337.

18. TJ to JA, August 1, 1816, *AJL* 2:485; TJ to Josephus B. Stuart, May 10, 1817, L & B, *WTJ* 15:113. The "become my own biographer" letter is quoted in Brodie, *TJ*, 600–601.

19. Francis D. Cogliano, *Thomas Jefferson: Reputation and Legacy* (Charlottesville, Va., 2006), 75–77.

20. TJ, Explanations of the 3 volumes bound in marbled paper, February 4, 1818, in Padover, *CTJ*, 1204. The "Anas" itself can be found in ibid., 1212–88.

21. TJ's Autobiography can be found in Padover, *CTJ*, 1110–94. The quoted material can be found on page 1119.

22. Quoted in Staloff, *Hamilton, Adams, Jefferson*, 359.

23. The literature on TJ and slavery is enormous. The following are good starting points: Paul Finkleman, "Jefferson and Slavery: 'Treason Against the Hopes of the World,'" in Peter S. Onuf, ed., *Jeffersonian Legacies* (Charlottesville, Va., 1993), 181–21; Lucia Stanton, "'Those Who Labor for My Happiness': Thomas Jefferson and His Slaves," ibid., 147–80; Adam Rothman, "Jefferson and Slavery," in John B. Boles and Randal L. Hall, eds., *Seeing Jefferson Anew: In His Time and Ours* (Charlottesville, Va., 2010), 103–25; John Chester Miller, *The*

Wolf by the Ears: Thomas Jefferson and Slavery (New York, 1977); the groundbreaking essay by William Cohen, "Thomas Jefferson and the Problem of Slavery," *Journal of American History* 56 (1969): 503–26; and Robert McColley, *Slavery and Jeffersonian Virginia* (Urbana, Ill., 1973), 2.

24. TJ to John Holmes, April 22, 1820, Ford, *WTJ* 10:157. (For what TJ actually said in this letter, see Finkleman, "Jefferson and Slavery," in Onuf, *Jeffersonian Legacies*, note 138, page 221.)

25. TJ to St. George Tucker, August 28, 1797, *PTJ* 29:519.

26. Monroe to TJ, February 13, 1802, *PTJ* 36:576; TJ to King, July 13, 1802, ibid., 38:54–55; Douglas R. Egerton, *Gabriel's Rebellion: The Virginia Slave Conspiracies of 1800 and 1802* (Chapel Hill, N.C., 1993), 153–62. On TJ's estimate on the cost of colonization, see William Cohen, "Thomas Jefferson and the Problem of Slavery," *Journal of American History* 56 (1969): 503–26.

27. Edward Coles to TJ, July 31, 1814, *PTJ: Ret. Ser.*, 7:503–4; TJ to Coles, August 25, 1814, ibid., 7:603–5.

28. TJ to Coles, August 25, 1814, *PTJ: Ret. Ser.*, 7:603.

29. JA to TJ, December 21, 1818, February 3, 1821, *AJL* 2:551, 571; TJ to John Holmes, April 22, 1820, Ford, *WTJ* 10:157–58.

30. Finkleman, "Jefferson and Slavery," in Onuf, *Jeffersonian Legacies*, 212. For a survey of the modern censure of TJ for race, see Gordon S. Wood, "The Trials and Tribulations of Thomas Jefferson," ibid., 396–98; Scot A. French and Edward L. Ayers, "The Strange Career of Thomas Jefferson: Race and Slavery in American Memory, 1943–1993," ibid., 418–56; Cogliano, *Thomas Jefferson*, 170–229. See also Paul Finkelman, "The Monster of Monticello," *New York Times*, November 30, 2012.

31. Philip D. Morgan, "Interracial Sex in the Chesapeake and the British Atlantic World, c. 1700–1820," in Jan Ellen Lewis and Peter S. Onuf, eds., *Sally Hemings and Thomas Jefferson: History, Memory, and Civic Culture* (Charlottesville, Va., 1999), 58. On the wages of craftsmen, see Sean Wilentz, *Chants Democratic: New York City and the Rise of the American Working Class, 1788–1850* (New York, 1984), 50–51. TJ once remarked that he cared "for the happiness of those who labor for mine." See TJ to Angelica Church, November 27, 1793, *PTJ* 27:449.

32. Finkleman, "Jefferson and Slavery," in Onuf, *Jeffersonian Legacies*, 181–221; Edmund S. Morgan, *American Slavery, American Freedom: The Ordeal of Colonial Virginia* (New York, 1975), 375–85; Joseph J. Ellis, *American Sphinx: The Character of Thomas Jefferson* (New York, 1997), 144–52; Ari Helo and Peter S. Onuf, "Jefferson, Morality, and the Problem of Slavery," *William and Mary Quarterly* 60 (2003): 583–614. See also Peter S. Onuf, "'To Declare them a Free and Independent People': Race, Slavery and National Identity in Jefferson's Thought," *Journal of the Early Republic* 18 (1998): 1–46; Onuf, "Every Generation is an 'Independent Nation': Colonization, Miscegenation, and the Fate of Jefferson's Children," *William and Mary Quarterly* 57 (2000): 153–70; and Henry Wiencek, *Master of the Mountain: Thomas Jefferson and His Slaves* (New York, 2012). Other important works on TJ and slavery include Cohen, "Thomas Jefferson and the Problem of Slavery," *Journal of American History* 56 (1969): 503–26; and Miller, *Wolf by the Ears*. For an especially thoughtful piece on TJ and slavery, see Andrew Burstein, *Jefferson's Secrets: Death and Desire at Monticello* (New York, 2005), 113–49. For Rakove's important essay, and the citation of the "evil of a kind" quotation, see Jack N. Rakove, "Our Jefferson," in Jan Ellen Lewis and Peter S. Onuf, eds., *Sally Hemings and Thomas Jefferson* (Charlottesville, Va., 1999), 228.

33. TJ to Coles, August 25, 1814, *PTJ: Ret. Ser.*, 7:603.

34. TJ to Joseph Cabell, February 7, 1826, Ford, *WTJ* 12:451. On the sale of TJ's library to the Library of Congress, see Kevin J. Hayes, *The Road to Monticello: The Life and Mind of Thomas Jefferson* (New York, 2008), 546–63.

35. Quoted in Brodie, *TJ*, 464. Some quotes are from Rebecca L. McMurry and James F. McMurry Jr., *Anatomy of a Scandal: Thomas Jefferson and the Sally Story* (Shippensburg, Pa., 2002), 70. On Callender, see the insightful essay by Joshua D. Rothman, "James Callender and Social Knowledge of Interracial Sex in Antebellum Virginia," in Lewis and Onuf, *Sally Hemings and Thomas Jefferson*, 87–113.

36. TJ's denial was in an 1805 letter in which he acknowledged his improper behavior toward Betsy Walker, but added: "It is the only one founded in truth among all their allegations against me." See TJ to Robert Smith, July 1, 1805, in *Thomas Jefferson Correspondence. Printed from the Originals in the Collections of William Bixby* (Boston, 1916), 115.

37. Annette Gordon-Reed, *The Hemingses of Monticello: An American Family* (New York, 2008), 648, 657–60.

38. TJ to Thomas Mann Randolph Jr., December 30, 1809, *PTJ: Ret. Ser.* 2:110.

39. TJ to Augustus B. Woodward, April 3, 1825, Ford, *WTJ* 12:408.

40. The foregoing paragraphs on TJ's retirement draw on Cunningham, *TJ*, 322–49. For an excellent brief essay on the subject, see Andrew Burstein, "Jefferson in Retirement," in Cogliano, *A Companion to Thomas Jefferson*, 218–33. The section on TJ and education draws from Harold Hellenbrand, *The Unfinished Revolution: Education and Politics in the Thought of Thomas Jefferson* (Newark, Del., 1990), 136–69; and Cogliano, *Thomas Jefferson*, 157–59. On TJ, religion, and death, see TJ to JA, November 13, 1818, April 11, 1823, *AJL* 2:529, 592. On TJ's thought on life in the hereafter, see Andrew Burstein, *Jefferson's Secrets: Death and Desire at Monticello* (New York, 2005), 257–63.

41. TJ to Priestley, March 21, 1801, *PTJ* 33:393–94.

42. TJ, First Inaugural Address, March 4, 1801, *PTJ* 33:149–50.

43. Quoted in Gar Alperovitz, *America Beyond Capitalism: Reclaiming Our Wealth, Our Liberty, and Our Democracy* (Hoboken, N.J., 2005), 11.

44. Funeral Oration, [July 14, 1804], *PAH* 26:325–29. Morris's diary entries, including his acknowledgement of AH's opposition to republican government, can be found in ibid., 26:324n.

45. Malone, *TJ*, 6:498–99; Cogliano, *Thomas Jefferson*, 137.

INDEX

A NOTE ON THE AUTHOR

John Ferling is professor emeritus of history at the University of West Georgia. A leading authority on American Revolutionary history, he is the author of ten books, including *The First of Men: A Life of George Washington*; the award-winning *A Leap in the Dark: The Struggle to Create the American Republic*; *Adams vs. Jefferson: The Tumultuous Election of 1800*; *Almost a Miracle: The American Victory in the War of Independence*; *The Ascent of George Washington: The Hidden Political Genius of an American Icon*, named one of the best books of 2009 by the *Washington Post*; and *Independence: The Struggle to Set America Free*. He and his wife, Carol, live in metropolitan Atlanta.